The Force of Prejudice

# Contradictions

Edited by Craig Calhoun
*Social Science Research Council*

Volume 13  Pierre-André Taguieff, *The Force of Prejudice: On Racism and Its Doubles*

Volume 12  Krishan Kumar, *1989: Revolutionary Ideas and Ideals*

Volume 11  Timothy Mitchell, editor, *Questions of Modernity*

Volume 10  Giovanni Arrighi and Beverly J. Silver, *Chaos and Governance in the Modern World System*

Volume 9  François Dosse, *History of Structuralism*, volume 2, *The Sign Sets, 1967–Present*

Volume 8  François Dosse, *History of Structuralism*, volume 1, *The Rising Sign, 1945–1966*

Volume 7  Patricia Hill Collins, *Fighting Words: Black Women and the Search for Justice*

Volume 6  Craig Calhoun and John McGowan, editors, *Hannah Arendt and the Meaning of Politics*

Volume 5  Gérard Noiriel, *The French Melting Pot: Immigration, Citizenship, and National Identity*

Volume 4  John C. Torpey, *Intellectuals, Socialism, and Dissent: The East German Opposition and Its Legacy*

Volume 3  T. M. S. Evens, *Two Kinds of Rationality: Kibbutz Democracy and Generational Conflict*

Volume 2  Micheline R. Ishay, *Internationalism and Its Betrayal*

Volume 1  Johan Heilbron, *The Rise of Social Theory*

# The Force of Prejudice
## On Racism and Its Doubles

Pierre-André Taguieff

*Translated and Edited by Hassan Melehy*

Contradictions, Volume 13

 University of Minnesota Press
Minneapolis
London

The University of Minnesota Press gratefully acknowledges translation assistance provided for this book by the French Ministry of Culture.

Copyright 2001 by the Regents of the University of Minnesota

Originally published in French as *La force du préjugé: Essai sur le racisme et ses doubles,* by Pierre-André Taguieff. Copyright 1987 by Éditions la Découverte.

All rights reserved. No part of this publication may be reproduced, stored in a retrieval system, or transmitted, in any form or by any means, electronic, mechanical, photocopying, recording, or otherwise, without the prior written permission of the publisher.

Published by the University of Minnesota Press
111 Third Avenue South, Suite 290
Minneapolis, MN 55401-2520
http://www.upress.umn.edu

Library of Congress Cataloging-in-Publication Data

Taguieff, Pierre-André.
 [Force du préjugé. English]
 The force of prejudice : on racism and its doubles / Pierre-André Taguieff ; translated and edited by Hassan Melehy.
   p. cm. – (Contradictions ; v. 13)
 Includes index.
 ISBN 978-0-8166-2373-0 (pb)

 1. Racism. I. Title. II. Contradictions (Minneapolis, Minn.) ; 13.
HT1521 .T313 2001
305.8–dc21
                                                                2001000523

The University of Minnesota is an equal-opportunity educator and employer.

To the memory of Pierre-Paul Grassé, Victor Nguyen,
Michel Pêcheux, Léon Poliakov, and Mitsou Ronat.
For Jean Leca and Gérard Lemaine, with my gratitude.

# Contents

Translator's Preface ix
Introduction: Doubts about Antiracism 1

**Part I**
**CRITIQUE OF ANTIRACIST REASON**

1. Heterophobia, Heterophilia: The Definitional Antinomy 19
2. "Racism": Ordinary Uses and Scholarly Uses, from the Word to the Notion 31
3. Births, Functionings, and Avatars of the Word *Racism* 81
4. An Ideal Type: "Racism" as an Ideological Construction 110

**Part II**
**GENEALOGY OF THE DOGMATIC CRITIQUE OF PREJUDICES**

5. The Theories of Prejudice and the Meanings of Racism 141
6. Antiracism and Antiprejudice Ideology 180

Part III
RACISMS AND ANTIRACISMS:
PARADOXES, ANALYSES, MODELS, THEORY

7. On Racism: Models, Ideal Types, Variations, Paradoxes     197
8. The Specter of *Métissage:* The Mixophobic Hypothesis     213
9. On Antiracism: Ideal Type, Ideological Corruption, Perverse Effects     230
10. Elements of a Theory of Ideological Debate     259

Part IV
BEYOND RACISM

11. Pessimism: Philanthropy in Spite of Humanity     281
12. Ethics: The Infinite of the Law above the Law?     287
13. Republican Metapolitics: Universalism or Barbarism? Universalism without Barbarism?     303

Notes     317

Index     405

# Translator's Preface

The work of translating Pierre-André Taguieff's *The Force of Prejudice* has involved not only rendering its meaning into English but also translation in the etymological sense of carrying across, in this case from one social and intellectual setting to another, transporting it from the French context in which it was executed to the anglophone one in which it will now be read. One would hope that Taguieff's overarching purpose, to strengthen the position of the active antiracist intellectual, is not lost in the translation. The subtitle of Taguieff's work, *On Racism and Its Doubles,* suggests the problem involved in this broader task of translation: whereas Taguieff's object is primarily the French discourses of racism and antiracism and the ways in which they mirror and implicate each other, the translation must to the greatest degree possible address the "doubles" of these discourses in the anglophone world. And it must speak to a community of readers whose disciplinary backgrounds and dispositions may be quite different from those of French readers.

One is struck by the sheer range of racist and antiracist discourses, both scholarly and popular, that Taguieff analyzes. In his "Critique of Antiracist Reason" (part I), he shows the ways in which antiracism has tended to conflate the many forms racist discourse may take, which he sees as having two major logical bases: an "inegalitarianist" logic, which is linked to the series "inequality, domination, exploitation" (the kind of racism practiced in colonization); and a "differentialist" logic, linked to the series "difference, purification, extermination" (exemplified by Nazism). In each case, but in very different ways, the Other is "racized" — discursively made into a racial grouping and discursively separated from the dominant group. In all cases, racialization is the effect of an exclusionary discourse. Far from complicating the work of translation, the scope of the book facilitates it, in that Taguieff is quite interested in key aspects of racism and antiracism in the United States. He devotes a good deal of space to examining racist discourses from the United States, mainly concerning African Americans, and it is remarkable how much light this analysis sheds on French racisms. The latter range from the anti-Semitism that divided the country in the first half of the twentieth century to the colonial and postcolonial situations in the wake of which France has seen vehement discrimination against North African immigrants and their descendants. For those interested in French racisms and their antiracist counterparts, *The Force of Prejudice* is a very rich resource.

What may be most astonishing in both anglophone and French contexts — and what has made the book a subject of controversy in France — is Taguieff's turning the analysis to the discourse of antiracism in order to reveal the ways in which the latter may be exclusionary and even racizing. Moving from dictionary entries to scholarly monographs to newspaper articles, in chapter 3 Taguieff examines the two different senses that the word *racism (racisme)* carried: first in the 1890s, when it was used as a self-designator (for those speaking of the supreme qualities of the French "race"); then in the 1930s, when it was used as an other-designator for the German who was "racist" through self-designation (in German, *völkisch*). At this point Taguieff has already signaled, in chapter 2, racizing tendencies with regard to regionalist slurs about Jean-Marie Le Pen, the charismatic leader of the neo-Nazi National Front and a native of Bretagne, whose career was surging in the 1980s. (Since the first publication of Taguieff's book, Le Pen's position has been eroded by infighting in the National Front.) Indeed, it was the sudden rise of a number of "new rights" (Taguieff is careful to put the term in quotation marks to indicate their status as terms in polemical discourse) and the rapid growth of a popular antiracist movement in France in the 1980s to which Taguieff was responding. A philosopher and political scientist of vast erudition,

Taguieff plays a role that in France is quite different from its U.S. equivalent, that of public intellectual — the intellectual whose work constitutes an effective intervention in public debate and policy making. Taguieff declares his task that of strengthening the antiracist camp by pointing out what he sees as a serious problem, a tendency to engage in discursive strategies of condemning the racist Other that all too often resemble the latter's exclusionary discourses, the very reason for the condemnation. Hence, in his treatment, antiracism can become a "double" of the racism that it opposes.

According to the traditions of intellectual activity in France, Taguieff seeks the underpinnings for contemporary attitudes, positions, and ideologies through a hermeneutic relation with philosophical works of the past. It is here that his book may seem quite different from its analogues from the Anglo-American social sciences, whose basis remains predominantly empiricist. And it is here that the work of translating *The Force of Prejudice* was also a work of editing: the French original is more than one-third longer than this translation, and I omitted certain sections because I judged them to belong primarily to French intellectual traditions. For example, I chose not to include a section in which Taguieff lucidly identifies the methodical doubt of René Descartes (1595–1650) as the source of the intellectual attitude of ridding oneself of prejudice, and another in which he presents Michel de Montaigne (1533–1592) as founder of modern demystifying critique. Such exercises might seem, in the anglophone world, to be tasks for specialists of French literature or the history of European ideas. Of course, Taguieff's linking of present discursive practices with intellectual predecessors runs throughout his work, and his thoroughness in the portions of the book that appear here offers sufficient explanation for such linking. I made the decision to include especially those sections relevant to the U.S. context and to provide notes where parallels could be made (such as in the case of the career of the English word *racist*).

It is worth noting that there have been phenomena in the anglophone world quite similar to the racisms and the antiracisms that Taguieff addresses. The United States and the United Kingdom also saw, in the 1980s, the rise of various "new rights," both populist and elitist. Although there has not been as cohesive an antiracist movement in the United States as S.O.S. Racisme, the largest popular antiracist organization in France in the 1980s, the progressivist reactions to the resurgent conservatism of the 1980s and 1990s are still a vivid memory. There was much talk, around the turn of the past decade, of "political correctness": although its unity was largely fictional, a figment of various polemical imaginations, the restrictive measures associated with it, ostensibly designed to combat a wide array of discriminatory discourses, were and still are quite real. Such progressivist discourses have their own precursors in the various strands of American liberalism, a history that Taguieff's analysis touches on in places, and which his book may hence be seen as addressing in the context into which it is being translated.

*Introduction*

# Doubts about Antiracism

## The Metamorphoses of the Ideological Field

> *Action! action! is a call that resounds on many sides, but is uttered most loudly by those who cannot get ahead with knowledge.*
> Friedrich W. J. Schelling

Our objective may be defined, according to an allegory that Rudolf Carnap was fond of, as the attempt to repair a ship that can never be brought into dry dock and so that must be worked on while afloat in the ocean. Let us add that the ocean is rough from a storm and that the ship is showing a few troubling signs of instability. Indeed, today the ship of antiracism is fragile; it is drifting as well as can be expected since the defeat of National Socialism. Since the robust vessel of the 1950s has become a lightweight raft inflated by media spectacle and political rhetoric, some are advocating a scuttling. This is moving too quickly and applying a treatment of the Cartesian type — destroying everything to its very foundations in order to rebuild it — to an evolving reality that it would be better to redirect. It is time once again to hear Schelling's counterappeal: finally to suspend the obligation to act at any price, even if in a great hurry, as long as one acts.

In the seething of contemporary activism, we propose a moment of pause: by voluntarily failing to obey the imperatives of the emergency, we will disengage from the Manichaean norms brought on by ideology. For the end of ideologies is not the death of ideology: the pseudoethical terrorism of action first and foremost is what has come to fill the void left by the defection of the great doctrines.

1. The debates surrounding racism define a situation of *ideological exacerbation* due to a breakdown of consensus on the very terms of the problem, as well as to the newness, the object of a more and more acute perception, of the stakes. The ideological appeasement of the 1970s was linked to the concentration (even the confinement) and stabilization of the debates in the realm of the biological sciences, in which authoritative argument (what does science say, and through which of its authorized representatives?) could decide and institute a thought majority (governed by the antiracism of the geneticists: Albert Jacquard, André Lwoff, François Jacob, Jacques Ruffié). This period of relative ideological appeasement has given way, since 1983-84, to a symmetrical rise in the extremes. The rhetorical heat has greatly increased, at the same time that actors in the debate have been transforming: the committed *politicians* and *journalists* tend to substitute for the interventionist *scientists*. The dominant problematic of the 1970s may be summed up by the question of its qualifications of scientificity, asked of what is perceived as "racism." The antiracist conclusion was then simple: racism, as an ideological parasitism of the bioanthropological sciences (the "hard" sciences), has no scientific validity. At that point the debate could only stop, for want of a theoretical legitimacy for the positions termed "racist": antiracism placed itself before racism as the authority of science in the face of perverse and archaic deliria. But the assumption and claims of "racism" (as selfdesignation) had at the same time become rare and marginal things. Antiracism, a component of the basic democratic consensus inherited from the Enlightenment, could claim to spread over the grounds of living Reason, consigning to the darkness of the irrational or of irrationalism its troubling subject, its clearly designated enemy. The fundamental presupposition of such an ideological optimism resides in the belief that racism is essentially a *theory of races,* the latter *distinct* and *unequal,* defined in *biological terms* and in *eternal conflict* for the domination of the earth — a conception as publicly inadmissible as it is refuted by science. Now, the serene evidence transmitted

by such an ordinary definition has been shaken by the recent offensives of national populism, setting in motion, after the fashion of the New Right (the GRECE),[1] arguments that do not respond to the expectations of the ordinary antiracist, based on the received model of "racism" since the 1930s.

2. The first flaws appeared when the scientific community made public its internal divisions: the partisans of hereditary determinism, recognized Nobel Prize–winning scientists, regrouped and formed a pressure group rivaling that of the declared antiracist scientists. The nonscientific public was much troubled by this, at least at the beginning: if scholars could not agree among themselves, how could members of the public form a clear and distinct idea of the question? The period of hegemonic antiracism after 1945 hence seemed to come to an end. This breakdown of scientific consensus could itself be variously interpreted:

- The problem might be *more complex* than one thought, so not yet concluded.

- Perhaps the problem was scientifically *poorly framed*, whence the cleavage in the heart of the community.

- The problem *did not really exist,* was only a false problem, stemming from the ideologico-political parasitism of some scientific research. This interpretation enabled the choice of a third way, a neutral position, beyond ideological oppositions, and a return to the ideological convictions from before the crisis: settlement within true science. Little by little the ideological majority has stood on such a terrain, not without conserving a few traces of its past disturbances: choosing the camp of the good scientists was choosing the party of true science, and it was also satisfying the humanitarian requirements (which cost nothing and involved nothing: "I, sir, am an antiracist," and so on).

In this way the debate over the New Right (1979–80) ended. The New Right was itself the principal vector in France of the hereditarian thesis, through an exclusion of what was likened to the diabolical tradition par excellence, *Nazism* (therefore *racism*). But the damage was done: the uncertainties and disturbances had to persist.

3. The appearance of previously unseen forms of "racism" occurred in two time periods, and on two different registers of discourse, in French ideological space.

- The formation and diffusion of *differentialist* ideology by the GRECE and the Club de l'Horloge[2] in the *metapolitical* field during the 1960s. This was the first source of confusion, the latter due to the fact that the New Right had simultaneously constituted a doctrine of (interindividual) inequality, elaborated an elitist theory, and taken the side of the hereditarian psychologists in the controversy over heredity and environment. Under pressure, the observers therefore believed that this was just a matter of a new version of *inegalitarian racism,* based on a *biological* scientism, whereas something quite different was being constituted, a *differentialist* racism, on *culturalist* bases.

- The formation and diffusion in the *political* field, since 1983, of an ideology of *identity* by national populism, around the National Front (le Front National — FN). Here again, the confusion and the mixture of ideas masked the novelty of the modes of racialization:[3] it was no longer, in the national racism of the FN, only a matter of reactivating colonial racism, which was authoritarian and paternalistic, but rather of integrating into a populist discourse the thematic, hitherto reserved for scholarly (New Rightist) discourses, of the defense of *peoples' right to identity* (see chapter 7).

To simplify the question, one may distinguish three fundamental operations, three great shifts of basic concepts, arguments, or dominant attitudes in racizing ideology since the early 1970s:

race → ethnicity/culture;

inequality → difference;

heterophobia → heterophilia.

These three ideological and rhetorical operations, which have characterized the novelty of racist discourses in the French language (although the phenomenon has a European dimension) for almost two decades, have important consequences for the shaping of the controversies around racism and antiracism.

1. The "racialization" of the lexicons of culture, religion, traditions, and mentalities, even specific imaginaries, has produced a surge of a great variety of reformulations of racism that are not expressly biologizing. The racist discourse has, so to speak, been "culturalized" or "mentalized" by abandoning (in a sometimes ostentatious fashion) the explicit vocabulary of "race" and "blood" and therefore by leaving behind the ritual biological and zoological metaphors. But, in being substituted for the zoological notion of "race," the notion of

"culture" implies a shift of problematic and a complete refashioning of the antiuniversalist argument. Cultural anthropology and/or ethnology are thus called on to legitimate the neoracist prescriptions of avoidance of intercultural contact, of separate development (in full "equality in difference," of course), of phobic rejection of any "crossing of cultures." Most often, a "classical" antiracist subject, trained in the struggle against the biozoological variant of racism (on the Nazi model), remains speechless in the face of the "culturalist" reformulations of racism. Not only does such a subject risk not recognizing the latter as "racist" (in the absence of biologizing indicators), but his argument from the "antifascist" tradition (that is, the antiracist tradition that targets Nazi ideology), out of touch with the ethnopluralist problematic, is also completely inoperative. From then on commemorative antiracism plays the role of screen and obstacle in the face of "culturalist" neoracism.[4]

2. The reformulation of "racism" in the vocabulary of difference, which tends to do away with that of inequality and hierarchy, and the correlative shift, on the rhetorical plane, from the inegalitarian argument (the classic indicator of "racism" in the antiracist vulgate) to the differentialist argument — that is, the exclusive affirmation of "differences" — have brought about a recentering of the racizing imaginary onto the fear of the specter of *métissage* (interethnic crossing and "cultural *métissage*")[5] and brought to the forefront the norm of an unconditional preservation of the community entities as they are (or as they should have remained, and should once again be) with all their particular characteristics, a norm whose other side is an anguish centered on the vision of a final destruction of collective identities. It is the return of the catastrophical imaginary: the neoracist discourses are fed by the common representation of an effacement of the diversity of the human world, of an imperceptible and irreversible passage from good cultural and ethnic heterogeneity to the crepuscular homogeneity of individuals and cultures. A culturalist and differentialist vision of the "end of the world." We propose the name *mixophobia*, an unrelenting fear of the specter of mixture (see chapter 8), henceforth the dominant form of racism integrated into nationalism, in all its contemporary variants corresponding to the following three levels: that of the infrastate (ethnicisms: regionalism, movements for autonomy and independence), that of the state (nationalism in the strict sense), that of the suprastate (Europeanism, for example). A kind of

division of the labor of formulation and diffusion is discernible, in France in particular: the vulgate of such a national racism is propagated by the national populist discourse of the National Front,[6] while its scholarly legitimation is furnished by the differentialist doctrine formed in the 1970s by the two schools of the New Right (the antiliberals of the GRECE and the "liberals" of the Club de l'Horloge). But the hard core of "racism," or rather the presupposition of any act of racialization, persists in its new formulations: the absolutization of specific heritages or of differential heredities. Today radical cultural pluralism is at the basis of the most acceptable modes of racism — acceptable because they are the most clandestine. Polylogicism has replaced polygeneticism in the scholarly legitimations of racism. It would of course be necessary to move the ideology of difference into the twofold frame of its appearance: the contemporary, hegemonic forms of individualism (a "narcissistic" and hedonistic centering on "oneself": the ego, one's own body, private life) and the periodic reactions of ethnopluralism, both gentle (regionalism) and violent (terrorism for independence). The postmodernist forms of individualism and the ethnicist reactions have the common postulate of absolutely impugning the universal. Every universalist position or requirement is, in such an ideological space, devalued as a presumed expression of a devastating imperialism, as a destroyer of community identities, as terrorist, ethnocidal. In the name of the fight against the devouring abstraction of the universal, there appears a *fundamentalism of difference.* This twofold functioning of differentialist fundamentalism permits an understanding of its current hegemony: the plays of analogy, the interactions, and the crossings of the interindividual and intergroup levels authorize a judgment of the differentialist motive as one of the aspects of the individualism interpreted as a total social phenomenon.[7] The hypervalorization of difference as well as the theme, central to the "political" fringes of the postmodern imaginary, of difference "against" hierarchy attest to the effective convergence of arguments and basic evidence. Here let us simply look, following Louis Dumont, at the illusory character of prescription, received without criticism, of "equality in difference": for there is no difference that, in the cultural context of any human society, is not interpreted as a difference of value and therefore as a hierarchy, explicit (in traditional societies) or implicit (in modern societies, living under a sky of individualist and egalitarian values).[8]

3. The systematic use of the strategy of "retortion" with respect to the words and values of antiracism, whose ideology was fixed on the motif of the praise of difference, has contributed to making the new racism of difference unrecognizable and hence ungraspable. We define the rhetorical operation of retortion as a triple procedure of reprise-reappropriation, of misdirecting and redirecting an adverse argument (set in motion by an adversary), an operation likely to engender a twofold effect of self-legitimation and of the delegitimation of the adversary — the latter being dispossessed especially of her own arguments, deterritorialized from her problematic and her ordinary lexicon. The racialization of the "right to difference" and of the ethnopluralist thematic will represent the first important ideological achievement of the strategy of retortion set in motion by the "New Rights" in France. Two modes of formulating racism then appear in competition, these modes likely to change places with each other: praise of difference (heterophilia) and rejection of difference (heterophobia). Racizing statements shift indefinitely to the interior of the genre of discourse that Aristotle called epideictic (that which bears on praise and blame); they oscillate from one pole to the other, from exaltation to abasement, from the celebration to the exclusion of difference — the latter understood either as the different term or as the pure differential relation (see chapter 1).

The debates and controversies are therefore recentered on the intersecting questions of collective identities and of their defense, of the rights of peoples (the right to be oneself as the very first), of the mixture and/or crossing of cultures, of the intercultural and the transcultural. Discourses of racizing intention and militant antiracist discourses meet in using the same language games, in taking recourse to the same foundational evidence, and in aiming for the realization of the same values. This is an eminently paradoxical situation, where dialogues of the deaf arose (and still arise) from a singular agreement on words, from a strange consensus on values and norms (around "equality in difference"), from a sharing of the same differentialist problematic. Then there appears, in the antiracist camp, a fundamental contradiction in the setup of requirements and prescriptions: the antiracists demand *both* absolute respect of collective differences, therefore claiming the right to difference, and passage to the act of tasting the interethnic and intercultural mixture, hence calling for the right to community indifference and sometimes affirming the imperative duty to efface differences, the supposed sources of racism. One will note that since the mid-1980s, the ideological imperative of *métissage* tends to make minor that of "difference": with the new praise of *métissage* (quickly inscribed in the fashionable "young" discourse) returns the requirement of equality, in the form of the equality of rights — supplied by "Beur"[9] militants. Strangely, the heterogeneity and even the logical contradiction of the two series of requirements went unnoticed in the antiracist community, completely immersed as it was in its exaltation of the plural, the diverse, the multiple, married to the praise of mixture, of confusion, of crossing, of *métissage* (see chapter 9). A hegemonic confusion between confusion and distinction, perhaps too crude to be visible.[10]

This fundamental antinomy of contemporary antiracism comes from the clash, the shock, of two antiracist logics whose incommensurability we assume, logics founded respectively on two distinct anthropologies and apparently irreconcilable in their systems of values. I will call the first *individuo-universalism,* illustrated by the claim of the rights of man, the denunciation of values belonging to communities "closed" as racist, the ideal of abolishing community identities and "particularist" traditions as obstacles to "progress," the prescription of the universal mixture of individuals beyond national and ethnocultural borders. I will call the second *traditio-communitarianism,* illustrated by the right to difference (cultural, ethnic, even racial: "Negritude," "Judaity," and so on); the rights of peoples to persevere in their own traditions; the ideal of preserving group identities (up to and including the duty of peoples to remain themselves); the denunciation of "racism" as being confused with universalism, exterminator of differences, ethnocidal, genocidal. It will be understood that if there are two distinct racisms (universal-inegalitarian racism and communitarian-differentialist racism), then there are, symmetrically, two antiracisms with contradictory values and norms — individuo-universalist antiracism and traditio-communitarianist antiracism (see chapter 10).

A large portion of the contemporary difficulties with antiracism stems from the misrecognition of one's own argumentative heterogeneity, linked to the fact that one's discourse of foundation and denunciation is constituted in the course of a historical struggle against an advancing adversary whose face is relatively uncovered — National Socialism — and that professes an explicit ideological racism (a "doctrine" or a "conception of the world"), deriving from "mystical" biological materialism. Today it must be recognized that this antiracist setup has undergone an arrested development in being institutionalized (antiracist leagues), in being integrated into common sense, and in being diluted by consensual values and norms.

The adaptation of antiracism to the new forms of racialization, recentered on the twofold thematic of identity and difference, and proceeding from indirect discourse, from oblique reference, and from generalized implicitness, is not yet complete. There is a lag in the antiracist setups with respect to the new practices of racialization, doubled by that of the modes of theoretical analysis in the face of previously unseen procedures of legitimation. But the preliminary task is to provide a philosophical foundation for the unconditional rejection of racism, of all racisms (see chapters 11, 12, and 13).

## Polemics and Functional Obscurity

Two simple pieces of evidence run through this book, which strives to elucidate their ideological conditions of appearance and functions.

These pieces of evidence are neither a point of departure nor a conclusion, but little by little they have imposed themselves on the sequence of sometimes laborious analyses. They are the following: antiracism is above all and essentially a *war machine* in the everyday sky of ideologies; racism is an *obscure notion,* a poorly constructed term for schematizing without precision an indeterminate reality.

Now, the polemical machine of antiracism functions insofar as it allows one to believe that racism is something well defined, or at least quite definable. Thus racism can only avoid and mask the questions provoked by the obscurity of the notion it functionally presupposes. An attempt at elucidating what one names "racism" fatally runs up against the locked gate put in place almost a century ago in Europe by the antiracist vulgate.

In Europe, but by way of France, the Dreyfus Affair[11] constitutes the first crystallization of "antiracist" ideas, even before the appearance of a camp, a trust of political parties and gathering of ideological families. At that moment the antiracist idea takes shape, is institutionalized, even professionalized. Since the end of the nineteenth century, the French intellectual class has tended to recognize itself here as though in its ideal image.

It is the case that French intelligence has historically been educated on the basis of the great Cartesian rationalism, the militant and "progressive" rationalism of the Enlightenment, the ideology of the Saint-Simonian and Comtian positivisms, and finally the Republican synthesis. The French mind, if it is not melded with it, ideally identifies with critical rationalism, that destroyer of idols, breaker of prejudices, eradicator of illusions. Antiracism derives its permanence and its power, its force of evidence as much as its incoercible vigor, from the fact that it is rooted in this rationalist tradition, lives by this paradoxical tradition of antitradition: the spirit of unlimited free examination, the reign of immoderate critical reason. But it has made of the latter the setting of a new dogmatism with hegemonic claims, the spiritual alibi of a doctrine as closed as it is summary: *a new obscurantism.*

That is why, as this obscurantism has only been able to smash us against the "misery of antiracism,"[12] we have had to begin analyzing it. This is only a beginning. For it would also be in order to consider the surprising powerlessness of antiracism, its ideological omnipresence, and its insolence in the media, which are avowed to be socially and politically crippled, and to analyze the conditions in which this takes place, even the reasons for it. Between the enemy camps, racism and antiracism, one may once again see what Lucien-Anatole Prévost-Paradol described concerning the singular relations of hostility between the Restoration and the Revolution: the former "preferred to declare an impotent war on the Revolution, a war of words, for it was not in its power to return to things, and it could only alarm and irritate its enemies without destroying them."[13] Dominant antiracism has also declared war on an unknown (because undeclared) racism, a war as absolute as it is powerless, for it lives only to assume the existence of its designated enemy; having no interest in the latter's disappearance, it can only avoid acting on the real causes of what it claims to combat. A simulacrum of a war decorated with the prestige of the "combat for man."[14]

This book does not escape the shadow cast by modernity: it was born from an exercise in critical reason. Nothing is more derisory than the latest contemporary claim to being situated beyond the principle of critical examination, which is one with thought, even if the latter cannot be reduced to it. Our postcritics are never anything but ex-critics turned hypercritical of their past roles, past because out of fashion. We pay no heed whatsoever to fashion, as some will perhaps see. The critical reason at work is the engagement in a struggle against what the classical thinkers called "prejudices." With respect to the latter, our position is at once inside and outside, comprehensive as much as critical. For, if we assuredly propose to flush out and reduce certain sets of prejudices called "racist," we no less analyze the programmatic idea of a world without prejudice as a fiction engendering harmful utopias.

The idea of "prejudice" therefore appears both indispensable for approaching the question of "racism" and sufficiently obscure so as to be itself submitted to a critical interrogation. Thus we have allowed ourselves certain exploratory detours through the great modern rationalist tradition, whose objective has been to struggle against prejudices until they are destroyed, by means of critical analysis, which alone enables one to know them (see chapters 5 and 6).

## Racism-as-Ideology

One of the singularities of *racism*, as an ideology prone to appearing in various doctrinal forms, is related to its seeming rivalry with the great ideologies, such as socialism, liberalism, anarchism, and nationalism, without for all that being graspable on the same plane as they are. The great mother ideologies are first of all doctrinal identifications and partial to themselves: their names designate conceptions of the world and programs of social reconstruction assumed by more or less isolated social groups or actors — such as "authors." To the contrary, *racism* designates, from the moment the word first appears in the French language (1925), a stigmatized doctrinal ensemble, a sum of positions and propositions presumed to be blameworthy, attributed solely to the hereditary enemy, the German (see chapter 3). *Racism* is one of the names of what is commonly and violently rejected, in the inventory of possible ideologies. The word *racism* designates the ideology of the adversary, of an adversary, in any case of an individual or collective actor opposed to the subject who, as speaker, uses it. Racism, it will be objected, is formally well defined — as dictionaries bear witness — in the manner of a great ideology: on the one hand, it is supposed to be a system of explanation or interpretation of the historico-social world (the "theory of races"); on the other hand, it is described, to borrow Durkheim's formulas on socialism, as a "plan for the reconstruction of societies, a program for a collective life which does not exist as yet or in the way it is dreamed of, and which is proposed to men as worthy of their preference."[15]

Racism-as-ideology may essentially be broken down into two aspects. In the first place, given as a conception of the world or a metaphysics of history claiming to state the truth of what is (or of what is important to man), it may be defined as a *racial theory*. In the second place, posed as an ideal, oriented toward the future, a project of social recasting on a racial basis, racism is a system of values, norms, and imperatives; it is then blended with a morality and a politics. But it is at this point that the parallel with the great matrix-forming ideologies ceases. For, besides the fact that racism is a stigmatizing characterization of the positions of an adversary — it is therefore a polemical notion — not all of its assumed doctrinal variants present the second aspect, the axiological, normative, and prescriptive one that we have brought out. The racial metaphysics of history, as incarnated in Arthur de Gobineau's *Inequality of Human Races* (1853–55), for example, is concerned not in the least with what must be, but rather with what was (the golden age of Aryanism) and with what is (irreversible decline): there is literally nothing to be done, because there is no longer anything to hope for, in the space opened and closed by Gobineau's narrative of the progressive disappearance of the creative elements of civilization. Gobineau's pessimistic and nostalgic "racism" may certainly be deemed, following the example of socialism, "a cry of grief, sometimes of anger, uttered by men who feel most keenly our collective *malaise*."[16] But, pushed by the aristocratic despair of the old romantic, the cry of grief is not accompanied by a method of salvation or a prescription of remedies: there is nothing beyond the moanings of the sick person but resignation in the face of the inevitable end. Neither the constructivist stance, nor the programmatic disposition, nor social and political demiurgy or surgery[17] may be found in the "racist" conceptions of nostalgic romanticism. Now, "racism" is most often illustrated by Gobineau's theory,[18] a retrospective utopia of the racial sublimity that is forever lost, precisely deprived of the projective and prescriptive component accorded to racism in general. The classical theory of races, which is supposed to incarnate the ideal type of racism, therefore does not usher in imperative statements: it neither recommends nor prescribes any "racist" conduct; rather, it is content to diagnose evil, to describe its infallible genesis and universal extension, and preaches a wait for death. But this ultimate version of *amor fati* is not in the least joyful, and even less Dionysian: here resignation is only the sobered accompaniment of absolute sadness. The dominant passion of Gobineau's system is unlimited sadness, foundational of an inaction troubled by nostalgia: we are at the antipodes of the activism of "racist" militants, doctrinarians, or politicians who propose to change life or to transform the world in their own way, even in their own image.

But it will be objected that racism, like the other matrix-forming ideologies, is "above all a ferment which affirms itself, although it may eventually ask Reason for the reasons with which to justify itself."[19] The pairing of passion and rationalization is effective here, as everywhere in the social imaginaries. And one of the polemical instruments common to all antiracisms consists precisely of denouncing racism as a pseudoscientific system, of delegitimating it by exhibiting the (negative) passion that would inspire it, that would surround itself with arguments appearing to be scientific so as better to perch its authority on opinion — this passion is assumed to be sensitive to scientistic decorum. Antiracist polemic concentrates on the unveiling of the strictly polemical function of the scientific apparatus possibly set in motion by "racist" authors. Combative antiracism postulates that "racist" theoreticians, when they appeal to apparently scientific facts, observations, or laws, hence do nothing but "establish a doctrine that they had previously conceived,"[20] the latter deriving from an affective base often presented as pathological. Such is the dominant refutational method of the antiracist crusade: demystifying criticism essentially effects a reduction of racism to a rationalization of negative passions (hatred, contempt, envy, resentment, and so on), which would have "real" social and economic origins, a body of symptoms willingly donning, in its public formulations, the deceitful mask of a scientific theory. Reason could therefore intervene in the vicinity of "racism" only as the legitimating façade of an "irrational" thrust or blaze.

These combat characterizations are misunderstood because they are "well known," interiorized so well that they are not known for themselves and resist objectifying analysis. Antiracism derives its symbolic effectiveness essentially from the presentation and treatment of its adversary, "racism," as a social and ideological fact, endowed with the nature of a symptom: it objectifies its adversary by characterizing it as pathological. In this way it excepts itself from the field of objects it claims to describe and analyze, even explain, and in so doing it monopolizes the legitimate function of the neutral gaze par excellence, distanced from the phenomena. Hence antiracism fills a function of absolute exclusion in the form and through the effect of an absolute denunciation attributed to racism. That is why it must reserve its nature, protect from criticism the reasons for its own critical position, hence keep itself out of the analytic gaze, which would risk taking it as an object in turn. The most effective way of protecting oneself from criticism is to monopolize the critical function.

These considerations lead us to an unimpeachable piece of evidence: it is *antiracism* that most presents structural and functional similitudes with the mother ideologies — liberal or anarchist antistatism, socialist anticapitalism, nationalist anticosmopolitanism. Like all the great ideologies, antiracism is a twofold setup: it is a system of representing the world, even of explaining its being and becoming; and it is a system of norms and imperatives. Henceforth, antiracism falls, better than racism — its continual invention and its condition of existence — under the general definition it gives to its designated enemy. For antiracism, contrary to unassumable, undeclarable "racism," declares itself, assumes itself, claims itself, holds itself up as the legitimate exclusive conception of the world and as the universal method of salvation, in the face of the other ideologico-political final solutions that henceforth enter into competition with it (liberalism, socialism, nationalism, anarchism). Thus do the great mother ideologies strive to assimilate antiracism, this newcomer that upsets the transideological system, to incorporate its dominant passions and typical arguments, to integrate its most strongly "rallying" motives. A struggle for the exclusive appropriation of antiracist exclusivism has been unleashed in the political field, a struggle whose stake is the monopoly on the right to the antiracist denunciation of the adversary. Let us give just one example: the rhetoric in use in socialist and communist milieus involves the denunciation of a kinship or complicity ("objective" or conscious), even of a profound identity, between racism and nationalism, on the one hand (essentially by the mediation of the anti-individualism and the antiuniversalism they would have in common, as well as by the tendency to "biologize" their conceptions of the collective), and between racism and liberalism, on the other hand (essentially by the mediation of "social Darwinism"). It is well known that liberal theoreticians have hardly any trouble retorting that the "classism" (centered on class hatreds) inherent in socialism presents troubling likenesses to "racism" (centered on the struggle and hatred of races among themselves) and that socialism can in many ways be considered a communitarianist (or "holistic") reaction symmetrical to racism in the space of modern ideology, which is at heart individualist and egalitarian.[21] For their part, intelligent nationalist doctrinarians can always denounce in return the "racist" will to destroy "natural" (or naturalized by history, second-nature) national identities, shared equally by "liberal" and "socialist" imperialisms, the twin enemies of ethnocidal universalism.

Since 1945, the struggle for the monopoly on the antiracist denunciation of the adversary has extended over the planet as it has intensified. In extending and diversifying, through mimicry and reversal, antiracism has become a complex field of themes and arguments, in which most of the great ideologies and doctrinal traditions have crossed paths and run up against each other. For the political actors, such an effective method of delegitimating the adversary could not be abandoned to the free-for-all of organized (and most often politically instrumentalized) antiracist militancy, and even less to potential adversaries or possible competitors. Antiracism has hence become a stake of importance in ideologico-political struggles.

The hypothesis whose statement we have been trying to justify is quite simple: *antiracism* is a great ideology in formation, which postulates the existence of an absolute enemy named *racism;* but *antiracism* is also, in the current conjuncture, a transideological stake, involving conflicts of legitimacy. So that, far from provoking any appeasement of the cultural and ideological wars, antiracism reanimates and stirs them up, hence giving the lie to its declarations of intention with its real effects.

*Part I*

# Critique of Antiracist Reason

## One

# Heterophobia, Heterophilia: The Definitional Antinomy

*Personally, I am of the opinion that no means in the world is too "pedantic" to be inappropriate when it comes to avoiding confusion.*
Max Weber

## The Fundamental Antinomy

Let us go to the heart of the matter. Our object is "racism" as it is defined, or rather as it may be defined, on the basis of the postulates incorporated in the spirit of the time, which envelopes something like a basic antiracism.[1] The fundamental antinomy of racism, as conceived by antiracism, arises from the shock of two positions, both held and defended by the authorized spokespersons, the militants, and the sympathizers. These contrary positions equally attributed to "racism" characterize without distinction (or in succession) attitudes or dispositions, representations, and evaluations, no less than behaviors. It is sufficiently suggested that the flowing and undefined alternation between *heterophobia* and *heterophilia* presents an obstacle to any attempt at cold and careful analysis. Such holistic characterizations of "racism" are neither true nor false: the "rejection of difference/praise of difference" pair, if it has little recognition value, has an ideologically determining face. It engenders the conceptual indeterminacy necessitated by the undefined pursuit of debates and controversies: conflicts of legitimacy, combats for legitimation.

1. Racism is the absolute negation of difference; it is fundamentally defined as *heterophobia*,[2] which proposes a negative evaluation of all difference, implying an ideal (explicit or not) of homogeneity. The troubling element is represented by what differs, by the fact of the relation of difference (between Self and Other) or that of the attribute of difference (of the Other). For heterophobia is a confused idea, as phobia bears as much on the differential relation among groups as on the difference (or some difference) attributed to the Other as a characteristic. In the first case, heterophobia signifies the desire to abolish the difference between Us and Them: either by a dialogue led by the finality of consensus (communicating makes commonality, engenders a community of minds or hearts); or by assimilation of the representatives of the collective "Them," reduced in the preliminaries to individuals without marks of belonging, to models of Us; or by the extermination of all the representatives of the collective "Them."

In the second case, heterophobia aims either to efface the differential trait of which the racized collective is supposed to be the bearer (the eugenic or educational solution) or to efface the existence of the Other through a rigorous separation (making him invisible or blinding oneself to his existence) along the lines of apartheid. Hence the concept of heterophobia lumps together various modes of the "racizing" treatment of groups of others: the gentle racialization of encompassing others in and through persuasive dialogue (dialogical anthropology), the terrorist racialization of the destruction of others (genocidal anthropemy), the clean racialization of separate development (tolerantist anthropoemia) — to use systematically the metaphorical distinction between anthropophagia and anthropemy, recently introduced by Claude Lévi-Strauss.[3]

To consider from the outside judiciary and penitentiary customs, Lévi-Strauss advances a distinction between two types of society:

> Those which practice cannibalism — that is, which regard the absorption of certain individuals possessing dangerous powers as the only means of neutralizing those powers and even of turning them to advantage — and those which, like our own society, adopt what might be called the practice of *anthropemy* (from the Greek *emein*, to vomit); faced with the same problem, the latter type of society has chosen the opposite solution, which consists in ejecting dangerous

individuals from the social body and keeping them temporarily or permanently in isolation, away from all contact with their fellows, in establishments specially intended for this purpose. Most of the societies which we call primitive would regard this custom with profound horror; it would make us, in their eyes, guilty of that same barbarity of which we are inclined to accuse them because of their symmetrically opposite behaviour.[4]

Applied to racism, the schematization allows one to distinguish between imperialist/colonialist racism, or the racism of assimilation ("anthropophagia"), and differentialist/mixophobic racism, or the racism of exclusion ("anthropemy"). In the first, one aims to make someone similar to oneself, in the second to preserve the fact of difference by the rejection of that which differs — two distinct strategies of resolving the conflicts termed ethnic or racial. A distinction whose physiological basis is susceptible to infinite variations in the collective imaginaries: absorb/eliminate, ingest-digest/reject — a formal distinction between including and excluding. We must reconsider the double correlation between the operation of assimilation/inclusion and the cult of universal power, imperial mythology, on the one hand, and between the operation of elimination/exclusion and the sacralization of roots, rhizophilic mythology, on the other hand.

A philosophical modelization of the distinction may be found in the classical opposition between dialectical logic (in the Hegelian sense of the reconciliation of contraries) and formal logic, the latter founded on the principle of the excluded third term, the former on the principle of the third term included by the synthetic operation of "sublation" (according to the double meaning of *Aufhebung, tollere* and *conservare*). From these two irreconcilable logics, one may deduce the two modes of racialization that we have schematized: racism of exclusion, analytic and formalist (exclusive disjunction: "either one or the other"), and racism of inclusion, synthetic and dialectical (positive conjunction, even fusion of opposites: "both one and the other").

2. Racism is absolute affirmation of difference; it is defined by the absolutization of difference,[5] the naturalization or the essentialization of differences,[6] either perceived or imagined. As these attempts at philosophical conceptualizations do not, with just a few exceptions (Raymond Aron figures as the most notable among them), come from philosophers, they generally resort to terms used without rigor. "Essentialist thought" appears as a mode of perception and categorization

of human groups that is at once summary and eternalizing: it condenses and congeals attributed characteristics; it eternalizes the latter by fixing them as stereotypes ("race characteristics").

Racism, as essentialism, would arise with the intervention of the vocabulary of race borrowed from zoology through the mediation of physical anthropology: "races" are so many distinct "essences" allowing human groups to be classified, in agreement with practical classifications, and increasing the evidence of spontaneous social perception. This essentialism implies a "naturalist" disposition, in that the idea of nature synthesizes the attributes of "race": the latter concern the given, the involuntary, the fixed, the eternal, the insurmountable.

In the field of the social sciences, "essentialism" is therefore the scholarly characterization of racism that, for two decades, has seemed self-evident; it defines racism's first definitional evidence as the common and perhaps only conceptual trait of all the particular approaches. Hence the ethnologist Michel Adam believes he can grasp "the properly ontological unity of racism," in contrast to its phenomenal diversity.[7] But, the author recognizes, "if racism...may be generally understood as an 'essentialism,' if everywhere it bears witness to a behavior of exclusion and objectification of a collective 'other,' its manifestations are so diverse that they each seem to derive from a particular order."[8] Indeed this is the basic difficulty: there are hardly any satisfying conceptual mediations between the too broad outfit of the general heading of "essentialism" and the many social practices (attitudes, behaviors) that may be termed "racist." To state it briefly, it may be that the determination of racism by the trait of "essentialism" itself derives from said "essentialism": "racism" would run the risk of being conceived as an eternal ideological and behavioral essence, attributed to an invariable human type, incarnating an immutable specific nature. One should not then be surprised that such a substantial type never enters the realm of the observable and seems forever to glide above empirical variety.

In order to go deeper into the "essentialist" theory of racism, let us proceed to a detour through several recent texts by sociologists. In his "Essay on the Controversy between Max Weber and Werner Sombart," in *Judaïsme et capitalisme*, Freddy Raphaël applies the critical model of "essentialism" to the sociological theory of Sombart: "The approach of Werner Sombart is strictly 'essentialist,' since it encloses human groupings in a specificity that no member may avoid, thus legitimating their alienation."⁹ Now, essentialism conceived as the first method of racialization, in the form of an exclusive (or dominant) appeal to the essence of an affinity group with pseudoexplanatory aims, absolutizes alterity: "It may henceforth no longer be eliminated, for it is constituted as an irreducible core."¹⁰ If racism is the ideological system that makes race, according to Colette Guillaumin, "an intellectual and perceptive category of priority," it presents the functional peculiarity of allowing the foundation in nature of the total inclusion of individuals in biological classes that are at once closed and irreducible, no less than of the domination and exploitation of the supposedly inferior races. Essentialism, when it appeals to a kind of scientific legitimation, becomes a naturalism or an integral biologism: human groups are assigned the status of *natural groups*.¹¹

We should nonetheless note that, in racizing arguments, "naturalization" itself has no value except as a means to an end, which is the "fatalization," so to speak, of the psychosomatic characteristics of race: everything happens as if the racist posited (or presupposed) several distinct *human natures,* hence abolishing the nature/culture *split* (there is only the natural) at the same time as he would suppress *common* human nature (whether it is interpreted as a universal anthropological substance, an ethical requirement, or a regulatory idea). A link has often been perceived between the operation of naturalization/fatalization of factual social groups and the legitimation of the social division as it is. Jean-Claude Passeron notes:

> It is surely the notion of human nature, with all its ideological effects, that they [the psychological and biological concepts introduced without examination into sociological analysis] reintroduce into the arguments, since, in coupling social differences, even if by way of multiple mediations, with a foundation other than social, they reactivate the legitimating power of the established order that is always concealed by a forgetting of the social arbitrary in favor of the "nature of things" and, correlatively, the transmutation of historical necessity into a destiny that escapes the history of human beings.¹²

This brief detour through sociological discourse confirms our hypothesis on the present structuration of what may conveniently be called the scholarly antiracist vulgate by the guiding idea of "essentialism," a central critico-demystifying category. What racist theories ("biological sociologies" in general, especially the anthroposociology of Georges Vacher de Lapouge and Otto Ammon) are therefore currently reproached for, by the dominant sociological tradition (as a scholarly tradition, whether obedient to Durkheim or individualist-methodological), is effecting at once a *naturalization* of the cultural and/or the social, treated as biological realities, and a *fatalization* of the course of human history, with contingency travestied/converted into necessity and necessity transformed into destiny.

We again find the critical concept of essentialism in Pierre Bourdieu's sociological analysis of racism in general. Essentialism appears here as a fundamental characteristic of racism, the latter approached on the basis of class positions and strategies of legitimation. Essentialism plays the theoretical role of a model that is both descriptive and functional. "Every racism is an essentialism,"[13] postulates Bourdieu. Essentialism henceforth defines the ideological core common to all racisms, if it is true that there are "as many racisms as there are groups who need to justify themselves in existing as they exist."[14] But essentialism characterizes only an invariable mode of legitimation of a dominant position; it is inseparable from the legitimating function it fulfills: essentialism, in any form of racism, is the "metaphysical" foundation of the sociodicy that a class domination of any kind would be unable to do without. Hence essentialism may appear at the foundation of a rhetoric centered on the positive self-racialization of various fractions of the dominant class ("We are the best") and possibly carried into the scholarly language of psychometric tests (the elite made up of those with an IQ of more than 120): "The racism of intelligence... is what causes the dominant class to feel justified in being dominant: they feel themselves to be *essentially* superior."[15]

One may go further and, rather than remaining at the static category of essentialism, state the hypothesis of an eternalizing essentialization as an act accompanying any designation of a scapegoated victim. A discernible set of humans incarnates the essentialized victim, treated by self-legitimating inversion as the aggressor-subject[16] onto which may be concentrated all the hate of the group in whose name one speaks and that one claims to be defending. In certain cases pure hate appears, without practical reason and without pragmatic interests, a hate targeting the essence of the racized, bearing on what the latter is supposed to *be*. The invention of an absolutely bad collective entity defines the object to which a pure or ontological, nonpragmatic hate may be applied. Vladimir Jankélévitch presented such a model in a text published in 1942, in which he clearly showed the specificity of anti-Semitism:

> Among all the fascist impostures, anti-Semitism is not the one that reaches the greatest number of victims [this was written in 1942!], but it is the most monstrous. Perhaps for the first time men are officially tracked down *not for what they do, but for what they are.* They expiate their "being" and not their "having": not acts, a political opinion, or a profession of faith like the Cathars, the Freemasons, or the Nihilists, but the fate of birth. This gives all its meaning to the immemorial myth of the cursed people, the scapegoated people, condemned to wander through the nations and bear the latter's sins on their backs.[17]

The anti-Jewish hate of the Nazis ("fascists") aims at the very *being* of the Jews, whatever they might *do*, whether as a people or as individuals. What the anti-Jewish subject here brings to light is his absolute rejection of any possible similitude of his own being with the being of the Jew. Pure hate is best deployed in relation to rivalry, that is, in a space representable as egalitarian and competitive: the anti-Jewish subject assumes as his imperative task the destruction of this rival but intrinsically bad being, this inverted double that threatens his own identity. At issue is making any resemblance impossible — a resemblance whose possibility is always implied by competitive egalitarianism, the supreme threat of nondifferentiation from the corrupt and corrupting element.

Affective ambivalence is not to be neglected here: the mimetic rivalry that follows egalitarian schismogenesis can be abolished only by the suppression of the adversary, precisely because the latter tends to be recognized as a partner in the interaction. Only the extermination of the rival-Other can put an end to the struggle, for in this case there is no possible stabilization in defined places on the scale of values. The destruction of the rival-Self is the general price to pay in the polemical space of the egalitarian type, by its very principle prohibiting any hierarchization considered to be legitimate and hence indefinitely reinitiating mimetic rivalry and hate. Jankélévitch noted, "The relations between the 'Jew' and the 'Aryan' are ambivalent relations of passion that would require a very painstaking description: we believe that, without this description, the extraordinary sadism of anti-Jewish persecution, its unforeseen refinements, and its diabolical inventiveness could not be understood."[18]

Pure racialization targets the racized individual as any representative at all of a group that is supposed to confer on her its substantial being, its "essential" identity. This derealization of the individual as such assumes the existence of a sociopolitical space in which the modern individual, as a subject endowed with rights and responsibilities in a legitimate state, and individualist ideology have emerged; for racist derealization applies to the legitimate subject (the person, the citizen) and to her ideological foundation. Particular persons (this Jew, that Arab, and so on) are racized as incarnating their respective collective types: this Jew as the Jew, that Arab as the Arab, and so on. The operation may be observed with regard to other types of collective entities. "Kill the Jews!" — this explicit imperative is made implicit and is open to variations, for example in crimes termed "sexist." In a text that develops the analogy, "Sexisme et racisme," Emmanuèle de Lesseps commented on the murder of a woman following her rape and torture: "This woman was killed *because she was a woman*, died for belonging to a specific human group.... Men are not murdered any less often than women, but they are not murdered 'for no reason' (as is said for a woman), that is, as males! Their maleness does not bring them into any danger."[19] It remains that ontological murder, in this case, is mixed with a pragmatic murder, linked to the erotic interest of rape. Any woman is certainly killed as a woman, but the murder follows and finishes, or "signs," the rape, bearing on the object of desire. The analogy is valid only between the feminized woman (according to the norm of an erotic interest) who is "sexized" and the racialized group (according to the norm of an economic interest) that is "racized." In the framework defined by such a restrictive clause, every representative of a category of "victimizables" — blacks, Jews, Arabs, women — may be termed destructible as such.

But let us come back to the unconditional and hyperbolic praise of difference, as a rhetorical pivot common to a certain antiracism and a certain racism.

*Heterophilia*[20] presupposes that differences are as such positive. Racism is henceforth based on the sacralization of difference; it implies a "second religiosity" of difference. The disturbing element here is the absence of difference, the threat of nondifferentiation. Heterophile racism is fundamentally antiuniversalist: the universal is reduced to only a homogenizing, unifying, standardizing machine. And it is denounced as an imposture consisting of raising a particularism to a universal norm:[21] travestied ethnocentrism, imperialism with a humanist face. The requirement of universality is condemned as a privileged instrument (because masked by its sublimity) of an enterprise of eradicating the good differences, those that symbolize life itself. Henceforth, leveling antiracism is stigmatized as cultural mass murder, as ethnocide that would proceed from an ethnocentrism that is dangerous inasmuch as it is touted as universal. Universalist antiracism would then be the true racism, the only racism. The denunciation of ethnocide and of the imposture of universalism in general spontaneously grafts itself onto a catastrophist vision of evolution toward the homogeneous. Let us borrow a description of such a picture of a gray world, conceived as a perverse effect of the ideal of assimilation, from the ethologist Irenaüs Eibl-Eibesfeldt, as the conclusion of a study of five so-called primitive tribes:

> In most cases one observes an assimilation in which all that emerges is a caricature of the model. The loss of outside civilization is rapidly succeeded by mental civilization, and all those who unscrupulously favor this evolution are guilty of ethnocide, even if they act with good intentions. The argument is often advanced that only a unitary worldwide civilization, involving the total mix of all races, would resolve the tensions and conflicts among groups. That does not seem to me either necessary or desirable. If one teaches man to be tolerant — that is, to be ready to understand and accept other styles of life as much within specific civilizations as among different peoples — then ethnocentrism will find itself forestalled, without it being necessary for the groups to abandon their cultural particularities and the pride in their civilization. The pacification of humanity should not leave in its wake the corpses of civilizations and races.[22]

The differentialist formula of antiracism is simple: the right to the difference of community and active tolerance between cultures (mutual familiarity, reciprocal interest, dialogue). Here the two basic principles of the "spontaneous" professional ethic of ethnologists will be recognized.

The antiracism that follows the trace of heterophobic racism is therefore defined by what it believes it must essentially denounce and combat, that is, the imperial universalism that aims for the assimilation of all others to the selfsame. The antiracism that posits heterophile racism as its enemy can only reaffirm the value of the requirement of universality, by denouncing this deceptive substitution of transcendence that is difference raised to the absolute. There is, on the one hand, an antiuniversalist and differentialist antiracism and, on the other hand, a universalist and antidifferentialist antiracism — an interlacing of antiracisms that echoes the chiasmus of their respective racisms. At issue here is an antinomy, an insurmountable contradiction that necessarily reproduces itself, on the basis of the same presuppositions, on two levels: that of racism as *it* is defined, that of antiracism as it defines *itself,* as it is sketched on the horizon of primary pieces of evidence concerning "racism," which are its own.

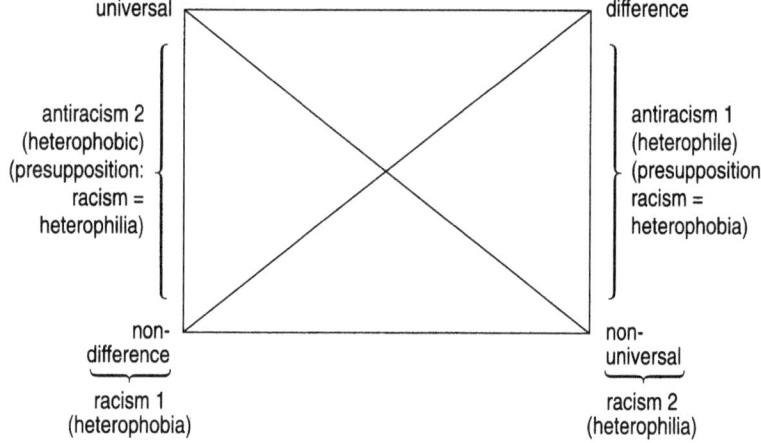

## Principles and Hypotheses

- Each antiracism (AR) has its own racism (R): AR1 → R1; AR2 → R2. Each racism has an antiracist double.

- The positions are determined by the double play of oppositions of the antis and the philias/phobias.

- The dominant antiracist discourse is a formation of compromise (unstable, even "explosive") between antiracism 1 and antiracism 2, which may be considered ideal types (illustrated nonetheless by positions perceived as "extremist").

## Axioms and Definitions

1. If racism is defined by heterophobia, then antiracism is defined by heterophilia.[23] The founding theme of antiracist slogans is that differ-

ence signifies richness: the ethnic and cultural diversity of humanity is presented as the natural capital of the entire species, an inalienable treasure that must be defended at any price. Difference *is* humanity, and its most precious capital. The praise of difference has been the first element of the dominant and majoritarian antiracist discourse since the 1960s. Type 1 antiracism is based on the conviction that differences are good, the gift of nature or God. This is the differentialist option in general.

2. If racism is defined by heterophilia, then antiracism is defined by heterophobia, which ordinarily presents itself through an affirmation of the universalist requirement. This heterophobia, a basic distrust in the face of differences, presupposes by an assumed derivation two mixtures of ideas, which are found at the basis of type 2 antiracist slogans: differences engender inequalities, which institute injustices; differences engender hostility, which feeds the drive to aggression, which manifests itself in wars. The two themes tend to appear together in the militant commonplaces: the struggle against inequalities and injustices — egalitarianist themes; the struggle against war and the "arms race" — a pacifist theme. Certain authors, often scientific types endowed with bad conscience, let it be known that differentiation leads to discrimination.[24] Other authors, radicalizing the antiscientific inspiration that they have retained from the Christian vulgate, advise us not to judge, as judging is differentiating, and so evaluating, and so hierarchizing according to value. Radical egalitarianism and total pacifism are the prerogative of minoritarian groups, either sects of millenarian ideology or front organizations manipulated for political ends (they constitute ideological reserve armies and instruments of provocation). Pacifist egalitarianism constitutes the second element of the dominant antiracist discourse, in spite of the fact that, taken in the isolated and "pure" state, it derives from the dominated and minoritarian antiracist discourse.[25]

3. The antiracist vulgate is produced by the synthesis of the differentialist thematic and the egalitarianist/pacifist thematic: its ideal-typical slogan is "equality in difference." Pacifism here appears as something presupposed: for there to be equality among different groups, one (the antiracist) says that it is enough that difference is simply observed, before being the object of praise, an occasion for mutual enrichment, a source of appeasing dialogue, a foundation of solid friendships, a provocation to beneficial exchanges. Is being content

with observing differences even possible? The question comes down to wondering if one is able not to judge, able to abstain from evaluating by differentiating, absolutely to keep oneself from referring to some scale of values.[26] The ideal sketched in such prescriptions is the very one indicated by the impossible synthesis of equality and difference,[27] which at once demands that one recognize or welcome differences and that one carefully blunt them, that one celebrate them, but all of them at the same time and just as easily; in short, that one distinguish without judging the distinctions. This linking of phobias — of the vertical, of degree, of conflict, and of the undifferentiated — defines the core of the antiracist vulgate. The typical slogan must therefore be rewritten in the developed state: "Equality in difference, to achieve universal peace: friendship among peoples, dialogue among cultures, exchanges among nations." Here we may recognize the basic formulas of the rhetoric of international civil servants: the dominant ideological form is also a professional jargon. But the latter is no less a political stooge language and instrument of propaganda, of adverse propagandas. Its instrumental value in ideological warfare partially explains the astonishing blindness of the antiracist intelligentsia in the face of such a paradoxical requirement, one that is impossible to satisfy: appreciate without preference. It is understood that it must engender a specific bad conscience, that of the fatally unhappy antiracist.

# Two

# "Racism":
# Ordinary Uses and Scholarly Uses, from the Word to the Notion

> *A vocabulary is words, but it is also thoughts, a logic, a philosophy, indeed a metaphysics; the one who accepts it, even to fight against the latter, is already occupied, attacked from inside.* Henri Massis

What does one think of "racism" when one stands outside and against the supposed field of racism? What are the elements of the antiracist representation of "racism"? Do they enable one adequately to know the phenomenon of this name and to combat it with the desired effectiveness? It is for both theoretical aims and practical objects of ideological struggle that we may take a detour through the exploration of the antiracist representations of "racism." The latter are to be reconstructed from the words, language games, and strategic uses of discourse, and they refer to a first agency, which is a principle of legitimation and a matrix of evidence; we will propose to call this agency *antiracist reason*. Our hypothesis is simple: the knowledge of antiracism, as a system of representations and reserve of preconstituted arguments, is one of the conditions of the knowledge of racism, if such a thing, categorizable as such, is endowed with a determinable mode of existence. Self-knowledge of antiracism, as will and as task, is the good faith in action of the humanist doing his best to be an effective, and positive, antiracist. For struggling against racism assumes a certain idea of what is not racism, of what escapes it absolutely, and authorizes a marking of boundaries, even if they are unstable and always to be redefined. That is why the optimism of the humanist who believes himself capable of "struggling against racism" must be submitted to a merciless critical examination. We should not avoid a critique of antiracist reason, of a cold exploration of its first pieces of evidence and spontaneous arguments, of a dissection of this *polemical* reason as it has been historically constituted for around a century, by sedimentation, through crises, debates, combats, and all-out wars.

## "Racism": Strange Uses

We therefore propose to contribute to an analysis of the representations that supposed nonracists and "antiracists" (the current self-designation) make of the object of their disapproval or their struggle: *racism, racists*. By the producer of the discourse termed *antiracist* (nonracist by presupposition) we must understand, more extensively than in the current usage — that is, the militant committed to the struggle against racism at the heart of a specific organization or in relation to it — any enunciator who, taking lexicological or encyclopedic distance with respect to what she names *racism*, either is content to refuse to assume the theses she describes, takes a reproving stance toward *racism*, or, stigmatizing racist actors and behaviors, declares herself an enemy of *racism*. The images of the racist Other are constructed, conveyed, reproduced, displaced, and transformed by words in the position of the discourse of blame. These words designate the object of blame: the enemy, the abused, the manipulated, the ignorant, the lunatic, the potential or real basher, the victim of an illusion. These images are assumed by the constitutive arguments of the "struggle against racism"; they themselves contribute to acts of social instituting in a symbolic field where racism and antiracism enter into a polemical relation. From words to thought, from arguments to ideology, from discourses to systems of representation: paths to be followed, objectified, conceptualized.

Our analyses are not devoid of all concern with preparation for action: there is no effective struggle at all against racism once it is made into a fictitious representation, once antiracism is constituted as the specular image of the racist myth. Racizing in return those whose racizing behaviors are stigmatized is nonetheless a paradox that is part of the everyday of racism, and one of its failings.

A few discursive examples of racistoid antiracism (and its polemical simulacra) will enable us to take stock of the ideological phenomenon. A graffito dating from June 1986 (Paris, Café Le Rostand) illustrates a spontaneous polemical reversal (by all appearances) of the racism involved in the selective xenophobic (anti-Maghrebian) nationalism of the 1980s in France. The formula of such an argument of retortion is the following: "[Jean-Marie] Le Pen, dirty buttfucking Breton, not even French." Many graffiti appeared, in the same period, that illustrated this typical argument of reverse-racism, "antiracist" racism: they put in play offending formulas, "dirty racist" (or "dirty race," racist/antiracist — a reciprocity of offending labels), "dirty Frenchman," or "dirty fascist." This obscenization of the enemy cannot be dissociated from the very ordinary procedure of reversing polemical metaphors, whether bestializing, criminalizing, or pathologizing: the animalized racist as a "wild" or "furious animal," racism treated as an illness (mainly of the viral type: "the racist virus"), the racist denounced as an exemplar of the criminal type (devoted to perpetrate or favor crimes called "racist").[1] We must also account for the formulas of explanation of racizing antiracism, through polemical redirection. A retorting parody of the racizing antiracist statement, which illustrates the meritocratic variation, is offered by the following graffito: "Dirty French people out! France for those who deserve it!" (École Polytechnique, December 1986). The anti-antiracist intention of such a parodic redirecting is here quite clear — not the case with all the statements using the discursive markers of antiracism (the simulacrum capable of appearing "truer" than the original). The scandalous presupposition ascribed to the antiracist from which is produced a statement of radical type is that the French "of old stock" do not deserve France, as they do not realize its ideals. Hence the polemical simulacrum allows an unveiling and a denunciation of an ulterior motive of the antiracist adversary, presented as wishing for the replacement of the "bad French" (of the old stock) by foreigners who better conform to the values presumed to be French (for example, those of the Republic). The denunciation of ulterior motives is a normal mode of delegitimation. An anti-antiracist statement of the same type, the polemical simulacrum comprising an anti-Jewish theme, is offered by this next graffito: "Indigenous French people out! France for the Jews who make it prosperous and proud"

(École Polytechnique, December 1986). Here the redirection allows us to attribute to Jews the ulterior motive of exclusive domination, even the absurd will to colonization to the point of substituting for the population. What is understood in the statement conforms to one of the ritualized anti-Jewish stereotypes: the Jews, a proud and dominating people, are anti-French racists who dream of sending the (non-Jewish) French out of France. A less radical suggestion also appears: anti-French racism, which is postulated as existing and incarnating true racism, is either favorable to the Jews or profits them or satisfies them in some way.

These conflictual interactions in the ideological field show how much the question of racism remains imprisoned in mythologizations and countermythologizations: in such a mythopolemical space, all arguments may be redirected, all themes circulate, all stereotypes are reversible. Antiracist discourse functions precisely under the condition of a misrecognition of the paradoxes linked to the mimetic rivalry of racism and antiracism. The latter may deploy its social effects (limited to the prohibition of the explicit speech of "racists") only by remaining blind to the racistoid presuppositions and constructions of its discourse of denunciation. Here is a first limitation of antiracism, which authorizes a certain pessimism with regard to the possibilities it has of evolving toward a radical reform of its methods. But we must raise a second limitation, concerning the epistemic conditions of effectiveness of antiracism. For, being content with fictionalizing the Other, even the *racist* Other, one is condemned to miss him: not to know him at all, never to reach him except in forms filtered by uncriticized preconceptions.

If the shortest path from racism to antiracism is well represented by continued and inverted myth, it is certainly not the best path. One of our objectives has been to take some distance with regard to the descriptions, narrations, and characterizations of racism that are acceptable in the "camp" that is our own ("antiracism"), to extract critical discourse from the mythology that takes its place, to demarcate the discourse on and against racism of a certain antiracist vulgate, the involuntary and abused double of ordinary racism. Before moving on to the study of assumed racist discourses — themselves distributed in a heterogeneous field — it has therefore seemed necessary to interrogate the discursive and argumentative procedures by which the system of our representations of *racism* and of the *racist* (the *racists*) is constructed. "Our" representations: I assume and claim this "we" implicated in and by analysis. For us, indeed, who do not accept racism, who even claim to combat it, the discourse on racism can be only a discourse against racism. Even then one must know what one is talking about, if one is going to speak well on something, and on the same thing, and if what one says is observable, verifiable, or refutable. Unavoidable questions of meaning, of reference, of communication, and of the efficiency of critical discourse arise, to be approached head-on. It has seemed to us imperative to bring the critical discourse targeting *racism* out of the circle formed by the repetition of incantatory and conjurational formulas....[2] Thus we must begin by self-analysis, apply ourselves to driving out the mythical element at the very heart of the discourses that "we" engage in, we who want ourselves to be, not without some presumptuousness and naïveté, the "Others" of racism, its foreigners and flawless enemies. First undertaking the deconstruction and critique of our own discourse, aracist and antiracist, is to accept the inevitable and seemingly necessary task of polemicizing a series of texts in which *racism* is named, described, defined. We also want this analytical series to be a search, aiming to pinpoint the arguments underlying the statements referring to racism. We are assuming that the analysis of rhetorical (argumentative) structures, if it may inform us as to modes of ideological functioning, would be conducted profitably only if brought into a hermeneutic perspective, which is characterized by the effort in view of understanding the intellectual debates and combats inscribed in the political in their sociohistorical contexts, while the hermeneutist does not remove himself from the field he is trying to understand. He can do so only on condition of moving forward in the understanding of his own "prejudices," of becoming conscious of his forenotions and preconceptions, of placing in the forefront, in plain sight, his "hidden thoughts." To sketch a political geography, a rhetorical history, and an archeology of discourses ("nonracist" or declared as such), in the French language (a quite provisional and methodological restriction), that bears on "racism" before and after the lexicographic appearance of the vocable (1932): such is the theoretical horizon of the study presented here. Antiracism lacks a knowledge of itself, which is required to constitute the knowledge of its other, "racism." Here again we will encounter the hermeneutic circle: there is no understanding without self-understanding, and the reciprocal is also true.

It has seemed to us that we should finally take seriously, on the question of racism, these remarks by Pierre Bourdieu: "One always ends up paying for simplifications, all simplistic thinking, or making other people pay for it.... Slogans and anathemas lead to every form of terrorism."[3]

## The Word in Use

*Racism* is a problem word, a word with a great number of questions hung onto and tied to it.

In the 1970s there appeared various derived forms, indicative of the extension of its uses, of the term *racism*. On the basis of a definition of classical construction, by proximate genre *(racism)* and specific difference (introduced by the prefix "anti-" followed by an anthropomorphic collective noun: *Jew, black, Arab*), lexical entries were formed that illustrated the paradigm: "antiyouth," "antiage," "antiwoman," "anti-immigrant (anti-Maghrebian)," "antiredhead," "antibald," "antibourgeois," "antiworker," "antiboss," "antiunemployed," "anticop," "antihomosexual" racisms, and so on. The denomination *racism*, in the normal usage of such lexical derivations, only reinforces (by recuperating) the connotation of hostility evoked by *anti-* and, by anchoring it in a cursed memory (that of Nazism), whose magico-polemical image is that of mass massacre, achieves an operation of delegitimation of the subjects to whom such and such a variant of "racism anti-X" is imputed. Denouncing "antiboss racism" is hence to delegitimate the attacks against management by likening them to the absolute evil that racism is supposed to be; it is correlatively rehabilitating the bosses who are supposed to have been the victims (by definition innocent) of racism. We must account for the appearance of a second model of derivation: "the racism of X." Thus are imposed fixed forms, such as "the racism of intelligence"[4] or "the racism of age."[5] In both cases, it is a matter of denouncing a privilege, a dictatorship, an abusive form of power — in short, an illegitimate right.

Such lexical entries carry with them the presupposition that there exists an open set of groups of Others, posited as generally different and submitted to some devaluation or exclusion by the representative of the "anti-" racism being considered, each collection of Others treated "as" a "race" (a biological metaphor) and submitted to a categorization analogous to — or of the same type as — the racist operation (an insistence on the difference and incommensurability of "specificities" or "essences"). Any group at all, differentiated in nature from the group to which the "racist" enunciator belongs, then devalued, excluded, and/or dominated by the latter's discourse, may thus be called "racized." The extension through analogy and metaphorization of *racism*, by way of the constitution of paradigms of derivation, in some way finds its theoretical respondent in the concept of "racialization." The latter should allow a substitution of a constructed model of the act of "racizing" and of the modes of "racialization" for the burgeoning polemical uses of the word *racism*, which tend to prohibit it from having any cognitive value. Henceforth, the moral (let us say moralizing) connotation of *racism* would be neutralized to the advantage of an enlightening value accompanied by a critical force, of which the model of *racialization* would be the proof. Youth, the elderly, the unemployed, homosexuals, women, bosses, Jews,[6] and "cops" would be categorizable "as" sorts of "races" or "as" equivalents of "races," such as "species." The problem of racism is thereby shifted onto a terrain that may be observed with some rigor: the social modes of perception and construction of Others. In this perspective, we assume that there are quite a few sociological quasi-races, engendered by processes of pseudospeciation. *Racism* as well as *race* are certainly eponyms; but through construction they enable a schematization of mental operations linked to social classifications whose importance should not be underestimated. By giving a name to an object of cognition, they call it into being, that is, to scientific attention. But schematization, forgetting its critical intention imposed on cognition, is exposed to limitation or is parasitized by polemical aims: hence we speak of "anti-X racism," not in order to know some process of racialization in a definite context but rather to disqualify radically the designated bearer of said "racism."

The act of racialization implies an operation of "racialization" of the racized collective entities: referring to "youth" as though they formed a race, that is, a "natural" human grouping characterized by the common possession of physical traits (statistically distributed and having psychological effects) transmissible by heredity. The absurdity of a literal application of the concept of race to the whole of "youth" leaps out. And nonetheless, this logical absurdity does not amount to a sociological absurdity. Henceforth it is a matter of determining the meaning of the operation of "treating as a race." Doing so assumes a certain knowledge of what a race is.[7]

In another respect, we come back to posing the problem of borders, that is, that of the line of rupture between the literal meaning of the descriptive and classificatory term (the *races* of physical anthropology, concepts scientifically authorized at least within the limits of the discipline in question, and supposedly referential human groupings that are factually observable) and the effects due to the symbolic imagination tinkering with this supposedly natural base (the engendering of metaphorical "races," when the social and political imaginary comes into discourse). In short, by aiming to legitimate through presupposition the racial carving up of humanity, one authorizes the differentiation of humankind into *races* presumed to be natural (their origin) and scientifically distinct (their fact or functioning).

If we indeed agree that *the young* constitute a specific category of "racized" persons, we do not see how we could a fortiori deny that *Jews* or *blacks* respectively form a racial category, a *race* par excellence, in the literal sense. In other words, the paradox implied by the use of expressions that are supposed to designate pejoratively a group characterized by a collective behavior (antiyouth racism, and so on) is to base, by a fortiori argument, the correct usage of the word *race* in expressly bioanthropological ("serious," "scientific," "neutral") discourses. The stereotyping of social groups ("youth," "the unemployed," ...) reinforces the stereotypical assignation of individuals to racial groups, which are supposedly natural.

Another way of making acceptable the indefinite extension of the word *racism* to designate any act or behavior (discursive or not—the nondiscursive being only what may become discursive) that is the object of a repudiation, for the enunciator, consists of taking recourse to an implicit biologization in any operation of differentiation that turns into an act of exclusion or domination: "Any discourse that aims to reject from the human species a fraction of the latter conceals an implicit biology, as confused as it may be."[8] The difficulties arising from such a postulate seem insurmountable. Once there is an implicit biology, there is a no-less-implicit racism. Nothing further hinders the affirmation of the connaturalness of "implicit racism" and the human, if implicit "biology" and "racism" follow like their shadows all human acts of discrimination, rejection, aggression, domination, and hierarchizing classification. Group hostility is even thereby "naturalized" as an act of biologizing the Other (the unknown, the different, the foreign), which is then supposed to be a defining feature of humanity. In 1977, Georges Mauco rightly observed,

> The word *racism* tends to assume such an extension that it is applied to every conflictual situation. There ends up being talk about antiyouth or antielderly racism, racism between bourgeois and proletarians, between religious sects, and between political parties — such that *the word racism today expresses less the reality of a race than the intolerance of a foreigner*, of that which is different, inferior, or threatening with regard to the specificity of the group or even the egoism of the individual.[9]

The word *racism*, in the working antiracist vulgate, has thus been desemanticized and resemanticized through abusive generalization, an operation institutionalized by the law of July 1, 1972, unanimously passed by the French National Assembly and the Senate. Racism here appears as designating "any discrimination, hate, or violence with respect to a person or a group of persons for reason of their origin or of their affiliation or lack thereof to an ethnic group, race, or religion."[10] It hardly seems necessary to insist on the indeterminacy of the term thus defined. The generalized use of the word *racism*, in the antiracist vulgate, produces a dissolution of its value as a concept, as an instrument of cognition, by making it designate any conduct or attitude of aggression or hostility toward an individual perceived exclusively as a member of a definite group.

An investigation into "the intellectual youth of both sexes," published in 1962 with the significant title *La Nouvelle Race*, furnishes us with a good example of the positive *racialization* of a social category: the young (we should not forget that "the young" may be no less the object of a negative racialization, for example when they are accused, as a collective subject, of "antielderly" or "anticop racism"). This positive metaphorization of the young comes from the pen of Michel de Saint-Pierre, a celebrated essayist in traditionalist Catholic circles. The last chapter of the book, elegantly titled "The New Race," presents a characterization of the latter that sets two distinct traits in motion: one trait produced by the biologization of the category of the young ("mutants") and another engendered by the metaphor of radical extraneousness ("aliens on earth"). A biological metaphor: "One may ask if young people today do not form in some manner a new biological species. Perhaps they are mutants."[11] A politico-cultural metaphor of the absolute (extraterrestrial) alien: "Our young people...are mutants. Has a leap just occurred in the human species?...Such a leap would doubtless explain why young people today are aliens on earth."[12] There would be a "new race" for reason of the twofold "fact" that the class of "young" individuals would be irreducible to any other class of individuals. This irreducibility is legitimated by a coupling of metaphors: that of absolute "novelty" implied by the analogy of the appearance of an unknown "species," that of a radical lack of resemblance suggested by the assignation of a distant, even unknown origin (they come from elsewhere). It remains that these mutants and aliens are a good race, that the new race seems to the enchanted observer better than his own: "I much prefer the new race to our own."[13]

In 1977, Christian Delacampagne was able to diagnose and deplore an "abusive extension of the suspicion of racism."[14] A realm particularly invested with the ideology of suspicion, in the 1970s and 1980s, was that of the conflicts among social categories or groups. The latter were submitted to a racialization that functioned as an instrument of legitimation/delegitimation. In the discursive production that accompanies and utilizes social conflicts, it is standard to meet with the accusation of "racism" or the denunciation of an adversary as "racist." The "antiracist" stigmatizing of the adversary as "racist" targets behaviors, attitudes, or dispositions toward certain social categories, which are distributed according to three types: biosocial, socioprofessional, and religious. The extremes of the age spectrum are particularly targeted (the young and the elderly). But the most exposed categories are women, homosexuals, immigrants (especially from outside Europe), the disabled (even the mentally ill), the marginal (the homeless, drug addicts, the unemployed), followers of "sects" (including "fundamentalists"), communists, the police ("cops"), and let us not forget the workers (the "riffraff"). We must take account of the categories resulting from synthesis: such as the composite type incarnated by the young immigrant (or the son of an immigrant, bearer of "stigmata" that mark him socially) who is a worker or an unemployed person suspected of being delinquent and drug-addicted (some will recognize the negative ethnotype of the "Beur"). Here it is possible to advance that "racism" is the name given to exclusion inasmuch as it treats as a natural grouping — that it "biologizes" — a set of individuals who are supposed to belong to the same social category. To this provisional hypothesis may be added a second: there are as many racisms as types of legitimation required by the specific passions (hate, rivalry, contempt, fear, and so on) of which the social groups in conflict are the bearers. These two hypotheses may be transformed into postulates of the extensive uses of the word *racism:*

- There exist as many racisms as attitudes of *exclusion* or hostile othering that target specific groups, with the reservation that there exist excluded social categories.[15] (On this point, common sense and ordinary usage are met by the scholarly analyses [Guillaumin and Bourdieu].)[16]
- Social categories are racized when they are the bearers, are declared or supposed to be the bearers, of a *biological marker,* a corporeal stigma; racialization applies to "institutional categories vested with the biological marker."[17]

Everything therefore happens as if the generalized ideological use of the word *racism,* with ends of delegitimation, were repeated as an echo and theorized in the discourse of the social sciences from a perspective of social critique. We will retain the paradox of such a consensus on certain characteristics of the antiracist vulgate (which authorizes the indefinite extension of the term's use) between ordinary users of the polemical term and analysts belonging to the scientific community. We may therefore state the consensual definition as follows: there is racism or racialization whenever there is, in the conflictual interaction of the different social categories, a *mode of exclusion* and a *biological* (or "naturalist") *marking* being applied to a category (to what is supposed to constitute one). A functional approach, leading to a critique of society (whatever the theoretical reference may be), distinguishes three fundamental elements in racism: *othering* or racized categories (but racialization would begin with categorization), *biologization* (an attribution of "biological" stigmata), and *oppression* lived by the victims right up to the interiorization of the racistoid mental forms.[18] The requisite of such an approach may be deemed hardly satisfying: it fits in with the identity of treatment of the various categories of those excluded/biologized/oppressed, identified equally, indeed without distinction, as *victims* of racism (or of specific racializations). It is henceforth difficult to avoid engendering what may appear as a combination borrowed from ideological functionings that we nonetheless choose to undo: the effect of a lack of distinction among the various objects of hate, among the various categories of victim. As if all the categories of the excluded, as the excluded, came under one genre: classes = sexes = races = socioprofessional categories = categories of marginals = minority groups (religious, political, and so on) = classes of age = oppressed nations or ethnic groups — and so on.

Next we must bring out the two presuppositions of such an approach, whose Manichaean simplism recasts scientific analysis in the field of ideological debates:

- The racizers are the dominators, the oppressors, even the exploiters or "genocidal ones." Such analyses work with pairs of opposites that themselves function in ideological life: dominant (dominant group, dominant class, and so on)/dominated, majoritarian/minoritarian.

- The racized (the oppressed and excluded) are innocent victims; at least the responsibility for the exclusion should in no way (nor to any degree) encumber them.

The racized is by definition not responsible, and here there is a risk that she is understood to be irresponsible. The affective disposition that such analyses both presuppose and confirm, or reinforce, is compassion, whether the latter becomes sympathy and active pity or empathy moved by guilt with respect to the victims. Compassion may take the form of behaviors of solidarity, actions in defense of rights (or for the acquisition of new rights); it may go toward the legitimation of behaviors of self-defense on the part of racized groups (groups perceived as such).

This task of critical theorization thus engenders a conversion of values: the racized group, as such, is the object of an unconditional positive valorization, and it tends to be idealized and sublimated (the purity of absolute innocence). The explanation Delacampagne has sketched — he was followed on this point by many other authors during the 1980s[19] — is based on the existence of the West's feeling of guilt. If what has appeared as "the capital sin"[20] since 1945 is a defining characteristic of the West, if racism is the "absolute evil" of contemporary westerners, and if our bad conscience postulates its existence everywhere and in everyone, then we will no longer be surprised at the indefinite flight forward in the process of denunciation, unmasking, driving out. The philosophy of suspicion (Nietzsche, Marx, Freud) is only the speculative tip of the ideology of suspicion, which is governed by the amoral categorical imperative of tracking and tracking down, hunting, unveiling, denouncing, demystifying, surprising, spotting, and identifying what is most hidden. Racism itself is assumed to lead an obscure existence and to uncoil its condemnable effects from hidden places — whence the appearance of the intellectual who specializes in hunting for racists. For this ideological mercenary, the philosophy of suspicion is the only possible philosophy: an accomplished nihilist, this hunter of ideological premiums has the goal of piercing the secrets, bringing into the full light of day, before everyone's eyes, latent, veiled racism, what is implicit about racism. This is the postulate of antiracist conviction of the militant decoder: racism is all the more real and harmful when it is imperceptible, when it is a matter of the unsaid, when it is nested in the depths of the shameful, the one presumed reason of the unsayable. Thus "racists," in the world marked by Auschwitz, play the role of new witches: they incarnate the new type of heretics to be hated absolutely, required by democratic consensus. It is necessary that an enemy who incarnates absolute evil be posited outside the consensual circle so that the latter may legitimate itself. "Racism's" only serious competitors, in the political imaginary of the 1980s, are "totalitarianism" (or "communism") and, a latecomer, "terrorism."[21]

## Scholarly Description
### The Theory of the Three Levels of Heterophobia

It is not without theoretical benefit to distinguish, following certain contemporary studies, three levels of use of the categorizing term *racism*. We thus isolate three registers on which the discourse called racist is deployed, which correspond to three modes of racialization. A synthetic exposition of these various attempts at clarification will show how much the initial definitional difficulties tend to multiply in the critical metadiscourses that propose to surmount them. The identification of the recurrent paradoxes — as if they could not be eliminated, in that they would be engendered by the ordinary problematic of "racism" — to us seems to be a theoretical objective worthy of our study. A scale of heterophobic prejudices may thus be elaborated, in view of the degree of distancing of the empirically verifiable references — from malevolent "realism" to accusatory "delirium," from "commonsense" belief to "murderous madness."

*"Primary Racism" and Ethical Antiracism.* Primary racism,[22] or "otherism," the supposed foundation of "heterophobia,"[23] otherwise denominated as "panekhthrism"[24] — from the Greek *ekhthros,* "enemy" — would designate a very general psychosocial phenomenon, and perhaps a universal reaction: the feeling of distrust toward the Other or any stranger whatever, the "spontaneous" perception of the unknown Other as an enemy, unleashing flight or aggression.[25] This encyclopedic sort of description, bearing on states of things in the world — here the subclass of living beings reacting in a certain manner, what ethology is supposed to establish scientifically — entails information on behaviors susceptible of manifesting themselves discursively through statements we will call more "spontaneous" or "immediate" among those who disparage the Other as such. Certain expressly "antiracist" presentations thematize this prime hypothetical phobia, a species of Rousseauist "conjecture" on origins, as an instinctual foundation, a "basis," a "primitive reaction" of "hatred," a natural melody on which history and its avatars would come to improvise diverse variations, more or less elaborated. Pierre Paraf, an antiracist militant and a "committed" writer, does not hesitate to present the sketch of a naturalist theory of racism as spontaneous, universal, and immemorial hostility: "History has revealed to us the complexity of the problem: *at the root, the instinctive hate* of the man of the clan for those who are near or far, but different from and weaker than him. This reaction has been affirmed for millennia against the foreigner."[26]

The argument is developed through the definition of a criterion concerning the reception of the accounts of "primary racism," through reference to a scale of verisimilitude. In the terminology proposed by Gavin I. Langmuir, affirmations on "the Jews" are called "realist" or "empirically well founded" so that they may "attract attention to certain aspects of the real behavior of Jews."[27] It would be less equivocal to characterize such affirmations by the high degree of *verisimilitude* that they represent. For once one isolates a "realist" level of racizing enunciation, one accords it a certain legitimacy; one distinguishes degrees of acceptability parallel to the discerned stages of realism — by speaking of "more or less" realistic statements, for example. Thus Maxime Rodinson can affirm that, in European anti-Semitism, "the anti-Semitic myth is founded either on accusations without the shadow of a foundation, or on the results of a situation that has been *imposed* on the Jews."[28] The foregoing runs the risk of being thus paraphrased:

anti-Semitism is either ungrounded (in the historical reality in question) or relatively grounded. An essential concession.... It is thus that to such a class of "realistic" statements (according to Langmuir), the discursive referent of the conceptualizing designation "primary racism," there would correspond a high degree of verisimilitude due to an effect of empirical foundation, to a possible observation reference. Here is a classic example, in which abusive generalization is already at work: "Jews are most often merchants or intellectuals."[29] Statements of this type are not necessarily perceptible as blaming a definite human group. But, for the very reason of their effect of descriptive neutrality, they constitute the best conductors of implicit racialization.

We may note that the marking off of this first level is scientifically authorized by a discourse of the Darwinian tradition, which leads to recognizing an instinctual (or genetic) basis for the following pair: preferential self-defense and mutual aid reserved for the members of the group of belonging — rejection of the individual who is foreign to the proper group. The scientific legitimation of this pair, besides that it derives from a selectionist paradigm, is part of the professional ideology of naturalists of strict Darwinian obedience[30] — the ethology of Konrad Lorenz, the sociobiology of Edward O. Wilson.[31] Henceforth, "racial prejudice" — xenophobia and racial discrimination — may be presented as a bioanthropological universal. Thus the sociobiologist William D. Hamilton (Wilson's "precursor") posits the following hypothesis:

> I hope to produce evidence that some things which are often treated as purely cultural in man — say racial discrimination — have deep roots in our animal past and thus are quite likely to rest on direct genetic foundations. To be more specific, it is suggested that the ease and accuracy with which an idea like xenophobia strikes the next replica of itself on the template of human memory may depend on the preparation made for it there by selection — selection acting, ultimately, at the level of replicating molecules.[32]

But the idea that individuals belonging to a given cultural group proceed to their choices according to a self-centered scale of values is shared by authors whose problematics are quite heterogeneous: these range from nationalist xenophobic doctrines[33] to a universalist perspective nuanced by a certain relativism of "good sense,"[34] by way of ethologist biopolitics.[35] The praise of sociocentrism, as the "natural" tendency for a group to identify itself with the whole of humanity, occurs equally in the lexicons of race, the nation, and culture.[36]

Each of the terminological propositions inventoried presents its own theoretical difficulties. Thus Albert Memmi proposes to reserve the use of the word *racism* to "biological exclusion" and to resort to the word *heterophobia* to designate any form of phobia of the Other in *his* differences, any phobia "that is transformed into a refusal of the other and leads to aggressiveness."[37] But the terminological confusion is not for all that overcome: the racism of colonial exploitation, for example, is in no way based on the "refusal of the other" or on her "exclusion," but on her subjection in view of a profit in the name of a number of rationalizations, variations on the duty of "civilizing" inferior or primitive peoples. The racialization implicated by the colonial form of one imperialism or another is a matter not of aggressive hostility but rather of a specific system of exploitation.

The concept of "panekhthrism" is also not free of ambiguity. Maxime Rodinson introduced it in this way: "A unity of intention and direction in all concrete forms of hostility is assumed.... It is a process parallel to the one represented by paranoia in individual psychology."[38] Such a definition of panekhthrism, referring to a certain ideological elaboration of perceived hostility (the myth of a global conspiracy), spans the two extreme levels, the inferior and the superior, of racism ("primary" and "tertiary" racism) — that is to say the theoretical difficulties that show through in the terminological paradoxes. Let us return to the statement, "Jews are most often merchants or intellectuals." How do we assure ourselves that it derives from primary racism? One of the criteria of taxinomic gauging is that the statement may be proffered and/or taken up by any enunciator of a referenced group (one Jew out of "the Jews"). Such a condition is of course questionable, referring to thorny problems of reflexivity and borders. We know that the problem has been posed, for modern anti-Semitism, in the too simple terms of "self-hatred" *(Selbsthaß)*: a racized person may with perfection speak the language of the racizer, and anti-Jewish discourse, for example, does not in the least bar its assumption by a supposedly "Jewish" enunciator — whether he mistakes this about himself, rejects his religious affiliation, presents and comes to terms with himself as being of Jewish origin or association but as having no religious allegiance, or expressly adheres to Judaism as a religion.[39] It follows that the criterion of acceptability, for a representative of a group targeted by the act of identifying-disparaging reference, is hardly convincing.

*Can One Struggle? How?* If we postulate that the Darwinian problematic is theoretically satisfying, two distinct positions appear in the face of "primary" racism: on the one hand, a certain antiracist pessimism, manifested by the unhappy consciousness of the ideologue persuaded of the existence of universal "racist" guilt; on the other hand, the antiracist optimism of those who believe that they read in the Darwinian conceptuality, if not in the writings visible to the common eye, the foundations of a surpassing of the doctrine of fighting and of "selection by death." The pessimists, convinced of the insurmountability of the drives to combat and exclusion, appeal to a radical rejection of human nature, the latter "Darwinian"; as for the optimists, they see no necessary rupture at all in the natural processes, the latter having in themselves what it takes to convert to moral behaviors. We will begin by examining several assumed implications of Darwinian theory in the ethical and political orders, before presenting the two dominant antiracist positions: the antinaturalist ethic of the pessimists and the naturalist ethic of the pro-Darwinian optimists.

Let us start with the simple hypothesis that the conditions of antiracist struggle are determined, at least partially, by the antiracist conception of racism. "All these manifestations of racism and anti-Semitism require from us a permanent vigilance and a systematic education so as to uncover *'the beast' that sleeps in each of us* and to learn together to combat it."[40] Thus speaks the pessimist antiracist as a matter of course, she who postulates that "we are all racists," that this racism belonging to human nature results from an innate genetic nucleus (phylogenetically acquired or not) or from the inheritance of an original flaw — with versions from Christian theology or from neo-religious psychoanalysis: "Racism is anchored in the unconscious."[41] This pessimism, linked to a conception of racism as a fateful attitude or behavior, results in the corruption of the principle of antiracist wakefulness or vigilance in permanent guilt, in generalized suspicion, as much with respect to oneself as to others. One's neighbor is the potential racist: suspicion establishes a nightmare world by making racism into a destiny that, in the best of cases, is a matter of individual therapeutics. (The irresponsible victims, those sick persons incapable of controlling their racist drives as normal subjects do, must go to see someone.)

It would be an illusion linked to the demonization of the ideological adversary to attribute the thesis of the universality or the "primariness" of racism to racists alone or, for example, to the sociobiologists whose theory would contain, in the virtual or latent state, a genetic legitimation of racism. Sociobiology "leads to" or "results in" consequences judged to be absolutely undesirable, summarized and characterized by "racism": such is the normal polemical manner of delegitimating sociobiology, by criminalizing it — the imputation of "racism" suggesting that of "genocide." Hence Pierre Thuillier declares, basically without nuances, despite certain rhetorical precautions:

> Wilson, it is certain, is not a partisan of racism; his ideas are "liberal." But he elaborated a theory that may favor and legitimate certain forms of racism. If the purpose of life is to ensure the propagation of genes, it might well occur that the carriers of certain genes decide to eliminate the populations that carry other genes.... Here we again find the Darwinian theme of the "struggle for life." In the nineteenth century, it served to justify war and competition in the extreme. In the logic of sociobiology, ideas of the same kind are likely to appear. And it is even truer that Wilson strongly suggests that xenophobia has a genetic basis — in a few words, that racism is "normal."[42]

According to the same logic of lumping together, by the reduction of the meaning of a theory to undesirable effects imputed to it as ineluctable, a journalist believed he could declare, in the fall of 1979, "All or almost all has been said about the segregationist racism *that results from the sociobiology of the New Right.*"[43] Let us pass through the journalistic ritual illusion concerning the definitive treatment of the problem: a prolonged campaign, or a proclaimed "case closed," engenders the quite professional conviction that "everything, or almost everything, has been said" on the question at issue. What we must especially note is that Julien Brunn, in a phrase, combines a *petitio principii* with a factual error. Indeed one should first of all show, precisely, in what way sociobiology — and what an example! — must necessarily (logically, even fatefully) "result" in "segregationist racism":[44] this is by no means done. One should then avoid attributing to "the New Right" in general, taken as a homogeneous ideologico-institutional entity (the first confusion, the principle of polemical lumping together), a theory or a doctrine that, for example, the top thinker of the GRECE,⁴⁵ Alain de Benoist, has expressly criticized and impugned in many respects.⁴⁶ Rather than renewing stereotypes and hasty likenings, at issue would be recognizing various tendencies and positions, at the very heart of the GRECE, on the question of sociobiology: such a differentiating analysis would show the ideological heterogeneity of the historical matrix of "New Rights" in France (among them the GRECE) with the exception of a single theme, absolute antiliberalism (or antieconomism). Yves Christen, for example, is not only a good vulgarizer of Wilsonian sociobiology but also one of its heated partisans:⁴⁷ his positions should not be likened to those of Alain de Benoist. The divergences in sociobiology are again met within the broader field of "New Rights," neoliberals (the Club de l'Horloge), or antiliberals (the GRECE): the common theme, and the differentiating criterion, could be the proximity or even the kinship between these conceptions of radical economic liberalism and sociobiological analyses (competition, maximization of profit, individual interest identified as genetic interest, and so on). That is why the economic liberalism of the Club de l'Horloge is quite well accommodated with biopolitical, biosocial, and bioethical foundations borrowed from Lorenzian ethology or Wilsonian sociobiology.⁴⁸

But the same postulate of universality is also too often joined with antiracist proposals that are as vague as they are bland. At the UNESCO conference in Athens, March 30–April 3, 1981, Habib Tawa did not hesitate to affirm that "the existence of racist prejudices is a universal given and [that], from one civilization to another, even from one country or region to another, the popular sayings cast the same reproaches at one another.... It is on this basis of primary xenophobia that collective or individual racism, of peoples or of persons, gains strength or withers."⁴⁹ Tawa postulates, on the one hand, the universality of primary racism, which he identifies with xenophobia; on the other hand, the existence of a continuity between xenophobia and elaborated racism.⁵⁰ It follows, he says, that antiracism must oppose itself to racism on an identical drive-oriented basis, in somewhat astonishing fashion: "It is on an analogous basis of human solidarity that good sense, just as popular, invites tolerance and fraternity. From Kong Fu Tseu (Confucius) to Jesus Christ, great minds have proclaimed it."⁵¹ All that remains is to oppose ritually "the universalist humanism of science" to the "sacred egoism of a few,"⁵² to hold up as a normative model the "absence of intellectual prejudices" that marks scientific analysis, in order to stigmatize the "racist societies of narrow and forced appearance" and to celebrate "progressive and pluralist society."[53] Who would not agree? The character of such proposals, as confused as it is flat, gives a certain idea of the "diplomatic" antiracism of international conferences on the question of racism.

It was enough for us to note the appearance of the evidence that racism is a universal disposition. It seems that the principal intellectual origin of such ideological evidence may be discerned in the vulgarization of Darwinism: on the basis of a hypothesis of Darwinian style, that a survival value is attached to the fear of the unknown or to the rejection of the different, one tends to set up as a functional mechanism the universal hostility in the face of the Other, the unknown, the stranger, whose appearance would necessarily entail flight or aggression. There are many recognized antiracist authors who base their analyses on this axiom, which has been thematized as a slogan: "Difference instills fear";[54] "the truth is that there is fear of what is not understood, of the unknown, therefore of differences.... I suppose that that comes from the history of the species: the unknown may be a source of danger."[55] The half-truths of common sense thereby simply become truths; the all-purpose explanations are converted, by the accommodating echo of the text, into scientific truths.

Following Gordon W. Allport, we may identify six types of behavior that involve the rejection of "out-groups" and hence define five degrees of "racial discrimination" in the broad sense, from the least intense to the most violent:

1. *Verbal rejection,* or antilocution: this involves the hostility manifested by insult or joke, inscribed in the modes of verbalization of "prejudices." "Most people who have prejudices talk about them. With like-minded friends, occasionally with strangers, they may express their antagonism freely."[56]

2. *Avoidance:* "If the prejudice is more intense, it leads the individual to avoid members of the disliked group, even perhaps at the cost of considerable inconvenience. In this case, the bearer of prejudice does not directly inflict harm upon the group he dislikes. He takes the burden of accommodation and withdrawal upon himself."[57]

3. *Discrimination* in the strict sense: the first act is to refuse to accord a person or a group of persons, for reasons of their ethnic background, treatment equal to that given the dominant group or groups:

Here the prejudiced person makes detrimental distinctions of an active sort. He undertakes to exclude all members of the group in question from certain types of employment, from residential housing, political rights, educational or recreational opportunities, churches, hospitals, or from some other social privileges. Segregation is an institutionalized form of discrimination, enforced legally or by common custom.[58]

Apartheid is the extreme example of this.

4. *Physical attack:* all forms of violence against persons and belongings, insofar as they are exercised for reasons of the ethnic background of the individuals. "Under conditions of heightened emotion prejudice may lead to acts of violence or semiviolence. An unwanted Negro family may be forcibly ejected from a neighborhood, or so severely threatened that it leaves in fear. Gravestones in Jewish cemeteries may be desecrated. The Northside's Italian gang may lie in wait for the Southside's Irish gang."[59]

5. *Extermination:* "Lynchings, pogroms, massacres, and the Hitlerian program of genocide mark the ultimate degree of violent expression of prejudice."[60]

Next Allport simplifies this scale of intensity, reducing the five degrees of exclusion or rejection to three:[61]

1. Verbal rejection.

2. Discrimination, which includes segregation. Allport feels he should be precise: "We often separate ourselves from people whom we find uncongenial. It is not discrimination when we do so, so long as it is *we* who move away from them. *Discrimination comes about only when we deny to individuals or groups of people equality of treatment which they may wish.*"[62] As for segregation, the definition is "a form of discrimination that sets up spatial boundaries of some sort to accentuate the disadvantage of members of an out-group."[63]

3. Physical attack, in all degrees of intensity, from "riot" to genocide.[64]

Allport's theorization possesses an undeniable descriptive value and presents numerous theoretical difficulties that we cannot consider here. We will content ourselves with looking at one of his postulates, whose place is in a naturalist conception of prejudice linked to a continuist or monist vision of the five (or three) degrees of intensity of rejection. On the one hand, Allport advances that "man has a propensity to prejudice" and that this propensity "lies in his normal and natural tendency to form generalizations, concepts, categories, whose content represents an oversimplification of his world of experience."⁶⁵ On the other hand, he assumes that "words betraying antagonism come easily"⁶⁶ and especially that verbal rejection and discriminatory practices are necessary conditions for any racist aggression. He thereby postulates a link between hostile opinions or attitudes (the first three degrees) and the forms of passing to the act (the last two degrees): "Violence is always an outgrowth of milder states of mind. Although most barking (antilocution) does not lead to biting, yet there is never a bite without previous barking."⁶⁷ Translated into ordinary language: the penchant for racist murder is present in each of us; the genocidal drive is natural in humanity, as it is already at work in prejudices (hate-prejudices), which arise spontaneously in the world of humanity's common experience.

We have briefly characterized the pessimistic, neo-Christian ("We are all guilty of racism") or para-Freudian ("We all have a racist unconscious and racist drives") variants, as well as the humanitarianist or wavering variant. Dualist antiracism is constituted around the idea that to be a human being worthy of the name implies that one struggles against oneself, engages in hand-to-hand combat, at every moment, with the "vile beast" crouching in each of us. To be antiracist is to be truly human, to refuse the animality that represents a natural component of human nature. But this ethical solution that extols the denaturing of humanity is not the only one. It is close to a naturalist solution, founded on some of Darwin's notations. This one has been most strongly formulated recently by Patrick Tort, on the basis of what he has called "evolution's effect of reversal," the mainspring of this antiracist extension of the Darwinian morality of sympathy.⁶⁸ In *The Descent of Man* (1871), Darwin thus poses the problem of a morality that would not be distinguishable from evolution and that consequently would not be opposed to it:

> As man advances in civilization, and small tribes are united into larger communities, the simplest reason would tell each individual that he ought to extend his social instincts and sympathies to all the members of the same nation, though personally unknown to him. This point being once reached, there is only an artificial barrier to prevent his sympathies extending to the men of all nations and races.... Sympathy beyond the confines of man, that is, humanity to the lower animals, seems to be one of the latest moral

acquisitions.... This virtue, one of the noblest with which man is endowed, seems to arise incidentally from our sympathies being more tender and more widely diffused, until they are extended to all sentient beings. As soon as this virtue is honored and practiced by some few men, it spreads through instruction and example to the young, and eventually becomes incorporated in public opinion.[69]

Patrick Tort rightly remarks that "the broadening of *sympathy*, a consequence of the *advancement of civilization,* which is in turn a consequence of evolution — that is, of the selection of *useful* behaviors — is a *fact of reason, and therefore of nature.*"[70] The moral feeling is therefore an effect of selective evolution, which seems to contradict natural selection: "We [could not] check our sympathy, even at the urging of hard reason, without deterioration in the noblest part of our nature."[71] Tort furnishes an enlightening conceptualization of this strange inversion of the law of natural selection achieved in and by the universal extension of sympathy: "*The effect of reversal* produced by civilization, even though it is a consequence of selection, ends up contradicting the laws of the latter in the field of nature."[72] By favoring the indefinite increase of the social instincts, for which sympathy provides the model, natural selection has thus progressively selected its opposite, civilization, which rests "on the *selection of antiselective behaviors.*"[73] Through such an effect of reversal,

> *civilization* appears *naturally* as the state at the heart of which selection demonstrates that it has, without for an instant having ceased to act selectively, *progressively reversed itself,* to favor, instead of the extermination of the weak, behaviors of aid and assistance toward the least capable; instead of the decline of those least armed for struggle, their rehabilitation through compensatory technologies...; instead of the eternalization of natural hierarchies, sympathetic assimilation; and instead of egoism, solidarity.[74]

By privileging some of Darwin's notations in this way, by treating them as principles of a universalist morality of sympathy, Tort triumphs in finding the author of *The Origin of Species* innocent of the capital sins of "racism," "social Darwinism," or "eugenicism," even of any rightist position.[75] Darwin becomes the partisan of a kind of ethics of universal fraternal solidarity; and the "social Darwinists," those partisans of fierce competition, of the law of "tooth and nail," become false disciples of the master. We must of course recognize that there may be found in Darwin's text the theoretical bases of a naturalist antiracism, bearing relation to a transcendence, to a super- or supranatural rejection of racism. But we must also recognize that here there is just one possible morality among all those for which Darwinian conceptions may be called on.[76] The direction of the extension of sympathy is neither more nor less orthodox than the direction of the improvement of the biological quality of the population and of the struggle against all forms of degeneracy.[77] The theory of evolution by natural selection authorizes just as much a humanitarianist morality of the effect of reversal as it does a moral of the indefinite pursuit of the struggle for life (the "gladiatorial theory of existence," as Thomas Huxley termed it)[78] or a bioethics of eugenic obedience, which proposes to invent and politically apply substitutes for natural selection in society (to substitute directed and mastered, eugenic social selections for the blind social counterselections, engendering a dysgenic evolution).[79] Such is the ambiguity of "moral progress" as it may be interpreted according to *The Descent of Man*, an equivocal text that sketches at least three possible orientations: growing sympathy and fraternity, interindividual competition and struggle for life (social Darwinism), and voluntary social selections (eugenicism). Extending mutual aid and solidarity, extolling the laissez-faire attitude and promoting competition, mastering human evolution: three directions that diverge radically but that are presented together in Darwin's text.

There is one other critical consideration that may be applied to the "Darwinian" morality of extensive sympathy and of the predominance of "social instincts." It is in the force of such an autonomy from a transcendent principle that evolutionist morality encounters its limits and its central weakness: this morality is in fact grounded on the postulate that what is given in and by evolution (or natural selection, including the effect of reversal) is morally "good," without the possibility of justifying such an evaluation[80] except by circular reasoning (the product of evolution is morally good because it is a product of evolution) or by an appeal to common sense and its "truths" (the extension of sympathy and altruism are worth more than the pursuit of the struggle for existence and selection by death). The integral biological morality of Konrad Lorenz presents the same characteristics: rationalist immanentism with regard to foundations, the universal law of love and friendship with regard to practical maxims. It is the transition from the innate system of the "great instincts" (hunger, fear, love, territory), indissociable from the law of selection, to a universalist ethics of brotherly love that poses a problem.[81] In more general terms: any naturalist morality is presented as formed through a deduction from scientific statements bearing on the real; it presupposes that the system of knowledge suffices to ground the system of values and norms. Such a scientism is not thereby hindered from turning into a prophetism: Western biologists, since Darwin, have imperceptibly transformed their imperial tendency to resorb the entire field of the human and social sciences into the power to reveal the true, to state meaning, to predict the future (as it will be and as it must be).

*Ethical Antiracism.* Now we can directly take on the position of the pessimist antiracists, whose basic conviction is that one cannot and will never be able to have confidence in human nature.

The antiracist struggle, in this naturalistic and pessimistic problematic, may be defined only as an ethical movement against human nature — a supposedly fixed and eternal nature — or as a reaction against nature. The dogmatically naturalistic perspective is hence reversed to become an antinaturalist position, once it has tried to ground the rejection of racism as a tendency inscribed in a presumed ground of drives. Questioned on the unanimous "great antiracist leap" that followed the incident on the Rue Copernic (October 1980), Vercors[82] refused any display of optimism that was not based in heroism of the will: "Racism is deeply ingrained in living species, and antiracism is what isn't natural. The beaked dolphin pursues the humpback dolphin. Man doesn't escape this instinct deeply ingrained in his genes, and only through thought, through will, may he overcome it.... It is an ongoing struggle. But it is the nobility of the human species to wage this combat and to wage it without hope — I mean, with successive victories but also with successive relapses."[83] The naturalization of racism logically leads to the imperative of an endless struggle of the mind against nature, inside us and outside us: the inchoateness of antiracism, an endless task, responds to natural, infernal repetitiveness.

Such is the presentation of ethical antiracism, according to its three constitutive moments: the naturalization of racism, the pessimism of intelligence, the heroism of the will. Antiracism is henceforth opposed to racism as the norm to the fact, as what ought be to what is, as what ought to be done to the spontaneous inclination. This occurs in such a way that humanity, to make itself human, must denature itself, make an effort to lose its fondness for the animal kingdom from which it inherits its first racist nature. For example, Vercors proposes to show schoolchildren that "racism is the very contradiction of what ought to be human."[84] But if one must always struggle against racism, it is the case that it constitutes an a priori determination of human nature, as the universal and necessary inclination that could not be destroyed once and for all without abolishing humanity itself: "Racism is specific to the search for a scapegoat. And it is unfortunately a universal phenomenon. Will we see an end to it? In the long run, in the very long run, racism will finish by disappearing. Perhaps."[85] Let us provide a Kantian translation of this ethical perspective: the human world without racism is a regulative Idea, such that it could not be integrally realized in existing human societies without setting to work a terrorist utopia. The dream of purification would risk provoking the nightmare of purity. Antiracist maximalism could only engender the minimal perverse effect of a "witch-hunt." If the nobility of the mind obligates us to refuse any racist inclination, in ourselves and in others, the modesty of critical reason must guard us from the extravagance of dogmatic antiracism, which acts as if it were possible and desirable to extirpate from the social and human world — here and now, once and for all — all "trace" of racism.

Ethical antiracism defines its task specifically as a long and difficult march, presents it as an authenticating conquest of the humanity of man in his struggle against his persistent animality, always susceptible of rebirth. Ethical antiracism oscillates between the obsession with the rebirth of the Beast in man — "racism" — and the phobia of the natural in man, since racism is supposed to derive from nature, which antiracism strives to reduce, even to eliminate. The antiracist dream par excellence is that of a human world absolutely "denatured," denaturalized, a world of pure culture from which "unfriendly" or polemical drives, tendencies, desires, and passions have disappeared, completely giving way to the peaceable forms of the social bond: mutual aid and solidarity, dialogue and mutual understanding, friendship for all.

The pathetic dialectic of the natural racist and the human antiracist is formulated as follows by Albert Memmi, as the conclusion of an article in which he summarizes his model: "It is racism that is natural and anti-racism that is not; anti-racism can only be something that is acquired, as all that is cultural is acquired."[86] The alliance of a radical pessimism of intelligence with a moderated optimism[87] of the will distinguishes the ethical, scholarly variant of racism from the political variant. The legitimate intellectual could not engage in the same discourse as the one responsible for an agitprop system, whose activist mythology relies on a permanent catastrophism (the diagnosis of the "return of what we saw during period $x$ or $y$") destined to initiate the appeal to "vigilance."

We should not be surprised to note that the interpretation of racism as a natural phenomenon may be found in the tradition of the naturalist theory of races. Georges Vacher de Lapouge thus declares, in the preface to *L'Aryen:* "The conflict of the races openly begins in nations and between nations, and one wonders if the ideas of the fraternity and the equality of men really do not go against the laws of nature. One begins to suspect that sentiments have just a sentimental value, that the evolution of peoples is ruled by inflexible laws."[88] Responding in advance to the imperatives of ethical antiracism are the prescriptions of scientific racism: "The idealist sentimental politics of Christianity has lived its life. To the fictions of Justice, Equality, and Fraternity, scientific politics prefers the reality of Forces, Laws, Races, and Evolution. What misfortune for the peoples who will remain caught up in dreams!"[89]

On the basis of a common axiom bearing on the mixed nature of man, half-angel and half-beast, natural being and supernatural (or even antinatural) being, scientific racism and ethical antiracism are constituted as two systems of values and norms, each the logical inverse of the other. For scientific racism, the ethical prescription is reduced to following the path indicated by evolution, a fact of nature. In the Lapougian perspective of a selectionist monism, at issue is either prolonging natural selection or correcting its "unpleasant consequences." True morality and true politics must agree to achieve one and the same positive end: "To multiply the types accepted as the finest and the best,"[90] to favor the increase of the eugenic. A negative task is thereby implied: to favor the disappearance of inferior elements, the elimination of the dysgenic. Human beings must stop taking themselves for angels. They are only living beings, among others, submitted as such to natural laws: the determinism of race, the law of struggle, the reign of force, and the principle of might.[91]

For ethical antiracism, the central prescription is to favor in man the dominance of the angelic portion over the beastly portion. Albert Memmi bases antiracist morality on a Manichaean conception of human nature: "Humans being what they are, the job can and should be undertaken. People are both angels and beasts; the angel must be assisted in prevailing over the beast."[92] Angelicize man and/or denature him: this is the antiracist task. For racism is postulated as the most natural and spontaneous behavior in the human world,[93] while also the least human of human behaviors. And for the same reasons: racism is both the most natural and the least human behavior because it is the way of ease, of greatest comfort;[94] in short, the behavior "ready to hand." To be antiracist is to the contrary to opt for the difficult way, to choose respect for others, which is "the essence of morality." At stake is "our honor as humans."[95] Ethical aristocracy is thus shrouded in well-conceived antiracism: if the racist is the first to come, the commoner of humanity who is barely human, the antiracist is the nobility of humanity, the salt of the human earth. The implicit conclusion of such a self-grounding argument is never stated, and with good reason: for antiracism presupposes a hierarchical conception of the human world, with the superior beings (the individuals endowed with a higher degree of humanity) represented by the antiracists and the inferior beings by the racists, endowed with the least humanity, close to the animal kingdom. Hence antiracism implies an internal contradiction: it presupposes an inegalitarian doctrine of humanity, which ends up contradicting the proclaimed egalitarian ideals.

But why should we bet on nature rather than on antinature, and vice versa? Why should we take the side, with antiracism, of the angel against that of the beast, if we are angels and beasts and if the muzzle of the beast awaits the one who tries too hard to be an angel? We have an antinomy of value systems: the choice of one axiology over the other can be justified only at the very core of the chosen axiology. There is an unsurpassable circularity of the values that dispose us to choose one system of values and the one we are in. There is no third term that could take the form of a universal, rationally based axiology, with the capacity to guide our faculty of choosing in total security and in exclusive fashion.

*"Secondary Racism" and Rationalist Antiracism.* "Secondary racism" assumes an ideological makeshift that bears on the materials (affective, discursive, and notional) given by "otherism." André Langaney defines it as follows: "A rationalization of primary racism in the name of arguments stemming from economic or political competition

among human groups,... a convenient means of reorienting aggressiveness."[96] This first elaboration of the heterophobic reaction, made explicit in discourse especially as a rationalization of "residues" (in Pareto's sense: displays of the feelings or the instincts), corresponds to what one designates, in ordinary language, by the terms *xenophobia* or *chauvinism* and, in scholarly metalanguage, by the term *ethnocentrism*. But the designated psychosocial phenomenon may be correctly characterized only by the pair ethnocentrism/xenophobia, which refers to two sides of the same process: closing in on oneself, exclusion of others. Such a process is analyzed as assuming an act of historical reference (fictional or verifiable) accompanied by the so-called sophism of abusive generalization implicated by statements such as "Jews all stick together" and "Jews are miserly."[97] The sophism of abusive generalization quite often appears in the form of the sophism of the accident, which especially consists of moving from what is relatively true to what is absolutely true in order to form the conclusion. Hence, from the statement "Some Jews are miserly," one moves to the statement "Jews are miserly," that is, from an accidental to an essential one.[98] The examples we have mentioned illustrate what may be called ordinary Judeophobia, the set of attitudes verbalized or of opinions set by discursive stereotypes that form a subcategory of "ordinary racism," which is manifested without explicit recourse to a self-legitimation at the heart of a determined and accepted ideology. Such convictions by themselves achieve justifications of past, present, or future practices. A statement of constative appearance, such as "The Jews killed Christ," by way of generalizing typification ("the Jews") and the effect of realism engendered by the historical reference presupposed, by its very force accomplishes a justification of any act directed against the Jews taken as a group, whether it involves authorizing an attack or rationalizing it after the fact.[99] In no way is there an implication of the too strong hypothesis that the act necessarily derives from the opinion expressed (see chapter 5, pp. 160–61).

Ethnocentrism is most often presented as a "universal attitude," coextensive with all of humanity, as the tendency of any social group to believe itself better than others: the only true humans, the excellent ones, the perfect ones.[100] This valorization of oneself is in general understood, in a functionalist perspective, as a condition of self-preservation of the group: a condition of the cohesion and permanency of the group, assuming in this perspective a relative exclusion of others (individuals or groups), would be a certain impermeability to the systems of values and beliefs of outside groups.

The later synthetic formulations of Claude Lévi-Strauss should be cited here, for their exemplarity and for the minimal equivocation they display. The first question concerns the border between racism and ethnocentric attitudes:

> People tend more and more to confuse racism in the strict sense of the term with attitudes that are normal, even legitimate, and in any case unavoidable. Racism is a doctrine that claims to see the mental and moral characteristics of a group of individuals (however the group may be defined) as the necessary effect of a common genetic heritage. One cannot put in the same category, or impute automatically to the same prejudice, the attitude held by individuals or groups that their loyalty to certain values makes them partially or totally insensitive to other values.... Such relative incommunicability... may even be the price to be paid so that the systems of values of each spiritual family or each community are preserved and find within themselves the resources necessary for their renewal.[101]

The condition of cultural diversity is therefore the relative enclosure within itself of every culture, a sociocentrism that implies a certain dose of xenophobia: "To a large extent, this diversity results from the desire of each culture to resist the cultures surrounding it, to distinguish itself from them — in short, to be itself."[102] If therefore a certain "intolerance,"[103] a certain mutual "deafness,"[104] or a certain impermeability[105] represents the price to be paid to assure that intercultural differences are maintained, there must be a denunciation of the common confusion between racism, "a false, but explicit theory,"[106] and what the ethnologist characterizes as "common inclinations and attitudes from which it would be illusory to imagine that humanity can one day free itself or even that it will care to do so."[107] In short, Lévi-Strauss's legitimation of ethnocentric-xenophobic attitudes is presented as both a naturalization of heterophobia on the cognitive level and a particularization of ethics, reduced to a system of values and norms centered on the self-preservation of a group. It follows that Lévi-Strauss can conceive the forms of interethnic hatred — of the affective attitude of war — only as a corruption of the legitimate self-preferential attitude of each group, a deviation through excess or exacerbation of a natural system of attitudes and inclinations: "Since these inclinations and attitudes are in some degree consubstantial with our species, we have no right to deny that they play a part in our history: always inevitable, often fruitful, and even dangerous when exacerbated."[108]

The argument that consists of resorting to the factual universality of the xenophobic sociocentric attitude in order to legitimate the latter characterizes the spontaneous political philosophy of the culturalist and structuralist schools of ethnology, whose professional ideology involves the norm of absolute respect for the ways of being, thinking, and doing of the studied cultures. The differentialist conservatism of the ethnologists tends to interpret factual universality as a necessity: universal "prejudice," such as ethnocentric prejudice, is worthy of respect for the fact that, as universal, it cannot have the function of enabling the survival of distinct cultural forms. And what is necessary is in turn interpreted as desirable or preferable. If every cultural entity tends to persevere in its being, and must persevere in its differential being, and if ethnocentric/xenophobic prejudice is the minimum safety belt of each cultural identity, then one must rehabilitate the prejudice against the hypercritical attitude of the moderns — for this attitude aims to destroy every society's systems of self-representation, that is, to suppress its primary conditions of self-conservation.

But one may still recognize the universality or the naturalness of ethnocentric/xenophobic prejudice without for all that affirming its necessity or, a fortiori, its desirability. In 1894, Bernard Lazare thus remarked on anti- and philo-Semitism: "The ethnologic prejudice is universal, and those who suffer from it are its most tenacious upholders. Antisemites and philosemites join hands to defend the same doctrines, they part company only when it comes to award the supremacy."[109] In the historicist perspective, mixed with the progressive and revolutionary faith that he maintained, Lazare accords by hypothesis a functional, historically situated value to "exclusivism" or to "national egotism": "Having come to a certain stage of development, primitive societies were in favor of isolation, exclusivism, mutual hatred; as national characters were being formed, they avoided any shock, any alteration, and exclusivism was perhaps necessary for a certain time to the constitution of types."[110]

But Lazare does not think according to the norms of the cultural relativism of twentieth-century ethnologists. If there is, as he believes, progress in history, then exclusivism and "ethnological prejudice," which have had their hour of necessity, must henceforth disappear.

But they remain, and this is typical of a relic or a passing regression, a nuisance that can be only provisional:

> Today, exclusivism or national egotism is manifested in the same way, and it is still just as much alive as the family egotism of which it is but an extension; one may even state that, by a sort of regression, it is currently [in 1894] affirmed more forcefully. Every people seems to want to erect around itself a Great Wall of China, one speaks of preserving the national patrimony, the national soul, the national spirit.... Immigration is opposed, foreigners are even expelled when their number becomes too great, they are regarded as a danger for national culture, which they modify; it is not noted that here is found a condition of life for this very culture.[111]

Hence, on the basis of the same recognition of the universality of ethnocentric/xenophobic prejudice, the partisan of progressive evolution will opt for the necessary and desirable suppression of "exclusivisms," whereas the partisan of relativism or cultural differentialism will advocate the preservation of intercultural "impermeabilities."

Ethnocentrism, for certain authors based "on a refusal of differences and a feeling of distrust toward the other,"[112] involves xenophobia in that "the Other" is perceived as foreign, even as a "potential enemy."[113] Xenophobic sociocentrism appears as a variant of panekhthrism. The boundary between primary and secondary racism henceforth tends to disappear.

Ethnocentrism is deliberately presented as leading to hatred or the designation of scapegoat victims, in the final analysis on a deterministic ground (that of a more or less explicit Marxism) through socioeconomic factors. Anthropobiologist Jean Hiernaux thus declares:

> There exists in man a general tendency toward ethnocentrism, which is easily transformed into a sort of feeling of superiority. This may go to the point where societies seek scapegoats among all those who present a certain form of alterity, political, religious, or social, in order to project onto them the causes of everything that is not going well. The hate for foreigners is a good executory for all the social tensions that may exist in a country.[114]

In the problematic of the class struggle, "racial prejudice" appears as both a symptom and a means of diversion; it is defined as an ideological veil and an instrument of legitimation to which the dominant and exploiting class resorts.[115] Such is the most ordinarily received representation of ethnocentrism in the antiracist circles of militant biologists.

This brief look at the representations of "racial prejudice" and the exploration of the reasons put forth as the basis of the distinction between the two levels of preideological racism show a wavering between two explanatory systems: (1) "Racial prejudice" is grounded in "a general tendency" of human nature and forms something like an instinctual a priori, the object of a general anthropology. (2) "Racial prejudice" is engendered in history by a mechanism of domination and economic exploitation. Most of the authors (such as Hiernaux) propose syncretic versions, mixing anthropological and socioeconomic theory, the latter privileging exploitation, of "racial prejudice."

It will also be noticed that the practical conclusion of ethnocentrism thereby defined is not necessarily attack, persecution, exclusion, or war: it may be a reaction of avoidance,[116] well known among ethologists. The sure criterion of the movement from ethnocentrism to racism remains the explicit biological interpretation of factual somatic and cultural differences and the correlative fiction of the existence of quite distinct races among which the boundaries are uncrossable. The scholarly discourses on racism therefore grant to racial biologization the status of an operator of racialization. That hardly seems to surpass the *petitio principii,* as long as one is left saying, tautologically: racism, which is defined by the biologization of "objective" (by virtue of their social origin) differences attributed to racial differences, begins as soon as there is a racial biologization of "objective" differences.

*"Tertiary Racism" and Critical-Demystifying Antiracism.* As soon as the "biological" vocabulary of race (marked by borrowings from and references to physical anthropology or raciology) intervenes in discourse and argument in constitutive fashion, and the scientific modes of legitimation (the recourse to categorizations and classifications that refer to a supposedly natural order) are invested in it, a *tertiary racism* appears, which presupposes the first two levels or degrees in that it integrates them. The notion of tertiary racism seems to refer to all the elaborated forms of the ethnocentrism-xenophobia pair, involving modes of theorization borrowed from the biological sciences. But through analysis, it is admitted that tertiary racism designates two sets of distinct phenomena of value-beliefs. On the one hand, it allows a marking of the specificity, in relation to the first two levels, of the ex-

plicit racist ideologies — that is, of the theories or doctrines presenting themselves as such, offering themselves as coherent and complete, endowed with a power of explanation (of history, of the social), taking the title of "scientific,"[117] sometimes even claimed to be verified by experiment. On the other hand, in Langmuir's terminology, modern racist scientism corresponds, not without posing numerous problems, to the level of statements categorized as chimerical, consisting of affirmations concerning the Other stemming from phantasmic projections, without reference to any empirical observation whatsoever. One may remember this classic example of a chimerical statement, presenting itself as a historico-anthropological certainty: "The Jews are guilty of ritual murder."[118] Or again, this medieval statement, put back into circulation by Nazi propaganda, before returning again through a certain "anti-Zionism": "The Jews poison wells."[119] But this class of statements cannot be given closure by the criterion of the modern recourse (taken since the end of the eighteenth century) to the biological paradigm, under scientific authority, in which difference of "race" was interpreted as the determining cause of cultural diversity and as the principle of a hierarchical scale ordering the differences. As soon as we accept, in spite of the hold of scientism[120] on our minds, an enlargement of the class of theoretico-"chimerical" affirmations through an inclusion in it of those stemming from the traditional principle of authority (the theologico-religious dimension), the modern biologico-scientistic discourse does not appear as differing in nature, functioning, and function from the traditional discourses of disqualifying exclusion. In all cases, it is the absolute adherence to a general conception of the world (of a religious, ideological, or scientific order), the unconditional belief (religious faith, ideological conviction, or scientific evidence) in the truth value of the Theory, that has the power to authorize the operation called, in the broad sense, *racist*.[121] The extension of the concept of racism is in this case maximum. Any act of racialization backed up by a general speculative construction that can be made explicit may hence be situated at this third level, that of elaborated racism, whose self-justifying argument is reinforced and crystallized by integration into a conception of the world. If it is true that extreme systematism and paranoid delirium carry on intimate relations, then chimerical statements of racialization never achieve their concept except in the contemporary biologico-scientistic mode, which describes a self-sufficient natural world, enclosed in itself and governed by supposedly eternal immanent laws. It is enough to enter the hypothesis of a change of the paradigm of transcendence, from the mathematical infinite to the miracle of what is living, that is, to the empirical and transcendental fact of difference (variation, individual diversity, genetic polymorphism). This hypothesis is attested by the emergence of difference, in the most unrelated discursive genres (the discourses of biology and advertising, of the everyday and politics in the media, of ethnology and philosophy), into a new object of praise, into a value of accepted values, into a motif celebrated for its own sake.

We encounter the following aporia: tertiary racism may be marked either as the ideological makeshift characteristic of modernity (from the mid-eighteenth to the mid-nineteenth century) or as the specific elaboration of "xenophobia" in general, appearing when the behavior of "phobia" toward the Other is integrated into an encompassing concept that gives its meaning and its titles of symbolic capacitation (biologization). It remains undecidable whether this hypothetical third level, this racist world of a third kind, refers to a historical third estate of racism—through a "law of three estates," reviewed and adapted—or describes the highest degree of a conceptual elaboration. The most operational criterion that may be retained to "save" the third racism seems to us to be twofold: first, a *sophistication* of xenophobic argumentation, that is, the pursuit of the process called "secondary racism"; second, the setting to work of the scheme of *diabolical causality*,[122] which marks a point of rupture with the heterophobia that is well tempered by the criteria of acceptability in effect, specifying the second level. In the latter case, the statements of racialization are hyperbolical and characterize the racized one by making him equivalent to a personified abstraction—an individual characterized as a Jew is thus identified as representing the abstract singular "Evil"; any exemplar of the Negro type is identified as representative of "Animality," even of the "Bestial."[123]

The three levels of racism distinguished by scholarly antiracism in fact define three levels of what may conveniently be named *xenophobia*, according to a scale spanning from the most simple, the most "natural," and the most determined (elementary reactions) to the most complex, the most "cultural," and the most undetermined (an oscillation between scientistic dogmatism and paranoid delirium). The fact remains that such a hierarchical typology of the modes of exclusion of the Other/foreigner risks engendering a perverse effect: legitimating, by naturalizing, the xenophobic mechanism thus analyzed.

This theorization of levels is based on a postulate of continuity of the "racisms" distinguished, which implies that among them there is only a difference of degree. Now, this is precisely one of the theoretical points in question, which we will approach later on, according to various problematics (Lévi-Strauss, for example, refuses to categorize ethnocentrism and racism as a unity). Besides, several interpretive hypotheses may be put forward in the face of this theory of levels. The first hypothesis, centered on the first level, could be that racism is everywhere in human attitudes and behaviors: racism, as an encompassing category, makes the link between elementary tendencies and elaborate systems of representation. The second hypothesis, centered on the heterogeneity of the racisms called primary and tertiary, could be that racism nowhere appears in a clear and distinct fashion and that we lazily call *racism* those phenomena the knowledge of which would improve in that they are modelized differentially. The third hypothesis could be that only the third level distinguished allows one to mark and then to define racism in opposition to elementary defensive reactions, the feeling of belonging to a community, the designation of one or more enemies (an act implied by the essence of the political), and sociocentrism in general. In this last perspective, one would be unable to speak of primary and secondary racisms. But if racism in the strict sense is situated on the level of "tertiary racism," one stands before an aporia: one calls racism at once an explicit doctrinal construction and a vague set of statements that, according to the authors, result from a chimera or delirious fiction, from the unverifiable or the false, from lying and willful falsification. The simplest way to overcome the aporia consists of an assessment of analogy with paranoid behavior: racism, as a system of coherent, closed, and "explanatory" representations at the same time as an incoherent bunch of chimeras, errors, and lies, is presented as a paranoid image of the world. We must admit, then, that scientific gain is slight.

The "theory" of levels enables a problematization of the current representations of racism, stemming just as much from ordinary as from scholarly discourse; this is its positive aspect. The illusion that it furnishes a satisfying theoretical model of racism defines its negative aspect. The hierarchy of levels, in being presented as an encompassing theory, only gives a pseudocoherency to the heterogeneity of the uses of the word *racism*. An ideological makeshift, the "theory" of levels does not allow one to clarify the ideological debates, for it is a part of these; it does not and cannot bring any conceptual clarity into the theoretical discussions other than that which is involved in ordinary language acts. It is thus that it reproduces, on the level of the overlegitimate discourse of science, the old confusion among group aggressiveness, ethnocentrism, xenophobia, nationalism, and racism; it is thus that the latter characterizes attitudes, behaviors, or systems of belief and value.

## The Theoretical Antiracist Discourse: Its Genres and Its Limits

The "theory" of levels sketched in the foregoing proposed to answer a question: What is racism? One may search for the reasons for its unsatisfying character through the analysis of the different theoretical constructions by means of which the antiracist specialists in racism ground their racism by producing ideal types and models of racism. After the inventory of the descriptive definitions of racism, we are continuing that of the stipulative definitions of racism, which was begun with the "theory" of levels.[124] Numerous authors have distinguished, in the field of scholarly antiracism with explanatory claims, two attitudes with respect to the concept of "race" in research in human biology: (1) the moderates propose to *limit* the scientific use of the term *race* by furnishing explicit criteria of what may be designated by it; (2) the radicals do not hesitate to *deny* any scientific usefulness for the term and, in prescribing its definitive abandonment, denounce as pseudoscientific any use of the notion of race in the study of man.[125]

These two epistemological attitudes correspond, in our typology, to genres 1 and 2 of scholarly antiracism. But as soon as the theoretical elaborations of the specialists in the social sciences are taken into consideration, other types of attitudes appear that may be defined differentially. In a more precise and systematic fashion, the multiplicity of scholarly antiracist arguments may be reduced to six genres of denunciatory discourse:

- the denunciation of the illegitimate uses of the scientific concept of race (genre 1);
- the denunciation of the scientific illegitimacy of the common notion of race (genre 2);

- the denunciation of the naively (or strategically) racial or raciological interpretation of racism, as much by racists as by antiracists, a position of which two variants may be distinguished, the first noticeable as early as the end of the nineteenth century, the second appearing in the 1960s and 1970s:
  - the sociological determination of ethnic factors involving the denunciation of the primacy of the determinism of group heredity in the social sciences (genre 3);
  - the psychosociological shift of the question to the social meanings of "race," which are to be decoded (genre 4);
- the denunciation of the deceptive uniqueness postulated by the expression *racism* and the reduction of pseudobiologism to modes of self-legitimation of social groups, always held in a structure of domination, real and symbolic (genre 5);
- the denunciation of the biological and sociological models of the racisms, whose diversity one aims to reduce by effecting a correlation with a typology of universal families, at the heart of a general politico-cultural anthropology (genre 6).

These six genres of theoretical antiracist discourse are presented as explanatory discourses that, following analysis, prescribe the rejection of racism in the name of one or another science, even in the name of science itself. They claim, each having its refutational and self-legitimating argument, to answer the question of why and how to combat racism in the field of knowledge. This assumes that one has a certain idea of what one is claiming to combat and that one applies oneself to elaborating it at the heart of one or another scientific problematic. Now, the stipulative definitions of racism first vary with the disciplinary specializations of the scholarly antiracists.

1. *Physical anthropology*, as it is conceived by its moderate representatives, who do not claim to reduce the sciences of man to the study of the human races. But anthropologists, by postulating a realism of race, argue as follows: races exist in the field of experience; they must be observed, described, and classified according to criteria linked to comparative measurements.

2. *Genetics*, and in particular the genetics of populations: with regard to the human races, contemporary geneticists are rather nominalist and tend to deem that, if race is only a classificatory term, it is poorly formed as a concept and stripped of objectifiable reference—

an empty and useless word that must be abandoned, so as to be done with racism.

3. *The sociological problematics* that impugn the recourse to race as an explanatory concept and postulate that race is a social product to be explained.

4. *Interpretative psychosociology,* the critical and demystifying hermeneutics inspired by psychoanalysis: the hypothesis of latent social meaning grounds the task of deciphering its indices, legitimates the indefinite interpretation of ambiguous signs of "racialization," racism referring first to the unsaid in all observable social conduct, verbal and nonverbal.

5. *A critical sociology* that, integrating into a determinist conception of a "sociologistic" type the Marxist hypothesis of a reduction of racizing practices to class behaviors, is applied to an analysis of the modes of legitimation/illegitimation, as they are achieved or presupposed by what is called racism.

6. *A familial anthropology* that, grounding a typology of racisms on a typology of families, sketches an anthropological map of the ideological variants of "racism" (a cultural and ideologico-political relativism in an anthropofamilial universalism).

These various ideal types and models of intelligibility may be placed in relation with the different types of public, or the various classes of addressees, that they specifically target: the effectiveness of their respective arguments, their persuasive force, is limited by the domains of receivability and acceptability that mark off the values and beliefs admitted by their listeners (the hypothesis may be made that each genre of scholarly antiracist discourse has its ideal listener, who is not necessarily herself a scholar).[126]

## Removing the Science of "Race" and of Racism from Legitimate Science

Racism is first of all denounced as false science, with the assumption of the existence of a normal and legitimate science by reference to which the diagnosis of falsity is pronounced. The antiracist speaker removes the problem of the existence of human races from that of racism, accepting the anthropological artificiality of racial differentiation, which he opposes to the placement of the diversity of "natural" groups on a hierarchical scale.[127] Such an act of hierarchizing assignation characterizes only racism. The hierarchization at issue would itself remain neutral, situated on this side of the disjunction of racism and antiracism. The addressee of this antiracist discourse, whom I will call "reasonable," is representable by a subject qualified by his knowledge, either empirical (the man in the street) or scientific (the expert).[128] It is a matter of persuading this empistemic subject not to go beyond the level of the observable, to convince him to keep to what he knows truly, without going further. The objective of the argument is to set the precise limits beyond which legitimate racial discourse becomes illegitimate racial discourse — and, in most democratic societies, illegal. In the first place, the point of rupture between the racial and the racist is an inverted symmetry, the specular image of the already classical epistemological break, interpreted according to the positivist model of ideological prehistory (errors, illusions, deliria, myths) to which the history of well-grounded science puts an end. From this comes the analogy of underlying proportionality: the knowledge of races is to racism what science is to ideology or false science, to its ever-threatening prehistory. The speaker thus assumes the position of ambient scientism, the keystone of modern ideological normality. In the second place, what brings about the greatest difficulties is that scientific knowledge, that of physical (essentially classificatory) anthropology, is set on an equal footing with the good sense of the subject who (clearly) sees the differences (first and foremost, the variations and color of epidermis). This discourse of antiracist exhortation, entailing a continual blame of a stigmatized subject ("the racist") and of a twofold object, impugned as such (racism-as-theory and racism-as-behavior),[129] is therefore directed to an addressee who greatly resembles the average man endowed with infallible good sense, susceptible to reasoning and to "rising" culturally by receiving the lessons of specialists authorized in the material. This is a naive and well-intentioned antiracism, in that it begins by accepting the representations and values current in its society of reference (the contiguous attitudes of respect, which are even like cults, toward *fact* and toward *science*, each reinforcing the other).

When it appears among sociologists, discursive genre 1 is often grounded in the distinction, classical since Max Weber, between judgments of fact and judgments of value:

> We have just seen to what point racial theories may be criticized. That obviously does not mean that there are no races. But these

theories have the grave defect of mixing random judgments of value with the observation of facts, some of which are indisputable and others of which are contradictory. These theories effect an arbitrary choice from among these facts, rejecting for no good reason those which do not fit them.[130]

Since the Nazi uses of the study of human races, physical anthropologists have become at once more conscious of the possible ideological drifts of their knowledge and more cautious in the face of statements that may be interpreted as racist. The core of their explicit rejection of racism contains a definition of racism that corresponds to the received one: they in fact apply themselves to impugn, in the name of scientific caution, the hypothesis of a universal, unique, and general scale of the aptitudes determined by race. The definitional evidence is that racism is essentially an inegalitarian doctrine of races. It will suffice here to quote Henri-V. Vallois:

> Certain authors have believed that they had to distinguish "superior" and "inferior" races, the first, more evolved from the somatic and psychic points of view, thereby all being designated to direct and command the others. *It is this notion that is the basis of racism.* But it does not rest on any proof. From the somatic point of view, each race has more evolved characteristics, others more primitive ones; the Australoids themselves, in whom certain primitive characteristics are particularly visible, are very evolved with regard to a series of others. From the psychic point of view, on the other hand, we have seen ... that it is impossible, at least for the moment, to differentiate that which, in the intelligence of an individual or a group, comes down to education or environment from that which may come down to race. The notion of superior and inferior races must disappear (see the UNESCO publication [on this subject], 1960).[131]

*The Impossible Neutrality of Differentiation.* A less recent example of the legitimation of the concept of race, in a context marked by scientific caution and under an authorized signature, will allow an indication of how discriminating among races, as neutral as it may try to be, involves metaphorical effects that are not dominated, and perhaps not masterable, by a principle. At the end of the preface to his hefty volume of encyclopedic synthesis, *Race and History,* Eugène Pittard obligingly warns the reader: "I have used the word race in its common acceptance, without pedantic scientific Byzantinism, as meaning simply a collection of like individuals of the same blood sprung from the same stock."[132] Refusing any "discussion" on the taxonomic questions posed by the uses of the word *race*, this professor of anthropology at the University of Geneva in 1924 allowed himself a borrowed definition:

> The following definition of race, by Boule, admirably suits this volume: "By race we should understand the continuity of a physical type, expressing affinities of blood, representing an essentially natural grouping, which can have nothing, and in general has nothing in common with the people, the nationality, the language, or the customs corresponding to groupings that are purely artificial, in no way anthropological, and arising entirely from history, whose actual products they are."[133]

No attempt at explanation follows the defining expressions "continuity," "physical type," "blood affinities," or the division of groupings as "essentially natural" and "purely artificial," the metaphorical effects of which are rejected in the evidence of what is admissible without discussion. Clarity in the defining argument barely appears except by the affirmation of the nature/history opposition — the "natural" (the biological given) as opposed to the "artificial" (the human construct) — in which it seems to have taken refuge; but again, in the form of first evidence. We thus find ourselves before an implicit analogy: "race" is to the set "people-nationality-language-mores" what "nature" is to "history"; a *petitio principii*, because the nature/history distinction, the unique source of classification, being merely affirmed, itself remains obscure, or at least problematic. "Race" is, by such a definition, naturalized, inscribed in the natural element that precedes the anthropological element; by this definitional act, it is legitimated as a scientific concept. Hence science joins common sense, and the promotion of good sense — for, as it may be said, "nature is nature."[134]

## The Scientific Delegitimation of the Concept of Race

> *And we think, with Jean Hiernaux, that the term race is, for humanity in the present, empty of signification.* Jacques Ruffié

The speaker refuses to accord the concept of "race" the least scientific legitimacy; and, assuming the foundation of racism to be the division of the human species into distinct races, he thus thinks he eliminates the argumentative basis of racism. Since the term *race* henceforth has no scientific use, since it belongs to the lexicon of political ideologies and modern myths, it is believed possible to conclude that eliminating the word constitutes an effective antiracist therapeutic. The core of the argument is simple: as the scientism of the last century credited the idea of "race" with a scientific value, today it is sufficient to discredit, in the name of science, the idea of "race" to delegitimate racism. This is the position defended by the geneticist Albert Jacquard, on the basis of an analysis of correlative acts, belonging of course to the natural logic of humans, of categorizing classification (defining distinct "races") and of hierarchization (establishing a scale of values among the "races"), in which he marks the cognitive foundation of all racism.[135] He does not find it difficult to conclude, once "the [genetic] distance between two persons of the same race is on the average 7 percent less than the distance between two human beings chosen at random from all of humanity,"[136] that for the geneticist of populations "the word *race* has practically no content."[137] From this, there is the proposition that stems from a hygiene and surgery of language, aiming to extirpate those of its terms loaded with potential ideological excrescences: "In view of the biological implications that so many writings, doctrines, and policies have indelibly hung on the word *race,* would it not be prudent to eliminate it, as we would a useless and dangerous tool?"[138] The solution to the problem thus seems to be reduced to a lexical and semantic purification. Its privileged and perhaps exclusive addressee is identifiable in the figure of the scientific researcher who, armed with epistemological prudence and a self-critical faculty, is committed in militant fashion to the camp of an "enlightened" humanism whose universalism takes its arguments from a certain state of science. The risk here is of addressing hardly anyone, in convincing fashion, but colleagues and minds already won over to the antiracist ethic. The force of such argumentation is reduced to its value of confirmation. It has hardly any persuasive force in the face of a listener who does not admit the same system of values — let us call it that of "scientific" humanism.

In a brief clarification of "Biology-Racism-Hierarchy,"[139] François Jacob begins by recalling that every living organism, every individual, is "the end result of a constant interaction between his [genetic] program and the environment in which he lives." Besides, each individual differs from all others, "from both the program he has received and the adventure he has lived."[140] The "normal reaction of the scientist" is to "seek to account for these differences by classifying the members of the same species in groups sufficiently homogeneous to be considered as distinct and definable entities,"[141] even if only on the basis of the more or less great frequency of certain physical traits in such and such a group. This classificatory activity assumes the existence of types, of typological or essentialist concepts of the groups thus classified (species, races, and so on). Now, this essentialist way of thinking has been "totally rejected by modern biology."[142] The individuals of a given or posited set can no longer be scientifically considered expressions of the same type, exemplars of an archetypical idea.[143] The vague Platonism postulated by such a theoretical system no longer has operational value: stereotypical fixity henceforth lacks scientifically gaugeable types. Jacob recalls that "the biological distance between two persons of the same group, of the same village, is so great that it renders insignificant the distance between the averages of two groups, *and this removes all content from the concept of race.*"[144] Otherwise stated, essentialist thought is incapable of accounting for the "extraordinary variability...of the characters that we can specify."[145]

The racist claim to hierarchize the races, for its part, is denuded of all scientific legitimacy: first from the fact that "the concept of race has *lost all operative value,* and can only freeze our vision of a reality ceaselessly in motion"[146] — hence the lack of the very elements of the hierarchizing enterprise; then from the fact that genetic predestination, presupposed by hierarchical racialization, is only a "legend," of the same status as the empiricist fiction of the tabula rasa.

Biology therefore permits only the affirmation of the absolute uniqueness of each individual, which from the outset hinders any attempt at the hierarchization of individuals among themselves as races proclaimed among themselves. "The only richness is collective: it is made up of diversity. All the rest is ideology,"[147] concludes Jacob. Science and ideology are thus very classically opposed as reason and the passions: "It is not the ideas of science that engender the passions. Rather, the passions use science to support their cause. Science does not lead to racism and hate. Rather, hate appeals to science in order to justify its racism."[148] On the basis of this sidelining of science, which is assumed neutral in relation to the field of the general and dominant passions that constitute ideology, two extreme types of positions are possible in which science and racism are joined: either racism is impugned in the name of science, which, for example, would no longer confer conceptual power on the word *race* (Ruffié, Jacquard, Jacob), or racism is authorized in the name of science, by reformulating, according to the current norms of scientific discourse, the theses said to be racist, today centered on the intellectual inequality between whites and blacks (C. Burt, H. J. Eysenck, A. R. Jensen). But who is to decide on and to authorize one or another mode, racist or antiracist, of scientific legitimation of the discourse on man?

## Race as a Social Product

The principle of the classical sociological critique of the theory of races is simple: racial difference should not be a principle of explanation because it is only a socially produced effect, and therefore sociologically explainable. The general thesis of race-as-result is common to the social psychology of Gabriel Tarde and the disciples of Frédéric Le Play. For Tarde, race is defined as a social construction, a historico-cultural product: "Every given civilisation...creates in the long run the race, or races, in which it is for a time embodied; and the inverse of this is not true, namely, that every race makes its own civilisation."[149]

There results an inversion of the determinist postulate of the "philosophy of race": it is the cultural type that engenders the racial type. The determinist explanation is therefore not put in question: the social psychologist is content to put the modeling force of the cultural milieu in the place held by the factors of race in the "theory of race." Tarde's position is then also moderated: it is not, when race takes its place of social effect, a matter of impugning its reality or neglecting its effectiveness. "I must not be accused of the absurd idea of denying...the influence of race upon social facts. But I think that on account of the number of its acquired characteristics, race is the outcome, and not the source, of these facts, and only in this hitherto ignored sense does it appear to me to come within the special province of the sociologist."[150]

In his work on social geography, *Comment la route crée le type social,* Edmond Demolins, a disciple of Le Play, states at the outset his refusal on principle of any explanation of human diversity by racial factors and puts forward what he deems the correct solution of the problem thus posed:

> There exists on the surface of the terrestrial globe a population of infinite variety.
> What is the cause that created this variety?
> In general, the answer is race.
> But race explains nothing, for it still remains to be discovered what produced the diversity of races. Race is not a cause, but rather a consequence.
> The first and decisive cause of the diversity of peoples and the diversity of races is *the road that the peoples have followed.*
> It is the road that created race and that creates the social type.
> The roads of the globe have in some way been powerful stills, what have transformed, in one manner or another, the peoples who have set out on them.[151]

The inversion of the causal order, in the sense of a sociogeographic mesologism, thus makes possible the sketch of a theory of race as effect: racial difference is a product of the diversity of environments. Strict biological determinism is answered by a no-less-strict sociogeographic determinism. The modelizing and differentiating force of the "road" must be understood as the effectiveness not only of the "regions crossed by the migrations of peoples" but also of the "place where those peoples settled." Let us take western Europe: "The Scandinavian, Anglo-Saxon, French, German, Greek, Italian, and Spanish types are also the product of the roads on which our ancestors were scattered in order to arrive at their current habitat. The diversity of these roads alone explains the diversity of the peoples of the West and what is too conveniently called the national genius of each of them."[152] If geography, ceasing to be only a nomenclature of names or an image of the earth's relief, "explains the nature and social role of the various roads and consequently the origin of the various races,"[153] "it also becomes the primordial factor in the constitution of human societies."[154] Social science may thenceforth formulate "social laws" from whose rigor man would not be able to remove himself, but to which he could, in knowing them, accommodate himself, that he could even "put to his service." History, for its part, "ceases to be the narrative of often unexplained and unexplainable events"; "it is coordinated, it is raised, it results in the highest and most exact of philosophies."[155] Demolins thus proposes a fictional experiment: "No sooner than you modify one or another of these roads, raise it or lower it, make it produce one material instead of another, and hence transform in one direction or another the form and nature of the labor, the social type is modified and you have another race."[156]

But if social science has discovered laws, then one may go "further: if the history of humanity were to begin again without the surface of the globe being transformed, that history would repeat itself in its general features."[157]

It remains that sociogeographic argumentation draws its explanatory force from taking into consideration only "historical races" and "zoological races." Now, "historical races," being social types fashioned by the environments in their specific histories, are more easily explained by the diversity of the latter than the "zoological races" of physical anthropology. In short, Demolins tends to confuse, by placing them on the same plane, the great races with peoples, nations, or ethnic groups: in his social typology, he speaks without distinction of the "Negro type" and "the Arab type," of the "Indian type" and the "French type," of the "Phoenician," the "Roman," or the "Germanic." These types seem to differ only by degree of complexity: "As I go I put forward, as it is suitable, from the simplest to the most complicated types, consequently from eastern Europe to western Europe."[158]

We will finally note that Tarde, severe toward the advocates of strict racial determinism,[159] was no less so for the inverse dogmatic bias, that is, all-encompassing explanation by "environment":

> There is a fetish, a deus ex machina that the new sociologists utilize like an "open Sesame" each time they are perplexed, and it is time to indicate this abuse, which is becoming really disquieting. This explanatory talisman is *environment*. Once this word is uttered, everything has been said. *Environment* is the all-purpose formula whose illusory profundity serves to cover the emptiness of the idea.[160]

The history of debates and controversies in the twentieth century seems to justify a posteriori Tarde's methodic distrust of dogmatic explanations, whether hereditarianist/racist or environmentalist.

## Thesis of Racialization with or without "Race"

The critical analysis of racism presents itself here as involving the decoding of a reciprocal presupposition of "race" and the racizing act. This is the first hypothesis of the method put to work by Colette Guillaumin as early as the mid-1960s.

The first three theoretical positions that we have presented develop an antiracist argument on the basis of a rationalizing and realist conception of science; the latter is presumed to be neutral with respect to ideologico-political values and passions or to have to keep itself in check by an always reinitiated ascesis, onto which a supplement of humanism is grafted in the form of a universalist ethic received without critical reflection. The insurmountable obstacle inevitably encountered by such a conception, linking racism and impertinent or false cognition of race, whether or not it otherwise admits the scientificity of the concept of race, in *socially functional reality* has to do with the overarching idea of race, or with racism without "race(s)." In other words, racism could first exist as racist attitudes and practices that, though susceptible to resorting to the word *race*, do quite well without it, as much as do scientific legitimations of racism, which depend on physical anthropology or genetics. It follows that the word *race* can no longer be taken for the exclusive (or best) indicator of the modes of racialization. If there is racism inside and outside the discourses on race, if there is racism with or without the invocation of race, it means that there is a complex social sense of what is called racism behind what is ordinarily designated as such — that is, the outer marks of racism (from public insult to publicly confessed murder).

"Racism is not a biological concept," Emmanuel Lévinas once remarked. He added, "Anti-semitism is the archetype of all internment. Social aggression, itself, merely imitates this model. It shuts people away in a class, deprives them of expression and condemns them to being 'signifiers without a signified' and from there to violence and fighting."[161] Here the question of racism in general is socialized. The question of whether racism is the model of all "classism," or the inverse, is and will be the object of debates and controversies. But the fact is that most of the basic mechanisms are analogous. Hence the hypothesis may be made that racist exclusion is the *ratio cognoscendi* of classist exclusion, on condition of assuming the possibility of the reciprocal hypothesis. But it is important to recall that what is named "racism" bears this recent name only from an incidental crossing, indeed from a meeting just as accidental as it was productive of misunderstandings — that is, an incursion into the domains of the newborn anthropological sciences, a bit too proud of their methods of objectification of the human given. This meeting today seems to have brought about a chaotic history that may quite well be only a parenthesis, from now on almost closed. This is to suggest that racism today must be observed elsewhere than in the explicit theoretical discourses claiming to legitimate it. An anthropobiologist such as Jean Hiernaux also suggests that the genesis of "racial prejudices" is strictly social: "It is clear that racial prejudices, like practices of racial discrimination, have no biological foundation."[162] Certainly, but where does the symbolic effectiveness of racial categorizations come from? Biologists have nothing biological to say about the question.

It is in the perspective of a critical sociology of science that the rationalist/humanist positions characterized above impose themselves: either one saves race in order better to impugn racism; or one condemns race and racism equally by assuming their continuity; or one reverses the determinism of culture by race. To be done with the scientific concept of race or with its methodological primacy, we see, is not at all equivalent to eradicating the symbolic effectiveness of race. Not only may the functional independence of racism with respect to the scientific evaluation of the term *race* be discovered, but it is right to assume that what is important here, in the first place, is "the perceptive organization of the unconscious."[163] Now, from the fact that unconscious processes do not recognize negation, it is easy to state the hypothesis that "an affirmed fact and a denied fact have exactly the same degree of existence."[164] This observation goes a long way: as soon as denying or affirming the scientific value of the category of "race," for the primary processes, comes down to the same thing, any attempt that aims to "show the inconsistency of such a category in the scientific domain is insufficient to make it disappear from the mental categories."[165] This means that the reality of "race" is social and political: it is "a *social* category of exclusion, of murder."[166] More precisely, the existence of acts of racialization is only social, and they arise from other modes of authorization than the mere scientific acceptability of a term. It is again from Colette Guillaumin that we will borrow the formulation of a paradox that indicates the major blunder of the antiracist vulgate, which today applies itself to giving praise to difference as such: whereas the neoracism of the New Right is constituted, without the aid of the word *race* and even by integrating the denunciation of "racism," around the sacralization of difference, the antiracists believe they can oppose it through a no-less-differentialist discourse, which barely distinguishes itself except by a certain insistence on the "enrichment" represented by differences.[167]

In short, racism and antiracism risk admitting positions of discourse that today have become indiscernible, mimetically accepting the same primary and positive value of difference and sacralization. Struggling through the praise of difference against the neoracism that gives praise to difference: here is the paradox, laden with consequences, that demands to be seriously interrogated. If ideology resides in what is perceived even as evidence,[168] then the contemporary praise of difference manifests one of the common cores, perhaps the most imperceptible, of the ideological functionings that think within us, without our knowledge. Such an iconoclastic and untimely (in the Nietzschean sense) analysis today seems to us ready for a listener who would go beyond the restricted class of specialists. It indicates a beyond of the mimetic rivalry of racism and of a certain antiracism that still remains to be invented.

## *Three*

# Births, Functionings, and Avatars of the Word *Racism*

> *The dictionary is charged with a political mythology.*
> Pierre Bourdieu

At issue now is to approach the question of the conditions of engenderment of the act of lumping together that is at the center of the polemical discourse that stigmatizes "racism." This lumping together may be represented by the linking of the following pejorative nouns: racism/anti-Semitism/(pan-)Germanism/Nazism/fascism/extreme right/right. The following are added to this series: eugenicism, genocide, crimes against humanity. Our working hypothesis is that "racism" is a part of a functional ideological whole, endowed with a geopolitical space of distribution and with a relatively graspable temporal development.

In this perspective, we propose to reconstruct the linkage of the constitutive propositions of the *metadefinition* of "racism" (see chapter 4). We state the hypothesis that this metadefinition furnishes an analogical model of the general and implicit conception of "racism" that is assumed by the definitional reformulations observable in "a-" or "antiracist" discourses since the appearance of the word in the French language.[1] Its ideological and political context is well defined: that of the first European echoes of the populist-racist *(völkisch)* campaign conducted by the nationalist organizations of the extreme right, among them the National Socialists and the groups founded by General Erich Ludendorff, in Germany from 1919 to 1933. The model of lexical creation by reference to the emergence of a new sociopolitical phenomenon in Germany, whose qualifying self-designation *(völkisch)* was transposed into the French language, may be confirmed by the entries "racism *[racisme]*" and "racist *[raciste]*" in the *Larousse du XX<sup>e</sup> siècle* dictionary, published in 1932. If the designator *racism* is therein defined as "position, doctrine of racists," *racist* is encyclopedically defined as "the name given to the German National Socialists."[2] In short, the class of "racists" is presuppositionally defined as a class comprising only one element, the latter being a well-defined collectivity ("the German National Socialists"). In French-language texts, the qualifier *racist* is most often found as a mention (in quotation marks or italics) around the mid-1920s, in contexts defined by reference to the active "racist" groups under the Weimar Republic.

## The Two Incommensurable Appearances of the Word *Racism* (1895–97, 1925)

Whether it is a matter of an attitude or disposition that may be verbalized (which is stigmatized by the expression "race prejudice": racism-as-*attitude*), of discriminatory behaviors (racism-as-*conduct*), or of elaborated doctrines ("theories" or "philosophy of race," numerous explicit conceptions of the world in the second half of the nineteenth century: racism-as-*ideology*), racism surely preexisted the appearance of the word *racism*.[3] The tendency, the idea, the conception, and the empirical behavior, contrary to the illusion common to all historical materialisms of the lexical index,[4] have no need at all for the word that, designating them, fixes the concept, in order to arise in a social formation. But the establishment of a conceptualizing term such as *racism* is capable, through a retrospective effect, of achieving an integration of the multiple meanings hitherto designated by distinct terms. Such a semantic recollection does not take place without producing certain confusions, linked to the effect of assimilation, even of retrospective identification, of phenomena held to be different before the synthesis accomplished by doctrinal denomination ("racism"). The ordinary use of the name of a doctrine in fact suggests that it refers to a field of notions that are relatively homogeneous and coherent among themselves, and hence to a continuity, a permanence in time through the conjunctural variations. To say "racism" ("was born...," "has its intellectual origins in...," and so on) is to draw on a set of elements of various orders (discursive, sociopolitical, and so on) whose unity and persistence are in some manner postulated: the descriptive model of intelligibility henceforth risks being taken for the substantial reality that it is supposed to illuminate. If "racism" is considered to be the name of a descriptive model that enables a simplification of the representation of a real at once ideological and practical, the illusion begins with the "realist" identification of the schematizing instrument constituted by the model with the empirical (historico-anthropological) morphology to which it refers. The means of improving the description is likened to the object described.[5] This is of course a classical confusion; but, for "racism," it engenders effects that are regrettable inasmuch as the term is endowed with two principal functions that interfere with each other: a gauging function in the language of the social and human sciences (a function of *cognition*) and a *polemical* function in the field of the great contradictory and adverse ideological discourses (liberalism, socialism, nationalism, anarchism, racism, and so on). Now, since the end of World War II, the label *racist* has been a powerful instrument of delegitimating any adversary in ideological warfare. The function of cognition, linked to the construction of ideal types or descriptive models of intelligibility, has then tended to be evacuated in favor of the polemical function: it is no longer a matter of knowing and making something known, but rather of having something believed and suggesting in order to vanquish an adversary in combat. *Racism* is, with *totalitarianism*,[6] which it preceded by several decades in such a use, a *consensual* operator in the disqualification of an adversary, whoever it may be — that is why, even as antiracists go to battle waving a flag, "racists" are rare beings, always disguised and therefore to be deciphered, driven out, hunted down. Racism is always attributed solely to the person of whom one speaks (the person absent from the interlocutive relation, excluded from dialogue) and to whom one does not want to speak.

What interests us in particular is what we may learn from the study of the relation of anteriority of racism-as-ideology to the word *racism*. This movement from the ideological factuality of "theories," "doctrines," or "philosophies" of race to the polemical characterization by the term *racism* as an operator of criticism and delegitimation of the adversary, this movement from the various ideological facts to the presumed unity of a conception of the world — the latter defined by an unequivocal partisan choice — marks a rupture that is a point of no return. The movement from the "philosophy (doctrine, theory, and so on) of race" to "racism" is seen in the ideology and politics of the late nineteenth century and in the full profile of the twentieth. Here the evolution of the vocabulary is a testimony to and a reflection of, as well as a factor and an actor in, general ideological evolution. Our hypothesis, based on a highly intense exploration of texts and documents, is that the descriptive-polemical meaning of the word *racism* is fixed only in the second half of the 1920s, for reasons that have to do with political history (the prelude to World War I and anti-German nationalism inscribed in a discourse of propaganda), with the history of ideas (the appearance of "racist" authors and trends), with the history of the biological and social sciences (the constitution, in certain cases — especially Germany — the institutionalization, of schools professing the "theory of race"). The following act of lumping together of homonymic racisms occurs: racism as a political doctrine attributed to an adversary (the German, the pan-Germanist, and so on), racism as an orientation common to certain literary circles and ideological tendencies, racism as a basic scientific model claimed by various schools of learned tradition, the latter recognized as such. This lumping together could operate *only* in the polemical discourse that the (French) victors conducted over the (German) vanquished. So here is what is essential: this lexical event, the establishment of the word *racism* during the years between 1922 and 1930, achieves a mutation that is at once semantic and ideologico-political. It is the case that *racism* henceforth no longer designates only a philosophy of history based on the primacy or the dominance of ethnic factors (the ethnohistorical metaphysics of Gobineau furnishes the examined model), the bases in the biological sciences that a school of sociology or political science claims to draw on (the "anthroposociology" or the "selectionist monism" of Otto Ammon and Georges Vacher de Lapouge),[7] or a system of preconceived opinions and received prejudices ("race prejudice," stigmatized as early as the second half of the nineteenth century by the ancestors of the contemporary universalist antiracists). Rather, it designates an exclusivist, elementary conception of the world (on the level of the slogan incorporated: "racist reactions") or an elaborate one (on the level of "[supposedly] racist theories"); this conception of the world is judged to be as false as harmful or dangerous, even scandalous or monstrous, and attributed to an enemy declared as such. In the ideological configuration of the appearance of *racism* -as-term, the foreign/enemy people to whom the latter has been exemplarily directed, we have insisted, has been *Germany,* caught in a complex network of pejorative connotations.

To move to the postpolemical stage of the history of racial doctrines, it must be admitted that *the Franco-German War has been over for a long time* and that it continues only on the fringes of the political imaginary dominated by ressentiment. Only then will scholarly studies no longer be kept out of publication by the warming-over of hatreds offered to the taste of the moment, and have some chance of no longer being parasitized by the stored-up remains of discourses of propaganda dating back more than a century. The Germanophobic era opened by the defeat of 1870 will finally be at an end.

## The Prenotion of Racism (1895–97, 1902): Being Racist, Being French

The counterproof of our hypothesis on the conditions of the crystallization of the contemporary meaning of *racism* is furnished by a brief analysis of the preliminary appearance of the neologism *racist,* in quite another ideologico-political context, showing the rupture of signification occurring between the end of the nineteenth century and the 1920s. We thus find the adjective *racist* penned by Gaston Méry, in the November 18, 1897, issue of *La Libre Parole,* founded and edited by Édouard Drumont: "It is truly time, in popular meetings, that truly French — truly *racist* — voices oppose their eloquence to the rhetoric of internationalist boastings."[8] In such a use, the adjective *racist* effects a positive characterization of being authentically French, in opposition to the cosmopolites[9] or internationalists: the French "voices" are those of the French "race," the true Frenchman and the being rooted in the permanent substance of France, the mooring place of the French "race." The word *racist* intervenes here as an anaphoric and reinforcing adjective to "French" and as such achieves a hyperbolic redoubling. The ideological context presupposed is respresentable by the encounter with the controversies around the Dreyfus Affair (anti-Semitic nationalists against Jewish or "Judaized" cosmopolites, in the *anti-Dreyfusard* perspective) and the debates on the "scientific" theory of race, which then furnish a legitimating support and setting to the nationalist-anti-Semitic pamphleteers.[10] We are still, in the years that close the nineteenth century but whose ideological orientations will be prolonged until World War I, in the notional and political space preceding the one that sees the appearance of racism-as-term in the contemporary sense, proper to the twentieth century, in the 1920s and 1930s. A testimony by Charles Maurras authorizes the placement of the appearance of the word *racist*, endowed with the same signification, before 1895: he is "racist" who believes in the existence of the "French race" and wants to preserve its integrity. Its ideological context is the anti-Semitic nationalism of the 1890s: the position then said to be "racist" does not refer back to the "scientific" theory of zoological races but rather to the traditio-nationalist conception of "historical races." In his report on a conference held on March 25, 1895, at the Sorbonne by the Society for National Ethnography, Maurras notes: "Race in the physical sense is a great subject for smiles. I believe that it is given an inflated importance. And nonetheless I myself am also 'racist'! Elsewhere I had the occasion to say so to my distinguished colleague M. Gaston Méry, who at a point became a Knight of the Race and coined the epithet 'racist.' Like him, I believe that there is a French race."[11]

The prenotion of "racism" reappears in 1902, the form *racism* clearly being introduced as the nominal substitute for "the idea of race" and created by analogy on the following model of derivation: "the idea of tradition" → "traditionalism." At issue is a polemical text by A. Maybon published in the *Revue Blanche:*

> What, in fact, is the basis of the *Félibrige d'action?* On what general theories does it erect the monument of its ignorance? This *félibrige* places at its origin the grand ideas of race and tradition. These words recur in all the speeches of these puerile theoreticians. "Bring the beauty of the race to flower again," "work toward the blossoming of the race" — these are the simplest expressions (because ordinarily these people are more emphatic) that endlessly come to their lips.... And, by these traits, do they not resemble theorists of nationalism? Do the writers of *L'Action Française*, eager to ground philosophically their miserable, purely political doctrine, not regard the ideas of race and tradition as the substratum of nationalism and monarchism?... It is not up to me to restage the trial of *racism* and traditionalism.[12]

It is again in 1902 that one may find a use of the adjective *racist* to qualify the program of a return to the origin that was attributed to a certain form of nationalism: "The racist idea goes further than the nationalist idea and would be, once in action, a return to savagery. Where do the Latins end and the Germans begin, and where is the exact line of demarcation between Germans and Slavs?"[13]

*The Notion of Racism*

Now we pass from the ideological "prehistory" of racism to its "history" as we still live it. The latter may be defined as the *hegemonically antiracist period,* in France, of the general history of theories of race. This singularity illuminates considerably the field of debates and controversies around "racism" in the first half of the twentieth century in the West.

"*Racic Theory" in 1921.* Before the semantic and ideological rupture of 1922–25, lexically marked, we thus find ourselves in the "prehistory" of *racism.* A counterproof of this may easily be furnished: before the explicit denunciation of the "racist" Germans, the adjective *racic [racique],* used concurrently with *ethnic,* does not seem to be exclusively seized by the polemical intention of delegitimating the adversary — the hereditary enemy so termed. An exemplary text by Louis Le Fur attests to this; published in 1921, this text (which had its own ideological importance) proposed to substitute the term *racic,* presented as a neologism strictly belonging to the domain of race (in the "proper," zoological sense), for the term *ethnic,* suspected of being equivocal in that it referred to an intermediary domain between race and people/nation, situated between bioanthropology and history.

In his 1921 critical study "Race et nationalité," Le Fur impugns what he names "racic theory"[14] for being "antiscientific,"[15] for constituting "a doctrine of social regression,"[16] and even for representing "a regression for humanity."[17] The recurring twofold thematic in the high-cultural French antiracist tradition is quite present: the theory of race is stigmatized, on the one hand, for its unscientific character, even for its nature as a pseudoscholarly imposture; and, on the other hand, for the reason that its effects are judged to be harmful, supposedly provoking a return to the past, a "regression," a movement contrary to progress. But what interests us most particularly here is the mode of denomination that Le Fur utilizes and glosses — let us emphasize the date — in 1921. The expression "the theory of race" appears in competition with the expression "*racic* theory"; this qualifier is presented as a neologism necessary for avoiding certain ambiguities. Le

Fur thus poses the problem of the relations between "race" and "nationality": "It is far from the case that the unity of race (in the proper sense of the word) and national unity are one and the same thing; rather, two opposing theories here confront each other: *racic theory*, which is located on the terrain of the physical and natural sciences, and nationalitarian theory, which is located on that of the political and social sciences."[18] The recourse to neologism is thus justified in a note: "I use this neologism ['racic'], as the term 'ethnic,' which comes from *ethnos* (people), is ambiguous, the notion of 'people' being nearer to that of 'nation' than to that of race."[19] "Racic theory" remains, thus designated, quite ambiguous to the retrospective gaze, which benefits from two relatively distinct expressions that authorize certain nuances: "racial theory" (theory of race) and "racist theory" (racism).[20]

But one may still note, in the 1950s, certain euphemistic uses of the word *racic*, which allow one to avoid the connotations of blame attached to the qualifier *racist*, even to *racial:* "To attribute to the riots of Leopoldville a political or *racic* character is to confuse cause and consequence."[21]

In 1950, after recalling that "the antagonisms so frequently manifested between certain races oppose one of the most serious obstacles to the constitution of humanity as a whole society,"[22] Théodore Ruyssen, one of the pioneers of a cosmopolitan society, notes: "The religious feeling may at times attenuate *racic animosities*, mainly among Christians, but political propagandas may also exploit and exacerbate them; anti-Semitism has perhaps been the most powerful driving force of Hitlerian National Socialism."[23]

*First Appearances of the Notion: "Racist" (1922) and Racism (1925).* In a book published late in 1922, *Relations between Germany and France,* the Germanist historian Henri Lichtenberger[24] introduced the adjective *racist* in order to characterize the "extremist," "activist," and "fanatical" elements in the circles of the German national and nationalist right as they had just recently been manifested by the assassination in Berlin, on June 24, 1922, of Walther Rathenau:

> The right indignantly condemned Rathenau's murder and denied any connection with the murderers. A campaign was even planned to expel from the Nationalist party the agitators of the extreme right known as "Germanists" or "racists," a group *(deutschvölkische)* whose foremost leaders are Wulle, Henning and von Graefe, and whose secret inspirer is supposed to be Ludendorff. Henning was expelled from

the party at the end of July by a vote of the parliamentary section. But they were careful to warn the public that the motive of this exclusion was not the deputy's adherence to the "racist" movement but his own personal political activity. The head of the party obviously tried to avoid breaking with the extremists, who evidently asserted a rather extensive influence over the party.... One can hardly help feeling a certain skepticism as to how far the opponents of the Nationalists will avail themselves of the general indignation caused by the murder of Rathenau to deal more rigorously with the subversive plots of the fanatics of the right and to strengthen the republican order.[25]

The context of the term's appearance is significant: the description of the behavior of the "German nationals" and more precisely the "activist," "extreme right" fraction. The adjective *racist* is clearly presented as a French equivalent of the German word *völkisch,* and always placed in quotation marks. In addition, it arises to conclude the narration (as if to exhibit the latter's "reason") of a long series of murders committed by the German national right, which is said to excel in the art of exploiting, in particular, "the fear of Bolshevism" and "the anti-Semitic passions."[26] The term, having only just appeared, is already charged with criminalizing connotations.

In 1925, in his reference book *L'Allemagne contemporaine,* Edmond Vermeil expressly reintroduced the adjective *racist* to translate the "untranslatable" German term *völkisch* and suggested the identification, which became trivial in the 1930s, of (German) racism with nationalist anti-Semitism or with the anti-Jewish tendencies of the nationalist movement in Germany in the 1920s:

> It is in this way that the National German Party has little by little split into two camps. *The "racist" (völkisch) extreme right* has separated from the party. *Racism* claims to reinforce nationalism, to struggle on the inside against all that is not German and on the outside for all those who bear the name German. Its doctrine is coupled with that of Hitler in Bavaria. Today it flourishes in all the German states, in which it is everywhere in open struggle with the more moderate elements of nationalism.... The Populist Party ... also believes itself to be patriotic, as German as the National Germans or *the racists.*[27]

At the same time, in a report on Germany that appeared in the February 15, 1925, issue of *La Revue Universelle,* René Johannet qualified as *racist* the militants and partisans of certain German political organizations: "Ludendorff's *racists*" (in italics in the text).[28] The notion appears more often as an adjective ("to be racist," "the racist N," and so on), but the use of the collective term in the plural ("the racists [of N]") begins to be attested. What is significant, in 1925–27, is the rarity of the form "racism," of the recourse to the name of the doctrine. The polemical lumping together of the theory of race in general and the German "racist" positions was in the course of formation, and the pejorative designation was not yet ritualized. This is confirmed by the analysis of an anonymous study published in the same revue, two years later, titled "The Patriotic and Military Organizations in Germany."[29] The latter extended the usage of the qualifier *racist*, without for all that using the designator *racism*. Henceforth the term is applied in order to characterize a party, such as "the racist party" of the same General Ludendorff, no less than its members or sympathizers ("the racists"), as well as certain attitudes or behaviors (some manner of conduct would be called "racist and anti-Semitic"): "General Ludendorff, by founding *the racist party,* showed himself to be violently anti-Jewish and anti-Catholic, and many veterans, his blind admirers, adopted the anti-Semitic insignia of the swastika or *Hakenkreuz* (⊹)."[30] The form "the racist N" appears at the same time as the form "the racists": "The leadership of the Stahlhelm [Steel Helmet], supported by the majority of members, refused to follow *the racists* down this road."[31] The adjective continues to appear in various uses ("is racist," "racist GN"), in co-occurrence with the collective noun in the plural ("the racists"): of the Front (Frontkämpferbung) founded by Ludendorff, it is said that "the political manner of conduct is officially *racist* and anti-Semitic (Jews are excluded from it), without there being a direct submission to one of the *racist* parties (the Nationalsozialistische Freiheitsbewegung [National-Socialist Freedom Movement] or the Deutsch-Völkische Freiheitspartei ['Racist' Freedom Party])"; "we have seen the failure of the *racists* of the Stahlhelm, of which the majority maintained its former manner of conduct, *the racist minority* splitting off to form the Front. The opposite happened in the Wehrwolf [Werewolf], of which the great majority went over to the *racist camp*"; "with other reactionary associations of a certain importance, one may cite the Rossbach and Ehrhardt organizations, the Wiking association..., the Oberland Line, the Bund der Frontsoldaten [League of Front-Line Soldiers], the Ludendorffbund, *an ultraracist union.*"[32]

The political designation *the racists* appears without quotation marks, in the same manner, in a study on "the political parties in Germany" published by the *Revue d'Allemagne* in April 1928. After enumerating the seven "main German parties," the author, Ludwig Bergstraesser, a member of the Reichstag, specifies:

> We are intentionally leaving out several small political parties that either are not represented in the Reichstag or have no real importance. Among these also figures a party to which an importance it does not have has been attached, abroad and especially in France: we mean *the racists*. They showed themselves markedly only in the elections of May 1924.... But... since then this party has not only dissolved, it has also divided into two factions. There is nothing astonishing about the decadence of this party. The only part of its program that attracted attention and formed a certain tie among its adherents was *a very pronounced anti-Semitism*.[33]

The co-occurrence of the words *racists* and *anti-Semitism* here has only an indicative value for an analysis of ideological representations: the main attribute of the "racist" is "anti-Semitism"; it is understood that the "racist" is a German "nationalist," most often called "extreme right." The identifying sequence is therefore the following: German, extreme right, nationalist, anti-Semitic (anti-Jewish), racist/racism. In the same study, with regard to the "nationalists" of the "National German Party," termed "of the extreme right" and characterized as "reactionary and legitimist," the author stresses the mimetic rivalry between "nationalists" and "racists,"[34] directly tied to the existence of a common border zone and overlapping to target electorates: "The nationalists have even less renounced their vehement racist speeches now that they also have as neighbors *a party of the extreme right, the racists*, and believe that they can retain only by such speeches those of their electors who feel attracted by that party."[35]

*French "Nationalism" against Germanic "Racism" (1927, 1937).*

> *It is true that nationality is not a phenomenon of race. It does not follow that it is the artificial result of the act of a contracting will.*
> Charles Maurras

In the "Preliminary Discourse (1900–1924)" of his *Enquête sur la monarchie*, Charles Maurras approaches the question of race with a certain caution:

> Practically, as scientifically, race appears to be a general factor one must consider. It is too poorly conceived to serve as the basis for any

law, but it furnishes the theme of physical and moral observations that politics utilizes. The type of a race of men that is keen and devoted to command is no more negligible than the type of a race of racehorses or hunting dogs. We needed to do lengthy experiments on mice... for it to be accepted that there is hereditary transmission of certain intellectual sensations...; that allowed us to admit that there are natural dynasties of artisans, scholars, and artists. The spontaneous wisdom of humankind has long recognized... that, as the powerful saying of [Frédéric] Mistral goes, blood pulls men far more than cables do, and finally there exist dynasties of leaders. That influence is complex and still poorly determined does not reduce us to closing our eyes and refusing attention to those born majesties.[36]

Maurras's position is clear: we do not know *what is* the hereditary transmission of racial characteristics (the *quid sit* question), but we do know *that it is,* that it takes place (the *an sit* question). We must therefore consider it. But we should not ground the laws of politics on that ill-defined reality of races,[37] that is, on physiological hereditary. That is why Maurras had harsh words for Gobineau as a theoretician of a political history grounded on physiological race: "The inept Gobineau, a genteelish Rousseau."[38] For Maurras, the "physiological" theory of race is German stuff, too German to be acceptable. In 1927, Marie de Roux posed the problem well, not without a certain propensity to hagiography:

> *Racism,* of which there is no trace in Maurras, is the most acute form of this *subjective nationalism* that is only posited as an opposition and becomes the justification for the excesses that seem to contradict it. Intellectual *pan-Germanism* is detestable because, instead of trying to give what comes from the German spirit to the treasure of world culture, to the contrary it sticks to opposing to the latter the defects and lacunae of the former, as though these were its most prized possessions.[39]

Subjective nationalism is characterized by the fact that it is "tied to cultivate the ways of being that distinguish it and that oppose it to the rest of the world."[40] It is opposed to integral nationalism, which is patriotism conceived by reason: "Every man must love his country as his mother; but he must imitate the latter only for its virtues. Thus is added to patriotism a particular and reasoned recognition that is due only insofar as national civilization makes us participate in the highest humanity."[41] Latin civilization enables precisely, according to Maurras, this fine alliance between nationalism and universality, through the work of reason. And the commentator is well grounded in concluding: "Such a reasonable nationalism can hardly flourish as *xenophobia*, if at issue is defending French culture, or as *imperialism* and *warmongering*, if at issue is foreign policy."[42] Thus there results the sloganized opposition between German barbarism and French civilization: "The wild fruit preferred to the fruit of the grafted tree, brute instinct to culture, under the pretext that the wild is no longer itself, no longer original — such is the philosophy of *pan-Germanism*."[43]

In 1927, therefore, a writer for *Action Française* proceeds to an equivalence of the terms *racism, subjective nationalism,* (intellectual) *pan-Germanism, xenophobia, bellicosity,* and *imperialism:* doing so, he ideologically constructs the German type, installs him in the wild lands of excess and of the absence of temperance (or of reason), invents the absolutely negative mythical figure of his collective enemy. This polemical lumping together, later established as a stereotype and distributed as various clichés, is constitutive of what is conveniently termed *French antiracism*, which is indiscernibly an anti-German doctrine — and the discourse of *Action Française* here only makes more visible, by gathering them in a synthesis of propaganda in which a general tendency is reflected, a multitude of dispersed and partial acts of lumping together aiming to delegitimate the figure of the German enemy. The differential characterization of antagonistic national spirits is set: *French nationalism against German racism.* "Racism" is a name properly attributed to the enemy and assumed to be inapplicable, by definition, to the French tradition. If therefore French nationalism is radically distinct from German racism, identified with pan-Germanism, it is also the case that German nationalism is a pseudonationalism, a nationalism corrupted by the excess of instinct or subjectivity, and by the absence of reason.

Ten years later, in 1937, Marie de Roux published a pamphlet called *Le Nationalisme français*, in which he again took up the question, integrating new identifying references (to the Aryan dogma, Hitlerism, National Socialism, the mystique of the chosen race) into the same system of stigmatizing the enemy. If racism, the German doctrinal specificity, consisted of setting up particular characteristics as universal norms and inflating oneself into an imperialist and warmongering enemy, French nationalism was characterized by a sense of measure that is just as much that of the universal and that merges with a force of peace. If the adherence to proper national characteristics, or the "determined preference for what is good for the nation to which one belongs,"[44] defines the foundation of all nationalism, there are "two ways of conceiving the adherence to the characteristics."[45] We will privilege the description of racism:

> One may ascribe to [national characteristics] such a value that one makes them into the measure of human values, the canon by which one judges all things, even those whose nature is to be universal. The people that has such pride, that believes itself to be the chosen race (the mystique of race completes that of language), through a logical deduction ends up believing that it has the right to impose by force, on the rest of humanity, the superior human form of which it is the exemplar. The best elements are assimilated, the others subjugated. This is racism.[46]

But specific to "German racist theory" is that it "constructed an Aryan dogma by which it judges the world": "National Socialism is the outcome of this mystique.... The sentiment of the German race thus expressly becomes the standard, the measure of universal moral values."[47] Now, it is "a disorder to want to submit them to the particular sentiment of a people."[48] Racism is the lack of measure that results in the imperialist will to impose a particular truth as absolute. In the view of *Action Française,* the racist says: "The particular way of thinking in my country, the way of feeling that belongs to it, is the absolute truth, the universal truth, and I will not rest or pause before I have ordered the world by law, that of my birthplace."[49] Now, insists Roux, *"racism is completely foreign to French nationalism,"*[50] which sets in motion "exactly the opposite notion: in order to love a woman, it is not necessary to believe that she is the most beautiful creature in the universe; our happiness may be tied to her gazes without the need to impose on all eyes the shade of hers."[51] French nationalism, *"in its most acute, most demanding form..., is permeated with the sense of the universal, and that is the intimate reason that makes it a force of peace."*[52]

In his *Lectures,* a posthumous collection of articles published in 1937, Jacques Bainville reduces the doctrine of National Socialism to its two essential components, "racism" and nostalgic "naturism," to which he believes he can deny any Germanic specificity, at least with respect to intellectual provenance. His interpretation of "Germanism" therefore apparently differs, on this point, from that of Maurras, who insisted on the Fichtean origins of "racism." On the subject of a 1933 issue of the *Nouvelle Revue Française* on the National Socialist doctrines, Bainville writes:

> The elements of Hitlerian doctrine, in analysis, are nonetheless weak. There is nothing in it that is not known and even that French books have not furnished. Gobineau is the source of racism. Hitler's Minister of Public Education the other day cited as a bible the book of a professor of anthropology at the University of Rennes, Vacher de Lapouge. I remember very well that this book *L'Aryen* was published around 1900 [actually, in 1899] and that Charles Maurras put the very young reader that I was on guard against the reveries of a pure race. Another element of National Socialism is a sort of naturism, of an agricultural golden age, of an artisanship raised on the debris of machines. It is precisely on this point and by the refusal to accept the materialist conception of history that this socialism is anti-Marxist.[53]

The doctrine of races imputed to Gobineau thereby plays, in recurrent fashion, the role of a repulsive myth, identified with the German faction in France: "We are just as much with Fustel as against Renan, as against Gobineau, before the mad admiration that the latter two show for Germany," declares Maurras.[54] The mind behind integral nationalism vigorously refuses to be placed "in the school of a visionary toward whom we have never experienced anything but an indifference tempered here and there by a just horror."[55] The difference holds up on one essential point: heredity and the political tradition cannot be reduced to physiological heredity.[56] To think otherwise, like Gobineau and Germanic racism, is to founder in the most pernicious idolatry:

> Quality, birth, race, privilege, thus conceived, thus separated from the profession of serving the state, become ridiculous and incomprehensible anachronisms: they are made into little divinities as strictly personal, as false, and as mendacious for a Gobineau, for example, as the idea of duty could have been for Kant or the idea of right for Rousseau.[57]

We have analyzed the two appearances, in the French language, of the word *racism* in their respective lexical and ideological contexts. In so doing we have seen how much the history of vocabulary, overdetermined by general intellectual history and political history, participated in these histories. The analyses presented seemed to us to justify the distinction introduced between the "prenotion" (1895–97, 1902, and subsequent years) and the "notion" of racism (1922–25 and subsequent years). These two ideological and semantic configurations correspond to two epochs or two regimes in the evolution of the term *racism*. They are inscribed in two successive ideologico-discursive spaces that may be considered *incommensurable*, in spite of the appearances brought on by the continued presence of the lexeme *racism/racist*. But the same signifier is joined in two systems of signification that are themselves incommensurable: from the simple equivalence of the qualities "French" and "racist" (1897) to the node of traits "pan-Germanist"/"anti-Semitic"/"German" (enemies of France)/"extreme right"/"Nazism," and so on, in the 1920s and 1930s, one moves from the preracist meaning of the term (the adjective *racist* may be considered, from 1895 to 1897, a singularity, if not a hapax legomenon) to its meaning as fixed in the general vocabulary, the latter including an oscillation between two poles: the theory of race (an explanatory model of historical evolution on the basis of a racial determinism, in a perspective that is either inegalitarianist/universalist or differentialist/particularist) and the relations of rivalry/hate among the "races" (as either zoological or historical collective entities: peoples, nations, ethnic groups, and so on).[58] These are the Gobinean and the "social Darwinist" poles, but their "antifascist" acts of propagandistic lumping together efface the distinction: "Nazi racism" is situated without distinction in the Gobinean lineage or in that of "social Darwinism," regularly confounded with eugenicism or selectionism. (The conjunctures of the two traditions pose various problems of interpretation that their lumping together, indeed their identification, magically suppresses, prohibiting any other approach than that dictated by denunciation and condemnation.) Propagandistic discourse really did nothing but reflect the confusion of the ideological heritages that was achieved by official National Socialist doctrine, a mix of elitist and competitive individualism, of communitarianist racism and universalist/inegalitarian racism (imperialism), of eugenic scientism and neoromantic, "organic" populism.

## The Preparation of the Ideologico-Discursive Field (1914–18) and Its Completion (1936–38)

*German Universalism or Barbarism*
*(a Polemic of* Action Française, *1915)*

> Ancient Greece never succeeded in becoming a state and, in that privileged corner of the world, the question of races, from the very first testaments, was as complex as in modern Europe; nonetheless those interests defined well everything by which a Hellene was opposed to "stammerers," to the barbaroi, and we ourselves believe we still feel something of the immense treasure that was represented for those men by "Hellenism," that is, the language with the thought that it favored and conveyed. Georges Dumézil

A call to German intellectuals, *Appeal to the Civilized World (Aufruf an die Kulturwelt)*,[59] dated October 3, 1914, contains in point 5 (*"It is not true* that we wage war in contempt of people's rights") the following statements: "Those who ally themselves with the Russians and the Serbs, and who do not fear inciting Mongols or Negroes against the white race, thus offering to the civilized world the most shameful spectacle imaginable, are certainly the last to have the right to claim the role of defenders of European civilization."[60]

Louis Dimier, commenting on this text, impugns its arguments one by one, before turning against his adversary the accusation of barbarism:

> The accusation of barbarism for a nation has nothing to do with the greater or lesser civilization of its allies, and no more (and this is something else altogether) of the race and color to which they belong.... What classifies a nation as barbarous is its acts. To those who denounce attacks, massacres, and pillages, it is ridiculous to respond that they have allies who are barbarous. This response alone accuses of barbarism the one who enacts it, because the essential barbarism consists of being incapable of conducting one's thought, of not understanding what one says.[61]

Besides that he sophistically resorts to the etymology of the word *barbarous* in order to term his adversary barbarous in return (the one who conceives poorly speaks poorly), the historian of *Action Française* invokes factual proofs (real acts) against racial prejudices: barbarism is not a property enveloped by the essence of such and such a people but rather a trait revealed by its mode of existence and manner of thinking or speaking. In the face of a people, one does not ask who it is but rather what it has done: in Talcott Parsons's terminology, Dimier argues according to the variable of the performance, against that of quality. Such a reformulation of the problem, involving a redefinition of barbarism,[62] allows the polemicist to reassume the offensive position in the accusation. It is enough for him, henceforth, to bring in the proofs that the Germans pillage and massacre for barbarism to be inferred from the facts that reveal it, the visibility of the latter confirming the evidence of "barbarism" of thought and language.

The polemicist historian proceeds to another type of argumentation on the specific question of "Negroes," distinguished from that of "Mongols," who are unveiled as in reality referring to "a nation like the Japanese, organized in the genre of those of Europe" — the objection of Eurocentric style is thereby destroyed. But the "Negroes" pose a problem: Dimier is from now on going to circumvent the adverse argument, is not going to treat the "Negro" theme as such, is going to shift the question onto the terrain of the leadership and mastery of those backup "troops." "It is no less vain to object that there are Negroes in the French army.... Who *directs* these Negroes? Who *commands* them? To what *discipline* are they submitted? Is France not present in this discipline and in this command? Are they themselves not *trained* by a long arm to accept this direction?" Here is the content of the response to the objection: the "trained Negroes" present no danger; they are only instruments of war of which it would be stupid to deprive oneself. In this fashion Dimier can conclude, putting in play the logic of total warfare, "We do not see what reason would require France to deprive itself of the extra troops that are hers, in a war that calls on the deployment of all her forces."[63]

The following point from the *Appeal* will allow its commentator and adversary to conduct a universalist argument against one of the themes of the German propaganda text: the invocation of the threat weighing on "German civilization" *(deutsche Kultur)*.[64] Point 6 of the *Appeal* develops the particularist theme thus, along the lines of the argument of legitimate defense:

> *It is not true* that the struggle against what is called our militarism is not directed against our culture *[unsere Kultur]*, as our hypocritical enemies claim. Without our militarism, our civilization *[die deutsche*

*Kultur]* would have been annihilated long ago. It is to protect our civilization that this militarism was born in our country, exposed like no other to invasions that have continued over the centuries. The German army and the German people are one and the same.... To you who know us and who have been, like us, the guardians of the most precious possessions of humanity, we shout, Believe us! Believe that in this struggle we will continue to the end as a civilized people *[als ein Kulturvolk]*, as a people to whom the heritage of Goethe, Beethoven, and Kant is as sacred as its soil and its hearth.[65]

Dimier's argument is effected in two strokes: first of all he puts in doubt the value of "German culture" as such, and then he impugns the very idea of a German culture-civilization. On the first point, Dimier is formal: " 'German culture,' taken in itself, apart from the men of merit who have been born in Germany, is as detestable as German might, as German militarism.... It is true that our friends the Germans have difficulty understanding that. The idea does not occur to them that someone might simply speak ill of something as fine as their civilization."[66] But how does one justify absolutely such a negative evaluation? For it is a matter not only of retorting that German culture-civilization does not have the value with which the *Appeal* graces it, but much more radically of denying it any value. This is the second point of the critical commentary, whose argument consists of relating the proclaimed "German civilization" to the superior interests of humankind. The polemicist of *Action Française* takes a stance on the "highest" level: that of "civilization," involving a universalist or "catholic" perspective expressly opposed to any particularist point of view — here all particular determination is a negation of the essence of humankind. "For what interest would humankind have in conserving German civilization? On the contrary, how could its interest not demand that this civilization not be wiped *[getilgt]* from the face of the earth? Do intellectuals not see that these words alone, German civilization, *deutsche Kultur,* express a usurpation?"[67] Here is the center of the argument, isolated in negative fashion: if there is a usurpation, if the invocation of a "German civilization" is only an imposture based on an obscure idea, it is the case that civilization is one and universal. *Civilization:* the expression must remain in the singular, for it refers to a unique and unitary attribute of humankind, susceptible of participation (each man or each people may claim to participate in civilization), but not of fragmentation into specific unities, as "original" as they are heterogeneous. The switch to the plural can in this sense be only mystification, nourished on prejudices. Dimier's strictly universalist argument is the following:

> Either civilization is nothing, or it is something common to all nations. It should therefore not, as such, bear a national mark. It may consist only of the discovery, application, practice, and habit of principles of value for all men. Local prejudices, particular moods, and ethnic determinations are not part of it. So there is not, there should not be, German civilization *[deutsche Kultur]*, any more than French or English civilization, or Italian civilization, any more than Bushmen's or Turkish civilization.[68]

Germanism has held up as absolute its cultural nationalism: here is the fault against the universalist spirit that Dimier denounces. What Germany has baptized "German culture" or "German civilization" is only a set of particularities issuing from the very "tastes," "fantasies," and "moods" that should have been precisely "regulated...on the common model of the just, the proportionate, the reasonable," to enable access to civilization. But Germany has aimed for the impossible and achieved a monstrosity: it has "tried to have a civilization that would be all its own."[69]

This refutation assumes a conception of the universal history of civilization that gives it its meaning. If there is in fact a single history of civilization, the latter has successively been incarnated in those wholes ordinarily baptized with the name "civilization" (Greek, Latin, of the Renaissance, and so on). This phenomenon must be correctly understood: civilization is the eponym of "civilizations"; it is from civilization that the latter get their common name. "Civilizations" are thus termed only in that they illustrate more perfectly, in a given historical epoch, civilization in general: "Among the modern nations, if one of them has at some time given its name to an epoch of civilization, it was...because the latter carried higher than the others these traits of common civilization. Hence was it said that the civilization of the Renaissance was Italian, that the civilization of the eighteenth century was French."[70] The various "civilizations" have meaning only in designating the different epochs of civilization. Dimier thereby tries to sketch a philosophy of history in which the universality of human nature and of its main attribute ("civilization") are projected onto various epochs, according to the degree of participation manifested by these "civilizational" epochs.

If, therefore, one must impugn the exorbitant claim of the partisans of "German civilization," "that does not mean that one nation may not hold up as its work, either as a whole or in part, the civilization that humankind enjoys: nothing prevents the fact that what is suited to all is the discovery, the result of the efforts of one."[71] The "civilizational" character of "civilizations" comes to them from the quality of their respective "contributions" to civilization: "Thus immense contributions to civilization have been furnished by Rome and Greece, and it is in this way that there has been talk of Greek civilization and Latin civilization."[72] It remains that the institution of such peoples as models of civilization has assumed a labor of these peoples on themselves, by which they have been reformed, purified, raised to the status of the most faithful images of civilization. To speak of Greek or Latin civilization "does not signify that Greek or Latin prejudices, Greek or Latin moods have suddenly become the rules of reason." It is "on the contrary ... by correcting these prejudices, by subordinating these moods, ... that they have deserved to become the instructors of humankind."[73]

The instructing civilizations are therefore those that preach by example, by setting themselves up as universal types by virtue of the effort of humanization to which they have attested through themselves. The "civilizational" models imitate each other insofar as they are in themselves imitations of civilization as a single and ideal form. It is therefore necessary to remain classical, to imitate the Greeks and Romans: "The understanding of their doctrine, the majesty and fullness of their examples, the naturalness of their imagination, has subjected men to them; by *imitating* them, men have not had the feeling of transforming themselves into Romans or Greeks, but rather of entering into *participation* with the common good of humanity."[74] In this way, the true alternative is the following: either civilization, whose nature is to be universal (in which one may then participate), or German barbarism, based on the fiction of a civilization that would be only German, accompanied by the claim of imposing it on the world, and borne by the will to conquest.[75] This development by Dimier illustrates the classicist variant of modern universalism, while showing how much the latter is constituted in and by the polemic directed against all forms of cultural or "civilizational" particularism (nationalism, racism). It should just as much be recalled that the nationalism of *Action Française* is conceived within the horizon of universality: integral nationalism is for itself only an epoch of catholicity, held in its historical image. For if it is true that the nation designates the supreme reality in the order of political ideas,[76] "spiritual goods are indivisible and common to the human spirit."[77] The suggested alternative follows: either one is a man or one is German — a formula of universalist exclusion.

## "German Nationalist Ideology" through the Lens of French Antiracist Ideology (a Talk by Edmond Vermeil, December 19, 1936)

In a talk given on December 19, 1936, the Germanist Edmond Vermeil began by characterizing "postwar German nationalist ideology" by the fact that the latter "claims to be, in general, at once *revolutionary* and *conservative:* revolutionary in the sense that it tries to mop up the influences that the democratic West or communist and Marxist Russia have exercised on Germany; conservative because it intends to return to healthy German traditions."[78] Vermeil next applies himself to defining "postwar nationalist ideology" according to the "three phases" of its development, the common objective of all the trends being the quest for a new order. "Discontent with the pseudo-revolution of 1918, [nationalist ideology] invariably proposes to define the true Revolution..., that which will transform Germany and enable it to accomplish its mission in Europe."[79] This true and truly German revolution is what Vermeil sets out to seek, in the link between the "revolutionary conservatives" and the National Socialists: "Its first prophets or announcers, such as Walther Rathenau and Oswald Spengler, then the somewhat coherent group formed by Moeller van den Bruck and the editors of *Tat* — Carl Schmitt, H. Zehrer, F. Fried, G. Wirsing, and others — and finally the Hitlerian leaders themselves, all of them seeking a new order."[80] This is the first assimilation on which Vermeil's critical argument rests. By the authority of his scientific personality, it will quickly become a piece of basic ideological evidence in the study of National Socialism, its intellectual sources, and its cultural contexts. Here the vulgate is grasped at the moment of its inaugural scholarly formulation in France. Vermeil continues, adding to the thesis of similitude that of doctrinal continuity, indeed identity:

> The schema is always the same. It is, from the critical point of view: (1) anti-Western protest; (2) anti-Marxist and anti-Communist

protest; (3) protest against the influences that Germany has undergone. And from the positive point of view, it is: (1) a definition of German and National "Socialism"; (2) a definition of the state that will serve as its instrument; (3) finally, a definition of the goals that must be those of the foreign policy of the Reich.[81]

The diagnosis that Vermeil gives is that "German nationalism is the result of a tragedy," which presents three faces: "An economic and social tragedy, a constitutional and political tragedy, an intellectual and moral tragedy — these three tragedies are one and the same."[82] Thus the study of "the reality and the notion of the *Volk*, of the people always in search of itself and of its own destiny," would be articulated around three theses:

> (1) that the state called "totalitarian" already virtually existed in Germany around 1930; (2) that here its more or less hidden presence made parliamentary procedure absolutely impossible; (3) that a middle bourgeoisie and peasantry, deprived of traditions and political education, found themselves driven back by their own distress into *an elementary and brutal racism* that, exempting them from thinking, brought to them, with the simple solutions that they needed, a sort of dictatorial "decisionism" that worked to galvanize them in view of the coming militarism.[83]

Here is what Vermeil believes he may characterize as "the arrival of dictatorial biologism,"[84] that is, of a state racism whose origins are confounded with the history of the notion of the *Volk*:

> *Volk, Volkstum,* race, National Socialism: these constitute the eternal *Ersatz* that Germany invents for itself in the face of ideas that, next to and in front of it, have blossomed into homogeneous and successful, and thereby stable, civilizations — whether it is a matter, for the West, of the Roman Catholic idea, the French laic and democratic idea, the Calvinist and Anglo-Saxon idea, or, for the Russian East, the Marxist and Communist idea.[85]

The polemical opposition is set: on the one hand, the bad German, unstable, and undefinable principle of race, bearer of all convulsions to come; on the other, the good, stable, and founding principles of "homogeneous and successful... civilizations."

Hence Germany appears to be a particular case, in resonance with its own hyperbolic affirmation of its national particularism. Vermeil opposes German nationalism, with its main attributes — relativism, nihilism, biologism, racism, and Caesarism — to "eternal humanism," whose existence he postulates in the metahistorical vision of a scene in which positive and negative values confront each other. Presupposed in the interpretation is that the German bourgeoisie is "deprived of traditions" and that this explains its palinodic instabilities: "Bourgeois thought in Germany... is ferociously turning against the values to which it owes its existence. It is annihilating all the values by which man tries to put his mark on the long period and to establish a society of peoples, all of which is a matter of eternal humanism."[86] Concerning the latter, Vermeil enumerates the following definitional traits: "Historical criteria, the transcendence of Christian salvation, the progress of the Enlightenment, the messianic hopes of Marx."[87] This is the set of key ideas that, in and through German nationalism, "collapses into a nameless relativism, into a terrible nihilism whose secret and whose full bitterness Nietzsche knew."[88] The encompassing procedure of the Germanist historian is evidently a component of the polemical genre to which these analyses belong. The postulate of continuity, the evidence of a direct lineage between Nietzsche and Hitler, by way of Sombart and a few others, unveils the bias of the scholar engaged in the antifascist propaganda of the epoch. There is a continual progression, therefore, of Nietzschean "nihilism" to pan-Germanism and Hitlerian racism:

> The war may approach, the war may come, followed by defeat and the subsequent hardships, and we will then see the triumph of the most elementary biologism and the most brutal racism. At that time, all the values of the past will be treated as "ideologies." There will no longer be belief in instinct or the unconscious. Everything will be used for this demonstration: the late philosophy of Nietzsche, Freudianism, indeed Bergsonism. And this crude objectivism, reduced to the dimension of vitalist simplism, will turn against the West with more fury than ever.[89]

The logic of lumping together leads the scrupulous historian to such excesses that, fixed as primary evidence and basic schemes of interpretation, have become tradition. Hence the political historian Zeev Sternhell, to cite only one author among so many others, begins in the 1970s and 1980s from the same presuppositions, which are those of a discourse of propaganda whose particular circumstances disappeared forty years ago.[90] The conclusive axiom of such an interpretive schema is that once "the psychological and intellectual 'climate' in which racism must triumph"[91] has been determined, through the history of its origins, the historian is able to foresee, not without some prophesying, the future of Germany, which can be only very somber. The premonitory explanation is done by "atmospheric" causes, that is, by the ideologico-cultural environment:

> Everything will be ready for Caesarism. The atmosphere has been created in which racism will be fruitful at its leisure. What is important to us, from this point of view, in the subtle distinctions that Sombart, in his *Deutscher Sozialismus*,[92] establishes between a nation and a *Volk*, or in the enumeration of all the meanings that this term may take, or in the patient study of terms such as *Volkstum, Völkheit, völkisch*, and so on? Let it be sufficient for us to have determined with some precision the ambiance in which German racism has formed and developed. Once its historical, intellectual, and religious origins are known, the rest follows.[93]

What here characterizes the analysis that Vermeil presents is that it fuses the university tradition of the erudite Germanist historian and the polemical disposition and ties the study of origins and causes with the critical intervention destined to combat the enemy who is confounded with the object of analysis. That is why the patient and cautious genealogical procedure of the historian of ideas is degraded to summary explanation by the "atmosphere," the "climate," the "ambiance," brought back to their "historical, intellectual, and religious origins" considered to be sufficient causes ("the rest follows"), whereas, correlatively, the scientific ideal of distinction is abolished in the polemical practice of lumping together. To paraphrase Vermeil, we will see that then everything is ready for one to liken, without empty nuances, a Sombart to a Hitler, or even a Fichte to a Rosenberg.... But Vermeil in his time had no small excuse: National Socialism appeared to be the real enemy that it was; the appearance of Nazism then coincided with its essence. Nazism was not yet that fictional object populating almost single-handedly the permanent collective nightmare of the liberal democracies, before finding itself in competition with communism, indeed dethroned by it — but never completely, so much is the specter of Nazism (neo-Nazism, the resurgence of the "vile beast") ideologically maintained by international communist propaganda. With Vermeil's contributions, the scholarly variant of the French antiracist vulgate is set, on the left and anti-German. In 1936 and 1937, antiracist ideology of French tradition, covering a field extending from the communist left to *Action Française* (not including dissidents), was definitively constituted and formulated.

*Spengler Nazified (1933–36).* Let us take another example of a treatment through lumping together. In a study published in 1936, Lucien Febvre approached the "case" of Spengler under the title "Oswald Spengler: The Greatness and the Decadence of a National Socialist Prophet." The author of *The Decline of the West* is henceforth stuck with his infamous label, which authorizes contempt and irony with regard to the "ideas of the prophet, . . . the one who does not hesitate at all to proclaim himself the 'Copernicus of history.' "[94] The classical method of the polemical genre, the teleological reduction of a work of thought, may turn up as early as the announcement of a program of analysis: "Let us try to understand him, plainly — and that means, in this case, to situate his book and its success in relation to the needs of a Germany from that time on gestating what was going to become Hitlerian National Socialism."[95] Spengler's philosophical thought is next stigmatized for being only a "totalitarian history," in a manner that draws out the identifying metaphor, Spengler/Hitlerism. In 1933, Henri Massis had already hit on the formula in his study "Spengler comme précurseur du national-socialisme": "The Romans, for Spengler, are barbarians without a soul, without philosophy, without art, *racists* to the point of brutality."[96] In his interview with Mussolini in September 1933, Massis again raised the issue of racist barbarism in an ironic remark: "Do they [the German historians who, in 1933, put forward the analogy between the Prussians and the Romans] not see in the Romans *barbarians, racists* to the point of brutality, shamelessly adhering to practical successes?"[97] Brutality and lowly practical materialism are thus imputed to the Prussian sort of racist barbarian. Spengler's recourse to the analogy proves, according to Febvre, the unscientific character of this philosopher's thought, which is reduced to the seductive use of "vividly colored imagery" or of "these fine words, these vitalist metaphors: the birth, flourishing, and death of cultures — old material renewed."[98] Spengler's success is thus due to his use of the old "vitalist" arsenal in the service of an analogical pseudohistory. Of course Febvre can only pick out Spengler's violent National Socialist critiques and positions. What does it matter? This "Prussian or Saxon petty bourgeois," "shaping himself into a prophet,"[99] is no different from the "strictly obedient Nazis":[100] it is enough to mention "the political programs of a man who counted, they say, among the very first adherents of National Socialism."[101] If, beginning in 1930, Spengler "lost the general esteem of Nazi circles,"[102] it is not in the least from the fact of a change in his attitude: it is to the contrary "because his tenacious prophecies ceased to be in accord with the ideology of the triumphant party,"[103] which was given over to active optimism. But the supremely ridiculous prophet "continued to offer himself to the Nazis as their true leader — or, at the very least, as their true adviser."[104] The execution was supposed to be definitive, and it has been so at least until now, the late 1980s. But hasty Nazifications appeal to unscrupulous de-Nazifications.

## The Two Cores of the Definition: Purity and Inequality

In the article in the 1932 *Larousse*, the reference given for the designator *racist* sets a restriction of its extension to the "German National Socialists," determined by the attribution of an aim characterized as follows: they "claim to represent the pure German race, by excluding the Jews," and so on.[105] One of the two constitutive metaphorical cores of the definitions of racism appeared thus in 1932, with regard to an identifying reference to National Socialism before its establishment as a regime: *purity of race*. In the *Supplément* of 1953, the second metaphorical core, the *superiority of race,* appears in contiguity with the first, in the same definitional formula for *racism:* "Theory whose purpose is to protect the purity of the race in a nation and that attributes to it a superiority above all others."[106] The self-attribution of racial purity and superiority is hence the act described as grounding the racism of the National Socialists. This twofold qualification of a racism specific to the political history of the twentieth century was generalized and normalized to become both poles, used in conjunction or not, of all the definitions of racism. The latter therefore presuppose the system of evaluation, standardized by self-designated racists, referring to the race called "pure" and "superior." To the two pivots copresent in the 1953 definition are joined two complementary characterizations of racism: the self-attribution of a superiority grounding an absolute right of conquest[107] and the self-qualification as a pure race that grounds a categorical imperative of the preservation of identity with itself. "Purity of blood" is the property of the proper identity, threatened by any contact with the outside — the latter because it is impure, is the supposed source of impurity. This self-defense of blood represents the primary duty and defines the most legitimate of sacrifices in the stigmatized ideological space — to preserve the purity of the proper race and to fortify the superiority of origin:

> The German National Socialist leaders did not recoil before any sacrifice to impose on the views of the German people the obsessive image of the ideal biological type of the German race. To preserve one's body and blood from any soiling, to fortify one's body through sport to make it the instrument of a virile will and of a fruitful maternity — these are the duties that an unflagging propaganda inculcated from the early school years on.[108]

In 1953, the *Supplément* to the *Larousse du XX$^e$ siècle* also broadened the field of the historical moorings of racism, synthesizing various elements of encyclopedic presentation of the phenomena into a model that, in 1988, still seems to be in use in the antiracist vulgate, Gobineau's *Inequality of Human Races* (1853–55) posited as grounding tradition. Gobinism is reduced to the assertion of the absolute superiority of "the pure white race alone, the Aryan race"; post-1870 Germany is denounced as a privileged welcoming ground for Gobinean racism, fertilized by "Nietzsche's theory of the overman" and by Wagnerism to legitimate the claims of pan-Germanism, then of National Socialism; the relationship among Aryanist racism, eugenicism (or racial hygiene), and anti-Semitism is assumed to be natural;[109] the concept of racism is extended to pan-Slavism, Mussolinian fascism, and the eugenic concerns of the Anglo-Saxon countries.[110] What finally appears in this article is the normalization of the mode of *scientific refutation* of racism, whose two argumentative axes, presented from the very beginning as naturally implying each other, are outstandingly summarized in the following statements:

> Permeated with the idea that they owe their supremacy to their racial purity, certain peoples assume the right to impose their conceptions on others. Now, this theory does not seem defensible from the scientific point of view, for pure races disappeared from our planet long ago, and, besides, it is not possible to speak of the superiority of one race, even if it is blond and dolichocephalic; each has its proper qualities, and it is the peoples of strongly composite origin that have most contributed to the progress of civilization.[111]

The paradox, and the irony of ideological history, here stems from the fact that, on the first point (the disappearance of the pure races), Gobineau was in perfect agreement; and from the fact that contemporary neoracism[112] has made the second point (the irreducibility of incomparable differences) the principle of its apologetic elaborations on ethnopluralism, in which "difference" is presented as an "antitotalitarian idea" and therefore as an egalitarian one.[113] These are avatars of the legitimating use of science: before the occurrence of the genocidal act of Nazism, the scientist balance seemed in some regards to tilt in favor of the theory of race, if not of "racism"; today, with Nazism the object of a universal impugnment, although the speakers termed scientific are divided on the question, the mass of discourses produced on the theory of race, likened to racism, seems to define a majoritarian antiracist position of scientific society.[114] Is this a change in the norms of ideological conformity or a decisive rupture in the history of the life sciences, with repercussions in the field of the anthropological sciences?

*Four*

# An Ideal Type: "Racism" as an Ideological Construction

### The Racism of Antiracism

One may represent, by a sequence of clear and well-illustrated propositions, the connected series of operations put in play in the corpus of definitional statements considered (1932–1987),[1] which, from the "simple" to the "complex," from the presupposition to that which presupposes, construct the common meaning of "racism." The fourteen characteristic traits noted below, which include the representations, beliefs, and judgments presupposed (or expressly posited) by the standard antiracist usage of the word *racism,* enable the construction of an ideal type of "racism" as fundamental evidence of antiracist ideology.

1. Racism is described as taking the form of an affirmation, which may be made explicit as that of a "belief"[2] or an "admission."[3] Belief marks the principle of racism. Doubt is not racist. Racism is of the order of believing.

2. Next may be noted the existence of a conceptual forming of the affirmed belief: "theory,"[4] "doctrine,"[5] "system,"[6] "ideology,"[7] "myth."[8] There is theorization, notional jury-rigging that, on the basis of an absolute conviction, brings about the construction of an edifice of coherent appearance.

3. Racist conceptual elaboration is sometimes termed "political."[9] Most often, the political character of the "theory" remains on

the level of suggestion. The involved or interested nature of the "theory" is often discredited by its designation as a set of "prejudices."[10] There is, in racism, an argument bearing on primary material, the heritage of words and ideas, which have to be justified by "good reasons." Racism appears to be a dogmatic construction, resting on a base of rationalizations.

4. Racism is often stigmatized as a "mental illness,"[11] a set of "perverse" theories,[12] and a "paranoid reaction."[13] Militant discourse willingly imagines and denounces it through the metaphor of "leprosy": "It is a recurrent illness of modern times. Or better: an *epidemic,*" declared Léopold Sédar Senghor in 1964.[14] Certain authors extend the pathological metaphor by proposing to identify in racism, "as in an illness, several degrees of evolution," from mere abusive generalization (prejudices, stereotypes) to extermination (genocide), by way of segregation (apartheid):[15] the polemical images and metaphors thus enable the construction of a coherent representation of racism, its figures (designated by antiracist stereotypes) supposedly appearing on a single continuum. In a no less general fashion, racism is presented as a "scourge" *(fléau)*: the "racist scourge"[16] is denounced in the same way as drugs or terrorism (more recently, around the mid-1980s). This coinscription in the metaphorical class of "scourges" is quite interesting. A scourge is, says the *Robert* dictionary, a "calamity that befalls a people": a scourge may be natural (such as a tidal wave) or cultural (such as a plague or a war). Racism is hence presented as a fundamentally harmful, disastrous, fearsome phenomenon, something analogous to a cataclysm or a catastrophe. Antiracist argument often reworks the classical scheme of the corruption of governments through a cascade of "scourges": racism would be, for example, a corruption of nationalism or a perversion of ethnocentrism. In 1868, Lucien-Anatole Prévost-Paradol thus affirmed that democratic government is inclined to "slide first toward the scourge of anarchy, then soon after toward the shame and the scourge of despotism."[17] A general madness or natural/cultural scourge, racism is no less a figure of "barbarism," like terrorism, blind or targeted. The association SOS-Racisme is now giving itself the right to condemn in the same way racism and terrorism, these two faces of modern barbarism: "this murderous and bloody barbarism" (its characterization); "the peril that weighs on our freedom to live in a democratic and sovereign society" (the definition of its danger); "the undersigned appeal to the unity and cohesion of all

those living in France, whatever their origin, to vanquish the scourge of terrorism."[18] Such likenings are based on a postulate in the form of an alternative: democracy or barbarism. The difficulty of such a vision is that the designated figures of barbarism are also products of modern democratic society. From abarbarous democracy derives the barbarism to which democracy is absolutely opposed.

The behaviors and representations called racist are therefore willfully described according to metaphors borrowed from mental pathology.[19] Racism is rejected as irrational, erroneous, delirious, demented. Three preferential metaphorical treatments are discernible: the racist is either psychiatrized, criminalized, or demonized. The racist is the abnormal one who scandalizes. Through its composite representation of the racist adversary, projected into the disturbing universe of madness, of the demonic, and of the anomic, the discourse is presupposed as conducted in a sure and normal world by a mentally healthy subject, who is at the same time an honest citizen and a virtuous being.

5. The existence of human groups separable by the summation of at least observable distinctive traits is an object of belief. There are differences among the human groups that are ordinarily named "races."[20] It happens that critical analyses are encountered that present as evidence the thesis of a necessary and direct relationship between racial categorization and racist thought. The statutes of the Study and Information Group "Races and Racism" in 1937 included this description of the primary objective of the association: "to study scientifically the notion of race and the doctrines that proceed from it."[21] From the perspective of the sociology of science, today there is a willing insistence on the constructive, and not only descriptive, act represented by cutting humanity up into "races": doing so, scientists "suggested a vision of the world, a conception of humanity — and therefore an ethics and a politics."[22] The assertion of difference is most often presupposed by that of inequality, of a "hierarchy,"[23] of a "superiority,"[24] of a "supremacy."[25] It remains that the position of a difference is logically distinct from that of an inequality and precedes it in any explicit argument.

6. The affirmation that these differences are inseparably physical, moral (values, interests, beliefs), and intellectual (the capacity to know, to understand, to explain) — in short, that they are in play at all levels of the human, that they extend to all dimensions of the anthropological field.

7. The conviction that there exists a stable correspondence between the physical and the mental. The relationship between the corporeal and the psychic components of man is either posited or presupposed. This psychosomatic relationship may be designated as the physiognomic condition of racist thought.[26] It is the affirmation of a coincidence, a parallel, an analogy, or a similitude between man's physical appearance and his mental organization that is perceptible only in its effects.[27] The stability of the psychosomatic correspondence assumes the fixity of the terms of the relationship, the permanency of the "races" or "types" distinguished. The sign of difference, race, is "the sign of permanency" in racism.[28]

8. The practice of the hermeneutist's gaze and/or of the deciphering of indices: the faculties of the inside are supposedly readable by the visible appearances, the mental unveiling itself in some fashion in the corporeal. More precisely: the forms and forces of the mind are revealed in the perceptible forms of the body. The body is the generalized figure of the mind: its metonymical index, its metaphor, its resembling image, its allegory. One will recognize here what Carlo Ginzburg named the "paradigm of the index," an epistemological model whose emergence he has shown in the field of the sciences of man and of society over the course of the last thirty years of the twentieth century: the stigmata of degeneracy identified by the psychiatrists, the morbid symptoms of medical semiotics, the policing indices (the criminal gives himself away with his fingerprints), the failed acts decoded by the method of psychoanalytic interpretation, the method of attributing pictorial works perfected by Morelli (marking the significant details), and so on — all these illustrate the broad distribution of the paradigm of the index. The racist perception of humans, besides the fact that it fulfills a function of social categorization, itself puts into play the technique of that "base intuition" comprising the decipherment of indices.[29]

9. The hereditary transmission of physical differences is postulated. Observable differences are thus brought into a strictly natural lineage. It is life itself that is said to bear the power to reproduce differences by designing discontinuous continuities — the differential heredity of lineages or races. Each group is supposed to transmit its own differences, hence persevering in its being. Heredity is henceforth posited as a productive and reproductive cause of human somatic organization.

The individual is perceived only as some representative of the type, who alone really exists. It follows that racism is anti-individualist. First, with the individual as only the exhibitor of the race, the individual is treated as the specimen of a racial type and thereby even negated as such. "If you've seen one, you've seen them all," goes one formula that circulated a lot before the appearance of the word *racism,* one of whose content traits it nonetheless makes explicit:[30] the illusion of uniformity. Next, it is not individuals who are said to be unequal, at least at first; it is rather the fixed classes of humans that are called races. There is a specific equality of those above, an equality of individuals taken as representatives of the race presumed to be superior. Here is a fundamental difference between racism and elitism, which is individualist by definition — as elitism defines legitimate inequality within the strict limits of democratic reason, implying equal opportunity for all at the start of the competition. Racism is then situated at an equal distance from a radical nominalism, that implicated by the sociopolitical model of liberalism, for which only individuals engaging in interaction really exist, and from a universalism by which humanity, as a single species and a moral idea (to be realized), possesses its own mode of existence. This is neither individualist nominalism nor religious or profane "catholicism" (the latter would be socialist internationalism). The ethical corollary of the negation of the individual as an anthropological dimension is the lack of worth of persons insofar as they are not referred to their racial affiliation. Julien Benda, in the aftermath of World War II, thus denounced "the violation of the person in racism, insofar as it invalidates a human being for the nature of his blood, that is, for a fact in which the will of his person counts for nothing."[31] The fixity and the exclusive determinism of heredity constitute two correlative postulates of racism: "Racist sophism consists... of accepting that the fate of a being is fixed at the same moment as its hereditary constitution."[32] The "crime" of an individual recognized for being of such and such a "race" is being what he is: "The crime of Isaac Tarrab? He was Jewish,"[33] notes Marc Kravetz, reporting the facts surrounding the murder in Beirut, on December 31, 1985, of a seventy-year-old man, a retired teacher. It is an "essentialist" crime, assuming that the individual exists only as some exemplar of his group of affiliation, hated by his killer, who believes he is bruising the body of the group. A reflection by Max Horkheimer brings into view the essentialist postulate common to the praise and the blame of the Jew: "It is hardly less suspect to me if someone says that he simply loves 'the Jews' than if he reproaches them with something false."³⁴ Racialization consists of taking being for doing, taking the generality of racial affiliation for the singularity of the person.

10. The reinterpretation of the physiognomic relationship (coincidence, parallel, analogy, similitude) in terms of productive causality. If the somatic refers to the psychic, it is because it carries on with the latter a necessary relation of cause to effect. Each somatobiological organization strictly corresponds to a specific mental organization that it engenders. One may thus speak, on the level of historico-epistemological metalanguage, of a "naturalization" of anthropological differences, and more precisely of a "biologization." The foundation of the anthropological difference as such is henceforth of a "biological" order — before it is of a "genetic" order, in the early twentieth century. From the physiognomic postulate to the biological causalism in which racism as theorization begins, one moves from a phenomenology of differences to a reductionist ontology. The operation may be described in terms of a "totalitarian and syncretic" attitude, in the framework of the genetic psychology of Henri Wallon, who postulates that "syncretism quite naturally tends toward myth." Hence the following definitional statement: "Racism is the syncretism of the biological, the psychological, and the social."³⁵ Racist explanation is reduced to an absolute biological determinism: "[Racism] tends to explain the whole individual by the blood that flows in his veins. No more individual consciousness or thought, but rather an amalgam in which all the elements are melded together and in which it is, definitively, the most removed elements, in which anthropology becomes directly determinant on each individual."³⁶ Racism is defined as a determinism and a reductionism, to the point of being impugned as "materialist" from the perspective of Christian metaphysics.³⁷ A Catholic mind willingly stigmatizes it as a "religion of blood," which he defines as "a biologism that lowers some of the human races almost to the level of the beast, and that makes blood an august entity that is held up as a 'foundation of society.' "³⁸ A transversal definition is put in place concerning Nazi racist nationalism, one of the rare objects of blame on which a consensus traversing political and religious divisions has arisen. What is absolutely condemned in the ideology of National Socialism is biological or zoological materialism,³⁹ in that it is directly opposed to both historical materialism and Christian spiritualism.

11. If differences of mental faculties are reproduced by the reproduction of somatobiological differences, they themselves correspond to differences in the mode of social and political existence of humans, considered as distinct, categorizable, and classifiable groups. The common underpinning of "psychological" and "sociological"[40] differences is hence defined as biological and placed in a position of causation. This relationship is contained in the affirmation that the social order "depends"[41] on the racial order, that race and society are in a relationship of cause to effect, that the doctrine of race provides the key to social science, that it even illuminates universal history.[42] "Gobineau's system" is ordinarily mentioned as the doctrinal example par excellence.[43] In epistemological metalanguage, one may speak of the biological (or genetic) determinism of all human productions and achievements (scientific, artistic, technical, religious, political, moral, military, and so on). This is the fundamental postulate of contemporary "sociobiology" in the strict sense[44] and, more broadly, of bioanthropological thought in the nineteenth and twentieth centuries. Until now, we should note, conceptualization has operated synthetically only on the ideas of *difference* and *hereditary transmission*. This is the first speculative layer of racism elaborated as a doctrine, whose nationalist application may thus be summarized: a people or a nation derives its difference or the principle of its becoming only from its racial (ethnic...) composition.

12. The projection of (bio-psycho-social) differences onto a hierarchical scale. Interracial differences are thus interpreted according to the model of inequalities measurable in that they are referred to places on a single scale of values, structured by the bipolarity of the high (superior) and the low (inferior). This interpretation is therefore an evaluation: one assigns to each presumably different group a fixed value that is supposed to synthesize the natural aptitudes with which it is endowed. It is by definition comparative: there is inequality of one group only in relation to another (or to more than one other) group, by which it is measured. The statements reconstructed and serially enumerated until now are explicit *constative* and *evaluative* statements. But racist discourse is not reduced to the phrastic realization of the referential and expressive functions — the enunciator saying something about herself, in a meliorative mode, by affirming something about what, in the human world, is represented by her as other than her. The nationalist application of the hierarchization of combined and

quantified differences may come down to a commonplace: peoples are as valuable as races.[45]

13. The theoretical component of racism involves a representation of the practice that it grounds. This practical ideology presents itself as at once an ethics, a politics, and a strategy (cultural, military). The statements of the practical component are of a programmatic type, schematizable by modal forms such as the "ought to be" and the "ought." The definitional formulas of dictionaries discursively treat the "ought to be" by military and medical metaphors: that of the *defense* of proper identity by separation from the others,[46] that of the *preservation* of the singular unity of the "Us" (threatened by the action of the others),[47] that of the preservation of the superior race against any crossing,[48] of its protection against any mixture, that is, from *métissage* that is always thought to be an abasement of the superior through its (con)fusion with the inferior. The self-valorized race, in such a perspective, takes as its first imperative the duty to conserve its proper identity; this act assumes the existence of a natural homogeneity and purity of the self ("Us") that is to be preserved from the impurity of any other self ("Them"). It is said of the race of the one who speaks in the name of his race that it ought to be itself and nothing but itself — to remain itself, to regain itself, indeed to become itself.[49] The imperative of separation is the practical analog of the positivist (then scientist) observation of the real separation of the races (in the zoological sense), by which the axiom of separability is authorized. What follows is an effect of legitimation: it is "normal" or "natural" to want to separate in the social state the "races" that are factually separated in the state of nature.

The thesis of real difference is linked, on the one hand, to the postulate of a causal relation between racial diversity and cultural diversity, and, on the other hand, to the determination of *métissage* (above all *métissage* between blacks and whites) as the supreme misdeed against race, whose essence is self-identity: unstained purity — what in National Socialist doctrine plays the role of primal definition. Alfred Rosenberg pleads cultural diversity to affirm the diversity of "bloods," that is, of races conceived as quasi-species, and infers from it the ontological identity of "blood" and of "character," two equally legitimate translations of the same deep "reality" *(Wesen)*, two manifestations of the same primordial substance:

We believe that the greatest discovery of our time is to be found in the experience and the strictly scientific proof that it is no accident, if on this globe human beings of different species *[verschiedener Art]* wander, if out of the conditioning by these particularities arise different states, cultures *[Kulturen]*, and forms of life *[Lebensformen]*, that blood and character are thus only different words for the same essence *[Wesen]*.[50]

Hence the diversity of races is inferred from the diversity of cultures by the principle of sufficient reason: the difference of race must be the productive cause of cultural difference, because the scientific principle of absolute determinism (nothing happens by chance or without an assignable cause; the same causes engender the same effects, in the same conditions), to which is added the postulate of heredity, excludes the explanations that bring in the aleatory. In addition, the supposed effect is identified with the presumed cause, such that there is only one reality, viewed in two different aspects — the uniqueness of the primordial ontological language. Monocausalism is consonant with monism: an agreement of the theory of knowledge with the theory of being. Here racism appears as a biocultural or sociozoological monism.

But one must insist on the establishment of white/black *métissage* as a maximal transgression of the system of racist values and norms (see chapter 8, pp. 213–15). In *Mein Kampf*, Hitler describes the "original sin of humanity," in attributing it both to the spirit of vengeance of the French and to a plot hatched by the Jews:

> The poisoning through negro blood along the Rhine, in the heart of Europe, corresponds just as much to the sadistic-perverse hate of this chauvinistic arch-enemy of our nation as to the cool-blooded reasoning of the Jews, who want to start in this way the bastardizing of the European continent right in the center, thus depriving the white race of the basis for its sovereign existence by mixing it with a lower type of people.
>
> *The present acts of France, instigated by her own hatred and carried out under the leadership of the Jews, constitute a sin against the existence of the white race and will some day turn loose upon that nation all avenging spirits of a generation, which has recognized degradation of race to be the original sin of humanity.*[51]

The most official National Socialist discourse thus intersects, in its presentation of the theory of race, with the statement of a naturalist monism, the typological vision of races and species, the principle of

*An Ideal Type* 119

determinism, and the postulate of the differential heredity of faculties (hence that of their unequal distribution). The classical argument put in play is that of the adequacy to nature or to its deep-rooted extensions, reinforced by the modern argument of positivist/scientistic guarantee (the facts are such that...; scientific knowledge teaches us that...). Such argumentation derives from the class of "arguments based on the structure of reality," as Chaïm Perelman has defined them in their specific mechanism: to make use of the structure of reality in order to establish a solidarity between admissible judgments and others that one seeks to promote.[52] On the one hand, the causal link is put in play, the one that connects the individual of race X with the latter, as the effect to its cause, said cause being productive from the outset.[53] On the other hand, there intervenes the liaison of coexistence between the race set up as essence and its individual manifestations, on the model of the relations between a person and his acts.[54]

14. The fundamental racist imperative may also be formulated as an "ought" bearing on the relation between oneself and others, collocated on a hierarchical scale. The racist enunciator, speaking in the name of his race, calls it superior and grounds on this superiority his right, then his duty, to "dominate the others,"[55] to "subordinate the others."[56] Racism is thereby often presented as a mechanism of legitimation of the right of conquest and, more recently, of "imperialism." Hence, the politics deployed in the early 1960s against the Soviet Communist Party by the Chinese Communist Party, defending itself against accusations of "racism" made against it, involved an instrumental definition of racism:

> Having used up all their wonder-working weapons for opposing the national liberation movement, the leaders of the CPSU are now reduced to seeking help from racism, the most reactionary of all imperialist theories. They describe the correct stand of the CPC in resolutely supporting the national liberation movement as "creating racial and geographical barriers," "replacing the class approach with the racial approach," and "playing upon the national and even racial prejudices of the Asian and African peoples."... When they peddle the "theory of racism," describing the national liberation movement in Asia, Africa and Latin America as one of the coloured against the white race, the leaders of the CPSU are clearly aiming at inciting racial hatred among the white people in Europe and North America, at diverting the people of the world from the struggle against im-

perialism and at turning the international working-class movement away from the struggle against modern revisionism.[57]

The "racist" ought may be understood in a descriptive statement of "theory" followed by an allusion to the (not expressly qualified) conduct that derives from it.[58] The class of those self-designated as "superior" says of itself that it has the right and the duty to manifest its natural superiority by a conduct of domination (oppression, exploitation) of the members of the class of those other-designated as naturally "inferior." It must be specified that any hierarchizing difference said to be natural is reworked in a scientistic argument of legitimation: science is said to guarantee the naturalness of inequalities and to do so by naming, measuring, quantifying, comparing, and ordering them on a supposedly universal scale. "From our point of view, we do not exclude, but rather *classify*," affirmed Maurras,[59] believing that he was thinking outside the field of the theories of race, even while he was affirming and putting to work one of its basic schemes. These fourteen traits to us seem to constitute the metadefinition of racism according to the antiracist vulgate.

## Inequality and Difference: The Two Logics of Racialization

*The center of every racism is to be found in the belief in a natural difference, and in the postulate that nature determines cultural traits.*
Colette Guillaumin

*Human beings are afraid of the Same, and that is the source of racism.*
Jean-Pierre Dupuy

The preceding reconstruction does not bring about the appearance of a distinction that seems fundamental to us and that will permit us to clarify a number of questions at the expense of an explosion of the unitary representation of "racism." We will posit the distinction between two logics of racialization. The first is made explicit by the following series: self-racialization/difference/purification/extermination. And the second by the following series: other-racialization/inequality/domination/exploitation. This is the trait that is missing from the ordinary representation of racism — this is the conceptual distinction whose absence engenders most of the confusions and obscurities perceptible in public debate (or spontaneous conversation).

The valorization of difference may operate in two ways: either by *self-racialization,* the affirmation of proper racial identity and (secondarily) of one's own superiority, or by *other-racialization,* the affirmation of racial difference centered on the inferiority or malfeasance of the Other. Whereas other-racialization is finalized by the relation of *domination,* itself reinforced by those of oppression and exploitation — a logic of interest and profit[60] — self-racialization is finalized by the relation of *exclusion* that, by a paradoxical logical procedure, ends in the extermination of the "other" agency, that is, by the destruction of the differential relation as such.

Our hypothesis is the following: the normal regime of racism, as it is incarnated in the inegalitarian ideology of colonization and of modern slavery, is grounded in the process of *other-racialization,* which presents two aspects, or which may be analyzed in two linked pieces of evidence, representable by two propositions:

- "We are the best"; that is, the fact of our race (our collective identity) is bound up with its superior value.[61] The attribution of inferior quality to the others, which suggests a relation of domination between Them (the dominated) and Us (the dominant). *Axiom of inequality.* It is the others who are racized to the point of inferiority.

- "We are humanity"; that is, we (the set of those who resemble us) and we alone incarnate humanity itself; we represent the essence of humanity. It is on this point that other-racialization best justifies its name: the "we" is forgotten as such, arising spontaneously and naively equaling humankind. *Axiom of universality.*

The "best," those who have power, hold the means of domination (social control, the monopoly on legitimate violence) and perceive themselves as *racially unmarked:* it is not they who are of a particular race, but rather the others. Jeanne Hersch has excellently described this first piece of evidence: "Those who hold power do not really have the feeling of belonging to a particular 'race,' even a superior one. They belong to humankind. It is the others who present that particularity, partially or totally negative with regard to their humanity, of having the characteristics proper to a certain race, exposed by their bodies for all to see."[62] Other-racialization therefore involves two correlative attributions: of the quality of universality to the representatives of "Us" and of the racial quality (particularity) to the representatives of the others. The universalist point of view on which such a racism is grounded may be briefly stated as follows: "In summary, the others commit the wrong of belonging to a race, whereas they themselves are the universal."[63] To the *inequality* among races is added the *objectivity* of the class of affiliation named "race," which must be conceived as "an essential characteristic of race: it is objective, it concerns the other, the objectified human being, the human being as object. Not 'me.' "[64] "Race," before being called inferior, is that of the Other, is attributed to the Other, is even defined as the very characteristic of the Other. Race is the Other.

One may see the difference between such a process and that of *self-racialization,* which is elaborated not on the attribution of racial qualities (marks of inferiority) to others ("not-Us"), but rather on the definition of oneself as being Race itself. The representation of oneself (of the representatives of "Us") involves bringing to the forefront the *difference* between those who are the Race (and/or who have "race") and those who are outside the "raced" group: inequality may certainly support or hold up the principle of difference; the latter is primary. Those who are "Us" do not claim to represent the human universal at all: on the contrary, they define themselves *against* the whole of humanity, for example divided into undermen (total animality) and Jews (monstrous rivals, whose essence is determined by the radical absence of naturalness). Self-racialization postulates the negation of the anthropological universal. The "Us" affirms itself not as identical to the universal of Humanity (we the Humans), but rather as expressing a different species, either resistant to erosion (of which *métissage* is the main factor) or in the process of formation through evolutionary differentiation or voluntary and systematic (eugenic) selection. The value of values is here the commonality of blood, reflected by a specific cultural/spiritual identity, of "Us." Collective self-identification does not occur through expansion (Us = humankind itself), but rather through contraction, by the isolation of a particular essence.

In this case, the *principle of objectivity* applies in exemplary fashion to the proper race: the true Aryans are defined as real Aryans — in the face of the false or inauthentic pretenders to Aryan racial affiliation. But the presumption of the objectivity of race is a conviction common to the two modes of racialization. Race is assumed to be a really existing block, a real being endowed with a quasi-personal identity and a permanency in time.

We can specify certain implications of the distinction between other-racialization and self-racialization. In the axiological space instituted by other-racialization, the supreme misdeed is the revolt of the inferiors against the situation given them for the very reason of the inferiority imputed to them: the claim of equal rights (political, economic, social, "cultural") for anomic behaviors (the refusal to work or obey, desertion, and so on). In the axiological space of self-racialization, the supreme misdeed is incarnated by *métissage;* the mixing of the pure (Us, the Race) with the impure (Them, the "raceless") defines the capital sin.

To the pair inequality/universality, which characterizes other-racialization by its presuppositions, is opposed the pair difference/(particular) commonality. These two pairs constitute the respective cores of the two ideal-typical "racisms" that we respectively term individuo-universalist and traditio-communitarian.

## *The Logic of Exterminability*

Self-racialization derives its energy from a specific passion: the unconditional fear of the Other,[65] the anguish identifiable with the feeling of absolute insecurity. It constitutes the therapy accorded to the infinite threat projected onto the Other: it reassures self-identity, achieving the function of self-assurance through overvalorization of proper identity. By first focusing argument on the defense of proper purity, by centering it on the imperative of the conservation of absolute difference, by next refusing any inegalitarian gauging of Self and Other on a common scale, by identifying the bad Other (the Other as intrinsically bad) as a representative of counternature or of the absolutely dangerous perverse spirit,[66] the death principle directed against Self, the ideology of self-racialization develops an argumentative logic whose ultimate conclusion may be only the *total destruction* of the Other.

Let us again take the example of the racialization of the Jew, with an eye to the identifying reference as such. "The Jew," a designator that functions as an absolute categorematic term, is analyzable as a concrete generic term on which a personification is applied; this operation enables the description of the designator as the simulacrum of a proper noun, a "proper noun of speech," as Bally has defined it: "Any concept that has been actualized and that may, from one case to another, designate a different individual."[67] If to individualize a concept "is at the same time to localize and quantify it,"[68] the actualization making "a concept of a thing into a proper name of speech,"[69] the lexical item "the Jew" is semantically analyzed according to two components. As for localization, the typical image of "the Jew" tends toward the image of the species — to speak like Gustave Guillaume[70] — and presents the semes of spatiotemporalization "everywhere" and "always" ("the eternal Jew"). As for quantification, the lexical item "the Jew" is the syncretism of "all the Jews" (an analysis in extension) and of "every Jew" (an analysis in comprehensiveness); it therefore operates through reference to all the representatives of the type (total qualification). But through the generic use of the substantive in the personification "a presentation of the genus as a personified entity,"[71] it moreover presents an existing entity with one exemplar: the unique representative of a singular class having universal value — "the Jew" as singular universal, or the type in person.

The elimination of others achieves the status of conclusive evidence only at the heart of a space of competition in which two rival agencies fight to the death, one good, the other demonic,[72] bound together by the relative equality of the specular behaviors. Symmetrical schismogenesis,[73] a type of interaction deployed at the heart of such a space, assumes the representation of an exclusive disjunction, which founds a practice of total war, in which anything goes, according to the normative principle "It's Us or Them" — the "Them" who are the Same, the unbearable images of the Same — a disjunction ratified by the alternative "life or death." Henceforth, the unique, paradoxical path of stabilization, of the relation between Self (the legitimate Self-same) and the Other (the rival Same, the useless, uncertain, dangerous Double) is represented by the abolition of any relation. The logically remaining outcome is genocide,[74] the systematic and total extermination of the Rival-Pervert, the type of the inverted double, the absolutely maleficent countertype. Genocide hence presents itself as a right, but more profoundly as a duty.[75] It is the logical conclusion of a certain mode of construction of alterity, of which the Jew demonized by Hitlerism remains the paradigm: "The Fascists [read: 'the Nazis'] do not view the Jews as a minority but as an opposing race, the embodiment of the negative principle. They must be exterminated to secure happiness for the world."[76] The specular mechanism engenders the Jew as the symmetrical negative of the good principle incarnate (the Aryan): as the pure power of the negative, the Jews are treated as the chosen people.[77] It is the same referential being that constitutes the object of blame and praise, without determination. Absolute blame may henceforth include and be submitted to praise, and the latter may become the very instrument of blame.

In most dictionary notes, there is a pointed lack of distinction, which is nonetheless central to Hitlerian racism, between the treatment of enslavement applied to the Slavs (and to the Russians in particular) and that of extermination reserved for the Jews. In a late statement, Hitler recognized, even while using a euphemism, the singularity of the treatment directed against the Jews in the racist ideology taken on as such: "Our racial pride is not aggressive except in so far as the Jewish race is concerned."[78] The singularity of anti-Jewish racism conforms to the incomparable nature of the "Jewish [pseudo-]race," according to Nazi ideology in Hitler's presentation: "We use the term Jewish race as a matter of convenience, for in reality and from the genetic point of view there is no such thing as the Jewish race.... The Jewish race is first and foremost an abstract race of the mind."[79] Hitler's reformulation is followed and finished by assigning an essential content to this paradoxical race, to this type that resembles only itself: "A race of the mind is something more solid, more durable than just a race, pure and simple.... The Jew remains a Jew wherever he goes, a creature which no environment can assimilate. It is the characteristic mental make-up of his race which renders him impervious to the process of assimilation."[80] The irreducible and disturbing difference of the Other is hence internalized, mentalized, so as to be identifiable as absolutely singular and absolutely intolerable. The Other who *cannot be made inferior*, that is, acceptable within the strict measure of his allocation to an inferior place on a common scale, may be defined only as *exterminable*. The genocidal logic imposes itself on the basis of the Other's incapacity to be ranked on a hierarchical scale. It constitutes the necessary steering of the perception of the Other as uncategorizable (unclassifiable, anomic), posited in his pure Difference, threatening proper identity.

Let us take a quick detour through an author who has been forgotten today, but whose focus on the relations between science and the racial question, in 1919, presented the interest of intersecting the position of the boundary between Us and Them with the distinction between difference and inequality. Jules Sageret, approaching the "race question" at the end of the Great War, notes that it "is burning only because of the European races,"[81] as few people would dare contest the evidence "that there is a true difference of race between a Fuegian and a Belgian, for example."[82] It must therefore be asked of "the science of these races,"[83] anthropology, to enlighten us on the proclaimed "question of race";[84] this comes down to "instructing us on their 'souls.' "[85] The response received from anthropological science is simple, almost a truism: "Collective beings differ. When they say to each other, 'I am not of your race,' it is only one way in a thousand of expressing that they feel this difference. That is the entire real meaning of race."[86] The secret of the racial question is contained in the fact of the perceived or lived difference among human groups and in that of its natural affirmation — we *are not* you/them, you *are not* us/they *are not* us. But such a differentialist solution is valid "for the European populations alone, or those of European origin,"[87] so within the circle traced by an "Us." Beyond the horizontal differences among European groups appear the vertical, hierarchical differences between Europeans and non-Europeans. There are differences among us, and inequality between us and the others. So if difference is not absolutized, if to the contrary it may be reduced to the distinction between collective self-perception and other-perception of a collective Other, within this community of equals that the white race is, it is the case that inequality, reserved for the relation between whites and nonwhites, tends to be assumed as absolute (concerning all the faculties, and insurmountable, like a destiny). Here we are well within the ideological universe of the racism ordered on the legitimation of colonization (Us-superior vs. Them-inferior).

### Paradoxical Self-Racializations

We would like to open a parenthesis on a paradoxical phenomenon that, to our knowledge, has not been approached from the angle that interests us here: *antiracist self-racializations*. Self-racialization of the National Socialist type (the proper race being bound up with the *völkisch* ideal of the maximal rooting of the peasant-warrior in his pure race) has its symmetrical inverse in the self-racialization of the "intellectuals without ties," who are precisely defined by the negation of the traits of the rooted type — they are described as being stripped of the "soul of race," and so disconnected from the particularist, "bounded" perspectives deriving from this soul, and starting out as though able to claim to escape the ethnic and/or cultural determinations of cognition. Epistemic salvation is then obtained through deracination: cultural disaffiliation, independence with respect to the sociocultural conditions of knowledge — this would be the express condition of scientific lucidity in the social sciences. Now, this self-attribution of a superior epistemic power has worked in a fashion parallel to that of antiracist self-racialization, whose primary conviction may be translated in this way: the superior "race" (*Us*) is determined by the lack of enclosure in one or another "race." Corresponding to the type of the intellectual without ties in the order of cognizing is the "race" of minds without race in the order of action, the type of the militant without roots. The good revolutionary, from such a perspective, is the deracinated, decommunitarianized subject: imagining itself as such is what must really be named the "superior" intellectual "race," endowed with an uncommon power of sociological vision.

The postulate of absolute antiracist racism is that the universal is reached only by radical detachment from any particular community. The corresponding vulgate is well known in its slogans, based on the praise of the stripping of "heavy" or "blinding" affiliations, on the praise of decentering and displacement, in short, of deracination. While certain contemporary authors, in the late echo of a polemical illusion characteristic of the 1930s (and "justified" in this singular conjuncture), set the zero-root intellectuals up as by nature bearers of truth and sovereign decoders of the social,[88] a certain antiracist militantism extols the man without definite qualities or affiliations, projects him as the ideal. Responding to the New Right celebration of rooting is the "lefty" sublimation of deracination. The deracinated sociologist becomes the "man without a country," proud of being so in his fief, the social sciences: supposedly not belonging to any sociocultural system in particular, he is assumed to be able to know all of them in their truth. The idealization of those "who are homeless"[89] or the sublimation of the *heimatlos* intellectual:[90] such is the symbolic scheme that is nearest to the ideal type of the intellectual as a modern cultural figure, characteristic of the system of individuo-universalist values. The roots of the intellectual without ties may be reduced to her requirement of universality, her collective identity bound up with her universal horizon, which shifts with her: this subject is a pure agency of posing problems valid for all and for no one in particular. But one may wonder if one does not stand before the specific illusion of the "intellectual without ties or roots," the core of the professional ideology of intellectuals.[91] The *Us* of antiracist/antifascist intellectuals is projected as the essence of humanity, posited as the incarnation of the thinking race. If the essence of man is to think, then the type of the pure intellectual defines the most faithful representation of the essence of humankind.

The modern intellectual, like everyone, poses problems, but under a transcultural (universal) sky and for a universal audience. The postulate common to all of her statements is that one may (and must) refer to a transcultural rationality, whose real condition of existence is the self-detachment of the subject from her community, the abolition within herself of the desire for ethnocentric solidarity[92] — and this implies a certain ferociousness directed against oneself, a hatred of oneself. It would be easy to do the inventory of other modes of positive racialization of the zero-root human type, that of fuzzy, indeterminate affiliation: besides the great communist hope in the "midwife" power of the proletariat that, as "nothing," can be "everything," one may note the Sartrian praise of the "bastard,"[93] the "antiracist" praise of the virtues of *métissage* as an eraser of definite cultural identity or of the immigrant without assignable national identity, an icon (in spite of himself) of the absolute innocence[94] of which the bad Western conscience makes great use.

It is not without interest to come back to Hayek's critique of the presumption of gnoseological superiority that belongs to the first school of the sociology of knowledge (Karl Mannheim):

> To derive from the thesis that human beliefs are determined by circumstances the claim that somebody should be given power to determine these beliefs... involves the claim that those who are to assume that power possess some sort of super-mind. Those who hold these views have indeed regularly some special theory which exempts their own views from the same sort of explanation and which credits them, as a specially favored class, or simple as the "free-floating intelligentsia," with the possession of absolute knowledge.[95]

The mind without community qualities, stripped of particular ethnocultural solidarity, identifies with the universal and confers on itself thus the faculty of universal theoretical vision. The quality of being "free-floating" is interpreted by the "detached" mind as grounding superiority in the ability to cognize, that of a pure subject that, though incarnated, represents nothing intermediate, nothing other than the universal. Here again is the classical figure of the philosopher as lover of general and necessary truths alone; he is thus authorized to be set up as a "functionary of the universal" (Husserl). This is the philosophical heritage of "critical" sociology. Hayek places the accent on the equivocality of the claim to the vision of hidden causes, attributed to himself by (or that one attributes to — the two subjects are generally only one) the free-floating intellectual: "While in a sense this movement represents thus a sort of super-rationalism, a demand for the direction of everything by a super-mind, it prepares at the same time the ground for a thorough irrationalism."[96] At issue is a singular "race of the mind" believing that it derives its epistemic superiority from its total lack of any quality of race, an absence hyperbolically affirmed, often claimed with arrogance. *The ruses of self-racialization:* once more, antiracism proceeds by a simple inversion; the effect of this process is to institute it as the double of racism. The hypercritical sociologist proceeds to a mere inversion of the modern anti-Jewish denunciation of "cosmopolites" and others "without ties" (the type targeted is that of the *heimatlos* of Drumont),[97] which is turned around as an apology. But the same figure remains, which is the object common to both blame and praise: a vicious circle in the epideictic genre. Moreover, in both cases, the operation presupposed is the same — that is, self-attribution, possibly mentioned in a discourse of praise, of an absolute superiority in the order of cognizing (true thinking, without "false consciousness," and so on).

Let us take another example of the superior epistemic type constructed in the field of the social sciences: the ethnologist. Her conviction of superiority is grounded on the coupling of two certainties about herself: (1) she attributes to herself the power to see (to know) well without being seen (known); and (2) she accords herself the power to free herself from prejudices, thus excepting herself from the field of ethnocentric forces to which the common mortal is subject.

Michel and Françoise Panoff affirm with serenity: "More accustomed than his colleagues (economists, agronomists, and so on) to outwit the traps of ethnocentrism, he may, free of any prejudice, approach certain facts from a new point of view."[98] How can anyone not be an ethnologist?! The latter is in fact elevated to the enviable rank of citizen of the world of cognition without prejudices, as the exemplary type of the social scientist. To believe the same happy ethnologists, egalitarianist ethics would be implicated by the very exercise of the profession and would condition the realization of the goal of cognition. There is a supplementary privilege to the ethnologist's knowledge: it would be, as an exemplary exception, based on the model of the contract freely passed between equals, which assumes a reciprocal recognition. Here, then, is a type of knowledge that, by its very realization, by profession, would constitute an ethical act. Again one finds the professional ideal of "equality in difference," the unsurpassable because unthinkable horizon of the contemporary ethnologist:

> In truth it is ethnology itself, as a mode of knowing, that is struck by prohibition once equality ends. It is not that a moral requirement comparable to the Hippocratic oath, for the medical profession, is in question here; but this occurs because the Other exists as such only if he is first recognized as an equal. Only on this condition can the differences separating the observer from the observed be perceived.[99]

But, as Jeanne Favret remarks, "one does not see, moreover, why equality would condition the perception of alterity."[100] The ethnologist's self-racialization appears as a particular case of a paradox characteristic of modern ideology (in Louis Dumont's sense — the evidence of egalitarian individualism): the egalitarianist subject affirms superiority over others from the egalitarian point of view. The ideological parasitism of the knowledge of anthropologists is here exemplary of the attempts of modern science, in particular of the social sciences (but the life sciences are not an exception), to show their a posteriori (described as such) agreement with the modern values of individuality and equality and even to present it as a condition of the constitution of knowledge (the postulate of an a priori harmony). Still at issue is effacing the break between knowing and the "ought," of filling in the abyss between knowledge and moral action.

## The Two Ideal-Typical Racisms

The dictionaries consulted hardly allow the reader who is not already in possession of their scheme to distinguish between the two distinct logics of racialization:[101] *other-racialization,* on the principle of a logic of domination and exploitation that strives to conserve the life of the Other — an inferior, of course, but a source of profit; *self-racialization,* which commands a logic of radical exclusion whose finality is the abolition of difference as such, by the total extermination of the Other, so that proper identity may be conserved. The Race is the essence of the Us: identity with oneself here grounds the inequality between oneself and the Other. It is because we are the Race, to which the others are by definition exterior, foreign, and of which they are already deprived, that the others are "inferior." But they are such only in that they are in some way outside the system, situated on the exterior of the common scale of values presupposed by other-racizing (universalist and inegalitarian) racism. As absolutely "inferior," they (Them) escape the Us-Them relation; they become incomparable with the Race (Us). Them and Us are constituted as incommensurable entities. If the very relation between Us and Them thus disappears — that which makes possible comparative evaluation and inegalitarian judgment (we are more X than they are) — there is nothing more of significance to say on what is not Us. The world of the Us is the only world, the limits of the Us define the limits of the world. As the "Them" are absolute foreigners, no new bridge may be built to span the abyss of the distance. The limit is certainly no longer a line, but rather a zone; the borders are deprived of interfaces. The very community of the borders becomes unthinkable, unrepresentable. And nonetheless the Us can posit itself only by opposing itself to the category of nonexistence, Them: a relation between Us and Them is hence reintroduced, by the polemical condition of existence. The total absence of relation is not a property of the human world as we know it.

Let us return to the thread of our argument: the single meaning of the self-definition of Self as an absolutely superior race threatened by the Other is therefore genocide, the total extermination of the Other. From now on the *racism$_1$ of domination* should not be confused with the *racism$_2$ of extermination:* inegalitarian logic, that which gives way to the Self-Other relation on a hierarchical scale, results in the struggle of the master and the slave, that is, in a dialectic whose very principle has been accepted; the logic of identity, that which refused any Self-Other relationship, and thereby all dialectization, can result only in the achievement of the desire for proper purity by the elimination of the unique source of impurity, the Other. Racism$_1$ and racism$_2$ have respective and striking historical illustrations, which enable one to distinguish them clearly: *colonialist racism* and *National Socialist racism.*[102]

Colonialists, as racists, "*above all* wanted to continue to exploit their victims, and they justified this exploitation with the aid of a racist prejudice, that of the intellectual inferiority of the exploited."[103] Here the victim should not represent a hyperbolic threat — but rather just a danger of deterioration, degradation, "mediocrization" through a sequence of crossings with inferior, passably animalized beings. The victim, not intrinsically perverse, may hence be spared and put to forced labor. Colonialist racism fulfills first a function of diversion and legitimation, in the service of the economic function: it is not in itself its own end, but is rather only an organon, constituting an instrumental ideology.

Hitlerian racial policy, to the contrary, in the battle waged against the Jews, presented explicitly as such,[104] "always used as an affective force the envy inspired by the Jews, to whom racial prejudice ascribed a dangerous intellectual superiority."[105]

Hitlerian racism, culminating in the anti-Jewish struggle, is in itself its own end; it is autotelic and realizes its own values. In so doing, it fulfills a function of assurance, in the first place, valid by its own effects. Enslavement is of value here only as a well-defined category of others: the European races, inferior because not "Aryan" or "Nordic,"[106] to the exclusion of the Jews, who are without any possible economic or political use. A tract published by the Central SS Office of the SS Reichsführer thus describes the relation between the "underman" and the "eternal Jew":

> The underman, that natural creature who, biologically, is apparently very similar..., is nonetheless a quite other one, a frightful creature, he is but a trace of a man.... Man was becoming close to God! But the underman also lived. He hated the work of others.... He associated with his fellows. The beast called to the beast.... And this underworld of the underman found its leader *[Führer]*: the eternal Jew! He understood, he knew, what the underworld wanted.[107]

The zoomorphic metaphorization applies to the "undermen," who, under the leadership of the diabolical Jew, represent the bad world struggling against the human and good world. The *under-other* may struggle against man in an exemplary fashion only when commanded by the *demonic other,* the "counterrace" that is, in the negative mode, the *over-other*. Hence, whereas colonialist racism could not, without functionally destroying itself, aim for the annihilation of its exploitable victims, Nazi racism, a racism of combat essentially directed against "the Jew," the singular name of the demonic other, had to go to the point of destroying without a trace the absolute enemy in order to realize its objectives. One of the arguments of the proclaimed "revisionism" of the history of World War II, represented mainly by Arthur R. Butz (the United States), Wilhelm Stäglich (the Federal Republic of Germany), and Robert Faurisson (France),[108] consists of likening the two racisms by imperceptibly applying the functional schema of the racism of exploitation to the explanation of the anti-Jewish racism of the Nazis. All this may be summed up by the following reasoning: since it is contradictory to destroy the physical persons of those whom one exploits, it is impossible to believe that the Nazis, who like all exploiters obeyed the logic of exploitation, could have exterminated the Jews, an important segment of manpower, in the course of total warfare; therefore, the extermination could not have taken place. The central point of the paralogism is contained in the imperceptible movement from the difficulty of believing in the possibility of a historical fact to the affirmation that it did not take place, from theoretical doubt to the certainty of the historical nonexistence of the genocidal fact.

## Evading or Conceptualizing

*Crises are not overcome by a few hasty and nervous attempts at suppressing the newly arising and troublesome problems, nor by flight into the security of a dead past.* Karl Mannheim

What is targeted by the denomination "racism," a supposedly observable phenomenon that is objectifiable through conceptual analysis — the construction of models or ideal types — proves to be, at the end of an examination of texts that propose to define it encyclopedically without being subject to it, such a variable extension and so indeterminate that one almost no longer knows what one is talking about, nor if what one says is true. The lexical definitions scarcely permit a surmounting of the equivocations and contradictions stemming from the historico-encyclopedic articles, bearing on the thing "racism." Here there is a dual identification through contiguity: racism and anti-Semitism, racism and National Socialism (often with Hitler as the eponym), but also the coexistence of mutually substitutable lexical items: racism, prejudice of race, prejudice of color. The racism linked to the anti-Semitism of the Nazi regime illustrates the definitions in the same way as the racism linked to the Western colonization of "peoples of color." Now, if anti-Jewish racism diabolized the Other in aiming for his eradication, antiblack racism zoologized the presumed inferior in aiming for his exploitation (from slavery to its neocolonialist successors and variants). Such a functional difference does not seem to have struck the semanticists and encyclopedists to excess. The play of historico-political exemplifications indicates the two mythical poles that, cast in discourse through ritualized metaphors, are constitutive of the heterogeneous whole denominated "racism"; they are self-identifying elements that the definitions take as their motto by being content to invert their values, to move from the racist praise of oneself to the antiracist blame of the Other: the *pure* (oneself, the proper, identity, difference) and *inequality* (superiority/inferiority, hierarchy). These may be named the two distinct cores present in the given definitions of racism, on the basis of which these definitions are constructed, without for all that always requiring each other. A difficulty stems from the exclusive presence of one of the cores of conceptualization (purity *or* inequality) or from the copresence of both (purity *and* inequality). One of the origins of the confusion seems to be found in the ordinary illustrative reference to Nazism (the ideology, the movement, and the regime), in which the mythology of purity is interwoven with the ideology of inequality, to the point of discursively manifesting itself as indiscernible. A discourse most often signals itself as antiracist by affirming as positive the values of mixture or (ethnic, cultural) *métissage,* wavering between the praise of mixed marriages and that of a "multiracial France," and by declaring itself for equality among human beings and therefore between nationals and foreigners, citizens and others. This simple inversion of the two cores of the racist axiology in the lexicographical or encyclopedic reformulations reproduces the chiasmus of the two racializations, of what has appeared to us as two operations susceptible of encountering each other in ideological and political syncretisms, yet remaining distinct. For as little as there has been an elaboration of a general theory of racializations grounded on the irreducibility of the racism of identity/difference and inegalitarianist racism, one will have to be content with concluding that racism cannot be conceptualized — in the mode of satisfying insufficiency: "We know what it is, but we can't say"; or in the more modest mode: "We know that it is, but not what it is." But if there is such a phenomenon, as soon as it derives from the unconceptualizable real or from the unsayable notional, "racism" strongly resembles "life," "existence," "the soul," and "race" itself: one experiences it, one feels it quite well, one touches it without understanding it, without being able to define it. A threatening paradox for any discourse striving to be "antiracist," the designative and stigmatizing expression *racism* risks, in order to be endowed with meaning, appealing for the latter to intuition, to a singular illumination, to a specific alertness, to a trained eye — more simply: to accepted representations and values, outlining the ideological space in which one knows what racism is. Hence the definers place themselves in a dialogical relationship with their eventual readers, who are supposed to share with them the same ground of opinions and beliefs in process, in which the meaning and reference of the word *racism* are conjointly given in the mode of evidence. "Racism": the denomination and qualification of the bad Other, who should be denounced, accused, driven out, condemned. The discursive act of identification by "racism" aims to hinder the return of the bad *Other*, most commonly figured by "Nazism": naming is valuable for prohibiting positive revalorization (from the "banalization" to the praise of Nazism, of which "racism" is the synecdoche); naming "racism" is equivalent to denouncing and removing its threat. At issue of course is an evasive designation. It is this functioning as a disqualifying label, a word indeterminate in its meaning and reference, but filled with its representations and associated negative values, culled from the cultural preconstructed, that scholarly definitions have a tendency to redirect and authorize. To condemn "racism," to stigmatize "racists": these are speech acts in which and by which, in ordinary conversation, one affirms that one is antiracist, by instituting oneself as such. It is antiracism in the mirror of racism: "Dirty racist!" And lexicographical metalanguage, which aims to define "racism" by taking the distance required to degrade it, on the primary material of the self-referential terms of "racism" (purity, superiority), is applied to disqualifying its object, either by the latter's pathologization (irrationality, delirium, illness, poison) or by the typizing recollection of its most highly and universally condemnable consequences (the Hitlerian genocide of the Jews and Gypsies).

It seems to us urgent to free antiracist discourse from demonology, at once a system of illusions and a propaganda device. Beyond the classic lumping together of "racism," "anti-Semitism," "Nazism," and "fascism," a basic operation in the polemical discourse of the left (of the lefts), there has appeared in international agencies, under the combined influence of the communist camp and the "Third World" sphere, a synthetic demonological discourse of which it is sufficient for us to furnish the following illustration: "Major obstacles to the implementation of the goals and objectives set by the United Nations in the field of the advancement of women include imperialism, colonialism, neocolonialism, expansionism [sic], *apartheid,* racism, Zionism...."[109] Such a ritualized discourse of denunciation is now taking its place alongside international catchphrases; there is no doubt at all that its sole target is represented by the Western liberal democracies. And there is a need to specify that this targeting in no way authorizes the idealization of the latter, nor the advance legitimation of just any Western crusade.

The preceding observations, and the interrogative distance that issues from them, come down to the following observation, which one may hope will be the starting point of more in-depth and less disappointing analyses: by saying whatever one will about "racism," in the contexts in which it is attributed to the *Other* of the enunciator, one does not conceptualize but rather evades. "Racism" functions as the proper name of a threat that should, in naming it and by the fact of denominating it, be removed, driven out, abolished. Outside the still indistinct limits of some evasive act of naming, beyond the immemorial behaviors of defensive magic, racism, an observable social phenomenon and a conceptual construction, remains to be conceived. Let us be pardoned for the weakness of believing, as a legacy of the old rationalism in its positivist formulation, that it is necessary to know in order to foresee, in order to be able to do something. We hope to contribute, by the present study, to making antiracism one day no longer an easily manipulable, collective phenomenon of mental regression, as through the effect of a fascination exercised by its adversary and model, racism.

One should begin by setting in motion one of the four mechanisms of control defined by Talcott Parsons: the "denial of reciprocities,"[110] which implies the refusal to respond to hostility with hostility, to anxiety with anxiety, to fantasy with fantasy, such that the vicious circle of "deviance" is broken. Let us finally stop evading.

And how vain is the antiracist verb that attracts admiration by the denial of things whose originals are no longer noticed, still alive and well: "a paradox of our time, namely that the virtuous lip-service most of us pay to the ideals of equality and fraternity among men in no way helps decrease the population of dog-faced cannibals we imagine lurking at every street corner."[111]

To evade is to persist, through commemorative discourse, in the relation of mimetic rivalry: magic without effect, symbolic inefficacy. To conceptualize would be to change ground by targeting at once the conduct of a rigorous theoretical analysis and the foundation of a deideologized humanism — the one way of an "antiracism" that would no longer present itself as a double of "racism."

*Part II*

# Genealogy of the Dogmatic Critique of Prejudices

*Five*

# The Theories of Prejudice and the Meanings of Racism

*We would spare ourselves questions and troubles if finally we were to determine the meanings of words in a clear and precise manner.*
Jean Le Rond d'Alembert

The main characteristic of the antiracist vulgate, a result of anticolonial and anticapitalist ideologies, is that it mixes together several negative themes that it always presents as necessarily linked. The classical anticolonialist model of racism assumes that the thesis of inequality among races has the dominant function of legitimating a process of exploitation, of making it ideologically possible or acceptable for the exploited as well as the exploiters. Such a functional conception of "inegalitarian prejudice" assumes that the latter is represented as part of the "strategies" of maximizing the profits expected by the agents of exploitation. Certain authors, Marxists, present racist/inegalitarian ideology as part of an apparatus of "overexploitation."[1] Racism would essentially be the extension of an economic exploitation involving a political domination and of an ideological legitimation, the condition of acceptability of exploitation and domination. This has been the most widespread model in Western antiracist circles (since the 1930s) and in international antiracism (since the 1950s); it is a model that seems at once to describe faithfully a real situation and to explain correctly the formation of "racist ideology" no less than its supposed essential function (to justify, legitimate the capitalist mode of exploitation).[2] This model corresponds to the first type of the "theory of prejudice" distinguished by Gordon W. Allport and that he even named the "historical approach": racial prejudice is here defined as a mode of rationalization of economic advantages.[3] More precisely, it incarnates the Marxist variant of the "historical approach," that is, the " 'exploitational' theory" of prejudice,[4] as the famous work of Oliver C. Cox, *Caste, Class, and Race: A Study in Social Dynamics,* presented and developed it in 1948. The "legitimating" model of racism-as-prejudice or as a set of prejudices serving to justify domination and exploitation of groups declared "inferior" — in the system of slavery, historical capitalism, or the colonial system — this model of racism as rationalized exploitation[5] presupposes the lack of distinction between racism-as-ideology (racism) and racism-as-opinion (racialism, racial prejudice)[6] and rests on the axiom that what is rationalized is the proper interest of the superior classes.[7] In this perspective, it is posited that "race prejudice ... is a social attitude propagated among the public by an exploiting class for the purpose of stigmatizing some group as inferior so that the exploitation of either the group itself or its resources or both may be justified."[8] To complement this demystifying psychology of interests (of the superior class), there intervenes the postulate that "*class* difference (i.e., the exploiter-exploited relationship) is the foundation of all prejudice; and that all talk about racial, ethnic, and cultural factors is mostly verbal mask."[9] Henceforth, an imperative task imposes itself on the convinced antiracist: to destroy the material conditions of the class society that engenders racism. The theoretical reduction of "racist prejudice" through economic monocausalism implicates the communist "ought" par excellence, the abolition of the inequality of classes, that is, classes as such. In 1935, in the preface to a book that battled the racial biology and hygiene of National Socialism, Marcel Prenant declared:

> The part of the book that is richest in teachings to me seems to be that in which the meaning of racism in the point of view of the class struggle is revealed. At issue here is no longer to proclaim the superiority of the German people, but rather to accept that of the most powerful capitalists — the Krupps, the Thyssens, the Hugenbergs — who are ex officio incorporated into the Nordic race. At issue is installing company ownership by a biological divine right. But if a capitalist is Jewish, the "Aryan paragraph" will bend in his favor,

and he will be accepted, just like an Aryan, as the Führer of his employees. It is there, taken from the Hitlerian texts themselves, the finest justification of Marxism, according to which class takes precedence over race.... [We must also draw attention] to the passages in which [Theodor Balk] touched on other racisms, beginning with those of antiquity and up to those which, close to us, undertook to justify the enslavement of blacks and colonial conquests.... There is a place for racism in any regime in which a class imposes its domination. Any racism is impossible in classless society, and that is why it is only there that the science of races will be developed without risk of interested falsifications.[10]

This type of explanation and representation of racism not only has not disappeared (it logically derives from the fundamental categories of Marxism) but has also been, since the 1930s, instituted as a hegemonic conception of "racism," as a store of evidence ready to hand for ideological use, of which even the adversaries of Marxism are great consumers — when they want to be antiracist and must advance some explanatory formula so as to be credible.

A note of explanatory nature, taken from a polemical essay by Henri Alleg on the United States, will place us before most of the elements of the vulgate: "Racism, 'legal' or de facto segregation, and exclusions 'for reason of color' are not only the 'cultural' heritage of prejudices of the past but also the fruit of a society that, based on exploitation and profit, naturally (so to speak) involves inequalities."[11]

If militant discourse is in general content to repeat this standard description or to proceed to small variations on one or another of its motifs, in what way might the social sciences, whose common boundaries with the ideologico-political field remain blurred, also do so when they approach the question? The centrality of the notion of "prejudice" is a fact of observation. But "prejudice" is also an interchange of representations and beliefs between modern ideology in general — egalitarian rationalist individualism — and the encyclopedic space of the social sciences. In addition, the mediating character of the idea of prejudice is found even within the elaborate ("scientific") problematics in which there appear various conceptualizations of "racism," which through analysis opens up into three distinct notional fields: ideological construction, attitude, and social behaviors or functionings. Here we will be able to give only a general idea of some of the dominant analytical orientations, as sociology, economics, ethnology, social psychology, and political science manifest them in their attempts at conceptualization. For just to present the principal studies done on the question by the social sciences in the West for over a century would be the task of an entire work. In particular, the vast American literature that stems from "ethnic studies," which approaches interethnic relations in all their aspects, cannot here be the object that begins the analysis, any more than the impressive corpus of (essentially American) studies in social psychology on "attitudes" and "prejudices."[12]

## The Scholarly Meaning: Racism, Racial Prejudice, and Discrimination

Let us begin with a simple observation bearing on the modern discursive use of the term *prejudice*, preliminary to any analysis of the idea of prejudice: everyone — every school, every party, every "camp" — has her own use of the term *prejudice*, that she reserves for qualifying her adversary in order to disqualify him. The term *prejudice* is in essence polemical: it first serves to delegitimate an opinion, a thesis, or a theory that the subject does not share, but rather impugns. Before the contemporary disqualifying uses of the word *racism*, the expression *race prejudice* was employed by the adversaries of any sociopolitical or sociohistorical doctrine of race in order to designate its conceptually inconsistent core or the nonexistence of its scientific basis. In particular, if a continuity is postulated between the position of the existence of distinct races (in the zoological sense) and the affirmation of racism, if the hard core of the idea of race is characterized by the notion of a *hereditary transmission* of the (supposed) differential qualities of race — so if racism assumes a *hereditarianist* position — then the rejection of racism implies a position of an *environmentalist* type.[13] That is why American antiracism, for example, was constituted around Franz Boas on the basis of a rejection of "biologism" in the social sciences. Such an antiracism, grounded on both the rejection of the primacy of factors of racial heredity and the abandonment of the idea of a unilinear evolution (so of a universalist conception of the "degrees" of civilization), had to constitute for itself a positive theory of the differences among human groups around the axiom that a culture can evaluate itself only in relation to its own values and beliefs: *cultural relativism* was the price one had to pay for avoiding the monocausal biologization of collective differences, even while refusing to deny the massive fact of cultural differences. There is a moderate cultural relativism in Boas, from the fact that he did not exclude, among cultures that were in principle autarkic, borrowings and the diffusion of cultural forms:[14] such a dialectic of the closed and the open is still a fecund model for any reasonable antiracism that refuses to constitute itself as a position symmetrical to the extremism that it denounces. To the Marxist and rationalist antiracisms, culturalist antiracism has added its basic positions and values: "The refusal of biological fatalism, the reiterated affirmation of plasticity, the hostility to the explanation of the differences among ethnic groups by other than sociocultural factors."[15]

But in spite of an incontestable homology in the polemical uses, the psychosocial realities thus designated according to a stigmatizing intention should not be assimilated to one and the same phenomenon, "racism." It is known that the polemical aim tends to reduce the heterogeneous set of adversaries (and/or of detestable things that they are or represent) to a single, homogeneous class. It will therefore be necessary to put forth and justify several elementary distinctions on which there appears a relative consensus in the field of the contemporary social sciences. We will hence distinguish *racist ideology* (doctrine, conception of the world, view of history, theory, philosophy), *racial prejudice* (attitude, affectivo-imaginary disposition, linked to ethnic stereotypes and coined as "opinions" and "beliefs"), and *racial discrimination* (observable and indeed measurable collective behavior, linked to certain modes of social functioning).

This tripartition of the broad and indistinct phenomenon named "racism" is especially encountered in an already classic book by the sociologist Michael Banton, published in 1967.[16] The author identifies three ideal types of conflictual interracial relations ("racial tensions"), to which it seems one might assign most discourses and positions, attitudes, and behaviors termed "racist": *racism-as-ideology, racism-as-prejudice,* and *racism-as-discrimination.*

## *Racism-as-Ideology*

The first type of conflictual social relations among groups perceiving themselves as "racially" distinct may be said to have as its basis "racism" in the strict sense, gauged according to the criterion of *ideology,* as an *explicit* system of representations and judgments (evaluations), formulated, susceptible of being presented in the form of a view of the world or of a general conception of history, and fulfilling a main function of legitimation. Racism would designate *stricto sensu* "the doctrine that a man's behaviour is determined by stable inherited characters deriving from separate racial stocks having distinctive attributes and usually considered to stand to one another in relations of superiority and inferiority."[17]

Racism is hence defined as a theoretical elaboration containing three principal elements, corresponding to three distinct and correlated theses:

(a) the statement of *biological* (or genetic) *determinism* of human behaviors;

(b) the statement of the hereditary determination, according to the "racial" lines or lineages, of behaviors (on the psychological, social, and cultural levels): the postulate of *biophysical* or *differential biocultural heredity;*

(c) the statement that the differences among racially defined groups must be interpreted as relations of *inferiority/superiority,* that is, of *inequality.* This is the affirmation generally maintained by common opinion and privileged by the antiracist vulgate: racism is the idea that the races are by nature unequal among themselves from all points of view, or at least from the points of view that matter.

To these three expressly posited traits may be added the trait presupposed by them, that is, that there really exist *distinct races,* that biocultural collective entities may be distinguished according to criteria of a scientific type (involving measurement, statistics, and so on).

There hence proceeds the following ideal-typical definition of racism-as-ideology:

Differentiate
1. There exist distinct *races.*
1'. These races are biocultural collective entities that tend to reproduce themselves *ne varietur.*
2. All races are subject to a dominant biological determinism.
3. Each race has its differential heredity, which determines both its proper "world" and its specific system of aptitudes.

Hierarchize
4. Differential racial heredity necessarily defines, in its sociocultural expressions, a superiority or an inferiority.

Racism is therefore "an explicit ideological system";[18] it most often takes the form of a theory of scientific appearance and accompanies the deliberate acts legitimated by it. Racism confers a *logic* to any act of violence or discrimination, without being conflated with the violence that it legitimates by doing so.[19] The murderous logic of racism, notes Hannah Arendt, comes from the fact that "it objects to natural organic facts — a white or black skin — which no persuasion or power could change; all one can do, when the chips are down, is to exterminate the bearers."[20] This is to resort to judgment by quality, as Talcott Parsons defines it in his model of the structural variables of action: a social object judges itself either according to the criterion of performance (what it does, produces, or accomplishes) or according to that of quality (what it is in itself).[21] Racizing evaluation involves considering individuals only for what they are supposed to be (their racial affiliation), to the exclusion of all that they can do. And the racial being that defines a destiny for each is indicated by some trait of his bodily appearance, always socially "clothed": the individual would henceforth not escape from the fateful category to which his mode of appearance assigns him and that is deciphered through too many sensory indices (visual, auditory, and so on). Scholarly racism very logically resorts to the "paradigm of the index,"[22] from which it constitutes one of the most successful avenues to the ideologico-political field.

Even before the appearance of the word *racism* in the general vocabulary, Max Weber intervened in the scientific community in order to submit to an exemplary epistemological critique the "racial theories" of the "racial biologists" of his time, of which Alfred Ploetz, founder of the German school of "racial hygiene," incarnated the type. This dense critical analysis brought into evidence the first two traits noted by Banton (*a* and *b*):

> Two things are necessary before racial theories would even merit a discussion: the observation of undeniable differences that would be always present, psychophysically definable, precisely measurable, and provable as hereditary: differences ranging from a "reaction" to "excitations" (to express it technically), for it is not the cultural contents of our consciousness but rather the psychophysical apparatus of our consciousness that is the object of heredity. And then, the second point: incontestable proof that these difference have a causal significance for the specific and different peculiarities of cul-

tural development. At present, we do not possess a single fact of this kind.[23]

Weber brings his critical examination to bear less on the theorems of biosociology than on the conditions of scientific arguability of these statements in general. This critical distancing is in addition centered on differential racial determinism and more precisely on the type of causal determination that may be formulated as follows: "this biological race, this culture (and/or civilization)." On both points, Weber remarks that experimental proofs are lacking. Since 1912, the general form of the situation has hardly changed: the more or less violent controversy between partisans of a sociology of biological basis (or integrated into the life sciences) and the adherents of the "continental" autonomy of the social sciences—this controversy between "biologists" and mesosociologists has endured. In certain ways, it has even aggravated its effects, by broadening the field of its ideologico-political implications. This is therefore the strange observation before which one must really pause: the polemical situation has scarcely changed since the beginning of the century, and nonetheless scientists, in their great majority (if one does not distinguish between the hard sciences and the others), have not ceased retracing the paths of Weber's critique! This is the index that a problem is posed through the unstoppable resurgence of its polemical effects—in any case, that the question has still not been scientifically addressed or even sufficiently illuminated.

### Racism-as-Prejudice

In the strict sense, we must distinguish racism (ideology, doctrine) from racial prejudice; the latter may be interpreted on the continuous line extending from attitude and disposition to opinion and evaluative judgment. This is to state the difficulty encountered in any attempt at a univocal definition of the terms. In one sense, it is social psychology as such that may be defined as the scientific study of attitudes,[24] if by *attitude* is understood "a state of mind of the individual toward a value"[25] or "the way in which a person situates herself with respect to objects of value";[26] the study of attitudes is thereby placed within personality theory.[27] Around the 1930s, the concept of attitude had been adopted, since it was the property of no school, as a "peaceful concept":[28] "Escaping the nature-nurture controversy"[29] (an interminable debate, inherited from Francis Galton), the concept of attitude was "useful to sociologist and psychologist alike, and susceptible of 'measurement' and statistical manipulation both relative to the individual and on the larger scale of public opinion and the like."[30] The study of attitudes, by means of measuring techniques, showed its fecundity by permitting the construction of numerous attitude models, "from baking powder preferences to race, war, religion, sex, radicalism, etc."[31] In his famous 1935 study, Gordon W. Allport proposes this definition: "An attitude is a mental and neural state of readiness, organized through experience, exerting a directive or dynamic influence upon the individual's response to all the objects and situations with which it is related."[32] An important characteristic of attitude, as it implies "a neuropsychic state of readiness for mental and physical activity,"[33] is that it prepares the individual to react in a specific way: an individual's attitude toward something contains "his predisposition to perform, perceive, think and feel in relation to it."[34] On this point, Klineberg gives an example:

> An attitude of hostility against the Negro... predisposes the individual to participate in activities in which such hostility is expressed, whether it be merely the perception and recollection of unfavorable news items in the newspapers, the expression of arguments against the Negro, or actual participation in some violent overt act. Even when this person is engaged in some perfectly harmless activity which does not concern the Negro in any way, we still speak of him as having an anti-Negro attitude because of his readiness to respond in a hostile manner.[35]

This last remark recalls to us both that opinions are strictly tied to attitudes[36] and that attitudes are not necessarily manifested in practices, which henceforth cannot be considered as the only indices of attitudes (dispositions, opinions, prejudices). There thus results this proposition of clarification: "It would be desirable to reserve the word *attitude* to indicate what we are prepared to do, and *opinion* to represent what we believe or regard to be true."[37] From the same perspective, Jean Stoetzel distinguished four characteristics of attitude in social psychology in order to specify its functional signification: attitude is "an inferred variable, not directly observed or observable"; it designates "a specific preparation for action." It implies the idea of polarity: "An attitude is always an attitude for or against something." The latter specification comes down to postulating that "attitudes are charged with affectivity, or that they are the subjective correlatives of values"; "attitudes are acquired and susceptible of undergoing the effects of external influences."[38]

It is clear — and this obscures the definitional boundaries — that these characteristics of attitude may be attributed to prejudice, which henceforth appears as a subclass of attitude. Racial prejudice is definable as a preconceived negative judgment, appearing among groups that differ from one another in various respects.[39] One may insist on the hypothesis that prejudices are acquired through apprenticeship, especially through "the acceptance of attitudes current in the social environment";[40] it is the problem of the impregnation with or the interiorization of dominant attitudes, according to the problematics. Once in place, prejudices model the experience of the individual, hence acquiring a functional value of the perceptual or epistemic type, reinforced by an instrumental value (a means-to-ends relation) of a social, economic, or affectivo-imaginary type (the designation of a scapegoated victim).[41] From the moment that it is assumed that prejudices accomplish certain ends, incarnate certain "vital" values (useful to the existence of the individual in society), their functional aspects come into evidence. Woodard excellently posed the problem in 1947:

> When the psychoanalyst quits attacking the symptom and works with the meaning-giving context until the total field is realigned — the symptom disappears of itself. One of the important strides in psychiatry came with the recognition of the function of the neurotic symptom itself, vicious, haltingly *accommodative,* and blocking a fully integrating adjustment though it might be. So with social problems, including prejudice and bias (racial and religious prejudice are rising steadily, thriving as does the hysterical symptom on direct attack).[42]

The *functional* character of racial prejudice marks the limits of any psychological explanation that would apply to it and would claim to account for it through a genesis centered on the following conceptual pair: aggressive affectivity/rationalization after the fact.[43] Like stereotypes or commonplaces, prejudices are anticipated cognitive and affective schemata, preexisting in "public opinion" before an individual makes them her own:[44] prejudices "are to informed judgment what clichés are to direct perception."[45] In the second place, prejudices "localize certain unconscious drives"[46] and are accompanied by justifications of rational appearance. In the third place, prejudices fulfill a function of accommodation in the society or group in which they are active.[47] The understanding of this last characteristic is essential for defining the conditions of effectiveness of a strategy of "reduction of prejudices" that does not sink down into sublime prattling, the moralizing sermon always let down by its addressees, or criminalizing denunciation ("antiracist" propaganda, judicial proceedings). It is therefore not in flushing out and tracking down prejudices (in general among others) that they may be uprooted, for their deep roots are conflated with the social setting in whose functioning they take place. One may change the "functional alignment" on which the position of the subject of an attitude depends only by "altering the 'field' with reference to which its position is functionally aligned."[48] Woodard specifies the conditions under which prejudices disappear:

> Like the neurotic symptom, although vicious and blocking full adjustment, prejudices also have their accommodative function from the center of reference of those who hold them. They persist until real changes are made in the complex of conditions that gives rise to them — freedom from insecurity, some real solution of conflicting interests, some genuine achievement of communal interests giving body to the verbalizations of idealized brotherly identifications, or some equitable, orderly, and effective mode of processing out irreducible conflicts. Then prejudice, no longer needed for tension release or as a folk-weapon of in-group solidarity, disappears.[49]

Such an orientation of social therapeutics remains in the tradition of modern technology: to act on the causes to modify the effects, by the light of a science grounded on the principle of determinism, implying the knowability of the necessary (or highly probable) relations between some system of causes and some system of effects. Such an orientation to us seems to be as seductive (because deriving from a paradigm of action on things that has become ordinary in the modern world) as it is utopian: it is situated in the long series of dreams of social surgery that seem to be infallibly inferred from the progress of science and technology. The sociological and functional point of view nonetheless keeps a core of "truth" shedding light on possible action on social reality. For intervention in (rather than on) the social may not be reduced to the violence and illusion stigmatized by Hayek.[50]

The social sciences, abandoning all naive technomorphic scientism in the area of sociopolitical intervention, may assume more moderate objectives and begin realistically by proposing to shed light on the settings on which action must bear. It is such a practical route, induced from sociological explanation, that certain analysts of interethnic relations in the Western democracies have been following,[51] from the moment that they felt called on to intervene in the very field of their research. If the realist imperative commits to transforming the real conditions of social existence and coexistence, then the questions of cohabitation and cooperation in everyday life come to the forefront of a "concrete" program of struggle against "ordinary" (it is well named) racism, of which racial prejudices are a functional element. One should not transform ordinary perception and cognition through sermons and judicial proceedings on the basis of legislative measures: this is the juridical illusion that belongs to the modern legal states, of which juridico-political antiracism is only a variant. The current forms of antiracist action target all of the *acts* — that is, the symptom, to extend the psychopathological metaphor. The high visibility of "racist acts" allows the ungraspable "prejudices" to be forgotten, of which the social invisibility and unsayability may be overcome only through techniques of investigation that are compromised and thus contestable in their results. The acts are recognized as racist by the antiracist leagues and those who recognize said leagues: a refusal of accommodation, housing, parking; discrimination in employment, competition at work; segregation, discrimination, refusal of contact; opposition to mixed marriage; provocation, mockery, insult; oppression, exploitation; physical violence, torture, genocide; explicit affirmation of chauvinism and xenophobia (or of such and such a doctrine of race).[52] This list (which is not exhaustive) shows very well that ordinary antiracist action can target racist prejudices (which it nonetheless assumes) only insofar as they are verbalized and declared, indeed proclaimed. The infernal underground of "racist prejudices" by its very principle escapes the juridico-political type of antiracist action, which can scarcely do more than denounce, according to proven rhetorical rules, that over which it has no control. It wheels out its evasions, masking the real impotence of juridico-political antiracism. The latter may nonetheless act in view of achieving equality before the law, of provoking a recognition of the political rights of immigrants working in France, of instituting equal employment and housing opportunity. But ethnic stereotypes and resistance to "mixed marriages," for example, are so widespread, as much among the dominated (or the victims) as among the dominators, that denunciations and judicial proceedings would here risk criminalizing society as a whole. Here is the main difficulty of antiracist action: How does one get at the underground drives and beliefs? How can one know and transform the deep structures of the "racizing" imaginary? One must recognize a certain impotence in antiracism, which is certainly capable of seeing the problem but remains deprived of the instruments required to "treat" it effectively. Hence there is the retreat into denunciative rhetoric and juridical formalism, not to speak of the scandal par excellence, from an ethical perspective: the political instrumentalization of antiracism, reduced to just a "cause" for commitment, in which one expects various gains — from electoral calculations to strategies for political and media attention, by way of the new techniques of ideological recuperation of "humanitarian causes" by the "show biz" system.

The second type of conflictual racial relations therefore stems from *racial prejudice*, that is, from a certain predetermined *attitude* of individuals or from no-less-preconstituted feelings. The scientific use of the term *prejudice* cannot fail to appeal to its modern scientific meaning, set in place by Cartesian rationalism, of preconceived opinion, ready-made idea, or judgment made hurriedly without critical examination *(prévention)*. The norm postulated here is that every opinion must be submitted to methodical doubt. To treat racism in terms of "prejudice" (of race, racial, racist) is to set in motion a *rationalist* representation of racism, which is reduced to a precritical attitude, formed without sufficient information or critical reflection, an opinion lacking the stamp of rationality or scientificity. Rationalist opinion, henceforth self-evident, is rarely marked as such: it appears as the theoretical core in the given definitions of prejudice. To be rationalist is here to grant prevalence to the idea that prejudice is a "retrograde" opinion, issuing from "barely evolved" (or "barely cultivated") minds, a judgment condemned as "irrational" by science (and so stated by ignorant persons alone), on the traditionalist idea that prejudice is "a sort of unknowing reason."[53]

It is necessary here to insist on the existence of a *nonrationalist*, indeed antirationalist, conception of prejudice, according to which the latter envelopes a living (functional) but hidden (implicit) rationality, constitutes a treasure of wisdom accumulated over time, and conceals a social or existential rationality that abstract reason does not know — that it does not know out of principle, by the simple fact that it must turn its back on this rationality in order to know what it may know.

For the traditionalist legitimation of prejudice, from Edmund Burke to Hyppolite Taine,[54] is linked to an "evolutionist"[55] conception of history and to an empiricist epistemology of a "sociologistic" type (nothing is in the understanding that does not come from social perception), susceptible to agreement with a functionalist redefinition of prejudice. If one imputes to the latter a social function of regulation or accommodation, it thereby acquires a status of normality, indeed of rationality, in the social system.[56]

Moreover, there must be noted a surprising support brought to the partisans of the functionality of prejudice by the late reflections and positions of Claude Lévi-Strauss on the question of "racism." The ethnologist's objective is to distinguish formally what stems from "racism," an illegitimate and harmful biodeterministic ideology, from what must be attributed to what he characterizes as "attitudes that are normal, even legitimate, and in any case unavoidable"[57] — the attitudes ordinarily said to be ethnocentric and/or xenophobic will be recognized. If racist doctrines do not have a universal distribution and seem, in the strict sense, to be attributable only to the modern West, "these inclinations and attitudes," declares Lévi-Strauss, with ethnocentrism and xenophobia in mind but not naming them, are "consubstantial with our species."[58] As they are universal and necessary, they appear to be a priori of the human condition: the ethnologist, by "naturalizing" collective attitudes and inclinations such as enclosure within oneself, self-preference, and opposition to others (those who do not resemble one, who are unknown, foreign), gives a legitimate foundation to ethnocentrism and xenophobia. Of course, the polemical disconnectedness effected between racism as a "situated" doctrinal elaboration and universal autocentric/heterophobic attitudes seems to prohibit the relocation of the leader of scholarly antiracism of the 1950s onto the side of the subtle defenders of racial prejudice (New Rights, hereditarian psychologists, and so on). But one might just as well remark that Lévi-Strauss thus only reformulates and redefines in not only acceptable but also positive terms a type of attitude that most observers continue to name "racial prejudice." Henceforth, Lévi-Strauss's analyses would seem to be a euphemizing instrument in the service of a quite understandable, professional will, the last avatar of the myth of the "noble savage," to save from the grievance of "racism" so-called primitive societies, those objects that are innocent by nature. The Lévi-Straussian distinction would be valid only as an argument linked to a professional ideology and to an important segment of the contemporary social imaginary, illustrated by neoromantic utopias of a pure origin: by legitimating, from the perspective of the right to difference and identity, ethnocentric and xenophobic attitudes, Lévi-Strauss reactivates a modern myth while saving from the capital sin of "racism" an object of research that it seems necessary to deem, out of principle, fundamentally "innocent." The positive reformulation of racial prejudice as it functions "normally" in the societies studied by ethnologists is presented as follows: "The attitude held by individuals or groups that their loyalty to certain values makes them partially or totally insensitive to other values," as "such relative incommunicability... may even be the price to be paid so that the systems of values of each spiritual family or each community are preserved and find within themselves the resources necessary for their renewal."[59] The self-preferential attitude therefore has a survival value in the struggle for the life of the identity of a culture; distrust of "others" (cultures, men, and so on), indeed the rejection of them, is what here enables the conservation of distance, the marking of the difference between self and nonself, the presumed condition of survival of communities. "A certain deafness"[60] and a "somewhat impermeable"[61] condition are presented as required for the preservation of cultural diversity: "This diversity results from the desire of each culture to resist the cultures surrounding it, to distinguish itself from them — in short, to be itself."[62] Every culture posits itself by opposing: this is the law of the survival of identity, the respect for which implies respect for ethnocentrism and xenophobia, those natural and necessary attitudes — above all when they appear outside modern Western space, in which they tend to stem from "racial prejudice."

It is hardly by forcing the thought of Lévi-Strauss, at least as it presents itself in the analyses summarized above, that one understands that the alternative it assumes may be stated as follows: *either ethnocide or xenophobia*. A people or ethnic group would have the choice between cultural death through an excess of openness to others (dialogue, tolerance, reciprocal knowledge, communication, and so on) and preservation in its distinct being in opposition to others, beginning with self-enclosure. Either (1) the irreversible disappearance of cultures through a lack of differentiation or a confusion or (2) ethnocentrism and heterophobia, indifference to the Other possibly accompanied by intolerance and rejection. It is difficult to engage in a more respectable discourse on the cultural imperative of exclusion of the foreigner and avoidance of any mixture with the latter's ways of being and thinking. It is even more difficult not to note that such positions and evaluations encounter, to the point of conflation with them, those of national populism, on the one hand, and those of the New Right, on the other hand.[63] One may conclude from this either that the great ethnologist has imperceptibly moved, with the help of experience, to the camp of doctrinal nationalism (subject to applying it only to the societies studied by ethnologists), or that the antiracists had abusively termed "racists" authentic defenders of cultural identities threatened by a process of uniformization, which alone would be properly racist. In both cases, the ideological representations of the ideological positions must be revised. The conflict of interpretations has just begun....

Let us come back to the rationalist, classical, pre-ethnological conception of prejudice. For an "enlightened" mind, racist prejudice may only be a quality of the ignorant one or the effect of stupidity: it is a return to a prescientific mentality at the same time as it is a survival of mentalities from before 1789, an archaism. In short, the domain of prejudice is that of obscure and confused ideas, of dubious judgments (abusive generalizations and so on). But if the Cartesian meaning has not disappeared in ordinary contemporary uses, it has also been well integrated into the operative definition conferred on "prejudice" by the psychosociological tradition. In Henri Piéron's *Vocabulaire de la psychologie,* Robert Pagès gives a synthetic definition of prejudice: "Favorable or unfavorable attitude toward any object (for example a person) that is formed in the absence of sufficient information (belief), specific (a stereotype or abusive generalization), and resistant to information (rigid)."[64] Similarly, but in an empiricist problematic in which the exclusive criterion of the true (that is, nonprejudice by definition) is the reducibility of the statement to a perceivable fact, Banton posits that one must understand by *prejudice* "a generalization existing prior to the situation in which it is invoked, directed toward people, groups, or social institutions, which is accepted and defended as a guide to action in spite of its discrepancies with objective facts."[65] Prejudice is defined as an empirical judgment that is unfounded — "false," according to the empirico-realist determination of the truth — but that responds to a need for practical orientation.

Prejudice is therefore an *affect* and as such is endowed with a function of regulating action (a pragmatic function); it is characterized by its *rigidity,* or its irrefutability, its resistance to any attempt to demonstrate its falsity. It is a judgment impervious to facts: "When someone tries to demonstrate that an opinion is false, prejudiced people do not modify their views but, indeed, often twist the new evidence to fit their preconceptions."[66] For prejudices are rooted in stereotypes imprinted on the unconscious. One may give a definition of prejudice centered on the social effects (discrimination) that it is supposed to produce or on the ideological function of legitimation that it fulfills:

> It is a set of feelings, judgments, and, naturally, of individual attitudes that provoke or at least favor, and even sometimes simply justify, discriminatory measures. Prejudice is linked to discrimination. There exist prejudices of sex that discriminate between man and woman, prejudices of class that discriminate between proletarian and bourgeois, and finally prejudices of race or ethnic group. But each time, what is at issue are attitudes, feelings, and judgments that justify or provoke these phenomena of the separation, segregation, and exploitation of one group by another.[67]

Roger Bastide identifies two invariable functions of prejudice, such that it "always appears as an act of defense by a dominant group against a dominated group or of justifications for exploitation."[68] Finally, certain authors tend to echo common sense by giving a stigmatizing definition of prejudice, identified and reproved as the product of a summation of lacks, which would be equivalent to the cumulative nonincarnation of three types of "ideal norms" implied in the definitions of prejudice: the norm of rationality, the norm of justice, and the norm of humanity. Racial prejudice would hence be defined as the consequence of either a *lack of rationality,* a *lack of justice,* or a *lack of humanity* on the part of an individual in her attitudes toward the members of another ethnic group.[69] Here scientific discourse is imperceptibly made normative, to the point of transforming into a discourse of denunciation of the individuals who do not conform in their opinions or into a moralizing description of a negative social type.

What is striking in all of these definitions is the permanence of strong evidence, inherited and shared by most of the authors in the field of the social sciences, evidence that forms the core of the classical theory of prejudice and particularly of pre-Cartesian theory, as Francis Bacon's *Novum Organum* (1620) formulated it in a nearly definitive fashion: prejudice is an error toward which one leans and to which one holds, a "favorite opinion," that is, an illusion of knowledge that fulfills a desire. Let us read Bacon:

> The human understanding, when any proposition has been once laid down (either from general admission and belief, or from the pleasure it affords), forces everything else to add fresh support and confirmation; and although most cogent and abundant instances may exist to the contrary, yet either does not observe or despises them, or gets rid of and rejects them by some distinction, with violent and injurious prejudice, rather than sacrifice the authority of its first conclusions.[70]

The contemporary stigmatizing definitions of "racial prejudice" contribute to this privileged instrument of breakage with a speculative past of the Baconian theory of "prejudice," as a deceptive anticipation engendered by the accumulation and storage of successive experiences not submitted to the methodical critique of which Descartes furnished the classical characterization, "methodical doubt,"[71] radicalizing Bacon's mitigated rationalism by purifying it of all sensualism.[72] In Descartes, prejudice *(prévention)* becomes one of the two principal causes of error, the other being haste.[73] In the Cartesian conception, as is well known, prejudice is opinion passively received during childhood, inculcated by early education. Prejudice is what is opposed to the evidence that alone offers certainty; it is that with which evidence breaks in order to appear in all its glow. Either evidence is perceptual and arises from sensible intuition (the empiricist criterion), or it is rational and arises from intellectual intuition (the rationalist criterion). As evidence is the very mark of the true in the Cartesian tradition, the field of prejudices covers exactly that of untruth. True judgment is either founded on the evidence of the ideas that compose it or compellingly demonstrated — on the model of mathematical demonstration. Such is the logical conclusion of the strict definition of the true given by classical rationalism, which impugns as false any opinion subject to controversy, any opinion that would be an object of debate (discussion, deliberation) and so submitted to argumentation. The "least doubt" is here a sufficient reason for exclusion outside the domain of the acceptable.[74] Indeed, the strictly empiricist definition of prejudice, as judgment not founded on sensible experience, does not exclude a priori the possibility of arguing in favor of racism, insofar as the latter infers a number of its theses from the immediately perceptible aspects of human individuals (skin color, language, accent, and so on). Hence the antiracist prescription of leaving aside the perceptual evidence of color, for example (the example par excellence), is contradictory to the gnoseological presuppositions of empiricism. It follows that only one rationalist position can ground with assurance the "struggle against racial prejudices" by which antiracism is defined. For to do justice to the antiracist demand to suspend all judgment toward the cultural signification of apparent (perceptible) individual differences, one must place oneself on the terrain of rational abstraction, which alone can legitimate the preeminence accorded to the unity of humankind, the ultimate product of a series of abstractions. In order to legitimate a declaration of total war against racial prejudices, one must assume that prejudice is irrational through and through,[75] even as one places oneself in the exclusive camp of the rational.

The antiracist choice therefore involves the choice of the abstract against the concrete, that of the rational against the perceptual, and that of the universal against the particular. But perhaps error is not, according to a maxim by Braque, the opposite of truth. In addition, if it is true that prejudice is the best shared thing in the world,[76] the immoderately democratic recourse to the principle of the majority risks ratifying it, conferring on it, by some procedure or other (on the model of the referendum), the letters of nobility that it lacks. It is not in the name of the legitimacy founded on number, but rather in that of the qualitative legitimacy founded on reason, that prejudice may be impugned as illegitimate. The difficulty then comes from the fact that, in modernity, instrumental reason, oriented toward technical solutions, has become hegemonic: How can the rationality that is part of the reign of quality confront the primacy of quantity? The effective antiracist, who is philosophically demanding, is hence not yet at the end of his troubles.

## Racism-as-Discrimination

In committed (expressly scholarly) studies, one often finds the postulate of a continuity between racist attitudes and acts, indeed the affirmation of a causal relation between prejudices and discriminatory practices.[77] The causal interpretation of the correlations between attitudes and acts is in all likelihood abusive and barely more than the effect of ordinary ideological evidence, which consists of explaining behaviors by the "ill intentions" of the actors. A certain number of contemporary studies have established that phenomena of social or racial segregation do not necessarily result from segregationist attitudes, that is, that some situation of segregation or discrimination may be the "perverse" (in the sense of an effect of composition) result of attitudes or behaviors that are not in themselves segregationist.[78] He who analyzes racism in order to act against it projects the teleological character of his analysis onto his object, thus ascribing to the racist actors conscious racist objectives that would suffice to explain their behaviors. Klineberg has proposed a table with four compartments that allows a representation of the types of relations between prejudice and discrimination (as seen in the following figure).

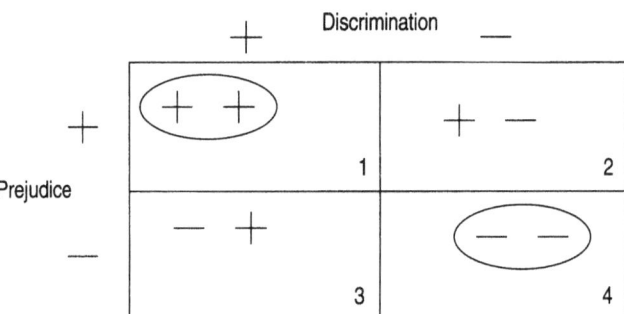

If the individuals of compartments 1 and 4 are the most numerous (a strong positive and negative correlation between prejudice and discrimination), the two other types of situation are not negligible. The situation defined by compartment 2 may be illustrated by the case of the "prejudiced" individual who, leaving California to mingle with a society without discrimination against Asians, must adapt himself to this new social environment, nevertheless without his prejudice disappearing. Defined by compartment 3, we find the situation of an inhabitant of [apartheid-era] Johannesburg who has no racial prejudices but who nonetheless must submit to the laws of his country.[79] The hypothesis of a circular reaction between prejudice and discrimination, which Klineberg has borrowed from Gunnar Myrdal, appears to be more satisfying than that of a determination of the second by the first. Let us recall that Allport, in his model of the five degrees of the behavior of rejection, placed discrimination after verbal rejection (antilocution) and avoidance and before physical attack and extermination.[80] Discrimination must not be confused with the mere avoidance of people whom we find disagreeable: it "comes about only when we deny to individuals or groups of people equality of treatment which they may wish."[81] Discrimination refers to measures of exclusion targeting the members of a group outside our own, segregation being "a form of discrimination that sets up spatial boundaries of some sort to accentuate the disadvantage of members of an out-group."[82]

In Michael Banton's typology of racial relations, the name *discrimination* is given to the third category distinguished. Discrimination defines a supposedly observable and relatively measurable *behavior*: it resides in the fact that persons are treated differently insofar as they are classified in one or another social category. Social categorization becomes racial discrimination when a population is treated differently according to criteria of ethnic/racial affiliation or of presumed ethnic origin: one racial group is thus placed as such in a subordinate position, indeed put in the service of or subjected to negative stereotypes maintained by the dominant "race."[83] Discriminatory laws or decrees are susceptible to abolition or modification either by the effect of a movement of opinion or by that of systematic state propaganda. But discriminatory practices, like the mentalities ("prejudices") and mores tied to group *interests,* strongly resist attempts at transformation.[84] There is therefore racial discrimination when ethnic affiliation is determinant (or at least dominant) in the assignment of individuals to their places in the social hierarchy. Individuals may not, in this case, overcome the visible destiny represented by their phenotype: skin color, for example (the example par excellence), in spite of the variable and socially constructed character of its perceived meaning, plays the role of a fixed point in the set of indices deciphered by the actors as race traits.

*Recapitulation.*

*First distinction:* the three principal types of conflictual interracial relations.

| Cognitive operations | Subcategorization of racism | Characterizations | | | |
|---|---|---|---|---|---|
| Perceive (judge) | 1. Racial prejudice | Attitude, feeling, disposition | Rigid affects (verbalizable: ready-made opinion) | Regulation of action (orienting abstraction) (passions) | Latent hostility |
| Classify (separate and hierarchize) | 2. Discrimination | Behavior, practices, actions | Classification and exclusion | Satisfaction of group interests (survival function) | From subordination to enslavement (domination, exploitation) |
| Explain (justify) | 3. Racism | Ideology | Explicit system of representations/ evaluations (interpretation) | Legitimation of actions | Violence: justified after the fact or engendered |

*Questions on Discrimination.* Now that this clarification of basic theoretical distinctions is done, we would like to sketch out a critical discussion of the falsely clear notion of discrimination, whose sole function until now has been to allow the establishment of a third domain of signification for the word *racism*. The ordinary notion of discrimination is in fact sufficient for a mere formal *marking* of said domain, without giving us the means to *know* it. In real social interactions, it must be specified, discriminatory theorizations, attitudes, and behaviors interact, implicate each other, fit together, and reciprocally reinforce each other. But if discriminatory practices are formally distinguishable from attitudes and ideological modes of legitimation, the first difficulty encountered comes from the fact that the word *discrimination* is used in very diverse contexts and with very different significations.

The analysis of what is named racial discrimination is indissociable from the studies of particular, empirically given societies, such as South Africa and its system of apartheid beginning in 1948[85] or the United States of America, especially on the basis of the practices of segregation in the southern states (the Jim Crow laws, that is, the set of segregation measures taken against the blacks of the southern states and their long-term effects).[86] These studies stem from the sociology of interethnic relations, involving complementary approaches concerning the juridical, political, demographic, and economic dimensions.

Pierre L. van den Berghe thus characterized the similarity between apartheid and Jim Crow: these two systems represent

> conscious experiments, on a grand scale, that aimed to establish a new modus vivendi among racial groups in the aftermath of profound social and economic changes. These two experiments constitute a deliberate effort, on the part of government agencies, with the goal of creating and maintaining a *spatial distance* between racial groups in order to preserve one of the basic elements of the social structure in the two societies in question. This basic element, in both cases, is the uncontested superiority of "Whites" with respect to other racial groups.[87]

Moreover, a comparative and international perspective today seems to impose itself on the question of ethnicity, of "race," and of "racism." In the framework of the following brief sketch of a problematization, we will be content to refer to some of these (now classic) studies of a monographic type, as well as to the recent efforts of comparative analysis (such as those of Thomas Sowell), without ourselves entering into the detail of the discussions.

We can of course begin by accepting the hypothesis that segregation "is integral racism, since it is the affirmation of the absolute superiority of whites, in official and institutionalized fashion to boot."[88] As soon as one refuses to be taken in by the lures of official euphemisms ("separate development," "multinational development," "pluralistic democracy," "vertical differentiation," and so on), the word *apartheid* must be translated, as Marianne Cornevin has proposed, as "unequal separation based solely on skin color."[89] A minimal suspicion here indeed seems necessary to us. Apartheid is at once the mode of legitimation, as ideology, of the political and economic supremacy of the white race in that it assumes the latter's absolute superiority, the condition of possibility of white domination as a regime, and the sociopolitical expression of a system of discrimination. It is known that euphemizing the assertion of superiority by the more acceptable affirmation of "difference" appeared in South Africa, in the public sphere, in the late 1970s.[90] But the lexical camouflage is here too obvious: the thematics of "diversity" (of peoples, ethnic groups, races) masks that of absolute inequality, imprinted on the social system. Gérard Chaliand has recently posed quite well the general problem of apartheid, which is one of political morality:

One may not conjure away the problem of apartheid by recalling that South African blacks have a higher level of life than those of the other states of black Africa. Poverty, in any case, is judged only in relation to the country in which one lives, but the problem does not lie therein: it resides in the fact that apartheid involves not only a separate development but also and especially that *blacks are deemed inferior by their very essence.* In this sense, the South African regime is the most unacceptable in the world.[91]

This maximal unacceptability stems from moral judgment and should in no way be substituted for a precise analysis of the interactions of ethnic, political, and economic facts. Moral condemnation must also not serve as a pseudoethical setting or a virtue-like supplement to a summary version of "exploitation theory," the prime example of which would be Marxist theory.[92] But it is undeniable that the "major contradiction" of South Africa is the fact of a "white minority, more and more minoritarian over the years, which has arrogated itself a racially instituted hegemony over a black majority on which it depends for manual labor."[93]

The economic dysfunctions provoked by racism (or rather by the measures it dictates)[94] are added to the social and political contradictions that it engenders — apartheid hence appears more and more as an unfortunate attempt at solving the problems posed by interethnic relations, an effort that has failed — and to the ethical scandal, even if the current regime [apartheid-era: Taguieff is writing in 1987. — Trans.] has never really been gripped by a "South African dilemma" on the model of the "American dilemma" that Gunnar Myrdal declared in 1944. To the contrary, basic consensus occurs in South Africa, in the absence of an assimilationist and universalist credo, on the segregationist model and the values that this model assumes.[95] All this should not make us forget that it is precisely the democratic ideal of the Americans that "made it ... necessary to justify the treatment of blacks by a racist ideology more sweeping than anything found in less democratic societies, such as those of Latin America or even South Africa."[96] The economic cost of apartheid may thus replace, in South Africa, the moral cost of the American laws of racial segregation. Marianne Cornevin characterizes very well the politico-economic contradiction, which seems insurmountable without the destruction of the system: "Whilst recognizing the necessity for the economic integration of the blacks, apartheid ... is utterly opposed to their sociopolitical integration."[97] Hence the structural instability of the regime and of the type of society that it upholds in a military-police fashion, and increasingly to boot. There is a great risk of a reduction of political power, now deprived of authority, in the sole exercise of the force of repression. Such a power, with no influence, should not remain for long by the edge of a sword alone.

Generally, what is understood by racial discrimination is the fact of excluding certain individuals from sharing in certain social goods, by virtue of their race or of a group affiliation perceived as being of racial type (according to the somatic or cultural indices). In addition, one must distinguish among discrimination in everyday life, which is imprinted on mores, institutional, legal, and administrative discrimination (discriminatory measures and laws), and the discriminatory applications of laws. In all cases, one meets with the perception of a *lack of respect* for a defined group and with the feeling of an *injustice* in the distribution of goods, advantages, rights, or duties. In modern, democratic, and liberal-pluralist societies, social and economic inequalities, and even more so inequalities of political rights, are perceived as forms of injustice, intolerable forms, at least if these inequalities bear on fundamental rights (or rights considered fundamental) and are legitimated by fixed natural characteristics such as the distinctions based on sex, age, race, or culture.[98] This attitude, in its common ideological expressions, assumes a favorable prejudice toward the most disfavored[99] — a normative judgment that defines one of the common spaces of ethico-political antiracism, according to ideas said to be from the left, and of a certain Christianity that has rediscovered the poor through political commitment. The maximal rejection, according to this liberal-democratic state of values, bears on the society of hereditary castes, in which social rank is biologically determined, with the social bond founded on blood ties. All this marks very well the relative and ethnocentric character of the modern impugnment of all "discrimination": the imperative of struggling against discrimination in general is founded on an exclusively modern and Western system of values and norms, which requires the condemnation of every other form of sociopolitical organization as discriminatory and segregationist. Individualist values and norms imply both the requirement of equal socioeconomic opportunity and the equality of political (and educational) rights. Hence the two major social indices are defined, in the common modern perception of racial discrimination: unequal opportunity and unequal rights. Thus, in such a perspective, the caste system can only be likened, in the same sort of stigmatization, to a racist system.

John Rawls indicates the central difficulty quite well:

> There are questions which we feel sure must be answered in a certain way. For example, we are confident that religious intolerance and racial discrimination are unjust. We think that we have examined these things with care and have reached what we believe is an impartial judgment not likely to be distorted by an excessive attention to our own interests. These convictions are provisional fixed points which we presume any conception of justice must fit. But we have much less assurance as to what is the correct distribution of wealth and authority.[100]

In short, Rawls attributes to moral common sense (whose existence he presupposes) the absolute conviction that racial discrimination is an injustice. The difficult problems begin with the construction of a theory of justice that includes the conditions of its applicability; for equal opportunity is not to be confused with either equality of conditions (which would be achieved by the utopian program of a thoroughgoing redistribution) or the equality of consideration or respect. Transideological consensus seems to occur on the increase of social mobility, involving "a policy for reducing inequality between groups (the initially advantaged and the initially disadvantaged) without reducing inequality between individuals."[101] It remains that the requirement of equality is manifested, in modern social reality, by measures to reduce inequalities that mainly aim, in conformity with the system of values of liberal-pluralist societies, to establish the conditions of equal opportunity. One may attempt to achieve such a change, as in the United States during the 1960s and 1970s, through various types of compensatory programs: the policy of school integration (busing), preferential hiring (which gives priority in recruitment and promotion to members of groups against which there has been discrimination), affirmative or positive action (designating "positive" measures aiming to involve members of groups that have been victims of discrimination), and reverse discrimination (discrimination in the encounter with individuals or groups that have discriminated against another group). The recourse to judicial constraint and the busing mandate have really contributed to breaking the tradition of segregation in the rural South of the United States.[102] These various modes of antidiscriminatory action all aim to establish (or to reestablish) equal opportunity for all the individuals of the given society, the criterion being the effective inclusion in the meritocratic system of individuals born in "disadvantaged" or "unfavored" groups.[103]

Thomas Sowell, after recalling that "racism is a term used to cover so many different kinds of behavior that it is difficult to pin down a specific meaning,"[104] rightly points out: " 'Racism' can be used legitimately as a term of moral denunciation of racially discriminatory behavior, and no confusion results so long as that is understood to be its sole purpose and significance."[105] Insofar as it attests a subjective state of blame for the practices said to be discriminatory, the word *racism* correctly describes a state of fact of a social order (the reaction of an indignant subject in the face of what he perceives as a form of injustice). Sowell adds, and here again we will willingly follow him, that "confusion and illogic result when this general usage alternates with a more specific designation of racism as a belief in the genetic inferiority of various peoples."[106] Now, many historical systems of discrimination, no less than the system of slavery, appeared independently of all biological theories of inequality among races. On the one hand, the Chinese and the Jews have been the object of discrimination and violence in numerous countries and over many centuries, without anyone generally believing in their biological inferiority.[107] If racism is defined as involving a genetic theory of the inferiority of those who are racized, then it is neither necessary nor sufficient to explain discrimination. On the other hand, it is a historical fact that

> blacks were not enslaved because of theories of biological inferiority. Such theories followed in the wake of slavery, and were not even the first rationalization used. Only after religious rationalizations for slavery began to run into difficulties were biological rationalizations substituted, both in South Africa and in the United States.... Non-racist slavery was common in the ancient Greek and Roman worlds.[108]

Here is the not inevitable paradox that arises from the *"shifting definitions"*[109] that are too often provided (or, more exactly, assumed) of racism: "From the standpoint of moral culpability, South Africa must surely be one of the most racist nations in all history. But such racial policies in South Africa long antedate any general concern with, or awareness of, genetic theories, and even today genetic theories or beliefs do not play anywhere near the role in South Africa that they did in Nazi Germany or the American South."[110] It must finally be noted that "discrimination and exploitation are two different phenomena, and evidence of the former is not evidence of the latter."[111] On the one hand, in fact, a group "may be very much discriminated against — blacks in South Africa, for example — without necessarily being exploited."[112] On the other hand, as illustrated by the prosperity of the Chinese in Southeast Asia, in spite of the many forms of discrimination of which they were the object, lack of economic success cannot be explained in general by ethnic or racial discrimination, assumed to engender or legitimate exploitation. The same goes for the history of the Japanese in the United States, which may be summarized in two words, "tragedy and triumph,"[113] marking two successive steps. Another fact will be noted, the interpretation of which can only comfort the hypothesis: even though racism in the strict sense is less marked in Brazilian society than in the United States, and although interracial relations are (and have been) easier (less conflictual) there, Brazil "has larger black-white disparities than the United States in education and in political participation."[114] In fact, blacks "are extremely rare in high professions or other high-level occupations in Brazilia."[115] Hence, in spite of more strongly marked racial discrimination, the socioeconomic disparities are less great in the United States than in Brazil.[116]

If therefore racism accompanies discriminatory situations, which constitute one of the obstacles to the individual's rise on the social scale, it would not by itself explain the economic and social differences between whites and blacks.[117] The moralist approach[118] can here only denounce and condemn, preach the redress of injustices or revolution; it can explain nothing. But the virtuists, who especially extol redistribution, assume "a posture of partisanship to the poorer and currently less productive segments of society, or of the world community — providing incentives for them to *remain* less productive and to become a growing portion of mankind."[119] Doing so, the upholders of social justice work for little more than themselves and the short term: "The only clear long-run gainers from such policies are those who feel noble or who gain politically by advocating them, or who gain power and prosperity from administering them."[120] The antiracist "victimization" of the individuals and groups situated at the bottom of the

## The Theories of Prejudice and the Meanings of Racism 169

socioeconomic scale is only the simple reversal of the racist blame of those who are "incapable" by nature. These two symmetrical and rival discourses share a negative passion, guilt, and an operation, the projection onto others of the defect, the imputation of malevolent intentions to some category of "others."

We can follow Sowell up to this point. At issue again is not to founder in amoral or immoral cynicism. If, in fact, the virtuist degradation of analysis is one of the main obstacles as much to the understanding of phenomena of ethnic interactions as to the search for concrete solutions, the question of ethics is not for all that addressed by abandonment and assimilation to instrumental moralism. But the ethical perspective bears on the final ends of action and can play a role only on the level of regulatory ideas. It is not to be confused with either cognition of the social real or the search for pragmatico-technical solutions stemming from instrumental reason. In denouncing the virtuist substitute for knowledge and practical treatments, we are not impugning ethics; rather, we are purifying the recourse to it.

Toward the end of the "Overview" of his important book *Ethnic America*,[121] published in 1981, Thomas Sowell notes: "Many discussions of group differences in income or occupation freely invoke such terms as 'discrimination' or the even more emotionally charged (and empirically elusive) term 'exploitation.'"[122] We will here limit ourselves to a critical investigation bearing on the meaning of the word *discrimination*, which "varies across a spectrum, from underpaying individuals for their current capabilities to the existence of historic barriers that inhibited the development of capabilities."[123] In his work published two years later, *The Economics and Politics of Race*, starting with the observation that "one of the most common concepts encountered in discussions of race and ethnicity is *discrimination*,"[124] Sowell proposes a semantic analysis of the term, resulting in an inventory of six distinct significations, with only the first four bearing on situations of racial discrimination properly speaking:

1. Paying one group less for a given economic performance than another group would receive for the same economic performance, quantitatively and qualitatively.

2. Charging one group more for an economic good with a given production cost than would be charged another group for the same good at the same cost of production.

3. Refusing to engage in transactions at all with one group while engaging in transactions with another group offering no better terms nor performing any better economic service.

4. Perceiving individuals from different groups so differently that they are offered different terms — or one is offered terms and the other is not — even when they are objectively the same.

5. Paying or charging different amounts to individuals from different groups, regardless of the reason.

6. Different "representation" of different groups in different jobs, colleges, jails, or other institutions, regardless of the reason.[125]

When income gaps are ordinarily attributed to the discriminatory attitude of employers, it is suggested that a given group is underpaid with respect to its effective capacities. It is, however, quite rare to encounter theoretical efforts that furnish the means to measure effectively these postulated capacities. Whatever the case, the presupposition of the affirmation that there is exploitation is that the exploited group, being thus underpaid, is so with respect to the fair price of its real possibilities (in general, the question of compensation for current productivity is set aside).[126] But discrimination on the part of the employer (definition 1) "cannot...explain large income differences among various segments *within* a given ethnic group."[127] The situation corresponding to definition 2 is that of discrimination in the consumer sector, expressed by the formula "the poor pay more."[128] Sowell shows that the ideological evidence of the formula especially masks "differences in crime rates...[that] affect the cost of running a store in many ways, leading to different prices for the same item in different ethnic neighborhoods."[129] An analogous remark may be made concerning the situation corresponding to definition 3: ethnic groups are not differentiated solely as such or by their income level but also by their degree of solvency. Definition 4, Sowell specifies, is "a special case of 'unconscious discrimination' (sometimes called 'institutional racism') in which the discriminator is consciously treating everyone alike whom he regards as having the same qualifications, but is simply biased in his assessments of qualifications of individuals from different racial or ethnic backgrounds."[130] The most general characterization of the discrimination affecting a group consists of saying that the latter is broadly judged unfavorably (certain disadvantages and certain inconveniences are thus entailed) or that it is underpaid.

Systematic analysis of the uses of the term allows one to specify this characterization.[131] It must first of all be noted that the first three definitions are coherent among themselves, but incompatible with the last two. In addition, the first four definitions come down to treating similar entities in a dissimilar fashion (groups or individuals as members of such and such a group), whereas the last two come down to not treating in a similar fashion entities (groups or individual representatives of such and such a group) *that are similar or not*. The last two definitions bear on the egalitarianist representations of discrimination: to discriminate is in this case to treat groups or individuals unequally. There is here postulated a type of "arithmetic" justice, in opposition to the type of "geometric" or proportional justice postulated by the first four definitions. Sowell holds that the latter may be combined into a single one "as *the offering of different transaction terms — including no terms at all — to groups who do not differ in the relevant criteria* (skill, credit rating, experience, test scores, etc.)."[132] As for situations 5 and 6, often accepted as presumptions of discrimination, Sowell holds that they "do not in themselves constitute discrimination,"[133] without for all that specifying the source of their interpretation in terms of discrimination: egalitarianist ideology (and its hold). The appeal to good sense and common experience here seems sufficient to him: "No one regards the over-representation of black Americans on professional basketball teams as constituting discrimination against white Americans."[134] But it will be noted that situation 6 may imperceptibly slip toward situation 4 or even result from it: instead of speaking of "discrimination" against a group, the legitimators of the situation will speak of "preference" for another group. Now, "preference" and "discrimination," Sowell rightly notes, are but the same thing expressed in two ways: "preferences for A, B, and C constitute discrimination against X, Y, and Z."[135] It is not useless to insist on the recourse to such euphemizing lexical substitutions in political discourse: in France, the imperative of the National Front since 1985, "national preference," illustrates the affirmative transformation of a proposition of exclusion, linked to xenophobic attitudes — the strategic shifting of an explicitly discriminatory statement toward the statement of a difference or an acceptable preference.[136]

Hence, a demanding analysis of the uses of the word *discrimination* shows the plurality of its significations, brings into evidence the difficulty of giving it a precise meaning in reference to such and such an empirical situation perceived as "discriminatory," and raises skepticism over the possibility of finding a semantic core common to all the meanings inventoried (as Sowell's six definitions are themselves susceptible of subcategorization). In other words, denouncing "discrimination" or standing up to "all discrimination" risks being only a conceptually empty principled position, a formal moral attitude, applying to all possible social situations and to none in particular (or precisely). Just like the denunciation of "exploitation" in general, that of "discrimination" stems from the virtuist pose (to be moral is to profess ideas perceived by the majority as moral at a given time and place), which especially has the function of steering away the denouncers who analyze real situations by substituting an indeterminant moralizing condemnation. Moral conformity of the left remains conformity, which is a functional blindness.

One may wonder if situations analyzed poorly or not at all and problems diagnosed poorly or not at all do not imply costs more important than an effort of analytic lucidity, which is not scared off a priori by the possible consequences. This is a position that in no way excludes, as we have emphasized, an ethical perspective, but rather gives it its just place and proper, noninstrumental value, beyond all ideological manipulation. The public antiracist sphere is encumbered with individuals of soft mind and hard heart, who take advantage of a reputation usurped from pure hearts. With Jacques Maritain, we will affirm this completely different demand: "We must be firm of mind and soft of heart!"[137]

*"Theories of Prejudice"*

If one reduces the difference between racism-as-ideology (racism) and racism-as-opinion (racialism, racial prejudice) to a difference of degree of elaboration (with racist ideology as only an organized set of racist opinions), then the analysis of racism is a subsection of the analysis of opinions and prejudices in general. But prejudices are analyzed from different perspectives, and one may state the hypothesis that the types of explanation or causal analysis of prejudices are not necessarily dialectizable, a fortiori synthesizable.

Gordon W. Allport distinguishes six types of "theories of prejudice," in relation to as many different levels of causal analysis.[138] This typology may be compared with the one that Klineberg proposes,[139] which differs from it only in points of detail, while proposing to lay "more stress... on the interdependence of the various levels."[140] Allport insists rather on the necessity, for the researcher, to accompany his free decision in favor of a type of approach with a recognition of the set of the other possibilities of modelization. Allport thus presents a diagram of the different existing approaches to prejudice (see the following figure).[141]

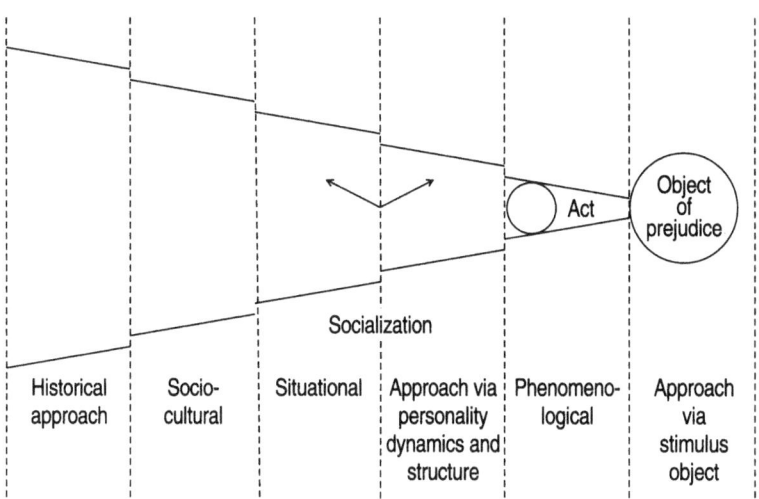

1. *The historical approach* is illustrated by the "exploitation" theory of prejudice, which is approached essentially as a mode of legitimation of economic advantages.[142] Prejudices are defined, in the framework of this instrumental theory, as means in view of a practical end[143] — that economic profit, for example, be linked to colonialism or slavery: racial prejudice here effects justification, rationalization, compensation, veiling.[144]

2. *The sociocultural approach* treats prejudice on the basis of factors stemming from culture and subculture.[145] The same thus applies to anti-Semitism, studied as a reaction to urbanization: the Jew becomes the symbol of the cosmopolitan, modern big city and is even its personification.[146] From the same perspective, Klineberg notes the mechanism of scapegoating as a pseudoexplanation of misfortunes and hardships — with gnoseological gain added to economic motive.[147]

3. *The situational approach* may be illustrated by the theory of the "atmosphere," that is, the set of external forces that act on the individual, the various sedimented influences exerted on the child in

her social/familial environment.[148] The situational approach considers all the effects of social mobility: situations of economic competition, unemployment, interethnic contact.[149] Prejudices are here defined as "learned":[150] they constitute one of the aspects of the process of apprenticeship and set in motion cultural representations without natural foundation (skin color) or real causes (concerning the traits of stimulus object). Klineberg, following Emory S. Bogardus, insists on the passive adoption of ethnic stereotypes and, in reference to a study by Hartley, on the hypothesis that prejudices may develop in the absence of any personal experience concerning the targeted groups.[151] In this way one may reverse the ideological evidence by privileging the process of legitimating imputation: "It is not the characteristics of the immigrants which cause them to be disliked, but rather that those characteristics are ascribed to them which give the dislike an apparent justification."[152] Prejudices here appear linked to the ritualized collective imaginary rather than to the characteristics of the social real: the attributed ethnic traits are the effect rather than the cause of prejudices. But on the model of the automatic fulfillment of "prophecies,"[153] one may fear that ethnic prejudices engender the conditions of their own verification.[154] Following Robert King Merton and Allport,[155] Klineberg notes the importance of "self-fulfilling prophecies" in the realm of interethnic relations: "Negroes are regarded as inferior, therefore they are not given adequate educational opportunities, therefore they do in fact become inferior — not in potentialities, of course, but in terms of their average accomplishments."[156] The two fundamental problems are therefore first that of the modes of inculcation of "prevalent attitudes" and received ideas and then that of the implications of the circular relation between prejudice and discrimination, an interaction that Gunnar Myrdal brought to light in 1944.[157] Between prejudice and discrimination, one should not be content to posit a relation of cause and effect, even if there exists a strong correlation, both positive and negative, between one and the other. But if one can legislate against prejudice, it is possible to eliminate discrimination: "Hence prejudice will be diminished by this, when the symbols of supposed ethnic inferiority have disappeared."[158]

4. *The approach via personality dynamics and structure* (or the psychodynamic approach): it assumes, like the situational approach, the centrality of the process of socialization and inculcation. The hypothesis according to which prejudices constitute a dimension of the

personality[159] is at the foundation of the research on the "authoritarian personality" of the late 1940s,[160] whose well-known results seem to attest a strong correlation of attitudes: "On the whole those subjects who dislike Jews also dislike Negroes and other minorities, and show excessive patriotic responses."[161] Hence the possibility of constructing this "new anthropological type": the authoritarian personality, especially containing the traits of ethnocentrism, anti-Semitism, hostility toward minorities, (politico-economic) conservatism, traditionalism (adherence to conventional values), and taste for authority (submissiveness and aggressivity).[162] One of the weaknesses of this program of research is to postulate that the object studied, which is also an adversary (and a foil), stems from pathology.[163] Allport cites Hobbes to illustrate a variant of the psychodynamic approach to the causes of prejudice in general, with the roots of the latter to be sought in the "bad instincts" of man, in his unlimited, insatiable desires: "In the nature of man, we find three principal causes of quarrel: First, competition; secondly, diffidence; thirdly, glory."[164] This is the "frustration" theory of prejudice.[165]

5. *The phenomenological approach* targets the system of responses to external stimuli that conform to the conception of the world borne by the subject;[166] in other words, it is interested in the manner in which the individual perceives the stimulus object. Klineberg contends, not without argument, that to the phenomenological approach there corresponds a distinct level of causal analysis:[167] the subjective-ideological interpretation of the social real by one actor may be conceived as an effect rather than a cause. This would occur when it is not the group targeted by prejudice that is the stimulus object but rather a set of inculcated and internalized representations attributed to this group.

6. *The approach via stimulus object,* starting therefore from the real characteristics imputable to the various ethnic groups.[168] This would be the empirical core that cannot be eliminated from prejudice, one of the materials on the basis of which ideological jury-rigging operates. Here the existence is therefore postulated of real conditions with an acquired reputation, which would be, at least for a portion, "earned." In any case, the existence is posited of an interaction on the causal level: prejudices would be coengendered by the nature of the stimulus and by considerations foreign to stimulus, by characteristics added onto those of the real object (the search for a

scapegoated victim, the projection of guilt, stereotyping, conformity to tradition).[169]

It seems to us necessary to conclude this rapid exposition of the various "theories of prejudice" with the evidence, obtained by analysis, that prejudice is multidimensional, in that it "may satisfy a number of different motives [and] may be the result of several different factors operating together."[170] This multidimensionality of prejudice should be found in the models of intelligibility that we are constructing. This fact might weaken the two antagonistic fortresses that split the ideologico-political approach to prejudice: that of the partisans of naturalness and the eternity of racial prejudices (the pessimists "on the right") and that of the partisans of their historical limitation to capitalist and imperialist modernity (the optimists "on the left").

## The Popular Meaning: Centering on Hatred, Contempt, and Inequality

In ordinary discursive practices, the word *racism* increasingly tends, by simplification, extension, and generalization, to designate "attitudes that aim to create or maintain unequal relations between racial groups,"[171] indeed to "racize" any group by a contemptuous, aggressive, or hostile attitude. The definitional circle is patent: through a derivation of the name *racism* is constructed a verb, *to racize,* that designates the act of submitting the Other to racism; this verb is then redefined so as to designate any known act of hostility and exploitation, hatred, contempt, and domination of victim groups (the "racized"). To be a victim, as a member of a racized group, is therefore to be "racized": the individual is "racized" inasmuch as she is a victim by the sole fact of being categorized as a member of the "racized" group, by instantiation. It is in this way that the discourse on racism comes to merge with the contemporary discourse of victimization, which gives it a supplement of affectivo-imaginary acceptability in becoming a new vector to it. In ordinary discourse, as in its journalistic occurrences (which formalize and ritualize it in return), there is now a tendency to call "racism" the set of acts of which one disapproves, that one reproves or condemns absolutely, when these acts place in relation a group perceived as "battering" or racizing (exploiting, dominating, abusing, discriminating, hating, attacking, and so on) and a group perceived as the "victim." The relation of racialization is from then on defined as intersubjective, and intersubjectivity as conflictual. The specificity of racism as an institutional ideology, attitude, or practice is thereby effaced, to the advantage of the indefinitely extendable relation to which it henceforth refers, illegitimate batterer/innocent victim, in which the typological opposition of the wicked and the good shows. On this simplification is grafted a mythologization with two faces: on the one hand, the demonization of the racizer, the absolutization of the wickedness of the "racist" (the "eternal" type of the "pure" wicked one, who is that way gratuitously, disinterestedly); on the other hand, the absolutization of the innocence of the victims, the racized, abstracted or isolated from any social context, angelicized, as it were. It is in this way that "the racist" is driven out of humankind as a foreign body is expelled, presumed absolutely dangerous for the body of the victims (who are innocent by definition, either as a dominated and repressed minority or as an exploited majority, discriminated against). The dehumanization of the racist "enemy," indeed his negative superhumanization, allows one to understand antiracist propositions of this type, put forth in the name of the best of causes (antifascism) by a historian who is also a filmmaker and a teacher, endowed with the required legitimacy (he combated fascism directly): "I am among those who fought the last war. We were confronting the fascists.... To fight against those people, one must isolate them morally, politically, and ideologically."[172] One (an antiracist worthy of the name) should not negotiate with "those people," who are excluded from antiracist dialogue. One must be content with making them unable to contaminate "Us," that is, unable to harm (as their essence is to harm: they are, literally, "harmful ones"). Let us not insist on the obvious resemblance between the discursive treatment of the "racist" by the antiracist and that of the Jew or the Negro by the racist or anti-Semite.

The nonscholarly use of the word *racism* therefore develops, in almost exclusive fashion, the themes of hostility, hatred, contempt, and inequality (or social injustice), bearing either on numerically minoritarian groups, designated as "victims" by their weakness, or on majoritarian groups, made socially, economically, and politically minor (the South African apartheid regime). When one committed scientist declares that "to be racist" is to hate the other in the name of her affiliation with a group[173] — this group that is definable by very diverse criteria (from skin color to one or another socially visible index stemming from cultural patrimony) — he is only reworking, by legitimating it through his position as a recognized scholar, the current definition in what is assumed to be public opinion. He reflects the common meaning and the ordinary knowledge of "racism," giving them the nobility of scientific thought. He "dignifies" and magnifies the ideological ordinary, for which one is grateful to him (such a discourse is heard over and over again in the media — it is the discourse of the media). There would be, from this perspective, as many "racisms" as manners of *legitimating* contempt or exclusion.[174] It is in such a problematic that the scholarly neologism *to racize* arises, conferring on this indefinite extension of the word *racism* a conceptual value (or an appearance of scientific legitimacy), in the terminology of the social sciences (more precisely, of a hypercritical social psychology).[175] The word *racism,* as a denominator supposedly common to the set of lexemes that it totalizes and supplements, is an archilexeme. A new word appears in this way, when the complex figure (metaphor and metonymy) is lexicalized: no more "Nazism-racism" (theory of race, extermination of inferior races, and so on) but rather "hatred/contempt/exclusion/exploitation–racism." Contemporary Western leftist discourse, denouncing "racism" or "racisms" in a broadened and indefinite fashion, here only pushes to the extreme an observable tendency in the hegemonic use of the word *racism*. That is why, only in the case of the denunciation of racism, one observes a curious basic consensus, from leftism and institutional communism to the liberal and conservative right, the national populists (the National Front) declaring themselves foreign, indeed hostile, to racism. By condensing the extremes, the most abstract ("the rejection of the other") and the most concrete (everyday insults and injustices), "racism" in the ordinary sense can engender a consensus on its absolute rejection. Antiracism, which is the ideology of this rejection, mixes no less high moral abstraction (respect for the other, tolerance) and the everyday lived experience of values and norms (the defense of the rights of one immigrant, in some discriminatory situation).

Hatred or contempt felt by a racist subject for victims he believes (wrongly) to be dangerous (so having to be rejected) or inferior (so exploitable and masterable): such is the general form of the popular definitions of racism. Whether the racized are interpreted as threatening enemies in a relation of confrontation or as inferiors exploitable in a relation of subordination, the racizing prescription is the same: to avoid getting involved, mixing with them. In both cases there is prescribed an avoidance of a phobic type of contact with the dissimilar, which is either demonized or animalized. The "spontaneous" antiracist argument, which reverses the mixophobic attitude characteristic of racism in general, for its part tends, not without naïveté, to prescribe mixture as the miracle solution and, in doing so, to set mixophilia up as the foundation of a system of values.

What defines the core of racism in the "popular" sense is the evidence that there is a necessary relation between the ethnic identification of individuals generally effected by inference on the basis of their skin color and the dominance of negative passions such as hatred or contempt. Hence, in his book *Colour Prejudice*, Sir Alan Burns defines race prejudice in the following way:

> The unreasoning hatred of one race for another, the contempt of the stronger and richer peoples for those whom they consider inferior to themselves, and the bitter resentment of those who are kept in subjection and are so frequently insulted. As colour is the most obvious outward manifestation of race it has been made the criterion by which men are judged, irrespective of their social or educational attainments.[176]

*Six*

# Antiracism and Antiprejudice Ideology

## How Does One Struggle? Utopian Orientations and Solutions

*On Racism as a False, Deceptive, and Outmoded Theory*

In the introduction to his book *The Rape of the Masses,* dated May 1939, Serge Chakotin approaches the question of "racism" (which he does not denominate as such) in a fashion that can be held up as a model of the naive progressive interpretation of racism, accompanied by moral stigmatization: the theories of race, at once scientifically false and, politically, as deceptive as they are dangerous, are only *survivals* of a now-surpassed stage or mental state of humanity. The enunciator thus sets himself up as at once the bearer of scientific truth, the representative of the meaning of history, and the exemplar of a (morally and intellectually) superior type of humanity. For such an "evolved" observer, incarnating the party of Good, Truth, and Meaning, racism can only illustrate a cultural regression, a historical step backward, a return to the past: racism achieves an involution. At the same time, the return of such an archaism as racism becomes difficult to understand: if there is in fact a progress in history, according to the necessary laws, how does one explain the failure to eliminate what has been definitively surpassed? Only a conspiracy theory of mystification, of the "rape of the masses by propaganda," may then bring the semblance of an answer in the name of "scientific" psychology. So what does such an absolutely legitimate subject see in 1939?

> We are faced with a...current of ideas noisily proclaimed and manifestly false, since they are in contradiction with the biological laws of evolution — that there is a fundamental difference between the races of mankind, that natural selection ultimately produces pure races, that such races exist, that they have a right to deprive other races of their liberty.... Are not these theories resurrections from a lower stage already passed by humanity, are they not a retrogression to a period resuscitated in camouflage for the benefit of a few selfish usurpers — an attempt, foredoomed to failure, to reverse the course of history? The attempt is doomed because it is in flagrant contradiction with all the causes of human progress — science, technology, the idea of society.[1]

The progressive conviction is identified with the tranquil certainty that is born from the evolutionist conception of history: if one does not stop progress, then any effort to stop it is evidently "doomed." And nonetheless it stops.... That is why the melioristic optimism of this disciple of Pavlov, when he despairs of the return of history to its progressive legality, reverses to a catastrophist pessimism: "If a chance combination of circumstances should enable this misdirected effort to get the upper hand of normal healthy evolution, if it were not combated and overcome like a contagious disease, all humanity would be menaced with destruction."[2] To struggle against racist regression is therefore to aim to put the train of history back on track, to bring it back to its true meaning and "natural" direction: "A new and true revolution is now preparing..., an unrest that is a collective reflex against the attempt to impose on humanity a reversal of its natural evolution toward liberty and material prosperity."[3]

*What Is to Be Done? A Scientistic Utopia of Antiracist Conditioning and Indoctrination.* In the face of "the Fascisms," Chakotin declared in 1939, concluding his book, "There is no choice but to act; [they] must be destroyed."[4] Not by prohibiting organizations or persecuting movements — that would only create martyrs — but by opposing deceptive propaganda with a truthful though no less violent propaganda: one must therefore "meet [the Nazi and Fascist movements] with violent propaganda,...counteract their tendency to psychical rape by equivalent action on the psychism of the masses, but without recourse to lying."⁵ But the task of propaganda will have to be to accompany an enterprise of reeducation, destined to make definitively impossible any regression on the scale of progress: "It will be necessary to build up in men's mentality, in the functional structure of their mechanisms of behaviour, reflexes which will render impossible a return to the state in which humanity is at present desperately struggling."⁶ It is from Pavlov's "objective psychology" that the scientific methods permitting the realization of such moral ends must be borrowed:

> The great ideas of Freedom, Peace, Love of all that is human, must become integral parts of our nature, reflexes anchored deeply in every human being. How can this be done?
> According to Pavlov, we now know: by a judicious formation of appropriate conditioned reflexes, by propaganda, and above all by education.⁷

Hence Chakotin is led to summarize his reeducation program for humanity, sketching a progressive catechism in three points, following the triad of superior values: Equality, Peace, Liberty. The treatment of the value of equality is quite interesting: in Chakotin's text, "the idea that all human beings are equal"⁸ takes over from "Love of all that is human." The egalitarianist ethic comes to be superimposed on the philanthropic norm, to the point of being identified with the latter: love of humanity, or the disposition of universal fraternity, is to the order of feeling what egalitarian conviction is to the order of knowing. To be able to love all human beings equally, one must assume — or better, be convinced — that all human beings are equal. Such is the circle of egalitarianism and philanthropy: one must believe in the fundamental equality of human individuals in order to be able to love without regard to differences of race, religion, culture, and so on. Chakotin, with just as much emotion as blindness, presents his antiracism as a program of anti-inegalitarianist education, thus postulating that the essence of racism is the belief in the inequality of the races:

> The fact that in the Soviet Union, in all the numberless schools, millions of children, from the tenderest years upwards, have had inculcated in their cerebral mechanisms the idea that all human beings are equal — that a black, a yellow, and a white man have the same rights to life and well-being — this single fact has already so vast a

bearing that it will totally change the world. The idea of equality, now the conditional excitant of a reflex, will determine for life the behaviour of nearly two hundred million men and women. That is the path to follow.⁹

The politico-pedagogical program is unequivocal: the humanity of tomorrow must be conditioned to the egalitarian reflex, by means of proven methods. What is striking here, of course, is the complete blindness of a mind struggling for "Liberty" with regard to the terrorist utopia that he is sketching out and positing as desirable. To the racist totalitarianism of the Nazis, the Pavlovian antiracist can oppose only another totalitarianism, in which the absolute norm of equality replaces that of inequality.

The other two points of the program are defined by the same operation: to inculcate from childhood onward the positive dogmas of Peace and Freedom. This surprising proposition of a systematic indoctrination, in the very name of "progressive" values, is stated as follows:

> Another idea, that of Peace, is of no less importance: war must be described to the youngest children as abominable and a crime, and not glorified as is done by the Fascisms. Finally, the myth of Liberty, the sublime idea of the French Revolution, must be spread. Its sparks, at a distance of more than a hundred years, lit the great liberating flame of the Russian Revolution.¹⁰

It is in this way that the progressive, antifascist, and antiracist catechism meets up with the revolutionary catechism.

## Limits of Antiprejudice Ideology
### Doctrines and Uses of Prejudice

> *According to Nietzsche, the theoretical analysis of human life that realizes the relativity of all comprehensive views and thus depreciates them would make human life itself impossible, for it would destroy the protecting atmosphere within which life or culture or action is alone possible.* Leo Strauss

In order to relativize the rationalist determination of prejudice, let us briefly sketch out a typology of the doctrines of prejudice, taking our inspiration from some of Leo Strauss's propositions. The "struggle against prejudice" has to vary in its reasons and its means according to three doctrinal versions distinguished as follows:

- the *positivist* version: arising from prejudice is any synthetic proposition (bearing on the real, or supposedly doing so) that is not susceptible of empirical verification or refutation, that is, any proposition conceived as not reducible to statements or states of perceptible things;

- the *scientistic* version: arising from prejudice is any synthetic proposition situated outside the field of propositions considered legitimate or valid — "scientific" — by normal (institutional) science at the moment when that proposition is pronounced;

- the *historicist* version: arising from prejudice is any synthetic proposition claiming a transhistorical or universal (or objective: situating itself in an intelligible world, in a field of eternal ideal objects) value, whether of a philosophical or a scientific order.

There exist only expressions whose signification and value, for a historicist, are strictly determined by their epochs and their places of appearance. Idealities must always be reducible to the spatiotemporal conditions in which they arise.[11] Ideas and judgments, insofar as they depend on their spatiotemporal context, are therefore of limited value: the historicist axiom is the affirmation of the historical character of every thought. But the idea that every idea is only a mortal temporal creation itself lays claim to a supratemporal value: this is the internal contradiction of historicism[12] from the very moment of its formulation. Thus historicism itself appears to be a system of prejudices belonging to the epoch of its formulation, a modern prejudice par excellence.

Let us take the example of philosophy. It is willingly said that a philosophy is *determined* by the prejudices of its time, that no mind may leap above its time, that every mind is of its time, only of its time. A philosophy can only *express* the prejudices of its time. But such a historico-determinist conception of philosophy implies a basic blindness to the philosophers' strategies of writing, a misrecognition of the rhetorical dimension implicated by any public philosophical act, in a world that is sooner hostile to the search for the truth, because dominated by opinion — the latter tied to the teaching of the useful, ordered by the ends of society. For the philosophical expression of prejudice, as it is attested in a world in which opinion is the norm, may signify any of the following:

- espousing them, sharing them;
- showing respect for them;
- giving the semblance of sharing them in order to persuade the listener, either by otherwise showing their absurdity or by bringing into evidence their undesirable consequences.

One must therefore account for the strategies of staging and/or divulging the true, if the latter is susceptible of being scandalous and hence of provoking a dangerous situation for its speaker. The latter must very normally resort to the oblique way of unveiling, which may borrow the technique of veiling or of dissimulating what one aims to *make understood*. One lets something be understood, then, rather than bringing it to understanding, one suggests rather than declares. Here is the foundation of the imperative of a reserved, secret, "gnostic" transmission of "disturbing" knowledge or of "scandalous" inquiries, either by way of initiation — oral transmission from master to disciple — or by way of indirect, symbolic scriptural communication that makes use of analogy as a strategic instrument. A philosophy is inseparable from the strategies of dissimulation that allow it to bypass obstacles ("prejudices") and to thwart the traps of its adversaries. That is why, notes Strauss, "esoterism is the necessary consequence of the primary meaning of philosophy, if we admit that opinion is the element of society."[13] It follows that there will exist an esoteric core in every genuine philosophy, at least while humanity itself does not become a philosopher: the mark of a philosophy is that it resists vulgarization. It proves itself as a philosophy by testing itself as a rebel against mass communication.

## *The Inversion of Denunciating Plays: Antiracism as Prejudice, Tolerance, and Exclusion*

Let us briefly pursue the historicist hypothesis in order to explore a few variations on the explicit discourse of denunciation of *antiracist prejudice*. We will thus call on all forms of negative characterization, in polemical contexts, positions aiming to denounce "race prejudice" or "racism": the antiracist denunciation of racism has regularly engendered its *anti-antiracist retortion*. This reaction of defense/attack, on the part of the "racists," assumes their self-representation: they define themselves as at once victims of the dominant prejudices and bearers of forbidden truths, too shocking for received ideas. They are victims because they are invested with the light of the true. In our examples, we will designate by "racists" (a constructed term, though sometimes used in self-designation) the bearers and defenders of the traditio-communitarianist conception of the world, either in its materialist-biological or in its spiritualist-culturalist variant, paradoxically legitimated by recourse to the ideology of scientific progress. Scientifico-technical modernity is here polemically turned against social and political modernity: the impugnment of modern humanitarianism, accused of resisting the truths of scientific racism, is effected in the name of the advancements of knowledge. This would be a "reactionary" usage, as it were, of the Enlightenment: it is in the name of science that the principle of equality (among individuals as among races) is impugned as a fiction, radically contradictory with respect to the data and laws of scientific knowledge. These few explorations will lead us to the intellectual origins of anti-antiracism: they are a first sketch of a genealogy of scholarly anti-antiracism (or constituted within the scientific community, according to the logic of the norms of the controversy recognized as scientific).

Our first counterdenunciative play of discourse is constituted by a "news brief" published in *L'Appel,* February 5, 1942:

*A Just Reparation by the Church*
Pope Pius XII has authorized the celebration, in 1942, of the third centenary of the birth of Galileo. It will be remembered that the latter was persecuted and denied by the Church for two centuries for his astronomical discoveries, which did not correspond to *the prejudices of the past.*
A belated reparation? Political savvy?
In any case, let us rejoice for the future. There is hope that modern scholars will one day be recognized for their works by the pomp of the Vatican. Let us hope that Gobineau and Vacher de Lapouge will later have the favor of being honored by a pope who is finally an adherent of racism. [My emphasis]

Besides this somewhat heavy shaft of irony against the church, one will note the recourse to argumentative analogy: the author of the text pleads a recent palinode by the church in order to bring to understanding that Gobineau and Vacher de Lapouge, the official founding fathers of "French racism" (rather than of racism in France), are identifiable, to sum up the argument in a metaphor, as the Galileos of racism. The suggestion is clear: the ingenious and misunderstood initiators of "scientific" racism, persecuted today, will one day be recognized and celebrated. The identification with Galileo is of course excessive: its objective is to emphasize the scientificity of the French fathers of racism, that the prejudices of today (1942!), echoing the "prejudices of the past," cause misunderstanding. So here we see denounced religious obscurantism and opportunism, equal to themselves in the face of any new spot touched by the light of science. After the science of nature, it is the science of man that is their victim.

Our second example of "scholarly" anti-antiracist denunciative discourse is a note excerpted from the *Journal des tribunaux* that, shortly after the publication of the second work of Vacher de Lapouge,[14] exhorted one to read it, under the title "Law and Race": "We signal to our readers the following important work, of extreme interest to all those concerned with the problem of race, increasingly on the agenda of minds that, *stripped of religious or childishly humanitarian prejudices,* apply themselves to solving it according to the data of positive Science."[15]

To the denunciation of religious prejudices is added that of humanitarian prejudices: the reference to the humanitarianist partisans of the innocence of Captain Dreyfus is transparent here. Positive science is supposed to respect only its own logic, which is that of discovery: God and humanity are the two powers of the past that are opposed to the advancement of the knowledge of the future. The struggle of the Enlightenment against Darkness, of data against fiction. Let us note, for our part, that one may wonder if the so-called question of race may be treated only "according to the data of positive Science," according to an orientation that is either "racist" or "antiracist"; for the debate, from this perspective, is inevitably enclosed in the antinomy "races exist"/"races do not exist (or are negligible, and so on)."

Our third example of the turning around of the rational-positivist denunciation of "prejudice" is to be found in several remarks by Vacher de Lapouge, characteristic of the scientistic style that belongs to the French selectionist school, founded on a supposedly scientific anthropology. This is a fine illustration of the strategy of retortion: in 1926 a reputedly "racist" author denounces the prejudices of those who contradict him, opposes the scientificity of his procedure and its results to the preconceived opinions of his adversaries. For the "racist" Lapouge, the "prejudice" par excellence (which today we would call "antiracist") is believing that the concern with preserving and improving the "superior" elements of a given population (which comes down to favoring the "better" lineages to the detriment of the "less good") stems from "race prejudice." The Lapougian defense is simple: it therefore returns to the sender his accusation of "prejudice." Here we find very well illustrated a central difficulty of the antiracist theory of "racist prejudice": its reversibility. Let us begin by quoting an observation from a later text, dating from 1926, bearing on the lack of awareness and foresight of the political and scholarly elites with regard to the qualitative future of the French population:

> As Americans and other peoples were taking their measures to increase eugenicism and suppress cacogenicism, here in France all those in official positions, the academicians as well as the rhetoricians in Parliament, were rising against what they called *race prejudice*. They counted, for raising the average and furnishing superior men, on *education* and what we would today call *mutations*.[16]

In the name of eugenicism and the theory of race, Lapouge thus denounces what he thinks represents, in 1926 (but in fact since long before), an essential component of dominant ideology in France, what today we call antiracism. The scientific concern with explanation by real causes and the concern with effectiveness are opposed to ideological blindness, which consists of abandoning oneself to the twofold belief in miracles and in chance, while proceeding to the official denunciation of improprieties summed up as "race prejudice," which shocks republican universalism, philosophy, and the "republic of professors." The demystifying critique in which the "racist" Lapouge engages therefore bears on what he thinks are the two grand ideological illusions of the partisans of the struggle against "race prejudice," the ancestors of the antiracists:

- the belief in salvation (collective progress, the formation of elites) by the influence of the educational environment: now, this instructionist mesologism is the mere effect of an ignorance of the determinism of heredity and above all maintains such an ignorance that it poses an obstacle to the correct scientific representation of the production of "eugenic persons." This is to believe in miracles: the belief in the possible scholarly transmutation of individuals, whoever they may be, is the modern version of the alchemical belief in the possibility of converting lead into gold;

- the belief in salvation by chance, which is only the modern version of the lazy argument, that is, of abandonment to destiny.

To the first belief, Lapouge shows no ambiguity or leniency. In 1909, he thus summed up the epistemological rupture that, he said, threw onto the trash heap of the prehistory of science the meliorist ideology of the Enlightenment: "There was a period in which, without closer examination, it was believed that a remedy to all the ills of society, as well as the principle of an unending progress of humanity, was to be found in instruction and education."[17]

Now, with the celebrated Weismanian distinction (between somatic and germinal cells) and the rediscovery of Mendel's laws, "all the hopes grounded on the heredity of acquired qualities vanished with the belief in this heredity.... Educationism collapsed along with Lamarckianism, and selectionism remained master of the field."[18]

The great hope of the Enlightenment is therefore disappearing, sapped in its foundations. Also disappearing is the alliance between mesologist conviction (along with its activist aspect, educationism) and progressive optimism.

In the face of the latest leaps, which are really only jolts, of the obscurantism that is as religious as it is enlightening (the Enlightenment obscures...), Lapouge celebrates the cold lucidity of the unprejudiced gaze, grounded on the lessons of science alone. Science points to the following orientation: systematic selection, as the true method of antidecadence, through the scientifico-technical mastery of the destiny of the races. In the opening lecture of his course on anthropology, given in 1886–87 at the school of science in Montpellier, Lapouge declares:

> The theories on heredity, on atavism, on crossings, on variations, on selection, and the struggle for existence are today demonstrated, established, and ordered for the future among the *conquests of science*. These theories are in formal opposition to an infinity of vulgar notions, some old, some of recent date, that form the basis of most of *our prejudices* in the areas of politics and society.[19]

Hence the truths conquered by the theories of transformist biology are destructive of the "prejudices" that until then formed the basic evidence of philosophy, ethics, politics, law, and so on.

These are "the consequences established by the recent conquests of biology":[20] to provoke a rupture with the apriorities of old beliefs ("chimerae") and to establish the new era of the scientific mastery of the destiny of man. The scientifico-technical optimism of the Cartesian tradition may thus ground the "scientific" theory of races and legitimate its project of struggling against the biological degeneracy of peoples: man must in turn become "as master and possessor" of *his nature*,[21] which includes his race characteristics. The mastery of the race in himself, and of the races in general, is an integral part of the Promethean project of modern science. Racism may thus legitimately, in a certain period of the history of science, take advantage of science.

A fourth example of the "racist" critique of the prejudices linked to the nebulous antiracist ideology is furnished to us by Julius Evola's impugnment of evolutionist racism, whose specific "prejudices" are attributed to a definite ontology and epistemology: zoological materialism and biological scientism. Evola explicitly distinguishes between biological or naturalist racism and spiritual racism;[22] he affirms the metaphysical superiority of the latter over the former, going so far as to declare: "Our racism goes well beyond the limits of these disciplines (biology and anthropology), which... are even, because of their positivistic and scientistic spirit, diametrically opposed to the true racist idea. True racism, more than a particular discipline, is a *mentality*."[23] Evola's attempt at the "rectification" of racism along the lines of a traditional metaphysics[24] must pass through the phase of a critique of certain prejudices. The first of them is the prejudice "that would like racism to remain entirely in a chapter of natural sciences."[25] Evola's argument consists of driving out the "progressive" or "enlightened," let us say "modern," elements of the most common forms of racism. In other words, one again finds certain prejudices characteristic of the ideology from which racism derives at the very heart of the racist positions (or those claimed to be so) — such as the rationalist and evolutionist prejudices. If one may distinguish, and hierarchize, three forms of racism — racism of the body, racism of the soul, racism of the mind — it is in the order of the research relative to racism "in the third degree" that there appear the most resistant obstacles, from the fact that they proceed from the evidence belonging to modern, "progressive," and "materialist" (or "positivist": in general Evola neglects the distinctions at this level of the critique) ideology. Hence the following prescription: "we must introduce revolutionary criteria into the disciplines [of 'third-degree' racism] and resolutely remove a certain number of prejudices belonging to the scientistic and positivistic mentality that, favored by a now outmoded historical school, persist no less in the most widespread forms of general education."[26] Evola is addressing present and future teachers. It is striking to note that a "traditionalist" and expressly antievolutionist thinker can himself resort (or not be able to avoid resorting) to the theory of "survivals," or of the persistence of what is "surpassed" in the present, a conception that assumes an evolutionist, indeed historicist, problematic. Evola continues: "It is first of all fitting to *surpass the evolutionist prejudice* in the name of which, in strict relation to the progressive and historicist prejudice, one interprets the world of origins and of prehistory as the dark and savage world of a semi-bestial humanity that, little by little, painfully, became 'civilized' and capable of possessing culture."[27]

What interests us here is the form of the argument rather than its content (the "theses" defended are those of original racial purity and of the raw intelligence of the spiritual world): at issue again is surpassing prejudices, a rationalist procedure par excellence, but one that is always susceptible of being turned back against rationalist "prejudices."[28] Evola argues the following: evolutionism is only a historically situated school and is now "surpassed" — But how can one conceive this "surpassing" once one has radically impugned any necessitarianist conception of progress? Here there is an ineffectiveness of the philosopher of Tradition, perhaps linked to a strategy of persuasion targeting minds modeled by the ideology of progress (Evola would then adapt his language to his addressees). The rejection of evolutionism may be translated quite particularly by a total impugnment of Darwinian theory, as much of natural selection as of the views on the "ascent" of man:

> As for...the general framework of the problem termed "descent," *one must resolutely take a position against Darwinism.* The original source of humanity — to which the superior races, whether ancient or contemporary, belong — does not derive from the ape or the ape-man of the glacial era (Mousterian or Neanderthal Man, and Grimaldi's Man), a fact that the nonracist specialists have more and more of a tendency to recognize at the present moment.... It is absolutely necessary to understand the living significance of such a change of perspective for racist conceptions: *the superior does not derive from the inferior.*[29]

One must therefore oppose to the evolutionist and progressive conception, and substitute for it, the traditional conception of the fall or descent through four phases corresponding to the four castes forming the social system common "to all ancient civilizations of traditional type":[30] the spiritual leaders, the warrior aristocracy, the "bourgeoisie" (the merchants), and the servant caste. This is a conversion of the metaphysical view of the history of the world, which must be conceived according to "a process of degradation, involution, or falling."[31] To be racist is first of all to defend the thesis of the splendor of Nordico-Aryan origins, of which the type, far from having been engendered by natural selection, was already at the outset entirely self-identical.[32] But to be racist is not only to have a sound and clear vision of the originary type; it is also to draw the practical and normative consequences from such a superior knowledge of the superior: "Such a position *commits:* from theoretical racism, the latter leads us to active and creative racism, that is, to the racism that consists of bringing about, in the general Italian type that is so differentiated today, the extraction and affirmation in always more substantial and precise fashion of the physical and spiritual type of the eminent race."[33] Committed racism is defined in this way: (Nordico-Aryan) noblesse oblige. Racial education is summed up by a certain interpretation "of the principles of our ancient wisdom: *Know thyself and be thyself*"; "fidelity to one's own nature, that is, to one's blood and one's race,"[34] and therefore just as much to the soul and spirit of the proper race. The idea of heredity is central: "We are bearers of a heritage that has been transmitted to us and that we must in turn transmit."[35] This is a threefold heritage, for it is distributed over the three hierarchical levels: the race of the body, the race of the soul, the race of the mind. The Evolian conception illustrates very well the cultural/spiritual variant of traditio-communitarianist racism, with its denunciation of the "prejudices" of biological materialism and its exaltation of the organic community conceived as the joining of three specificities (of blood, of soul, of spiritual values): "Racism conceives and valorizes... the individual as a function of given community: whether in space (as a race of living individuals) or in time (as the unity of a lineage, of a tradition, of a blood)."[36] Here, then, is the essence of racism: to conceive and want, "not the man *in abstracto,* but the man as representative of a race, just as corporeal as spiritual."[37]

The reaction against the "prejudices" targeting the theory of race is also found in Houston Stewart Chamberlain when, in 1902, he responded to the criticisms and objections provoked by his 1899 book, *Foundations of the Nineteenth Century:*

> In many places my book treats of the influence of Judaism and, through this intermediary, of Semitism, in the broadest sense of this term, on the innate religious instincts of the Slavo-Celto-Germans. I did not carelessly take hold of merely a wasps' nest, but of an entire colony of them! For it happened that, in expressing my ideas on this subject, I ran up against Catholic, Protestant, Jewish, and also antireligious prejudices. Such prejudices are all the more difficult to overcome if it is the case that, for example, the Protestant is also a Jew or the Jew an enemy of religion.[38]

Under the Vichy regime, the doctrinaires of "racism" willingly presented it as involving a struggle against ("antiracist") prejudice. In 1941, Louis Thomas, in his apologetic book *Arthur Gobineau, inventeur du racisme*, devotes a chapter to the theme of "the battle against prejudice." Here Gobineau is from the outset presented as an "iconoclastic" thinker, an enemy of "intellectual conformism," located at the antipodes of the "blind submission to a credo": "It was with constancy, with tenacity, ... that he would state theses that were most opposed to the honored gospels of his time."[39] The chapter ends with classic anti-Jewish attacks (which are, moreover, off the subject of Gobineau):

> If Gobineau makes certain prejudices related to the dissolution of peoples into a tabula rasa, it is because he wants to demonstrate that the degeneration of societies comes from the mixture and corruption of races. And what more corrupted race than that which allows itself to be invaded by the Jews? Gobineau is therefore a quite shocking spirit: he hits head-on the great Jewish conspiracy based on the unity, equality, and similarity of races and of men. And how were the Judaified criticism and academe to let him get away with that?[40]

In the same way, but in a less delirious tone, Jacques Boulenger introduced the "racist thesis" two years later:

> In France the racist thesis inspired very great enmities, because it was violently opposed to egalitarian passion and the romantic optimism of 1848.... "The principle that the democratic school denies the most strongly," [Ernest] Renan would write in 1871, "is the inequality of races and the legitimacy of rights conferred by racial superiority." Thus it is that after the end of the Second Empire and the foundation of the Third Republic that aristocratism and the hard determinism of the racist theses inspired the enmity of our democrats.[41]

Thus the denunciation of the *prejudices of the adversary* appears as an indefinitely reversible mode of polemical argumentation: "racists" and "antiracists," when they battle through discourse, exchange between them this typically modern reproach, inherited either from Cartesian rationalism or from British skeptical empiricism. The construction of the *adversary as a mind subject to prejudice* is a basic mode of delegitimating modern ideological controversies.

Can the circle of denunciations and accusations be escaped? First one must return to the caution of Descartes when he affirms that universal doubt must be reserved for minds that can make good use of it. Doubt is an intellectual weapon liable to turn against its user to make him dizzy, an instrument that is not to be put in just anyone's hands, where it would be dangerous — as though the democratization of doubt posed the threat of engendering a properly democratic phantasm. "The simple resolution to abandon all the opinions one has hitherto accepted is not an example that everyone ought to follow."[42]

*Part III*

# Racisms and Antiracisms: Paradoxes, Analyses, Models, Theory

## Seven

# On Racism: Models, Ideal Types, Variations, Paradoxes

> *If one defined as racist those opinions that proclaim the superiority of one race over another and claim particular rights for the superior at the cost of the inferior, then the value of a legal interdiction would be trivial, for the really definitive forms of racism in societies with racial conflicts are only seldom expressed in this manner; in the United States, the first victim of such a law would be the Black Muslim movement.* Leszek Kolakowski

## A Theoretical Model of Racism

In order to clarify as much as possible what is conveniently named "racism," it is not poor method to venture to construct its ideal type through a systematic inventory of its definitional traits. Let us emphasize the conventional aspect of the use of the word *racism*: this word will be maintained only for reasons of language convention, founded of course on the historical conditions of appearance of the modern theory of "race," which today hardly intervenes except in court or under erudite or militant scrutiny. Let us recall one of the results of the preceding analyses: "racism," as it operates socially, in no way assumes an explicit theory of "race"; there are even forms of "racism" that expressly reject any conception of "human races." Henceforth, speaking of "racism" will facilitate communication while reorienting a set of received ideas of which we should be rid — not in order to deny the phenomena poorly designated and conceptualized by the term *racism,* but rather in view of extracting the latter from the ordinary polemical field by constituting it as a conceptual instrument. This operation involves *neutralizing* the connotative burdens accompanying the ordinary uses of the term and consequently suspending its affectivo-imaginary effects.

At issue, therefore, is constructing the concept of "racism." By insisting on the necessity of a construction, we are trying to place in evidence our refusal of any substantialist, or metaphysical, conception of what we will call "racism." A good model of such a conventional, axiologically neutral construction is furnished by Vilfredo Pareto's presentation of the concept of an elite. In his *Mind and Society,* Pareto thus sums up the constitution of his sociological concept of an elite: "So let us make a class of the people who have the highest indices in their branch of activity, and to that class give the name...of *élite.*"[1] We propose, in analogous fashion, to form a class of individuals whose indices are the highest in the realm of the following relational behaviors: distance (avoidance of contact), rejection or exclusion, abasement (contempt), domination and exploitation, indeed extermination, targeting individuals insofar as they belong (or are supposed to belong) to groups perceived as different from the proper group of the "racist" subject; this difference is represented as a difference in nature (itself susceptible to a multiplicity of interpretations) that has precisely taken the historical form of a racial difference. The latter is made twofold according to the perspectives of the racizing and the racized: on the one hand, there is a self-perception of one's own group of affiliation as racial, self-racialization; on the other hand, there is a perception of the other's group of affiliation as racial, heteroracialization. In this asymmetrical relationship, the very opposite of a dialogue, self-racialization is effected in the manner of praise, whereas heteroracialization is necessarily incarnated in a discourse of blame. We will therefore give to the class of individuals presenting such attitudes the name *racist(s).* "Racism" may then be defined as the set of typical (implicit or explicit) attitudes manifested by the individuals said to be "racist." It follows that racism is never completely incarnated, incorporated, or realized, in an individual or a group. One assigns the name *racist* to a concept, a formal/abstract object, a class term that subsumes dissimilar individuals. The racism attributable to these individuals varies in intensity, manner, depth of assumption, cognitive level, and so on. One may thus define an ideological core of racism that is analytically presentable as a series of statements ordered according to the rule of nonreciprocal presupposition (where trait 1 is presupposed by traits 2, 3, 4, and 5, but does not presuppose them).

In addition, we have proposed to place in parentheses, explicitly, the pejorative connotations of the word *racism*. More generally, the *epokhē* of axiological, normative, and deontological presuppositions to us seems required by the project of avoiding any risk of reproduction, by way of a translation into a scholarly lexicon, of the dominant ideological representations associated with "racism" in ordinary language. It is again the conventionalist or algebraic model advocated by Pareto that indicates our direction: "Any other name [than that of *élite*], and even a mere letter of the alphabet, would be just as appropriate to the end we propose to ourselves."[2] In the same way, what we denominate as "racism" might just as well be denominated "ethnicism," "culturalism," or "nationalism," according to the case — indeed, according to the three possible axes: identitarianism, differentialism, and otherism.

And the suppression of the habitual connotations must be accompanied by a neutralization of the historico-metaphysical and scientific memory of the term at issue, *race*. Here, Viggo Brøndal shows us the method in action, on the old question of the parts of speech. Reworking the four universally recognized categories of "substance, quantity, quality, and relation" in the framework of his philosophy of language, Brøndal specifies the two conditions that these classical transcendental categories must satisfy in order to become effective: "First, they must be stripped of any metaphysical or absolute character.... Then, the fundamental concepts must... be defined in a strict interdependency."[3] It is the first condition that interests us here: the theory of racism must "remain entirely neutral or agnostic," as much as the philosophy of language, according to Brøndal, which is nonetheless elaborated by means of tool-terms endowed with old memory.[4]

We must therefore begin by constructing an ideal type of racism-as-ideology, which we will approach less as a definite doctrine (as Gobinism, for example) than as a set of representations, values, and norms presupposed by the "theories," "doctrines," or "philosophies" that are historically attested and consensually judged to be "racist."

Our analyses will here be able to take as their object only the question of racism-as-ideology.

We will understand by "racism" the ideology, incorporated in practices or incarnated in behaviors, made implicit in "prejudices" or made explicit in speech acts, the cores of which, susceptible as they are to variable focalizations (from the antiuniversalism of strict differentialist racism to the universalism of inegalitarian racism), may be described by a series of positions or mental acts, according to an order that proceeds from that which is presupposed to that which presupposes:

1. the rejection of the universal;

2. the set categorization of individuals;

3. the absolutization of collective differences;

4. the naturalization of differences, either by scientific biologization or by ethnicization or "culturalist" fixing;

5. the inegalitarian interpretation of differences, projected onto a universal scale of values.

1. The *rejection of the universal* is manifested, in the attested discourses, according to two modalities that may be linked but not likened to each other: the rejection of the unity of the human race or the rejection of the regulating idea of a human community that forms the beyond of all collective differences. The antiuniversalist position comes down to taking the exclusive side of what is — the concrete of collective identities (racial, ethnic, cultural, national) and their irreducible plurality — against what is not and what would be expressed by the abstraction implied by any universal form of ethics. Multiplicity opposed to unity, the concrete to the abstract, the real to fiction: these are the three polemical acts presupposed by the impugnment of any nonreligious "catholicity." The latter characterizes modern ideology, engendered by the secularization of the catholic idea: the laicization and humanization of Christian universalism. Thus must be noticed the antimodern meaning taken by the first manifestations of the rejection of universalism, the latter conflated with the project of an "emancipation" of all human beings, beyond their affiliations and whatever their identities may be (heritages, traditions, mental forms). But antiuniversalism appears with just as much force in the neobaroque currents that occupy a not negligible place in what

is conveniently named the "postmodern condition": the celebration of difference, of the plural, of singularities, and of dissemination is committed to the abandonment of the "unitary myth" of universalism. These two strategies of antiuniversalism, though fundamentally different, can approach each other at the heart of certain doctrines: they thus represent the two intellectual poles of the New Right.[5] Antiuniversalism is stated in at least two senses.

The rejection of a horizon of universality or of a universal norm especially leads to the denunciation of "human rights" as useless, even harmful, fictions — for every declaration of human rights is universal. But the impugnment of humanitarianism as imposture indicates an essential ideological correlation between universalism and individualism: the one and the other may be condemned equally and in the same gesture because they represent the two doctrinal faces of the *spirit of abstraction*. The antiuniversalist position therefore involves a struggle on two fronts. On the first front, it must defend the thesis that there is no anthropological universalism either in a substantialist perspective,[6] which would in some way postulate the existence of a "human nature" (for example, represented as a common store of biopsychosocial characteristics), or in a normative sense, which would indicate an *"ought"* and an *"ought to be"* of humanity in general, that is, a certain anthropological ideality endowed with a regulatory power over behaviors, from the fact that it incarnates a constellation of positive values. On a second front, the antiuniversalist position must confront one of the most powerful ideological pairs of the modern world, which we have proposed to name individuo-universalism.[7]

Finally we will note that, in the political vulgate, the antiuniversalist position tends to be formulated in the form of the denunciation of "cosmopolitanism" and "globalism," counternatural tendencies supposedly aiming for the abolition of the diversity of the races, a fact of nature or of divine creation. Most of the texts that come from the so-called extreme right groups (from Catholic traditionalism to national populism)[8] link together the condemnation of globalism (in its Janus-faced form, both capitalist and communist), the stigmatization of *métissage*,[9] and the denunciation of reverse-racism ("antiwhite racism"). These three ideological elements clearly appear in the following exemplary sentence: "On the level of race, globalism encourages *métissage* as a panacea, and produces the frenzied antiracism that is now in the process of transforming into antiwhite racism."[10]

One of the least questionable criteria of the position — which I will call racist — of a certain author is indirectly furnished by the attribution of the universalist thesis by the latter to his designated adversary. "Racist" authors tend to define the theoretical position of their adversaries by "the belief in the dogma of the unity of the human race."[11] Antiuniversalism willingly presents itself as an antidogmatism, cloaks itself in the signs of tolerance, of intellectual openness, and sometimes calls on the spirit of the progress of knowledge.

2. The *set categorization of individuals* is the second operation implied by every racialization and itself presupposes a *derealization* of the dimension of the individual. In fact, on the one hand, individuals are assigned to classes of humans that are supposedly stable (in a creationist perspective, for example) or stablilized in the course of an evolutionary process; on the other hand, the individual is treated as any representative whatever of her category of affiliation, presumed to be her original one, to which a certain fixity is attributed. By the "derealization" of the individual, we intend to designate the process of dissolution of the individual as such in a collective entity that would alone really exist, in a fashion that one might call permanent: "race," "ethnic group," "culture"/"civilization," "mentality," "people," and so on. The thesis of the fixity of individual affiliations presupposes the thesis of the permanency of the types of affiliation. Whatever shape it may take, the community of affiliation is posited as the value of values, at the same time as it is interpreted as the only true reality — as a substantial type or a first substance in the anthropological order. The type is a destiny: thus may be formulated the basic belief of supraindividualist ideology. The essentializing categorization of the individual implies the ineluctability and the insurmountability of the incarnation of the type. The individual has no other status than to be the epiphenomenon of the type, a moment of its epiphany. Hence the essential insufficiency of the individual echoes the existential inconsistency of the universal.

A second ideological operation, correlative with the derealization of the individual, may be gauged: collective identity, as a class of affiliation, is treated as an individual — *indivisum in se, divisum a quolibet alio,* according to the scholastic adage.[12] *The individualization of the collective:* a shift of individuality, or at least of its scheme, is thus effected, from the level of *the biological individual* (the singular living being) to that of the *community,* redefined as the only true individual.

In short, the ideological reaction named racism puts into play the very model of individualism that it at first sight seems to impugn but transposes it from the realm of the indivisible biological to the social totality, metaphorized into a great individuated organism or even the "organic community."[13]

Racism may be defined as a holistic reaction *against* modern individualism, but *within* modern ideological space, where it brings to bear the schemes borrowed from the conception of the individual. The mechanism of the analogical transposition of the individual is nonetheless found outside the specific domain of racial theories, as indicated by these critical remarks of Husserl: "All the fond talk of common spirit, of the common will of a people, of nations' ideal political goals, and the like, are romanticism and mythology, derived from an analogous application *[analogischer Übertragung]* of concepts that have proper sense only in the individual sphere."[14]

In the nationalist imaginary, the self-racialization of the nation contains a supplementary trait: the presumption of the homogeneity of the social body.[15] Vacher de Lapouge presented the observation of the nationalist/racist derealization of the individual, reduced to a mere abstraction of his community or lineage: "The individual is crushed by his race, and is nothing. Race and nation are everything."[16]

In many contexts, the individual is treated as half-informed raw material, whose complete form and final meaning are found only on a supraindividual level. In such a holistic perspective, any sufficiently typed (and therefore individualized on its level) collective entity is susceptible of playing the role of total and integrative Form, from regional community to race, by way of ethnic group and nation. The metaphor of the letter, as a minimal form in itself stripped of meaning, allows the forcible exposition of the elementarization of the individual: "The individual is a letter from the book of race; the letter has no meaning. But the book does."[17] Hence the meaning of the individual should be sought not in the fiction of some universal human or other but rather in the concretion of that great diasporic individual that is race. Racism is an ontology of the intermediate substances between individual half-beings and universal nonbeings. It matters little that these anthroposocial substances, alone posited as really existing, are denominated "races." Racism may not be reduced to a question of explicit vocabulary.

The elementarization of the individual may be stated through another play of metaphors: the individual is treated as the imperfect incarnation of a type that integrally exists only in its temporal deployment, as *lineage*. Here again we will have Lapouge speak, making explicit the representations and evaluations associated with the postulate of the determinism of heredity:

> Heredity weighs on and literally crushes us. It is far from the case that a man's value is individual; he hardly has any except by way of his ancestors, and his individuality is but one more or less happy and always complex assembly of elements borrowed from all his ancestral lineages. Reciprocally, each lives again in his descendants, and the most effective solidarity binds together members of a family, to such a point that in a lineage it is in a way descent that is the reality and the descendants who are the temporary and phenomenal manifestations of heredity, the successive incarnations of an imperfectly realized type.[18]

3. The third operation implied by every racialization may be represented by the *postulate of absolute difference* among the categories of affiliation: when the difference between "races" or "cultures" is absolutized, it then ceases to be a difference, and the two terms become incomparable.[19] What follows is the thesis of the *unassimilability* of the individuals of one definite "race" to any other "race." Irreducible, incomparable, and unassimilable, the human types that differ (the reasons for difference are infinite), moreover, may not communicate with each other, neither de facto nor de jure. The impossibility of a human community beyond the enclosures is the ultimate conclusion of the thesis of *incommunicability*. Hence the violent denunciations of "cosmopolitanism" or "globalism," processes and ideals that are supposed to destroy singular and closed communities, and, more profoundly and less distinctly, their "identity." Hence also the impugnment out of principle of interethnic crossing or "cultural *métissage*," identified as concerted modes of the same process of dissolution of collective identities, that is, of universal "café-au-lait-ization,"[20] a metaphor that renews the catastrophist figment of the "chaos of races"[21] that Houston Stewart Chamberlain attacked in his famous description of the fall of the Roman Empire, the "decadence of reference"[22] for the whole mythical history of Europe. The norm involved in the absolutization of difference is formulated either as an "ought-to-preserve" of proper identity or as an "ought-to-guarantee" of the purity of all identity.

If interethnic difference is absolute, it follows that the lack of differentiation that transgresses the law must engender an evolution of the better toward the worse, this evolution itself absolute: a decadence. The mixophobic argument has been expressed just as well, in clinical thought, through the concept of "divergent amphimixture," borrowed from the zoological tradition. The following reflections by Dr. Edgar Bérillon attest to this, exemplary as they are of a common manner of posing the problem of *métissage* and its pathological effects:

> It is not only in *métis* animals that one observes the states of instability that zootechnicians designate with the term *disordered variation* or *turmoil;* as little attention as one may pay to them, one observes these instabilities in human *métis*. If . . . the first sign of normal heredity is to resemble one's parents, one will understand the difficulty for the *métis* presented by the fact of resembling two types of very different character at once. . . . [Now], in the near totality of abnormal children and adolescents that, for the last thirty years, I have had the opportunity to examine and follow, I have been able to convince myself that intellectual and instinctual flaws and defects originate in *métissage*. In fact, as a result of the crossing of individuals of very differentiated races, the great majority of abnormal infants are found among the *métis*.[23]

It seems that one may posit a speculative correlation between two basic "differentialist" arguments that appeared in nineteenth-century anthropological thought: namely, ethnic crossings (that is, the nonrespect for the principle of absolute interethnic difference) as a general rule produce poor results (physical and/or intellectual "decadence," "decline," "degeneracy": that is, the movement contrary to the "perfecting of the races"); the human races are not (all) perfectible, and that comes down to holding that the permanency of types defines a destiny. The combination of the two alternatives that these arguments engage (perfectibility/nonperfectibility, crossing leading to decadence/not leading to decadence) permits the definition of an ideological boundary between "racists" and "nonracists," as represented in the following figure.

| Arguments \ Positions | "racist" | "nonracist" |
|---|---|---|
| The perfectibility of all human races | − | + |
| Interethnic crossings necessarily engender a form of decadence | + | − |

In the French anthropological tradition, Armand de Quatrefages de Bréau stands out by the aracist exceptionality of his theoretical positions:

- He is a universalist with regard to the question of the origin of the races, in the doctrinal debate that was denominated, in the 1840s, "the great controversy":[24] namely, monogenism or polygenism. His metaphysical option in favor of universalism implies that he maintains, in the field of anthropology, the monogenist thesis.

- He maintains the thesis of the perfectibility of every race, including the inferior races.[25]

- He refuses the thesis of fatal decline through interethnic crossing, either in its radical form ("any race crossing [is] followed by physical or intellectual decadence")[26] or in its moderate form ("distant crossings offer only poor results, and...pure races are superior to crossed races").[27] He even maintains the thesis, at that time ultraminoritarian, of a certain positiveness of crossings. In 1863, Paul Broca thus summed up the untimely views of Quatrefages: "Mr. de Quatrefages...thinks that, in many cases, crossing retempers the races, complements their instincts, develops their aptitudes, and sometimes even gives birth to aptitudes foreign to the primal races."[28]

4. *Naturalization,* which historically begins with *biologization,* of the differences among preliminarily absolutized collective "identities": cultural distances and national borders become impenetrable barriers. What will later be named genetic determinism is established in the second half of the nineteenth century: a determinism of differential heredity that is only the scientific and materialist version of fatalism, applied to human lineages — from family to race.[29] This was quite well seen by the all-too-forgotten Joseph-Pierre Durand (de Gros), the isolated Leibnizian of the late nineteenth century: "Determinism is the ancient doctrine of fatalism or predestination rejuvenated by biology."[30] Also to be noted, in addition to biologizing naturalization, is the more recent *culturalist naturalization* of differences and collective identities, instituted by an ideologization of the cultural relativism that appeared in the American ethnological school around Franz Boas, in the 1930s and 1940s; this tendency was radicalized by certain currents in the international community of ethnologists during the 1960s and 1970s, who professionalized, so to speak, the denunciation of ethnocide, identified as the racist act par excellence (in

the same way as genocide), and who correlatively fetishized cultural affiliations. For mental traditions, cultural types or heritages, supposedly specific imaginaries, or particular configurations of value may be *sacralized,* projected, and inscribed in a cultural nature posited as in itself and absolutely of value and may hence produce a "culturalist" mode of racialization. Naturalization is therefore either *biologizing* or *culturalist.* This analytical (and ideal-typical) distinction must not mask the fact that, in really produced discourses, the thematics of "race" and "culture" may appear simultaneously, the argumentative moves authorized by some coexistence that reinforces the power of resistance to criticism, and so the force of persuasion, of the discourses of racialization (responding, for example, to a critique of biologism by a culturalist profession of faith). In the 1970s and 1980s, we have lived[31] the passage to the political argument of the great culturalist wave of the modes of racialization, hitherto implicit and contained within the limits of scholarly debate broadened by the antiethnocentric commitment of an intellectual elite. A perverse effect: cultural pluralism, of antiracist intention, is at the origin of the new modes of racialization.

Through the combination of these four traits, *differentialist* ideology is at this point constituted, ready to be incarnated in its acceptable formulations: the "right to difference," the "respect for differences," or the "praise of differences" then comes to legitimate the prescription of separating what differs in nature. It is difficult not to discern here an incitement to apartheid, by other names, behind new cultural banners, and too often in the name of some identitarianist version of the humanist requirement: "rights of peoples," a legitimate defense of threatened collective identities, a respect for specific mentalities. These are so many ideological instrumentalizations of ethical requirements, which are thus placed in the service of racist intentions. These instrumentalizations willingly make use of the appeal to the authority of science: biology and ethnology furnish most of the grounding arguments.

Lapouge thus reinterpreted the Darwinian theory of evolution as a theory "of survival":[32] "The true law of the struggle for existence is that of the struggle for descent."[33] In Lapouge's "anthroposociology," as in contemporary sociobiology, the importance accorded to heredity is correlative to that accorded to differential reproduction, such that the social bond is reduced to blood ties and its normality to the preservation of race identity — racial mixture inevitably engendering "the rupture of the social bonds."[34]

The assignment of interindividual and interethnic differences to a differential heredity involves a valorization of temporality as the element of transmission of the "genetic patrimony." The outstanding quality of blood ties is essentially manifested in the concern for the lineage, for ancestry and descent: "The individual who dies without leaving descendants puts an end to the immortality of his ancestry. He finishes killing the dead."[35] The norm of conserving the identity of a blood community appears as an absolute: each individual is responsible for her descent and her ancestry, responsible before them. "That is why the absolute sin is infertility."[36]

5. The *inegalitarian interpretation of differences* recognized as natural, insurmountable, and "eternal." Paradoxically (from the point of view of ordinary racist opinion), the positing of an inequality among "races" or "cultures" reintroduces the universal into racist thought: for one must be able to *compare* collective "identities" in order to relate them to a common scale. *Inegalitarianist racism* thus appears as a derived and retrocorrective phenomenon of the fundamentalism of difference, the effect of a "reading" of differences by a thinking that classifies by hierarchizing, that therefore deabsolutizes them, confers a relativity onto them by submitting them to the act of comparison. The inegalitarian interpretation of differences, from the fact that it realigns the latter according to a universal hierarchy, corrects differentialist ideology. Any hierarchization postulates a comparability of hierarchized terms and suggests that they have a common nature. The logic of inegalitarianist racism is illustrated by domination and exploitation of the imperialist type, which are legitimated by a paternalistic project of education of "inferior peoples" — and their educability is thereby suggested. Whereas the logic of differentialist racism, centered on the imperative of preserving proper identity and governed by the phobia of mixture (*métissage*, and so on), is developed either as a politics and ethics of apartheid or as a racio-eugenic program of exterminating the irretrievable "waste" of humanity (less the "inferior" or "not as capable" than the "parasites" and other "harmful" figures of an animalized and demonized infrahumanity). It is hardly difficult to judge which of these two logics is the worst;[37] for one cannot avoid evaluating, if one is less than an angel.

# The Logics of the "Right to Difference" (Variations on a Text by Louis Dumont)

*What I maintain is that, if the advocates of difference claim for it both equality and recognition, they claim the impossible.*

Louis Dumont

If we agree to define modern ideology, with Louis Dumont, as the set of common representations characteristic of the modern world, a configuration itself definable as *individualist* in that it valorizes the individual (the moral, independent, autonomous, and extrasocial being) by neglecting or subordinating the social totality,[38] the question of the "struggle against racism" transforms into a necessary and preliminary critique of antiracism. For if racism results from the "dissociation" of holistic representation by individualism,[39] if it consequently presents constitutive individualist traits, and if racism implies the transposition of the scheme of individuality from the empirical singular being to the community, antiracism in turn assumes the individualist ideology, aligns itself in the space of the latter, naively takes on its essential postulates. The polemical difficulties of antiracism are to be related to its paradoxical speculative position: racism and antiracism uncritically share most of the statements that ground modern ideology as individualist. They represent two of its recurrent variants. This is the first motif of a critique of antiracism.[40]

A second motif appears once one takes note of the central political inadequacy of antiracism: the impasse in the *communitarian fact* no less than in the ethical and political questions to which it refers.[41] Antiracism in fact wavers between the focalization on the individual and the focalization on humanity — as if nothing very important existed between individual human beings and the human race: hence the twofold effect, contradictory on the background of shared values, of modern ideology. The latter carries, on the one hand, "a powerful universalist slant which leads to rejecting the differences, when actually encountered, from the cognitive domain":[42] a reduction of the intermediate dimension, which is collective or communitarian, between the individual and the universal, and so of intercultural or international difference. Antiracism inherits this bias toward the universal, holds it up as dogma, fixes it into combat formulas. The position that is in principle universalist hence becomes one of the basic arguments of the human-racism to which ordinary antiracist doctrine is reduced. But if individualist ideology, in this sense, prompts the privileging of the empirical individual as a representative of the species, it just as much allows the person, or the supposedly independent and nonsocial moral being, to be held up as the supreme value.[43] This is the humanist or personalist version of individualism, which must be compared with its racist version, which appears to be absolutely opposed to it. The ideology of the nation, in its German form, offers a striking preparation for racism: the nation, in Herder or Fichte, is less a collection of individuals than an individual on the collective level, facing other nation-individuals. The individualization of the collective responds to the moralization of the individual, in the same way as the logic of framing, of communion, of rooting replies to the logic of the emancipation of individuals.[44] Antiracism, then, only develops the two argumentative possibilities offered by modern ideology, in emphasizing one of the two terms of the individualism/universalism pair. In doing so, it reproduces the conditions of appearance of racism as a communitarianist reaction to the plays of individualism and universalism, in the very space of modern ideology. In short, antiracism and racism in some way form a system, feed each other with themes, arguments, metaphors.[45] It is such a vicious circle that is, by a twofold critique of racism and of the antiracist vulgate, to be deconstructed, in order to escape from it without falling back into the same field of recurring illusions, in other discursive dress.

The powerlessness of the antiracist vulgate to conceive the collective thus defines one of its several political weaknesses, which have been quite well confirmed by sociohistorical observation. There will be no more surprise before a now classical phenomenon: the nationalist right tends to seize on the *unposed problem* of community existence (from the "ethnic group" to the nation) and poses it in its own way, which most often includes the figment and the rhetoric of race. It must be recognized that such behavior is part and parcel of ideological warfare.

But in addition, the antiracist vulgate commits the sin of taking recourse to a fundamental postulate that is rarely made explicit, the origin of an illusion containing a speculative error. The fundamental antiracist demand is in fact to respect difference, to rehabilitate those who are (or are perceived as) in some way different, to recognize the Other as the Other. Now, the recognition of the difference of the Other, as Dumont remarks, may signify two fundamentally different things.

In the first place, it may signify the set of claims centered on obtaining equal rights, equal treatment, or equal opportunity.[46] If no theoretical problem appears in this first sense, a paradox immediately arises that stems from the fact that the "right to difference," by the very requirement of an egalitarian treatment of "those who are different," implies some reduction of difference, its subordination to the egalitarian imperative, indeed the long-term risk of an "erasing of distinctive characteristics,"[47] accompanied by a forgetting of the initial valorization of difference. Stated otherwise, egalitarian logic is susceptible of being captured by identitarian logic, and the valorization of difference of being correlatively turned around into the valorization of similarity, indeed of uniformity. The egalitarianist interpretation of the right to difference carries the risk of engendering such a perverse effect.

In the second place, the demand to recognize the Other may signify the recognition of the Other as the Other, the valorization of the Other as such, in her pure difference. The categorical imperative would then be: evaluate the Other as herself.[48] Stated otherwise: recognize her without placing her on a hierarchical scale. This is certainly a very widespread ethical ideal for the antiracist portion of humanity. The sole but decisive question that it commits one to posing is the following: Is a recognition of the Other as such even possible, without hierarchizing evaluation? Or again: Can one affirm the value of difference without presupposing any scale of values? The question comes down to that of the possibility of a judgment of value that would operate without hierarchizing values. The response is simple, even though it costs our dear vital illusions a great deal: if to recognize signifies nothing other than to evaluate or to integrate, and if to evaluate implies at once the distinction and the hierarchization of values, then the recognition of the Other can be only hierarchical. The antiracist vulgate henceforth turns out to be resting on a postulate that contains an impossibility or a contradiction in terms. We can only agree with Dumont's conclusion: "If the advocates of difference claim for it both equality and recognition, they claim the impossible. Here we are reminded of the American slogan 'separate but equal' which marked the transition from slavery to racism."[49]

The argument of the "right to difference" is distributed over three distinct and incompatible ideological regions.

1. *Egalitarianism,* whose logic leads either to a *petitio principii* (the "right to difference" = the right to equal rights) or to a production

of a perverse effect (the egalitarian treatment of difference = the latent devalorization of difference).

2. *Ethical differentialism,* whose prescription contains two contradictory imperatives or is grounded on the illusory possibility of an evaluative act without a hierarchization of values.

3. *Differentialist,* or mixophobic, *racism,* whose two possibilities of ideological manifestation must be distinguished: (1) Differentialist racism that is presented as the praise or tolerant affirmation of all differences and takes itself for a rejection of "all racisms" no less than of "all totalitarianisms."[50] In this perspective, the value of difference is exalted in that it is a condition of the *conservation of collective identities.* The hypervalorization of intercollective differences is in no way a position indicator in bipolar political space: an ultraleft that has denounced ethnocide since 1970[51] expresses it just as well as the New Right that impugns the West as a process destructive of identities or a "system for killing peoples."[52] One must no doubt note certain rhetorical variations that seem to operate between two limits: either one insists on "equality in difference," for which there can be no concept, or one applies oneself to demonstrating the incomparability of supposedly different collective entities (they may then be called "superior," each in its own genre).[53] (2) Differentialism may also appear as the tactical dressing of inegalitarian racism, as an *acceptable reformulation* making an appeal to an ideological keyword *(difference).* Such a use of the differentialist argument only follows a suggestion from ordinary language: everything happens as if one could not affirm a difference without at the same time affirming a difference of value.[54] So if differentiating, as a language act, comes down to hierarchizing, a continuous effort will have to be made to separate the two operations that are linked in verbal spontaneity — in other words, to go against the natural leaning of ordinary usage, which ceaselessly reproduces the obvious point that to differentiate is to hierarchize. Hence the constitutional weakness, so to speak, of differentialist antiracism, which must always climb against the leaning of the evidence that contemporary nationalist (or ethnonationalist) discourse is content to follow.[55]

*Eight*

# The Specter of *Métissage:*
# The Mixophobic Hypothesis

## The Rejection of *Métissage*

*Racism is the refusal to be further bastardized.*
                                    Abel Bonnard

Earl Finch, in the paper he gave at the First Universal Races Congress (London, July 26–29, 1911), "The Effects of Racial Miscegenation," began by recalling that "the followers of Gobineau, in France, and Morton, in America, have maintained that racial inter-mixture has had and can have only disastrous consequences."[1] To these two names one might of course add many others: Nott, Agassiz, Perier, and Dally, as Théodule Ribot indicated in 1873;[2] Davenport, Mjoen, Humphrey, Widney, Grant, and Stoddard, according to the inventory Frank H. Hankins made half a century later.[3] The Gobinean axioms are well known, as they have been crystallized in a vulgate since the end of the nineteenth century: "Nations die when they are composed of elements that have *degenerated*";[4] "Peoples degenerate only in consequence of the various admixtures of blood which they undergo;...their degeneration corresponds exactly to the quantity and quality of the new blood."[5] The received idea is that *métissage* is the fatal mediocritization of the species: the end of the human world would coincide with equality for all through resemblance, at the heart of a leveling by the lowest common denominator.[6]

The radically pessimistic hypothesis consists of stating that the crossing of races produces mulattos who are at once degraded ("degenerate") and infertile (in variable fashion), as the spreading of *métissage* risks bringing on an extinction of the species or an irreversible regression. This mixophobic pessimism was at the heart of anthroposociological doctrine at the end of the nineteenth century (Otto Ammon, Ludwig Woltmann, Georges Vacher de Lapouge).

The existing positions may be characterized as follows.

1. *Absolute mixophobes: métissage* is by itself the cause of infertility and degeneration (or degeneracy). Henceforth, the depopulation and extinction of the elites — with the corollary of a "relapse into barbarism"[7] — that is, the respectively quantitative and qualitative figures of demographic decline, may be explained by the crossing of races. Georges Vacher de Lapouge, an originator of the popularity of the theme of "hereditary shock," is quite explicit on this point, from his earliest scholarly interventions: "The mixing of classes and races results in infertility, in physical and moral incoherency, in the most regrettable atavistic blows, in the extinction through crossing of the exceptional races and families."[8] After the Anglo-Saxon prophets of the "passing of the great race"[9] and the theoreticians of "ethnic chaos,"[10] the National Socialist doctrinaires constructed their racial myth, a myth of blood, around the determination of *métissage,* especially between whites and blacks, as the supreme offense: "A sin against blood."[11] The sacralization of "race" assumes both that of the "laws of nature" and that of the "purity of blood": "France will henceforth be afflicted by an instinctual racial *Angst* which is the inescapable heritage of the crossbreed [in the French translation, *métis*] however superficially secure he may appear to be," affirmed Alfred Rosenberg in 1930.[12]

2. *Unconditional mixophiles:* it is they who preach "the gospel of amalgamation..., maintaining that intermixture between races so dissimilar as the whites and negroes would prove beneficial."[13]

3. *Moderate mixophiles:* they are characterized by the affirmation that *métissage,* in order to be positive, must be effected in moderation. Hence, either if it is produced in "favourable circumstances"[14] or if "differences [between the races] are not great,"[15] *métissage* must have happy results. Finch sided with this wise opinion: "While race blending

is not everywhere desirable, yet the crossing of distinct races, especially when it occurs with social sanction, often produces a superior type."[16]

4. *Moderate mixophobes:* following the example of Felix von Luschan, these last recognize, on the one hand, that "a certain admixture of blood has always been of great advantage to a nation"[17] — a thesis quite acceptable to the Gobineau of *The Inequality of Human Races.*[18] But, on the other hand, they adamantly affirm, in conformity with the Gobinean vulgate:

> We are all more or less disposed to dislike and despise a mixture of Europeans with the greater part of foreign races. "God created the white man and God created the black man, but the devil created the mulatto," is a very well-known proverb. As a matter of fact, we are absolutely ignorant as to the moral and intellectual qualities of half-castes. It would be absurd to expect from the union of a good-for-nothing European with an equally good-for-nothing black woman, children that march on the heights of humanity.[19]

It is from the same perspective that the racist eugenicists distinguish between "good" and "bad" *métis*.[20] Gustave Le Bon insisted, for example, on the condition of racial proximity for the production of "good" *métis:*

> There are doubtless quite different races — the White and the Black, for example — that happen to fuse together. But the *métis* that results from such crossings constitutes a population very inferior to the products from which it derives, which is completely incapable of creating or even continuing a civilization. The influence of contrary heredities dissociates their morality and their character.... Crossings may be an element among superior and neighboring races, such as the English and the Germans of America. They always constitute an element of degeneracy when these races, even the superior ones, are too different.[21]

The doctrinal presuppositions of the partisans of nonmixture are the following:

1. Each race corresponds to a human type presumed to be stable[22] — the postulate of the stability of types.

2. There are superior human types and inferior human types — the postulate of the inequality among the types.

3. To each type there corresponds a specific quality of "blood" — the postulate of racial "monohematism."

4. The value of a race resides in the purity of its blood,[23] and the racial value of a mixed population resides in the proportion of superior racial blood that it contains.[24]

5. *Métissage*, or crossing between races, is a mixture of bloods. Procreation is effected as a "blood transfusion" that is supposed to transmit skills and failings.[25] Immigration is itself conceived as "a massive ethnic blood transfusion,"[26] as much as "an interracial graft."[27]

6. Mixture irreversibly destroys the differential quality of "bloods" and therefore the specific values of the races that have been mixed. *Métissage* inevitably tends to be advantageous to the inferior race: it mediocritizes.[28] Agassiz, in an often-quoted remark, summed up this conception of *métissage* producing decadence as follows:

> Those who place in doubt the pernicious effects of mixing the races, and who are tempted by a false philanthropy to break down all the barriers placed between them, should go to Brazil. They would find it impossible to deny the decadence that results from crossings, which are more widespread in this country than anywhere else. They would see that this mixture destroys the best qualities of the White, the Black, the Indian, and produces an indescribable type of hybrid [*métis*], whose physical and mental energy is weakened.[29]

Moreover, *métissage* is incriminated because it would produce a war of self against self: "This battle of the soul is the battle of bloods."[30] Finally, *métissage* might engender only types that are in themselves heterogeneous and hence unstable, "anarchic" — a political metaphor prized for stigmatizing the disorder attributed to the nature of the *métis*. Madison Grant presented this last judgment as obvious to common sense:

> It is scarcely necessary to recall the universal distrust, often suspicion, inspired throughout the world by the hybrid of two clearly differentiated races. Physically belonging to the inferior race, but aspiring to be recognized as a member of the superior race, the unfortunate hybrid, in addition to a disparate physique, often gets an unstable brain from one of his parents.[31]

In the argumentation of political racism, the condemnation of *métissage* takes up the themes, in large part borrowed from the modern anti-Semitic tradition, that target beings "without ties," from nowhere, devoid of all rooting: being tied to nothing (neither soil nor tradition), they are foreigners par excellence, the very type of the universal foreigner; the typical indeterminate being is opposed to any type of determinate being and constitutes a threat to the latter. In the following, Abel Bonnard attempts to legitimate the mixophobic prejudice by presenting it as derived from the laws of human nature, an instinct common to man and animal:

> As for the *métis,* how can one disdainfully treat as a prejudice the widespread sentiment in all times and all races that he is a being less noble than those issuing from purer blood? He is tied to nothing, to no belief, he is adapted to nothing, save a shady life between peoples and races.... There is no doubt that the universal prejudice against *métissage* is justified.[32]

The first biopolitical imperative is to spare the races "from all sinking at once into a vile mixture."[33] That is why, the racist eugenicists conclude, "we must, by universal and inflexible laws, prevent mixed marriages."[34] The man qualified by his definite racial affiliation, the man of distinct racial quality — this is the type opposed to the man without quality incarnated by the *métis;* for the multiplicity of contradictory affiliations transforms into neutrality: "Racism therefore expresses the refusal to become just any man."[35] All this assumes a traditional — and pre-Darwinian — conception of a cosmos, of a hierarchical order of the world, in which each class of beings has a fixed place in a finalized system: "Every race has its qualities, even its charms, but without any doubt the mulatto is lower than the Negro. Each race has its place, but mixture is repugnant to all."[36] Mixture is the movement that displaces beings, it effects the error of category, it alters places, it brings disorder to the cosmic order. This racial metaphysics readily includes the polygenist thesis: "There are several humanities in humanity."[37]

These are the doctrinal presuppositions of the mixophobic prejudice, in the way it is stated and therefore expressed in order to be legitimated. The fundamental legitimation of the rejection of *métissage* consists of inscribing in the nature of the living, of making mixophobia into an instinct, an expression of the laws of nature, the instrument of a providential nature that tends to preserve differences. Now, the basis constituted by the first three postulates was strongly shaken as early as the beginning of the twentieth century. The postulate of the stability of types was questioned by Franz Boas between 1900 and 1910, as is recalled by the conclusion to his paper presented at the First Universal Races Congress in 1911, which bears precisely on the "instability of types": "The old idea of absolute stability of human types must, however, evidently be given up, and with it the belief of the hereditary superiority of certain types over others."[38] If therefore the types are not absolutely stable, the empirical conditions of a scientific comparison collapse; the result is that the relation of absolute inequality is no longer utterable. The related postulate of racial monohematism stems from the old "myth of blood," to which some of Aristotle's formulations gave a persistent legitimation[39] and that implies the fictional ideas of a "heredity through blood" and of a "community of blood." The myth is founded on a primordial identification, that of "race" and "blood."

To *métissage* is attributed not only the responsibility for the depopulation and extinction of eugenic beings (the disappearance of elites). It would also be, by the "shock of heredities" that it is supposed to provoke in the racio-eugenicists, at the basis of various pathological phenomena. It would play a role in individual pathology, in that it would be a factor in the production of abnormal children,[40] and would bring on mental illness.[41] It would also contribute to social pathology, in that it is one of the causes of the appearance of criminals and "degenerates."[42] Finally, as immigration is linked to *métissage* as though to one of its consequences, there will be no surprise that the selectionist criticisms are grounded on the rejection of *métissage*, an absolute rejection when it is a matter of crossing between whites and blacks.[43]

The myth of race-blood is a variant of the myth of the pure and the impure. One may of course think of it in a substantialist fashion, think of the pure as a proper essential identity threatened with disappearance or as an accumulated biopsychic treasure that risks being violated or stolen. But, more profoundly, at issue is a problem of categorization: the impure is first of all what is not in its place.[44] Hence the immigrant is impure in that she is displaced, the *métis* from the fact that he incarnates the impossibility of a twofold categorial affiliation. One may interpret such a conception through the scheme of a radical biologization of the model of caste society. Humans are, in this setting, represented as beings fixed by nature to one place or another, assigned to one category or another. The impure being is the decategorized (the "degenerate"), the overcategorized (the *métis*), the displaced, or the "acategorized" being (the immigrant). The core of the pure being is correlatively that which cannot be displaced, transmitted,[45] assimilated: the pure being is the unmixed, fixed, distinct, and definite type, the unicategorial being. The impure being is any being who transgresses the boundaries set by nature: the *métis* is the product of the transgression of "blood barriers" — a political mythology.

There is nonetheless a real problem, raised by the specter of *métissage* (and independently of the question of its universality, which will remain open). If in fact one sticks to the data of the life sciences alone, one arrives at the idea that interracial crossings inevitably bring on degeneracy or debility, mediocrity, sterility (infertility and the "extinction of the race" being especially put down to "the absence or weakness of the need to perpetuate oneself" among *métis*),[46] disharmonious phenomena (defects of proportion), or "instinctual" conflicts (somatic and psychic "incoherence").[47] This idea stems from myth and sets in motion, at the very heart of modernity, the categories of the "savage mind." And nonetheless, one must consider the symbolic effectiveness of such beliefs, an aspect of the persistence of "magic" representations. There is a psychosocial reality of the devalorization, even of the specter, of *métissage*, through the fiction of the mixture of "bloods." That such collective representations put in play certain elements of the myth of blood, in particular the (scientifically false) belief in heredity "through blood," does not in the least cut into their psychosocial value, which is measured by its effects in the system of attitudes and behaviors.

Here is the paradox of the mixophobic myth: On the one hand, to take account of the teachings of the life sciences, one may reaffirm, following Juan Comas,[48] that (1) *métissage* has existed since the dawn of humanity; (2) that it favors physical and psychic variations; and (3) that it is, from the biological point of view, neither good nor bad, and that it always depends on the personal characteristics of the individuals submitted to hybridization.[49] On the other hand, sociological observation cannot avoid considering the social effects of opinions and beliefs, especially through the phenomena of symbolic effectiveness studied under the name "self-fulfilling prophecy."[50]

After William E. Castle, Otto Klineberg insisted on the displacement of the problem posed by *métissage*: it would be less a matter of biology than of interindividual and social relations. The sociologization of the problem begins with a simple observation: "If there is a general objection to miscegenation [translated into French as *métissage*], and if as a consequence the hybrids find it difficult to fit into the social and economic life of either of the parent groups, the effect upon them as individuals may be very unfavorable."[51] As Célestin Bouglé understood it in 1904, the problem had to be taken up on the level of "opinion," that is, understood in terms of attitudes.[52] It is the *social identity* of the *métis* that is a problem: to which family, which lineage, which cultural tradition will he attach himself in order to be socially identified, in the framework of the constraints imposed on him by the play of intersecting rejections? The multiple collective identity of the *métis* runs the risk of turning into a suspended identity, his dual or complex affiliation that of being converted into a zero degree of affiliation. From that moment one again finds, in this neutralization of the social affiliation of the *métis*, in that he belongs to an absent category, the sociological equivalent of the naive biologizing conceptions of the racio-eugenicists (such as Lapouge, Grant, or Martial). The *métis* incarnates the indeterminate term that wavers between the complex pole (the one and the other) and the neutral pole (neither the one nor the other). The impossible assignment of the *métis* to a supposedly distinct ethnic categorization is at the basis of the difficulties of his social recognition, as Jacques Ruffié indicated in 1976:

> *Sociologically, [métissage]* poses serious problems. The multiethnic situation of the *métis* is often uncomfortable, for he runs the risk of not being recognized by any of the groups of which he is the outcome. He remains an unassimilated person. The situation may be still graver when a tension exists between these groups; the *métis* has no refuge against the discriminatory and aggressive behaviors that may come from both sides.[53]

Moreover, the fact must be considered that the scientifico-political myth of *métissage* as catastrophe has been bolstered, since the vulgarization of ethnographic studies, by the imperative of the "right to difference," itself inscribed in an eschatological myth of the "death of ethnic groups/cultures" through a lack of differentiation. Here we may recognize, transferred to the cultural level, the idea of a growing mediocritization, indeed of a disappearance of humanity in and by the "chaos of races." That is why a racist anticolonialism centered on the phobia of interethnic contacts could be constituted and become tradition, in the second half of the nineteenth century, around the prescription of the absolute rejection of white/nonwhite *métissage*.[54] In the mixophobic imaginary, assimilation incarnates the grievous error par excellence of Western colonialism. Mixophobia requires difference. And in racist thought, racial difference and cultural difference are two designations of the same phenomenon. The first word, a descriptive one, is difference. The last word, a prescriptive one, is also difference.

Again we find the logic of differentialist values, its appeal to the tolerance of given diversity and to the respect of racial differences, which derives from an ethics grounded on the sacralization of "nature." Abel Bonnard sums up very well the categorical imperative of racial bioethics: "Refusing mixture is not only the sign that one knows one's worth; it is not only a sign of pride; it is just as much a sign of respect for the other races."[55] We also find again the postulate of unassimilability, with its twofold formulation, both biological and cultural, and the plays of substitution between the argument of incompatibility of "bloods" and that of the heterogeneity of "mentalities." The arguments used today in national-populist xenophobia illustrate the process of euphemizing reformulation, of making the racist argument of "interracial graft" (Martial) acceptable. The stability of the argumentative metaphor of the "graft" is one of the indices of the fact that the cognitive presuppositions involved in making "immigration" a problem have remained relatively stable since the end of the nineteenth century in the West, where they were constituted.[56] In its "Responses to Immigration," in 1985, the *Lettre d'information* of the Club de l'Horloge approached the question of "French Identity and European Identity" on the basis of a biosurgical metaphor and legitimated its rejection of immigration by a reasoning reducible to a syllogism of the following type:

1. "For a graft to succeed, there must be compatibility between the identity of the receiver and that of the giver."

2. Now, "between the French and the planetary immigration that they undergo, there is no compatibility through culture, history, religion, or language."

3. "That is why the 'integration' of immigrants would turn France into a multicultural ensemble that would be able to last in history only at the price of a terrible mutual impoverishment in which the foreign communities, like the French nation, would little by little lose the essential values that define their proper character."[57]

One must therefore refuse immigration and give oneself the adequate means to put such a refusal to work. The preliminary is stated thus: "First revise our code of nationality" according to "the principle of national preference."[58]

The principle of absolute interethnic difference moves between the conception of nationality-citizenship and that of the desirable type of education. The idea (and the ideal) of an education specific to each race appeared in the sphere of influence of the polygenist school, as these remarks by Louis Agassiz, dating from 1850, illustrate:

> What would be the best education to be imparted to the different races in consequence of their primitive difference?...We entertain not the slightest doubt that human affairs with reference to the colored races would be far more judiciously conducted if, in our intercourse with them, we were guided by a full consciousness of the real difference existing between us and them, and a desire to foster those dispositions that are eminently marked in them, rather than by treating them on terms of equality.[59]

The polygenist thesis is congruent with the polylogical norm in education, as absolute cultural pluralism is distributed just as well in the pedagogical ideal as in the model of "acculturation." In this way is presented one of the first statements of the theorization, in the mid-nineteenth century, of the pluricultural model of education. Here is a provenance, which should well be called racist (seen from today), of the contemporary models of differential instruction according to ethnic origins — a provenance assuredly covered by forgetfulness.

In his evaluation of the "pragmatic reach of racial theories," Gaston Bouthoul proposed to distinguish "religious and political beliefs, even the most fanatical ones," from "racial beliefs." For the first are constitutive of doctrines that are open in that they cut the path of conversion, whereas the second are at the basis of the type of the closed doctrine par excellence, without bridge or gate (conversion), without a road to redemption, atonement, or salvation (perfectibility). And what the sociologist said about biological racism applies just as much to culturalist ethnicism: "Racial beliefs are without remission. There is no conversion or redemption for them. They negate human perfectibility, and consequently intellectual progress as much as moral redemption. And they do it all the more as they proscribe *métissages,* considered a crime against the race."[60] If every community affiliation is a quasi-destiny, racism has nothing to propose but an overdestiny.

## The Psychosociological Hypothesis of Pagès-Lemaine: The Desire for Physical Homofiliation

*If nature has created definite human races, she has unfortunately not created difficulties insurmountable enough to prevent their mixture.*
                                                                    Dr. Edgar Bérillon

*The Arabs say, "God created the White man and God created the Black man; the devil created the* métis.*"* Dr. Edgar Bérillon

What we call differentialist racism assumes the existence of an originary mixophobic phantasm that constitutes its psychosocial core. The singular treatment of the *métis,* and in particular the *métis* child, object of phobic repulsion, will be our guiding thread. In 1911, in her book on Nietzsche, Claire Richter noted the presence of this attitude in the philosopher:

> Nietzsche cites the fact, communicated to us by Darwin,[61] that Livingston one day heard someone say, "God created white and black men, but the devil created the half-castes." Nietzsche cites this adage in *The Dawn of Day* [§272], and since, by the example of Darwin in the passage cited above, he insists on the cruelty of *métis,* I am very much disposed to accept here a direct influence of Darwin on Nietzsche through the latter's reading of *Variation of Animals and Plants,* all the more so as Rütimeyer was full of admiration for this work.[62]

Again we find ourselves before a myth of purity/impurity, purity being distributed in the distinct and recognizable racial types, impurity being exclusively imputed to the mixed type, or rather to that typologically neutral, inoperative being, the *métis.*

The Pagès-Lemaine hypothesis allows an accounting for such a set of facts of avoidances, repulsions, and phobias aimed at the *métis.* It presents the advantage of conferring a psychosocial basis on what are called racist attitudes or race prejudices, the attitude being a theoretical construction by the psychologist that aims to objectify a disposition to behave in a certain manner toward others; this disposition is itself only one factor in observable behaviors. Our hypothesis of a mixophobia rooted in an unconscious core, the latter possibly linked to specific historical and cultural conditions, is henceforth confirmed and specified by its preferential point of application: filiation or descent, the love that leads to interracial procreation, and not the "mixed" sexual relationship. Mixophobic representations appear to be hinging on generation and are inscribed in the temporality of reproduction. In two articles published more than fifteen years apart,[63] Robert Pagès formulated the hypothesis according to which "hostility with regard to 'different' groups comes from the fact that one wishes to keep one's phenotypical identity or that one wishes to 'find oneself back' as much as possible in one's descendants."[64] It comes down to "assuming that a certain manifest *morphological perpetuation* constitutes, at the very least in contemporary Western societies of the conjugal family, one of the *motives of initiative or acceptance of procreation,* direct or passing through descendants."[65] Thus may be stated the hypothesis of the desire for *"physical homofiliation"* that may be postulated at the basis of the specter of *métissage,* of the fear of degeneracy through the effect of mixing races, of the fear of being soiled by foreign or immigrant elements, all of them bearers as such of a threat of impurity, of soiling, of an indelible "stain" that is supposed to be able to defigure proper identity forever (that of the individual and/or the group). The fear of sexual relations and "dirtiness"[66] here only appears as a particular case. If interethnic crossings are so often impugned with so much force, it is because the group desire for the *self-reproduction of the identical* is "deeply rooted, at least in our Western culture with the system of kinship that is ours."[67] Everything happens as if the reproduction of the identical were the ideal toward which the group must tend. If the black man represents the threat of the ineffaceable stain, the *métis* incarnates the being soiled by the destruction of the identity of the white group—a maximal soiling, since it is henceforth uncategorizable in the typological system of whites versus blacks. The *métis* have the status of foil: they seem to be, exemplarily in the American imagination, what whites refuse to become.[68] The imagination of descent, continuity, and permanence is governed by the "spontaneous" norm of the self-reproduction of "Us": "The members of the group, of the community, feel as a danger the introduction of the stranger if it will leave 'traces,' children who could not become one of 'us.' "[69]

Robert Pagès takes as a starting point Emory S. Bogardus's scale of social distance,[70] of which one of the lessons is that "entrance into the family calls on the final and strongest resistance to racial acceptance, that whose breakage hierarchically involves all the degrees of integration."[71] This "quasi-metric" description refers to a set of facts that seem to illustrate "a fundamental taboo, a law of racial endogamy that limits and complements, on the same level, the law of exogamy."[72] Its typical verbal expression is the rhetorical question, "Would you like it if your daughter married a native (a Negro)?" which seems to manifest an "insurmountable instinctive revulsion."[73] But why, then, is interracial marriage to be avoided at all cost? This social expression of the mixophobic attitude is indeed not self-evident: for, on the one hand, the physical proximity of blacks is not excluded in the family, if they are servants — the social barrier in the way of marriage — and, on the other hand, extramarital sexual unions are in no way forbidden by arguments such as the "smell" or the "filth" of blacks, that is, by the "legitimate" and legitimating forms of the argument of racial blemish.[74] Then, if the taboo does not apply to intrafamilial coexistence or to interracial procreation as such,[75] it may be defined only in that it aims to prevent the risk of an unwanted child: it *"bears uniquely on sexual acts, of white or black and especially male initiative, whose nature introduces a* métis *child into the white family."*[76] In one sense the principle is simple: the *resemblance* of the child to his ancestors allows the *recognition* of his *belonging* to the family, it confirms the authenticity of his *descent*.[77] The one who does not "look like a member of the family" (this is valid for every sphere of belonging, which is determined a priori) is identified as "allogenic": the proper identity of the lineage (or the ethnic group, the race) must be capable of expression and illustration through resemblance, which is the *ratio cognoscendi* of descent, which in turn is the *ratio essendi* of resemblance. Now, skin color seems to be the characteristic that determines racial discrimination in privileged fashion.[78]

If therefore the racist imagination is constructed around the specter of the indelible "stain," it is distinguished from the properly eugenicist imaginary centered on the specter of the "flaw."[79] This metaphor refers back to defects of the germ-plasm that characterize the inferior social categories, and pose a risk, as much from the fact of the greatest fertility of these categories as by the effects of crossings, of distribution in a growing portion of the population that incarnates a value to conserve and defend.[80] Here is the recurring image: the rising flood of inferior elements (degenerate, feeble: biosocial "waste") threatens to submerge all of society and hence to cause the best elements to disappear by substituting for them. When one encounters arguments made by racist eugenicists, one observes that the latter always present in them a certain combination of motifs borrowed, on the one hand, from the figment of the "stain" (impurity, soiling, shattered identity) and, on the other hand, from that of the "flaw" (inferiority, feebleness, subhumanity). In the representation of "waste" there coexist two types of beings that incarnate a threat to proper identity: the "soiled" and the "flawed." We also thus find here again, through this illuminating distinction proposed by Gérard Lemaine and Benjamin Matalon, the scheme of our distinction between differentialist racism and inegalitarianist racism. But one should not try to make the two distinctions correspond term for term: the one functions to differentiate the eugenicist orientation (the specter of the "flaw") from the racist orientation (the specter of the "stain"), while the other allows one to differentiate two orientations of racism, or two ideal-typical racisms. Now, if all eugenicists are meliorists and ground themselves on the basic convictions of the so-called progressive rationalist-constructivist project, not all racists are meliorists; indeed, many are not. Biopolitical voluntarism, artificialism, and interventionism characterize the eugenicist utopia: eugenics — as a science, a technology, and an ideology — belongs to modern ideology, even if one may find distant origins for it. To create "better" social material with scientifico-technological material cumulatively filling the roles of the political, the religious, the legislator, and the moralist: here is the very act, the "revolutionary" act, of the eugenicist. The sterilization, confinement, and extermination of the elements that constitute biosocial "waste" are the three solutions that offered themselves as possibilities at the end of the nineteenth century: the three were politically put in motion in the twentieth century. After the "pioneering" American attempts (in the early twentieth century), Nazism historically achieved the eugenico-racist synthesis. But the theoretical distinctions remain — and that is neglected out of principle by the antiracist propaganda discourse.

The common aim, a kind of categorical imperative that the differentialist racists, the eugenicists, and the "liberal" social Darwinists all share, is that one must define the conditions according to which the reproduction of the "unfit" and the "degenerate" would be hindered: a free play of natural selection (social Darwinism), sterilization (forced or voluntary), confinement ("democratic" negative eugenicism), and extermination (totalitarian negative eugenicism: Nazism).

An interpretative hypothesis, of historical order, has been formulated especially by Lemaine and Matalon: the destruction of a social order founded on a transcendence, a destruction characteristic of the modern world, opens the field of a total naturalization of man. Humanity is henceforth perceived as a natural species divided into races (the monogenist thesis), or as a group of distinct species in the zoological sense (the polygenist thesis). From then on, the legitimacy of the social order as it is becomes a problem, and group identities must be as strictly defined by science as they are designated as natural entities to be destroyed, conserved, or improved — an anthropological raw material. One may of course interpret this naturalist reduction of humanity to its biological being (an object of possible experimentation) as a figure of modern individualism in the broadest sense, which designates the ideology that, grounded on the "primacy of the relations to things over the relations among human beings" (Louis Dumont), may be characterized by the "general primacy of the individual as a value."[81] In the individualist perspective of modern Western societies, "essential human reality is to be found in man as an individual";[82] the real anthropological subject to which the triad of "liberty, equality, fraternity" is attributed is the particular human being represented by "individuals, independent beings who are in principle sufficient in themselves, existing in and for themselves."[83] The hypothesis of physical homofiliation precisely allows one to account for the resistances to the incarnation of individualist values and norms — these are grounded on a certain "dedifferentiating universalism" expressed by the pseudotautology that "a human being is a human being"[84] — that, on the one hand, imply the possibility and the normality of interracial marriages and, on the other hand, situate the legitimacy of the choice in the sphere of love of the romantic type (between two singularities there is established a tacit contract of love with no consideration but the pure reciprocity of passion).

In 1963, Pagès proposed a second hypothesis, that of *cultural homofiliation*, which comes down to assuming that "if the morphological perpetuation of familial identity constitutes a value for procreation and therefore for conjugal alliance, the perpetuation of the similitudes of various orders, in particular sociocultural ones, has an equally positive value within certain limits."[85] But the model of intelligibility remains the same: racism derives not from a residue (in Pareto's sense) that would be "the horror of differences"[86] — a psychological theory minted, since the 1950s, as the "refusal of the Other," in the language of ethics — but from a "horror," or a phobia, of repulsion of any rupture of identity, solidarity, and cohesion of the family group, a rupture that would be marked by a discontinuity in the phenotype. The hypothesis is that of a horror induced by the threat of an interruption in the continual transmission of the resemblance belonging to the lineage. It is a horror felt before the risk of an irremediable loss of the conditions of recognition of one's own descent as one's own. But if physical homofiliation seems to be absolutely opposed (as an ineducable, imperfectible residue) to crossings between races, cultural homofiliation might engender forms of resistance reducible to crossings, cultural differences tending to cancel each other out in being crossed, through the exchanges alone[87] — "racial prejudice" would then be attenuable, indeed reducible. For the "traces" left by intercultural crossings are not those who are exceptionally unassimilable, as *métis* children. But when the argument of cultural heterogeneity ("they are not made like us"; "they think and live differently from us") can no longer function, as in a situation in which intellectual equality and intimacy are added to juridical and socioeconomic equality (an ordinary case, for example, in American universities), then there is a risk that the specter of the rupture of biosomatic identity will appear in the foreground, as though stripped bare by the acquired relative equality of conditions.

If the ultimate foundation of racist attitudes, perhaps as much as of discriminatory practices, resides in the desire for physical homofiliation, and if the latter feeds on any distinctive trait that it holds up as a signaling index of incompatibility and as a symbol of threat, then only the utopia of a universal and integral *métissage* can furnish a "definitive" solution to the problem of the struggle for the extinction of racism. Such a radical action on the deep causes would be accomplished only in a world other than our own, unless the latter is one day under the hold of a totalitarian regime, a universal empire, in which interracial crossings would be made obligatory until the disappearance(?) of factors of discrimination. It would be a political regime incarnating the antiracist variant of negative eugenics, whose project would be to improve humanity in the moral sense defined by antiracism. This is an apparent truism: in order for intolerance to disappear, one must bring about the disappearance of all the causes of and occasions for intolerance. But one may propose the pessimistic hypothesis that there would then arise other factors of and occasions for discrimination and intolerance, as the human imagination is what it is, transforming the smallest trait into an index, a signal, a symbol of threatening alterity. Here again we find the same type of difficulty as with the frustration-aggression theory, inspired especially by psychoanalysis, and whose popular version is the theory of the scapegoat:[88] if the theory is true, one may predict that racial prejudice will disappear only in a cosmopolitan and planetary society in which causes of and occasions for frustration have disappeared. While waiting for this happy advent, one may be consoled by the following remark, tinged with bitter humor, that Robert E. Park made in 1924: "Every one, it seems, is capable of getting on with every one else, provided each preserves his proper distance."[89]

Back in our own world, it seems to us that one must also consider those supraindividual individuals, the different spheres of affiliation: lineages, nation-peoples, ethnic groups, even races (beyond bioanthropological entities of the same name), all half-real, half-fictional communities endowed, at least virtually, with a differential self-representation, that is, with a collective identity, an "Us."[90] The question is then the following: What remains after the disappearance of an absolute foundation of the sociopolitical order? Is this disappearance of the same nature as that of an absolute foundation of our knowledge? How does one then conceive a society and its order? What society does one want? Can one want here? What is to be done?

# *Nine*

# On Antiracism: Ideal Type, Ideological Corruption, Perverse Effects

## The Misery of Commemorative Antiracism (an Ideal Type)

*It is superstitious to put one's hopes in formalities.* Blaise Pascal

*Resistance confined to struggle against the future in the name of a past which is already decomposing is just wicked nonsense. It is surely a barren form of conflict which bases itself on ideas that have lost all efficacy.* Nicolas Berdyaev

*Retrospective indignation is also a way of justifying the present.*
Pierre Bourdieu

Understanding the contemporary forms of racism involves submitting ordinary antiracism to critical reason. Avoiding any analogical or metaphorical reduction of the present to the past (and to a certain past, one that nourishes an ever-effective political imaginary: the Dreyfus Affair, the Nazi genocide of the Jews...), engaging in an analysis without pity of the antiracist discourses on "racism" that seem to play the role of collective screen-memories: such are the conditions of an active departure from the circle of exorcising practices, pious ceremonies, and lazy repetitions of the same formulas of defensive magic.

Classical antiracism, a system engendered by the ideologization[1]

of the humanist tradition, hardened into a rhetoric that is today on the way to being totally instrumentalized by the political struggles for power (as well as for cultural hegemony), may be briefly characterized by a set of traits that sketch an ideal type.[2]

1. Antiracism represents the *functional survival* of an ideological apparatus brought into focus in the 1930s to fight against the National Socialist regime, its diffuse influence, and the growing power of its allies, beginning with Italian fascism. The latter underwent the misadventure, through the unfathomable paths of propaganda, of quite involuntarily giving its name to the *demonized/demonizing entity, fascism,* a term that lumps together all the contemporary motifs and objects of political hatred but that above all has few traits in common with Italian fascism as a historical reality.[3] A discourse of propaganda destined to fight against a state racism that represented a real danger for the European democracies no less than for the communist system, antiracist antifascism constituted the least common ideological denominator between pluralist democracies and Stalinist totalitarianism, a shared polemical position strictly tied to conjuncture. When the latter disappeared, antiracism had to find new negative objects, outside the communist field of influence, as by definition. As South Africa alone precisely corresponded to this model, antiracism after 1945 was slowly displaced from the preferential denunciation of "neo-Nazism" (from 1945 to the early 1960s) to that of the apartheid regime practiced by South Africa,[4] not without integrating, in its left wing (Third-Worldist and/or Christian-communist), the stigmatization of "Zionism," which was progressively demonized to the point of being likened to "racism" and to an apartheid regime, in the extension of Soviet and Arab propaganda.[5] The antiracist left allowed itself to be instrumentalized bit by bit by a complex of propagandas, while the antiracist right tended to reduce, as if by reaction, its field of investigation to a general struggle (but an expressly political one: anticommunism continued by humanitarianist means) against "anti-Semitism."[6] Now, the tendency to typify antiracism in general as "the struggle against anti-Semitism" may appear especially anachronistic and at the very least paradoxical. For, on the one hand, the new forms of anti-Jewish discourse no longer carry a racist legitimation (so no longer an "anti-Semitic" ideology in the strict sense) except as a remnant, and, on the other hand, the regime designated as the principal enemy (and sometimes, significantly, the only enemy) is incarnated by

the Soviet Union,[7] whose victims one risks reducing to the sole category of unassimilated Jews — that is, in essence, religious or "Zionist" Jews, in the broad sense.[8]

Let us summarize: the antiracist ideologization of humanism, an apparatus that remained unitary until the defeat of the Axis powers, has since evolved in the direction of a differentiation into two opposing camps, which may be schematized by the "anti-imperialist" and the anticommunist poles of antiracism. That is why it is perhaps not excessive to deem that today, in spite of the ideological homogeneity suggested by the term *antiracism,* the latter masks the reality of political scission and covers with a single and thereby equivocal name two rhetorical systems that are fundamentally heterogeneous and hence antinomic. Antiracism must be stated in at least two senses: antiracism is a homonymic term.

2. Antiracism puts into play a received idea, a first piece of evidence that it posits as a univocal and sufficient definition: racism is in its essence *the rejection of difference,* the refusal or impossibility of accepting another as different — that is, as not identical to nor resembling oneself. Antiracism limits racism a priori, by a primal definition, to *heterophobia.* It thereby even prohibits merely considering the racializations that proceed from the praise of difference, that build on anthropological pluralism in order to hold up factual cultural differences as supreme values and to prescribe their unconditional defense as a categorical imperative. So doing, antiracism first commits a grave error concerning the rhetorical functioning of ordinary language, in the order of what Aristotle called the epideictic genre:[9] for if praise and blame are continually converted to each other, then racism may indiscriminately be constituted by blame (of difference/differences) or praise (of difference/differences). But racism has a demerit whose practical consequences are graver: it dissimulates the functional ambiguity of the racism that proceeds in wavering between blame and praise; it prohibits its access to knowledge in the very name of the conviction of knowing its nature. The *illusion of knowing* is worse than ignorance. Thus the antiracist risks dreaming with his eyes open, sure of himself and accusing, laughing, or lamenting, never belied by the facts nor disappointed by his radical inefficacy.

3. Antiracism continually modulates a basic statement, which one will note is common to the left (communist or not) and to the liberal-democratic right: "Crisis breeds racism, which breeds fascism."[10] If

crisis breeds racism, it is because it leads to the designation of scapegoated victims.[11] Explanation by "crisis" is willingly stated as a law ("any crisis..."), and a causal law. Let us give two examples of statements of the *crisological formula,* the first restricted, the second developed. The editorial board of a socialist monthly posited, in November 1984, the following axiom: "Any economic crisis, by the disarray and anguish it incites, is accompanied by a rise in intolerance and xenophobia."[12] Thus is satisfied the mesological desire, the reduction of xenophobia to an effect of specific social conditions that are themselves achieved in being assigned to an economic determinism. In the framework of the ideology of the supposedly omnipotent middle, explanation by crisis tends to be presented as an explanation by *economic* crisis, which responds to the dominant, fundamentally economophile objectivist need. Hence the entry into circulation of ideological evidence: the phenomena of society considered aberrant may be only, in the last analysis, effects produced by economic dysfunctionings. The "roots" of xenophobia and racism are of an economic order, first and essentially by reason of the axiom that the economy is the real.

The developed crisological evidence carries within it the thesis of *victim solidarity,* the idea that all victims are equal by the effects of a single cause ("the crisis"), most often based on the memory of the Nazi massacres. In her report on racism and anti-Semitism (1982), Madeleine Barot summarizes this common view of social evil:

> Any period of crisis — economic recession and unemployment, external threat and war — breeds insecurity, fear, withdrawal into oneself, the rejection of the other. Explanations for the crisis must be found, guilty parties and, failing that, scapegoats; we quickly find ourselves in the realm of terrorism and racism. The history of National Socialism has shown all too well that Gypsies, Jews, *métis,* and all those connected with liberties are attacked together.[13]

A remarkable condensation of a great number of common stereotypes and clichés, this text shows very well the tie between the conviction of the "objective" solidarity of the victims — regularly "proven" by the misdeeds of Nazism — and the reduction of all the faces of evil to a single one. Hence "terrorism" and "racism" — that is, what is consensually reproved — are here reduced to a common denominator. The able antiracist subject makes it understood that it is always the same ones (the wicked ones typified by the Nazis) who do evil to the same ones (the victims predestined as such by their minoritarian nature, their supposed vocation of being oppressed and exploited minorities). The postulate of the mutual solidarity of the victims, or the presumption of their objective alliance, hinging on the lumping together of all supposedly victimizing forces, constitutes a recurrent theme of hegemonic, neo-anti-Nazi discourse.

Added to the definitional illusion is henceforth the illusion of an explanation by efficient causes, itself at the basis of an illusion on the order of practice: the antiracist who believes herself to be furnished with a powerful model of intelligibility of the phenomenon of "racism" is not going to waste her time studying the latter (that would be to obscure a clear knowledge) but is rather going to strive to elaborate outlines of solutions that derive from her explanation by "crisis." It is hardly difficult to deduce the general form of all the solutions imaginable to antiracist dogmatism: in order to act on racism-as-effect, one must act on its causes (the latter supposedly real — whence the dominant designation of "economic crisis," in conformity with contemporary economistic doxa). It then suffices to repeat the *crisological formula,* in return for small prescriptive variations: to fight against unemployment (especially that of young people, the latter being more prone to exterminate those marked as different when they have too much leisure time in which to do it), to make French products, to awaken the spirit of enterprise against the spirit of assistance, to have a revolution,[14] to reactivate republican values (for left and right volunteerists), to recover the use of reason.[15] In brief, the magical and pseudoexplanatory uses of the vocable *crisis* tend to be substituted for precise analyses of definite types of "crises," seized in determinate conjunctures.[16]

Referring to "crisis" achieves the most common incantatory naming of Evil (or of its favorable conditions: "in favor of crisis") in contemporary ideological space. An indistinct name, *crisis* signifies and designates without distinction the cause and the effect, the essence and the accident, the "seed" and the manifestation. A well-advised political scientist has accurately characterized the ideological advantage of such a great confusion: "Political vocabulary offers the term *crisis,* the most confused word in contemporary social thought. Because it has no content, because its use is not governed by any discipline, it may designate any situation at all."[17] But we might note here a general trait of political discourse, if it is true that the latter is constituted around a systematic avoidance of any precise definition of the terms it employs.[18]

The universalist antiracists stigmatize as "racist" the reactions that the supposed racists, who proudly designate themselves as "national" or "nationalist," describe as natural and legitimate: reactions of legitimate defense before the threat of an invasion or of a destruction of community identity, of a theft of work, or of a rape of the national body. Hence the same imperative, "We must defend against the foreign invasion" (certain foreigners constituting an invasion more than others), is interpreted in two rigorously opposite ways: as typically "racist" by the dominant group of antiracists and as a prescription for self-defense against "anti-French racism" (and the invasion that supposedly accompanies it) by the "racists" (those so named by the former). But the two opposing collective subjects, "antiracists" and "racists," agree on the broad diagnosis of "crisis," linking economic crisis (unemployment), social and moral crisis (values in crisis), and the identity crisis affecting France and the French.

What we have called the "crisological formula" applies perfectly to monocausal explanation by "economic crisis." At issue here is a sloganized form (thus calling for struggle against the so-called crisis) of the economic conception of the world, which must be conceived as a system of illusory explanation appeasing a specific *dogmatic need*. Now, economistic monomania long ago left the limited ideologico-political territory of the "materialist conception of history," in which Max Weber situated it exclusively at the beginning of the twentieth century. The liberal-socialist consensus on the primacy of the economy has instead been put forth as absolute ideological evidence: modernity is achieved as economolatry. In 1904, Weber perfectly identified this new axiom of the historico-social sciences, this economistic principle of sufficient reason that certain circles insisted on as governing the methodology of these sciences. Indeed, he stigmatized

> the peculiar condition that their need for a causal explanation of an historical event is never satisfied until somewhere or somehow economic causes are shown (or seem) to be operative. Where this however is the case, they content themselves with the most threadbare hypotheses and the most general phrases since they have then satisfied their dogmatic need to believe that the economic "factor" is

the "real" one, the only "true" one, and the one which "in the last instance is everywhere decisive."[19]

But we must carry the critique of economistic monocausalism to its very spiritual-cultural roots: we must in this sense conceive it as one of the ideologico-scientific figures of "the inevitable monistic tendency"[20] that, on the basis of some science or other (biology, physics, economics, and so on), claims to construct a conception of the world endowed with an explanatory omnipotence. This monistic presumption, thus postulated as an a priori of the human mind, characterizes "every type of thought which is not self-critical."[21] Incarnated by its "eager dilettantes,"[22] economistic dogmatism claims to reduce historical becoming in its totality, "in the last instance," to the rivalry of economic interests. Hegemonic antiracism does nothing but apply to its specific domain the scheme of economorphic gnosis.

4. Antiracism assumes a *manipulatory,* even *conspiracist, representation*[23] of racism. The rhetorical schema that subtends the antiracist representation of racism is the following: there exists a social power, anonymous or personalized, whose activity consists of dissimulating (in its objectives and tactics), of both inventing and diffusing erroneous models of interpretation of social and economic questions, of proposing illusory solutions based on the designation of those responsible (the racists) for "the crisis," in order to channel the dissatisfactions and hatreds in the direction of a scapegoated minority victim, foreign to the average (or ideal) type of the "homegrown" population. In short, racism would be an ideological and discursive device destined to get people to believe so as to get them to do, thus fulfilling a supplementary function: to camouflage the true problems, to turn attention away from the real causes of social discontent. (These causes waver between the class struggle and the welfare state, between left antiracism and right antiracism.) The placement in discourse of these interpretive schemes, which also play the role of arguments in ideological warfare, is most commonly effected by the metaphor of "orchestration" or according to the model of the "campaign," whether political or journalistic (or the conjunction of the two). The manipulatory representation of racism involves focusing on the power to deceive, on the mystifying agency that would be its true subject, the latter all the more dangerous since it would not itself believe in the racist propositions that it would banalize in opinion. This

mystifying and overpowerful subject is formally distinguished from the "racist" who practices in the open. The latter is only the "maneuver" of the former.[24] The "racist" of journalistic discourse is hence reduced, in the elaborate representation that antiracist "theory" gives of him, to the subaltern role of manipulated collaborator in a cause that he cannot know in its truth. Stated otherwise, the dominant antiracist view of racism assumes a distinction between the real and the apparent subject of racism, deceptive and deceived, abusive and abused, cynical and naive. But, even here, racism is no longer defined as an ideology (in spite of the usage of ideologistic vocabulary); rather, it is in turn reduced to the functional status of an instrumental myth, to a fiction of propaganda. Racism no longer stems so much from the spontaneous collective imaginary, from ideological production, as it does from an intention of and will to indoctrination, in the service of an occult politics. A recent antiracist text, "Themes for Reflection Submitted to All Members," for the preparation of the 1985 Congress of the MRAP, perfectly illustrates the manipulatory representation of racism:

> *Racism is not spontaneous,* at least in its social manifestations. It is a Machiavellian manipulation of opinion, destined to give true problems a false interpretation and to propose nonexistent solutions.... This mystification involves three personages: the designated victim, the mystified racist who attacks the victim, and the mystifier who designates the victim.... If, instead of objectively analyzing the data, the causes, and remedies of the crisis, one stupidly and spitefully attacks immigrants, it is because one true enterprise of falsification, orchestrated with enormous means, has been undertaken against them.[25]

The paradox is here formulated in remarkable fashion: the "one" that refers to the mystifying power is in some way extracted from the racist field, while the racist becomes in her own way a victim, deceived by the ruses of the intelligence of the supraracist power. It is a demonization of the hidden one responsible for racism, herself aracist; but also a correlative movement of the racist to the side of the victims, the innocents, and the "noble people" that "one" abuses and whose good faith "one" exploits. It is striking to recognize here a reinvestment of the populist myth of the "fat cats," those wicked and omnipotent anonymous persons who are supposed to *profit* from racism. To fight against racism and xenophobia is therefore to begin by denouncing the "real" responsible ones, behind the apparent ones, the latter reduced to mere puppets who insult, attack, or kill without quite knowing why, without ever knowing the ultimate *why* of their behavior. The recommended strategy and tactic derive from the received and posited definition of racism: denounce the inspirers, mystifiers, and conspirators, educate or reeducate the mystified and inspired ones. Police, justice, education: antiracist action claims to achieve in one blow the tasks of these agencies, for there exist at once criminals, perverts, and ignoramuses. To be antiracist is to declare oneself honest, normal, and cultivated. We see the threat that weighs on the postwar antiracist: conformism, self-categorization as a right-thinking person, through the placement in ideological evidence (received without criticism) that "racism" is a "bad" thing that one must avoid, that is rightly condemned.

The antiracist is therefore qualified as much by her virtues as by her competencies and faculties; she tends to present herself as a supremely honest polymath, an encyclopedist educator of wayward humanity, a hunter of ignorance and wickedness. The antiracist utopia consists of assuming as possible the achievement of a world of good and cultivated persons. For mystification immediately to cease being effective, it would suffice to make the mystifiers, the "racists," understand that they are abused by wicked profiteers. With this single and sufficient condition, racism would disappear. It will easily be observed that it still has fine days ahead of it....

5. Antiracism tends to serve as a *means of diversion,* insofar as the denunciation of racism[26] is susceptible of turning public attention away from real social, economic, or military problems. This ideologization and politicization of antiracism confer on it an instrumental function in an ideological war of which one objective is to paralyze the adversary through disinformation. That is why the tactical function of antiracism is willingly brought into evidence by conservative ideologues and anticommunists, whether "nationalists" (the National Front) or "liberals" (who express themselves in *Le Figaro* or *Le Quotidien de Paris*). Antiracism may in certain cases be denounced as a method of intellectual terrorism, an enterprise of obfuscation and blinding. On the side of xenophobic nationalism, the affair has long been understood, inasmuch as some trait of antiracism remains one of the rare ideological means of confronting it. In the following, François Brigneau devotes himself to disqualifying antiracism for the reason that the latter would target only a "straw man": "Today, the straw

man is racism. Even if the word cannot be applied to reality, it sounds out the sweeties and rounds up the cuties."[27] Its function of rallying the lefts would enable an understanding of racism as the last means of "blackmail" and of "intellectual terrorism of the left." The first "straw man" was clericalism, which, under the Third Republic, was denounced only to serve to rejoin the bloc of lefts. The second "straw man" was fascism, whose proclaimed threatening return, brandished like a flag, allowed one "to forget the Soviet Union." The third "straw man," finally, is racism, which is stirred up in order to effect "a particularly repugnant operation against French nationalism."[28] It will be noted in the passage that the defensive argument for nationalism is able to integrate one of the real characteristics of antiracism. But if the argument does not reproach the latter for a fictional property, it nonetheless integrates the motif of the instrumentality of antiracism in a *conspiracist* grand narrative in which the enemy is, as if in a mirror, demonized: "We are in the presence of a vast incantation against the French France and its natural defenders."[29] The reaction to the anti-Maghrebian and anti-Jewish murders and incidents of late March 1985, instigated by SOS-Racisme, is interpreted in the framework of this paranoid vision of the world:

> Menton. Miramas. Paris. The bomb at the Jewish festival (eighteen slightly wounded) whose sound drowns out the small echo from Guadaloupe (a bomb at a National Front café owner's): the campaign of feigned indignation and real intimidation unleashed by the anti-French racists touches on delirium. By their clamors, their denunciations, their displays, their acts of lumping together, they want to provoke the worst. We leave them with the responsibility for their undertaking. We see perfectly its mainsprings and tricks.[30]

Among ex-communists who have become conservatives and anticommunists, who are particularly sensitive to the techniques of ideological instrumentalization (they know them from the inside), the critique of antiracism is also based on the grievance of obfuscation/ diversion: "By continuing to struggle 'against racism,' we are in the process of falsifying, distorting, occulting the diversity of motives that command individual and collective decisions."[31] But what is essential is elsewhere for "systemic" anticommunism: antiracism is only understood in the framework of the communist strategy in western Europe that, "based on a union with a possibly radicalizing social democracy," would strive to "revive the 'progressive' tradition of the 1930s."[32] Antiracism is reduced to a single element in the discourse of communist propaganda. After analyzing the linked acts of lumping together implied by communist antiracism/antifascism, Annie Kriegel moves on to decoding the "struggle against anti-Semitism":

> The "struggle against anti-Semitism" was drowned and diluted [by the MRAP and similar organizations] in a struggle against racism or rather "against all racisms," one of which was Zionism. It is in this way that, by an apparent broadening of a single theme — from the struggle against anti-Semitism to the struggle against all racisms — the communists were successful with the tour de force, for example after the incident on the Rue Copernic, of lining up the leaders of the Jewish community behind a banner that, implicitly, for the ones who read it from the communist point of view, included the state of Israel among the purveyors of hatred against the Jews.[33]

The critical argument is quite simple: generalized and generic antiracism (which subsumes all humanitarianist "struggles") is advantageous to international communism, its true initiator and sponsor. Unfortunately for our desire for objectivity, the mythical slant of such a demystifying critique is quickly revealed, as much through the neglect of empirical "details" (we are content with a few striking illustrations of "theory") as through a singular speed of elevation to the great anticommunist view of the world, a new paranoid picture that has no cause to envy the old communist view. The simplism of conspiracist pseudoexplanation (to whom is this advantageous?) in fact blocks scientific investigation. The renewed communist imaginary remains within the limits of diabolical causality. Good analyses are not done with disappointment, resentment, and vindictive recycling.

6. Antiracism is founded on a *postulate of exteriority* of the antiracist spectator-actor with respect to the racist, that is, of the one who designates "racist" in the face of the one who is designated as such. The antiracist, having the power of qualification, therefore presupposes himself, by the fact of spotting a "racist" and qualifying her as such, as a subject situated on the exterior of the racist world, or at least the world of racists. This is the *postulate of radical separability* of the antiracist and the racist, to which is surreptitiously added a *postulate of inequality*: for the antiracist does not doubt for an instant that his antiracist position is superior to the racist position he stigmatizes. Here is a paradox of egalitarian ideology in general, which necessarily

arises in the particular field of antiracist egalitarianism: one may not affirm the value of equality to be superior to that of inequality without postulating a hierarchical scale of values; in the same way, one may not affirm antiracist values without assuming them to be superior to racist values, therefore without putting into play an inegalitarian relation (between the antiracist and the racist types) that one otherwise impugns absolutely, precisely as an index of racism.[34] But the antiracist representation of the racist goes beyond the relation of inequality: the racist tends to be treated, by an only slightly elaborated rhetorical reversal, in the very same way the racist treats the racized. The racist — as the Other rejected from the world of properly human values, excluded from dialogue, likened to a delinquent — tends to become the representative of that demonized entity who bore the names, in the racist tradition, of the "inferior race" or the "antirace."[35] We see an inversion of the process of racism: the racist is *demonized,* after being thrown off into inhumanity.[36] The operation of designating the racist enemy, implied by the "fight against racism," thus enables the antiracist to exclude himself from what he blames and, absolutely innocent, to hold himself up as a tribunal for a set of behaviors that he judges to be infrahuman, indeed satanic.

A typology of antiracist attitudes may be sketched according to the types of "racists" distinguished or blamed.

*a. The ignorant racist:*[37] if racism is measured and produced by ignorance, the antiracist struggle will merge with the task of education and upbringing. This is an optimistic postulate: no one is a racist voluntarily. The antiracist is an educator. His mission is twofold: on the one hand, to teach differences, to make them "known" and "liked"; on the other hand, to teach that differences are negligible and that what alone is worthy of absolute respect in each human being is shared by all human beings. This is a pedagogical hesitation inherent in contemporary antiracism, revealing the antinomy that it cannot surmount by its own means (see trait 8 below).

*b. The wicked racist:* it is no longer ignorance, a mere lack, but rather hatred, negative power, that is designated as the source of racism. To fight against racism is to disqualify and isolate it, to keep it from doing harm — to the point of excluding it: "I judge it unacceptable," declares Bernard-Henri Lévy, "that Le Pen is considered a politician like the others.... I am a partisan of the exclusion of the bearers of xenophobic thoughts and racist ideology."[38] The antiracist realm is populated with rituals of counterexclusion, according to the simple logic of give-and-take: "The only just attitude, in the face of Le Pen: exclude him by all possible means from the family circle of established politics. The only imperative: draw around him the ideological and ethical line that, alone, will keep him out of action."[39] As Leszek Kolakowski has duly noted, at issue here is one of those arguments most often invoked against tolerance, which presupposes the uniqueness of the supreme value of each domain of value in question: there is only one truth, only one good, only one type of beauty. Besides an unwavering axiological dogmatism, such a position illustrates almost as a caricature the relationship of mimetic rivalry (everyone excludes everyone), practiced as unsurpassable (or normal) while offering a good example of a phobic attitude: one must avoid contact with the group of plague victims or lepers; one must mark off the distance, separate, even differentiate — in a word, discriminate. In pseudoethnographic terms adorned with vague psychoanalysis, the antiracist will demand that taboo be restored, that there be respect for the border that absolutely separates the legitimate-respectable ones from the untouchables. That which is feared is displayed as a submersion in the "mud," the rising mire. Lévy explained and prescribed, in November 1985:

> I insist on the case of Le Pen. The base of the affair, of course, is the taboo that has leaped out of the way. It is the lock that has come undone. It is that old mud, held back for years, that rises all at once, oozes into consciousness. And in the face of this oozing, in the face of this flood..., I believe we must no longer be afraid to call things by name — nor to call, literally, for *a restoration of Prohibition.*[40]

The wicked one is hence rejected, under the blow of metaphors, into the muck, the mire, the muddy element from which he should never emerge. This is an unconditional norm: the antiracist must protect herself from that which soils, covers with stains; she must be sufficiently vigilant not to fall into the (racist) mud, where there is risk of getting bogged down and dirtied, indeed of getting sucked in. Not only does the antiracist attribute to herself the monopoly on good intentions, but she also captures the superior position (she may fall into the mud if she is not careful) and the possession of purity, far above the muddy swamp in which the subhumans wallow, vile and corrupt. We should therefore be done, according to the distinguished antiracist, with a certain laxity toward the presumed bearers of racism: they are dangerous because they are endowed with a power of contamination, which is deployed every time they are allowed to come up from the bottom of this muddy marsh that is their natural element. We should in some way lock back up the sites of access to terra firma and clean air. The program is clear, simple. But is it not a transparent *petitio principii?* Just what is the prohibition that must be restored? Is the law of July 1972 insufficient? By which new and firmer means must we exclude the presumed racists? And how do we identify them without too much risk of being deceived? For the clandestine racists are legion.... This is precisely the question: for antiracist legislation to be effective, it should be applicable to all forms of racism, especially including those which in no way resemble the recognized and therefore recognizable forms. That is hardly possible: ineffectiveness seems to be guaranteed. Thus, to demand the restoration of prohibitions, and all the more so of Prohibition, is to speak and say nothing — at least nothing other than a barely shameful dream of the authoritarian organization of society. This is a wholly literary activism, a flagging antiracism.

In his essay "Diktatur der Wahrheit: Ein quadratischer Kreis," reprinted in the book *Der revolutionäre Geist,* Leszek Kolakowski approaches in depth this type of argument, so often invoked against tolerance, always in the name of better reasons and for good cause.[41] Let us first of all specify that Lévy's antiracist plea is a good example of *intolerance by conviction,* which Kolakowski distinguishes from intolerance by indifference.[42] In the case of intolerance based on the ethic of conviction, the dogmatic moralist proceeds by denunciation and condemnation of what he considers to be absolutely unacceptable; he preaches intolerance because he is convinced that he holds the truth or that he is there to stay in the camp of the Good. The sociopolitical application of the dogmatic argument against tolerance takes the following form: tolerance must not extend to the enemies of tolerance under penalty of destroying itself. In its most current contemporary ideological form, it now appears that the following rhetorical question is asked: Does tolerance mean freedom for Nazi activity? It is asked in order to legitimate all possible practices of intolerance, by invoking the fact that it aims for attitudes or doctrines that are either "false," "anti-," or "in-human."[43]

Kolakowski designates well the limits of any legislation termed antiracist:

A law that summarily prohibits organizations and ideologies having some connection to National Socialism, to Hitler's doctrine, or to the National Socialist system is absolutely justifiable. But the value of such a law is trivial if the solution of political problems is at issue; for the groups that openly acknowledge their relations with the Nazi tradition in no way hold social power and are not really dangerous. Such a law, which prohibits organizations with National Socialist names, symbols, and slogans, would have a clearly symbolic value; in order to be effective, the ideological content of the forbidden movement and organizations would have to be formulated.[44]

Racism in the legal sense henceforth covers only a tiny (and negligible) part of real racism. The latter may be defined by its social and political efficacy, as well as by its high degree of implicitness, which make it unrecognizable and do not unleash social mechanisms of inhibition or rejection. Antiracist laws therefore find their first limit in the difficulty of their application to the dominant forms of racism, which are not socially negligible: they risk being unable to function except in the case of declared and hyperbolical forms, the latter all the more decodable for being provocational, belonging to minority and marginalized groups in the political field. Let us say that they are applicable to the nostalgic racism of old fighters and militants, to reactive racism, a compensation for real social impotency or for individual isolation. One may synthetically formulate an uncertainty principle in the antiracist struggle, which is just as much an impotency principle: either antiracism is based on a precise and restricted definition of racism, and the antiracist struggle has no real social reach (in truth only applying to marginal forms of racism), or it is based on a broad and less precise definition, which covers a very large number of scenarios, and the legislative texts tend to be inapplicable by the very fact that they apply to too many social situations. These may range from ordinary xenophobic behaviors to an apology for violence, for intolerance, for tyranny, which are evidently encountered beyond the field that may be defined as "racist," even according to quite broad criteria. Either antiracist law is well applied but stripped of effectiveness by the restriction of its zone of applicability, or it is practically inapplicable in virtue of its will to be of extensive applicability. Thus may be formed the "crux" of politico-juridical antiracism.[45]

It is not only vain but also dangerous for freedoms to be directed at suspending the principle of tolerance, at impugning its application to individuals or groups whose existence is considered intolerable. The perverse effect is of very classic craft: in the name of a will to the maximalization of virtue (as one defines it), one risks favoring ideological despotism, installing a heightened control over opinions and behaviors. One may only agree with Kolakowski when he declares, in conclusion to his essay on tolerance: "All attacks on the principle of tolerance can only strengthen the really dangerous tendencies to make bureaucracy independent of society — but that would mean that they would only contribute, despite an expressly different intention, to the totalitarian organization of society."[46]

c. *The mad racist:* in a certain way a mentally ill person (moving between neurosis and psychosis), the racist must be vigorously cared for. Racism, without referring to a type of mental illness, designates the set of symptoms distributed in the nosographic field. The antiracist is a polymorphous therapist. Let us take an exemplary text by Roger Ikor, whose intransigent democratic individualism draws on a militant rationalism whose polemical tendency is to pathologize any attitude perceived as irrational. By defining racism as "a flight, a fear, a hatred that attempts to find a justification and an excuse," Ikor believes he can explain that "this madness, specific to modern man, can be only furious."[47] Hence the hardly amenable description of the racist, at once bestialized and pathologized: "Yes, at the start, the racist is simply a beast who is afraid of his emerging soul and whom fear makes mad."[48] And the illness of this mad beast becomes a threatening epidemic: "Virus, terrain: there remains the opportunity that may unleash the illness."[49] In the racist are condensed the ordinary figures of threat, from the "dangerous madman" to "the proliferation of the racist cancer."[50] Antiracism has its own version of the catastrophist myth, with its obsessional and phobic anxieties.

d. *The stupid racist:* the grievance of stupidity ("he's a moron"; "he's a simpleton") has the advantage of unconditionally disqualifying the racist, but the disadvantage of being unable to be specific or to justify except by recourse to an inegalitarian theory of intelligence that, in antiracist milieus, is in general likened to racism and eugenicism (there are many slogans based on this chain of equivalence: elitism = eugenicism = racism = fascism). To fight against stupidity is first to ridicule it, thereby to exclude it from legitimate dialogue, to render it shameful and speechless. The antiracist is part of the intellectual elite that detests the racist, that weak and narrow mind.[51]

*e. The ill-bred racist:* racism may be the effect, no longer of a lack of education, but of a poor upbringing. The racist is the one who says things that should not be said, who makes inappropriate remarks. And also the one whose thoughts are supposedly dominated by "prejudices," "stereotypes," "clichés." The antiracist henceforth makes an effort to teach her methodical mistrust before received ideas; he will apply himself to reeducate her to speak correctly, for words are bearers and vectors of "racist prejudice." At issue is inculcating her with good habits, which begin with the right choice of denominations: the most virtuist will advise that one not say "Negroes" but "blacks," no longer say "Jews" but "Israelites" ("French people of the Israelite faith"), or Israelis, when that is the case; no longer to speak of "races" but rather of "cultures" or "ethnic groups"; to term "different" the peoples one tends, spontaneously and very inadvertently, to declare "inferior," "primitive," or "savage" (these qualifiers must always be preceded by the cautious adjective *so-called*), and so on. The racist must reeducate one to speak, to think, to behave appropriately, by way of the standardized euphemisms in the use of which may be socially recognized the distinguished antiracist. The height of antiracist euphemization is the suspension of judgment: it is necessary to teach human beings not to judge and above all to *abstain from judging* what differs from "Us" — and to abstain all the more as the intended individuals belong to "otherized" or "excluded" categories, as they incarnate victimizable types. The reeducated antiracist must be able to content herself with affirming that there is difference, while adding that one must respect, indeed love, differences — in such a way that the antiracist offers himself as a reeducator without borders, part teacher, part police officer, part master of ceremonies.[52]

The disadvantage of such an antiracist attitude is that one may too easily come under the grievance of conformism: the antiracist becomes the right-thinking person who is shocked by racist behavior, thus held up as a member of an oppressed minoritary, inventive and on the fringe, a martyr to the contestation of the last taboos of postmodern society.

*f. The racist as social symptom:* the status of "symptom" makes the racist radically innocent, reduced to a mere effect of structure. The presupposition in question is that society as a whole is in a state of dysfunction, that there is discontent in civilization, and so on, the causes of which, once recognized, may be modified in order to act on the effects. As the racist is reproached as *nouveau pauvre*, unemployed person, and delinquent by social fate, his disappearance will of itself be effected, with all those effects of a bad society, once the latter is improved. The most common schema is the masterpiece of socialist-communist utopia: to be a consequential antiracist is to bring on revolution in order to destroy the class bases of racism. A revolutionary dream: in a classless society, racism will disappear for lack of function, like an organ that has become useless. "The cure for anti-Semitism will only be found in the complete transformation of the societies in which we live," declared Daniel Cohn-Bendit in 1978.[53]

7. Antiracism effects a *placement in evidence and in relief of the "racial," "ethnic," or "cultural" identity* of individuals, which it likens to an unsurpassable origin. This operation comes down to legitimating, of course involuntarily, the racist reduction, which one claims to combat, of the individual to a fixed class of affiliation, which is confused with his "origins" (racial, ethnic, cultural). Racist fatalism is hence renewed, comforted, confirmed. This perverse effect of antiracism turns up again in the reclaiming of identity, from the moment it absolutizes the differences and identities of origin.[54] In short, whether one calls oneself "racist" (rarely) or "antiracist" (commonly), one legitimates the racial criterion of differentiation among humans; one tends to present it as the principal and determining criterion of the classification of individuals. It is such a "cementing" of collective differences, flowing into the exclusive vocabulary of race, that constitutes the dominant perverse effect of antiracism. To the antiracists' "Live together with our differences"[55] responds the racists' "Live separately with our differences." It is clear that the reference to racial differentiation represents a presupposition common to the declared ideological enemies, which envelopes a second and implicit postulate: differences are treated as unsurpassable or as uncrossable boundaries. In brief, everything happens as if it were within the same circle of prejudices that the fraternal enemies confront each other, agreed on a "differentialist" reductionism and fatalism.

On this point, one may only be in agreement with these remarks formulated by Annie Kriegel:

> The "fight against racism" is currently led in such a manner as ineluctably to end up in a "panracialization" of the social bonds: unduly privileged and even held up as the only significant factor is

the dimension of personal identity that stems from the affiliation with one or another ethnic community. This is an extraordinarily questionable and dangerous trend: ethnic identity — a prudish qualifier to designate race — is not and should not be the constitutive criterion of the intermediary groups that a complex society such as French society is made up of.[56]

8. The ideological hesitations manifested by the store of slogans produced for a number of years now throw a certain light on the *major theoretical contradiction* of the contemporary antiracist vulgate. The analysis of slogans and watchwords in the sphere of influence of what is conveniently called spectacle antiracism, originating in the recruitment of the confirmed stars of "humanitarian" causes and the selection of a new generation of media personalities, indeed enables a placing in evidence of a contradiction between the two principal demands formulated by the antiracist actors endowed with a spokesperson's legitimacy.

a. On the one hand, *to call for the respect and safeguard of difference,* to practice the praise of difference against the supposedly heterophobic "racists." The partisans of "multiracial," "pluriethnic," or "multicultural" society develop the logic of good multiplicity and presuppose an absolutely positive valorization of interracial/ethnic/cultural difference. The slogan launched in the spring of 1985 by the MRAP, "Live together with our differences,"[57] illustrates it as much as that of the marchers in "Convergence 84": "For a rainbow France that recognizes the diversity of rights and cultures."[58] The basic axiological postulate here is that difference is good in itself and of itself.

b. On the other hand, *to call for mixing, hold up* métissage *as a method of salvation,* as at once the hybridization of ethnically diverse populations and "intercultural exchanges" that must result in a new culture. Numerous statements illustrate such a praise of *métissage*, presented as the new royal road to the ideal of assimilation through the radical abolition of the distinctive traits of ethnocultural groups, these characteristics being implicitly evaluated as so many stigmata destined to be erased. Two slogans in the form of definitions of France, launched on the occasion of the second March for Equality (1984), bear witness: "France is like a moped: to move forward, it needs a mixture";[59] "Great! France moves toward mixture."[60] The axiological postulate is here that difference is not as good as exchange and mixture, which tend toward a lack of differentiation. The latter seems desirable insofar as difference is evaluated as a source of nonequality: the primacy accorded to the requirement for equality implies the position of the final abolition of differences, holds up the state of the lack of differentiation as the horizon of antiracist desirability. The normative and prescriptive statement that "*It needs* a mixture" is itself propped up on a constative statement: "France is like a moped: to move forward, *it has always needed* a mixture."[61] The basic argument is that mixture has already taken place, that there is a precedent of mixture, that France has always "moved forward" toward mixture. The constative legitimates the normative and the prescriptive: mixture is needed because mixture has already taken place. "To 'each in his own home,' we respond with the mixture that already exists."[62]

The inegalitarian interpretation of difference functions as the founding ideological evidence of the production of such slogans as this one: "Different, that is, unequal."[63] It follows that difference may not be claimed as a positive value and norm. From this moment on it is understood that "resemblance" tends to be substituted for "difference" in antiracist statements: "Let us live in equality with our similarities, whatever our differences."[64] But the ideological indeterminacy remains, marked by the hesitation renewed by the spontaneous remarks of one marcher or another: " 'Convergence' means a crossroads. A crossroads of men and women who fight for the ideal of Equality.... Equality with our similarities, Equality with our differences."[65] We see a wavering between the primacy of the mixed and the primacy of difference, a norm of interethnic mixture and a prescription of respect for ethnocultural diversity, an ideal of assimilation through the similarity of all to all (pure egalitarian reciprocity: a state of absolute lack of differentiation) and a celebration of the "multiracial" or the "pluricultural":[66] these figures of hesitant ideological steps reproduce and renew the fundamental antinomy that has structured ideological debates in France since the French Revolution; these two series of demands, contradictory to each other, are two contemporary variants of the antinomy formed by the *logic of assimilation* and the *logic of differentiation*.

The logic of assimilation is not linked to one or another instrument of sociopolitical realization; rather, it may resort, simultaneously or successively, to the operators of uniformization of language, the legal system, mores, or *métissage*. In all cases, assimilationist antiracist action has as its final cause the ideal of a lack of differentiation through similarity, through the sharing of bloods and cultures,[67] through equal distribution/allotment of all traits of all to all: it is the case that similarity is the relationship in which the ideal of egalitarian reciprocity is best incarnated. From such a valorization of the homogeneity of the population, one will easily find formulations on the left and the right. We must insist on the fact that the positive valorization of *métissage* is currently received as one of the surest criteria of the absence of racism: the criterion of decisive identification of the antiracist attitude is the praise of *métissage* pronounced by the subject in question. That *mixophilia* is hence held up as a major index and in the essence of antiracism constitutes an absolute piece of evidence belonging to the *individuo-universalist* view. "All the same not racist because Élie Faure believes in the virtue of *métissage*," notes for example Pierre Guiral after a quotation from the philosopher-doctor that may be rather disturbing to a convinced antiracist.[68] The positive value of *métissage* is sufficient to remove the diagnosis of "racism" concerning the subject who offers proof of it (that is, who *declares* his mixophilia, whatever his other judgments may be). The mixophile affirmation plays the role of absolute proof of antiracism.

As for the logic of differentiation, let us say that it is expressly opposed to what is generally perceived as the "Jacobin" model of centralizing and authoritarian integration: differentialist antiracism is elaborated on the basis of the federalist countermodel of regionalisms or ethnicisms — whose right and left versions interfere with each other and are sometimes confused.

Two distinct types of evaluation may therefore be gauged in the corpus of contemporary antiracist statements.

*a.* Difference is better than nondifference (leveling of cultures, destruction of collective identities, lack of respect for what is "other," and so on): *differentialist antiracism*.

*b.* Mixture, as exchange and sharing of ethnic as well as cultural traits, is better than the refusal of contact (communication, communion, fusion); *métissage* is infinitely better than "each in his own home": *assimilationist antiracism*. Two political versions of this type of antiracism must be distinguished: either one extols the mixture of all with all as the surest means of realizing the "Jacobin" ideal of the assimilation of individuals in a national body; or one expects that generalized *métissage* will shake up the basic consensus on which the republican ideal of assimilation rests. Moreover, it will be noted that this mixophilic formulation of assimilation appears, in the discourses, to be concurrent with a mimetic formulation: the similarity of all to all is the normative state that gives its meaning to antiracist action. An "amusing" illustration of the mixophile vulgate is furnished to us by an editorial in the monthly *Latitudes*. It is a culinary version of the celebration of mixture — one gains access to salvation through the exchange of specific "foods":

> A living society is a society that *brews* ideas, businesses, cultures, human beings. When a twenty-year-old man shoots a Turkish worker and declares, "I don't like foreigners," there is in this gesture an absolute despair, an absurd refusal of *life*. In fact, today one cannot wish to leave a crisis by refusing to *breathe the air of the world*....I, on the contrary, rejoice in it [the presence of foreigners]!...They come with *their rhythms* and *their cooking,* and that interests me!...Yes, dancing to Caribbean rhythm or listening to raï — the new music of Oran — all that is part of my culture, just as couscous and paella have naturally gained citizens' rights on my table! You take yourself — and it happens that I take myself — for *the salt* of the earth. They, the Blacks, the Beurs, are the *pepper* of the earth. *Let's pepper ourselves:* it heats us up and gives us energy!⁶⁹

The drawn-out metaphor of the exchange of culinary and rhythmic specialties is of course here a caricature; even so, it does not reveal any less to what point antiracist discourse of propaganda contributes the fixed idea of mixture and how much the universe of such an imaginary "mixed person" is wanting for images, which are reduced to sempiternal clichés and stereotypes. This materialism of cooking in truth achieves as it is chanted a mise-en-scène, which tries to be convivial, of twin slogans, "Friendship among peoples" and "Dialogue among cultures," to which will be added "exchange" among ways of being and doing (but what a thing to be and do!). It is admitted that the great Mardi Gras of the world of which Nietzsche dreamed is only an eclectic, backroom brew, and one whose air would surely be unbreathable to whoever would try it. But let us be wary of the form of argumentation. A deduction is effected from the "to be" to the "must be": from the ontocosmological axiom "Life is a mixture (a brew)," it is inferred that one must mix in order to live, to live well or truly. For, as there is no true life without "pepper," symbolized by "Blacks" and "Beurs," one must call on "Black" and "Beur" in order to live. Now, the being of pepper communities, what makes up their "cultural specificities," is reduced to the most standardized and sweetened export products (the sweeteners offered by the new noble savages: couscous, paella — and why not pizza and bananas?). Victor Segalen dies a second time from it: "essential Exoticism" is here degraded into exoticism of the inessential, into immediately consumable merchandise, whose sound is heard and which is eaten. Let us say it without amenity: at issue here is a vulgar neotouristic antiracism, adorned with Kodak ideas about the dear "others," and grafted onto a *mixist populism* that is as unengaging as the purist populism of nationalist xenophobes. It is a new avatar of what Segalen named the "degradation of Exoticism," "the diverse going bland."

It remains that these types of evaluation have a common axiological and normative presupposition: *equality* is the supreme value that defines the final cause of antiracist action. Respect or praise for difference and prescription for mixture or for making similarities common constitute diversified means enabling the realization of a single ideal, that of the radical equality of all individuals.

The central and constitutive difficulty of contemporary antiracism derives from the conflictual duality of the means it gives itself to achieve a single aim: differentialist ideology and assimilationist (or mixophilic) ideology are not only heterogeneous but also incompatible, and together form an antinomy.[70] The dominant antiracist vulgate, in its "marginalist" contestatory version (that of the "Beurs" who ostensibly refuse the star system) or in its spectacular and consensual version (SOS-Racisme), is traversed by an insurmountable (by its own means) contradiction between an axiology of difference and one of equalizing mixture. Let us add that "good feelings" and "just causes" do not of themselves furnish the elements of an analysis of the social field nor the principles of a practicable politics. Hyperbolic moralism even risks prohibiting its conditions of appearance. The critique of the illusions of hypermoralism nonetheless makes sense only in that it makes possible the definition of a scientific model of acts of racialization and finally makes thinkable the ethics presupposed by the empirical antiracist positions, lived in the conflict of values.

In an incisive semiautobiographical study, "My Negro Problem — and Ours," published in 1964, Norman Podhoretz openly posed the problem and perceived the principal difficulties. The latter may be summed up by a tragic paradox: one may surmount racial hatreds only by reversing the barriers of race through unconditional and systematic *métissage,* which runs into racial barriers. Let us reread Podhoretz:

> The tragic fact is that love is not the answer to hate — not in the world of politics, at any rate. Color is indeed a political rather than a human or a personal reality and if politics (which is to say power) has made it into a human and a personal reality, then only politics (which is to say power) can unmake it once again. But the way of politics is slow and bitter, and as impatience on the one side is matched by a setting of the jaw on the other, we move closer and closer to an explosion and blood may yet run in the streets.
>
> Will this madness in which we are all caught never find a resting-place? In thinking about the Jews I have often wondered whether their survival as a distinct group was worth one hair on the head of a single infant.... What does the American Negro have that might correspond to this [that is, to the chosenness of the Jewish people that requires them to survive as a people]? His past is a stigma, his color is a stigma, and his vision of the future is the hope of erasing the stigma by making color irrelevant, by making it disappear as a fact of consciousness.
>
> I share this hope, but I cannot see how it will ever be realized unless color does *in fact* disappear: and that means not integration, it means assimilation, it means — let the brutal word come out — miscegenation. The Black Muslims, like their racist counterparts in the white world, accuse the "so-called Negro leaders" of secretly pursuing miscegenation as a goal. The racists are wrong, but I wish they were right, for I believe that the wholesale merging of the two races is the most desirable alternative for everyone concerned. I am not claiming that this alternative can be pursued programmatically or that it is immediately feasible as a solution; obviously there are even greater barriers to its achievement than to the achievement of integration.[71]

9. Antiracism presents a ninth trait, borrowed from *pacifist ideology:* it defines its final objective by the idea of an achievement of peace in the world. Antiracist discourse is regularly accompanied by a denunciation of conflict in general, by a condemnation of the principle of war, by a violent reproof of the passions that are supposed to lead to fighting among human beings. Hatred and contempt are the two passions most often stigmatized — to the point of a symptomological practice that seems characteristic of antiracism: the latter believes it can recognize the presence of racism in the manifestations,

verbal or not, of hatred or contempt. This belief implies a certain ability to decipher ambiguous indices. This violent denial of conflict, which is reduced to an antivalue, identified with radical evil, this *polemophobia* may not be expressed without paradoxes: hatred of hatred (in the objective genitive), contempt for contempt, an intellectual fight against the idea of fighting, war against war. The specter of the polemical element is willingly presented under the positive appearance of an absolute love of peace and of a position taken in favor of "friendship among peoples."[72] The self-representation of antiracism integrates the will to concord, the desire for pacific exchanges, the wish for an amicable planetary dialogue. Several dominant figures of the ideal of universal sympathy may be inventoried, according to empirical models transposed analogically. The model of the couple: the difference of the sexes at the origin of a union of complementaries. The model of familial relations: a primacy of sentiment, a centering on love as a gift. The model of intracommunity relations: the mutual aid and solidarity of the members of the same grouping, friendship. The model of commercial relations: exchange in order mutually to enrich, a presumed factor of peace. The more general model of the complementarity of parts or agencies in interaction: differences are good for the sole reason that they are the occasion to make ties, to form new series, to institute networks of groupings, among those who are different and complementary. Such is the horizon of empathy or sympathy that antiracism must hold up as a regulatory ideal of its action. If racism is violence, its legitimation, and its cult, antiracism is nonviolence.

The nightmare of the war of all against all is hence reversed into the dream of universal and perpetual peace. The ideal of the total and definitive pacification of humanity is imposed as the last finality of antiracist action. Now, the achievement of peace on earth involves the abolition of differences that are not reducible to the various types of treatment reserved by antiracism. The bad differences, those that cannot cash themselves out as fertile complementarity or enriching cooperation — these negative differences must be eliminated. For they would be able only to impose oppositions that would lead to war, which must be avoided absolutely. What governs the imaginary and axiological universe of antiracism is therefore not the mere consideration that war is not desirable; it is rather the idea that war is what should be *unconditionally avoided*. The total abolition of conflict in all its forms furnishes the content of the categorical imperative that antiracism presupposes.

It follows from such an ideal of absolute pacification that one must declare war on war and that it is necessary to dedifferentiate the part of humanity that presents differences irreducible to the criterion of nonpolemical complementarity. Antiracist pacifism hence unveils its normative dream of a unified, homogenized human universe or of a humanity absolutely reconciled with itself. But there must be a preliminary surgical operation: to amputate from the body of humanity the members suspected of provoking and maintaining the gangrene of conflict. To trim, to clean, to scrub up by the destruction of germs of opposition: the pacifist ideal reveals its hidden thanatological motor, its fundamental distrust with regard to the world of life, populated with impure contradictions, made up of troublesome oppositions. Thus antiracism founders in the inconsequence of engaging in total war against its enemy ("racism," "the racists") while legitimating its action of an absolute condemnation of war. Total pacifism henceforth appears to be the most effective means of self-legitimation of a warlike action, insofar as it absolutely delegitimates its enemy.

It seems that we must distinguish, in antiracism, the two types of pacifism that it involves. Beginning with a proposal by Raymond Aron, one may in fact sort out the multiplicity of pacifisms into two principal types: on the one hand, a pacifism that tends to be reduced to the unconditional attitude of nonviolence, a quite negative pacifism in that it is defined by an absolute opposition to war and the absence of a theory of the causes of war;[73] on the other hand, a pacifism that grounds "on a theory of wars a pacific or belligerent action with a view to perpetual peace,"[74] which therefore seeks to suppress the supposed causes of war. In globalist virtuism, the dream of a pacified, unified, amicable, and dialogic world, contemplative pacifism will be recognized, the type 1 pacifism that resides in the attitude determined exclusively by the ethic of conviction.[75] Absolute love of peace substitutes sentimental abstraction, humanitarianist enthusiasm,[76] and tenderness for the sober consideration of war, for the analysis of the forms and meanings of violence. From the absence of a theory of war and its causes derives that of a theory of peace, capable of orienting concrete political action.[77] In the pacifism of conviction, peace cannot be the object of a will that gives itself the means to its objectives; peace is only the object of vague desire. The pacifist dreams of mutual aid, of mutual cooperation and friendship: he would very much like to make this dream come true, but he is powerless to represent the means of doing so to himself. Heterotelic action henceforth appears, as if by an immanent historical judgment: as absolute pacifism is a doctrine of "all or nothing," it is particularly apt to reverse itself into a call to force, into a praise of final violence, that which is supposed to put an end to all violence.[78] Faced with political reality, the vague pacifist desires metamorphosis through total reversal: the *unrecognized enemy* is held up as the *absolute enemy;* the war that has remained unthought becomes total war. Pacifico-dialogic ideology is transmuted into activist demonology. But the powerlessness remains the same throughout this conversion. The "racist," once discovered in her resistant reality, becomes the "dirty racist" that one must annihilate in order to cleanse the world or scrub up society. Projecting onto the "racist" the metaphors of dangerous beast, of parasite, or of contagious impurity is a particular case of the treatment of the enemy who goes unrecognized in the framework of humanitarianism. "When a moral or humanitarian ideology becomes sovereign, [the enemy] becomes an intrinsically guilty being, such that a service is rendered to humanity when he is made to disappear — by euphemism it is said, when he is immolated."[79]

The boundary between type 1 and type 2 pacificism is not easy to determine in all cases. It remains that, contrary to absolute pacifism of conviction, "realistic" pacifism expressly has the objective of acting on social conditions in view of eliminating the presumed causes of wars[80] by depending on a theory of war. The will to act on causes in order to modify effects involves a certain dose of the ethics of responsibility as well as of pragmatism. But utopianism may be found in the determination of final aims, which may be summed up by the idea of perpetual peace.[81] And the demonization of the enemy remains latent.

The fundamental presupposition of humanitarian pacifism is the position of a *politics without an enemy* as the sovereign good. But the idea of a politics without an enemy constitutes the very negation of the essence of the political.[82] Antiracism presents itself as a "fight," a "combat," but it denies the political dimension of this combat by affirming itself as aiming to establish "friendship among peoples" or universal concord, an abstraction made up of the "characteristics of every politics, such as war, violence, and fear."[83] Antiracist pacifism also makes an abstraction of the political meaning of the differences that separate human beings: racial, religious, economic, scientifico-technological, and so on. It makes an abstraction of them either by considering them a priori to be positive (*petitio principii:* there are differences, and they are good) or by neglecting them in favor of similarities (humanitarianism as the love of "everything with a human face" — that is, of what is de facto shared by every human being: the external characteristics of the human race).[84] But if there is a proclaimed antiracist pacifism, there is also a practiced antiracist warmongering (the "fight against racism"), just as racist pacifism (the absolute mutual respect of ethnic differences) is matched by racist warmongering (the struggle of the races for world domination).[85] The political dimension of its combat is hence at once unrecognized, denied, and assumed in the denial by racism.

The moralism practiced in diplomacy contains a pacifist profession of faith whose echo may be found in the basic antiracist position: in the rhetoric of international agencies, anticolonialism, anti-imperialism, pacifism, and antiracism are the object of a nearly unanimous celebration. This antiracist universal consensus is surely suspect: it "does not in the least prevent certain nations from practicing a fundamentally racist politics while rallying with ardor and bombast to world public opinion."[86] But it indicates a general ideological evaluation characteristic of modernity, the unveiling of which has been accelerated by the horror of Hitler's racial exterminations: the condemnation of racism as an intrinsically and absolutely bad end of political action, which follows the condemnation of slavery and tends to be substituted for it during the twentieth century. In many respects, in fact, doctrinal racism has taken the cue from the traditional legitimations of slavery: the being considered inferior (exploitable, detestable, negligible, and exterminable if she becomes "useless" or "harmful") is supposed to be so *by nature.*[87] Here is the scandal par excellence in the eyes of the Moderns. Racism, since it seems to imply both the idea of an inferiority by nature of certain categories of humans and the praise of combat or war involving massacres and genocides, henceforth holds the place of the doctrine that is bad in itself, as such absolutely condemnable. This situation of racism justifies all the means employed to fight against it. But in a paradoxical reversal, "racism" thereby risks becoming the main attribute of the type of the ultimate victim, the one against whom a total war is declared, with the most certain awareness of being on the right path and on the right side.

The modern exaltation of "love of humanity," as it is deployed in humanitarianism, philanthropy, or absolute fraternalist pacifism, seems very much to be the work of ressentiment, and, as Max Scheler has shown, may be understood only as a movement of struggle and protest against the love of the spiritual person (or of one's "neighbor") and of God, on the one hand, and against the love of one's country, on the other hand.[88] That is why the ideal of universal peace involved in antiracist humanitarianism and its "love of humanity" "has very often been *employed* polemically ... from motives of ill-will."[89] Nothing indicates that the situation has been perceptibly modified since Scheler described it as such in 1922 or that it is going to evolve in the world to come. Pacifist humanitarianism remains one of the most effective weapons of ideological warfare, since it appeals to a disposition that is deeply anchored in the mind of the Moderns.

In the conclusion to his talk in January 1927 titled "The Idea of Peace and Pacifism," Scheler impugned the pair formed by *instrumental pacifism,* an explicit discourse as much as a hypocritical position, and *implicit* and shameful *militarism*. We will willingly follow him in this terrain: "We must repudiate the old forms of militararism as well as all types of properly instrumental pacifism. Pacifism of conviction and instrumental militarism, with furtherance of all efforts toward perpetual peace: thus is our requirement."[90] In the same way we think that any form of instrumental universalism is given over to ineffectiveness; its sole reason for existing is thereby destroyed. What remains is to determine the conditions of a requirement of Perpetual Peace that cannot be reduced to a mode of ideological legitimation of a warmongering project.

*Ten*

# Elements of a Theory of Ideological Debate

> For the Ideational mentality, the Sensate mentality is but illusion and blasphemy; for the Sensate mentality, the Ideational mentality is but prejudice, superstition, or pathological disturbance.
> Pitirim A. Sorokin

> It must be concluded that there are as many specific pieces of evidence as there are values that are absolute or considered to be so.
> Eugène Dupréel

## Principles of a Conceptualization

After postulating the existence of two distinct kernels of racialization — inegalitarian (heteroracialization) and differentialist (self-racialization) — we applied ourselves to constructing an ideal type of "racism" on the basis of five traits (chapter 7), in which we found the distinction between two racisms (inegalitarian and differentialist). But in our ideal type, the construction of inegalitarian racism caused a difficulty to appear, expressed in the following paradox: if the rejection of the universal defines the first trait of racism, how does one conceive the possibility of a *universalist racism* without contradiction? For racism, defined as the theory of the inequality of races that grounds that of cultures or civilizations, is well situated within the framework of universalist values and norms. We had a first solution in the hypothesis that inegalitarian racism constitutes only a *pseudouniversalism,* the appeal to universal values in this case stemming only from a strategy of self-legitimation through adaptation to the values accepted in modernity (in the West, it should not be forgotten). But, more profoundly, it appeared to us that we had to state the hypothesis of the irreducibility, indeed of the incommensurability, of two first "conceptions of the world," of two ideologico-discursive universes, each containing a system of specific beliefs and values. It seemed to us that the ideological debates between "racists" and "antiracists," most often dialogues of the deaf, are such only because the arguments in conflict stem from heterogeneous axiological and normative universes: on the one hand, the world of individuo-universalist values and, on the other hand, the world of traditio-communitarianist values (see the figure on p. 275). Between these two worlds, communication is at once inevitable and destined to misunderstanding, to the tightly knotted conflict of absolute evidence. Henceforth, inegalitarian racism would no longer have to be interpreted as a pseudouniversalist variant of racism, which by definition would be traditio-communitarianist. Our hypothesis is that, on the level of systems of (axiological) values, two broad types of racism are distinguished and opposed, according to a regulated mutual misunderstanding: the metaracism grounded on the absolute modern values of individual and universal, "individuo-universalist"; and the metaracism founded on the "holistic" values of belonging to a certain community, distinct from any other by its beliefs and its ways of being and doing. If inegalitarian racism may be conceived only in an individuo-universalist system, differentialist racism may be grounded only in a universe of the traditio-communitarianist type. We have therefore returned to and reformulated the distinction between *Gesellschaft* and *Gemeinschaft* (the "fundamental categories of pure sociology," according to Tönnies), reconceived by Louis Dumont as opposing modern (individualist, universalist, economico-egalitarian) ideology to the holistic or traditional conception, as well as the structural variables of action by which Talcott Parsons attempted to make explicit and to formalize Tönnies's dichotomous model: universalism versus particularism (the first dilemma), performance versus quality (the second dilemma), affective neutrality versus affectivity (the third dilemma), and specificity versus diffusion (encompassment).

Here we can only indicate briefly the anchoring points of our analyses in the sociological tradition. On the horizontal axis, on which we situate the systems of values according to the principle of the various meanings given to existence, it seemed to us necessary to add an axis on which to situate the conceptions of what is (ontology) and the mode of cognition (gnoseology); the second axis, that of spiritualism/materialism, cuts vertically through the first. The figure on p. 277 allows us to show the existence of the following four types of racism: (1) *Universalist/spiritualist racism* ($R_1s$): the evolutionist conception of the progress of civilization and the civilizing mission of the superior and hence more evolved races (the French version is republican colonial ideology); intellectualist and educational racism (Jules Ferry). (2) *Bioevolutionist racism* ($R_1m$): to legitimate the colonization-domination or extermination of the inferior races, which are unsuited to progress (Ernst Haeckel, Clémence Royer). (3) *Communitarianist/spiritualist racism* (or "idealist" or "cultural" racism) ($R_2s$): each race incarnates a spiritual/cultural type that is absolutely different from any other; this type must be preserved (Oswald Spengler, Julius Evola, Ludwig Ferdinand Clauss, Houston Stewart Chamberlain). (4) *Materialist/zoological racism* ($R_2m$): the races are quasi-species; polygenism and polylogism — between them there are neither doors nor windows, and there can be none because of interspecific barriers (Gustave Le Bon, Georges Vacher de Lapouge).

We state the complementary hypothesis that to these four elementary types of racism there polemically correspond four types of antiracism (see the figures on pp. 274 and 276): (1) $AR_2m$, opposed to $R_1s$ (polemical structure 1); (2) $AR_2s$, opposed to $R_1m$ (polemical structure 2); (3) $AR_1m$, opposed to $R_2s$ (polemical structure 3); and (4) $AR_1s$, opposed to $R_2m$ (polemical structure 4).

The debates between racists and antiracists, after being governed by polemical structure 4 alone (that of the partisans of the indefinite progress of the Enlightenment against materialist polygenists), today seem dominated by a composite polemical structure: (1) $AR_2s$ against $R_1s$ and $R_1m$ (the differentialist antiracism of the New Right, against "imperialist racism"), seen by the neoracist "right"; and (2) $AR_1s$ against $R_2s$ and $R_2m$ (the universalist antiracism of the "leagues" against the cultural racism of the New Right and the zoological racism of the "neo-Nazis"), seen by the antiracist leagues.

## The Shock of Rhetorics: The Impossible Dialogue between Margaret Mead and James Baldwin

The example we propose to analyze is a fragment of conversation between Margaret Mead and James Baldwin from a book published in 1971, *A Rap on Race*.

In this dialogue, continued in spite of the difficulties encountered — a truly impossible dialogue, given the lack of common interlocutional space (the a priori of any dialogue) — Mead, a good-willed antiracist anthropologist, summarizes the classical position of the antiracism of the individuo-universalist type, whose base postulate is the total suspension of judgment with respect to race affiliation. The type 1 (individuo-universalist) antiracist argument in fact contains the unconditional prescription of *forgetting race* in general, my own and that of whoever comes into the position of other. The *epochē* of the racial dimension appears as the condition of the antiracist attitude: an antiracist subject worthy of the name recognizes herself in the fact that she unrelentingly practices this ascesis, which consists of placing in parentheses her ethnic perception of herself and others. The antiracist perception of humanity is defined as ethnically adiaphoric.

Let us read this fragment of conversation:

> MEAD: I was speaking in those days about three things we had to do: appreciate cultural differences, respect political and religious differences and ignore race. Absolutely ignore race.
>
> BALDWIN: Ignore race. That certainly seemed perfectly sound and true.
>
> MEAD: Yes, but it isn't anymore. You see, it really isn't true. This was wrong, because —
>
> BALDWIN: Because race cannot be ignored.
>
> MEAD: Skin color can't be ignored. It is real. When we said ignore race... and I was so proud — you know, we were all proud whenever we forgot it.[1]

The reminder that Margaret Mead states concerning the universalist type of antiracist prescriptions shows quite well its internal difficulty.

Whereas, on the one hand, it is a matter of respecting, indeed celebrating, differences (the good collective differences: "cultural," "political," "religious"), on the other hand, it is a matter of suspending all judgment concerning the bad collective differences, which are reduced to racial differences. Forgetting race is the antiracist operation par excellence. But can one forget at will, by an act of will governed by the duty to forget? And how does one justify the duality of the treatment of differences? Why are the ones ("cultural") good and the others ("racial") bad? A first series of aporias hence appears that will not cease to arise in the conversation, that will strive in vain to define "solutions," to open paths that may put aside the difficulties encountered.

Two remarks may be made at this point: (1) The two interlocutors take their distance with respect to the method of "eliminating the question of race," which demands that one perceive only individuals without ethnic affiliation. But the *evidence* of perception (secondary qualities: *color* first of all) imposes itself and continues to impose the question of race. (2) The method of antiracism thereby proposed fails from the fact that it is founded on an empirically false belief: believing that one can *decide* to dissipate a "prejudice" or an "illusion," that theoretical reason has the power to suspend systems of representation inscribed in one recurrent perception or another, which ceaselessly "awakens" the ethnotype one wishes to neutralize and requires the subject continually to take an attitude of unbearable and impracticable self-surveillance. This is a magic belief characteristic of militant rationalism (or of ideologico-political "Cartesianism"): that critical awareness (which is by definition self-critical) and the will to judge only rationally (according to the evidence of theoretical reason or the latest "truths" of "science") suffice to destroy "prejudices." The will based in rationality would have the power to eliminate the productions of the "irrational" involuntary, that is, those issuing from the affectivo-imaginary dimension of humanity. This is the persistent illusion of the antiracism of the enlightened will: the antiracist subject manifests a strangely voluntarist belief on the basis of immoderate rationalism (that theoretical reason can and must govern human behaviors).

Bernard Lewis has duly noted the difficulty in Malcolm X's narration of his pilgrimage to Mecca. On the one hand, the American Negro leader expressed his amazement at the indifference of the Islamic world to the prejudice of color:

> The *color-blindness* of the Muslim world's religious society and the *color-blindness* of the Muslim world's human society: these two influences had each day been making a greater impact, and an in-

creasing persuasion against my previous way of thinking.... There were tens of thousands of pilgrims, from all over the world. They were of all colors, from blue-eyed blonds to black-skinned Africans. But we were all participating in the same ritual, displaying a spirit of unity and brotherhood that my experiences in America had led me to believe never could exist between the white and the non-white.[2]

But, on the other hand, as an "acute and sensitive observer"[3] Malcolm noted what he had seen with surprise during the same pilgrimage, as though alongside aracist fraternity: "There was a color pattern in the huge crowds.... Being from America made me intensely sensitive to matters of color. I saw that people who looked alike drew together and most of the time stayed together. This was entirely voluntary; there being no other reason for it."[4] Nonetheless, Malcolm does not examine the antinomy of the "spirit of unity and brotherhood" and the "color pattern" as such: he simply places the second observation (on drawing together according to racial similarities) after the first (on the neutralization of racial differences). This keen observer of differences and similarities still sketches the problem, "though the beliefs which he had acquired and still cherished at that time prevented him from realizing the full implications of what he saw."[5] In fact Malcolm examines the apparently unconstrained and unprescribed character of this ethnic redifferentiation as very much within the transracial fraternal unity, foreign to all discriminatory practice: "Where true brotherhood existed among all colors, where no one felt segregated, where there was no 'superiority' complex, no 'inferiority' complex—then voluntarily, naturally, people of the same kind felt drawn together by that which they had in common."[6] Malcolm therefore describes redifferentiation by color as a process that appears "natural" and "voluntary": thus is posed the difficult and very delicate problem of the foundation of "race prejudices," on the basis of the exemplary problem of "color prejudice." Is the latter a universal and necessary tendency, whether of "natural" or "cultural" origin? Or again, is it only a psychosocial construction, a particular and contingent one, of which one may define the sociohistorical conditions of appearance and disappearance?

How are we to understand this strange coexistence, in the Muslim crowd, of a realized interracial utopia and a differential racial reorganization by color? This is the same aporia that Baldwin and Mead run up against: antiracism, whether religious-moralist or laic-progressive, requires the neutralization of racial differences that do not cease to reappear in unexpected ways. We know very well the simple and brutal solution to the problem, for it constitutes one of the commonplaces of the antiracist vulgate: because the perception of colors revives or reactivates racist drives, and seems to engender a differential ethnic rallying, then one must propose the objective of radically abolishing differences of color by the one morally practicable means, the *métissage* of all with all. In order to avoid a rebirth of racism, it is proposed to *erase ethnic differences* through universal interethnic crossing. But the latter may fully achieve its aim only in presenting itself as a categorical prescription: the mixing of races must be practiced *by all*, unconditionally, in order to arrive at the expected result.

All this assumes the establishment of an international consensus on this type of solution or the founding of a global antiracist empire whose task is to erase the visible differences between human groups. This is a more than authoritarian vision of relations among human beings: it is a totalitarian utopia. We must henceforth seek another way, at a distance from the dangerous illusions set in motion by antiracist slogans. Here we are stating one of the reasons why antiracism must be seen as an ideological obstacle to be surmounted.

Let us come back to the exemplary conversation between Margaret Mead (representing AR1) and James Baldwin (representing AR2). It illustrates the antinomy of individuo-universalism and traditio-communitarianism as it is manifested in the different ways of being antiracist. So as to simplify the analysis, let us differentially characterize the respective positions of the two types of antiracist: (1) Mead (AR1s): a fight against segregation and for the assimilationist integration of individuals, whatever their groups of ethnic affiliation; and (2) Baldwin (AR2s): a fight against alienation, for the "cultural" identity and authenticity of the ethnic group.

Between positions 1 and 2, there appears no common term; no third way seems to offer the possibility of a synthesis. The incommensurability of 1 and 2 implies an irreducible deafness of each of the two participants in the dialogue to the arguments of the other. The fundamental antinomy of antiracism is expressed by the shock of two undialectizable rhetorics: that of human rights, centered on the individual and humanity (humankind); and that of communitarian identity (ethnic, cultural, national), of the right to difference, centered on the group (whether it is itself defined as ethnic/racial, cultural, or national — see the figure on p. 275).

We could not do better here than to address and develop the analysis that Roger Bastide proposes in his preface to the French translation of the book by Mead and Baldwin. We will distinguish two aspects of the problem: the characterization of two types of antiracism and the sketch of a modelizing reduction of the diametrically opposed antiracist positions.

## The Two Antiracisms

Even though he avoids presenting too abruptly the irreducible kernels of the dispute, Roger Bastide poses the problem extremely well by identifying the respective positions:

> Communication is not identification. It does not necessarily lead to communion. It may allow only reciprocal understanding. Of course, Baldwin and Mead both want integration, but they do not conceive of it in the same way. At bottom what Mead attempts, beyond the differences of color that are only somatic differences, is to find a cultural field that is common to whites and blacks. She defines this common cultural field according to the model of miscegenation: blacks must claim their white ancestors, and whites must also share their ancestors with blacks. Thus hate would disappear, for one will have repaired, on this commonality of ancestors, familial unity. But Baldwin, while accepting to be "American" and not "African"..., cannot accept supporting integration, since it is unilateral and requires blacks to become white; there must be struggle...even more against alienation than against segregation, against the loss of a Negro identity more than against the isolation of Negroes in society. Integration, yes — but in the acceptance of cultural differences, not in assimilation to white values. Mead is first and foremost concerned with the political problem that whites hold the reins of power and do not want to give them up; and Baldwin with the problems of personality: he does not want to lose his authenticity.[7]

The opposition between manners of arguing is clear: on the one hand, the issue is the primacy of assimilation through equal rights and treatments; on the other hand, it is the primacy of the conservation or development of the constitutive characteristics of an "authentic" identity.

## The Dualist Model

The dissension we have observed between Mead and Baldwin is itself not of a particularist type; rather, it has a universal value. That is why the identification of their respective positions enables the elaboration of two ideal types of antiracism, which are opposed in a dualist model derived from the pairing of society and community (Tönnies) specified by the opposition between universalism and particularism in Talcott Parsons's general theory. Such a modelization involves the consideration of the *metaphysical* foundations of the type 1 and type 2 rhetorics.

Bastide begins by defining Mead's trans- or metacultural perspective, which may well be considered the professional ideology of the "liberal" or "progressive" ethnologist: individuo-universalism, to which there corresponds a politico-educational treatment of the problem posed by "racism" — a centering on the *equal rights* of all citizens. Egalitarianism and individualism are the ideological kernels presupposed by the universalist view on the racial question:

> Margaret Mead, because she is an individualist, is also a universalist — as universalism is, as Parsons showed very well, a consequence of individualism. For her, every racism...rests on the same basis: the belief in the superiority of one group over others. The white man...bears, as the expression goes, the same "burden," that of considering himself master of the world and responsible for the progress of humanity.[8]

Baldwin's antiracist positions presuppose an ethnopluralist perspective, which lays out a particularist treatment of the problem: a claiming of the rights of cultural minorities, an affirmation of differential communitarian identities. Thus is sketched the framework of a nonuniversalist, indeed antiuniversalist, antiracism: "To the contrary, Baldwin is situated in a particularist perspective; he gives more importance to social and cultural contexts, which vary according to place and time, than to the general traits of human nature."[9]

It is the case either that one emphasizes the similarities, even if it means reaffirming the primacy of "human nature" over the diversity of ethnocultural diversity (AR1), or that one emphasizes the differences and denounces any universalist perspective as accompanying an enterprise of dispossession and "alienating" uniformization (AR2).

Bastide considers the two views of the human world in opposition to each other: the "external" view (from the outside) of anthropology, which studies differences, marks down similarities, and takes the comparative position derived from the distantiation required by scientific objectification; and the "internal" view (from the inside) of the spokesperson, the spontaneous sociologist of a particular group (his own) he who does not want to see from above the whole field of differences, but rather wishes to express the defining character of a collective identity. Two epistemologies stand in opposition:

> In short, Mead's arguments are situated within the framework of an anthropology: if racism comes from the idea of the superiority of one race over others, it may be made to disappear through education. Baldwin's are situated in the framework of sociology: each expression of racism poses a particular problem, and one must, each time, seek a singular response to it. It is the case that Margaret Mead speaks in the name of a white elite that has molded a transcultural thought. James Baldwin, to the contrary, speaks in the name of a Negro group that...wants to remain faithful to a communitarian culture.[10]

Two ideological kernels appear that enable a better distinction between type 1 and type 2 antiracism: (1) AR1 is centered on the relation of *inequality* (superior/inferior), whose legitimacy it impugns and which it presupposes to be a fundamental element of racism in general. Its conception of racism is that of a doctrine of inequality among racial groups, affirmed by the racial group (or the racial groups) that defines itself as superior. Now, the pairing of equality and inequality has no meaning or value except in the individuo-universalist universe in which AR1 is situated. (2) AR2 is centered on the relation of *difference* (between proper collective identity and all the other identities), which is assumed to be not only legitimate but also endowed with an infinite value. Its conception of racism is based on the idea of a negation of difference, which comes down to the abolition of collective identities in favor and in the name of some universal model.

We are now in possession of the elements that permit a systematization. If in fact we have been able to distinguish two antiracisms (AR1 and AR2), we can also distinguish two racisms (R1 and R2) according to the ideologico-discursive universe that they respectively presuppose: R1 and AR1 are elaborated on the bases of the evidence and prenotions furnished by the archi-ideology that we have named *individuo-universalism;* R2 and AR2 are constituted on the ground

Elements of a Theory of Ideological Debate    269

of evidence and prenotions furnished by *traditio-communitarianism,* the ideal type of a set of representations and arguments irreducible to individuo-universalism. Such a dualist model of racisms (R1 and R2) and antiracisms (AR1 and AR2), besides that it separates supposedly homogeneous ideological discourses, effects a fundamental *relativization* of the qualifications *racist* and *antiracist.*

The specter of an ideology of substance inscribed in antiracist polemical discourse is at this point removed: the illusion of a substantial subject ("the racist," the one whose being is to be racist) is definitively dissipated. The act of naming the "racist" is in a parallel gesture deabsolutized: everything is relative, including racism and antiracism — that is the only absolute. We will see that such a decline of the racist and antiracist absolutes opens a new space of problems, specifically the classical problems of relativism, perspectivism, and historicism. We will therefore come back to it.

Let us meanwhile proceed to several complementary clarifications of the polemical structure that links type 1 and type 2 racisms and antiracisms, according to the figure of the chiasmus (see the figure below; see also the figure on p. 276).

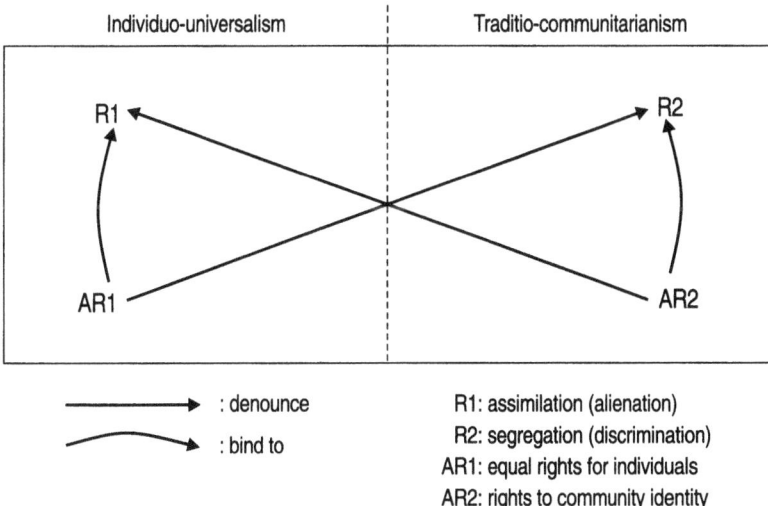

1. In each of the two ideologico-discursive universes, the field of visibility of the antiracist genre has a blind spot: AR1 does not see R1, and AR2 does not see R2. But R1 willingly presents itself as AR1

(universalist), and R2 ordinarily poses as AR2 (differentialist): they have intersecting ideological strategies.

2. Each type of antiracist genre is blind to the other: AR1 does not see AR2, which in turn does not see AR1.

Let us recall that the proposed schematization represents, in the form of a model, what really happens in the conflictual field in which "racisms" and "antiracisms" confront each other (accuse, mutually denounce each other). But the agencies represented do not themselves possess the encompassing representation of the real functioning of their interactions. It might be that the principle of unawareness and the absolutization of each point of view (its exclusivist closure on itself) constitute conditions of appearance and functioning of the two "antiracisms" and their respective "racisms."

3. Everything happens as if each of the two "racisms" were the troubling dream of the specific antiracism that it targets, its negative representation, its waking nightmare: AR1 "dreams" R2, which it denounces, as AR2 "dreams" R1, which it denounces.

4. According to AR1, whose dominant self-image is the defense of human rights — that is, equal rights for every human being (the requirement of universality whose point of application is the particular individual) — "racism" (R2) is a theoretical elaboration of sociocentrism or ethnocentrism. "Racism" is produced by a radicalization of the self-centering of the group, which implies a self-attribution of superiority (most often absolute, but susceptible of being relativized). This individuo-universalist conception of racism is based on the postulate of the continuity between ethnocentrism and racism, one of whose implications is that the central objective of antiracism is the total elimination of ethnocentrism. This is the image of the *Other;* these are the traits of the one to whom "racism" is imputed, when he is seen in the type 1 spiritual-cultural world: ethnocentrism, self-preferential inegalitarianism, the naturalization of the scale of values. The indices of racism are then the following: exclusion, segregation, discrimination — that is, all the sociopolitical forms derived from the combination of inequality and hostility toward those presumed inferior. The difference is as such suspect, as soon as any manifestation of "racism" assumes a process of differentiation among individuals according to their groups of affiliation. Heterophilia is considered to be racizing, and the dominant opinion is that the roads to racism are paved with good differentialist intentions.

The praise of difference would be only the ruse of inequality, the mask of the intention to discriminate. The characteristics attributed to "racism" are elaborated forms of nonintegration, of nonassimilation. What follows is one of the specific traits of the self-image projected by AR1: the requirement of integration, the ideal of assimilation.

5. According to AR2, whose dominant self-image is the defense of the right to intercommunity difference, "racism" (R1) is an elaboration of the legitimating ideology of the majoritarian and dominant group, which is characterized by its hegemonic tendency, its assimilationist claim, and its will to make uniform the modes of cultural existence. "Racism" is "intensionally" defined by the will to eradicate communitarian identities and extensionally defined by the practice of a leveling imperialism. Universalism is decoded, demystified as the principal mode of legitimation of "racism," the latter a monster feeding on living differences. But these differences, once devoured and assimilated, are not reborn: a decadentist and catastrophist imaginary accompanies the conception of "racism" as a process with two sides, heterophobia (from insensitivity to communitarian differences to their rejection) and heterophagia (assimilation of differences by their reduction to a dominant model). Heterophagia is here only the instrument of heterophobia: one makes differences disappear only by making them similar to oneself. The requirement of equality is from this moment suspect; it is unmasked as a ruse of the will to dispossession, as a pseudomoral mode of legitimation of the enterprise of the dedifferentiation of ethnocultural wholes. These are the main presuppositions of type 2 antiracist evidence, the intransigent claim of the right to collective difference.

## Aporia and Dialogue

If one reduces dialogue to an exchange of arguments, on the general model of conversation, then dialogue between Mead (the enunciating subject of AR1) and Baldwin (the enunciating subject of AR2) has taken place; it is therefore possible, though difficult. But here is the zero degree of the dialogic process: interlocution becomes dialogue not only through the exchange of arguments founded on the agreement to converse but also through the position of a common finality considered to be superior to the positions of each of the interlocutors. The finality of dialogue is, in its general form, a third way, defined by an agreement on principles and produced either as the exclusive choice of one of the two positions (the one or the other) or as the synthesis of the two (the one and the other), as their negative conjunction (neither one nor the other) assumed by the invention of a completely other position. Commenting on the conversation between Mead and Baldwin, Bastide recognizes this, willingly albeit implicitly, from the fact of a conception of dialogue that is not strict:

> Dialogue is therefore possible, not communion. For two worlds collide, or, if one prefers, two irreconcilable value systems, the universalist spirit and the communitarian spirit, the elimination of the past (let the dead bury the dead) and to the contrary the recovery of the past (one exists only insofar as a proper lineage is created).[11]

If no third term may be envisaged, if synthesis is absent by principle, if reconciliation on principles seems prohibited, it is the case that we find ourselves before an *antinomy:* there are two opposing theses that seem to be endowed with equal legitimacy once they are brought back to the spiritual-cultural universe that their foundations confer on them. Let us accept that there is dialogue, but *aporetic* dialogue. We see this more clearly: conversation has the real function of bringing to light the hiatus between two incommensurable positions. But the meeting of the two positions does not engender a process of elevation; conversation is not grasped by an ascensional dynamism: agreement seems achievable only on the reasons of profound discord.[12] In the framework of such a dialogue, consensus therefore intervenes only on the conditions of dissension. Nonetheless, let us not believe that this is a vain agreement: it is the "indispensable prelude to a peaceable meeting in which one accepts coming to terms with the other in order to produce meaning."[13] At least it is the object of a wager: *eirēnē* against *agōn*, the dialogal virtue of irenism against the agonistic transposition of violence.[14] For the practical problem rests in an observation and an interrogation: there are differences, there is alterity. How does one relate to them without violence? Here one can only bet. Here there is a specific tragic element: the tragic appears in neither the individuo-universalist nor the traditio-communitarianist framework, but rather in their shock, in the common experience of their reciprocal extraneousness. These two universes seem to have to exist in parallel, to remain unknown to each other, to shock each other. They seem devoted to being mutually unaware of each other or to running up against each other in the dispute: the chiasmus of denunciations is engendered naturally — according to a natural logic — by the intersection of misrecognitions and the insurmountable fact that each universe is a scandal for the other. To know such a process is to be removed from it in an objective gaze, but not to be removed as a living subject: we live in only one spiritual-cultural universe, in which we think, know, evaluate, believe, project.

Before moving further, let us note an important aspect of dualism, which Bastide duly brings to bear: the placement in parentheses of the *past* by any argument of individuo-universalist type, which tends to devalorize absolutely the past belonging to one or another community. The past is always surpassed or to be surpassed. Opposed to this attitude of indifference or hostility toward the pairing of past and community is the affirmation of the incomparable foundational value of the past in an argument of traditio-communitarianist type. The self-affirmation of a communitarian identity may be made only in relation to a past assumed as such, that is, to a heritage, alone authorizing a self-foundation. This heritage, to invoke a Kantian distinction, has no price, as its value is situated beyond any price: the infinite value of community heritage is the collective equivalent of the incomparable dignity of the person. There is hence a specific value of community life. More profoundly: moral value is as a whole enclosed in the *duty of self-preservation* of the living community, encompassing its memory and its desire for descent. The morality of individuals, of particular persons, is such only in that it represents collective morality. In truth, here there are no more individuals in the strict ("modern") sense but only representatives of the whole, "I's" without identity other than that of the "we" that they represent more or less faithfully and with participatory intensity.

Here there is an axiological language that is perhaps untranslatable into an individuo-universalist language, which accords infinite value only to particular persons (all "equal" as such, by their "dignity") or to Humanity as an Idea.

Let us reformulate the antinomy found at the heart of the debate, by taking account of the particular circumstances and the idiosyncrasies. Antiracist thesis 1 is defended in the name of a decentered, transcultural individualism, by a "white" intellectual refusing to act as such, aiming to free herself of all sociocentrism and striving to represent the point of view of the universal, to be only a neutral functionary of Humanity. Antiracist thesis 2 is defended by a "black" intellectual proceeding to a self-affirmation of his ethnic identity, presenting himself as spokesperson for a minority (threatened, oppressed, "victimized," or "victimizable") group, therefore clearly assuming his ethnocultural affiliation. Militant communitarianism, reflected and declared ethnocentrism: here is what is presented as the method of liberation. It is a radical negation of all collective identity, of all particularism, on the one hand; and a hyperbolic and exclusive affirmation of a collective identity, on the other hand.

## Ideal Types and Models of Intelligibility

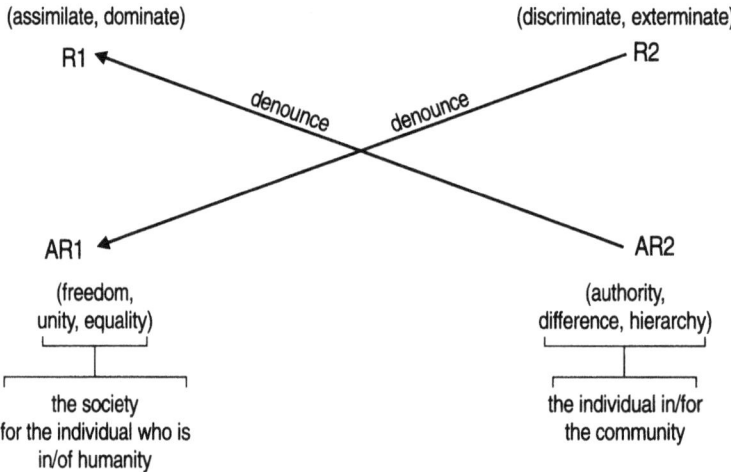

The engendering of antinomic antiracisms:
*ethic/economic antiracism* (AR1)
and *ethnic/traditionalist antiracism* (AR2)

# The dualist model of ideologico-discursive universes
## (the two incommensurable axiologies)

| IDEOLOGICAL POSITIONS | RHETORICAL TYPES | | |
|---|---|---|---|
| | **1** *Arguments of the society type: individuo-universalism* | *Mixed forms* | **2** *Arguments of the community type: traditio-communitarianism* |
| **Racism (R)** | R1 (racism according to AR2) ethnocentric universalism (planetary uniformity/lack of differentiation): the global empire led by the most "civilized" <br> { homophilia <br> { heterophobia <br> { "anthropophagia" <br> R of assimilation (genocide = destruction of collective identities, dissolution of cultural specificities and ethnic types) <br> ← Franco-republican type (assimilate) <br> ← domination/exploitation <br> ← communism <br> ← imperial universalism | Inequality <br> Intolerance <br><br> Colonialism (oppress) <br><br> Apartheid (discrimination) <br> Totalitarianism <br> Nationalism | R2 (racism according to AR1) mixophobic differentialism <br> → (destitution of the universal/derealization of the individual): planetary apartheid <br> { homophobia <br> { heterophilia <br> { "anthropoemia" <br> → Anglo-Saxon type (segregate) <br> R of exclusion { differentiate <br> { purify <br> { cleanse <br> → separation, exclusion ────→ extermination <br> (genocide = collective massacre) <br> → Nazism <br> → community of people |
| **Antiracism (AR)** | AR1 <br> individualism (individual identity)/difference <br> egalitarianism <br> humanism <br> rationalism <br> human rights <br> chosen/invented identities <br> universalism (surpassing differences) <br> { against the confinement of the individual in a closed collectivity <br> { fight against segregation <br> respect human rights <br> abolition of group prejudices ↔ | Tolerance <br> Dialogism | AR2 <br> group identitarianism (collective identity/difference) <br> hierarchism <br> particularism <br> traditionalism <br> the right to difference (ethnopluralism) <br> prescribed/assumed identities <br> differentialism (preserve differences) <br> { preserve the identity and authenticity of the group <br> { fight against alienation <br> → respect the rights of peoples <br> → affirmation of group identities |

## The vicious circle of racisms and antiracisms

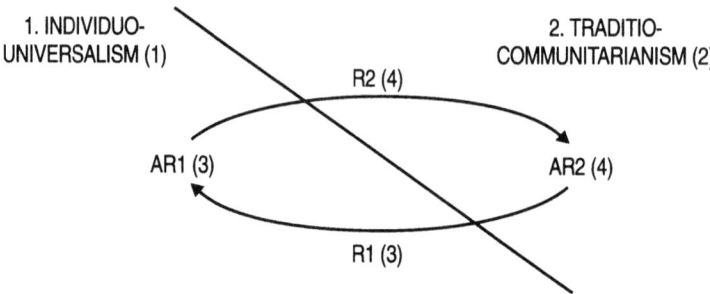

A reduction and modelization of the racism/antiracism controversies according to the fundamental dichotomy of "individuo-universalism versus traditio-communitarianism."

Hypothesis: the *irreducible duality* of type 1 racism (R1) and type 2 racism (R2), which are accompanied by their respective antiracist arguments (AR1 and AR2).

1. (*Gesellschaft*) (Tönnies); (universalism and performance) (Parsons); (modern ideology) (Dumont); (familial type: egalitarian nuclear/northern France) (Todd).

2. (*Gemeinschaft*) (Tönnies); (particularism and quality) (Parsons); (holistic conception) (Dumont) [amodern, premodern]; (familial type: authoritarian/ Germany) (Todd).

3. AR1 and R1: dominants and of the dominants (concurrent derivations of French ideology: liberty, equality) → R2 is the most visible racism, if not the only one.

4. AR2 and R2: dominated and of the dominated (France) (authority, hierarchy); dominants when values are those of the authoritarian family.

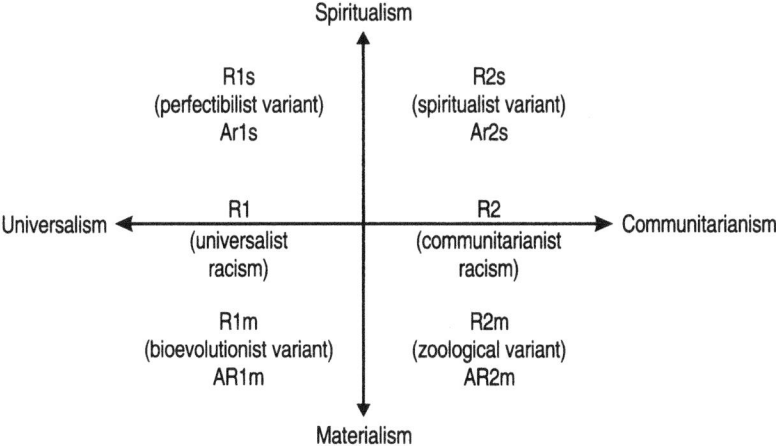

*Part IV*

# Beyond Racism

*Eleven*

# Pessimism: Philanthropy in Spite of Humanity

### Heroic Pessimism: Postoptimist Humanism

> *All deep thought must begin with despair.*
> Lev Shestov

There is little doubt that our considerations may be called pessimistic. This is first of all the case from the fact that our analyses, besides designating the irreducible spiritual-cultural dualism from which the antinomies between the individuo-universalist and traditio-communitarianist theses derive, authorize both the diagnosis of an inconsistency in the positions termed antiracist and the prognosis of their inevitable inefficacy. These positions are aggravated by the illumination of their racistoid (the arising of antiracist "racism," directed against the supposed "racists") or racistogenic (the engendering of "anti-antiracisms") perverse effects. A terrible thought: everything happens as though only racism "won" in the end — racism would be the term common to racisms and antiracisms. Our considerations are pessimistic also because our critique of the claims of critical reason logically leads to the conclusion that the thought of critical rationalism as such, with its ideals of emancipation tied to the much-exalted instrument of free judgment, is the bearer of dogmatic illusions and fanaticism just as much as its declared enemies (tradition, superstition, revelation, prejudices, and so on). There is a circle of corruption, drawn by interlinked ideological corruptions, a fatal circle on which the speculative will is broken, itself a tributary of the critical reason that is part of the circle. Only a radical pessimism is in accord with such views: the ethical requirements, of which that of liberty forms the essential type, appear not only as unrealizable in this world but also as engendering unforeseen, unwanted, and unacceptable effects. Nonetheless, this pessimism is absolute only in the speculative order, in which the ideals of reason turn back against themselves, destroy themselves; and also with regard to the possibility of "moralizing" in the empirical world of human beings, a place of the irrealization, derealization, and dysrealization of hopes and ethical requirements.

There yet remains a precarious refuge for optimism, of which Max Horkheimer said, "It consists in the fact that one must, in spite of everything, try to do and achieve what one holds to be true and good."[1] Is this "to be theoretically pessimistic and practically optimistic"?[2] The formulation of critical theory still seems to us naively optimistic. It illustrates the optimism that remains among those disappointed by historical optimism, that of revolutionary messianism. But optimism may be defended only after being "reduced," purified of all illusions issuing from the necessitarianist conception of progress. Optimism is the quality of the action that is affirmed only *in spite of* and never *because of*. The optimism that remains is an optimism not grounded in just any certainty. Situated beyond any necessitarianist assurance, it orients action without rational or historical legitimacy. That is why optimism is no longer tolerable except as a heroic attitude inscribed in the everyday. The vacillation of the modern gnoses engenders the existence of an everyday heroism. The hope is only the continued refusal to despair, a refusal without a *why* and in spite of all the good reasons to be resigned to despairing. There is therefore in humanity the means to resist good reasons, the means to go further than the disappointing view of universal evil — and the strength to refuse to kneel before the sole necessary truths. This metaphysical nostalgia gives humanity the fragile and firm assurance of being able to take distance both from the given and from logical truths.[3] I may not say what I am or who I am; I have the sole intuition that I am not only of this world. It is the sense of my metaphysical existence that grounds my ungrounded optimism, my heroism without a *why*. The limit-formula of such an extremely pessimistic optimism could be not to have any need at all to hope to act *as though* I were hoping. This ethic of the *as though* is surely the neighbor of skepticism, with which it shares certain positions and presuppositions. It is nevertheless separated from skepticism by an abyss. Its seriousness is situated at the antipodes of the smiling skepticism of the hedonist who has become one in order to step back from all doubts, and even to move to doubting the value of doubt itself. The seriousness of ethics, another name for the responsibility[4] to which the latter is an answer, digs out an infinite distance in the face of the amoral resignation of the absolute pessimism that has removed itself from "logical suicide" (Dostoyevsky) only in order to devote itself to the breeziness of conformist aestheticism.

That is why heroism is the virtue incarnated by such an optimism, the latter barely namable as such. Absolute pessimism is in fact normally accompanied by a radical skepticism that opens the way to the basest reconciliation with given reality. This skepticism that keeps itself at an equal distance from all values, an aesthetic nihilism, contains in itself the supreme ruse that leads to the total acceptance of what is: it finishes as conformism, which is certainly its secret. Why in fact distance oneself, scandalize oneself, revolt, why refuse the unacceptable, refuse resignation before the intolerable, if all things have value — if therefore the unacceptable and the intolerable are only troubling fictions, illusions harmful to the tranquil soul, secretly the last supreme value? Some would say for "peace," the supreme value that one should want at any price. But not everything has the same value. We do not know why. The meaning of value is without a *why*. If humanism is a still-open possibility, it can only be heroic.[5]

Perhaps one must be content with a pragmatic, "vitalist," or "existential" argument, in favor of hope. That was one of Malraux's lessons: "All seeds begin by rotting, but some of them germinate. A world without hope is...suffocating."[6] Hope is a transcendental determination of human existence, a condition of desirability of the human world, its condition of "breathability." Hope, that "weakness" (Montherlant) or that "cowardliness" (Spengler), appears as a condition of the meaning of life. Waiting for deliverance, the belief in a promise of redemption of this world,[7] faith in the possibility of a liberation: here is the part of the biblical heritage that is a component of our eternal (because inchoative) escape from nihilism. The story of the Exodus: the escape from Egypt and the end of servitude, crossing the desert, the Covenant at Sinai, the Promised Land. Michael Walzer, after showing the centrality of this thematic in Western thought, in its political culture, concludes his study as follows: "The 'door of hope' is still open; things are not what they might be — even when what they might be isn't totally different from what they are."[8] One must hope for "a better place, a world more attractive, a promised land,"[9] but with the firm assurance that "the way to the land is through the wilderness"[10] and that "there is no way to get from here to there except by joining together and marching."[11]

## The Failures of Abstract Universalism: Genocide and Deducing the Value of Cultural Differences

A conceptual distinction introduced by Richard Marienstras allows a clarification of the impugnment of abstract universalism, in the name of some elaboration of the differentialist perspective. In a study titled "Réflexions sur le génocide," Marienstras from the outset posits a distinction between two types of individual-to-collective human relation: (1) the individual's affiliation to the human *species*, without mediation; and (2) the individual's affiliation to human *kind*, through the mediation constituted by integration into a community.[12]

Marienstras proposes to term mediating communities "elementary collectivities," which he defines as the exclusive place of existence of the differences in which individuals find the resources of their will to live. To be is to be different, by living the constitutive differences of an elementary collectivity: "Human beings are what they are only through particular collectivities."[13]

> The relationship to *humankind* does not result from the fact that the human being belongs to the *human species;* rather, it results from his insertion into an elementary collectivity.... Insofar as they belong to humankind, and not only to the human species, human beings are what they are only through their differences, and abolished differences cannot be compensated.[14]

That is why genocide, as a mechanism of destruction set to work against the entire system of differences that give meaning, cannot simply be considered as historical fact — as absolutely scandalous by its horror, of course, but in the past. The inhumanity of genocide seems to be endowed with a power of persistence in the cultural memory of those who must be called survivors. And the latter, no more than the remaining exemplars of an animal species condemned to extinction, "cannot again find reasons to live or hope in the spectacle presented by the flourishing of neighboring, competitive, or rival species."[15] Genocide inflicts a definitive wound and effects an absolute rupture by the reflection it demands, engendering the suspension of the meaning of existence. Genocide is not reducible to a "mere" attack on the human race, from which the latter can only recover one day, in view of its resources. The "speceic" denunciation of "crimes against humanity" thereby authorizes an "indignation full of hope." But, notes Marienstras insistently, "the outrage committed against the human *species* brings one to forget — or allows one to forget — the crime committed against human*kind.*"[16] Now, the two types of attack may not be likened, nor may they be differentiated by the number of victims within the same class of crimes. Moreover, crime against the human race may, in the last analysis, be deemed to be "not irremediable as long as there are living human beings."[17] But the loss of a collectivity is irremediable, and the memory of its disappearance inconsolable. That is why it is not excessive to say that any prolonged meditation on genocide "can lead only to madness, or to that despair bordering on death that rips a being from his cultural, social, and genetic bases and places him in absolute solitude — a solitude that beats with extreme futility, with extreme inanity any project, any vision of the individual or collective future, any relationship with the rest of humanity."[18] In the perspective belonging to the destroyed community, the end of a world that is its own is equivalent to the end of the world. Empathy is thus required in order to comprehend such a collapse: "One must place oneself *in the perspective* of the destroyed collectivity, that is, in the total absence of perspective that, for the survivors of that collectivity, results from its destruction." For the internal perspective of the destroyed collectivity "represents the truth of *humankind* in the same fashion as the subjective perspective of the man facing death represents the truth of the *human condition.*"[19]

The consolations that fall from the sky of "speceic" universalism exert all their effects only on condition of encountering a system of values that is rarely made explicit, from the very fact that it is melded with the common axiological atmosphere. For further clarity, let us designate this atmosphere by names of doctrines: these values and norms of the ambiance of the modern world are those of the abstract universalism ("every human being is a human being") issuing from the ideologization of rationalism ("every human being is a being endowed with reason"). So why defend the right to existence of cultures, communities, collective identities? Why, for example, "re-create, perpetuate, or resurrect Jewish culture"? Marienstras answers with an admirable sobriety: "To this we must respond as Sartre did with respect to literature: the world can obviously do without the Jews and their culture. But it can do without man even better."[20] There is no *why*, because the question is always asked from the perspective of abstract universalism, which denies it any legitimacy. Collective identities have no status in the space, instituted by ideologico-political rationalism, in which the atomic individual recognizes himself in every other and perceives this formal recognition as a proof of universality, of a direct link with the human universal. The differences among cultures, in the individuo-universalist problematic, may be considered only as vestiges, survivals, and archaisms destined to be fatally and happily abolished by the march of progress. And the latter has a meaning, given by a direction that is sometimes made explicit: the final realization of the ethnic and cultural homogeneity of the human species, made possible by the total destruction of these obstacles to planetary homogenization represented by the cultural identities that refuse to disappear.

In the face of the arrogance of planetarianist ideology, one may reaffirm, with Marienstras, that "the will to live does not have to prove its right to life. It is the will to destroy and the acquiescence to death that must henceforth furnish their proofs."[21] If therefore the will of a collectivity not to allow the effacement of its differences is without a *why*, if it "is enough that the group exists, that it works to maintain, renew, and re-create its identity," the meaning of genocide is to abolish the cultural conditions of all meaning.[22] From that moment on, and "in spite of the ideologies of consolation, the death of collectivities is not fertile but rather sterile"; this death can only be the first act of a continually committed murder, because it is "the irremediable abolition of a quantity that has been."[23] And even so, there are some who have barely hesitated to dare "to affirm that it is progressive to level the ways of life, to annihilate the gestures and speeches on which, along with the multiple past of human beings, their present diversity comes to the surface."[24] The progressive claim here is only the most opportunistic means of seduction of the will to destroy humankind, by the terroristic achievement of the absolute cultural unity of the human species. Such is the universalism that must be refused absolutely. But imperial universalism should not be confused with the requirement of universality, of which its is precisely the *counterfeit*.

# Twelve

# Ethics: The Infinite of the Law above the Law?

> It is deplorable to see everybody debating about the means, never the end. Everybody thinks about how he will get on in his career, but when it comes to choosing a career or a country it is fate that decides for us. Blaise Pascal

## From Duty to Ends, and On Values (Kant)

> *Ethics does not give laws for* actions (justice *does that), but only for* maxims *of actions.* Immanuel Kant

> *It nonetheless remains true that there are acts to which we must absolutely say no, whatever their circumstances; and that is what constitutes the permanent value of Kantian formalism.* Jean Wahl

Let us begin with the second formulation of the categorical imperative: "Act in such a way that you always treat humanity, whether in your own person or in the person of any other, never simply as a means, but always at the same time as an end."[1] We already know that we may make universality, "universalizability,"[2] the sign of the action accomplished out of duty. A categorical imperative represents an action as objectively necessary, without any relation at all to a condition or another end, as good in itself.[3] The cited formula of the supreme practical imperative assumes that "man, and in general every rational being, *exists* as an end in himself, *not merely as a means* for arbitrary use by this or that will."[4] If humanity must be considered as an end in itself, it is because it is the form in which reasonable nature is given to us.[5] Man therefore has a value that is neither measurable nor conditional, and this fact distinguishes him absolutely from "all the objects of inclination" that "have only a conditioned value."[6] Man, certainly, but as a reasonable being: this point must be insisted on in order to avoid any anthropocentric and empiricist misinterpretation of Kantian ethics. Kant is nonetheless as clear as he is firm on the question: "Suppose...there were something *whose existence* has *in itself* an absolute value...; then in it, and in it alone, would there be the ground of a possible categorical imperative....Now I say that man, and in general every rational being, *exists* as an end in himself, *not merely as a means.*"[7] If the moral law must "hold for all rational beings..., and *only because of this* can it also be a law for all human wills,"[8] this means that "anthropology does not play any role, it must not and cannot play one when it is a question of grounding morals."[9] The absolute validity of the moral law means that it is valid for all reasonable beings, human or not, in all possible worlds.[10] That is why any naive interpretation, of humanist type, must be excluded from the second maxim: "It does not signify that the person as such is an end; it does not establish a humanism or a personalism....The end, here, is not the man but the humanity in him, that is, universal reason acting through goodwill."[11]

To reasonable beings, "persons," there must be accorded a *universal* (or unconditioned) *value,* while to "things" it is only necessary to attribute a *relative* (or conditional) *value.*[12] The distinction between things and persons is here fundamental:

> Beings whose existence depends, not on our will, but on nature, have none the less, if they are non-rational beings, only a relative value as means and are consequently called *things*. Rational beings, on the other hand, are called *persons* because their nature already marks them out as ends in themselves — that is, as something which ought not to be used merely as a means — and consequently imposes to that extent a limit on all arbitrary treatment of them (and is an object of reverence).[13]

The foundation of the supreme practical principle is that "rational nature exists as an end in itself";[14] we must understand by this such an end as may not be replaced by any other or subordinated to any other end for which it would be the means.[15] As reasonable beings must reciprocally treat one another as ends in themselves,[16] it is possible to conceive their systematic unification under common laws. Thus appears the ideal of the "kingdom of ends,"[17] if by *kingdom* we understand "a systematic union of different rational beings under common laws."[18] It follows that Kantian morality impugns any recourse to a cosmological or technical finality (an instrumental rationality)[19] but does admit finality in a strictly formal and "abstract" sense, as provided in the maxims of the moral rule. If in fact the subject is called on to act in such a way that the maxim of his action may institute a universal legislation — that is, in such a way that he may consider himself a legislator and subject in the kingdom of ends made possible by the freedom of the will — the supreme end of morality is to promote reason in the world, to cause reason to act or to exist, to institute the kingdom of the universal.[20] The kingdom of ends that must be instituted is only the kingdom of autonomous good wills. Thus may one conclude that "finality, that idea of reason in action, is reduced in Kant to universality."[21]

What is essential here is the introduction of the concept of humanity as an end in itself, as human nature is a "concrete specification of the reasonable being."[22] Now, a reasonable being "belongs to the kingdom of ends as a *member,* when, although he makes its universal laws, he is also himself subject to these laws."[23] He belongs to it, adds Kant, "as its *head* when as the maker of laws he is himself subject to the will of no other":[24] his will is then "a perfect or holy will."[25]

Let us place ourselves in the kingdom of ends: every action possesses a value there, but these values are different, presenting themselves on a hierarchical scale. "In the kingdom of ends everything has either a *price* or a *dignity,*"[26] affirms Kant, restating a distinction of Stoic origin.[27] It is a matter of conceiving well "the Idea of the *dignity* of a rational being who obeys no law other than that which he at the same time enacts himself."[28] For this to take place, one must more precisely determine, in their difference, the two modes of assessing value: "If [something] has a price, something else can be put in its place as an *equivalent;* if it is exalted above all price and so admits of no equivalent, then it has a dignity."[29] The first criterion of that which has a price is represented by substitutability or interchangeability: that *thing* has a price that is recognized in that, being commensurable with other "things," it is exchangeable with equivalent things. Among the things that simply have a price, that is, "a relative value," one must moreover distinguish between those that have a *market price (Marktpreis)* and those that have a *fancy price (Affektionspreis)*.[30] They have a market price when they are relative "to universal human inclinations and needs":[31] the same may be said for "skill and diligence in work."[32] Their relative or extrinsic value stems from the realm of usefulness, of the satisfaction of needs, or of the responsiveness to inclinations. Things have a sentimental price when, without even bearing on needs or penchants, they correspond "with a certain taste — that is, with satisfaction in the mere purposeless play of our mental powers."[33] Examples of things with a sentimental price are "wit, lively imagination, and humour,"[34] qualities esteemed outside any concern for usefulness, without consideration of material advantages.

That which has a value that is not reducible to the two categories of "price," that which possesses "an intrinsic value — that is, a *dignity*,"[35] is that which has no equivalent and that is therefore not exchangeable: for example, "fidelity to promises and kindness based on principle."[36] These qualities are moral in that they have an incomparable value: they bear directly on man as a moral subject[37] and have value by themselves. The value reckoned as dignity is "that which constitutes the sole condition under which anything can be an end in itself."[38] The question is to discover that which has an absolute intrinsic value. Now, as the first section of the *Groundwork* has established, only goodwill, considered in itself, may be called absolutely good.[39] The "only condition under which a rational being can be an end in himself" is morality, "for only through this is it possible to be a law-making member in a kingdom of ends."[40] The value of moral qualities consists "in the attitudes of mind — that is, in the maxims of the will — which are ready in this way to manifest themselves in action even if they are not favoured by success."[41] When our will, through a morally good intention, becomes identical to the law, "the value of such a mental attitude" is revealed "as dignity"[42] "and puts it infinitely above all price."[43] There is an incomparability and an incommensurability to the value of dignity: "it cannot be brought into reckoning or comparison without, as it were, a profanation of its sanctity."[44] Good intention confers on the reasonable being the faculty of "*shar[ing] ... in the making of universal law,* and which therefore fits him to be a member in a possible kingdom of ends."[45] Goodwill, action done out of duty, respect for the moral law, autonomy — the dignity of humanity in each person, his "sanctity," results as a common presupposition:

> Nothing can have a value other than that determined for it by the law. But the law-making which determines all value must for this reason have a dignity — that is, an unconditioned and incomparable worth — for the appreciation of which, as necessarily given by a rational being, the word *"reverence"* is the only becoming expression. *Autonomy* is therefore the ground of the dignity of human nature and of every rational nature.[46]

It is on the basis of Kant that the problem of value, according to a remark by Jean Wahl, may "be posed as a separate problem."[47] Kantian ethics in fact assumes that whereas "all the things that we desire have but determinate and conditional values ... alone, reasonable beings have an absolute value; they are and must be ends in themselves."[48] If the world of ends, the world of values, "is closed, according to Kant, to theoretical understanding," it is open to practical reason.[49] Such is the path followed, and that may always be followed, by the project of an ethical socialism: if "the legislation that belongs to the kingdom of ends, to the republic of wills, has everything estimated according to the dignity of the person, ... [it] authorizes only by subordinating them to this dignity the actions by which reasonable subjects are means."[50] To the question, "What are the ends that are also duties?" Kant responds with simplicity: "They are *one's own perfection* and *the happiness of others.*"[51] But he knew that the inversion of this twofold prescription is the most widely practiced thing in the world: human beings seek their personal happiness and take the perfection of another as their end.[52]

## The Rights of Another (Lévinas)

*Everything begins with the right of the other and with my infinite obligation toward him.* Emmanuel Lévinas

Of Abraham, "father of believers," Emmanuel Lévinas says that he was "above all the one who knew how to receive and nourish human beings: the one whose tent was open to the four winds."[53] This was so much the case that Abraham's descent "is of every nation: every man who is truly a man is probably of Abraham's descent."[54] This descent is to be conceived as made up of those "men whose ancestor bequeathed a difficult tradition of duties to another, which one is never done completing, an order in which one is never out of debt, but in which duty first and foremost takes the form of obligations with respect to the body, the duty to nourish and shelter."[55] In this sense human rights are first of all the rights of another, who should be recognized and respected up to his most elementary needs. The abstract universalist must be made to come down from her philanthropic ivory tower: it is less openness of mind and tolerance than openness of doors and the untallied gift that bear witness to the meaning of human rights. Thereby, already, doubt is cast on an ethic founded either on the pure reciprocity of interlocutive subjectivities in a dialogue or on the pure formal universality of the moral law. The ethical path of metaphysics, in Lévinas, is just as removed from the dialogic model illustrated by the philosophy of Martin Buber as from the Kantian model of "universalizability" of the maxim of my action. Hence the insufficiency of a principle of an ethics based on exchange, the relation of gift to countergift, or on the pure respect for the moral law: the primacy of Another and the infinite he brings before me are misunderstood in such systems.

My infinite obligation with regard to another is the meaning of my responsibility before quite another face, that of the stranger[56] — and whatever the inevitable ingratitude of the other may be. Thus appears the responsibility for another, that is, a responsibility "for what is not my deed, or for what does not even matter to me; or which precisely does matter to me, is met by me as face."[57] It is surely not enough to be content with giving, for "everything depends on the manner,"[58] adds Lévinas, linking up with a theme dear to Vladimir Jankélévitch.[59] Let us examine the insufficiency of dialogue, so very lauded in its virtues, the central value in the contemporary version of the wisdom of nations. The insufficiency of the dialogic relation is that of the structure of reciprocity as a model and foundation of the ethical relation: the reciprocity of the "I" and the "Thou" of the formalism of a meeting that "can be reversed, read from left to right just as well as from right to left."[60] The dialogic pieces of evidence (or the presuppositions) are the symmetry of the interlocutive positions, the perfect (as a norm) reciprocity and ideal reversibility of the discursive positions, the placement on the same level and belonging to the same spiritual-cultural space (a condition of the intended consensus) of the "I" and the "Thou." The objections made to the dialogic, or rather dialogal, philosophy of Martin Buber are all brought together in this critical motif: the risk of indifference to "dimension of height"[61] that affects another in the ethical relation. In the latter, from myself to another, I do not go from the Like to the Same. The alterity of Another must be thought beyond the egalitarianism that is perfectly realized in the dialogue that conforms to its concept: "Thou" is posited by "I" as like himself and on the same level as himself. But the ethical relation does not arise at the intersection of the principles of similitude and equality. Ethics begins "when the 'I' perceives the *Thou* as higher than itself": "Another is at once higher and poorer than I."[62] It follows that even the "pure spiritualism of friendship" — let us leave aside "the simple materialism of objective contact" — is lacking the ethical relation that subsists entirely in the access to the alterity of the Other through the latter's "dimension of height and human distress."[63] One must see beyond *philia,* beyond any sum, as fine as it may be, of exchange, reciprocity, and respect: "We may well ask ourselves whether clothing the naked and feeding the hungry are not the true and concrete access to the otherness of another — more authentic than the ether of friendship."[64] On March 11, 1963, Lévinas wrote to Martin Buber that Another is "always, *qua* Another, the poor and destitute one (while at the same time being my lord)."[65] The implication here is that the ethical relation is "*essentially* dissymetrical."[66] Now, there is in the ideal of dialogue — egalitarian exchanges, common projects, and a consensual horizon — a fundamental and hidden insensitivity to ethics: to think the relation with Another according to the dialogic model is to tend to reduce the other to a partner endowed with the same rights to speech as myself, as such just as respectable as myself; it is to grasp another as another "I" — an alter ego. Hence that abyssal misapprehension of ethics, incarnated by a certain interpretation of the imperative: "Love thy neighbor as thyself" — that is, as another "Thou," in virtue of the fact that he is just that. Lévinas invites us to hear quite another requirement: to love another rather than oneself, before oneself, to love him for and as himself; not to reduce the alterity of Another to an image of the Same, who is "I."

Ethics brings on a shattering of every speculative system through "the very impossibility, for a thinking that reduces all otherness to the same, of reducing Another."[67] This impossibility, which therefore merges with the "shattering of the system because of Another," correlatively places the "I" in question: "This putting in question signifies the responsibility of the 'I' for the Other. Subjectivity *is* in that responsibility and only irreducible subjectivity can assume a responsibility. That is what constitutes the ethical."[68] The "I" is redefined on the basis of its "placement in question...in the face of Another": "To be 'I' henceforth signifies not being able to rid oneself of responsibility.... The placement in question of the 'I' by Another leaves me in solidarity with Another in an incomparable and unique fashion.... The uniqueness of the 'I' is the fact that no one may respond in my place."[69] The deceptive moralities of the "I" conceived as prime mover and of its doubles show their inconsistency before "the responsibility that rids the 'I' of its imperialism and egotism."[70] Finally there arises "total altruism,"[71] beyond the ruses of egocentrism and egomorphism: "To discover in the 'I' such an orientation is to identify the 'I' with morality. The 'I' before Another is infinitely responsible."[72]

There had to be a positive break with the formalism of ideological moralities: generalized irenic dialogue, exchange and the goodwill of reciprocity, conformity to a universalizable existence, critical protest in the face of abuse, public denunciation of the forms of intolerability, and so on. These fine and good attitudes and practices involve only an "I" equipped with an ideal of the "I" and involve it only halfway. It is necessary to disengage the "I" from itself and to begin with a decentering in favor of the Other, with the dissymmetry ordained by the preeminence of Another. Solidarity and fraternity, let us say justice, do not begin with exchange and dialogue, in which the Infinite would not show. It is necessary to await the appearance of the face in its nakedness:

> If the face is the very facing, the proximity that interrupts the series, it is the case that it comes enigmatically on the basis of the Infinite and its inmumemorial past that this alliance between the poverty of the face and the infinite is inscribed in the force with which the near is imposed on my responsibility before any commitment on my part — the alliance between God and the poor person is inscribed in our brotherhood.[73]

The alterity of Another is infinitely different from that of an alter ego, for the infinite that is therein unveiled is an "unassimilable alterity, an absolute difference in relation to all that is shown, signaled, symbolized, announced, and commemorated."[74] Such is the path of the "humanism of the Other Man," shown by the "unusual meaning" of Jeremiah 22:16: "He judged the cause of the poor and needy;...*was not this to know me?* saith the Lord."⁷⁵

The ethic implied by biblical universalism is thus grounded on a fundamental intuition that is stated in the following apparent paradox: "Perceiving that I am not *the equal* of another."⁷⁶ But this proposition must be understood in a very strict sense: "I see myself *obligated* with respect to another; consequently I am infinitely more demanding of myself than of others."⁷⁷ This is the ethical interpretation of the chosenness of Israel, a chosenness "made up not of privileges but of responsibilities."⁷⁸ Here we see a paradoxical particularism, which conditions universality and which opens the way to it. The reciprocity of the ethical relation is thereby grounded on an original inequality: "For equality to make its entry into the world, beings must be able to demand more of themselves than of another, feel responsibilities on which the fate of humanity hangs, and in this sense pose themselves problems outside humanity."⁷⁹ This infinite responsibility, which gives universalism its essential content, is set up by the extraordinary fact that "a *self [moi]* can exist which is not a *myself [moi-même]*, a self viewed face-on."⁸⁰ As soon as a religion enables one to affirm, with Rabbi Meir, that a pagan who knows the Torah is the equal of the high priest, such a religion is universal, open to all. Hence the notion of Israel lets itself be separated "from any historical, national, local, and racial notion."⁸¹ Chosenness, as the cryptic indication of a surplus of obligations and exceptional duties, contains the promise of the abolition of differences among Jew, Hellene, and barbarian; but this promise is enveloped in the affirmation of particularism, and as a task it is always to be renewed.⁸²

Even though he had come from Lithuania, Lévinas spoke of his admiration for France as it appeared to him in 1923: "Through the teachers who were adolescents at the time of the Dreyfus Affair, a vision, dazzling for a newcomer, of a people who equal humanity and of a nation to which one can attach oneself by spirit and heart as much as by roots."⁸³ There is hardly a more enlightening commentary than the one that Alain Finkielkraut gives on these phrases:

> A people that equals humanity — this is a people that does not seek its specificity in local color, in the picturesque, in the affirmation of an original essence, but rather in attachment to universal values. A nation to which one is attached by heart and mind — this is a nation that lives itself as a collection of individuals united by a conscious and

rational adherence to certain principles, as the expression testifies: "France, homeland of human rights."[84]

It is difficult not to follow Rudolf Bultmann when he affirms that, for modern man, "the conception of a God that is above or beyond the world is either unrealizable or is perverted into a religiosity that would like to flee the world."[85] There nevertheless remains a door that may be opened, incarnated by "the conception of a God who can find, seek and find, *the undetermined in the determined,* the beyond in the beneath, the transcendent in the present."[86] The idea of a possible presence of transcendence in immanence defines one of the conditions of a humanism that would not be anthropocentric, would not boil down to a naturalism or complete immanentism making the human race divine as a race. It is the availability or the opening "at any time to *meetings of God in the world, in time,*" that now constitutes real faith, and not "the acknowledgment of an image of God, as just as it may be."[87] Nonegological humanism (Humanity being only the promotion of the ego through generalization and absolutization) may be summarized, according to Paul's remarks (Romans 13:9) on the Ten Commandments, in one word, that which says love. The religious foundation of ethics merges with the experience of the presence of eternity in time, as it is admirably illustrated in the picture sketched by Jesus of the judgment of the world (Matthew 25:31–46). Bultmann presents it with simplicity:

> The judge of the world gathers men before his throne, to the right and to the left. He speaks to those on the right: "I was hungry, and you fed me; I was thirsty, and you gave me something to drink; I was a stranger, and you took me in...." And if those called on ask, astonished, "When did we do all that?," the Lord will answer: "What you did for one among my smallest brothers, you did for me!"[88]

## Insight into an "Antiracist" Wisdom: The Indirect Route (Scheler)

Let us accord to hegemonic antiracism that racism gets its energy from the passions and drives that carry it. And let us ask this question: What is to be done? Max Scheler's thesis is known: "Spirit is originally devoid of power and efficacy, and the more this is so, the purer it is."[89] As spirit has none of its own energy,[90] we must "be much more modest [than those who espouse the classical theory] in our view of the influence of the human spirit and will upon the course of history."[91] Ideas, in order to be inscribed in history and mark it by their influence, must necessarily "have interests and passions behind them, that is, energies derived from the vital and instinctual sphere of man."[92] Ideas and values, stripped of originating power, must be "appropriated by the great instinctual tendencies in social groups and by the common interests that link them."[93] The spirit and the will of man can have no other role than *guidance,* that is, the "process of presenting ideas and values, which are then realized through the impulses," and *direction,* that is, the "inhibition" and "liberation" of instinctive impulses.[94] For "one thing the spirit cannot do [is] generate or cancel the instinctual energy."[95] The realization of the spirit assumes the mediation of the inferior forms of being, which it can only "sublimate." The process is the following: "The spirit as such presents ideas to the drives, and ... the will supplies to, or withdraws from, the drives (which must always be present first) such images and representations as may lead to the complete realization of these ideas."[96] Between the spirit and life, there is quite a difference in nature, but just as much a complementarity. What is excluded is to expect from the will alone as such a mastery of the passions and impulses: "A direct struggle of the pure will against the instinct is impossible."[97] Here Scheler foregrounds the unwanted effects of the voluntary act: when a direct struggle by the will is proposed, "it only strengthens the tendency of the drives to go in their own direction."[98] The powerlessness of the will and reason to originate brings it about that, when they claim to vanquish by themselves the drive forces, they engender perverse effects: "The will always achieves the opposite of what it intends, when, instead of aiming at a higher value, the realization of which attracts the impulse and makes us forget what is 'bad,' it is directed merely toward inhibiting and at struggling against the impulse whose goal is condemned as 'bad' by our conscience."[99] The analysis may be applied to contemporary hegemonic antiracism, which is voluntarist and rationalist: xenophobic impulses, the ethnocentric preferences of sentimental nationalism, when they are directly combated by antiracism, are thereby stimulated, radicalized, pushed to absolutize themselves and to seek legitimations whose assembly engenders the passage to racism-as-doctrine. The idealist-spiritualist illusion consists of believing that the vital impulses may be combated and vanquished by the "power" of the will enlightened by reason. But this "power" is a fiction, the fiction par excellence of modern intellectualism. That is why the only good path — not the best — consists of not fighting face to face the forces of impulse recognized as "bad," but rather of diverting them and surmounting them in indirect fashion. Homage must be done to Spinoza for having understood that reason is incapable of regulating the passions "except in so far as it becomes a kind of 'passion' through sublimation, as we would say today."[100] It is possible to discover in the *Ethics* the foundation of a doctrine of "nonresistance" to evil,[101] which is effective, stripped of rational-voluntarist presumptions. The wisdom that derives from such an orientation may be worded as follows: "Man must learn to live with himself and to tolerate even those inclinations which he recognizes as bad and perverse. He must not fight them directly, but he must learn to overcome them indirectly by investing his energies in worthwhile tasks which are accessible to him and which his conscience recognizes as good and decent."[102]

Faced with "racism" — that is, with the ensemble of passions and drives directed toward exclusion or discrimination — such a wisdom invites one first to tolerate what is intolerable in the eyes of the spirit; but then, in order better to affirm the contrary positive passions, to inscribe them in practices, and thereby indirectly to vanquish the phenomena said to be "racist." The paradox is the following: to vanquish racism and convince its "partisans," one must not "struggle against racism." One must rather return to the only true pedagogy, that of example: to offer to view successful types of existence emptied of "racism" and its antagonistic double, antiracism. Certain contemporary psychosocial studies thus describe successful experiments in everyday or professional life in which racism (and therefore antiracism) seem unknown, stripped of existential meaning. Antiracism exhausts itself in fighting against racism: the process cannot come to an end and resembles an infernal cycle. It is a matter of breaking the cycle — and of living outside that space of combat where the adversaries exist only on condition of reinventing each other at every moment.

## Human Rights, in Spite of Everything

We propose to sketch several arguments in favor of the affirmation and defense of a political rationalism and an ethical universalism that is, while *moderate*, of strong conviction, which to us appear to justify the invocation of human rights. No one would seriously question the fact that today human rights are necessary, more or less efficacious instruments in the struggle against totalitarian and authoritarian regimes, the organized practices of racial discrimination, and indeed the contempt for persons tied to state-technocratic sclerosis. If it is true that every generation, according to a remark by Max Scheler, has its "demand of the moment," a requirement of its own that never appears again,[103] the defense of human rights is the requirement that, today, impresses itself on us.

The question of rationalism, when it exceeds the strict limits of a theory of knowledge by furnishing values and norms to the different regions of its practice, has already been examined in its extreme, indeed extremist, forms (antifanaticist fanaticism). If *dogmatic rationalism* has a legitimate use for the limitation of the claims, otherwise self-destructive, of the skeptical forms of empiricism — but not such that it is substituted for them — if it allows one to recall the minimal requirements of the rational in the face of the recurrent offensives of antirationalism (traditionalism, emotionalism, aesthetico-romantic solipsism), if *critical rationalism* is well suited to accounting for the logic of scientific discovery in the modern sense (Karl Popper) and to permitting the foundation of morality by the delimitation of the proper domain of pure practical reason (according to the rule of universalizing the maxims of action), then it is a *problematic rationalism* that to us appears capable of best escaping the various forms of corruption of rationalism (orthodox rigidity, hypercritical fanaticism, dreams of dictatorship among the most rational people). As Catherine Kintzler recently suggested, it was Condorcet who opened the way without thinking it through and without himself being able to avoid its dogmatization.[104] The first requirements of such a problematic rationalism bear on the general progress of education and reflection, involving the perfecting of institutions. Its first historically incarnated form is the legal state that guarantees the exercise of the rights of man and the citizen.

Beyond the obvious claim of the subjectivity of the person (the "subject of rights") who affirms what she may allow herself and what she has ground to require, and so beyond the freedom of the person as a faculty of self-determination,[105] the properly modern claim of human rights has a precise meaning, which is still more or less hidden, that subsists in "the human privilege of perfectibility."[106] The affirmation of human rights expresses an aspiration that is a part of the defining character of humanity: on the one hand, a general need for improvement of the human condition,[107] of course; but just as much, on the other hand, the aim of a world of reconciliation of humanity with itself, in which the very idea of rights, being realized in mores, "would lose all significance."[108] The deep sense of human rights is that human beings are not devoted to the unending repetition of age-old behaviors, that the destiny of human beings is neither in the instinctual programs that determine them nor in the cultural codes that separate them. That enemy of the individualist principle of human rights, Auguste Comte, did not ask for anything else: "Make humanity predominate over animality"[109] — as well as over those substitutes of animality, closed communities, quasi-species. Human rights may be, in another perspective — a theological one — considered to be in tune with the requirement of a universality to be realized in the world, which must become "one world," be instituted as a universal legal community, a symbol, for Christians, of the universal community, the kingdom of God.[110] Berdyaev recalled the infinite distance between the symbol and the transcendental symbolized: "Democracy, in so far as it affirms the dignity of every man, expresses...truth. It errs, however, in emphasizing the material aspects [whose type is the state] of human existence.... Every society is Caesar's, whereas true communion is the Kingdom of God."[111] As soon as human rights, in spite of their metaphysical presuppositions (which come down to anthropocentric prejudices), in spite of their incoherencies or inevitable conflicts of legitimacy (right as freedom and right as belief, rights of individuals and rights of peoples, rights of individuals and rights of the living, and so on) as well as of their cynical political instrumentations, embody the hope suggesting that humanity does not coincide absolutely with the sad spectacle given by its empirical forms.

It remains that the requirement for justice should not be identified with human rights; this requirement would, by such an identification, be reduced to individual or collective *aspirations*. The latter would pretend to universality — by christening themselves, for example, "legitimate claims" or "the just fight for...."[112] The positivity of human rights must be discovered beyond their subjective character and their internal contradictions.

The specific corruption of human rights (the same goes for antiracism, which is only a variant on or an application of it) resides, on the one hand, in the *cult* of which they are the object, a cult involving sacred texts, mysteries, a clergy,[113] chapels, solemn celebrations, professional apologists and inquisitors.[114] In short, it resides in the institution of a community of the faithful that involves the excommunication of the infidels.[115] On the other hand, it resides in the attribution of rights to the abstract entity "humanity" as subject of inherence.[116] Humanity is presumed to be the "subject of rights." As such, the expression "human rights" is poorly worded, and hence the source of a misunderstanding. It appears to us, following Michel Villey, that rigor requires that one unveil and convey the positive content of human rights through the reformulation of *duties toward human beings*.[117]

Here is what obligates us to proceed to a radical decentering, to begin, no longer with my rights (or with our rights), but rather from the rights of another. Such a recentering on one other than the Ego (or its broadened image, the "We") does not occur without an ascesis. For there is, in a space dominated by the values of possessive and competitive individualism, a basic tendency to an egoistic hijacking of rights, no less than a propensity to reduce "rights of" to "rights to." Perhaps, then, ethical individualism is only a homonym of competitive individualism and hedonistic individualism (the latter exalted in its most gentle forms by the doctrinaires of the "postmodern"). The "person" may not be reduced to the self-idealization of the proprietor, the predator, the sensualist. The deep meaning of the rise of the individual as a person — that is, as a problem of the human person — is that "humans cannot be identified with any role they may assume in the world."[118] Now, "modern individualism, as it stretches from the Renaissance on..., was an attempt not to penetrate beyond and beneath every role but rather to play an *important* role."[119] That is why a demanding interpretation of human rights must break with the modern individualist cult of the role. Jan Patočka describes in profound fashion the avatars of this hypervalorization of the role: "Bourgeois revolutions battle over roles (equality is equality of roles! and freedom is the possibility to choose whatever role suits us!). Modern individualism is increasingly being unmasked as a collectivism (universalism), and collectivism as this false individualism."[120]

What does it mean to "defend human rights"? It is first of all to require that they are realized by a society calling on the values assumed by them. The spokesperson for human rights, then, in order to be consequential, must recognize a certain prophetic character: the humanitarianist prophet "defends" human rights by denouncing the lapses with respect to the values and norms that they envelope. As such, the defender of human rights may be likened to Joachim Wach's type of the "protest-within" (in opposition to the "protest-without"). At issue is a model of a prophet, of religious (biblical) or ideological (modern democratic) type, as a creator of dissonance.[121] The condition of appearance of such a type of humanitarianist prophet is that the renewed questioning of the social state as it is, effected by the "denunciator" through his speech (or his symbolic public acts), be made "in the very name of the values and beliefs attested by the group and whose current organization the latter presents as though it were its guarantor."[122] If therefore "protest-without," perceived as deviant, "paradoxically loses its dissonant character, in the sense that no reduction of it is ideologically thinkable,"[123] "protest-within" is the agency whose speech brings dissonance to arise and maintains it, with an eye to reducing it. Its type of intervention is grounded on the postulate that dissonance is reducible. The difficulty with human rights comes from the fact that their prophet-defender presents himself as the spokesperson of the ideal community formed from the group of their "faithful," a community whose first requirement is to constitute itself as universal, that is, as a group with no outside. But the axiological unification of humankind is precisely what is in question. Now, the condition of efficacy of the defense of human rights is the existence of a universal listener defined by her adhesion to the system of values and norms that the humanitarianist prophet "defends." But this universal listener is really a regulatory idea, an ideal to be incarnated to infinity.

# Thirteen

# Republican Metapolitics: Universalism or Barbarism? Universalism without Barbarism?

> *An emancipated society... would not be a unitary state, but the realization of universality in the reconciliation of differences. Politics that are still seriously concerned with such a society ought not, therefore, propound the abstract equality of men even as an idea. Instead, they should point to the bad equality today... and conceive the better state as one in which people could be different without fear.*
> Theodor W. Adorno

> *By their very essence there is no zoology of peoples.*
> Edmund Husserl

The marriage between pessimism and hope engenders the insurmountable evidence of the tragic. We have given certain reasons to assume that the antagonism of values is unsurpassable. How then do we conceive the political? The assumption of an insurmountable *axiological dispute* obliges us to posit universalism only as the correlate of a requirement. The universalist requirement is manifested in the political order as the idea of an endless task, the idea of politics as inchoative antitragic effort. That is what Michael Ignatieff has in his own way seen:

> The needs of human beings are contradictory; specifically,... the need for freedom and the need for belonging or *rootedness* are

theoretically irreconcilable.... Politics... is the perpetually renewed attempt to reconcile in practice what is theoretically irreconcilable, that is, the incompatibility of the human needs for freedom and for security, for individualism and for belonging.[1]

For the corruption of ideals and values threatens on two fronts, those of universalist barbarism and differentialist barbarism.

The antagonism of worlds of values is just as much expressed in the conflict between the great forms of solidarity, which their respective ideological corruptions exacerbate. On the one hand, *solidarities of blood*, which are ordered by the meaning given in a traditio-communitarianist world, are corrupted into the racism of exclusion and extermination. On the other hand, *solidarities of reason*, ordered by the meaning constructed in an individuo-universalist world, are corrupted into the racism of assimilation, into the inegalitarianist legitimation of imperialism. We cannot, as modern human beings, escape either solidarities symbolized by blood (the model of the family) or those symbolized by common reason (Humanity). But the solidarity between two diametrically opposed types of solidarity is in no way an entitlement; it designates a task. Its first condition of achievement is to avoid racistoid corruptions on two fronts. Type 2 racism consists of turning a group (an ethnic group, a nation, a people, a race) into a sort of family situated between the family and humankind (the latter derealized as major abstraction). Type 1 racism consists of explicitly derealizing any group whose extension is less than that of humankind, as if there were nothing (important) between the biological individual and the genus (or the species), as well as of surreptitiously holding up one or another group as the ideal type of Humanity, as the normative model to which it becomes "normal" to accord specific rights and duties. (To the representatives of "superior civilizations," those who bear the excellence of "Civilization," it comes down to bearing the "white man's burden," to take one example.)

The antagonism of values may be formulated in a less polemological fashion than in the Weberian tradition, by insisting on the difference among the regimes of discourse that belong to the ethnic and political spheres, on their *heterology*. It is thus that Paul Ricoeur, reworking the Weberian distinction between two moralities, posits the insurmountability of the gap and the tension between ethics and politics, yet forcefully reaffirms their interaction, which must be interpreted as an intersection and not as a subordination:

> It is because the morality of conviction and the morality of responsibility cannot completely merge that ethics and politics constitute two separate spheres, even if they do intersect.... It seems to me that there is a much greater danger today of failing to recognize the intersection of ethics and politics than of confusing the two spheres. Cynicism feeds on the apparently innocent acknowledgment of the abyss separating moral idealism from political realism.[2]

## The Indirect Value of Difference

*Would it not be deplorable if, because the music of Mozart is sublime, that of Beethoven did not exist?* Ernest Renan

What remains for a republican political philosophy is the task of rethinking its own founding universalism, which forms the basis of an effective antiracist position. The French intellectual community has recently rediscovered the tradition, or the republican idea,[3] that may be rethought, by way of the "return to Kant" that certain contemporary philosophers have sketched,[4] as an Idea of reason.[5] To rethink universalism, the horizon and requirement that certain ideologues had hastily buried with an ironic gesture — "that famous and hollow republican universalism," said, for example, Shmuel Trigano[6] — is just as much to dare to recover humanity, beyond two decades of Heideggerian-structuralist terrorism. But it was first necessary that critical reason fulfill two tasks. The first is to show that the insular conception of collective identity — that is, the inclination to make each type of ethnocultural affiliation a fortress and prison — boils down to a nationalist myth suited to legitimate self-defensive massacres indefinitely. The second is to distinguish authentic universalism from its instrumentalizations by Western ethnocentrism — in short, no longer to confuse the legitimate critique of the simulacra of the universal with the nihilist rejection of every requirement for universality.[7] Once such requirements have disappeared, there in fact remain only singular (individual and collective) forces that confront each other indefinitely in a space of pure violence, from which all other communication is on principle excluded. This is a world of brute facts and brutal forces: "The nationalist formula that engenders state reason, 'My country right or wrong,' illustrates in glaring fashion the fall of transcendent values into the immanence of plain facts."⁸ The universe governed by the nationalist principle is the reign of pure violence. And one of the great hoaxes of the century is the maintenance of the conflation of nationalist logic and the meaning of minority claims. In one of his fine, untimely texts, Jacques Ellul strongly indicated, against the ideological tendency, the incompatibility of nationalist terrorism and the rights of minorities:

> The truly poor are the minorities we forget about. That is the proper definition.... The history of the last thirty years allows us to state a general law: ethnic and cultural minorities have no right to independence, must be eliminated, and are always wrong.... The ideological scales have not been impartial when it has come to judging between the rights of minorities and the need of forming nations. Nationalism is the universal law of our time; everything else must yield to it.... Political views that fall within the spectrum of colors that are generally admitted are, strictly speaking, acceptable. But cultural minorities? Absolutely not. It is not admissible that in the name of a common past, a religion, rites, and principles, or a special language and customs, a group should refuse submission to a political organism that is national and seeks to unify by centralizing. World opinion is set; there is no recourse against it. The cultural and ethnic minorities are condemned. Their members are the truly poor of our century.⁹

One must think in the opposing direction, and doubly so. One must first conceive the rights of cultural minorities other than by the dominant nationalist model: this is already a difficult task. And then one must do everything to keep members of minorities from sinking into nationalist mythology: an even more difficult task. One must do this even when the ideological history of the twentieth century abounds with examples of couplings between absolute nationalism and the totalitarian reduction of "particularist" entities whose regularity may suggest that they are manifestations of a law authorizing every modern nationalist politics. A case in point is the alliance of state racism with the radical homogenization of the national body in Nazism. Let us here be content with instructing ourselves through the admiring descriptions of a committed witness, Robert Brasillach. Brasillach brought strongly to the fore, in the new imaginary installed by Hitler's Germany, the imperative of a total stripping by "the fascist man" of any regional, religious, or cultural "particularism," that is, of any minority stigma. He did so on the basis of a pairing of the myths of unity and purity:

> We have seen the birth of fascist man.... A human exemplar is born.... In Germany, I think in only ten years, we will see the true man of the Third Reich, rid of all Saxon of Bavarian particularity, tossed onto the fields with all the other Germans from the whole Empire.... [The young fascists] want a pure nation, a pure history, a pure race...; they believe a nation is *one*, in exactly the same way as a sports team is *one*.[10]

The analogy of the sports team is very enlightening here with regard to the reduction of societal forms to community forms that characterizes the National Socialist imaginary and its doctrinal elaborations. To hold up as an ideal society the model of the community and its various interpretations, wavering between the community of blood (the family) and the community of work or play (the team), all of which involve the idea of a community of destiny: here is what seems to define most deeply the axiology of racist nationalism, that is, of *integral communitarianism*. In this sense, one might hold that the conflation of community and society represents the fundamental illusion of racism as an antimodern ideology that has appeared in the modern world, the negative of the model of the "great society" and a regressive reaction directed against the latter.[11] Two forms of the illusion arise, illustrated by numerous historical examples:

- A community that takes itself for a society: such is the minoritarian illusion par excellence, fulfilling at once a self-defensive and a compensatory function in the modern framework of the nation-state. This is the illusion of the part that takes itself for the whole.

- A society that takes itself for a community: such is the majoritarian illusion by which a population whose imaginary is saturated by nationalist passions is represented and legitimated as an organic totality. The community's self-representation allows a national population threatened with "decomposition" (an "identity crisis," and so on) to recover a powerful collective identity. An effective mythological instrument of rapid social cohesion and self-identification, the communitarianist illusion fits in well with racist rationalizations: the National Socialist regime furnishes its most striking illustration.[12]

It is not superfluous to specify that the protoracist ideal of the community is that of the *organic* community, grounded on the dissolution of the individual in the element of the national body and on the maximal, self-sufficient intensity of the feeling of belonging, in opposition to the idea of the community mediating between the individual and the universal,[13] the *closed* community, in which individual choices are nearly abolished along with the freedom to come and go.[14]

All this leads us to distinguish two interpretive models of the "community," which may be called homonymous. On the one hand, there is the *community that mediates universality,* community integration appearing as a necessary condition of a horizon of universality for any subject — endowed with a trans- or metacommunity sky, the community of affiliation is not an end in itself, is not autotelic, but is rather transactional. On the other hand, there is the *self-sufficient community,* a totality that cannot be transcended, deprived of mediating function and of a horizon of universality: let us name it the *world community.* The idea of a nonviolent universalism thereby becomes thinkable.

The meetings between philosophy and humanism suggest the hope that the antinomy between nationalist/racist nihilism and humanitarian/racist moralism will find its solution. The declaration of the rights of human beings should no longer be prohibited by that of human rights. That is to say that cultural democracy[15] is always before us and that it must be so as an idea of reason. There is then the primary obligation to deabsolutize the principle of difference in order to integrate it as a factor of relativization into a nonethnocentric humanism.

This is the indirect value of difference, to borrow André Lalande's formulation.[16] Lalande has sketched a general philosophy, as it were a scientific ideology,[17] centered on the idea of assimilation held up as a fundamental principle of progress:

> The great *successes* of science have been, not differentiations, but rather assimilations.... In the moral order, it may hardly be doubted that the disappearance of ancient slavery, and later of that of blacks, have been changes *for the better,* that the same goes for the equality of citizens before the law, the reduction of privileges due to birth, the equalization of the rights of women with those of men.[18]

If similarities and assimilations are often valuable by and for themselves, and if one must be careful not to *exalt* the role of diversity and differentiation, one must nevertheless *recognize* the reality of differences. But one does so by specifying that "difference, in order to be a value, must be a compensation"[19] — indeed, as in love and friendship, it must intervene only as a supplement on a basis of similarity: "differences are like salt."[20] In such a philosophy of progress by growing assimilation,

> the value of differences is never intrinsic, and ... never categorical. Value only comes to them either from the fact that they serve to correct, compensate, or prevent the introduction of other differences, or from the fact that they constitute an individual superiority in the realization of other values, themselves apparently definable by a progress of assimilation.[21]

Lalande's personalism involves a twofold rejection: that of egoistic individualism, which makes an absolute of individual difference, and that of all forms of collectivism, which accords no value at all to the person as such.[22] There emerges a universalist ethics, grounded on the norm of subordinating differentiation to assimilation: "Work to dissolve the oppositions that bring war to individuals, parties, interest groups, classes, nations. One may believe, if one likes, that absolute value is not the end result, but the gradual movement from difference to identity."[23] Lalande's theory of values and norms thus presents one of the best approximations of the ideal type of an ethics of universal assimilation. It is lacking only the thought on the conditions of its passage to the political — a lack that may appear essential, inasmuch as a personalist would certainly have refused to envisage the establishment of a universal empire.

The thesis of the primacy of the universal in the ethical order, which implies that of the secondariness of difference, therefore allows a redefinition of *barbarism* on the basis of the absolutization of collective differences — allows that difference be thought as an attribute or intercommunity relationship. From the same perspective, Max Horkheimer noted the following in 1961: "To treat a human being a priori, not as an individual, a person, but generally and above all as a German, a Negro, a Jew, a foreigner, or a Mediterranean ... is barbarous."[24] It is clear that indeterminacy with respect to the community of the individual, which is produced by the neutralization or suspension of any assignation to a fixed origin, is the condition of her "elevation" to an infinite value. But empirical humans are only rarely embodiments of the ideal type of the person to whom the commandments of ethics are addressed. Embodied persons must not be respected any less in the historico-cultural forms of their embodiment. The nonrespect for this cultural "flesh" defines a *second barbarism,* engendered by the absolute negation of the second value of difference. Therefore one must *also* recognize the barbarism that derives from the absolutization of a scale of universal values. *The particularist barbarism of difference and exclusion must not make one forget the universalist barbarism of inequality and uniformization.* And still, it is on the horizon of universality that hope rises.

## The Republican Idea

We can only encounter anew the Kantian orientation[25] whose ethical universalism, far from substituting for thought on the political, enables an assignment to the latter of its norms and final, "cosmopolitical" purposefulness. The union of human beings among themselves, says Kant, is "an end in itself — ...the end that everyone *ought to have*"; it is "the first and unconditioned duty."[26] That is why the great criticist does not let the mockeries of the projects of perpetual peace in his time (just as we see them today) make an impression on him.[27] The idea of perpetual peace in fact defines "the first and last requirement of morality with respect to historical life on this earth: one must *found* the state of peace, the society of free states."[28] The postulate required by the will to achieve peace has been well formulated by Carl J. Friedrich: "The idea that law is distinct from power and strength is essential to a durable peace, for it rules our war as a means of regulating a conflict of ideas between men."[29] In his *Perpetual Peace*,[30] Kant suggests that the republican constitution is to be conceived as an Idea of reason, that is, as the indication of an ideal or the position of a regulating principle of our reflection on the human community in general. The regulative use[31] of the republican Idea, as the "Idea of a free, rational, and just society in which law would reign absolutely,"[32] is what allows "moral beings" or "men of goodwill,"[33] in serving them as measure and criterion, to take a position with respect to sociohistorical reality, that is, to judge it and thereby to orient it. That is why the republican Idea is that of an unending task. Our problem is to give ourselves the philosophical means to clear the horizon of the opiated fumes exhaled by the fetishism of difference: either in the form of the tribal particularism that posits itself as unsurpassable (the ideological homeland of racism) or in the form of the humanitarianist idolatry of the individual outside the social world (the default position of antiracist reaction). Now, the neo-Kantian perspective enables us to sketch a satisfying speculative solution. In the first place, the reference to the republican Idea "includes *a reference to the values of modern humanism since the Enlightenment,* for it refers to the supposition that the public space — the res publica — is *ideally* grounded on the possibility of rational communication between men."[34] We once again find the requirement of universal communicability, as the transcendental presupposition that communication is always possible by right at the heart of humanity.[35] Of the latter it must be emphasized, following Jürgen Habermas and with Luc Ferry and Alain Renaut, that it "in no way rules out respect for differences, but rather requires them."[36] Here is the authentic universalism, neither terrorist nor ethnocentric, for which we have searched and that we seek to ground.

In the second place, the reference to the republican Idea presupposes "the at least de jure *unity* of humanity in contrast to the barbarism that, whatever form it takes, always amounts to thinking of humanity as *essentially* divided (into races, classes, or even into heterogeneous cultures)."[37] Barbarism is exclusivist differentialism, whether it is expressed as the naturalist legitimation of slavery in a metaphysics of the hierarchical order[38] or as the scientific foundation of the exploitation, indeed the extermination, of populations defined as essentially inferior, dangerous, or harmful. From this moment on, the "right to difference," tainted with a constitutive ambiguity, must be submitted to critical reason: if it may serve, on the one hand, to *limit* the "totalitarian" claims of an imperialism with a universalist face, it tends, on the other hand, and more often, to *mask* the exclusivist contractions of one or another tribal particularism or to legitimate the headlong flight into nationalist and xenophobic passions. There must be agreement: the renunciation of the requirement of universality, involving the abandon (indeed the refusal)[39] of any reference to rights for humanity, opens the door to barbarism.[40] We designate as barbarism the state of humanity that does not recognize humanity in itself. The barbarian is the man who does not recognize himself in his humanity, that which he shares with those who are least similar to him.

## The Requirement of Universality: Heroic Humanism

*Therefore do not seek assurance and firmness.* Blaise Pascal

*The meaning of the transcendent is the core of every civilization, the very essence of humanity. A culture given over to the exclusive search for the "useful" is at heart only barbarism. The world takes sustenance in what surpasses it.* Abraham Joshua Heschel

Universalism or barbarism: such is the form of the alternative that it is proper, *in spite of everything,* to affirm in the face of the exclusivist celebrations of difference, in the face of the archeonationalists who proclaim "France for the French," or, in euphemized fashion, "The French first." That is the difficult question of tolerance: it is no sooner posed and celebrated than the aporias arise, the antinomies appear. In the problematic of the universal and difference, as we have attempted to elaborate it, the first antinomy is that between the universalist tolerance grounded on the abstraction of a one and only Reason and the differentialist tolerance whose commandment is absolutely to respect community differences. Here is the fundamental antinomy: the absolute respect for the person is opposed to the absolute respect for the community as such. It can be speculatively surmounted only on the basis of a *wager* for the universal, followed by the determination of the *limits* of the universalist requirement, in order that the latter may not be degraded into an aim for terrorist unification through imposed uniformization. The only danger, not a negligible one, of universalism resides in its tendency to immoderation: the requirement of universality must be the star guiding a quest, not the flag flying above the assurance that one is standing within the true and the good. That is why we will, in spite of everything, hold that the roads of least corruptible tolerance are not paved with irreducible differences and that they may be illuminated only by a recovered catholicity, beyond the dogmatic universalism of the triumphant petty reason of the Moderns.

If the analysis of the republican Idea enables a recovery of the meaning of the universal, that of democracy as a regulative Idea encounters the requirement of a global community,[41] beyond the idolatry of congealed affiliations, closed communities, and barred national identities. The Idea of a human community is that of complete democracy, no longer enclosed within the borders of a subject-people, those required by the nation-state. Moreover, the democratic Idea involves the rejection of racism inasmuch as it contains a requirement of universal equality: "The advent of democracy very much implies that there is no legitimate foundation for the hierarchy of social groups, and that human beings all belong by right to the same condition."[42] Equality overflows the (closed) circle of equals, the private club of peers: such is properly modern thought, proper to the modern idea of democracy, of equality, which is outstandingly stated in the utterance of a universal proposition, the first premise of the syllogisms of modern political thought — "all human beings are equal."[43] The egalitarian requirement, which in some fashion is a double of the properly modern delegitimation of the hierarchical model, is opposed to the doctrines and regimes that hold up as supreme value the bonds between humanity and the earth or the bonds of blood[44] and pretend to realize a homogenous society without further delay, a reconciled society, one without conflicts, identified with *one* people.[45]

In the face of difference and universality, the beginning of error is to take the side of one at the exclusion of the other, in maximalist haste. Here as elsewhere, the truth resides in the mixed, in the intermediary order — with apologies to the vague but exclusivist Platonism[46] that governs our spontaneous thinking. On the outer edge of cold analysis, the ideological war will continue to be waged on two fronts. On the one hand, one will face *anthropophagic racism,* a machine to devour human differences, a false messianic universalism with which every colonizing, reductive, predatory imperialism adorns itself. On the other hand, one will face *mixophobic racism,* that false respect for the Other with which the drives of exclusion today paint themselves, the twin myths of the pure blood, the homogeneous people, and the healthy national body, indeed the cult of the immaculate national culture, and their shared inverse, the specter of mixture — neither the reduction of the Other to the Same nor the protection of the Same from the Other with the long stick of the very noble *difference.* But salvation would not appear, by dialectical miracle, at the end of the negation of the mixophobic negation: obligatory physical and cultural *métissage* would be only a "revolutionary" illusion and no more. One does not construct a method of resolving problems by inverting an "against" into a "for," nor by converting a phobia into a philia.[47] That would be to confuse thinking with taking a position for or against an opinion: "Transposition from adherence to a party," was Simone Weil's diagnosis.[48] But the spirit of taking sides — that is, wavering between two opposite sides — is a consolation: "Contraries. Today we thirst for and are nauseated by totalitarianism, and nearly everyone loves one totalitarianism and hates another."[49]

"The tragedy of the modern democracies is that they have not yet succeeded in realizing democracy," affirmed Jacques Maritain in 1943.[50] The tragic element arises in the very political incarnation of modern optimism, which finally wanted to be foreign to the tragic and posited man as the sovereign master of his own destiny. The return to the tragic should not accommodate the vestiges of the naively anthropocentric humanism of the Enlightenment, of its dreamy philanthropy. Only a "heroic humanist," absolutely distinct from the individualist forms of humanism (competitive, hedonistic, and humanitarianist individualisms), may be at the height of the challenge launched by the sense of the tragic. For "heroism alone surmounts tragedy";[51] it alone commits us to pursuing with courage and generosity that great human adventure so poorly named by the word *civilization*.[52] But let us repeat: genuine humanism laughs at humanism, as genuine antiracism laughs at antiracism. The professionals of humanism or antiracism can be only impostors.

We have no more absolute certainties, not even that God is dead (the new foundation of a paradoxical dogmatic theology) or that the gods have fled, leaving us the language in which their absence speaks (the foundation of a negative atheology of writing or of a negative "polytheology" practiced by neopagan romanticism). We must live without dogmatic assurances (issuing from revelation, tradition, or reason), must even dispense with that supplemental reassurance of anthropocentric humanism, whose vestiges the fixed languages of the late twentieth century conjointly accommodate, by thus completing its ideological corruption. We must rather live *as though* God grounded the meaning of our existence. True meaning is only given under the horizon of the "as though." True meaning derives from the modern divinization of Humanity and is illustrated by its specific consequences. To the presumption of the self-sufficiency of humanitarianism there corresponds a definite inverse, the fact and the idea of "crime against humanity." The erasure of any absolute foundation, including the erasure of the erasure of any absolute foundation, leaves us in restlessness, in the state of wakefulness in which lucidity is a call to courage. That is why humanism must be heroic.

We have advanced several arguments that to us seem to legitimate our rejection of both skeptical relativism (the paradoxical placement in the perpetual wavering between contraries or the hedonistic wandering in the forest of differences) and cynicism, whether a realism of force and power or a pluralistic aestheticism. The dialogic orientation and the hermeneutic intention assume the requirement of universality in the place of a *first requirement*. Universality should henceforth be only the object of an unending requirement, beyond all certainty of "being right" or "being in the realm of the true." The first universalist requirement is at once the expression of an *aspiration* (justice), the motive for or the stake of a *wager* (freedom: reciprocal respect for the autonomy of everyone and openness of all to all), and the end or aim of a *hope* (brotherhood). One must wager for the universal, give our restlessness its metaphysical object and its first norm: the requirement of universality. For we are committed.[53] Born from restlessness, indeed in fear and trembling, the wager signifies a failure of reason: if in fact reason were capable of proving the existence or nonexistence of God, the existence or nonexistence of a set heaven of values, there would be no need to wager.[54] The wager is that by which the self-surpassing of restlessness may be effected. We have no other choice: either dogmatic slumber or the wager. The latter commits us to accept remaining uncertain about winning; this uncertainty is not the reward for the wager but the act of betting itself.

Everyone, within the strict limits of her system of values, sees barbarism only in the eye of her neighbor from the system on the other side. But barbarism is not located in one or another axiological universe. It resides neither in the ethical requirement of universality nor in the "cultural" requirement of identity, which can be only differential. Barbarism is engendered by the corruption of one requirement or the other, when each one is held up as absolute, denying through its exclusivism the very existence of the other requirement. The limit that may be imposed on barbarism is precisely the thought that a requirement other than my own exists and deserves to exist: the other requirement, that of another, is the limit of *my* requirement; without this relation, the latter can only be hated. Such is the "back-thought" that one must keep, an essential reserve. One must from here on accord to the differentialist arguments the functional value of a *principle of limitation* of the abusive claims of universalist *ideology*.

Tragic realism, which affirms the heterogeneity of values without rejoicing in it — indeed, which affirms their insurmountable conflict without for all that lamenting it — glimpses the twofold possibility of a universalist barbarism and a differentialist barbarism. Because of the acute awareness of this "crux" of ideological corruptions, we do not take the comfortable point of view of Sirius. We commit ourselves to the opposite, but after the disengagement made possible through understanding the principle of debates and controversies. The awareness of the principle as such eludes the grip of the principle. The subject that shows such an understanding of axiological dispute places itself at a distance from the manifestations of the latter in what makes up "ideological life." It is as wary as possible of intersecting exclusivisms. But the subject who knows and comprehends is not the whole subject, nor the whole of the subject. That is why the subject must wager, as the intellectual expression of the insufficiency of the power of the intellect. We see here what intelligence can do. The rest stems from chance and from the heart, from courage and from decision.

Pessimism is not necessarily conservative. For it obligates. It calls for living in spite of the understanding that depresses life and requires that one take on an insane hope. It brings on thinking on both contraries and contradictories at the same time. Hence it makes us philosopher, child, or novelist. Here is one of the half-certainties whose plain obviousness we would like to have shown, stated in the words of F. Scott Fitzgerald: "One should, for example, be able to see that things are hopeless and yet be determined to make them otherwise."[55]

# Notes

## Introduction

1. [GRECE: Groupement de Recherche et d'Études pour la Civilisation Européenne — Research and Study Group in European Civilization. — Trans.]

2. [The Club de l'Horloge is a French group largely made up of intellectuals, government employees, and businessmen whose raison d'être is to oppose socialism, on the grounds that the latter is "contrary to the republican values of liberty, equality, fraternity, and national sovereignty" (Le Club de l'Horloge, *L'Identité de la France* [Paris: Albin Michel, 1985], 351). — Trans.]

3. [The term *racialization* translates the French *racisation*, a neologism. In Taguieff's usage, it refers to the ideological or rhetorical operation by which a person or group is characterized by traits associated with the notion of "race." — Trans.]

4. In 1971, Maxime Rodinson clearly saw the necessity to make a distinction between "racism" and "ethnicism" ("Racisme, xénophobie et ethnisme," in *L'Histoire, I, de 1871 à 1971: Les Idées, les problèmes* [Paris: Bibliothèque du CEPL, Les Dictionnaires du Savoir Moderne, 1971], 392–411; the same text was reprinted in its entirety several years later: "Racisme et ethnisme," *Pluriel* 3 [1975]: 7–27).

5. [The word *métissage* refers to the process of mixing. In the racist and antiracist discourses that Taguieff is analyzing, it refers specifically to the mixture of "races" or ethnic groups such that offspring are a "mixture" of the groups to which the parents belong. The term for the person who is of such "mixed" "racial" background is *métis*, akin to the English word (of Spanish origin) *mestizo*. In many of the texts to which Taguieff refers, the words *métis* and *métissage* translate or are translated by, respectively, *hybrid* and *hybridity* or *miscegenation*; but I have preserved the two French words as often as possible because of the particular sense they carry in the discourses that constitute Taguieff's object. — Trans.]

6. On the discourse and ideology of "national populism," see the studies in which I

introduce and justify the expression and model: Pierre-André Taguieff, "La Rhétorique du national-populisme," *Cahiers Bernard-Lazare* 109 (1984): 19–38 (part 1); *Mots* 9 (1984): 113–39 (part 2); "La Doctrine du national-populisme en France," *Études* (1986): 27–46. On the "New Right," see my general study, "La Stratégie culturelle de la 'nouvelle droite' en France (1968–1983)," in *Vous avez dit fascismes?* (Paris: Arthaud/ Montalba, 1984), 13–152; see also my book *Sur la nouvelle droite: Jalons d'une analyse critique* (Paris: Descartes et Cie, 1994). For analyses and bibliographic orientations, see *Mots* 12 (1986), special issue edited by Simone Bonnafous and Pierre-André Taguieff, *Droite, nouvelle droite, extrême droite. Discours et idéologie en France et en Italie.*

7. Cf. Georges Vigarello: "Individualism becomes a total phenomenon, touching on the entirety of attitudes and social relations" (*"Le Deuxième Âge de l'individualisme," Esprit* [July–August 1984]: 64). But we do not follow Vigarello when he postulates that "the 'era' of the void precisely marks the end of transcendences, the systematic promotion of the present," for it is exactly "difference" that is erected into a new transcendence, doing away with the transcendence of the collective projects and the universalist programs of installing a "new man." On the "individualist" theme of "the affirmation of differences" (or the "respect for differences"), in the framework of an interpretation of the end of the universal as an entry to the postmodern, see Gilles Lipovetsky, *L'Ère du vide: Essai sur l'individualisme contemporain* (Paris: Gallimard, 1983), especially 9, 12, 24, 25ff., 129, 145.

8. Cf. Louis Dumont, *Essays on Individualism: Modern Ideology in Anthropological Perspective* (Chicago: University of Chicago Press, 1986): "The recognition of *alter qua alter*... can only be hierarchical.... Here, to recognize is the same as to value or to integrate.... What I maintain is that, if the advocates of difference claim for it both equality and recognition, they claim the impossible. Here we are reminded of the American slogan 'separate but equal' which marked the transition from slavery to racism" (266–67; see also chapter 7 in this book). During the National Conference against Racism (Paris, Maison de l'UNESCO, March 16–18, 1984), two independent contributions raised the question of the theoretical pertinence of the slogan "Live together with our differences," as well as its ideological significance: that of Farida Belghoul (*Compte rendu des Assises* [Paris: Éditions Différences, 1984], 18–19, 74) and my own (50). In the same vein, for a more elaborate analysis, the reader is referred to Jean-Pierre Dupuy's study ("Differences and Inequalities") published in the proceedings of the conference (Paris, December 10, 1983; proceedings published by Différences, 1984) and to Pierre-André Taguieff, "Les Présuppositions définitionnelles d'un indéfinissable: 'Le Racisme,'" *Mots* 8 (March 1984): 71–107. See also the penetrating remarks of Jean-Pierre Dupuy, "Libres propos sur l'égalité, la science et le racisme," *Le Débat* 37 (November 1985): 42–44 (in which the author reworks and develops the paper of December 10, 1983). We were followed in our critical analysis of "differentialist" arguments by Alain Policar ("Les Pièges," *Le Monde,* April 30, 1986, 2; "Absolutisation de la différence ou ambiguïtés de l'antiracisme," *Les Cahiers Rationalistes* 417 [November 1986]: 47–51). See also Alain Policar, "Racism and Its Mirror Images," *Telos* 83 (spring 1990): 99–108.

9. ["The word *Beur* was a *verlan* (backslang) expression formed by inverting and contracting the word *Arabe*. The term first entered public usage in 1981, with the creation of a local radio station based in northern Paris called Radio Beur run by young men and women from North African immigrant families" (Rodney Ball et al., "French in the World: From Imperialism to Diversity," in *French Cultural Studies: An Introduction*, ed. Jill Forbes and Michael Kelly [Oxford: Oxford University Press, 1995], 270). — Trans.]

10. As an example of the confusion, which is quite ordinary in the antiracist vulgate,

between the praise of difference (heterophilia) and the praise of mixture (mixophilia), we may read this conclusion to a study devoted to racism: "If therefore science has a lesson to offer us in the moral realm, what it teaches us consists above all of discovering the richness of what we call mixture, diversity, heterogeneity, difference, and of promoting their valorization" (Anouch Chahnazian and Jean-Luc de Meyer, "Le Racisme, mythes et sciences: Un Essai critique," *Revue de l'Institut de Sociologie* 3–4 [1982]: 540). When the antiracist intelligentsia notices the antinomy between the norms of mixture (destructive of difference) and those of difference (prohibiting mixture), it tends to come back to the norm of equality. But the differences then come back to the field of equality, which problematizes them; hence the formation of a new prescription that envelopes a reformulation of the antinomy "equality in difference" (see chapter 1 in this book).

11. [The Dreyfus Affair was a prolonged series of incidents around the turn of the twentieth century involving accusations of treason made against Captain Alfred Dreyfus of the French army. In 1894, Dreyfus was convicted on falsified evidence and incarcerated on Devil's Island for what was to be a life term. In the face of enormous public outcry and declarations of anti-Semitism, the government conducted an investigation that suggested that another officer, Esterházy, was the guilty party. After Esterházy was acquitted, public protest grew. The best-known document from this time, and perhaps the most famous piece of journalism in two hundred years of French history, is Émile Zola's *J'accuse*, published in *L'Aurore* in January 1898, in which the author attacks, with razor-sharp phrases, various officials of the army and the government for having condemned an innocent man on anti-Semitic motives. The Dreyfus Affair divided France into two very distinct camps. After several more investigations and the suicide of a colonel who had participated in the falsification of evidence, in 1906 Esterházy was finally found guilty, and Dreyfus was released and restored to his old rank. The consolidation of groups of the left over the Dreyfus Affair is often credited with giving strong impetus to the socialist movements that lasted throughout the twentieth century. —Trans.]

12. "The Misery of Antiracism" was the subtitle of a paper ("Commemorative Antiracism and Differentialist Racism") we gave at the meeting organized by the research seminar "Migrations and Pluralism" (Véronique de Rudder, René Galissot) on April 25, 1985 (at the University of Paris 1). Galissot found the formula sufficiently suggestive to use it as the title of a pamphlet, *Misère de l'antiracisme* (Paris: Arcantère, 1985). See also Pierre-André Taguieff, *Les Fins de l'antiracisme* (Paris: Michalon, 1995); Taguieff, *Le Racisme* (Paris: Flammarion, 1997).

13. Lucien-Anatole Prévost-Paradol, *La France nouvelle* (1868) (Paris and Geneva: Slatkine Reprints, 1979), 312.

14. Our apparent severity, we should specify, does not apply to the numerous militants whose devotion and good faith, bolstered by ethical conviction, we have sensed, not without admiration. But as Charles Péguy would say, if there are initiators pure of heart, there are also profiteers and exploiters, "crooks" who specialize in taking up "great causes." In addition, there are organizations, ideologico-political apparatuses such as leagues and parties, that obey specific, apsychological modes of regulation in the heart of the social system. From the outset, the fact of antiracism requires a threefold questioning, one that is ethical, political, and sociological.

15. Émile Durkheim, *Socialism and Saint-Simon*, trans. Charlotte Sattler (London: Routledge and Kegan Paul, 1959), 5.

16. Ibid., 7.

17. Cf. Jacques Julliard, *La Faute à Rousseau* (Paris: Seuil, 1985), 84–85: the sentiment common to the traditionalist and liberal families, in the nineteenth century, is

rightly characterized by the "horror of political and social surgery." This may be translated by the hate for social volunteerism: see Stéphane Rials, "La Droite ou l'horreur de la volonté," *Le Débat* 33 (January 1985): 34–48; the author's thesis is that "the horror of the will" is "at the heart of the metapolitical (and as a consequence political) positions that one can call *on the right*" (46).

18. The typical characterization is the following: "the first great doctrinarian of racism, Count Gobineau..." (Michel Leiris, "Race et civilisation," in *Le Racisme devant la science* [Paris: UNESCO-Gallimard, 1960], 236).

19. Durkheim, *Socialism*, 7 (the author thus characterizes socialism and individualism).

20. Ibid.

21. In the sense Louis Dumont has given to this general model.

## 1. Heterophobia, Heterophilia

1. [The term *basic antiracism* is in English in Taguieff's text.—Trans.]

2. Albert Memmi, *Racism,* trans. Steve Martinot (Minneapolis: University of Minnesota Press, 2000), 118–21: heterophobia, designating a general category of which racism is a "variety" (characterized by a biologizing ideology), is defined by "the rejection of the other in the name of no matter what difference" (121). The proposed model of racism is barely distinguishable from the commonsense notion. Cf. Christian Delacampagne: "That strange refusal of difference on which racism winds up grafting itself" (*Figures de l'oppression* [Paris: Presses Universitaires de France, 1977], 145). Joseph Gabel also answers the call for definitional evidence: "Racism is essentially heterophobia" ("Racisme et aliénation," *Praxis International* [January 1983]: 432).

3. On the metaphorical distinction between anthropophagia and anthropemy, which we here generalize and shift into a broader field (that of racist ideologies), see Claude Lévi-Strauss, *Tristes Tropiques*, trans. John and Doreen Weightman (New York: Atheneum, 1974), 387–88.

4. Ibid., 388.

5. Cf. Colette Guillaumin, *L'Idéologie raciste: Genèse et langage actuel* (Paris and The Hague: Mouton, 1972), 4: the peculiarity of racism may be defined "as a biologization of social thought, which attempts through this bias to posit as absolute any observed or supposed difference"; Memmi, *Racism,* 173–74: "[Placing a value on difference] is certainly one of the key elements in the racist process.... The racist will do his utmost to stretch the distance between the minus and the plus signs, to maximize the difference.... The ... difference must be made absolute..., it must be made radical." Bernard Dupuy retains the criterion of the focalization of difference: racism is "the attitude that consists of underscoring the difference of the other, instead of recognizing that the other is my fellow, my kin, the one who participates in a common *destiny* with me" (paper presented at the conference "Monotheism against Racism," March 29, 1981, B'nai B'rith, published in the proceedings: *Le Monothéisme contre le racisme* [Paris, 1984], 10).

6. Cf. Guillaumin, *Idéologie*, 13: "the essentialist perceptive system—that is, racist ideology"; see also Raymond Aron, *Progress and Disillusion: The Dialectics of Modern Society* (New York: Praeger, 1968), 55–57. Jean-Marie Mayeur and Madeleine Rebérioux note, on the Dreyfus Affair, "No doubt the racial analysis was often secondary. Sometimes anti-semites even officially denied the essential component in their racism" (*The Third Republic from Its Origins to the Great War, 1871–1914*, trans. J. R. Foster [Cambridge: Cambridge University Press, 1984], 201).

7. Michel Adam, "Racisme et catégories du genre humain," *L'Homme* 24, no. 2 (April–June 1984): 77.
8. Ibid.
9. Freddy Raphaël, *Judaïsme et capitalisme* (Paris: Presses Universitaires de France, 1982), 326.
10. Guillaumin, *Idéologie*, 44.
11. Colette Guillaumin, "The Idea of Race and Its Elevation to Autonomous Scientific and Legal Status," in *Sociological Theories: Race and Colonialism* (Paris: UNESCO, 1980), 44ff.
12. Jean-Claude Passeron, "Présentation" to Joseph Schumpeter, *Imperialisme et classes sociales*, trans. Suzanne de Segonzac and Pierre Bresson (Paris: Flammarion, 1984), 19.
13. Pierre Bourdieu, *Sociology in Question*, trans. Richard Nice (London: Sage, 1993), 177.
14. Ibid.
15. Ibid.
16. Cf. Pierre-André Taguieff, "Sur une argumentation antijuive de base: L'Autovictimisation du narrateur," *Sens* 7 (July 1983): 133–56.
17. Vladimir Jankélévitch, "Psycho-analyse de l'antisémitisme" (published anonymously), in *Le Mensonge raciste,* pamphlet published by the National Movement against Racism (Toulouse, 1942), 18–19.
18. Ibid., 19.
19. Emmanuèle de Lesseps, "Sexisme et racisme," *Questions Féministes* 7 (February 1980): 97.
20. Here I introduce the term *heterophilia* to designate the symmetrical inverse of heterophobia. Cf. Pierre-André Taguieff, "Le Néo-racisme différentialiste," paper presented at the Third International Conference on Political Lexicology, "Nationalism/Racism/Sexism in the Words of Contemporary Political Discourse," École Normale Supérieure of Saint-Cloud, September 10–13, 1984, published in *Langage et Société* 34 (December 1985): 69–98.
21. See, for example, Oswald Spengler, *The Decline of the West*, trans. Charles Francis Atkinson (New York: Knopf, 1932), 43–46 (the end of the universal as an illusion, giving way to a pluralism and radical relativism of values); on this point, see Pierre-André Taguieff, "L'Idée de décadence et le déclin de l'Europe," *Politique Aujourd'hui*, special issue, *L'Europe* (fall 1985): 26ff. In quite another problematic, see Immanuel Wallerstein, *Historical Capitalism* (London: Verso, 1983), 80–88 (universalism as an instrument of rationalizing the world to which historical capitalism is given over, and the planetary opium of the middle classes); universalism is hence reduced to a legitimating ideology of the global extension of capitalism: a "catch" (85), a poison gift of the powerful to the weak, a present imprint of latent racism. The "demystifying" critique of human rights, in the name of the proletarian revolution, proceeds in the same direction: see Régis Debray, "Il faut des esclaves aux hommes libres," *Le Monde Diplomatique* (October 1978) (the supplementary ingredient: the period's Third World remystification of the questions explored). The GRECE has not failed to denounce human rights as being "in the service of market capitalism" and the ideological instrument of a Western crusade of "monotheistic" origin, destructive of collective identities, see *Eléments* 37 (January–March 1981), report on human rights: 5–35 (the title of the report, on the cover: "Droits de l'homme: Le Piège" — "Human Rights: The Trap").
22. Irenaüs Eibl-Eibesfeldt, *Par-delà nos différences* (Paris: Flammarion, 1979), 246. Here we could have just as easily quoted Arthur de Gobineau, Claude Lévi-Strauss,

Konrad Lorenz, Robert Jaulin, or Alain de Benoist. This suggests how much the theme cuts across boundaries between discursive genres or disciplines, as well as philosophical and political divisions.

23. Albert Memmi, *Le Racisme* (Paris: Gallimard, 1982), 207: "This position is exactly the inverse of the racist's. Racism makes difference into something bad; I myself make it the possible occasion for a richness." [The recent translation of Memmi's *Le Racisme,* cited above, does not include the section quoted here. In references that Taguieff makes to this section below, I will refer to and indicate the French edition. — Trans.] The praise of difference as richness is common to antiracist positions as different as those of MRAP (Mouvement contre le Racisme et pour l'Amitié entre les Peuples — Movement against Racism and for Friendship among Peoples) ("Live together with our differences") or of LICRA (Ligue Internationale contre le Racisme et l'Antisémitisme — International League against Racism and Anti-Semitism), of differentialist feminism, of most regionalisms, of Lévi-Strauss (see Claude Lévi-Strauss, "Race and History," in *Structural Anthropology,* trans. Monique Layton [New York: Basic Books, 1972], 2:362; Lévi-Strauss, "Race and Culture," in *The View from Afar,* trans. Joachim Neugroschel and Phoebe Hoss [New York: Basic Books, 1985], 23–24), of a certain liberal and centrist or moderate right (see Bernard Stasi, *L'Immigration: Une Chance pour la France* [Paris: Laffont, 1984]), of the ethnopluralist Robert Jaulin, and of a part of the ideology of "Beur" organizations (which in general proceed to a coupling of equality and difference: "Equality with our differences").

24. See, for example, Rémy Droz, "Différencier et discriminer: Les Problématiques pouvoirs des tests psychologiques et des psychologues," in *Racisme, science et pseudo-science,* from UNESCO Conference, Athens, March 30–April 3, 1981 (Paris: UNESCO, 1982), 121.

25. The recentering of the discourse of "Beur" militants on the egalitarian claim is exemplary; see *La Ruée vers l'égalité (Mélanges)* (Paris, 1985), 17.

26. See the definition of racism adopted in 1979 by UNESCO, in *Racisme, science et pseudo-science,* introduction (quotation from the 1978 Declaration on Race and Racial Prejudices): "Any theory that posits the intrinsic superiority or inferiority of racial or ethnic groups that would give to some the right to dominate or eliminate the others, presumed inferior; or that bases judgments of value on a racial difference" (13). The last part of the definition implies the prescription that one must not judge when it is a matter of racial differences, which are presumed to be contestable.

27. See Louis Dumont, *Essays on Individualism: Modern Ideology in Anthropological Perspective* (Chicago: University of Chicago Press, 1986), 223–24.

## 2. "Racism"

1. See, for example Roger Ikor, "La Grande Question," *La Nef* 19–20 (September–October 1964): 11–40; we will return to this article (see chapter 9, p. 245).

2. The absolute exclusion of dialogue ("one does not debate with...") is realized in the reversible formulas of racizing the hated adversary, which often include parasitological and bacteriological metaphors. A prototype of these is given by this sequence of racizing evidence that, first appearing in modern (late-nineteenth-century) anti-Jewish discourse, is currently used by contemporary antiracist polemicists: "One does not debate with the trichina or the bacillus, one does not educate the trichina or the bacillus, one exterminates them as rapidly as possible" (Paul de Lagarde, "Mitteilungen" [1887], in *Ausgewählte Schriften* [Munich: Lehmann, 1924], 2:209). On such a protoracist statement, see Saul Friedländer, *L'Antisémitisme nazi: Histoire d'une psychose collec-*

*tive* (Paris: Seuil, 1971), 84; Jean Favrat, *La Pensée de Paul de Lagarde (1827–1891)*, thèse d'Etat, University of Lille III (Paris: Champion, 1979), 468; Eugène Enriquez, *De la horde à l'État* (Paris: Gallimard, 1983), 416.

3. Pierre Bourdieu, *Sociology in Question,* trans. Richard Nice (London: Sage, 1993), 6.

4. See especially Pierre Bourdieu's contribution to the MRAP conference (May 1978), "Le Racisme de l'intelligence," *Races, sociétés et aptitudes: Apports et limites de la science,* special issue of *Cahiers Droit et Liberté* 382 (1979): 67–71; published in English as "The Racism of Intelligence," in Pierre Bourdieu, *Sociology in Question,* 177–80. The expression "racism of intelligence" is a polemical metaphorization of class contempt. But hostility may mix with contempt: "Does there exist elsewhere than among us the sort of intellectual racism that inspires in every family of minds the desire to bully and dominate its rivals?" (François Mauriac, *Le Bâillon dénoué,* in *Oeuvres complètes* [Paris: Fayard, 1952], 447).

5. See, for example, this comment by Jean Ferré on remarks Evelyne Sullerot made on *Apostrophes:* " 'Now, we have to declare our age for any reason.... At thirty-seven you're offered a job you'd be refused at forty-four, even before being asked about your qualifications and abilities.... Except in the arts and politics, everyone is subject to the dictatorship of the notion of age.... Nonetheless we don't all age the same way.' Finally! Someone is publicly reacting to the racism of age!" ("Racisme de l'âge," *Le Figaro-Magazine,* January 18, 1986). Here the journalist applies the word *racism* to a mode of categorization that encompasses and reduces individuals, classed on the scale of ages, without accounting for individual differences (performances that vary from one individual to another). The expressions "anti-X (noun) racism," "racism of X (noun)," and "X (adj.) racism" have a performative value: in being said, they delegitimate the attitude to which they refer, by reducing it to a *prejudice* to be destroyed or overcome. Hence "anti-X racism" is denounced just as the "anti-X prejudice" is stigmatized: "a reaction of antisuccess racism" (*Le Point,* July 19, 1976, 7).

6. See Roland Gaucher, "S.O.S.-Racisme: Objectif 'melting-pot,' " *National Hebdo* ("Le Journal du Front National") 127 (December 24–30, 1986): 4.

7. Let us here recall the strict definition of "race" in the perspective of physical anthropology: the human groups called races "may be defined as 'natural groupings of men,' which present a set of common physical and hereditary characteristics, whatever their languages, mores, or nationalities may otherwise be" (Henri-Victor Vallois, *Les Races humaines* [Paris: Presses Universitaires de France, 1976], 4). *Races,* defined by sets of physical characteristics, are then distinguished from *nations,* groupings that correspond to political communities, and *ethnic groups,* groupings based on "characteristics of civilization, in particular a language or a group of identical languages" (5–6). To treat any group at all "as a race" implies that one attributes to it a set of "natural" characteristics, shared by each of its members, who are henceforth identifiable by a sum of "hereditary physical characteristics." But the analogy is rarely achieved in a rigorous fashion in everyday discourses. "Natural logic" cannot be reduced to either formal logic or codified rhetoric.

8. Christian Delacampagne, "Le Racisme ordinaire," *Le Genre Humain* 2 (1982): 66.

9. Georges Mauco, *Les Étrangers en France et le problème du racisme* (Paris: La Pensée Universelle, 1977), 192. "Intolerance," the criterion of "racism" in the generalized sense, is analyzed as *hostility* (hate, violence) and as *contempt* (hierarchy, discrimination). There remains the gap, unnoticed in the antiracist vulgate, between attitudes and behaviors: at one end, "antipolice racism"; at the other, "racist murders,"

defined as murders carried out through racism becoming act (the causal model, to which we will return in chapter 5).

10. Madeleine Barot, "Evolution du racisme et de l'antisémitisme," in *Racismes I* (Paris: Groupe "Racisme" de la Fédération Protestante de France, 1982), 7. The law of July 1, 1972, bearing on the struggle against racism, in its first and second articles reads as follows: "Those who, either by speech, shouts, or threats..., or by writings, printings, drawings, images, paintings..., or by signboards or posters exhibited for public viewing..., have provoked discrimination, hate, or violence toward a person or group of persons for reason of their origin or their affiliation or lack thereof to a determinate ethnic group, nation, race, or religion will be punished by imprisonment ranging from one month to one year...." (MRAP, *Chronique du flagrant racisme* [Paris: La Découverte, 1984], 111). Let us consider just two types of presupposition: (1) the reduction of individual identity, the categorization guided by the principle of "racism," is effected without distinction through ethnic, national, racial, or religious affiliation (an extension of racism beyond racial interactions); (2) the leveling of distinctions between discrimination, violence, and hate, which supposes a continuity between attitudes or prejudices and behaviors (on this point, see chapter 5 below). The movement of fundamentalist Catholics favorable to Le Pen published a pamphlet that analyzes and denounces "the antiracist law of 1972": *Le Soi-disant Antiracisme: Une Technique d'assassinat juridique et moral,* special issue of the journal *Itinéraires* (December 1983).

11. Michel de Saint-Pierre, *La Nouvelle Race* (Paris: La Table Ronde, 1962), 245.

12. Ibid., 246.

13. Ibid., 247.

14. Christian Delacampagne, *Figures de l'oppression* (Paris: PUF, 1977), 151.

15. Colette Guillaumin, *L'Idéologie raciste: Genèse et langage actuel* (Paris and The Hague: Mouton, 1972), 3, 7.

16. Bourdieu insists on the self-legitimation of the group with respect to its very existence and its specific modes of existence (see Bourdieu, *Sociology in Question*, 177).

17. Guillaumin, *Idéologie*, 3.

18. On othering, see ibid., 4.

19. Delacampagne, *Figures de l'oppression,* 150–52. See, for example, Pascal Bruckner, *The Tears of the White Man: Compassion as Contempt,* trans. William R. Beer (New York: Macmillan, 1986). On the "positive" aspects of this essay, according to the leader of the "New Right" (around the denunciation of self-hatred among Westerners), see Alain de Benoist, *Europe, tiers monde, même combat* (Paris: Laffont, 1986), 77–81.

20. See Étiemble, *Le Péché vraiment capital* (Paris: Gallimard, 1957).

21. See, for example, these declarations by François Mitterrand at Alençon, June 22, 1987, denouncing "barbarism": "There is no possible compromise with any of these forces of terrorism, racism, intolerance. Let us be attentive to the contagion" (*Le Monde,* June 25, 1987, 8).

22. André Langaney, "Comprendre l' 'autrisme,' " *La science face au racisme,* special issue, *Le Genre Humain* 1 (1981): 95–97. The whole analysis is based on the hypothesis that, "in racist behavior, the perception of difference has more importance than difference itself" (94). This implies a recentering of analysis on the racizing-racized *relation,* the discussion on the scientific legitimacy of the notion of "race" being thereby secondary. Antiracist argumentation is then placed on the sociological terrain of interactions in singular conjunctions, which nevertheless allow certain regularities to appear.

23. Memmi, *Le Racisme,* 205–10.

24. Maxime Rodinson, "Quelques thèses critiques sur la démarche poliakovienne,"

in *Pour Léon Poliakov: Le Racisme, mythes et sciences* (Brussels: Éditions Complexe, 1981), 318.

25. See Christian Delacampagne, *L'Invention du racisme: Antiquité et Moyen Age* (Paris: Fayard, 1983), 42; Langaney, "Comprendre l' 'autrisme,' " 96. "Primary" statements may in a certain measure be made homologous to "realist statements," defined by Gavin I. Langmuir as expressing the representation of a conflictual situation, by a group engaged in it. See Gavin I. Langmuir, "Qu'est-ce que 'les Juifs' signifiaient pour la société médiévale?" in *Ni Juif ni Grec: Entretiens sur le racisme*, ed. Léon Poliakov (Paris, The Hague, New York: Mouton, 1978), 179–80.

26. Pierre Paraf, *Le Racisme dans le monde* (Paris: Payot, 1981), 60 (my emphasis). Paraf is the honorary president of the Movement against Racism, against Anti-Semitism, and for Peace (Mouvement contre le Racisme, contre l'Antisémitisme et pour la Paix—MRAP, founded in 1949). The self-designation was modified in 1977 to the Movement against Racism and for Friendship among Peoples (Mouvement contre le Racisme et pour l'Amitié entre les Peuples). In the same vein, see Georges Mauco, *Les Étrangers en France et le problème du racisme* (Paris: La Pensée Universelle, 1977), 198.

27. Langmuir, "Qu'est-ce que 'les Juifs,' " 179.

28. Rodinson, "Quelques thèses critiques," 237 n. 119.

29. This example is given by Delacampagne, in Christian Delacampagne, Léon Poliakov, and Patrick Girard, *Le Racisme* (Paris: Seghers, 1976), 29.

30. See Charles Darwin, *The Descent of Man and Selection in Relation to Sex* (Chicago: Rand, McNally, 1874).

31. See Edward O. Wilson, *On Human Nature* (Cambridge, Mass.: Harvard University Press, 1978), 143–44, 232–33.

32. William D. Hamilton, "Innate Social Aptitudes of Man: An Approach from Evolutionary Genetics," in *Biosocial Anthropology*, ed. Robin Fox (New York: Wiley, 1975), 134. For a brief but enlightening presentation of the first "sociobiological" efforts of W. D. Hamilton in 1964, see Michel Veuille, *La Sociobiologie* (Paris: Presses Universitaires de France, 1984), 32ff.

33. See Jean-Marie Le Pen, *Les Français d'abord* (Paris: Carrère/Lafon, 1984), 170, 239 (on the "hierarchy of feelings and preferences" whose field of validity extends from the French family to the "white world," which is to be preferentially defended). See Jean-Paul Honoré's comments in "Jean-Marie Le Pen et le Front National," *Les Temps modernes* 465 (1985): 1852–54.

34. See Alain Finkielkraut, "La Dissolution de la culture," *Le Débat* 37 (November 1985): 23.

35. See Konrad Lorenz, *On Aggression*, trans. Marjorie Kerr Wilson (New York: Harcourt, Brace and World, 1966), 259. Robert Ardrey legitimates aggressive ethnocentrism in an evolutionist framework on the basis of a theory of "territorial instinct"; see Robert Ardrey, *African Genesis* (New York: Delta, 1963), 38–58.

36. According to a psychobiological and "evolutionist" conception of racial prejudice, the xenophobic attitude is assumed to be a universal of human nature, a phylogenetically acquired a priori of the human species, involving both the exclusion of the Other and the hierarchy of preferences. Thus Glenn Wilson defends the theses that there exists "an innate tendency to prefer people who resemble us" ("Review: Attitudes and Opinions by S. Oskamp," *British Journal of Social and Clinical Psychology* 17 [1978]: 287; quoted in Michael Billig, *L'Internationale raciste*, 164).

37. Memmi, *Le Racisme*, 209–10.

38. Maxime Rodinson, *Peuple juif ou problème juif?* (Paris: Maspero, 1981), 274.

39. I borrow this typology of "the Jews" from ibid., 19–22.

40. Madeleine Barot, *Racism and Anti-Semitism* (pamphlet, 44 pp.), presented by the "Racism" group of the Protestant Federation of France and the Ecumenical Group on Immigration, Paris (1982), 41 (my emphasis).

41. On the question of the characterization of racism as fateful by naive racism, Guy Laval makes good remarks, unfortunately soon spoiled by a series of psychoanalytical stereotypes and "psychosociological" generalities, in his article "Le Ça, le moi et la haine de l'autre," *Différences* 57–58 (June–July 1986): 34–35.

42. Pierre Thuillier, *Le Darwinisme aujourd'hui* (Paris: Le Seuil, 1979), 180–81.

43. Julien Brunn, *La Nouvelle Droite: Le Dossier du "procès"* (Paris: Nouvelles Éditions Oswald, 1979), 14.

44. The qualifier *segregationist* here has no conceptual value but intervenes to reinforce the strongly negative connotation of the word *racism*.

45. In the context of the previously cited article, the GRECE constitutes the most plausible sociological reference of the expression "the New Right."

46. Cf. Alain de Benoist, *Les Idées à l'endroit* (Paris: Libres/Hallier, 1979), 21–22: the author summarizes his critique of the "reductionist" tendencies of sociobiology, which misapprehends cultural diversity and the historical dimension by claiming to explain all human behaviors by the principle of the optimization of profit linked to genetic capital (87, 93). Benoist impugns all varieties of "biologism," beginning with the most famous, the very ill-defined "social Darwinism."

47. Yves Christen, *L'Heure de la sociobiologie* (Paris: Albin Michel, 1979).

48. Henry de Lesquen and the Club de l'Horloge, *La Politique du vivant* (Paris: Albin Michel, 1979).

49. Habib Tawa, *Aspects historiques de la question de la science face au racisme* (Paris: UNESCO, 1982), 62.

50. Immanuel Wallerstein to the contrary defends the thesis of the discontinuity between xenophobia and racism and insists on their heterogeneity. See his *Historical Capitalism* (London: Verso, 1983), 78.

51. Tawa, *Aspects*, 63.

52. Ibid., 71.

53. Ibid., 73.

54. Memmi, *Le Racisme*, 208.

55. Ibid. The author is pessimistic with regard to intelligence: "It is racism that is natural and anti-racism that is not" (196).

56. Gordon W. Allport, *The Nature of Prejudice* (Cambridge, Mass.: Addison-Wesley, 1954), 14.

57. Ibid.

58. Ibid., 14–15.

59. Ibid., 15.

60. Ibid.

61. Ibid., 49.

62. Ibid., 51.

63. Ibid., 53.

64. Ibid., 57.

65. Ibid., 27.

66. Ibid., 49.

67. Ibid., 57. Every (latent) attitude is presumed to be potentially manifest; every opinion is postulated as expressible; every verbal expression is assumed capable of engendering a physical attack — and not to be substituted for one, as a performative speech-act. See Monica Charlot's remarks in *Naissance d'un problème racial: Minorités*

*de couleur en Grande-Bretagne* (Paris: Armand Colin, 1972), 89 (the author otherwise sticks to the "reduction" of the scale of intensity to three degrees).

68. Patrick Tort, *La Pensée hiérarchique et l'évolution* (Paris: Aubier Montaigne, 1983), 188–89.

69. Darwin, *Descent of Man*, 119. In *Mutual Aid*, written in the form of articles from 1890 to 1896, Peter Kropotkin gauged quite well in Darwin's text the elements of an ethics of cooperation, fraternity, and solidarity, whose lack of sufficient development he deplored; see Peter Kropotkin, *Mutual Aid: A Factor of Evolution* (New York: New York University Press, 1972), 17–18.

70. Tort, *La Pensée*, 189.

71. Darwin, *Descent of Man*, 131.

72. Tort, *La Pensée*, 193.

73. Patrick Tort, in *Misère de la sociobiologie*, ed. Patrick Tort (Paris: PUF, 1985), 126.

74. Ibid.

75. "Darwin n'est pas à droite" (interview with Patrick Tort), *Enjeu* 18 (January 1985): 20–22.

76. See the remarks Gérard Lemaine and Benjamin Matalon make in *Hommes supérieurs, hommes inférieurs? La Controverse sur l'hérédité de l'intelligence* (Paris: Armand Colin, 1985), 26–28 (which are along the same lines as those of Kropotkin).

77. As every eugenicist begins by doing, Darwin deplores the dysgenic effects of the "instinct of sympathy" and of behaviors of assistance in "civilized" societies (*Descent of Man*, 130–31).

78. "Man, like every other animal, has no doubt advanced to his present high condition through a struggle for existence consequent on his rapid multiplication; and if he is to advance still higher, it is to be feared that he must remain subject to a severe struggle. . . . There should be open competition for all men; and the most able should not be prevented by laws or customs from succeeding best and rearing the largest number of offspring" (ibid., 612). It is difficult not to recognize in such a text the principles of social Darwinism, based on the evolutionary value of struggle and competition and advocating minimal state intervention. Strict liberalism [in its European version, which, different from American liberalism, is a liberalism favoring "free enterprise" — Trans.], the enemy of the welfare state, may find in Darwin a biological legitimation of its system of values and beliefs.

79. See George Gaylord Simpson (who cautiously but hopefully presents a selectionist program), *The Meaning of Evolution: A Study of the History of Life and of Its Significance for Man* (New Haven, Conn.: Yale University Press, 1949), 333–34.

80. Cf. George Gaylord Simpson: "All trend ethics demand the postulate that the trends of evolution, or some particular one among those, is ethically right and good. There is no evident reason why such a postulate should be accepted" (quoted in Theodosius Dobzhansky, *Mankind Evolving: The Evolution of the Human Species* [New Haven, Conn.: Yale University Press, 1962], 342).

81. Lorenz, *On Aggression*, 298–99.

82. [Jean Bruller Vercors (1902–91), known mainly by his surname: politically active intellectual who played a key role as a publisher for the Resistance, a founder of the Minuit publishing house. — Trans.]

83. Vercors, "À la longue, très à la longue, le racisme finira par disparaître: Peut-être . . . ," *La Croix*, March 28, 1981 (remarks reported by J.-P. Hauttecoeur). The norm of a tearing away from nature is most notably of Biblical origin; it defines the Jewish people as an ethical people, an "antinatural people," in Albert Cohen's expres-

sion (*Carnets 1978* [Paris: Gallimard, 1978], 135–40). In the same vein, see Vladimir Jankélévitch, *Le Pur et l'impur* (Paris: Flammarion, 1978), 205; and my comments, Pierre-André Taguieff, "V. Jankélévitch: Les Apories de l'éthique et la musique de la métaphysique," *Cahiers Bernard-Lazare* 113 (November–December 1985): 81–82.

84. Vercors, "A la longue."
85. Ibid.
86. Memmi, *Racism*, 196.
87. Memmi, *Racism*, 159: "Evidently, I am a moderate optimist. The struggle against racism will be long and probably never totally successful."
88. Georges Vacher de Lapouge, *L'Aryen: Son rôle social* (Paris: A. Fontemoing, 1899), vii.
89. Ibid., ix.
90. Ibid., 504.
91. Ibid., 509–10.
92. Memmi, *Racism*, 160.
93. Ibid., 139: "It is always ready at hand, in reach of all" (on racism as "one of the manifestations of aggression"). Cf. 129: "The temptation of racism is the best shared thing in the world."
94. Ibid., 139.
95. Ibid., 141.
96. Ibid., 161.
97. Delacampagne, *L'Invention du racisme*, 42–43. Gavin I. Langmuir also identifies "xenophobic" statements as representing the second level of racizing discourse (Langmuir, "Qu'est-ce que 'les Juifs,'" 182). The definitions of "xenophobia" hardly vary at all: "Hostility to foreigners and to everything foreign" (Poliakov, *Le Racisme*, 154); "hostility to what is foreign" (*Le Petit Robert* dictionary, 1967). "Xénophobe": "hostile to foreigners, to everything that comes from a foreign place" (ibid.). For example: "Jews are [all] usurers" — this is an abusive generalization as well as a falsification of historical realities.
98. We know that in formal logic one of the rules of the syllogism, concerning the terms, stipulates that no term must be taken into the conclusion with a greater extension than it has in the premise(s). If it were otherwise, one would affirm or deny more than would be right to do: there would be *abusive generalization*. See, for example, Maurice Gex, *Logique formelle* (Neuchâtel: Griffon, 1968), 177.
99. Delacampagne, in Delacampagne, Poliakov, and Girard, *Le Racisme*, 30.
100. Delacampagne (ibid.) assumes the analysis of Claude Lévi-Strauss ("Race and History," in *Structural Anthropology*, vol. 2, trans. Monique Layton [New York: Basic Books, 1976], 328–32), and he seems to take it as definitive. His commentary is passably justifying: the ethnocentric attitude "is so deeply anchored in the unconscious of human beings that it is mastered only with difficulty. Moreover, as a general rule, it is hardly dangerous" (31). On the continuity between ethnocentrism and racism, the author remains sibyline: he wavers between the affirmation of "a fundamental distinction between ethnocentrism and racism" (30) and the thesis that ethnocentrism "bears *perhaps in the form of a seed* a necessary condition of racism" (31; my emphasis). The summary that precedes the chapter titled "Racist Prejudice: Its Different Species" does not allow one to escape such an indeterminacy, confining one to the *petitio principii*: "We must not confuse ethnocentrism with racism: if the former is *almost* universal, the latter, on the other hand, has appeared only in determined circumstances" (29; my emphasis).
101. Lévi-Strauss, *View from Afar*, xiv. For a radically antiuniversalist reading of this

text by the New Right, see Pierre Brader, "L'Europe mystifiée," Eléments 51 (fall 1984): 13-14.

102. Lévi-Strauss, *View from Afar,* xiv.
103. Ibid., 20.
104. Ibid., 24.
105. Ibid., xv.
106. Ibid.
107. Ibid.
108. Ibid. We will come back to the analyses and positions of the "later" Lévi-Strauss in chapter 5, pp. 154-56.
109. Bernard Lazare, *Antisemitism: Its History and Causes* (London: Britons, 1967), 123-24.
110. Bernard Lazare, *L'Antisémitisme: Son histoire et ses causes* (Paris: Documents et Témoignages, 1969), 148. [The translation of Lazare's book cited above is an abridged version of the French original. — Trans.]
111. Ibid.
112. Delacampagne, in Delacampagne, Poliakov, and Girard, *Le Racisme,* 31.
113. Ibid.
114. Jean Hiernaux, *Races humaines et racisme* (Lausanne, Paris, and Barcelona: Grammont-Laffont, Salvat, 1976), 85.
115. Ibid., 87.
116. Delacampagne, in Delacampagne, Poliakov, and Girard, *Le Racisme,* 31. The indeterminacy of the analysis should be noted: the author moves from the hypothesis that a necessary condition of racism is "perhaps seeded" by ethnocentrism to the assertion that "racism *necessarily involves* the desire to bring down the other" (31; my emphasis).
117. Langaney, "Comprendre l' 'autrisme' ": "the racism that calls itself scientific." We must recognize that such a definition of racism through qualifying self-designation has found very few public discursive illustrations since 1945. The contemporary discourses that call themselves scientific or call on scientificity, stigmatized on the outside as "racist," such as that of the New Right, almost all declare themselves foreign to racism, even hostile to any racist thought. Cf. the self-representing slogan of the GRECE, "Against all racisms," introduced in 1974 (Alain de Benoist, "Contre tous les racismes," interview, *Éléments* 8-9 [November 1974-February 1975]: 13-23; reprinted in part, revised, and corrected in Benoist, *Les Idées à l'endroit,* 145-56); see also Alain de Benoist, "Le Totalitarisme raciste," *Éléments* 33 (February-March 1980): 13-20. The high degree of argumentative sophistication of neoracism (of what *we* designate as such), whose discourse integrates the call to "struggle against all racisms," renders the typology proposed by Langaney inoperative, of value only for the rhetorical state of racism before the defeat of Nazism.
118. Langmuir, "Qu'est-ce que 'les Juifs,' " 185.
119. Delacampagne, *L'Invention du racisme,* 49.
120. On the stereotype whose symbolic power is surprisingly persistent, see Léon Poliakov, *The History of Anti-Semitism,* vol. 1, *From the Time of Christ to the Court Jews,* trans. Richard Howard (New York: Vanguard, 1965), 104-7 (the rumor arose during the summer of 1321 in Aquitaine); Norman Cohn, *Warrant for Genocide: The Myth of the Jewish World-Conspiracy and the "Protocols of the Elders of Zion"* (New York: Harper and Row, 1967), 206, 211; Friedländer, *L'Antisémitisme nazi,* 119; Dominique Pélassy, *Le Signe nazi: L'Univers symbolique d'une dictature* (Paris: Fayard, 1983), 202. The statement may be found in *Mein Kampf* (New York: Stackpole, 1939), 651,

where at issue is "blood-poisoning" (281). The Hitlerian argument fuses the anti-Jewish stereotype of Christian origin and the biologico-scientistic mode of legitimation.

121. By *scientism,* I understand one of the most widespread ideologies in modernity, constituted by a set of highly acceptable assumptions: that "science" alone offers authority, that it is infallible, that it suffices for the approach to any object of cognition, that it has access to absolute truths, by which it is endowed with an unconditional power of legitimation of discourses and practices and with a grounding role that institutes it as the exclusive heir of theologico-metaphysical dogmatism. Scientism is the traditionalism of modernity. "Racists" and "antiracists" resort to it equally: a mimetic rivalry.

122. See Léon Poliakov, *La Causalité diabolique: Essai sur l'origine des persécutions* (Paris: Calmann-Lévy, 1980). In this work the author presents, synthesizes, and applies various attempts made to analyze the policing view of history or "conspiracy theory" — this "typical result of the secularization of religious superstitions," as Karl Popper defined it — namely: "The view that whatever happens in society — including things which people as a rule dislike, such as war, unemployment, poverty, shortages — are the results of direct design by some powerful individuals or groups" ("Prediction and Prophecy in the Social Sciences," in *Conjectures and Refutations: The Growth of Scientific Knowledge* [New York: Basic Books, 1962], 341).

123. See Léon-François Hoffmann, *Le Nègre romantique: Personnage littéraire et obsession collective* (Paris: Payot, 1973). It is especially on the basis of fictions on the sex lives of Negroes — immorality and lubricity supposedly characterizing it — that bestialization operates (37–38). The latter may always be reversed by the transubstantiation achieved through erotic exoticism (41). On personification and personalization, see Pierre-André Taguieff, "Le Titre, le type et le nom," *Cahiers de Praxématique* 8 (1987): 47–58.

124. On the classical distinction between descriptive or lexical and stipulative definitions, see for example Carl G. Hempel, *Philosophy of Natural Science* (Englewood Cliffs, N.J.: Prentice-Hall, 1966), 85–88. The first are the list of the various senses taken by a term in use (by taking account of semantic variations over time) and are classified by them: they proceed through an inventory of accepted significations or received meanings as well as prescribed contents. The second select one signification or another (or some semantic trait) among the inventoried significations, create an expression to which a technical meaning is attributed, or redefine a term by giving it a new or special meaning ("By X, we will understand... "). Genetic definitions (which construct their objects), ideal types, and models of intelligibility are species of the stipulative definition. Here is an example: "By *racism,* we understand... " (as opposed to "By *racism* is understood... ").

125. See Gloria A. Marshall, "Racial Classifications: Popular and Scientific," in *Science and the Concept of Race,* ed. Margaret Mead (New York: Columbia University Press, 1971), 149–50.

126. On correlative notions of receivability (the discourse engaged in must conform to a certain number of institutional practices) and of acceptability (likelihood, coherency, agreement), of a schematization in natural or "informal" logic, see Jean-Blaise Grize, *De la logique à l'argumentation* (Geneva: Droz, 1982), 30, 211–14.

127. This is, for example, the position defended by the author, who is a lawyer and a member of LICRA, of a book in the "Que sais-je?" series, whose pedagogical qualities have been successful: François de Fontette, *Le Racisme* (Paris: Presses Universitaires de France, 1981), 7.

128. "The negation of the racial fact is not in itself a possible attitude, for it consists of

denying reality, one of the greatest disturbances of the mind. It is to this effect that L. C. Dunn, a UNESCO spokesperson, wrote in June 1951: 'The anthropologist, as the man in the street, knows perfectly well that races exist; the former because he can classify the varieties of the human species; the latter because he cannot doubt the evidence of his senses'" (ibid., 8).

129. Cf. ibid.: "The scientific study of racism in which we would like to engage rests on a twofold examination, that of facts and that of ideas" (6); "the true racist is not ashamed" (122). Responding to unitary racism ("racism") is the essentialist *typification* of the "racist" — an operation otherwise denounced in the one called a "racist."

130. Gaston Bouthoul, *Traité de sociologie* (Paris: Payot, 1946), 263.

131. Henri-V. Vallois, "L'Anthropologie physique," in *Ethnologie générale*, ed. Jean Poirier (Paris: Gallimard, Encyclopédie de la Pléiade, 1968), 680–81 (my emphasis).

132. Eugène Pittard, *Race and History: An Ethnological Introduction to History*, trans. V. C. C. Collum (New York: Knopf, 1926), 3–4.

133. Ibid., 3–4; quoted in M. Boule, *Les Hommes fossiles*, 322.

134. The claim of joining science and good sense is an argumentative core common to racist and antiracist rhetorics. For example, we refer to this presentation of a collective book on racism, destined for a broad public: "In this book, Léon Poliakov and his collaborators bring *the scientific and sensible answers* to these often divisive questions (such as, Is humanity really divided into races?, and so on)" (Poliakov, Delacampagne, and Girard, *Le Racisme*, first preliminary page; my emphasis).

135. Albert Jacquard, "Biologie et théorie des 'élites,'" *Le Genre Humain* 1 (1981): 15.

136. Albert Jacquard, "À la recherche d'un contenu pour le mot 'race': La Réponse du généticien," in *Le Racisme: Mythes et sciences* (Brussels: Complexe, 1981), 36; see the critical remarks by Pierre Thuillier, *Les Biologistes vont-ils prendre le pouvoir? La Sociobiologie en question* (Brussels: Complexe, 1981), 257–58.

137. Jacquard: "this concept does not correspond to any objectively definable reality in the human species" ("À la recherche," 39).

138. Ibid.

139. François Jacob, "Biologie-racisme-hiérarchie," text of a talk given at a meeting of the MRAP, published in *Le Racisme: Mythes et sciences*, 107–9.

140. Ibid., 107.

141. Ibid., 108.

142. Ibid. See also, on this point, Jacques Ruffié, "Le Mythe de la race," in *Le Racisme: Mythes et sciences*, 357–61; Ruffi, *Traité du vivant* (Paris: Fayard, 1982), 38ff.

143. See Ernst Mayr, *Evolution and the Diversity of Life* (Cambridge, Mass.: Harvard University Press, 1976), 27–28.

144. Jacob, "Biologie-racisme-hiérarchie," 108 (my emphasis); cf. Jacques Ruffié, *De la biologie à la culture* (Paris: Flammarion, 1976), 375: *"in man, races do not exist"* (emphasis in original).

145. Jacob, "Biologie-racisme-hiérarchie," 108.

146. Ibid., 69 (my emphasis).

147. Ibid. In the same perspective, Ruffié arrives at the "absurdity of the racist-eugenicist program" ("Le Mythe de la race," 364); he then concludes that typological thought has been crushed and genetic polymorphism scientifically imposed (361ff.).

148. François Jacob, *Le Jeu des possibles: Essai sur la diversité du vivant* (Paris: Fayard, 1981), 12–13.

149. Gabriel Tarde, *The Laws of Imitation*, trans. Elise Clews Parsons (New York: Holt, 1903), xxi.

150. Ibid., 19n.
151. Edmond Demolins, *Comment la route crée le type social* (Paris: Firmin-Didot, 1927), 1:vii. Demolins (1852–1907) had as "teacher and friend" Henri de Tourville (1842–1903), "who was most completely the heir of Le Play's genius" (1:x–xi).
152. Ibid., 2:v.
153. Ibid., 1:ix.
154. Ibid., 1:x.
155. Ibid., 2:vii–viii.
156. Ibid., 1:x.
157. Ibid., 1:ix.
158. Ibid., 2:vi.
159. Gabriel Tarde, "L'Action inter-mentale," *La Grande Revue*, November 1, 1900, 319–29 (in which the anthroposociological theories of Georges Vacher de Lapouge and of Otto Ammon, based on the concepts of race and selection, are submitted to a concise critique).
160. Gabriel Tarde, *On Communication and Social Influence*, trans. N. Claire Ellis, Priscilla P. Clark, and Terry N. Clark (Chicago: University of Chicago Press, 1969), 124.
161. Emmanuel Lévinas, *Difficult Freedom: Essays on Judaism*, trans. Seán Hand (Baltimore: Johns Hopkins University Press, 1990), 153.
162. Jean Hiernaux, "La Biologie humaine face aux préjugés raciaux," *Raison Présente* 6 (April–May–June 1968): 101.
163. Colette Guillaumin, "Continuité et ruptures dans l'histoire d'une idéologie: Le Racisme, ses antécédents, sa postérité," text of a paper presented at the Hammamet Conference, 1971, 1. On Guillaumin's research, see Pierre Fiala, "Encore le racisme, et toujours l'analyse du discours," *Langage et Société* 34 (December 1985): 10–15. For a clear distinction between race as "an animal category that belongs to the field of the natural sciences" and the social phenomenon of "race," or racial categorization in society, see Colette Guillaumin, "Les ambiguïtés de la catégorie taxinomique 'race,'" in *Hommes et bêtes: Entretiens sur le racisme*, ed. Léon Poliakov (Paris and The Hague: Mouton, 1975), 201–11.
164. Collette Guillaumin, "'Je sais bien mais quand même,' ou les avatars de la notion de 'race,'" *Le Genre Humain* 1 (1981): 63.
165. Ibid. Guillaumin has given an exemplary analysis of a discursive mode of racialization playing on latent themes and implicit evidence in "Immigration sauvage," *Mots* 8 (March 1984): 43–51.
166. Guillaumin, "'Je sais bien mais quand même,'" 65.
167. Colette Guillaumin, "Le Chou et le moteur à deux temps: De la catégorie à la hiérarchie," *Le Genre Humain* 2 (1982): 35; for a more developed critique of the differentialist argument, "antiracist" or "racist," see Pierre-André Taguieff, "Le Néo-racisme différentialiste," *Langage et Société* 34 (December 1985): 69–98.
168. See Guillaumin, "Continuité et ruptures," 1.

## 3. Births, Functionings, and Avatars of the Word *Racism*

1. [The *Oxford English Dictionary* defines *racism* first as a theory of the superiority of one race over others and then as a synonym of *racialism*. The latter term is defined as a belief in the superiority of one race over another. *Racism* is used primarily in the United States and *racialism* primarily in the United Kingdom to designate racism as a belief or opinion. The first attestation of *racism* the dictionary provides is from the United States in 1936 (the link with the French *racisme* is suggested, whose first dictionary

definition is said to occur in 1935 in the *Robert*); in this attestation, the word is used as a self-qualifier in which the author is praising those who consider their own race to be superior. The first attestation of *racialism* is from the Canadian parliament in 1907, and it is used as an other-qualifier and a disqualification. — Trans.]

2. *Larousse du XX$^e$ siècle* (published under the direction of Paul Augé) (Paris: Larousse, 1932), 902. The reference word, in 1932, is the designating qualifier *racist*; it becomes, in the *Supplément* accompanying the editions after 1945 ([Paris: Larousse, 1953], 362), the doctrinal denomination *racism*, the definition of the noun and the adjective *racist* referring back to it ("partisan of racism"). The current use of *racist*, as adjective and substantive, may be found as early as 1930, whereas, in the same texts considered, the substantive *racism* remains rare, even unused. Cf. Paul Morand, *New York*, trans. Hamish Miles (New York: Holt, 1930), 242–43: "Am I not right in the heart of Germany?... Certain cafés are the meeting places of nationalist "racist" groups, as shown by the words 'no jews' written on the door." Cf. also B. Combes de Patris, *Que veut Hitler?* (Paris: Babu, 1932). On *Mein Kampf:* "the racist gospel" (15); "the true racist character of the Jewish community" (53); on certain imperial states: "the racist core that has shaped them" (126); "a state that... takes care of its best racist elements" (148). Neither *racist* (noun and adjective) nor *racism* occurs in Jules Romain's *Le Couple France-Allemagne* (Paris: Flammarion, 1934), in which the designation is used for "Nazism, persecutor of the Jewish race" (77). The same may be said of A. de Châteaubriant's apologetic essay *La Gerbe des forces (Nouvelle Allemagne)* (Paris: Grasset, 1937) (euphemism: "racic principle," 191).

3. Jacques Léonard recalls this concerning the word *eugenicism (eugénisme)*, which appeared in the French language as a derivative of *eugenics (eugénique)*: "As is often the case, the content of the notion precedes the word. Before the introduction of Darwinism in France, the idea existed of a medical interventionism in marriages and births" ("Eugénisme et Darwinisme: Espoirs et perplexités chez les médecins français du XIX$^e$ siècle et du début du XX$^e$ siècle," in *De Darwin au darwinisme: Science et idéologie*, International Congress for the Centenary of the Death of Charles Darwin, Paris-Chantilly, September 13-16, 1982 [Paris: Vrin, 1983], 187). In an analogous manner, Armelle Le Bras-Chopard, in her important study on Pierre Leroux, seems to presuppose that an ideological phenomenon can preexist its specific and distinctive denomination (*De l'égalité dans la différence: Le Socialisme de Pierre Leroux* [Paris: Presses de la Fondation Nationale des Sciences Politiques, 1986], 250). To denounce doctrinal wholes or systems of attitudes is to be in principle capable of gauging, analyzing, identifying, and evaluating them, and so on. But the author postulates what in no way constitutes a piece of evidence, that is, that it was the *same phenomena* that, unnamed in the mid–nineteenth century, would later be named, on the one hand, *anti-Semitism*, and, on the other hand, *racism*.

4. The basic lumping together here is: "The conditions of appearance of a lexeme are indistinguishable from those of the notion to which it is supposed to correspond."

5. Here I freely borrow, in quite a different context, certain remarks by René Thom on "description" as a scientific objective, especially in the framework of the structuralist enterprise, whose "only goal is to improve description" (*Modèles mathématiques de la morphogenèse* [Paris: Union Générale d'Éditions, 1974], 20, 131ff.).

6. There may be observed, in the 1970s and 1980s, a coexistence of two hegemonic vulgates, the antiracist and the antitotalitarian. The one and the other present many analogous traits and functionings — beginning with an understood identification of the rejected configuration, which remains functionally vague ("racism" or "totalitarianism"), with a weighty historical figure ("Nazism," "Stalinism," even "communism"

or "collectivism"). Toward the mid-1980s, we witnessed the settlement of *terrorism* in the hell of ideological values: "Terrorism is absolute evil. It is just as serious as Nazism; it must be fought by any means, to the exclusion of none" (Édouard Balladur, quoted in *Le Figaro,* September 10, 1986). A new figure of "absolute evil," terrorism joins racism (Nazism) and totalitarianism (communism or Nazism): a diabolical trinity of maximal antivalues, a triad of infernal ideological values. One may see here the confirmation of the gnostic hypothesis (E. Voegelin, A. Besançon): Manichaean dualism is the active center of modern political ideology in general.

7. On the anthroposociology of Georges Vacher de Lapouge, see Pierre-André Taguieff, *Dictionnaire des philosophes* (Paris: Presses Universitaires de France, 1984), 2559–65; Taguieff, *La Couleur et le sang: Doctrines racistes à la française* (Paris: Mille et une Nuits, 1998), 91–163, 193–204.

8. Gaston Méry, *La Libre Parole,* November 18, 1897; cf. Jean-Paul Honoré, "Le Discours politique et l'affaire Dreyfus: Étude des vocabulaires, 1897–1900" (thesis, University of Paris III–la Sorbonne Nouvelle, 1982), 154–55. Approaching the analysis of the "racist basis" of the vocabulary of anti-Semitism in the era of the Dreyfus Affair, Honoré notes that "two neologisms underscore this new dimension of the Jewish question: *racist* and *eugenicism*" (155). Some of Maurice Barrès's notes may be quoted in this connection: "I reflect. There is *national consciousness* and then *energy*. Having national consciousness, the feeling that there the country has a past, the taste for linking with this nearest past.... Now, there is energy. Eugenicism" (Maurice Barrès, *Mes Cahiers,* vol. 1 [Paris: Plon, 1929], 93–94; this text is dated June 1896). The influence of Vacher de Lapouge, even if Barrès does not cite him in the first volume of the *Cahiers,* is not to be missed here: the two criteria of the elite being are in fact, in *Les Sélections sociales* (Paris: A. Fontemoing, 1896), intelligence and energy (68). On this selectionist criteriology, see the remarks by Léon Winiarski in his critical study on anthroposociology ("L'anthroposociologie," *Le Devenir Social* 4, no. 3 [March 1898]: 193–232; reprinted in Léon Winiarski, *Essais sur la mécanique sociale* [Geneva: Droz, 1967], 130–61). This economist and sociologist of Polish origin, who became one of the representatives of the Lausanne school (Léon Walras, Vilfredo Pareto), puts in question the Lapougian criterion of racial superiority, namely, "not so much intelligence as character": "The apogee of eugenic projects, in the sense of men of character and energy, does not coincide with the flash of civilization, but only with that of struggles and exterior conquests. The flash of civilization begins only with the decadence of eugenicism thus understood" (159). It should be specified that the term *eugenic (eugénique)* (first an adjective, then a substantive noun) had been introduced into French by Georges Vacher de Lapouge in "L'Hérédité," *Revue d'Anthropologie* 1, no. 15:3 (1886): 512–21. Here Lapouge transposed with *eugénique,* in the scientific vocabulary of the French language, the [English] substantive *eugenics,* introduced three years earlier by Francis Galton, in his *Inquiries into Human Faculty and Its Development* (London: Macmillan, 1883). The terms *eugenics/eugenicism,* accompanied by *selectionism* (or by *human selection*), henceforth tended to substitute for the concurrent denominations: *viriculture, megalanthropogenesie, callipedie, anthropotechnie (zootechnie* applied to man), *hominiculture, eubiotics, orthobiosis,* and so on. In 1886, Lapouge introduced thus the biotechnical term as follows: "Mr. Galton's research has but one goal: to determine the practical means of producing eugenic beings, subjects hereditarily endowed, and to have humanity evolve without shocks or delays, by a continual substitution of the eugenic races for the inferior or mediocre races" (Lapouge, "L'Hérédité," 516). Whether it applies to individuals or races, the adjective *eugenic* qualifies "elite," "superior," or "well-endowed" subjects. As with the word *racism,* the dates furnished by the dictionaries are hardly

trustworthy — thus the *Robert* indicates 1912 for *eugénique* (noun) or *eugénisme*. (*Le Robert* is the brief designation of the *Dictionnaire alphabétique et analogique de la langue française* [Paris, 1953–1965].)

In the 1877 edition of Paul-Émile Littré's *Dictionnaire de la langue française*, one finds mentioned the words *eugénésique, eugénine,* and *eugénique*. But, whereas *eugénésique* refers to the improvement of the race, *eugénique* has no trace of the Galtonian sense that it took ten years later, especially through the efforts at adapting to the French scholarly tradition of the eugenicist idea, carried out by Vacher de Lapouge. The definitions from Littré are the following: *"Eugénésique.* adj. 1. Said of that which improves the race. Eugenesic crossings *[croisements eugénésiques].* 2. Eugenesic hybridity: hybridity in which the two orders of mixture are each limitlessly fertile to the other. *Revue d'Anthrop.,* v. 4, 243." (The term does not appear in Bescherelle's *Dictionaire national,* 16th ed. [Paris: Garnier, 1877].) *"Eugénine.* s.f. Term from chemistry. A crystalline matter that is spontaneously deposited in the water distilled from cloves." (The term also appears in Bescherelle, 1877.) *"Eugénique.* adj. Term from chemistry. Eugenic acid: a liquid with a spicy and burning flavor, with a strong odor of cloves." (This term does not appear in Bescherelle.)

Before the founding of the French Society for Eugenics (Paris, January 1913), the vocabulary is barely set, even in scholarly circles. The call inviting the organizational meeting of the society, held on December 22, 1912, in the main amphitheater of the school of medicine (under the presidency-in-honor of Léon Bourgeois, minister of labor and social welfare), ended with the following terminological specification: "To name the Society whose formation we propose to you, we think that we should keep the term 'eugenics,' which has become current in the English-speaking countries. It is in fact the dominant term, and no other has appeared to us appropriate to replace it. The future Society will therefore be called the *Société française d'eugénique*" (minutes of the sessions of the society, in *Eugénique* [organ of the French Society for Eugenics] 1, nos. 1–4 [January–April 1913]: 43). The constitution of the society followed by a few months the first International Eugenics Congress, held in London in July 1912 (ibid., 42). The Anglo-Saxon usage was therefore, in the choice of the scientific term, determining (the president of the society was a naturalist of considerable authority, Edmond Perrier, director of the Museum of Natural History, member of the Institute). But, during the organizational meeting, certain waverings in the terminology may still be noted. Senator Paul Doumer thus posed the problem: "The increase in well-being, the protection accorded to the weak and the disinherited, the substitution of inanimate forces for muscular force, and many other bits of progress due to civilization... tend to bring about the disappearance of the natural selection that, for centuries, regulated the growth of the human species. And new problems pose themselves: how does one hinder the ferments of degeneracy from developing?" (ibid., 44). Professor Pinard continued, and prescribed this remedy: "A misunderstood welfare reduces descent in both quantity and quality.... The evil comes from the fact that civilization is incomplete, as the man who procreates does not have sufficient consciousness of the loftiness of his mission.... We must combat the alcoholism and the poisons of the race. *Eugenetics [l'eugénétique]* must be taught, and we may to this effect put to good use the facts of genetics" (ibid., 44; my emphasis). Professor Landouzy (one of the three vice presidents of the society, along with Professors Pinard and Houssay) then added: "Our goal is *hominiculture:* to favor the birth of beings who will offer the cultivation of healthy and vigorous men — it is to this that those in medicine and hygiene have applied themselves. Civilization sometimes leads to a reverse selection, as we have the duty of caring for the wounded, the infirm, the weak. But science has seen the danger. The breeders have followed its directions.... Those in medicine... must see farther than the present sick man, must direct their attention to the son and the grandson, must pose an obstacle to all uncleanliness of body and mind" (ibid., 45; my emphasis).

9. It was the article by Maurice Barrès, "La Querelle des nationalistes et des cosmopolites," *Le Figaro,* July 4, 1892, that introduced into the general political discourse the Manichaean dichotomy of nationalist and cosmopolite. It will be noted that Barrès, far from taking the side of boastful and bellicose patriotism, in this article takes a stance against cultural chauvinism, as Zeev Sternhell recalls in *Maurice Barrès et le nationalisme française* (Paris: Colin and Presses de la Fondation Nationale des Sciences Politiques, 1972), 27. But with this came the establishment of the pair of opposites waiting to be invested with positive and negative values at the time of the Dreyfus Affair (cosmopolitan Dreyfusards and nationalist anti-Dreyfusards), in such a way as to form a relatively stable ideological opposition.

10. See the penetrating remarks by Anatole Leroy-Beaulieu, which show how racial theory gives a "scientific" basis to anti-Semitic passion: *L'Antisémitisme* (Paris: Calmann-Lévy, 1897), 27–29; Leroy-Beaulieu, *Les Doctrines de haine* (Paris: Calmann-Lévy, 1902), 111–14. See also James Hocart, *La Question juive: Cinq conférences, avec un appendice sur la charité juive* (Paris: Fischbacher, 1899), 35–43. In his fine study titled *La Croix et les Juifs (1880–1899)* (Paris: Grasset, 1967), Pierre Sorlin does not fail to note the significance and importance of the new ideological need for the scientific legitimation of politico-polemical positions (160). For his part, Michael R. Marrus notes that, in France from 1880 to 1890, the Jews themselves had incorporated into their discourse of community self-identification the vocabulary of "race," in spite of the dangers it carried: Michael R. Marrus, *The Politics of Assimilation: A Study of the French Jewish Community at the Time of the Dreyfus Affair* (Oxford: Clarendon Press, 1971), 26–27. On this point, see the complementary lexical remarks of J.-P. Honoré, "Le Vocabulaire de l'antisémitisme en France pendant l'affaire Dreyfus," *Mots* 2 (March 1981): 83–87.

11. Charles Maurras, in *La Gazette de France,* March 26, 1895, 1. Maurras partially incorporated this text into his *Dictionnaire politique et critique,* ed. Pierre Chardon (Paris: À la Cité des Livres, 1933), vol. 4, fasc. 19, 304; see Jeannine Verdès-Leroux, *Scandale financier et antisémitisme catholique: Le Krach de l'Union Générale* (Paris: Centurion, 1969), 111, 234.

12. A. Maybon, in *Revue Blanche* 223 (September 15, 1902): 146–48 (quoted in *Matériaux pour l'histoire du vocabulaire français: Datations et documents lexicographiques,* 2d ser., fasc. 15. [Paris: Klincksieck, 1978], 289–90).

13. Friedrich Stackelberg, *L'Inévitable Révolution* (Paris: Stock, 1903), 24 (quoted in *Matériaux pour l'histoire du vocabulaire français,* 2d ser., fasc. 26 [Paris: Klincksieck, 1985], 184).

14. Louis Le Fur, "Race et nationalité," *Revue Catholique des Institutions et du Droit,* published as a pamphlet (Lyons, 1921), 21, 22, and passim. Other occurrences of the qualifier *racic* may be found before 1921, as in certain texts of Georges Palante: "Many other *racic,* political, and ideological antitheses, which encumber an already obscure symbolism" (*Mercure de France* 450 [March 16, 1917]: 300; my emphasis). "At issue can be only an intellectual and moral regeneration, with the aid of the tonic of the noble philosophers, possible at most only for the happy few who survive the flood of *racic* mixture" (*Mercure de France* 462 [September 16, 1917]: 323; my emphasis). (These texts are quoted in *Matériaux pour l'histoire du vocabulaire français,* 2d ser., fasc. 18 [Paris: Klincksieck, 1980], 202.) *Racic,* in such contexts, is equivalent to *racial* rather than *racist*. That is not the case in the following polemical use of *racic,* penned

ten years later by Jacques Maritain, denouncing at once the humanitarianist corruption of universalism and (what *we* would call) the national-racist corruption of patriotism: "Humanitarian and *racic* naturalism are both alike hostile to the idea of patriotism and Christendom" (Jacques Maritain, *The Things That Are Not Caesar's*, trans. J. F. Scanlan [London: Sheed and Ward, 1930], 90; my emphasis). It will be noted that this twofold rejection defines the doctrinal position of the church in this area: the "true" sense of Catholicity is not in the least exclusive of "true" patriotism; rather, it implies it (as much as it does attachment to the family).

15. Le Fur, "Race et nationalité," 22–32.

16. Ibid., 32.

17. Ibid., 22.

18. Ibid., 21 (my emphasis).

19. Ibid., 21 n. 1. The *Larousse du XX$^e$ siècle* (Paris: Larousse, 1932) contains the entry *racic:* "adj. Ethn. Having a relation to race (when one speaks of peoples): *racic aggregation [l'agrégation racique]*" (902). The qualifier *racic* is polemically neutral, contrary to *racist*, defined as applying "to the German National Socialists who claim to represent the pure German race, by excluding the Jews," and so on (ibid., article entitled "Raciste").

20. If *racial* is integrated into the general vocabulary just after 1910 (the *Robert* dictionary suggests 1911), *racist* is integrated only progressively in the second half of the 1920s.

21. *Dernière heure*, January 8, 1959, 3 (quoted in *Matériaux pour l'histoire du vocabulaire français*, 2d ser., fasc. 22 [Paris: Klincksieck, 1983], 252).

22. Théodore Ruyssen, *La Société internationale* (Paris: Presses Universitaires de France, 1950), 3.

23. Ibid., 4 (my emphasis). The philosopher appeals to "experience" in order to hold that the human species is "one, if not in its *matter*, at least in its current *form*" (3). But it is still an indubitable fact that there is "the intensity of the passions that the diversity of races may incite" (3–4). On this question, the universal thinker states an unexpected hypothesis: "The reasons for these antagonisms [among races] are ... difficult to discern; perhaps it is less *reasons* that would conveniently be spoken of than a sort of instinctive repulsion that has so far been poorly studied" (3).

24. Henri Lichtenberger, *Relations between Germany and France* (Washington, D.C.: Carnegie Endowment for International Peace, 1923). In a preface dated November 11, 1922, the author specifies, "This book is a preface to the inquiry on the Germany of today, instituted by the Musée Social, the first volumes of which will be issued at the beginning of 1923" (xiii).

25. Ibid., 53.

26. Ibid., 50.

27. Edmond Vermeil, *L'Allemagne contemporaine (1919–1924): Sa structure et son évolution politiques, économiques et sociales* (Paris: Alcan, 1925), 55 (my emphasis). This passage is partially (until the words "not German") quoted in *Matériaux pour l'histoire du vocabulaire français*, 2d ser., fasc. 26 (Paris: Klincksieck, 1985), 184. It will be noted that the stated correspondence between *racist* and *völkisch* is lexicographically confirmed in 1929: "*Raciste.... pol.l.a.* deutschvölkisch. 2.s. Deutschvölkische(r)" (*Taschenwörterbuch der französischen und deutschen Sprache* [Berlin and Schöneberg: Langenscheidt, 1929]; quoted in *Matériaux pour l'histoire du vocabulaire français*, 2d ser., fasc. 15 [Paris: Klincksieck, 1978], 290).

28. René Johannet, "Relèvement et redressement de l'Allemagne," *La Revue Universelle* 20, no. 22 (February 15, 1925): 524. It should be recalled here that Johannet

had published, nine years earlier, a work whose erudition (passably compilatory) could not mask its nature as an anti-German pamphlet: René Johannet, *Le Principe des nationalités* (Paris: Nouvelle Librairie nationale, 1918). It was again Johannet who provided a preface to the no-less-polemical essay (criticizing both the theory of races and the tendencies of German science) by Louis Le Fur, *Races, nationalités, États* (Paris: Alcan, 1922). Johannet was a regular contributor to *La Revue Universelle*, which was founded in April 1920 by Jacques Bainville (director) and Henri Massis (editor-in-chief) and ceased publication in August 1944. See Eugen Weber, *Action Française: Royalism and Reaction in Twentieth-Century France* (Stanford, Calif.: Stanford University Press, 1962), 501–4; and the testimony by Henri Massis, *Maurras et notre temps* (Geneva and Paris: Palatine, 1951), 1:145ff.

29. "Les Associations patriotiques et militaires en Allemagne," *La Revue Universelle* 28, no. 24 (March 15, 1927): 646–50 (for what interests us).

30. Ibid., 646 (my emphasis).

31. Ibid., 647 (my emphasis).

32. Ibid., 650 (my emphasis).

33. Ludwig Bergstraesser, "Les Partis politiques en Allemagne," *Revue d'Allemagne* 2, no. 6 (April 1928): 496 (my emphasis). The context allows one to refer the designation *the racists* to the "nationalist" movements of which General Ludendorff was the figurehead.

34. Ibid., 499–500.

35. Ibid., 502 (my emphasis).

36. Charles Maurras, *Enquête sur la monarchie* (Paris: Fayard, 1937), xcvi–xcvii. Maurras conceives race according to the natural ("familial") model of filiation (a sequence of individuals with a single lineage) and suggests that he would be a partisan of these hereditary (so biologically grounded) castes, but he makes it clear that he is interested in them mainly for the dynastic question, as is indicated by the metaphorical usage of the term *dynasty*. What is important here is the continuity of superior "blood," that of the race of leaders.

37. See Marie de Roux, *Charles Maurras et le nationalisme de l'Action française* (Paris: Grasset, 1927), 224 (this commentator has a tendency to emphasize exaggeratedly the Maurrassian distrust of race factors). In 1937, Maurras cites one of his book reviews, "from more than thirty years ago": "I have, for my part, always been careful to separate the reflections on political and economic heredity from those vague, adventurous, and specious generalizations on strict physiological heredity" ("Le Nationalisme français et le nationalisme allemand," note published as an appendix to a study by Marie de Roux, *Le Nationalisme français* [Paris: Action Française, 1937], 29).

38. Quoted in Roux, *Charles Maurras*, 224 (see Charles Maurras, *Dictionnaire politique et critique*, vol. 2, fasc. 7 [Paris: À la Cité des Livres, 1932], 135). See also Charles Maurras, *La Démocratie religieuse* (Paris: NEL, 1978), 120, 292, 493; Maurras, *Quand les Français ne s'aimaient pas: Chronique d'une renaissance 1895–1905* (Paris: Nouvelle Librairie nationale, 1916), 197. In his "Mémorial en réponse à un questionnaire," Maurras still vitupérated "the stupid Gobineau, unworthy of being called French" (Charles Maurras, *Pour un jeune Français* [Paris: Amiot-Dumont, 1949], 96). A text dated January 12, 1905, reprinted in "Gaulois, Germains, Latins (Extraits)" (*Les Cahiers d'Occident* 1, no. 1 [1926]: 29–30), enables a measure of the distance carved out by the exasperation that Maurras bore toward Gobineau.

39. Roux, *Charles Maurras*, 224–25 (my emphasis).

40. Ibid., 218.

41. Ibid., 225–26.

42. Ibid., 226 (my emphasis).
43. Ibid., 225 (my emphasis).
44. *Larousse illustré,* s.v. "nationalisme."
45. Marie de Roux, *Le Nationalisme français,* with an afterword by Charles Maurras on French nationalism and German nationalism (Paris: Action Française, 1937), 12.
46. Ibid., 19.
47. Ibid., 20. In his afterword to Roux's study, Maurras comments thus on the encyclicals of March 14 and 19, 1937: "We now know that what is prohibited is Hitlerism, Hitler's Germanism, the religious metaphysics of soil and blood" (27) — that is, "what constitutes the object of a sort of completely aberrant historical, temporal, and terrestrial monotheism" (28).
48. Ibid., 20.
49. Ibid., 23.
50. Ibid., 20.
51. Ibid., 21.
52. Ibid., 25.
53. Jacques Bainville, *Lectures* (Paris: Fayard, 1937), 220. The March 15, 1908, issue of *L'Action Française* (536-39) includes the minutes of the February 15 meeting, at which "M. Berneval" gave a talk on "the theories of Professor Otto Ammon." Berneval seems to distinguish correctly both orientations, already for ten years called, respectively, "optimist" (Ammon: social selection is exercised along with natural selection) and "pessimist" (Vacher de Lapouge: social selection is exercised against natural selection), from the theory of selection and more broadly from anthroposociology (537). In the discussion, Louis Dimier "pointed out what is at once strong and dangerous in this counterrevolutionary position, which likens society to an organism" (538). If it helps to recall, on the one hand, that "the principles on which it rests are uncertain," it is necessary, on the other hand, to recognize that "this kind of mental state comes to us from Taine; now, it is to Taine's reaction that we owe our being here" (ibid.). That is why one should not say "too many bad things about this conception" (ibid.). Charles Maurras "speaks along the same lines.... He insists on the uncertain and drifting character of the premises and on the looseness in the adjustment of the doctrines in question" (ibid.).

Maurras quotes a section of this passage from Bainville (from "Gobineau..." to "pure race") in its entirety in his 1937 note (*Mes idées politiques* [Paris: Fayard, 1937], 28). But it is quite difficult to reconcile the absolute impugnment of "Germanism" as the specific mentality that chooses "racism" (Maurras's classic thesis) and the French claim of a doctrinal paternity (or anteriority) of racism (Bainville's thesis). Of course, the orientation of the argument of a French birth of racism may be reversed and may authorize a rehabilitation of Gobinian thought, the latter in its turn conditioning a positive reevaluation of racism. See Louis Thomas, *Arthur Gobineau, inventeur du racisme (1816-1882)* (Paris: Mercure de France, 1941), 7. In the same area, around the theme of a preceding French racism, one may refer to Claude Vacher de Lapouge, preface to Hubert Thomas-Chevallier, *Le Racisme français* (Nancy: Georges Thomas, 1943), ix ("Racism was born of French parents"); Alfred Fabre-Luce, *Journal de la France* (March 1939-July 1940): 228 ("There is a French pre-Hitlerism — and not only with Gobineau.... But by making ourselves forget a part of our tradition, we have sincerely forgotten it"). In his *Anthologie de la nouvelle Europe* (Paris: Plon, 1942), the same Alfred Fabre-Luce claims for France the honor of having many illustrious precursors of National Socialism: "Proudhon, Michelet, Quinet, sons of 1789 and militants of 1848, were already treating of the National Socialist themes: respect for power, opposing religion, cult of labor and fatherland.... Count Gobineau and Mr. Georges Sorel, two men who at first passed unnoticed in their country of origin, last year exercised a singular influence through the intermediary of their illustrious disciples, Adolf Hitler and Benito Mussolini" (iii). But Fabre-Luce adds a nuance and a restriction, insisting that the French mind would be held back by its "moderation" and would not, without refusing itself, adhere without reserve to biological racism (xv).

54. Maurras, *La Démocratie religieuse*, 493.
55. Ibid., 120.
56. Ibid., 120–21.
57. Ibid., 292.
58. On the distinction between zoological races and historical races, see especially Gustave Le Bon, *Lois psychologiques de l'évolution des peuples* (Paris: Alcan, 1894), 30–31, 57ff.; Vacher de Lapouge, *Sélections sociales*, 8ff. (Lapouge posits that "the notion of race is of a zoological order, nothing but zoological"; this idea leads him to propose the creation of the word *ethne* or *ethnie* [ethnic group] to designate non-zoological human groupings); and the critical remarks formulated by Léon Winiarski, "L'anthroposociologie" [1898], in *Essais sur la mécanique sociale,* and Alfred Fouillée, *Psychologie du peuple français* (Paris: Alcan, 1898), 26ff., 117ff. The question constituted, in the 1890s, one of the commonplaces of the politico-scientific debates and controversies: see, for example, Lucien Roure, "Races et nationalités," *Les Études Religieuses* 1 (January 1899): 5–20. The famous text by Bernard Lazare, *Antisemitism: Its History and Causes,* shows through the omission of the term *ethnic group (ethnie)* that the latter was not yet in circulation in the circles of university culture and had not moved outside the circle formed by the community of anthropological scholars. Lazare's arguments aim to impugn the thesis that the Jews are a "race" *(ethnos)*. After impugning the very fact of race in the zoological sense in human history (chapter 10, "The Race"), Lazare redefines the term and from there confers a certain "psychosocial" legitimacy onto what is called "race" *(ethnos)* by means of a phenomenalist or "hermeneutic" argument; a race is if it believes that it is, if it perceives itself as a race or is perceived as a race. In chapter 11, "Nationalism and Antisemitism," he affirms, for example: "Modern Judaism...is in reality an *ethnos*..., for it believes it is that" (136). This intermediary status, this quasi-race status, implies neither a zoological race nor a historical nation in the strict sense; the Lapougian term *ethnie* attempts to name it differentially — an attempt to conceptualize the ungraspable, the equivocal. It will also be noted that this type of self-racization is quite close to the process of formation of "quasi-species," according to certain contemporary authors: this applies to the "pseudospecies" analyzed by Erik H. Erikson (see, for example, *Identity: Youth and Crisis* [New York: Norton, 1968], 41–42, 298–99) and reworked in a different problematic by Konrad Lorenz (see, for example, *Behind the Mirror: A Search for a Natural History of Human Knowledge,* trans. Ronald Taylor [New York: Harcourt Brace Jovanovich, 1977], 191–96, 209; Lorenz, *Das Wirkungsgefüge der Natur und das Schicksal des Menschen* [Munich: Piper, 1978], 267–69; Richard I. Evans, *Konrad Lorenz: The Man and His Ideas* [New York: Harcourt Brace Jovanovich, 1975], 246ff.; each man tends to consider his group to be the human species itself and to perceive every other individual as a "nonhuman"). It will also be noted that before the attribution to Gobineau of the paternity of "racist ideas" and of "racism," so before the mid-1920s in France, the Gobinist conceptions were termed "ethnological," classified as "ethnology," a designation henceforth equivalent to "theory of race": "*The ethnological ideas* of M. de Gobineau did not obtain, at the time they were published, a very great success" (Maurice Kahn, *L'Européen,* August 19, 1905, 15; my emphasis). See also Jacques Duclaud, "Gobineau," *L'Action Française,* January 10, 1911.

59. This text had an official French version, passably different from the German original. [Its English title was *Call to the Civilized Nations*. — Trans.] See Louis Dimier, *L'Appel des intellectuels allemands* — official texts and translation with preface and commentary (Paris: Nouvelle Librairie Nationale, 1914), 45.

60. Ibid., 55 (text of the official French version).

61. Ibid., 141-42.

62. The qualification *barbarous* (the "stammerer," the one who neither understands nor speaks the language correctly) is the object of conflicts for the mastery of its exclusive usage; an operation of redefinition is thereby assumed. Cf. the now classic (but not, for all that, illuminating) argument by Claude Lévi-Strauss: "By refusing humanity to those who appear the most 'savage' or 'barbarous' of its representatives, one is only borrowing one of their typical attitudes. The barbarian is first and foremost the one who believes in barbarism" (*Race et histoire* [Paris: Gonthier, 1968], 22). In 1776, concerning the slavery of Negroes, Condorcet showed with irony a sure sense of the relativity of the qualification *barbare:* "It would be a horrible barbarism if these men were white, but they are black, and that changes all of our ideas" (*Remarques sur les Pensées de Pascal,* in F. Buisson, *Condorcet* [Paris: Alcan, 1929], 26).

63. All quotations are from Dimier, *L'Appel,* 142 (my emphasis).

64. The same word, *Kultur,* is used in point 6 of the *Appeal* in the German original when both *culture* ("our culture") and *civilization* ("our civilization") appear in the official French version (55).

65. Dimier, *L'Appel,* 55 (we have added the terms from the original German text in brackets).

66. Ibid., 57.

67. Ibid., 144-45.

68. Ibid., 146.

69. Ibid.

70. Ibid., 148.

71. Ibid., 147.

72. Ibid., 148.

73. Ibid., 146-47.

74. Ibid., 147 (my emphasis). Cf. Charles Maurras: "What I praise is not the Greeks, but the work of the Greeks; and I praise not being Greek but being beautiful" (*Athinéa* [Paris: Flammarion, 1942], ix).

75. See Maurras, *Mes idées politiques,* 83-84, 265.

76. Ibid., 257-59.

77. Maurras, *Athinéa,* vi.

78. Edmond Vermeil, "La Notion de *Volk* et les origines du nationalisme hitlérien," *Politique Étrangère* 1 (February 1937): 45. Edmond Vermeil, professor at the Sorbonne, originally presented the paper on December 19, 1936, with M. Eisenmann presiding, under the rubric of the activities of the Group for the Study of Germanic Questions. The journal *Politique Étrangère* was published by the Center for the Study of Foreign Policy, an association whose purpose was "the objective study of contemporary international questions." Its general secretariat was directed by Etienne Dennery and Louis Joxe, and its administrative council included personalities such as Célestin Bouglé, L. Eisenmann, L. Marlio, P. Renouvin, and A. Siegfried.

79. Vermeil, "La Notion de *Volk,*" 45.

80. Ibid.

81. Ibid., 46.

82. Ibid.

83. Ibid., 47 (my emphasis). The reference to Schmittian theory here is transparent. The analysis of the French reception of the thought of Carl Schmitt has unfortunately not been done, along two paths of diffusion (or rather of "resistance"): the debates in the community of peers (jurists, philosophers of law, political philosophers) and the polemics around National Socialism in the ideologico-political field. We will here be content to give several elements of clarification. In French-language discourses, between 1934 and 1936, the rare references to Schmitt, a jurist and political philosopher, appeared in the context of critical expositions of National Socialist doctrine approached in its juridico-political aspects (let us recall that Schmitt became a member of the National Socialist German Workers' Party in May 1933). See especially François Perroux, *Les Mythes hitlériens* (Lyon: Bosc, 1935), 28–29 (on the opposition between friend and enemy and the distinction between the public enemy and the private enemy), 88–89 (the reference to Carl Schmitt, *Staat, Bewegung, Volk* [Hamburg: Hanseatische Verlaganstalt, 1933], followed by a characterization of the "pesudoreligion of Hitlerism" through the involvement of "a voluntarist conception of the world"); *Le Droit national-socialiste*, proceedings of an international conference held in Paris, November 30–December 1, 1935 (Paris: Rivière, 1936), 31–32 (Schmitt is designated as "the official philosopher of the National Socialist right"), 40, 47–48, 60; Roger Bonnard, *Le Droit et l'État dans la doctrine national-socialiste* (Paris: LGDJ, 1936), 80 ("In an article aimed at justifying these bloody events [the executions of June 30, 1934, and the days following], Professor Carl Schmitt has invoked ideas analogous [to those of Adolf Hitler]"), 86, 88, 118. The principal academic source of knowledge of Schmittian conceptions, in the French intellectual sphere, was the important study by Kurt Wilk, "La Doctrine politique du national-socialisme: Carl Schmitt: Exposé critique de ses idées," *Archives de Philosophie du Droit et de Sociologie Juridique* 4, no. 3–4 (1934): 169–96 (171ff.: a good critical exposition of decisionism, in the theory of the state and constitutional theory). See also O. Kirchheimer, "Remarques sur la théorie de la souveraineté nationale en Allemagne et en France," *Archives de philosophie du droit et de sociologie juridique* 4:3–4 (1934): 251 (in the "decisionist" perspective, Schmitt "justifies the victor in a civil war"). It must be added that, in 1936, there had just appeared a partial French translation of *Legalität und Legitimität* (July 1932), thanks to William Gueydan de Roussel, *Légalité, légitimité* (Paris: LGDJ, 1936), following up on the no-less-partial translation of the essay *Politische Romantik* in 1919; 2d ed., 1925, trans. P. Linn (Paris: Valois, 1928); English translation, *Political Romanticism*, trans. Guy Oakes (Cambridge, Mass.: MIT Press, 1986). Cf. the reactions of Georges Gurvitch to the publication of *Légalité, légitimité* in *Archives de Philosophie du Droit et de Sociologie Juridique* 6, no. 6 (1936): 235–36. It will be noted that, in the same period, the expositions of National Socialism centered on the theory of race and the racist state do not mention (or mention very little, marginally) Carl Schmitt—the "authors" most often cited are rather Hitler, Rosenberg, Goebbels, H. F. K. Günther, and G. Feder. See, for example, Lawrence Preuss, "La Théorie raciale et la doctrine politique du national-socialisme," *Revue Générale de Droit International Public* (November–December 1934): 661–74 (no mention); Theodor Balk, *Races: Mythe et vérité*, French adaptation by Lydia Staloff, preface by Marcel Prenant (Paris: Sociales Internationales, 1935); Grete Stoffel, "La Doctrine de l'État raciste dans l'idéologie national-socialiste," *Archives de Philosophie du Droit et de Sociologie Juridique* 6, no. 3–4 (1936): 201–26; Otto Scheid, *L'Esprit du IIIe Reich* (Paris: Perrin, 1936); *Hitler et Rosenberg ou le vrai visage du national-socialisme* (Paris: La Bonne Presse, 1936).

84. Vermeil, "La Notion de *Volk*," 52.

85. Ibid., 53. That "the Marxist and communist idea" was assumed, in 1936, to be

the initiator of a "homogeneous and successful... civilization," in opposition to Nazi barbarism, is a blunder in large part explainable by circumstances, and thereby intellectually "excusable," as it may be. The illusion was very much shared in the "antifascist" circles, see Marcel Prenant: "There is a place for a racism in any regime in which a class imposes its domination. Any racism is impossible in the classless society" (preface to Balk, *Races*, 10). See also the declaration of the Alertness Committee of Antifascist Intellectuals after the denunciation of the Locarno accords by Germany: "If democratic France, overcoming its profound aversion to Hitlerian racism, accepts, in the superior interest of peace, to negotiate and deal, in the framework of the League of Nations, with the Third Reich, it cannot accord to the latter the right to pose as the champion of Western civilization and to refuse all contact with the USSR, a member of the League of Nations" (text signed by Paul Rivet, president; Paul Langevin and Alain, vice presidents; in *Non! la guerre n'est pas fatale!* pamphlet of the Alertness Committee [Paris, 1936], 6). What is, on the other hand, intellectually unpardonable, and morally scandalous, is to repeat such statements well into the 1980s.

86. Vermeil, "La Notion de *Volk*," 55.

87. Ibid.

88. Ibid.

89. Ibid. Recognizable here are most of the acts of lumping together established and conducted up to the present day by the "rationalist" dogmatic of the "antifascists," from Julien Benda to the hacks of "Free Thought," the pious caretakers of the remains of a prestigious patrimony. The radical critique of "vitalism," of "mysticism," or of "rationalism," borrowed especially from Benda and Seillière, and corrupted into criminalizing denunciation, is lumped together with the thematics of anti-German propaganda. Its final product is the recurring denunciation of "irrationalism," an intellectual attitude assumed to be the source of all the modern forms of barbarism (clericalism, pan-Germanism, racism, fascism, Nazism... up to the "sects"), in the perspective of degraded illuminism as it is found incarnated in the various leagues (should we say "sects"?) calling for "human rights" or "rationalism."

90. See Zeev Sternhell, *Maurice Barrès et le nationalisme français* (Paris: Colin and the Fondation Nationale des Sciences Politiques, 1972), especially 8–20 (antirationalism, antiscientism, biologization of the organicist or the Darwinian type, the "resurgence of irrational values," "neoromanticism," the "revolt against positivism," the impugnment of democracy, racism, anti-individualism, anti-intellectualism of the Bergsonian/ vitalist style, elitism of the Nietzschean style, and so on); and Sternhell, *La Droite révolutionnaire 1885–1914: Les Origines françaises du fascisme* (Paris: Le Seuil, 1978), especially the introduction (15–32) and conclusion (401–16), in which the acts of lumping together pile up, so to speak. The political scientist/historian insists on biologism of Darwinian inspiration, on the thematics of heredity and of selection, as well as on anti-Marxism (based on a mimetic rivalry between economic and biological determinism); Sternhell, *Neither Right nor Left: Fascist Ideology in France*, trans. David Maisel (Princeton, N.J.: Princeton University Press, 1986) (for a clear example of synthetic lumping-together, see 48–51). It is clear that in characterizing the French "precursors" or "founders" of "fascism" by means of the traits ordinarily used to characterize "fascism" and Nazism, one has every chance of finding at the exit what one left at the entrance: the classic illusion of teleological reconstructions. The ideological presuppositions of the historian are those of the critical rationalism of French tradition, the spontaneous philosophy of most of the "antifascist" intellectuals of the 1930s, whether Marxist, radical, or liberal. On the ritualized polemical usage of the word "fascism," travestied into a concept, see Pierre-André Taguieff, "La Stratégie culturelle de la 'nou-

velle droite' en France (1968–1983)," in *Vous avez dit fascismes?* (Paris: Arthaud/Montalba, 1984), 97–99.

91. Vermeil, "La Notion de *Volk*," 52.

92. Werner Sombart, *Deutscher Sozialismus* (Berlin: Buchholz and Weisswange, 1934), 176–85.

93. Vermeil, "La Notion de *Volk*," 55. Along the same lines, twenty years earlier, see Émile Boutroux, "Germanisme et humanité" (talk given May 2, 1915, at the Museum of Natural History), *Grande Revue* (August 1915); the text was republished in Émile Boutroux, *Études d'histoire de la philosophie allemande* (Paris: Vrin, 1926), 139–62. The guiding idea here is that "Germanism is surely a doctrine. It has presided, for a long time, over the education and instruction given to the German people. It has been applied to modeling intelligences and wills.... Germanism is not a sudden and accidental attack of infatuation and violence. It goes back to tendencies manifested by German peoples throughout the course of their history" (139–40). It will be noted that such a history of ideas assumes that there exist permanencies of the psychoethnic type: Germanism is a set of tendencies and representations attributed solely to Germanic peoples. See also, from the same philosopher engaged in intellectual warfare, "L'Évolution de la pensée allemande," in *Études d'histoire de la philosophie allemande,* 199–227; "L'Allemagne et la guerre," in *Études d'histoire de la philosophie allemande,* part 1, 117–36, part 2, 231–57. On pan-Germanism and its various ideological aspects, the most involved analyses, during the war years, were done by Charles Andler (they alone merited a study): see especially *Le Pangermanisme* (Paris: Conard, 1916), 4 vols. For locating this intellectual contribution in its ideologico-political framework, see Ernest Tonnelat, *Charles Andler: Sa vie et son oeuvre* (Paris: Les Belles Lettres, Publications of the Division of Letters at the University of Strasbourg, 1937), fasc. 77, 167–81.

94. Lucien Febvre, "De Spengler à Toynbee: Quelques philosophies opportunistes de l'histoire," *Revue de Métaphysique et de Morale* 43, no. 4 (October 1936): 574.

95. Ibid., 575.

96. Henri Massis, "Spengler comme précurseur du national-socialisme," in *Débats* (Paris: Plon, 1935), 1, 214 (the word *racist* is emphasized in the text). Massis published, as an appendix to his book *Allemagne d'hier et d'après-demain* (Paris: Conquistador, 1949), the French translation of the preface written by Abbot Georg Moenius, "Germanisme et romanité," to the latter's German translation of the famous essay by Massis, *Defense of the West,* trans. F. S. Flint (New York: Harcourt, Brace, 1928) (*Allemagne d'hier et d'après demain,* 101–46). Here Moenius strongly affirms that "Rome is a universal idea , not a 'racist' one: her foundation is Catholic and apostolic" (145).

97. Henri Massis, "Entretien avec Mussolini (September 1933)," *Les Amis d'Édouard* 166 (June 1937): 29 (my emphasis).

98. Febvre, "De Spengler à Toynbee," 576.

99. Ibid., 578.

100. Ibid., 579.

101. Ibid. "They say": the allusion to rumor, in and for the "case" of Spengler, seems sufficient to satisfy this historian's requirement for proof. His slim epistemological requirement brings him closer to the polemicist ideologues whom he is precisely working to denounce; for it is no longer a matter here of impartially evaluating a work and its field of influence, but rather of delegitimating a manner of writing history on the basis of explicit philosophical presuppositions and in an encompassing perspective.

102. Febvre, "De Spengler à Toynbee," 579.

103. Ibid., 580.

104. Ibid.

105. *Larousse du XXᵉ siècle* (Paris: Larousse, 1932), 902. In the aforementioned book by Combes de Patris, Hitlerian racism, unnamed as such, is thus designated: "a racist 'nationalism' " (12); the "capital point of the doctrine..., the thesis that inspires the entire movement..., this notion of race" (36); "the theory of races" (126); the "Hitlerian theories" (137); "the Hitlerian doctrine" (142); "Hitler's system" (143); "Hitlerian thought" (145). In one of the best French presentations on National Socialism, that of Otto Scheid, *Les Mémoires de Hitler et le programme national-socialiste* (Paris: Perrin, 1932), for *one* recurrence of the word *racism,* one encounters various formulations containing the adjective *racist:* "a new conception of the world, racism"; "racist ideas"; "racist philosophy" (129); "the racist conception" (135); "the racist state" (translation of *völkisch*); "racist aspirations" (89); "racist energies" (125); "racist forces" (132); "racist policy" (172); and so on.

106. *Larousse* (1932), 362.

107. The right of domination and territorial expansion is described in the following encyclopedic definition: "The dogma of the superiority of the Germanic race was adopted by the Germans to justify their pan-Germanism, which was exalted to the level of Teutonomania" (*Larousse, Supplément* [1953], 362). "For the National Socialist leaders, then, Nietzsche's theory of the overman was shaped into that of the superiority of race, and, in order to assure supremacy, anything was permitted" (ibid.).

108. Ibid.

109. "Racist ideology has served to justify *anti-Semitism* and *eugenicism*" (ibid.). The exclusion of the Jew was mentioned in the 1932 edition. That anti-Semitism is often given as an illustration in the contemporary expositions of "racism" is one of the effects of the inaugural and recurring presentation of racism by its Hitlerian illustration. Whereas the dominant anti-Jewish attacks, in Western history, in that they come from Christianity (the deicidal Jews, and so on), are foreign to biological stigmatization, Hitlerian anti-Semitism achieves in exemplary fashion the syncretism of an anti-Jewish discourse and of a racial ideology. "Racism (that is, anti-Semitism)...," wrote Brice Parain and Georges Blumberg in 1933 ("Documents sur le national-socialisme," *La Nouvelle Revue Française* 21, no. 239 [August 1, 1933]: 237). Of course, the overlapping of an anti-Judaism and a racist biologization of self and other is observable, as early as the 1880s, in the ideological effects of a nascent physical anthropology and of Darwinian selectionism. The *quid proprium* of Nazism is that it made exclusion of the Jews into a state ideology.

110. *Supplément,* 362. The names of authors cited — Francis Galton in Great Britain, Lothrop Stoddard and Madison Grant in the United States — are those of men of science who had become ideologues of "the improvement of the race," eugenicists and racists at the same time. Let us be clear that the eugenicist themes may be defended without implicating those of racism: the examples of Jean Rostand and Julian Huxley remain so as to keep us from any quick lumping together. It will be noted that in 1931, in a well-researched book, there is no use of the word *racism,* whereas the correlation between eugenicism and "racial pride" is denounced: "Eugenicism is capable of inspiring pride, egotism, and toughness of race" (Édouard Jordan, *Eugénisme et morale* [Paris: Bloud et Gay, 1931], 134).

111. *Supplément,* 362.

112. With this denomination, I target the differentialist ideology that, in the European circles of "New Right" intellectuals, claims to prop itself up on the results of the biological or ethnological sciences. See Pierre-André Taguieff, *Sur la nouvelle droite* (Paris: Descartes et Cie, 1994).

113. See Alain de Benoist, "La 'différence,' idée antitotalitaire," in *Les Idées à l'endroit*, 163–66; Benoist, "Le Totalitarisme égalitaire," 159–62.

114. Perhaps also for reasons of the behaviors of avoidance and taboo creation, and of individual strategies (as the label *racist* is difficult to bear). Let us here recall that the delegitimation of the theory of race began its establishment in and by the victory of the Dreyfusard camp. The anti-Nazi struggle only reinforced the pejorative assimilation of the theory of race to anti-Semitism and the identification of the scientific rejection of the idea of "race" to the impugnment of any anti-Jewish attitude or conduct — whence the constitutive polemical evidence of contemporary antiracist ideology: "the struggle against racism *and* anti-Semitism."

## 4. An Ideal Type

1. "The many faces of what is named by the name *racism*, which Hitler made popular" (Pierre Paraf, *Le Racisme dans le monde* [Paris: Payot, 1981], 5). "The term *racism* dates from around 1930: as with *anti-Semitism*, it arose to designate a new social reality, political campaigns on a grand scale; but no one will hesitate to term Gobineau or Disraeli racists retroactively" (Léon Poliakov, "Racisme et antisémitisme: Bilan provisoire de nos discussions et essai de description," in *L'Idée de race dans la pensée politique française contemporaine*, ed. Pierre Guiral and Émile Temime [Paris: Centre National de la Recherche Scientifique, 1977], 17). Let us insist on the assimilation, which has become current, of Nazi racism to anti-Semitism, its most striking illustration if not its only one, but to which most of the early descriptions of National Socialism reduced racism. See these remarks by a good observer of Nazi Germany: "this German racism is not what it claims to be; for, in reality, it boils down to a fairly broad anti-Semitism" (Roger Bonnard, *Le Droit et l'État dans la doctrine national-socialiste* [Paris: LGDJ, 1936], 11, 33; racism comes down to the exclusion of Jews).

2. *Larousse (Supplément,* 1953): "A theory whose purpose is..."; *La Grande Encyclopédie* (Paris, 1975): "a theory according to which..."; *Lexis* (Paris: Larousse, 1975): "A theory that attributes..."; *Logos* (Paris: Bordas, 1976): "A theory that affirms..."; *Grande Larousse de la langue française,* vol. 6 (Paris, 1977): "A theory establishing..."; *Polec: Dictionary of Politics and Economics* (Berlin: de Gruyter, 1967): "*Racist,* adj. One who adheres to the nationalism based on racial theory"; *Le Robert* (1962), entry for *racism:* "theory...based on the belief that..." The *Petit Robert* (1967) short-circuits foundational belief through a mention of the conclusion: "A theory...that concludes...."

3. André Lalande, *Vocabulaire technique et critique de la philosophie* (Paris: Presses Universitaires de France, 1956): "Doctrine that admits..."; *Larousse* (1932): "Doctrine of the racists..."; Paul Foulquié, R. Saint-Jean, *Dictionnaire de la langue philosophique,* 2d ed. (Paris, 1969): "A doctrine that affirms..."; *Alpha encyclopédie,* vol. 12 (1972): "A set of doctrines and attitudes..."; *Dictionnaire usuel illustré* (Paris: Quillet-Flammarion, 1981): "1. A doctrine that, originating at the end of the nineteenth century...2. *Curr.* An attitude of hostility toward different...human groups."

4. *Larousse* (1953), and so on.

5. Lalande, *Vocabulaire technique et critique de la philosophie*.

6. *Le Petit Larousse illustré* (1960): "A system that affirms..." (a designation again given in the following editions, until 1980); *Nouveau Larousse universel* (1969).

7. *Le Petit Larousse illustré* (1983): "An ideology that affirms..." (since the 1981 edition). From 1946 (the year of the lexeme's first entry) to 1959: "A theory that seeks to..."; "A theory that tends to..." (1948).

8. Cf. for example, these statements by Jacqueline Marchand: "For the Rationalist Union, we think that the use of reason enables one to drive out the most dangerous myths and to denounce pseudoscientific claims.... Scientific methods enable one to reject the exorbitant claim to the scientific justification of racism" (introduction to an interview with Albert Jacquard, "L'Hérédité de l'intelligence et le racisme," *Les Cahiers Rationalistes* 353 [September–October 1979]: 9).

9. *Le Littré* [dictionary] (1960): "A political theory of...." The entry *racism* is absent from Émile Littré's *Dictionnaire de la langue française* (1863–77). We quote the revised edition, edited and abridged by A. Beaujan (Paris: Éditions Universitaires, 1960).

10. *Dictionnaire Hachette juniors* (1980): "Many people are victims of racism, of prejudices that falsely affirm that a race is...."

11. Rudolf Siebert, "Le Phénomène du racisme," *Concilium* 171 (January 1982): 23. In a Christian context, racism is often stigmatized as an infringement of religious law: "error," "myth," "mysticism," "madness." See P. Charles et al., *Racisme et Catholicisme* (Paris and Tournai: Casterman, 1939); Canon Louis-Claude Delfour, *Le Mythe du sang et de la race* (Paris: Sorlot, 1939); Msgr. Bressoles, Robert d'Harcourt, and Yves de la Brière, *Racisme et Christianisme* (Paris: Flammarion, 1939) (42: "the mysticism of the chosen race").

12. Siebert, "Le Phénomène du racisme," 17.

13. Ibid., 23. The author blames equally "the false consciousness" (15) of racism and "the unconscious destructiveness" (18) of the racist, "racist narcissism" (16), "the absolute dementia of racism" (23). Cf. the pamphlet by Georges Lakhovsky, *La Civilisation et la folie raciste* (Paris: S.A.C.L., 1939): "Racism is a dangerous madness that threatens civilization" (140). As Raymond Aron has noted, racist essentialism and diabolization have an antiracist double (*Progress and Disillusion: The Dialectics of Modern Society* [New York: Praeger, 1968], 56).

14. Léopold Sédar Senghor, "Une Maladie infantile des temps modernes," *La Nef* 19–20 (September–December 1964): 7–10.

15. François de Fontette, *Le Racisme* (Paris: Presses Universitaires de France, 1981), 121–22.

16. Cf., for example: "Showing solidarity with all victims of the racist scourge..., the antiracists..." (Charles Palant, "Printemps de la fraternité," *Droit et Liberté* 259 [February 1967]: 5). The *Petit Robert* dictionary distinguishes three senses of the word *scourge [fléau]*, which are condensed into the metaphorical and polemical usage that the antiracist speakers make of it: "1. A person or thing that seems to be the instrument of divine wrath ('Attila, the scourge of God'). 2. A calamity that befalls a people ('the scourge of war, of the plague'). 3. That which is harmful, disastrous, fearsome (to be 'the scourge of society')." Through such a qualification, racism is held up as a quasi-natural phenomenon (indeed a providential one, for minds sensitive to the popular theology of guilt: "We are all responsible" for the "scourge") that has to be eliminated as one confronts and defeats a natural catastrophe.

17. Lucien-Anatole Prévost-Paradol, *La France nouvelle* (1868) (Paris and Geneva: Slatkine Reprints, 1979), 45.

18. SOS-Racisme, "Manifesto" (condemning terrorism), *Le Monde*, September 17, 1986, 11.

19. In the conclusion of a study on antiracism that is nonetheless very critical, Paul Dehem renews the pathologizing stereotype: "The individuals affected by racism are sick persons whom one does not cure by either incantations or reproaches, but rather by a scientific study of their illness, and above all by looking into their case with a comprehensive solicitude" ("De quelques écueils de l'antiracisme," *Esprit*, March 1965,

561). It will be noted that the antiracists turn the metaphor of leprosy, borrowed from the racizing tradition ("Jewish leprosy," and so on), against their enemy, the racists: "The authorities affirmed their resolution to combat this 'leprosy'" (Madeleine Barot, report titled "Le Racisme et l'antisémitisme," on the passing of the law of July 1, 1972, [Paris, 1982], 7).

20. Lalande, *Vocabulaire technique et critique de la philosophie:* "Doctrine that admits the existence of races in the human species...." Such a definition introduces a presupposition that makes it inapplicable to certain expositions of racism (see, for example, some of Hitler's texts): the acceptance of a relative *unity* of the human species, divisible into races. Célestin Bouglé presented the slogan of vulgar raciology as follows: "It is known how broad a position was occupied, in nineteenth-century literature, by the notion of the omnipotence of heredity.... The vulgarization of like theses ['Semites have a monotheistic skull,' and so on] gave credence to the opinion, to which the nationalism of today has made such a fine fortune, that 'the question of race takes precedence over everything'" (*La Démocratie devant la Science: Études critiques sur l'hérédité, la concurence et la différenciation* [Paris: Alcan, 1923], 37–38). Bouglé analyzes "the philosophy of races" (such as the anthroposociology of Vacher de Lapouge [38]) as one of the "main tendencies" of "naturalist sociology" (36).

21. *Races et Racisme* (Bulletin du Groupement d'Étude et d'Information) 1 (January–February 1937): 15. The designations of the ideological phenomenon stigmatized by the group are "racism" (1), "racist theories" (1), "these [racist] doctrines" (1), "racist ideas" (2), "the racist idea" (1), and "racist doctrines" (4).

22. Pierre Thuillier, *Darwin et C°* (Brussels: Complexe, 1981), 133.

23. *Le Robert:* "A theory of the hierarchy of races...."

24. *Le Petit Larousse illustré* (1960): "A system affirming the superiority of one racial group over others...."

25. *Le Littré* (1960): "A political theory of the supremacy of the Aryan race."

26. Cf. Otto Klineberg on the physiognomic glance, recalling the importance of the "spontaneous" (in truth culturally modeled) inferences made on the basis of visual indices in the racizing category: "If popular wisdom must be believed, the physical appearance of an individual is a good indicator of his psychological characteristics" ("Race et psychologie," in *Le Racisme devant la science* [Paris: UNESCO/Gallimard, 1960], 478). On the physiognomic preparation for racism, in a historical perspective, see William B. Cohen, *The French Encounter with Africans: White Response to Blacks, 1530–1880* (Bloomington: Indiana University Press, 1980), 89–94.

27. Johann Caspar Lavater (1741–1801), in his major book on physiognomy, identified a broad and a narrow meaning of the science: "Taking it in its most extensive sense, I use the word physiognomy to signify the exterior, or superficies of man, in motion or at rest, whether viewed in the original or by portrait.

Physiognomony, or, as more shortly written Physiognomy, is the science or knowledge of the correspondence between the external and internal man, the visible superficies and the invisible contents" (*Essays on Physiognomy: Designed to Promote the Knowledge and the Love of Mankind* [1775–1778], trans. Thomas Holcroft [London: Tegg, 1853], 11). On the "human physiognomy" of Jean-Baptiste Della Porta (1538?–1615), see Gérard Simon, "Porta, la physiognomonie et la magie: Les Circularités de la similitude," in *La Magie et ses langages,* ed. Margaret Jones-Davies (Lille: University of Lille III, Travaux et Recherches, 1980), 95–105; Michel Foucault, *The Order of Things* (New York: Random House, 1970), chapter 2, 17–45; F. Azouvi, "Remarques sur quelques traités de physiognomonie," *Les Études Philosophiques* 4 (1978): 431–48. Physiognomy, a popular art and the dream of a universal science, is based on a theory of expression whose principle may be thus formulated: "No exterior without an interior" (Alexandre Koyré, *Mystiques, spirituels, alchimistes du XVI^e siècle allemand* [Paris: Gallimard, 1971], 91 — on Paracelsus). See also Patrick Dandrey, "La Physiognomonie comparée à l'âge classique," *Revue de Synthèse* 3 (January–March 1983): 5–27; François Dagognet, *Faces, surfaces, interfaces* (Paris: Vrin, 1982), chapter 3, 89–131.

28. Colette Guillaumin, *L'Idéologie raciste: Genèse et langage actuel* (Paris and The Hague: Mouton, 1972), 77. A perfect illustration of the postulate of differential fixity in a supposedly racial discourse is given by the statements of Dr. René Martial, "in charge of the course on immigration at the Institute of Hygiene in the Medical School of Paris, professor of the open course on the anthropobiology of race": "he who says 'race' says duration. If race is prey to many vicissitudes ceaselessly renewed over the long course of the ages, it remains fixed in its mass like a rock that always dominates the ebb and flow of the tide" (*Vie et constance des races: Leçons d'anthropobiologie professées à la faculté de médecine de Paris* [Paris: Mercure de France, 1939], 9).

29. Carlo Ginzburg, "Signes, traces, pistes: Racines d'un paradigme de l'indice," *Le Débat* 6 (November 1980): 3–44. Research on the cephalic index draws on the paradigm of the index, but in addition situates itself in the "metrological" tradition, of either positivist or materialist tendency. On anthropometry and the anthroposociological school, see Frank H. Hankins, *The Racial Basis of Civilization: Critique of the Nordic Doctrine* (New York: Knopf, 1931), 101–40; Pitirim A. Sorokin, *Contemporary Sociological Theories* (New York: Harper, 1928), 233–51; Jean Boissel, "A propos de l'indice céphalique: Lettres de Durand de Gros à Vacher de Lapouge," *Revue d'Histoire des Sciences* 35, no. 4 (1982): 289–319.

30. "One who has seen an aboriginal American has seen all aboriginal Americans," quoted by Émile Durkheim, *The Division of Labor in Society,* trans. George Simpson (Glencoe, Ill.: Free Press, 1947), 134; variants of this statement may be found in Paul Topinard, *L'Anthropologie* (Paris: Reinwald, 1879), 458 (attributed to Marshall), and *L'Homme dans la nature* (Paris: Alcan, 1891), 346 (attributed to Morton); see also Célestin Bouglé, *Les Idées égalitaires: Etude sociologique* (Paris: Alcan, 1925), 155. This is an axiom that has often been repeated with regard to Jews in modern anti-Semitic discourse of Drumontian type.

31. Julien Benda, *Exercice d'un enterré vif* (Paris: Gallimard, 1946), 107.

32. Marcel Prenant, *Biologie et Marxisme* (Paris: Hier et Aujourd'hui, 1946), 189. Integral biology is here viewed as the modern metaphysics of destiny, a fatalism reconstituted in the name of science.

33. Marc Kravetz, "Vive la mort," *Libération,* January 2, 1986, 13.

34. Max Horkheimer, afterword to Thilo Koch, *Porträts zur deutsch-jüdischen Geistesgeschichte* (Cologne: Dumont, 1961), 277. [My translation. — Trans.]

35. Henri Wallon, "L'Étude psychologique et sociologique de l'enfant," *Cahiers Internationaux de Sociologie* 3 (1947): 13–14; reprinted in *Enfance,* special issue (1976): 111.

36. Ibid. (1976), 111.

37. Cf. Charles et al., *Racisme et Catholicisme,* 9: "Racism: its preparation among certain theoreticians of the nineteenth century; its materialist synthesis in the Third Reich."

38. Robert d'Harcourt, "La Religion du sang," in Bressoles, d'Harcourt, and la Brière, *Racisme et Christianisme,* 15. Cardinal Alfred Baudrillart, in a preface to the collective work, locates the appearance of racism "in a time of scientism and materialism" (7).

39. "In Germany, nationalism is built on zoological racism," notes Gaston Bouthoul

("Les Doctrines politiques depuis 1914," in Gaetano Mosca, *Histoire des doctrines politiques depuis l'antiquité*, trans. Gaston Bouthoul [Paris: Payot, 1955], 356).

40. Let us recall that the word *sociology* was created by Auguste Comte. It first appears in his *Cours de philosophie positive* only in 1839 (vol. 4, lecture 47), substituting for the expression "social physics."

41. The *Robert:* "A theory... based on the belief that the social state depends on racial characteristics...."

42. Lalande, *Vocabulaire technique et critique de la philosophie:* "Doctrine... that considers these differences to be the essential factors of history." The Gobinian postulate will here be recognized, stated as such in *The Inequality of Human Races* (1853–1855). See Hannah Arendt, *The Origins of Totalitarianism* (Cleveland: Meridian, 1958), 165–75. Arendt remarks, not incorrectly: "Nobody before Gobineau thought of finding one single reason, one single force according to which civilization always and everywhere rises and falls. Doctrines of decay seem to have some very intimate connection with race-thinking" (171). Léon Poliakov's studies allow the nuancing of such a judgment, see *The Aryan Myth: A History of Racist and Nationalist Ideas in Europe*, trans. Edmund Howard (New York: Basic Books, 1974), 224–38.

43. In 1930, it was not yet common usage to designate Gobinian doctrine, "Gobinism," by the word *racism:* "At the beginning of the twentieth century — the age of the great vogue of 'gobinism' — the works of Fustel de Coulanges... excluded little by little from French science *the notion of race, as a principle of historical development*" (Charles Singevin, "Autour de Gobineau," *La Revue Universelle* 42, no. 11 [September 1, 1930]: 627; I emphasize the definitional, cataphoric formula of Gobinian "racism").

44. This is the self-denomination of the neo-Darwinian science of synthesis made current by the title of the principal work of Edward O. Wilson, *Sociobiology: The New Synthesis* (Cambridge, Mass.: Harvard University Press, 1975).

45. Quoted in Bouglé, *La Démocratie devant la science*, 38.

46. The *Petit Larousse illustré* (1983): "An ideology that affirms... by advocating, in particular, the separation of the latter [the others: inferiorized] within a country (racial segregation)...." Cf. the definition from the 1946 edition: "A theory that seeks to fix the purity of certain races."

47. The *Littré* (1960): "A theory that tends to preserve the unity of a race." Cf. the *Petit Larousse illustré* (1948): "A theory that tends to preserve the purity of the race in a nation."

48. The *Robert* (1962): "A theory... that concludes with the necessity of preserving the 'superior race' from cross-breedings with other races...." The *Petit Robert* (1967): "A theory... that concludes with the necessity of preserving the race said to be superior from any cross-breeding...." Cf. the *Larousse du XX$^e$ siècle* (1932), *racist:* "Name given to the German National Socialists who claim to represent the pure German race, by excluding the Jews...."

49. *To become itself:* proper identity is the object of acquisition and creation from the eugenic perspective, projecting purity on the future horizon as the finality of a will mastering a technique of bioanthropological production.

50. Alfred Rosenberg, *Blut und Ehre: Ein Kampf für deutsche Wiedergeburt* (Munich: Eher, 1938), 37 (speech given at Nuremberg, September 1933). [My translation. — Trans.] See Edmond Vermeil and Pierre Gérome, *L'Hitlérisme en Allemagne et devant l'Europe* (Paris: Comité de Vigilance des Intellectuels Antifascistes, 1937), 20 n. 1.

51. Adolf Hitler, *Mein Kampf* (New York: Stackpole, 1939), 605. See Vermeil and

Gérome, *L'Hitlérisme*, 59–60. Let us recall that Hitler had already characterized France in this way: "France is and remains the inexorable enemy of the German people" (*Mein Kampf*, 600).

52. Chaïm Perelman and Lucie Olbrechts-Tyteca, *The New Rhetoric: A Treatise on Argumentation*, trans. John Wilkinson and Purcell Weaver (Notre Dame, Ind.: University of Notre Dame Press, 1969) 261.

53. Ibid., 263–66.

54. Ibid., 293–96.

55. *Le Petit Robert* (1967): "Theory of the hierarchy of races, which concludes... with its right to dominate the others."

56. Lalande, *Vocabulaire technique et critique de la philosophie*: "Doctrine... that grounds on them [the differences among races] a right for the superior races (or race) to subordinate the others to itself."

57. *Apologists of Neo-Colonialism — Comment on the Open Letter of the Central Committee of the CPSU (IV)* (Peking: Foreign Languages Press, 1963), 29–31.

58. *Dictionnaire du français contemporain illustré* (Paris: Larousse, 1980): "Theory that attributes a superiority to certain ethnic groups; behavior that results from it." The "behavior" is charged, by mere contiguity and anaphorization, with connotative semes of the defined word, *racism*, by which it is degraded.

59. Charles Maurras, *Kiel et Tanger, 1895–1905: La République française devant l'Europe* (Paris: Nouvelle Librairie Nationale, 1910), 371. To classify is to differentiate what is by nature different, and to put it in order on a scale of values.

60. See Memmi, *Racism*, 193.

61. See Jeanne Hersch, "Sur la notion de race," *Diogène* 59 (1967): 127: "Hence in race is achieved the lumping together of fact and value."

62. Memmi, *Racism*, 193.

63. Ibid.

64. Ibid.

65. Memmi, *Racism*, 193–94.

66. Cf. Hermann Rauschning, *The Voice of Destruction* (New York: Putnam, 1940), 241–42: "the Jew" is defined as "the anti-man," or the unique exemplar of the "counter-" or "antirace." On "the Jew" as "antirace" *(Gegenrasse)* in Hitlerian doctrine, see Saul Friedländer, *L'Anti-sémitisme nazi: Histoire d'une psychose collective* (Paris: Seuil, 1971), 144–45; Olivier Reboul, *L'Endoctrinement* (Paris: Presses Universitaires de France, 1977), 133.

67. Memmi, *Racism*, 192.

68. Ibid., 78.

69. Ibid., 80.

70. Gustave Guillaume, *Le Problème de l'article et sa solution dans la langue française* (Paris: Nizet, 1975), 22.

71. Bally, *Linguistique générale*, 81.

72. The Other, in the process of self-racialization, incarnates a Manichaean demon, that is, the absolute Pervert, master of every norm and every legality, obeying no set and discernible rule. He is unlimited wickedness and the strategic intelligence that uses any means to destroy his enemy. This characterization grounds the ethical imperative of his extermination in the name of legitimate defense against pure violence. On the Other as "enemy species," see Léon Poliakov, "Racisme et antisémitisme," 30. Norbert Wiener introduces the concept of the "Manichean demon" in *The Human Use of Human Beings* (Boston: Houghton Mifflin, 1950).

352    Notes to Chapter 4

73. In 1935, Gregory Bateson described a phenomenon of interaction that he named *schismogenesis* and defined as a process of differentiation of the standards of individual behavior resulting from a cumulative interaction among individuals ("Culture Contact and Schismogenesis," in *Steps to an Ecology of Mind* [New York: Ballantine, 1972], 61–72). Two models of schismogenesis may be distinguished. One, based on the maximalization of differences and the acceptance of a complementarity, results in a placement of individuals interacting on a two-position scale: dominant/dominated (above, authoritative subject; below, submitted subjet) — *complementary* interaction. The other, based on the competition and overbidding of individuals representing each other as equals in a position of rivalry, involves a mirroring behavior in the players, defining a *symmetrical* interaction. The latter is at the center of the anthropology of René Girard, developed according to the concepts of "mimetic desire" and "mimetic rivalry," in relation to a general theory of the mechanism of victimization. See René Girard, *Deceit, Desire, and the Novel: Self and Other in Literary Structure*, trans. Yvonne Freccero (Baltimore: Johns Hopkins University Press, 1965), chapters 1–3; Girard, *Violence and the Sacred*, trans. Patrick Gregory (Baltimore: Johns Hopkins University Press, 1977), chapter 6, 143–168; Girard, *Things Hidden since the Foundation of the World*, trans. Stephen Bann and Michael Metteer (Stanford, Calif.: Stanford University Press, 1987), books 1 and 3.

74. The *Petit Robert* (1967), entry for *génocide* (1944): "The methodical destruction of an ethnic group. 'The extermination of the Jews by the Nazis is genocide.'"

75. Lalande, *Vocabulaire technique et critique de la philosophie*: "Doctrine... that grounds on [the difference among the races] a right for the superior races (or race) to subordinate or even eliminate the others." The *Petit Larousse illustré* (1983): "Ideology that affirms..., by advocating, in particular,... or even by aiming for their elimination (genocide, racism of the Nazis)." The *Robert* (1962): "The racism of the Nazis, which results in genocide."

76. Max Horkheimer and Theodor Adorno, "Elements of Anti-Semitism: The Limits of Enlightenment," in *Dialectic of Enlightenment*, trans. John Cumming (New York: Continuum, 1995), 168. This radical demonization of the Jew is opposed to the progressive-liberal denunciation of the Jew as the incarnation of antitypical particularism or as the bearer of difference that does not conform to the universal model: "The existence and way of life of the Jews throw into question the generality with which they do not conform" (169).

77. Ibid., 168: "They are branded as absolute evil by those who are absolutely evil, and are now in fact the chosen race."

78. *The Testament of Adolf Hitler: The Hitler-Bormann Documents, February–April 1945)*, trans. Colonel R. H. Stevens (London: Cassell, 1961), 55 (statement dated February 4, 1945).

79. Ibid.
80. Ibid., 56.
81. Jules Sageret, "La 'Question des races' et la science," *Revue du Mois*, June 10, 1919, 155.
82. Ibid., 154.
83. Ibid., 155. The author mainly grounds himself on the works of Joseph Deniker, "Les Races européennes," *Bulletin de la Société d'Anthropologie de Paris* (1897); Deniker, *The Races of Man* (New York: Scribner's, 1900).
84. The expression, which had been standardized, is explicitly mentioned by the author: "The so-called question of race..." (Sageret, "La 'Question des races,'" 167).
85. Ibid., 155–56.

86. Ibid., 168–69.
87. Ibid., 169.
88. See, for example, Joseph Gabel, "Une Pensée non idéologique est-elle possible?" in *Sociologie de la connaissance*, ed. Jean Duvignaud (Paris: Payot, 1979), 13–22. A certain reading of Karl Mannheim results in the praise of the deracinated sociologist, who would be the best of sociologists. Quite often, the ideal type of the scientist "without ties" is incarnated by the figure of the diasporic Jewish intellectual, the agnostic and revolutionary Jew, citizen of the whole world, represented as an atomic individual (unmarried, without children). In the 1930s, it was understandable that, in the face of the "rooted" type incarnated by the *völkisch* or Nazi militant, the type of the intellectual Jew detached from his tradition, a maximal countertype in the anti-Jewish imaginary, could be held up as a normative ideal. But this was an invention of total ideological warfare.
89. See Friedrich Nietzsche, *The Gay Science*, trans. Walter Kaufmann (New York: Vintage, 1974), 338–40: "We who are homeless *(Wir Heimatlosen)*."
90. This is the simple evaluative inversion of the status of the Jew as *heimatlos* in Édouard Drumont. Cf. *La Libre Parole*, November 12, 1894: "These eternal *heimatlos*, sworn enemies of any home in which they are allowed to sit down." Jean-Paul Honoré relates the stigmatizing qualification *heimatlos* to the "nationalist basis" of 1890s anti-Jewish vocabulary in France: recourse to the German term, foreign par excellence, and so connoting maximal removal, enables a polemical condensation of the main enemies demonized in the figure of the "German Jew," the one without a country who hides the "German-Jewish band" ("Le Vocabulaire de l'antisémitisme en France pendant l'affaire Dreyfus," *Mots* 2 [March 1981]: 82). The cosmopolite is the one targeted: "the Jew — to use an energetic expression of the *Israelite Alliance* — adheres to an *inexorable universalism*" (Édouard Drumont, *La France juive: Essai d'histoire contemporaine* [1886] [Paris: Marpon and Flammarion, n.d.], 1:58).
91. See the critiques formulated by Pierre Bourdieu, *Sociology in Question*, trans. Richard Nice (London: Sage, 1993), 43; and also Bertrand de Jouvenel, *Les Débuts de l'etat moderne: Une Histoire des idées politiques au $XIX^e$ e siècle* (Paris: Fayard, 1976), 288–89.
92. Cf. Richard Rorty, "Solidarity or Objectivity?" in *Objectivism, Relativism, and Truth: Philosophical Papers* (Cambridge: Cambridge University Press, 1991), 1:21–34. The American philosopher identifies the two principal ways in which humans give meaning to their lives: "By telling the story of their contribution to a community" (21) (the desire for solidarity) or by "describ[ing] themselves as standing in immediate relation to a nonhuman reality" (21) (the desire for objectivity). The "realists," who "wish to ground solidarity in objectivity" (22), postulate the existence of a universal and transcultural rationality. Rorty, who as a "pragmatist" opposes the "realist," impugns such a postulate and defends an "ethnocentrist" position, which assumes the "admission that we are just the historical moment that we are" (30). It follows that "we cannot justify our beliefs to everyone, but only to those who, to a certain extent, share these beliefs...." This is the position of ethnocentric relativism.
93. On ethico-political (but intraliterary) salvation through bastardy, see, for example, Jean-Paul Sartre, "Of Rats and Men," in *Situations*, trans. Benita Eisler (New York: Braziller, 1965), 327–71. The "bastard" (the traitor, the guilty one, the desperate colonized one, and so on) is the type directly opposed to that of the "prick" (an honest person). On this point, see Jean-Paul Sartre, *Saint Genet: Actor and Martyr*, trans. Bernard Frechtman (New York: Braziller, 1963).
94. The antiracist idealization of the victim operates either on the type of the *métis* or

on that of the immigrant: the common archetype is the displaced person, the unclassified, the uncategorizable, and is absolutely valorized (as the type of the innocent).

95. F. A. Hayek, *The Counter-Revolution of Science: Studies on the Abuse of Reason* (Glencoe, Ill.: Free Press, 1952), 90.

96. Ibid.

97. See note 90, above.

98. Michel Panoff and Françoise Panoff, *L'Ethnologue et son ombre* (Paris: Payot, 1968), 13.

99. Ibid., 99.

100. Jeanne Favret, "En ethnologie, le crime ne paie plus," *Critique* 271 (December 1969): 1076.

101. In his *Hérédité et racisme* (Paris: Gallimard, 1939), Jean Rostand separates the two arguments and analyzes each one: first the argument based on *hierarchy*, grounding practices of domination (57–64); then the argument based on the *purity of identity* (64–66). A rigorous, abridged description of other-racialization is given by Guillaumin, *L'Idéologie raciste,* 224. The separation of the analyses concerning, respectively, maintaining difference (the conduct of setting apart) and the manifestations of hostility is fortunately sustained. Identifying differentiation is "already" racism (72–79).

102. Jeanne Hersch has grounded on their opposition her critical reflection on the "antiracist" usage (of the UNESCO type) of the terms *race* and *racism* ("Sur la notion de race," 127–28). The distinction between the racism of extermination and the racism of colonization has been taken up by Arthur Kriegel and related, in the history of ideas, to the distinction between two separate scientific traditions, physical anthropology and Darwinism (Arthur Kriegel, *La Race perdue: Science et racisme* [Paris: Presses Universitaires de France, 1983], 15–17, 145–47). It is difficult to follow the author in his enterprise of the radical "exculpation" of Darwinism, whose "innocence" (147) he affirms, in spite of the massive reinvestments of selectionist conceptuality in racist discourse, both scholarly and "popular," of exploitation as well as of extermination.

103. Hersch, "Sur la notion de race," 127 (my emphasis).

104. When, in the name of the Aryan race, an enunciator says that he must combat "the Jew" (for example, in *Mein Kampf* ), the act of this exhortation assumes a recognition of the real danger represented by "the Jew" and so an identification of the latter as a superior, though negative, power. "The Jew" is postulated as susceptible to defeat only by being destroyed, and not enslaved: this is to accord him the positivity of a Master, that which is projected onto the double, the symmetrical inverse.

105. Hersch, "Sur la notion de race," 127–28.

106. On the specific treatment of the properly "inferior races," of the "undermen," such as "the Slavs," to invoke the letter of Nazi vocabulary, see Heinrich Himmler, *Geheimreden 1933 bis 1945, und andere Ansprachen,* ed. Bradley M. Smith and Agnes F. Peterson (Frankfurt: Propyläen, 1974), 146–83. From the speech of October 6, 1943, Posen (on the campaign in Russia): "We need ... only treat the Slavs — whether Serbs, Czechs, or Russians — as all Slavic peoples were always treated throughout history by those who have actually dominated them" (165). [My translation. — Trans.] For an overview of the "grand Nazi plans," see Léon Poliakov, *Harvest of Hate* (London: Elek, 1956), 263–80.

107. Quoted in Léon Poliakov and Josef Wulf, *Das Dritte Reich und die Juden: Dokumente und Aufsätze* (Berlin: Grunewald, 1955), 217. [My translation. — Trans.] See also Norman Cohn, *Warrant for Genocide: The Myth of the Jewish World-Conspiracy and the "Protocols of the Elders of Zion"* (New York: Harper and Row, 1967), 179–80. On the indoctrination of Russian children, advocated in the perspective of enslavement,

see Reboul, *L'Endoctrinement*, 152–59; Henri Michel, *The Second World War*, trans. Douglas Parmée (New York: Praeger, 1975), 234; Dominique Pélassy, *Le Signe nazi: L'Univers symbolique d'une dictature* (Paris: Fayard, 1983), 158.

108. Arthur R. Butz, *The Hoax of the Twentieth Century* (Brighton, Eng.: Historical Review Press, 1977); Wilhelm Staeglich, *The Auschwitz Myth: A Judge Looks at the Evidence*, trans. Thomas Francis (Newport Beach, Calif.: Institute for Historical Review, 1986); Robert Faurisson, interview, in Serge Thion, *Vérité historique ou vérité politique?* (Paris: La Vieille Taupe, 1980), 171–212. See Pierre Vidal-Naquet, *Les Assassins de la Mémoire* (Paris: La Découverte, 1987); Pierre-André Taguieff, *Les "Protocoles de Sages de Sion": Faux et usages d'un faux* (Paris: Berg International, 1992), 1:315–63.

109. Original text of the final document, *The Nairobi Forward-Looking Strategies for the Advancement of Women*, discussed (harshly), amended (the series "*apartheid, racism, Zionism*" replaced with "*apartheid* and all other forms of racism and racial discrimination"), and adopted during the World Conference to Review and Appraise the Achievements of the United Nations Decade for Women: Equality, Development and Peace, Nairobi, Kenya, July 15–26, 1985 (paragraph 95, 26; French version quoted in *Le Monde*, Sunday–Monday, July 28–29, 1985, 16).

110. See Talcott Parsons, *The Social System* (New York: Free Press, 1951), 297–321.

111. Edmund Leach, *L'Unité de l'homme*, trans. M. Luciani (Paris: Gallimard, 1980), preface, 20.

## 5. The Theories of Prejudice and the Meanings of Racism

1. See, for example, Claude Meillassoux, *Maidens, Meals, and Mondy: Capitalism in the Domestic Community* (Cambridge: Cambridge University Press, 1981), 91–95, 135–37; Meillassoux, *The Anthropology of Slavery: The Womb of Iron and Gold*, trans. Alide Dasnois (Chicago: University of Chicago Press, 1991); Immanuel Wallerstein, *Historical Capitalism* (London: Verso, 1983), 76–80; Wallerstein, "La Construction des peuples: Racisme, nationalisme, ethnicité," *Actuel Marx* 1 (first semester 1987): 25–26.

2. See the synthesis by Oliver C. Cox, *Caste, Class, and Race: A Study in Social Dynamics* (New York: Doubleday, 1948); Gordon W. Allport, *The Nature of Prejudice* (Cambridge, Mass.: Addison-Wesley, 1954), 209–10. On the historicist explanation of racial prejudice through the needs of the capitalist system, see Kenneth L. Little, "Race and Society," in *Le Racisme devant la science* (Paris: UNESCO/Gallimard, 1960), 67–70 (Little here cites Cox). In a perspective analogous to that of Cox, see Marvin Harris, *Patterns of Race in the Americas* (New York: Walker, 1964), 65–89. Cox and Harris's theory of class is discussed in the following: Michael Banton, *The Idea of Race* (Boulder, Colo.: Westview Press, 1977), 129–34; Robert Miles, "Class, Race, and Ethnicity: A Critique of Cox's Theory," *Racial and Ethnic Studies* 3 (1980): 169–86; Michael Banton, *Racial and Ethnic Competition* (Cambridge: Cambridge University Press, 1983), 85–91.

3. Allport, *Nature of Prejudice*, 206–18, especially 209–10.

4. Ibid. (race prejudice as a mode of rationalization of economic advantages).

5. Ibid., 209.

6. [See chapter 3, n. 1, above.]

7. Allport, *Nature of Prejudice*, 210. See also Hugo Tolentino, *Raza e historia en Santo Domingo* (Santo Domingo: Editora de la Universidad Autonoma de Santo Domingo, 1974).

8. Cox, *Caste, Class, and Race*, 393; see also Allport, *Nature of Prejudice*, 209.

Along the same lines, see Wallerstein, *Historical Capitalism,* 78–79 (the recurring theme of the justification of inequalities); Wallerstein, "La Construction des peuples," 26 ("to legitimate the hierarchical reality of capitalism..." ).

9. Allport, *Nature of Prejudice,* 210.

10. Marcel Prenant, preface to Theodor Balk, *Races: Mythe et vérité,* French adaptation (from the German manuscript) by Lydia Staloff (Paris: Éditions Sociales Internationales, 1935), 9–10. The same type of argument (with Japanese businessmen replacing Jewish capitalists) is found in Wallerstein, "La Construction des peuples," 22. For several approaches to racism from a Marxist perspective, see Herbert Aptheker, "Imperialism and Irrationalism," *Telos* 4 (1969): 168–75; this article is listed by Louise Marcil-Lacoste in her invaluable catalog, *La Thématique contemporaine de l'égalité* (Montréal: Presses de l'Université de Montréal, 1984), 9; James and Grace Boggs, *Racism and the Class Struggle* (New York: Monthly Review Press, 1970) (see Marcil-Lacoste, *La Thématique contemporaine,* 22); Clarence J. Munford, "Ideology, Racist Mystification, and America," *Revolutionary World* 17–18 (1976): 57–85 (see Marcil-Lacoste, *La Thématique contemporaine,* 136).

11. Henri Alleg, *S.O.S. America!* (Paris: Messidor/Temps Actuels, 1985), 172.

12. For a bibliographical orientation, one may refer to the following books and articles, certain of which are now classics, which synthetically present the problematics, methods, and principal results of research:

*a.* Social psychology (research on attitudes and prejudices): Louis L. Thurstone, "Attitudes Can Be Measured," *American Journal of Sociology* 33 (1927–28): 529–54; Emory S. Bogardus, "Race Friendliness and Social Distance," *Journal of Applied Sociology* 11, no. 3 (January–February 1927): 272–87; Gordon W. Allport, "Attitudes," in *The Handbook of Social Psychology,* ed. Carl A. Murchison (Worcester, Mass.: Clark University Press, 1935), 798–844; Harry Bone, *Le Préjugé: Étude objective* (Paris: Hermann, 1935); E. L. Horowitz, " 'Race' Attitudes," in *Characteristics of the American Negro,* ed. Otto Klineberg (New York: Harper, 1944), 141–248; E. L. Hartley, *Problems in Prejudice* (New York: King's Crown Press, 1946); Gordon W. Allport and B. M. Kramer, "Some Roots of Prejudice," *Journal of Psychology* 22 (1946): 9–39; James W. Woodard, "Social Psychology," in *Twentieth Century Sociology,* ed. Georges Gurvitch and Wilbert E. Moore (New York: Philosophical Library, 1945), 218–66; Muzafer Sherif, *An Outline of Social Psychology* (New York: Harper and Brothers, 1948), chapters 9–13, 14; G. E. Simpson and J. M. Yinger, *Racial and Cultural Minorities: An Analysis of Prejudice and Discrimination* (New York: Harper and Brothers, 1953); Allport, *Nature of Prejudice;* Otto Klineberg, *Social Psychology,* rev. ed. (New York: Holt, Rinehart, and Winston, 1954), 481–548; Serge Moscovici, "L'Attitude: Théories et recherches autour d'un concept et d'un phénomène," *Bulletin du CERP* 11 (1962): 177–91; Theodore M. Newcomb, R. H. Turner, and P. E. Converse, *Social Psychology: The Study of Human Interaction* (New York: Holt, Rinehart, and Winston, 1965); Marie Jahoda and Neil Warren, eds., *Attitudes* (Harmondsworth, Eng.: Penguin, 1966); William J. McGuire, "The Nature of Attitudes and Attitude Change," in *The Handbook of Social Psychology,* ed. Gardner Lindzey and Elliot Aronson, 2d ed. (Reading, Mass.: Addison-Wesley, 1969), 3:136–314 (with an important bibliography, 272–314); Dana Bramel, "Attrait et hostilité interpersonnels," in *Introduction à la psychologie sociale,* ed. Serge Moscovici (Paris: Larousse, 1972), 1:192–238; Jean Maisonneuve, *Introduction à la psychologie sociale* (Paris: Presses Universitaires de France, 1985), 106–29; Michael Billig, "Racisme, préjugé et discrimination," in *Psychologie sociale,* ed. Serge Moscovici (Paris: Presses Universitaires de France, 1984), 449–72.

*b.* On "ethnic psychology" and the study of "national character": Otto Klineberg,

"Psychologie et caractère national," *Revue de Psychologie des Peuples* 3, no. 1 (1948): 14–26; Margaret Mead, "L'Étude du caractère national," in *Les "Sciences de la politique" aux États-Unis*, ed. Harold D. Lasswell and Daniel Lerner (Paris: A. Colin, 1951), 105–32 (bibliography, 127–32); Georges A. Heuse, *La Psychologie ethnique: Introduction à l'ethnopsychologie générale* (Paris: Vrin, 1953); H. C. J. Duyjker and N. H. Fridjda, *National Character and National Stereotypes* (Amsterdam: North Holland Publishing, 1963); Alexander Vexliard, "Le Caractère national, une structure en profondeur," *Revue de Sociologie de l'Université d'Istanbul* (1970): 17–51; G. Dingemans, *Psychanalyse des peuples et des civilisations* (Paris: Colin, 1971); Roy Preiswerk and Dominique Perrot, *Ethnocentrism and History: Africa, Asia, and Indian America in Western Textbooks* (New York: NOK, 1978); Edmond-Marc Lipiansky, *L'Âme française ou le national-libéralisme: Analyse d'une représentation sociale* (Paris: Antropos, 1979); Alex Inkeles and Daniel J. Levinson, "National Character: The Study of Modal Personality and Sociocultural Systems," in Lindzey and Aronson, *Handbook*, 4:418–506 (bibliography, 492–506). On the transposition, by Margaret Mead and her students, of the notion of cultural pattern onto "national character," in order to study modern societies, see Claude Lévi-Strauss, "Panorama de l'ethnologie (1950–1952)," *Diogène* 2 (April 1953): 117ff. The question of "national character" has recently been approached in a new way by Jean Stoetzel, *Les Valeurs du temps présent: Une Enquête européenne* (Paris: Presses Universitaires de France, 1983). On ethnic stereotypes: Daniel Katz and Kenneth W. Braly, "Racial Stereotypes of 100 College Students," *Journal of Abnormal and Social Psychology* 28 (1933): 280–90; Katz and Braly, "Racial Prejudice and Racial Stereotypes," *Journal of Abnormal and Social Psychology* 30 (1935): 175–93. (The last two articles were adapted and combined as "Verbal Stereotypes and Racial Prejudice," in *Readings in Social Psychology*, ed. Guy Swanson [New York: Henry Holt and Co., 1952], 67–73; on the 1933 article, see Klineberg, *Social Psychology*, 486–89.)

*c.* On political attitudes (in relation to opinions and prejudices): Theodor W. Adorno et al., *The Authoritarian Personality* (New York: Harper and Brothers, 1950); Richard Christie and Marie Jahoda, eds., *Studies in the Scope and Method of "The Authoritarian Personality"* (Glencoe, Ill.: Free Press, 1954); Hans J. Eysenck, *The Psychology of Politics* (London: Routledge and Kegan Paul, 1954); H. J. Eysenck, *Uses and Abuses of Psychology* (Harmondsworth, Eng.: Penguin, 1953), part 4, 243–313; Milton Rokeach, *The Open and Closed Mind* (New York: Basic Books, 1960); Jean Stoetzel, *La Psychologie sociale* (Paris: Flammarion, 1978); Guy Michelat and Jean-Pierre Thomas, *Dimensions du nationalisme* (Paris: Colin, 1966); Alain Lancelot, *Les Attitudes politiques* (Paris: Presses Universitaires de France, 1974); Michael Billig, *Fascists: A Social Psychological View of the National Front* (London and New York: Harcourt Brace Jovanovich, 1978); Madeleine Grawitz, "Psychologie et politique," in Madeleine Grawitz and Jean Leca, *Traité de science politique* (Paris: Presses Universitaires de France, 1985), 3:1–139 (bibliography, 119–39); Raymond Boudon and François Bourricaud, *A Critical Dictionary of Sociology*, trans. Petern Hamilton (Chicago: University of Chicago Press, 1989), s.v. "Authority."

*d.* From a politico-economic and comparative perspective: Thomas Sowell, *Race and Economics* (New York: David McKay Co., 1975); Sowell, *Markets and Minorities* (New York: Basic Books, 1981); Sowell, *Ethnic America: A History* (New York: Basic Books, 1981); Sowell, *The Economics and Politics of Race: An International Perspective* (New York: Morrow, 1983).

*e.* On the sociology of racial and interethnic relations: Edgar T. Thompson, ed., *Race Relations and the Race Problem* (Durham, N.C.: Duke University Press, 1939); M. Freedman, "Some Recent Works on Race Relations: A Critique," *British Journal of Sociology* 5, no. 4 (December 1954): 342–54; Herbert Blumer, "Recent Research on Racial Relations," *International Social Science Bulletin* 10, no. 3 (1958): 403–47; E. Franklin Frazier, *Race and Culture Contacts in the Modern World* (New York: Knopf, 1957); Brewton Berry, *Race and Ethnic Relations* (Boston: Houghton-Mifflin, 1958); Andrée Michel, "Tendances nouvelles de la sociologie des relations raciales," *Revue Française de Sociologie* 3, no. 2 (April–June 1962): 181–90; Robert E. Park, *Race and Culture: Essays in the Sociology of Contemporary Man* (Glencoe, Ill.: Free Press, 1964); Roger Bastide, *The Sociology of Mental Disorders*, trans. Jean McNeil (New York: McKay, 1972), chapter 7, 139–52; Michael Banton, *Race Relations* (New York: Basic Books, 1967); E. Franklin Frazier, *On Race Relations* (Chicago: University of Chicago Press, 1968); Pierre J. Simon, "Ethnisme et racisme ou 'l'école de 1492,'" *Cahiers Internationaux de Sociologie* 48 (January-June 1970): 119–52; Pierre J. Simon, "Notes sur la sociologie des relations interethniques et des relations sociales," part 1, *Pluriel* 2 (1975): 96–104, part 2, *Pluriel* 4 (1975): 87–96; Pierre J. Simon, "Propositions pour un lexique des mots clés dans le domaine des études relationnelles," part 1, *Pluriel* 4 (1975): 66–76, part 2, *Pluriel* 6 (1976), 77–90; Emerich K. Francis, *Interethnic Relations: An Essay in Sociological Theory* (New York: Elsevier, 1976); Anthony H. Richmond, "Migration, Ethnicity, and Race Relations," *Ethnic and Racial Studies* 1, no. 1 (1978): 1–18; William J. Wilson, *The Declining Significance of Race* (Chicago: University of Chicago Press, 1980); Thomas F. Pettigrew, "Race and Class in the 1980s: An Interactive View," *Daedalus* 110, no. 2 (spring 1981): 233–55; Michael Banton, *Racial and Ethnic Competition* (Cambridge: Cambridge University Press, 1983); Marc H. Piault, *Vers des sociétés pluriculturelles: Études comparatives et situation en France* (Paris: Office de Recherche Scientifique et Technique d'Outre-Mer, 1987).

*f.* On ethnicity (ethnic groups), the nation, and race: Gunnar Myrdal, *An American Dilemma: The Negro Problem and Modern Democracy* (New York: Harper and Row, 1944), 2 vols.; Herbert Blumer, "Recent Research on Racial Relations," *International Social Science Bulletin* 10, no. 3 (1958): 403–47; Pierre L. van den Berghe, *Race and Racism: A Comparative Perspective* (New York: Wiley, 1967); Fredrik Barth, ed., *Ethnic Group and Boundaries: The Social Organization of Cultural Difference* (London: Allen and Unwin, 1969); Pierre L. van den Berghe, *Race and Ethnicity: Essays in Comparative Sociology* (New York: Basic Books, 1970); Sami Zubaida, ed., *Race and Racialism* (London: Tavistock, 1970); Wsevold W. Isajiw, "Definitions of Ethnicity," *Ethnicity* 1, no. 2 (July 1974): 111–24; Nathan Glazer and Daniel Patrick Moynihan, eds., *Ethnicity: Theory and Experience* (Cambridge, Mass.: Harvard University Press, 1975) (the collection includes Daniel Bell, "Ethnicity and Social Change," 141–74, and Talcott Parsons, "Some Ethical Considerations on the Nature and Trends of Change of Ethnicity," 53–83); Frances Henry, ed., *Ethnicity in the Americas* (The Hague: Mouton, 1976); William A. Douglass and Stanford M. Lyman, "L'Ethnie: Structure, processus et saillance," *Cahiers Internationaux de Sociologie* 41 (July–December 1976): 197–220; Françoise Morin and Guy Pouget, "Langue et identité ethnique: Le Cas occitan," *Pluriel* 15 (1978): 9–26; Guy Michaud, ed., *Identités collectives et relations interculturelles* (Brussels: Complexe, 1978); Pierre L. van den Berghe, *The Ethnic Phenomenon* (New York: Elsevier, 1981); Roland J.-L. Breton, *Les Ethnies* (Paris: Presses Universitaires de France, 1981); Jean Cazemajou and Jean-Pierre Martin, *La Crise du melting-pot: Ethnicité et identité aux États-Unis de Kennedy à Reagan* (Paris: Aubier-Montaigne, 1983); Anthony H. Richmond, "Le Nationalisme ethnique et les paradigmes des sciences sociales," *Revue Internationale des Sciences Sociales* 111 (February 1987): 3–19; Ulf Björkland, "Ethnicité et État-providence," *Revue Internationale des Sciences Sociales* 111 (February 1987): 21–33; Immanuel Wallerstein, "La Construction des peuples."

g. In the perspective of discourse analysis: Marianne Ebel and Pierre Fiala, *Sous le consensus, la xénophobie: Paroles, arguments, contextes (1961–1981)* (Lausanne: Institut de Science Politique, 1983); Teun A. Van Dijk, *Prejudice in Discourse: An Analysis of Ethnic Prejudice in Cognition and Conversation* (Amsterdam: Benjamins, 1984); Van Dijk, *Elite Discourse and Racism* (Amsterdam: University of Amsterdam, 1984, 37 pp.); Van Dijk, *Communicating Racism: Ethnic Prejudice in Thought and Talk* (Newbury Park, Calif.: Sage Publications, 1987); Annette Paquot and Jacques Sylberberg, "L'Incantation québécoise," *Mots* 4 (March 1982): 7–28; Paquot, "Les Mécanismes discursifs de l'exclusion et de l'inclusion dans un corpus journalistique québécois," *Langage et Société* 34 (December 1985): 35–55.

h. In a psychoanalytic approach: John Dollard, *Caste and Race in a Southern Town* (New York: Harper and Row, 1937); John Dollard, "Hostility and Fear in Social Life," *Social Forces* 17 (1938): 15–26; Adorno et al., *The Authoritarian Personality;* Nathan Ward Ackerman and Marie Jahoda, *Anti-Semitism and Emotional Disorder: A Psychoanalytic Interpretation* (New York: Harper, 1950); Bruno Bettelheim and Morris Janowitz, *Dynamics of Prejudice* (New York: Harper and Brothers, 1950); Rudolph M. Loewenstein, *Christians and Jews* (New York: International Universities Press, 1951).

13. See Gérard Lemaine and Benjamin Matalon, *Hommes supérieurs, hommes inférieurs? La Controverse sur l'hérédité de l'intelligence* (Paris: Colin, 1985), 11–19.

14. Ibid., 107. See also Theosodius Dobzhansky, *Mankind Evolving: The Evolution of the Human Species* (New Haven, Conn.: Yale University Press, 1962), 9.

15. Lemaine and Matalon, *Hommes supérieurs*, 108; Woodard, "Social Psychology," 227 (on Allport's decision in favor of a mesological/educational position).

16. Banton, *Race Relations*, 7–8; see also Otto Klineberg, "Relations entre les groupes ethniques," *Bulletin de Psychologie* 226 (December 31, 1963): 467. In the very title of his contribution to the treatise on social psychology published under Serge Moscovici's direction, Michael Billig seems to announce that he will follow the tripartition of "racism, prejudice, and discrimination" ("Racisme, préjugé et discrimination," 449ff.). The formal distinction between prejudice and discrimination is in fact placed in evidence from the beginning (450). But the author later does not seem strictly to differentiate racism-as-ideology (racist theory) from racism-as-opinion (racist attitude, racial prejudice), nor to distinguish what stems respectively from attitude and from behaviors, as discrimination is conceived as the logical consequence of hostile attitudes. It remains that Billig rightly insists on the interactions between attitudes/prejudices and discriminatory practices.

17. Banton, *Race Relations*, 8. Cf. the characterization of "racist theories" as assumed in a description by Henri Atlan in 1975: "A genetic racial determinism, on the level of individuals, with the notions of superiority or inferiority tied to it" (Henri Atlan, "Variabilité des cultures et variabilité génétique," *Entre le cristal et la fumée: Essai sur l'organisation du vivant* [Paris: Seuil, 1986], 185–86). We again find the two basic traits of the scholarly definitions: a postulate of differential genetic determinism and a position of a unidimensional (and universal) scale of value, involving the "superior/inferior" classificatory scheme. We find the same definitional evidence in Leonard Lieberman, "The Debate over Race: A Study in the Sociology of Knowledge," in *Race and IQ*, ed. Ashley Montagu (Oxford: Oxford University Press, 1975), 27; here, to the traits of genetic determinism and inequality among races is very classically added that of justification (the functional definition of ideology).

18. Hannah Arendt, *Crises of the Republic* (New York: Harcourt Brace Jovanovich, 1972), 173.

19. "Violence always needs justification" (ibid., 174). This is one of the rare points of agreement between Margaret Mead and James Baldwin in their famous 1970 debate on race and racism: see Margaret Mead and James Baldwin, *A Rap on Race* (Philadelphia: Lippincott, 1971) (see chapter 10 in this book).

20. Arendt, *Crises*, 173.

21. On the "structural variables of action" (universalism/particularism, performance/ quality, affective neutrality/affectivity, specificity/diffusion, orientation toward oneself/ orientation toward the collectivity), see especially Talcott Parsons and Edward A. Shils, eds., *Toward a General Theory of Action* (Cambridge, Mass.: Harvard University Press, 1951), 76ff. On this fundamental component of racialization, see Vladimir Jankélévitch, "Psycho-analyse de l'antisémitisme" (published anonymously), in *Le Mensonge raciste*, pamphlet published by the National Movement against Racism (Toulouse, 1942), 18.

22. See Carlo Ginzburg, "Signes, traces, pistes: Racines d'un paradigme de l'indice," *Le Débat* 6 (November 1980): 3–44.

23. Max Weber, paper presented at the Second Congress of German Sociologists, 1912, in Léon Poliakov, "Max Weber et les théories bioraciales du $XX^e$ siècle" (introduction), *Cahiers Internationaux de Sociologie* 56 (January–June 1974): 117. Weber had intervened at the First Congress of German Sociologists in 1910 to impugn the raciological monocausalism of Alfred Ploetz, the founder, in 1906, of the International Society for Racial Hygiene; see Max Weber, *Gesammelte Aufsätze zur Soziologie und Sozialpolitik* (Tübingen: Mohr, 1924), 456–62. See Julien Freund, "Les Garde-fous et les miradors," in *Racismes, antiracismes*, ed. André Béjin and Julien Freund (Paris: Méridiens, 1986). See also Michael Pollak, "Utopie et échec d'une science raciale," in ibid., 170ff.; this article is complemented by the following very useful bibliographical orientation: "Aux origines de la politique raciale nazie: Le Rôle de la science et du droit," *Bulletin de l'Institut d'Histoire du Temps Présent* 27 (March 1987): 31–47.

24. See Klineberg, *Social Psychology*, 481; Woodard, "Social Psychology," 232. The primary references, for the analysis and then the measurement of attitudes, in particular of racial attitudes, are W. I. Thomas and F. Znaniecki, *The Polish Peasant in Europe and America*, 5 vols. (New York: Knopf, 1918–20) (see Théodore Caplow, *L'Enquête sociologique* [Paris: Colin, 1970], 22–27: this work centers on the idea of the "combination of value and attitude"); Emory S. Bogardus, *Essentials of Social Psychology*, 4th ed. (Los Angeles: Miller, 1923); Bogardus, "Race Friendliness and Social Distance"; Louis L. Thurstone, "An Experimental Study of Nationality Preferences," *Journal of General Psychology* 1, no. 3–4 (June–October 1928): 405–25. For a suggestive overview, see Myrdal, *American Dilemma*, 2:1136–43 (studies on racial attitudes and racial prejudices); Michel, "Tendances nouvelles," 181ff.

25. Klineberg, *Social Psychology*, 481.

26. Stoetzel, *La Psychologie sociale*, 194.

27. The model of this placement is the research of Adorno, et al., *Authoritarian Personality*, and that of Eysenck. On this type of analysis, see Lancelot, *Les Attitudes politiques*, 77–83, 89–98; Michel Lobrot, *Priorité à l'éducation* (Paris: Payot, 1973), 140–57; Billig, "Racisme, préjugé et discrimination"; Grawitz, "Psychologie et politique," 21ff.; Yves Christen, *Biologie de l'idéologie* (Paris: Pauvert/Carrère, 1985), 48–55 (a discussion of the typological models through the representative of the "biological scientistic" tendency of the GRECE).

28. Woodard, "Social Psychology," 229.

29. Ibid.

30. Ibid., 229–30. See also Klineberg, *Social Psychology*, 481.

31. Woodard, "Social Psychology," 230.

32. Gordon W. Allport, "Attitudes," 810 (quoted in Klineberg, *Social Psychology*, 482; Michelat and Thomas, *Dimensions du nationalisme*, 6).
33. Allport, "Attitudes," 810 (quoted in Klineberg, *Social Psychology*, 482).
34. Thomas M. Newcomb, *Social Psychology*, 118–19 (quoted in Klineberg, *Social Psychology*, 482).
35. Klineberg, *Social Psychology*, 482.
36. Cf. ibid., where Klineberg specifies: "Since what we believe to be true regarding an object or a group will obviously play a part in determining our readiness to respond to it in certain ways rather than others." A.-M. Rocheblave-Spenlé rightly recalls that Gabriel Tarde (see "Belief and Desire," in *On Communication and Social Influence*, trans. N. Claire Ellis, Priscilla P. Clark, and Terry N. Clark [Chicago: University of Chicago Press, 1969], 195–206) "may in some way appear to be a precursor to the studies on opinions and attitudes.... The relationship between opinion and attitude appears very narrow, such that at present they are taken together at times and such that one finds studies on opinion published under the heading of 'attitude measurement'" ("Gabriel Tarde et la psychologie sociale," in Gabriel Tarde, *Écrits de psychologie sociale* [Toulouse: Privat, 1973], 34–35; see also Jean Milet, "Gabriel Tarde et la psychologie sociale," *Revue Française de Sociologie* 13, no. 4 [October–December 1972]: 472–84).
37. Klineberg, *Social Psychology*, 482.
38. Jean Stoetzel, "La Conception actuelle de la notion d'attitude en psychologie sociale," *Bulletin de Psychologie* 16, no. 16 (May 13, 1963): 1004–5 (see Michelat and Thomas, *Dimensions du nationalisme*, 6).
39. Klineberg, *Social Psychology*, 544.
40. Ibid.
41. Ibid., 526–32.
42. Woodard, "Social Psychology," 233 (my emphasis).
43. Jean Maisonneuve, *Psychologie sociale* (Paris: Presses Universitaires de France, 1977), 112. Myrdal noted the functional character of racial prejudice as legitimating the rejection of "mixed marriages" by the invocation of an "innate repulsion" toward any physical contact between whites and blacks; see *An American Dilemma*, 2:590 (and 590 n. a).
44. Maisonneuve, *Psychologie sociale*, 110–11. Cf. Klineberg: "Prejudice refers to pre-judgment, a feeling or response to persons or things which is prior to, and therefore not based upon, actual experience" (*Social Psychology*, 511). It remains that one may study the mode of formation of national/racial stereotypes on the basis of the process of the *mythization* of persons or episodes: see, for example, Robert Minder, "Mythes et complexes agressifs dans l'Allemagne moderne," *Psyché* 3, no. 21–22 (July–August 1948): 783–94. Moreover, a sociology or ethnography of science cannot fail to study the modes in which some stereotype becomes the object of scholarly legitimations: hence the same applies to the "threshold of tolerance" (for foreigners) that backs up with sociological authority the received idea that, for example, as soon as one black settles in somewhere, others follow (see Véronique de Rudder, "La Tolérance s'arrête au seuil," *Pluriel* 21 [1980]: 3–13).
45. Maisonneuve, *Psychologie sociale*, 111. See also Sylvaine Marandon, "Français et Juifs dans la conscience anglaise, I: Stéréotypes nationaux et préjugés raciaux au XIXe siècle: Sources et méthodes à travers l'exemple anglais," in *Stéréotypes nationaux et préjugés raciaux aux XIXe et XXe siècles*, ed. Jean Pirotte (Louvain: Nauwelaerts, 1982), 5–6. Marandon adds to her study a useful "selection of works and articles on the methods of studying prejudices and stereotypes" (16–18). Let us note that, as

a general rule, prejudice encompasses a plurality of more or less coherent stereotypes: Maisonneuve concludes from this that "prejudice seems to constitute a sort of 'genotype' whose stereotypes are 'phenotypes,' more or less numerous and prominent, at times fuzzy or absent. As such, prejudice *strictly belongs to attitude* and even tends to merge with it" (*Psychologie sociale*, 137–38).

46. Maisonneuve, *Psychologie sociale*, 111.
47. Woodard, "Social Psychology," 233; Maisonneuve, *Psychologie sociale*, 113.
48. Woodard, "Social Psychology," 232.
49. Ibid., 233.
50. F. A. Hayek, *Law, Legislation, and Liberty*, vol. 1, *Rules and Order* (Chicago: University of Chicago Press, 1973), 8–34 (on the opposition between "rationalist constructivism" and "evolutionism").
51. See especially, for France, the new research on multiethnic cohabitation: Véronique de Rudder and Isabelle Taboada-Leonetti, "La Cohabitation pluriethnique: Espace collectif, phénomènes minoritaires et relations sociales," *Pluriel* 31 (1982): 37–54; Mustapha Saadi, "Cohabitation et relations interethniques à la Goutte-d'Or," *Pluriel* 31 (1982): 55–64; Véronique de Rudder, "L'Exclusion n'est pas le ghetto: Les Immigrés dans les HLM," *Projet* 171–72 (January–February 1983): 80–91; Rudder, "Le Logement des Maghrébins (racisme et habitat)," *Les Temps Modernes* 452–54 (March–May 1984): 1956–74; Michelle Guillon and I. Taboada-Leonetti, *Le Triangle de Choisy: Un Quartier chinois à Paris* (Paris: Harmattan, 1986).
52. See Paul H. Maucorps, Albert Memmi, and Jean-François Held, *Les Français et le racisme* (Paris: Payot, 1965), 110–35.
53. Hippolyte Taine, *Les Origines de la France contemporaine*, vol. 1, *L'Ancien Régime* (Paris: Hachette, 1876), 6 (Taine here defines "hereditary prejudice"). It may be deemed that the Tainian model of prejudice, between traditionalism and functionalism, finds one of its later versions in certain interpretations of prejudices and stereotypes given by psychologists of personality. For example, Raymond B. Cattell declares, "It looks as if what the sociologists wanted to consider as imaginary national 'stereotypes,' or even slurs, may have a substantial core of truth" (*The Scientific Analysis of Personality* [Harmondsworth, Eng.: Penguin, 1965], 261–62; quoted in Michael Billig, *L'Internationale raciste* [Paris: Maspero, 1981], 168). One also finds the idea of a hidden rationality of racial prejudice in H. J. Eysenck, in the framework of his "interest theory of attitudes": "It is true that colored immigrants cause problems to white working-class people; thus far the reactions of these people are 'rational' " (*Psychology Is about People* [New York: Library Press, 1972], 251; quoted in Billig, *L'Internationale raciste*, 169). Henceforth racial prejudice appears as no longer irrational or devoid of social function.
54. Edmund Burke, *Reflections on the Revolution in France* (New York: Bobbs-Merrill, 1965), 98–102. One should not neglect the influence of Thomas Carlyle's *The French Revolution: A History* (New York: Heritage, 1956); see Hyppolite Taine, *L'Idéalisme anglais: Étude sur Carlyle* (Paris: Baillière, 1864), 164ff.
55. In the sense in which F. A. Hayek opposes "evolutionism" to "constructivism" (*Law, Legislation, and Liberty*, 1:8–34).
56. Cf. John J. Ray, *Conservatism as Heresy* (Sydney: Australia and New Zealand Book Co., 1974), 267: racial prejudice derives its proper rationality from the fact that it is "simply a function of the varying stimulus properties of the groups concerned" (quoted in Billig, *L'Internationale raciste*, 166). Sir Arthur Keith (1866–1955) held, from a classically evolutionist perspective (in the "Darwinian" sense), that prejudices have a selective value, in that they condition the self-preservation of groups and preserve their specific modes of adaptation to the environment. This general defense of prejudice ap-

plies very particularly to racial prejudice, to the "feeling of racial belonging that nature has placed in us," and of which the "universal" repugnance to interracial cross-breeding would be an index of the innateness of the evolutionary function: "In the prehistoric world these [local, national, and racial] prejudices served a useful purpose.... I maintain that, for the ultimate good of mankind, we should nurse and preserve them" (*The Place of Prejudice in Modern Civilization* [New York: Day, 1931], 14; quoted in William C. Boyd, *Genetics and the Races of Man: An Introduction to Modern Physical Anthropology* [Boston: Little, Brown, 1950], 11; see also Jean-Pierre Hébert, *Race et intelligence* [Paris: Copernic, 1977], 24). Franz Boas replies to these two points by contesting, on the one hand, the innateness of racial antipathy and, on the other hand, that the maintenance of a "pure" racial stock must necessarily result in a physical and moral improvement (*Race, Language, and Culture* [New York: Macmillan, 1940]; see Boyd, *Genetics*, 13). These criticisms did not in the least hinder Sir Arthur Keith from coming back to the evolutionary virtues of prejudices based on nation, race, and class, in a late synthesis, *A New Theory of Human Evolution* (New York: Philosophical Library, 1949). Keith here proceeds to a classical scientistic and naturalistic legitimation of hatreds and phobias among human groups — once more in the name of biological anthropology. For a critical examination of Keith's racist as well as classist "social Darwinism," see also Ashley Montagu, *Man's Most Dangerous Myth: The Fallacy of Race* (Cleveland: World, 1964), 269–72; on the ideologico-political meanderings of the bioanthropologist, see Géza Róheim, *Psychoanalysis and Anthropology: Culture, Personality, and the Unconscious* (New York: International Universities Press, 1950), 410–12 (Róheim recognizes Keith's lucidity; before L. Bolk, Keith sketched the theory of man's fetalization [403–4]).

57. Claude Lévi-Strauss, *The View from Afar*, trans. Joachim Neugroschel and Phoebe Hoss (New York: Basic Books, 1985), xiv.

58. Ibid., xv. Along the same lines, Karl Popper presents xenophobia, to which he reduces a bit hastily Austrian anti-Semitism, as a very widespread trait in empirical humanity (*The Unended Quest: An Intellectual Autobiography* [La Salle, Ill.: Open Court, 1982], 105–6).

59. Lévi-Strauss, *View from Afar*, xiv.

60. Ibid., 24.

61. Ibid., xv. See Ludwig Ferdinand Clauss, quoted in Julius Evola, *Indirizzi per una educazione razziale* (Naples: Conti, 1941) (French edition: *Eléments pour une éducation raciale*, trans. G. Boulanger [Puiseaux: Pardès, 1984], 56–57).

62. Lévi-Strauss, *View from Afar*, xiv.

63. See Michel Giraud, "Le Regard égaré: Ethnocentrisme, xénophobie ou racisme?" *Les Temps Modernes* 459 (October 1984): 737–50. The author shows how the academically legitimate, or at least defensible, distinction between ethnocentrism/xenophobia and racism implies a naturalization of ethnocentrism — whose correlate is xenophobia — inasmuch as it is defined as the "product of inclinations consubstantial to the human race." It is in fact difficult here not to see a return, though certainly an elegant one, to the thesis of the innateness of racial prejudice. See also Emmanuel Terray, "Face au racisme," *Magazine Littéraire* 223 (October 1985): 54–55 (the author insists on the return to a "biological and organic model" in the recent thought of Lévi-Strauss and insists on the latter's "biological inspiration"); Tzvetan Todorov, "Lévi-Strauss entre universalisme et relativisme," *Le Débat* 42 (November–December 1986): 173–92 (a study centered on the critique of cultural determinism, as a substitute for racial determinism). Colette Guillaumin and Marion Glean O'Callaghan reacted sharply shortly after the publication of the study "Race et culture" (1971) (Lévi-Strauss, "Race and Cul-

ture," in Lévi-Strauss, *View from Afar,* 3–24): see "Race et race...La mode 'naturelle' en sciences humaines," *L'Homme et la Société* 31–32 (1974): 195–210 (an article written at the beginning of 1972). The integration of Lévi-Strauss's arguments into the discourse of the New Right would be interesting to study; see Alain de Benoist, *Europe, tiers monde, même combat* (Paris: Laffont, 1986), 216 (the differentialist thesis is legitimated by a reference to Lévi-Strauss's analyses in *View from Afar*). For a comparison with the racizing positions of the National Front, see Pierre-André Taguieff, "L'Identité nationale saisie par les logiques de racisation," *Mots* 12 (March 1986): 91–128; Taguieff, *Les Fins de l'antiracisme* (Paris: Michalon, 1995), 9–20; Taguieff, *Le Racisme* (Paris, Flammarion, 1997), 44–56.

64. Robert Pagès, in Henri Piéron, *Vocabulaire de la psychologie* (Paris: Presses Universitaires de France, 1979), s.v. "Prejudices." It is difficult to distinguish formally "prejudice" from "stereotype," if one defines the latter as a "a ready-made opinion that is imposed, as a cliché, on the members of a collectivity" (Piéron, s.v. "Stereotype").

65. William Vickery and Morris Opler, "A Redefinition of Prejudice for Purposes of Social Science Research," *Human Relations* 1 (1948): 419–28 (quoted in Banton, *Race Relations,* 8).

66. Banton, *Race Relations,* 8.

67. Roger Bastide, "Le Préjugé racial," in *Le Prochain et le lointain* (Paris: Cujas, 1970), 16–17.

68. Ibid., 23–24.

69. See John Harding et al., "Prejudice and Ethnic Relations," in Lindzey and Aronson, *Handbook,* 5:6. On the question of the "ideal norms" implied by the definitions of prejudice, the authors refer (5:3) to Robin M. Williams Jr., *American Society: A Sociological Interpretation* (New York: Knopf, 1960).

70. Francis Bacon, *Novum Organum,* book 1, no. 46, in *Advancement of Learning, Novum Organum, New Atlantis* (Chicago and London: Encyclopaedia Britannica, 1952), 110.

71. Cf. René Descartes, *Discourse on the Method* (1637), part 2, in *The Philosophical Writings of Descartes,* trans. John Cottingham, Robert Stoothoff, and Dugald Murdoch (Cambridge: Cambridge University Press, 1985), 1:120: the first rule of the method comes down to "to carefully avoid precipitous conclusions and preconceptions." One will note with surprise that André Lalande, *Vocabulaire technique et critique de la philosophie* (Paris: Presses Universitaires de France, 1956), has no entry for "prejudice."

72. Bacon asked that reason and experience be married. On the nuanced position of this empirical rationalist, see Victor Brochard, "La Philosophie de Bacon," in *Études de philosophie ancienne et de philosophie moderne* (Paris: Vrin, 1966), 309–10. If one locates oneself in a problematic of the Cartesian type, the empiricist origins (Locke, Hume) of racism become evident. On this point, see Harry M. Bracken, "Essence, Accident, and Race," *Hermathena* 16 (1973): 81–96; Bracken, "Philosophy and Racism," *Philosophia* 8 (November 1978): 241–60.

73. René Descartes, *The Principles of Philosophy* (1644), part 1, article 1, in *The Philosophical Writings of Descartes,* 193; see also articles 47 (208), 71 (218–19), 72 (219–20): prejudices come from childhood and education.

74. René Descartes, *Meditations* (1641), first meditation, in *The Philosophical Writings of Descartes,* vol. 2:12.

75. Cf., for example, Billig, *L'Internationale raciste,* 163: progress is defined as the process of the indefinite elimination of the irrational.

76. [The author is here alluding to the opening sentence of Descartes's *Discourse on*

the Method (1637): "Good sense is the best shared thing in the world: for everyone thinks himself so well provided with it that even those who are the hardest to please in everything else do not usually desire more of it than they have" (René Descartes, Discourse on the Method, part 1, 111).—Trans.]

77. See, for example, Maucorps, Memmi, and Held, 110. For a sociological critique of the hypothesis according to which there is a direct relation of cause and effect between racial prejudice or stereotype and racist behavior or politics, see Earl Raab and Seymour Martin Lipset, "The Prejudiced Society," in *American Race Relations Today: Studies of the Problems beyond Desegregation*, ed. Earl Raab (New York: Anchor, 1962), 29–55; George M. Fredrickson, "Le Développement du racisme américain: Essai d'interprétation sociale," in *Esclave = facteur de production: L'Économie politique de l'esclavage*, ed. Sidney W. Mintz, trans. Jacqueline Rouah (Paris: Dunod, 1981), 55; in English: George M. Fredrickson, *The Arrogance of Race* (Middletown, Conn.: Wesleyan University Press, 1988), 189ff.

78. On the mythical attribution of social ills to malevolent intentions and intentional acts, which are supposed to profit the actors presumed responsible, see Kingsley Davis, "The Myth of Functional Analysis as a Special Method in Sociology and Anthropology," *American Sociological Review* 24 (1959): 757–73, especially 770–71; Raymond Boudon, *Effets pervers et ordre social* (Paris: Presses Universitaires de France, 1979), 46–58. Boudon provides a brief summary of the studies of Thomas C. Schelling on the segregation engendered by perverse effects (54–68). See Thomas C. Schelling, "On the Ecology of Micromotives," *Public Interest* 25 (fall 1971): 59–99; Schelling, "Dynamic Models of Segregation," *Journal of Mathematical Sociology* 1, no. 2 (July 1971): 143–85. See also Schelling, *Micromotives and Macrobehavior* (New York: Norton, 1978) (on the effect of segregation engendered by the aggregation of individual demands). See also Philippe Bénéton, *Le Fléau du bien: Essai sur les politiques sociales occidentales (1960–1980)* (Paris: Laffont, 1983), 18ff.; Raymond Boudon, *Theories of Social Change: A Critical Appraisal*, trans. J. C. Whitehouse (Berkeley: University of California Press, 1986), 151–52 (on the racism of American unionists in the period following World War I, of which the classic analyses of Robert King Merton have shown that at issue was an effect of aggregation; see Robert King Merton, *Social Theory and Social Structure* [New York: Free Press, 1957], 421–36).

79. Otto Klineberg, "Relations entre les groupes ethniques," *Bulletin de Psychologie* 234 (June 1964): 1253.

80. Allport, *Nature of Prejudice*, 49ff. See also chapter 2 in this book.

81. Allport, *Nature of Prejudice*, 51.

82. Ibid., 53.

83. See Fredrickson, "Le Développement du racisme américain," 54 (*Arrogance of Race*, 189–90).

84. See, nonetheless, Arendt, *Crises*, 79–80.

85. The following are some reference works on racial segregation and apartheid in the Republic of South Africa (texts in French and English): Ian Douglas MacCrone, *Race Attitudes in South Africa* (Oxford: Oxford University Press, 1937); Gwendolyn Margaret Carter, *The Politics of Inequality* (London: Thames and Hudson, 1958); Pierre L. van den Berghe, "Apartheid: Une interprétation sociologique de la ségrégation raciale," *Cahiers Internationaux de Sociologie* 28 (January–June 1960): 47–56; Brian Bunting, *The Rise of the South African Reich* (London: Penguin, 1964); W. H. Hutt, *The Economics of the Color Bar* (London: Institute of Economic Affairs, 1964); Pierre L. van den Berghe, *South Africa: A Study in Conflict* (Middletown, Conn.: Wesleyan University Press, 1965); Michael Banton, *Race Relations* (London: Tavistock, 1967), chapter 8,

"White Supremacy in South Africa," 164-92; Serge Thion, *Le Pouvoir Pâle: Essai sur le système sud-africain* (Paris: Seuil, 1969); Heribert Adam, ed., *Modernizing Racial Domination: The Dynamics of South African Politics* (Berkeley: University of California Press, 1971); Marianne Cornevin, *Apartheid: Power and Historical Falsification* (Paris: UNESCO, 1980); Pierre L. van den Berghe, ed., *The Liberal Dilemma in South Africa* (London: Croom Helm, 1979); Robert Price and Carl Gustav Roseberg, eds., *The Apartheid Regime* (Berkeley: University of California Press, 1980); George M. Fredrickson, *White Supremacy: A Comparative Study in American and South African History* (Oxford: Oxford University Press, 1981); Odette Guitard, *L'Apartheid* (Paris: Presses Universitaires de France, 1983); Michael Banton, *Racial and Ethnic Competition* (Cambridge: Cambridge University Press, 1983), chapter 9, 209-38; G. Lory, ed., *Autrement* 15 (November 1985), special issue on South Africa; *Les Temps Modernes* 479-81 (June-August 1986), special issue on South Africa; Sowell, *Economics and Politics of Race,* 108-19, 142-44, 164-65.

86. On racial segregation in the United States (particularly the South): Dollard, *Caste and Race;* Allison Davis, Burleigh B. Gardner, and Mary Gardner, *Deep South: A Social Anthropological Study of Caste and Class* (Chicago: University of Chicago Press, 1941); Myrdal, *American Dilemma;* C. Vann Woodward, *The Strange Career of Jim Crow* (Oxford: Oxford University Press, 1957); Banton, *Race Relations,* 131-63; E. Franklin Frazier, *The Negro in the United States* (New York: Macmillan, 1971); Richard Wasserstrom, "Rights, Human Rights, and Racial Discrimination," *Journal of Philosophy* 61 (December 1974): 628-40; H. Adam and H. Giliomee, *Ethnic Power Mobilized: Can South Africa Change?* (New Haven, Conn.: Yale University Press, 1979); Fredrickson, *White Supremacy;* Banton, *Racial and Ethnic Competition,* 239-84; Sowell, *Ethnic America,* 183-224; Sowell, *Economics and Politics of Race,* 120-32.

87. Van den Berghe, "Apartheid," 47.

88. Arnaud Durban, in collaboration with Patrice de Comarmond and Claude Duchet, "Apartheid et assimilation en Afrique australe," in *Racisme et société,* ed. Patrice de Comarmond and Claude Duchet (Paris: Maspero, 1969), 56.

89. Cornevin, *Apartheid,* 25.

90. Ibid., 30-31.

91. Gérard Chaliand, *Où va l'Afrique du sud?* (Paris: Calmann-Lévy, 1986), 111.

92. See, for example, the following militant pamphlets: *The Political Economy of Apartheid,* 15 pp. (excerpt from *A World to Gain,* March 1985, London), which ends with: "Death to apartheid! Death to all forms of imperialist power in South Africa! Death to imperialism!" (15); *Apartheid-non!* special issue 49 (February 1983), *Afrique du Sud: L'Apartheid au programme,* 68 pp. (newspaper of the Anti-Apartheid Movement, Paris). For a recent example of the denunciation of Third World anti-imperialism by a neoconservative, see Jean-Antoine Giansily, "L'Afrique du Sud, tiers monde mythique," in Michel Leroy and the Club de l'Horloge, *L'Occident sans complexes* (Paris: Carrère, 1987), 141-60 (the author has been vice president of the Club de l'Horloge).

93. Chaliand, *Où va l'Afrique du sud?* 117.

94. Van den Berghe, *South Africa,* 183-216; Banton, *Race Relations,* 190-92.

95. Van den Berghe, "Apartheid," 56. On the cost of discrimination in a competitive market, which is measured by "the profits lost by passing up transactions that would otherwise be remunerative," see Sowell, *Economics and Politics of Race,* 179-80.

96. Sowell, *Economics and Politics of Race,* 121.

97. Cornevin, *Apartheid,* 137; see F. Gaulme, "Le Prix de l'apartheid," *Autrement* 15 (November 1985): 232-35.

98. See John Rawls, *A Theory of Justice* (Cambridge, Mass.: Harvard University Press, 1971), 99.

99. Let us insist on the fact that, in Rawls's theory of justice, the "difference principle" seems to concentrate on the fate of the most unfavored. See Philippe Van Parijs, "La Double originalité de Rawls," in *Fondements d'une théorie de la justice: Essais critiques sur la philosophie politique de John Rawls*, ed. J. Ladrière and Philippe Van Parijs (Louvain: Institut Supérieur de Philosophie, 1984), 20–23, 25; Michel Meyer, "Rawls, les fondements de la justice distributive et l'égalité," in Ladrière and Parijs, *Fondements*, 65–66. More radical in his critique is Jean Roy, "Liberté, égalité, fraternité 'revisited': Une Étude sur Rawls," *Cahiers de Philosophie Politique et Juridique de l'Université de Caen* 2 (1982): 216, 222, 224.

100. Rawls, *Theory*, 19–20.

101. Christopher Jencks, *Inequality: A Reassessment of the Effect of Family and Schooling in America* (New York: Basic Books, 1972), 195.

102. Ibid., 257–58.

103. On racial segregation and the compensatory and counterdiscriminatory programs in the United States, see Jencks, *Inequality* (Jencks illuminates the setting of the debates and dissipates several myths on the role of the school); Nathan Glazer, *Affirmative Discrimination: Ethnic Inequality and Public Policy* (New York: Basic Books, 1978) (the author presents arguments that call into doubt the effectiveness of positive discrimination, especially in that it risks engendering resentment); Nathan Glazer, *Les Différences culturelles et l'égalité des résultats scolaires* (Paris: OCDE, Education and Cultural and Linguistic Pluralism Project, March 1985), 25 pp.; Bénéton, *Le Fléau du bien*, especially 18–46 (a good synthesis of the American studies of neoconservative orientation); Louise Marcil-Lacoste, *La Thématique contemporaine de l'égalité* (Montréal: Presses de l'Université de Montréal, 1984) (a valuable repertory of many of the books and articles involved in the controversy over counterdiscriminatory measures).

104. Sowell, *Economics and Politics of Race*, 143.

105. Ibid.

106. Ibid.

107. Ibid., 15–49, 80–92.

108. Ibid., 144.

109. Ibid.

110. Ibid., 143–44.

111. Ibid., 163.

112. Ibid., 162.

113. Sowell, *Ethnic America*, 155 (see all of chapter 7, 155–79).

114. Sowell, *Economics and Politics of Race*, 103.

115. Ibid.

116. Ibid., 143.

117. Here is an exemplary declaration (August 1980), by Louis E. Martin, special assistant for minority affairs to President Jimmy Carter: "Racism is the No. 1 problem for blacks in that it infects so many areas of society. It is at the root of unemployment, of poor housing, of poor pay—everything affecting black life" (*U.S. News and World Report*, August 4, 1980, 51; quoted in Bénéton, *Le Fléau du bien*, 18-19).

118. Sowell, *Ethnic America*, 273–74.

119. Sowell, *Economics and Politics of Race*, 256.

120. Ibid.

121. Sowell, *Ethnic America*; section 6, "An Overview," chapter 11, "Implications," 273–96.

122. Ibid., 290.
123. Ibid., 290–91.
124. Sowell, *Economics and Politics of Race,* 159.
125. Ibid.
126. Ibid., 162.
127. Sowell, *Ethnic America,* 291.
128. Ibid., 292.
129. Ibid.
130. Sowell, *Economics and Politics of Race,* 160.
131. Sowell, *Ethnic America,* 291.
132. Sowell, *Economics and Politics of Race,* 160.
133. Ibid.
134. Ibid.
135. Ibid., 161.
136. Pierre-André Taguieff, "L'Identité nationale saisie par les logiques de racisation: Aspects, figures et problèmes du racisme différentialiste," *Mots* 12 (March 1986): 122ff.
137. Jacques Maritain, *Lettre à Jean Cocteau* (1926), quoted in Bénéton, *Le Fléau du bien,* 8.
138. Gordon W. Allport, "Prejudice: A Problem in Psychological and Social Causation," *Journal of Social Issues,* supplement series 4 (1950): 1–25, reprinted in Talcott Parsons and E. Shils, eds., *Toward a Theory of Social Action* (Cambridge, Mass.: Harvard University Press, 1951), part 4, chapter 1; Allport, *Nature of Prejudice,* chapter 13, "Theories of Prejudice," 206–18.
139. Klineberg, *Social Psychology,* chapter 19, 511–48.
140. Ibid., 536.
141. Allport, *Nature of Prejudice,* 209.
142. Ibid., 209–10 (Allport here summarizes *Caste, Class, and Race*).
143. Klineberg, *Social Psychology,* 526.
144. Ibid., 526–32.
145. Allport, *Nature of Prejudice,* 212.
146. See Arnold Rose, ed., *Race Prejudice and Discrimination* (New York: Knopf, 1951), chapter 49.
147. Klineberg, *Social Psychology,* 532.
148. Allport, *Nature of Prejudice,* 213.
149. Ibid., 214.
150. Klineberg, *Social Psychology,* 519–26.
151. Ibid., 520–21. See Emory S. Bogardus, *Immigration and Race Attitudes* (Boston: Heath, 1928); Hartley, *Problems in Prejudice.*
152. Klineberg, *Social Psychology,* 523.
153. In the sense of Merton's "self-fulfilling prophecy"; see Robert King Merton, *Social Theory and Social Structure* (New York: Free Press, 1957), 421–36.
154. See Klineberg, *Social Psychology,* 523–24. See also Hanna Malewska, "Crise d'identité, problèmes de déviance chez les jeunes immigrés," *Les Temps Modernes* 452–54 (March–May 1984): 1794–1811. The immigrant's behavior of overidentification has been finely examined by Georges Devereux, "Ethnic Identity: Its Logical Foundations and Its Functions," in *Ehtnopsychoanalysis: Psychoanalysis and Anthropology as Complementary Frames of Reference* (Berkeley: University of California Press, 1978), 136–76.
155. Allport, "Prejudice."
156. Klineberg, *Social Psychology,* 524.

157. Myrdal, *American Dilemma*, 1:75 (quoted in Klineberg, *Social Psychology*, 524): "White prejudice and discrimination keep the Negro low in standards of living, health, education, manners and morals. This, in its turn, gives support to White prejudice. White prejudice and Negro standards thus mutually 'cause' each other." This mechanism of colegitimation of prejudice and of its discriminatory practices, a socially incarnated vicious circle by which the dominated are maintained in their condition as dominated, therefore stems from a principle of cumulation. See Caplow, *L'Enquête sociologique*, 73; Otto Klineberg, "Relations entre les groupes ethniques," *Bulletin de Psychologie* 17, no. 20 (June 1, 1964): 1253.
158. Klineberg, "Relations," 1253.
159. Klineberg, *Social Psychology*, 532.
160. Adorno et al., *Authoritarian Personality*.
161. Klineberg, *Social Psychology*, 533. By *patriotism*, one must here understand "blind attachment to certain national cultural values" (Adorno et al., *Authoritarian Personality*, 107; Klineberg, *Social Psychology*): chauvinistic nationalism rather than attachment to one's country of birth or love of one's homeland.
162. On the historical context of the research that resulted in *The Authoritarian Personality*, see Martin Jay, *The Dialectical Imagination: A History of the Frankfurt School and the Institute of Social Research 1923–1950* (Boston: Little, Brown, 1973), 219–52.
163. See, for example, Henri Baruk, "Le Problème psychologique et psychopathologique de l'antisémitisme," *Bulletin de Psychologie* 6 (December 1952): 80–86; S. A. Shentoub, "Le Rôle des expériences de la vie quotidienne dans la structuration des préjugés (de l'antisémitisme nazi)," *Les Temps Modernes* 92 (July 1953): 6–71. From a differently nuanced perspective, accompanied by methodological caution, see Ackerman and Jahoda, *Anti-Semitism and Emotional Disorder;* Marie Jahoda, "Relations raciales et santé mentale," in *Le Racisme devant la science*, 493–532.
164. Thomas Hobbes, *Leviathan* (1651) (New York: Collier, 1962), 99; see Allport, *Nature of Prejudice*, 214.
165. Allport, *Nature of Prejudice*, 215.
166. Ibid., 216–17.
167. Klineberg, *Social Psychology*, 536.
168. Klineberg notes: "The occurrence of stereotypes [for example, concerning immigrants] without any kernel of truth does not permit us to conclude that they never contain any truth. This point is made by Allport [1950], who suggests that one of the most important research tasks that we should undertake is the discovery of the actual characteristics of the groups against whom prejudice is directed" (*Social Psychology*, 523). One may doubt not only that this is an "important task" but also that it is even feasible and, once done, capable of enlightening judgment of those subject to prejudices.
169. Allport, *Nature of Prejudice*, 217.
170. Klineberg, *Social Psychology*, 535.
171. Fredrickson, "Le Développement du racisme américain," 53 (*Arrogance of Race*, 189).
172. Basil Davidson, statement reported by Patricia Loué, *Le Monde*, supplement 12894, Sunday–Monday, July 13–14, 1986, 7. The immediate context shows that Davidson, by the words *racism* and *fascism*, targets the same referential group (the same types of personality, attitudes, behaviors).
173. Albert Jacquard, "La Science face au racisme," in *Racisme, science et pseudo-science* (Paris: UNESCO, 1982), 15.
174. Ibid.

175. See Colette Guillaumin, *L'Idéologie raciste: Genèse et langage actuel* (Paris and The Hague: Mouton, 1972), 3.
176. Sir Alan Burns, *Colour Prejudice, with Particular Reference to the Relationship between Whites and Negroes* (London: Allen and Unwin, 1948), 16. "Race prejudice" is here equivalent to a popular synthetic racism.

## 6. Antiracism and Antiprejudice Ideology

1. Serge Chakotin, *The Rape of the Masses: The Psychology of Totalitarian Political Propaganda* (London: Labor Book Service, 1940), xiii.
2. Ibid.
3. Ibid., xiv.
4. Ibid., 284.
5. Ibid.
6. Ibid.
7. Ibid., 284–85.
8. Ibid., 285.
9. Ibid.
10. Ibid.
11. See Leo Strauss, *Natural Right and History* (Chicago: University of Chicago Press, 1953), 26–29, 37–39. The reader is referred to the excellent commentary by Terence Marshall, "Leo Strauss, la philosophie et la science politique," *Revue Française de Science Politique* 35, no. 4 (August 1985): 616–19.
12. Strauss, *Natural Right and History*, 37.
13. Ibid., quoted in Michel-Pierre Edmond, "Persécution et politique de la philosophie," *Libre* 6 (1979): 70.
14. Georges Vacher de Lapouge, *L'Aryen: Son rôle social* (Paris: Fontemoing, 1899).
15. *Journal des Tribunaux* 1514 (1899): 1179 (my emphasis).
16. Georges Vacher de Lapouge, preface to Madison Grant, *Le Déclin de la grande race*, trans. E. Assire (Paris: Payot, 1926), 17–18 (my emphasis) (French version of Madison Grant, *The Passing of the Great Race; Or, the Racial Basis of European History* [New York: Scribner's Sons, 1916]).
17. Georges Vacher de Lapouge, *Race et milieu social: Essais d'anthroposociologie* (Paris: Rivière, 1909), xxx.
18. Ibid.
19. Georges Vacher de Lapouge, "L'Anthropologie et la science politique" (opening lecture in the course on anthropology of 1886–87, school of science at Montpellier, December 2, 1886), *Revue d'Anthropologie* (March 15, 1887): 6 (my emphasis).
20. Ibid. See Pierre-André Taguieff, *La Couleur et le sang: Doctrines racistes à la française* (Paris: Mille et une Nuits, 1998), 93ff.
21. [Taguieff is alluding to a famous passage, whose significance for the modern technical disposition was signaled by Heidegger, in Descartes's *Discourse on the Method*: "Instead of that speculative philosophy taught in the schools, we may find a practical one through which we could know the power and actions of fire, water, air, the stars, the heavens, and all the other bodies in our environment, as distinctly as we know the various crafts of our artisans; and we could thereby employ these forces in the same fashion for all the uses for which it is appropriate, and thus make ourselves *as masters and possessors of nature*" (part 6, 142; my emphasis). — Trans.]
22. Julius Evola, *Indirizzi per una educazione razziale* (Naples: Conte, 1941), French trans., *Eléments pour une éducation raciale*, 13; Evola, *Sintesi di dottrina della razza*

(Padova: Ar, 1978), especially 44ff.; Evola, *Il Cammino del Cinabro* (Milan: Scheiwiller, 1963), French trans. Philippe Baillet, *Le Chemin du Cinabre* (Milano and Carmagnola: Arché-Arktos, 1982), 145–48.

23. Evola, *Éléments pour une éducation raciale,* 14.
24. Ibid., 159.
25. Ibid. 15.
26. Ibid., 71.
27. Ibid.
28. On the antirationalist presupposition of well-understood, that is, "rectified," racism, see Evola, *Sintesi di dottrina della razza,* 18–22.
29. Evola, *Éléments pour une éducation raciale,* 72. Against the "superstitious world of life, becoming, and naturalism," from which "Nordism" should be "liberated," see Julius Evola, "The Restoration of the West in the Original Aryan Spirit" (presentation at Studienkreis, Berlin, December 10, 1937), published in French as "Restauration de l'Occident dans l'esprit aryen original," *Totalité* 21–22 (October 1985): 25; for the denunciation of "the Nietzschean and Darwinian caricature of the beautiful blond beast," see p. 33. For a broad critique of evolutionism, see Julius Evola, *Revolt against the Modern World,* trans. Guido Stucco (Rochester, Vt.: Inner Traditions International, 1995), 177–83. To illuminate the "traditionalist" critique of evolutionism, we must signal the Evolian journal *Totalité* 15 (fall 1982), special issue titled *Un Crime contre l'humanité: Le Darwinisme.*
30. Evola, *Éléments pour une éducation raciale,* 97.
31. Ibid., 73. For a systematic defense, grounded in an important body of scientific literature, of the hypothesis of a regressive evolution presented as conforming to the teachings of the church and opposed to that of progressive evolution ("the dogma of continual progress," indefinite progress, and so on), see Georges Salet and Louis Lafont, *L'Évolution régressive* (Paris: Éditions Franciscaines, 1943) (especially 93ff., 157ff., where reference is made to a book along the same lines — "to show that living nature is in degeneracy" — by Henri Decugis, *Le Vieillissement du monde vivant* [Paris: Plon, 1941]).
32. See Evola, *Éléments pour une éducation raciale,* 74–79.
33. Ibid., 79.
34. Ibid., 30.
35. Ibid., 31.
36. Ibid., 30.
37. Ibid., 32.
38. Houston Stewart Chamberlain, "Dilettantisme, race, monothéisme, Rome" (October 1902), second annex of *La Genèse du XIX$^e$ siècle,* trans. R. Godet (Paris: Payot, 1913), 2:1413–14. [I translate this passage from the French edition of *Foundations of the Nineteenth Century,* trans. John Lees (New York: Fertig, 1977), because the annex from which it is quoted does not appear in any edition of the book, German or English, that is available to me. — Trans.]
39. Louis Thomas, *Arthur Gobineau, inventeur du racisme (1816–1882)* (Paris: Mercure de France, 1941), 45. On Thomas, director of *Cri du Jour* (a Paris weekly) beginning February 1, 1934, see Jean Drault, *Histoire de l'antisémitisme* (Paris: Calmann-Lévy, 1942), 182–84. See also Pierre-André Taguieff et al., *L'Antisémitisme de plume 1940–1944* (Paris: Berg, 1999), passim.
40. Thomas, *Arthur Gobineau,* 50.
41. Jacques Boulenger, *Le Sang français* (Paris: Denoël, 1943), 329. Let us specify here that Boulenger, a collaborator on the Maurrassian bimonthly *La Revue Universelle*

(directed by Henri Massis), did not show any sympathy in 1940 for Hitler and Nazism, in conformity with the anti-Germanic line of Action Française: see Jacques Boulenger, "Le 'Moral,'" *La Revue Universelle* 80, no. 1 (April 1, 1940): 6–22 (as well as his "Lettres du Front," *Le Temps,* November 3, 1939).

42. René Descartes, *Discourse on the Method,* part 2, in *The Philosophical Writings of Descartes,* trans. John Cottingham, Robert Stoothof, and Dugald Murdoch (Cambridge: Cambridge University Press, 1985), 1:118.

## 7. On Racism

1. Vilfredo Pareto, *The Mind and Society: A Treatise on General Sociology,* trans. Andrew Bongiorno and Arthur Livingston (New York: Harcourt, Brace, 1935), nos. 2031, 1423.

2. Ibid.

3. Viggo Brøndal, *Les Parties du discours: Partes orationis: Études sur les catégories linguistiques* (1928), trans. Pierre Naert (Copenhagen: Munksgaard, 1948), 81.

4. Ibid., 82. Let us recall that the neutrality of theoretical knowledge does not imply a neutrality of ethical and political knowledge. Hence, in the Brøndalian perspective, the traditional concept of substance is reworked without its sedimented philosophical implications: "It makes no difference, from the point of view of languages, whether the objects on which it operates are real or imaginary, personal or impersonal, corporeal or incorporeal" (82). At a lower level of abstraction, one might say as much about "race" — that the groups of affiliation perceived as "races" may or may not be races in the view of biological knowledge. It is the social perception of racial quality that makes race, as well as the manners of stating the racial element. Hence the functioning of a pararacial lexicon, comprising the derivations of a set open to terms such as *ethnic group, culture, tradition, mentality, people, nation, religion,* and so on.

5. Belonging to the New Right in the restricted sense: the GRECE. To simplify the question, let us say that the position termed "nominalist" (not without risk of equivocation) by Armin Mohler and Alain de Benoist is in line with the tradition of ironic remarks on man in general as Joseph de Maistre formulated them in his 1797 *Considérations sur la France.* The ideal is that of an organic community (neither a separate individualism nor an abstract humanitarianism) and the norm that of rooting. This communitarian problematic, not clear of traditional elements (indeed of *völkisch* nostalgia), must be distinguished from the neoconservative and postmodern positions of a Guillaume Faye, whose imperial Europeanism is coupled with a technophilic enthusiasm. See A. Mohler, "Le Tournant nominaliste: Un Essai de clarification," *Nouvelle École* 33 (summer 1979): 13–21; Alain de Benoist, "Fondements nominalistes d'une attitude devant la vie," *Nouvelle École* 33 (summer 1979): 22–30, reprinted in Alain de Benoist, *Les Idées à l'endroit* (Paris: Libres/Hallier, 1979), 31–48; Guillaume Faye, *Nouveau Discours à la nation européenne* (Paris: Albatros, 1985), 58ff. (an impugnment of "rooting in the past"). On the idea of a "people," as opposed to the abstract universal of humanity, see *La Cause des peuples,* Proceedings of the Fifteenth National Conference of the GRECE (Versailles, May 17, 1981) (Paris: Labyrinthe, 1982). On the question of "nominalism" as an antiuniversalist doctrine, see Pierre-André Taguieff, "Alain de Benoist philosophe," *Les Temps Modernes* 451 (February 1984): 1440ff.

6. See Léon Husson, "Contenu et signification des notions de morale naturelle et de droit naturel," *Archives de Philosophie* 45, no. 4 (October–December 1982): 529–30.

7. See Pierre-André Taguieff, "L'Identité nationale saisie par les logiques de racisation," *Mots* 12 (March 1986): 111.

8. See, for example, Henry Coston, *La Fortune anonyme et vagabonde* (Paris: Coston, 1984).

9. Cf. J.-G. Malliarakis, "Rapatrions les immigrés," *Troisième Voie* 202–3 (September–October 1985): 11: the "revolutionary nationalist" leader castigates the "desire to make France, through a massive *métissage*, a new Brazil." We find the same obsessive fear of *métissage*, no less linked to the figment of an anti-French (and/or anti-white) plot, in the publications of the French Nationalist Party (founded December 10, 1983), and especially in the monthly *Militant* (see, for example, the editorial "Demain il sera trop tard," *Militant* 153 [November 1983]: 2, 5).

10. Alain Brenier, "Ésotérisme et mondialisme," *Jeune Nation Solidariste* (the organ of the Revolutionary Nationalist Movement [MNR]) 178–79 (July–August 1983): 24.

11. Dr. Edgar Bérillon, "Le Métissage: Son rôle dans la production des enfants anormaux," *Revue de Psychologie Appliquée* 36, no. 1 (January 1927): 4.

12. Indivisible in itself, divisible with regard to any other. On the medieval debates around the individual (*individuum, singulare*), see Camille Bérubé, *La Connaissance de l'individuel au Moyen Âge* (Paris: Presses Universitaires de France, 1964). On the individual in the nominalism of Ockham, see Paul Vignaux, *Nominalisme au XIV$^e$ siècle* (Paris: Vrin, 1981); Claude Pannaccio, "Guillaume d'Occam: Signification et supposition," paper presented at the conference "The Theory of the Sign in the Middle Ages," Cerisy-la-Salle, July 1977, 41 pp. On the adventures of the term *individual* in modern sociopolitical vocabulary (in the seventeenth and eighteenth centuries), see Anne Viguier, "Enfance de l'*Individu*, entre l'école, la nature et la police," *Mots* 9 (October 1984): 33–56.

13. Cf. Louis Dumont, *Essays on Individualism: Modern Ideology in Anthropological Perspective* (Chicago: University of Chicago Press, 1986), 118: "Cultures are viewed as so many individuals...; *cultures are individuals of a collective nature*. In other words, Herder... uses the individualist principle by transferring it to the level of compounds."

14. Edmund Husserl, "Philosophy and the Crisis of European Man," lecture delivered at Vienna on May 7, 1935, in *Phenomenology and the Crisis of Philosophy*, trans. Quentin Lauer (New York: Harper and Row, 1965), 184.

15. See Uli Windisch, *Xénophobie? Logique de la pensée populaire* (Lausanne: L'Age d'Homme, 1978), 173.

16. Georges Vacher de Lapouge, *L'Aryen: Son rôle social* (Paris: Fontemoing, 1899), 511. Here we cite Lapouge, whose work may in no way be reduced to a sum of "racist" statements, only insofar as his arguments illustrate then-current representations and evaluations in the complex ideological space in which the nascent science of anthropology effected a syncretism with the political projects of reform, revolution, and social recasting. Hence, in the quoted proposition, Lapouge seems to be caught in a conceptual confusion that he never ceased to denounce: the lumping together of "race" and "nation." The proposition is then less Lapougian than it is a faithful (and unfortunate) reflection of the dominant ideologization of the question in a given period.

17. Note by Vacher de Lapouge, undated (in the Lapouge Collection housed at Paul Valéry University at Montpellier, in the care of Professor Jean Boissel).

18. Georges Vacher de Lapouge, "L'Anthropologie et la science politique" (opening lecture, December 2, 1886), in *L'Aryen*, 166.

19. See René Zazzo, "La Comparaison," *Enfance* 4 (1982): 233–34.

20. See Henry de Lesquen and the Club de l'Horloge, *La Politique du vivant* (Paris: Albin Michel, 1979), 150–51. [The French expression *café au lait* is descriptive of the skin color of certain persons, especially of Caribbean origin, whose ancestry includes people of both European and African descent. — Trans.]

21. Houston Stewart Chamberlain, *Foundations of the Nineteenth Century*, trans. John Lees (New York: Fertig, 1977), vol. 1, chapter 4, "The Chaos," 258–328.

22. Pierre Chaunu, *Histoire et décadence* (Paris: Perrin, 1981), 199, 259.

23. Dr. Edgar Bérillon, "Le Métissage," 4–5. Immigration has been approached from the same psychopathological perspective, as an "interracial graft," by Dr. René Martial. See Dr. René Martial, *Traité de l'immigration et de la greffe interraciale* (Paris: Larose, 1931); and in particular Dr. René Martial, "Étude de l'aliénation mentale dans ses rapports avec l'immigration," *L'Hygiène Mentale* 28, no. 2–3 (February–March 1933): 29–71.

24. Paul Broca, *Histoire des Travaux de la Société d'Anthropologie de Paris (1859–1863)* (Paris: Masson, 1863), 39.

25. Ibid., 38.

26. Ibid., 36 (Broca here sums up the position defended by "several modern authors").

27. Ibid. (Broca here summarizes the position defended by Perier).

28. Ibid.

29. The biologization of differences implies the *hereditarianist postulate*, itself a central element in any definition of the concept of a "human race." The most widespread theoretical definition of racism is constructed around the postulate of genetic determinism. See, for example, Raymond Ruyer, *Les Nuisances idéologiques* (Paris: Calmann-Lévy, 1972), 95. It is true that the thesis of production, on a simple causal model, of culture by the factors of race (in the strictly zoological definition) has since 1945 become an ideological rarity. Few statements that come from "characterized" racism may be found today in public writings, such as this note to a study on the "metaphysics of blood" published in a "revolutionary-traditionalist" (the self-designation of the disciples of Julius Evola) journal: "The proportion of genes that come from the white population and make up a part of the genotype of contemporary black Americans is on the order of thirty-one percent — *hence* the recognized superiority of the American black among the other blacks" (Bruno Bruneau-Piaud, "À rebours" [supplement to "Metaphysics of Blood"], *Totalité* [for the European cultural revolution] 23 [fall 1985]: 78 n. 4).

30. Joseph-Pierre Durand (de Gros), *Questions de philosophie morale et sociale* (Paris: Alcan, 1901), 41.

31. [Again, the reader should keep in mind that Taguieff is writing in the mid-1980s. — Trans.]

32. Vacher de Lapouge, *L'Aryen*, 503.

33. Ibid., 501.

34. Georges Vacher de Lapouge, *Les Sélections sociales* (Paris: Fontemoing, 1896), 192. We owe to André Béjin's works the fact of having brought attention to these aspects of the Lapougian problematic: see André Béjin, "Le Sang, le sens et le travail: Georges Vacher de Lapouge, darwiniste social, fondateur de l'anthroposociologie," *Cahiers Internationaux de Sociologie* 73 (1982): 323–43; Béjin, "De Malthus à la sociobiologie: Les Formes de prise en considération des liens du sang," *Revue Européenne des Sciences Sociales* 69 (1985): 129–30.

35. Vacher de Lapouge, *Sélections sociales*, 306. An undated note from the Lapouge Collection at the Paul Valéry University at Montpellier reads: "Science against Democracy. The individual is the synthesis of his ancestors, modified by a particular environment." In his essay on "biopolitology," Yves Christen does not fail to insist on the ideal of genetic perennation, with various formulations of it found just as much in Lapouge as in Gustave Le Bon (Yves Christen, *Biologie de l'idéologie* [Paris:

Pauvert/Carrère, 1985], 104-5 [the author apparently cites Lapouge, following Béjin, "Le Sang," 338]).
36. Vacher de Lapouge, *Sélections sociales*, 307.
37. On the two models of racism, the differentialist and the inegalitarianist, see Pierre-André Taguieff, "Les Présuppositions définitionnelles d'un indéfinissable: 'Le Racisme,'" *Mots* 8 (March 1984): 71-107; Taguieff, "Le Néo-racisme différentialiste: Sur l'ambiguïté d'une évidence commune et ses effets pervers: L'Éloge de la différence," *Langage et Société* 34 (December 1985): 69-98. See also Taguieff, *Les Fins de l'antiracisme* (Paris: Michalon, 1995), 43-51, 253-327.
38. Dumont, *Essays on Individualism*, 17, 280.
39. Ibid., 166.
40. Ibid., 169.
41. Ibid., 154-58.
42. Ibid., 114.
43. Ibid., 61-62 (on the two senses of the notion of the individual).
44. Ibid., 128.
45. Ibid., 131.
46. Ibid., 265-66. Cf., for example, the interpretation that Henri Giordan proposes: "Our action finds its sense of progress in the affirmation of the right of all to equal dignity.... The right to difference must be understood as the cultural translation of the right of all to equal dignity. It specifies and concretizes the principle of equality among all human beings" ("Le Droit à la différence: Pour un nouveau dynamisme en France," *Nouvelle Revue Socialiste* 74 [March-April 1985]: 17, 21).
47. Dumont, *Essays on Individualism* 266.
48. Ibid., 266. (I am paraphrasing Leo Tolstoy's Christlike requirement: "Love thy neighbor as himself.")
49. Ibid.
50. Let us recall that the GRECE has produced one of the rare neoracist discourses that incarnates nearly to perfection the ideal type of differentialism. See especially Alain de Benoist, "Le Totalitarisme raciste," *Éléments* 33 (February-March 1980): 13-20 (the right to collective difference is here presented as the antitotalitarian weapon par excellence).
51. See Robert Jaulin, *De l'ethnocide* (Paris: 10/18, 1970). By *ethnocide*, Jaulin proposes to understand "the act of destruction of a civilization, the act of decivilization," or even "collective assassinations perpetrated against races or ethnic groups and their cultures" (Robert Jaulin, *La Décivilisation, politique et pratique de l'ethnocide* [Brussels: Complexe, 1974], 9).
52. The polemical identifying description comes from a pamphlet by Guillaume Faye, *Le Système à tuer les peuples* (Paris: Copernic, 1981). The book works to demonstrate that the technoeconomic "system" that has resulted from the domestic "American market order" destroys and homogenizes "ethnocultural and national entities" (22) — in short, that it kills peoples. This is the rightist version of the antiethnocidal ideology that Robert Jaulin and his friends spread in the 1970s. Cf., along the same lines, *Pour en finir avec la civilisation occidentale* (special issue on finishing up with Western civilization), *Éléments* 34 (April-May 1980). One will note in passing the circulation of the indeterminate syntagm "X for killing peoples," which marks the diffuse influence of the GRECE: "Immigration is a machine for killing peoples," one may for example read in a recent book by Jean-Yves Le Gallou and the Club de l'Horloge, *La Préférence nationale: Réponse à l'immigration* (Paris: Michel, 1985), 56.
53. Alain de Benoist sometimes defends a thesis stemming from a racism that is

at once differentialist and relativist: "*All* races are superior. All have their proper genius.... One may therefore say that each race is superior to the others in carrying out the achievements that belong to it" ("Contre tous les racismes," *Eléments* 8–9 [November 1974–February 1975]: 13, 14). This is a reformulation of racism in a nominalist (that is, antiuniversalist) problematic. See Pierre-André Taguieff, "The New Cultural Racism in France," *Telos* 83 (spring 1990): 109–22; Taguieff, "From Race to Culture: The New Right's View of European Identity," *Telos* 98–99 (winter 1993–fall 1994): 99–125.

54. The axiom that grounds Dumont's analysis may be thus formulated. It is insofar as this analysis does not *also* envisage a "pure" differentialist racism that we part ways with it.

55. See, for example, Jean-Marie Le Pen, *Les Français d'abord* (Paris: Carrère/Lafon, 1984), 167ff. See Pierre-André Taguieff, "The Doctrine of the National Front in France (1972–1989)," *New Political Science* 16/17 (fall/winter 1989): 29–70.

## 8. The Specter of *Métissage*

1. Earl Finch, "The Effects of Racial Miscegenation," in *Inter-Racial Problems: Papers from the First Universal Races Congress Held in London in 1911*, ed. G. Spiller (New York: Citadel, 1970), 108.

2. Théodule Ribot, *L'Hérédité psychologique* (Paris: Alcan, 1906), 346–47.

3. Frank H. Hankins, *The Racial Basis of Civilization: Critique of the Nordic Doctrine* (New York: Knopf, 1931), 328–51.

4. Arthur de Gobineau, *The Inequality of Human Races*, trans. Adrian Collins (London: Heinemann, 1915), 24. [This translation comprises only the first volume of Gobineau's hefty work. — Trans.]

5. Ibid., 211.

6. Arthur de Gobineau, *Essai sur l'inégalité des races humaines* (1853–55), in *Oeuvres*, vol. 1 (Paris: Gallimard, 1983), 1162–66 (the last pages of the conclusion of the work). In the same perspective, see Georges Vacher de Lapouge, "*Dies irae*: La Fin du monde civilisé," *Europe* 9 (October 1, 1923): 59–61. See Pierre-André Taguieff, *Les Fins de l'antiracisme* (Paris: Michalon, 1995), 53–81; Taguieff, *La Couleur et le sang: Doctrines racistes á à la française* (Paris: Mille et une Nuits, 1998), 21–58.

7. Finch, "Effects," 112. See Vacher de Lapouge, "*Dies irae*," 65–67; Vacher de Lapouge, "La Race chez les populations mélangées," in *Eugenics in Race and State* (Baltimore: Williams and Wilkins, 1923), 2:6. Vacher de Lapouge's mixophobic pessimism was shared by C. B. Davenport (with whom he had correspondence): see C. B. Davenport, "The Effects of Race Intermingling," *Proceedings of the American Philosophical Society* 56 (1917): 364–68 (cited in Hankins, *Social Basis*, 339n).

8. Georges Vacher de Lapouge, "L'Anthropologie et la science politique" (opening lecture, December 2, 1886), *Revue d'Anthropologie* (March 15, 1887): excerpt

10. On depopulation as an effect of *métissage*, see Georges Vacher de Lapouge, *Les Sélections sociales* (Paris: Fontemoing, 1896), 188ff. On the somatic and psychic disharmony of the *métis*, ibid., 178ff; Dr. René Martial, *Les Métis* (Paris: Flammarion, 1942), 43ff. On "hereditary shock," Martial, *Les Métis*, 60ff. See Pierre-André Taguieff et al., *L'Antisémitisme de plume 1940–1944* (Paris: Berg, 1999), 298, 304ff.

9. See Madison Grant, *The Passing of the Great Race; or, The Racial Basis of European History* (New York: Scribner's, 1916), 68–72 (on miscegenation as "a frightful disgrace to the dominant race" [74]).

10. See Houston Stewart Chamberlain, *Foundations of the Twentieth Century*, trans.

John Lees (New York: Fertig, 1977), 269–75. Dr. René Martial, faithful to the Gobinean tradition, speaks of "racial anarchy" (*Les Métis*, 61) or "anarchic *métissage*" (*Race, hérédité, folie: Étude d'anthroposociologie appliquée à l'immigration* [Paris: Mercure de France, 1938], 188).

11. See, for example, Alfred Rosenberg's analyses of the "bastardization" of France, *The Myth of the Twentieth Century*, trans. Vivan Bird (Torrance, Calif.: Noontide, 1982), 53–55, 403.

12. Ibid., 55.

13. Finch, "Effects," 108. Let us recall that contemporary antiracism, if we go by its explicit declarations, is a matter of unconditional mixophilia.

14. Ibid.

15. See G. Stanley Hall, *Adolescence: Its Psychology and Its Relations to Physiology, Anthropology, Sociology, Sex Crime, Religion, and Education* (New York: Appleton, 1904), 2:723; quoted in Finch, "Effects," 111.

16. Finch, "Effects," 112.

17. Felix von Luschan, "Anthropological View of Race," in Spiller, *Inter-Racial Problems*, 22. On the theory of the "infiltration of 'new blood,'" see the remarks by Arthur J. Toynbee, *A Study of History*, abr. ed. (Oxford: Oxford University Press, 1946), 249–50.

18. Gobineau, *Inequality of Human Races*, 208–10.

19. Von Luschan, "Anthropological View," 23. Along the same lines, see Vacher de Lapouge, *Sélections sociales*, 162ff.; Georges Vacher de Lapouge, *L'Aryen: Son rôle social* (Paris: Fontemoing, 1899), 488–89. See also the reflections by Abel Bonnard on racism as a natural expression of the "natural" repugnance to mixture ("La Question juive," in *Inédits politiques* [Paris: Avalon, 1987], 116ff.). For an anthropological discussion of the fertility of "hybrids," see Carl Vogt, *Lectures on Man: His Place in Creation, and in the History of the Earth* (London: Longman, Green, Longman, and Roberts, 1864), 436–41.

20. See Martial, *Race, hérédité, folie*, 131ff.

21. Gustave Le Bon, *Lois psychologiques de l'évolution des peuples* (Paris: Alcan, 1919), 59. See Pierre-André Taguieff, *Couleur et le sang*, 59–90.

22. "Each race-type, formed ages ago, and 'set' by millenniums of isolation and inbreeding, is a stubbornly persistent entity" (Lothrop Stoddard, *The Rising Tide of Color against White World Supremacy* [New York: Scribner's, 1921], 165). On the "immanent fixed character" of "the various races," see Vogt, *Lectures on Man*, 193–94.

23. "Blood" is therefore that whose purity must be preserved at any price: "One element should be fundamental to all the compoundings of the social pharmacopoeia. That element is *blood*.... It is clean, virile, genius-bearing blood, streaming down the ages through the unerring action of heredity" (Stoddard, *Rising Tide*, 305).

24. See Vacher de Lapouge, "La Race chez les populations mélangées," 4.

25. Martial, *Race, hérédité, folie*, 138; Martial, *Les Métis*, 61.

26. Martial, *Race, hérédité, folie*, 140 (and 101).

27. Dr. René Martial, "Etrangers et métis," *Mercure de France* 990 (September 15–October 1, 1939): 517ff. Martial had presented in detail the notions of "interracial graft" and "ethnic blood transfusion" introduced in *La Race française* (Paris: Mercure de France, 1934), 245ff. See also Dr. René Martial, *Français: Qui es-tu?* (Paris: Mercure de France, 1942), especially 94ff., 188ff.

28. Martial, *Race, hérédité, folie*, 135: "In a general fashion, from the point of view of blood groups and the biochemical index, *métissage* is more profitable to the less beautiful, the less intelligent, the less cultured, the less strong race; it depreciates,

to the contrary, the superior of the two races." Dr. Charles Richet affirmed the same opinion, with the authority of "Nobelized" science: see *La Sélection humaine* (Paris: Alcan, 1919), 82ff., 88ff.

29. Agassiz, quoted in Ribot, *L'Hérédité psychologique*, 346 n. 1. The same text is paraphrased in Le Bon, *Lois psychologiques*, 59 n. 1; see also Chamberlain, *Foundations*, 1:290-91n.

30. Martial, *Race, hérédité, folie*, 105.

31. Madison Grant, *Le Déclin de la grande race*, trans. E. Assire (Paris: Payot, 1926) 29-30 [introduction for the French edition]. [I was unable to find this passage in the edition of *The Passing of the Great Race* that I consulted. — Trans.]

32. Bonnard, "La Question juive," 116.

33. Ibid.

34. Richet, *Sélection humaine*, 89.

35. Bonnard, "La Question juive," 143.

36. Ibid., 131.

37. Ibid., 140.

38. Franz Boas, "Instability of Human Types," in Spiller, *Inter-Racial Problems*, 103. For more details, see Franz Boas, *Changes in Bodily Form of Descendants of Immigrants* (Washington, D.C.: Senate Documents, 1910-11). On the question, see George W. Stocking Jr., *Race, Culture, and Evolution: Essays in the History of Anthropology* (Chicago: University of Chicago Press, 1982), 161-94. On the role of Franz Boas, see the testimony of Gilberto Freyre, *The Masters and the Slaves: A Study in the Development of Brazilian Civilization*, trans. Samuel Putnam (New York: Knopf, 1946), 292-93. See also Elazar Barkan, *The Retreat of Scientific Racism: Changing Concepts of Race in Britain and the United States between the World Wars* (Cambridge: Cambridge University Press, 1992), passim.

39. See Julian Huxley, "'Race' in Europe," in *On Living in a Revolution* (London: Chatto and Windus, 1944), 163-80; Julian Huxley and A. C. Haddon, *We Europeans: A Survey of "Racial" Problems* (New York: Harper and Brothers, 1936), 18-23; Juan Comas, "Les Mythes raciaux," in *Le Racisme devant la science* (Paris: UNESCO/ Gallimard, 1960), 24-27. On the origin of the axiom of the continuity of blood between parents and their descendants, which resides in the false idea that the mother's blood is the *causa materialis* of the body of the child (and so that the mother determines race), see Aristotle, *Generation of Animals* 1.20, in *The Complete Works of Aristotle*, ed. Jonathan Barnes (Princeton, N.J.: Princeton University Press, 1984), 1130-32. On this conception of generation, see Joseph Moreau, *Aristote et son école* (Paris: Presses Universitaires de France, 1962), 104-5; Sir David Ross, *Aristotle* (London: Methuen, 1953), 112-28; L. Bourgey, *Observation et expérience chez Aristote* (Paris: Vrin, 1955), 86; É. Guyénot, *Les Sciences de la vie aux XVII$^e$ et XVIII$^e$ siècles: L'Idée d'évolution* (Paris: Albin Michel, 1957), 233.

40. Dr. Edgar Bérillon, "Le Métissage: Son rôle dans la production des enfants anormaux," *Revue de Psychologie Appliquée* 36, no. 1 (January 1927): 3-5.

41. On the "shock of heredities," see Martial, *Les Métis*, 60-61, 198ff.; Martial, *Race, hérédité, folie*, 105ff. Cf. the passably ironic remarks by É. Guyénot on the examples Martial provides of the production of insanity by *métissage*, in *Les Problèmes de la vie* (Geneva: Cheval Ailé, 1946), 139. On the persistence of the beliefs likening "blood" and "heredity," see William C. Boyd, *Genetics and the Races of Man: An Introduction to Modern Physical Anthropology* (Boston: Little, Brown, 1950), 39 (the biologist then submits to a critical analysis the correlative false idea of "hereditary mixture" or "mixture of blood," with a view to the particulate nature of heredity [39-45]).

42. Vacher de Lapouge, *Sélections sociales,* 184–185 (Lapouge cites Dr. Armand Corre, *Ethnologie criminelle* [Paris: Reinwald, 1894]); Le Bon, *Lois psychologiques,* 8.

43. See Martial, *Race, hérédité, folie,* passim; Dr. René Martial, *Vie et constance des races* (Paris: Mercure de France, 1939), passim; Martial, *Les Métis,* passim. See William H. Schneider, *Quality and Quantity: The Quest for Biological Regeneration in Twentieth-Century France* (Cambridge: Cambridge University Press, 1990), 230–55.

44. Cf. Mary Douglas, *Purity and Danger: An Analysis of Concepts of Pollution and Taboo* (New York: Praeger, 1966), 178: "Occasionally the odd species or individual gets out of line and humans react by avoidance of one kind or another." The *métis,* incarnating ambiguity in the framework of a system of expectations dominated by an identitarian and taxinomic logic, can only be an object of avoidance. (We thank Gérard Lemaine, who, in his teaching at the École des Hautes Études en Sciences Sociales, suggested to us the application of this hypothesis to the question of *métissage.*) The *métis* becomes the object of a phobia of repulsion, most often accompanied by reactions of fear, even though the phobic theme carries no danger (see Dr. Léon Michaux, *Les Phobies* [Paris: Hachette, 1968], 9–10). The dominance of the element of repulsion is also found in ethnic anthropophobias (43).

45. See Jacques Boulenger, *Le Sang français* (Paris: Denoël, 1943), 156.

46. Vacher de Lapouge, *Sélections sociales,* 190–92. On the Lapougian explanation of the decline in the birthrate by *métissage,* see Hervé Le Bras, "Histoire secrète de la fécondité," *Le Débat* 8 (January 1981): 83–84; André Béjin, "De Malthus à la sociobiologie: Les Formes de prise en considérations des liens du sang," *Revue Européenne des Sciences Sociales* 69 (1985): 130; Pierre-André Taguieff, "Face à l'immigration: Mixophobie, xénophobie ou sélection," *Vingtième Siécle* 47 (July–September 1995): 109ff.

47. Lapouge expounds this set of grievances in *Sélections sociales,* 155–96.

48. Comas, "Les Mythes raciaux," 27.

49. See Hankins, *Social Basis,* 342–43.

50. See Robert King Merton, "The Self-Fulfilling Prophecy," in *Social Theory and Social Structure,* rev. ed. (Glencoe, Ill.: Free Press, 1957), 421–36. We know that by way of the self-fulfilling prophecy "fears are translated into reality" (436).

51. Otto Klineberg, *Social Psychology,* rev. ed. (New York: Holt, Rinehart and Winston, 1954), 318. Julian Huxley presents the same thesis: "The disapproval of 'miscegenation' is primarily social, not biological" (Huxley and Haddon, *We Europeans,* 230). The de facto quasi-universality of mixophobia (as an attitude) then remains to be explained.

52. Célestin Bouglé, *La Démocratie devant la science: Études critiques sur l'hérédité, la concurrence et la différenciation* (Paris: Alcan, 1923), 80.

53. Jacques Ruffié, *De la biologie à la culture* (Paris: Flammarion, 1976), 467.

54. The tradition of differentialist anticolonialism has been especially illustrated by Gustave Le Bon's analyses, presented in his article "Influence de l'éducation et des institutions européennes sur les populations indigènes des colonies," *Revue Scientifique* 28 (August 1889): 225–37. For a critique of the assimilationist conception of colonialism (that is, of the universalist and missionary French model), see Gustave Le Bon, "L'Inde moderne: Comment on fonde une colonie, comment on la garde, et comment on la perd," *Revue Scientifique* 22 (November 20, 1886): 648–57, in which the accent is placed on the danger of *métissage* as a factor of racial instability and anarchy. Le Bon approaches the question of Algeria in his article "L'Algérie et les idées régnantes en France en matière de colonialisation," *Revue Scientifique* 23 (October 8, 1887): 448–57. On these texts, see the (too) brief remarks by Norbert A. Nye, *The Origins of Crowd*

*Psychology* (London: Sage, 1975), 50–51. See also Pierre-André Taguieff, *Couleur et le Sang*, 60ff.

55. Bonnard, "La Question juive," 117. This is a fine example of a tolerationist statement of racism.

56. The racio-eugenicist approach to immigration was formulated in rather definitive fashion by Vacher de Lapouge in *Sélections sociales* (1886), followed by Richet (who does not cite Lapouge in 1919), Martial, and Montandon (who cite him as a master). On the Anglo-Saxon position, see Edwin Grant Conklin, *Heredity and Environment in the Development of Men* (Princeton, N.J.: Princeton University Press, 1916), 423–25, 444–47.

57. *Lettre d'information du Club de l'Horloge* 20 (first trimester 1985), 3.

58. Ibid., 1.

59. Louis Agassiz, "The Diversity of Origin of the Human Races," *Christian Examiner* 49 (1850): 145, quoted in Stephen Jay Gould, *The Mismeasure of Man* (New York: Norton, 1981), 47.

60. Gaston Bouthoul, *Traité de sociologie* (Paris: Payot, 1946), 272–73.

61. Charles Darwin, *Variation of Animals and Plants under Domestication* (New York: New York University Press, 1988), 2:18.

62. Claire Richter, *Nietzsche et les théories biologiques contemporaines* (Paris: Mercure de France, 1911), 184–85. The neo-Lamarckian naturalist Rütimeyer, who was not hindered by his scientific choices from feeling close to Darwin, and who admired Carl-Ernst von Baer (himself admired by Nietzsche), met Nietzsche in 1869 at the University of Basel, where they were colleagues (Richter, *Nietzsche*, 14ff.). Nietzsche shared Rütimeyer's aversion to Ernst Haeckel (ibid., 15–17); see Charles Andler, *Nietzsche, sa vie et sa pensée* (Paris: Gallimard, 1958), 1:468. It was under Rütimeyer's influence that Nietzsche, once a Darwinian (especially through the reading of Lange's *History of Materialism*, as early as 1868), would lean more and more toward Lamarckianism (Andler, *Nietzsche*, 474). In reference to numerous texts (see, for example, Friedrich Nietzsche, *The Will to Power*, trans. Anthony M. Ludovici [New York: Macmillan, 1924], vol. 1, bk. 1, no. 395, 315–16), one may classify Nietzsche among the pessimistic selectionists (see Jean Granier, *Le Problème de la vérité dans la philosophie de Nietzsche* [Paris: Seuil, 1966], 407). See also Pierre-André Taguieff, *Les Fins de l'antiracisme*, 53ff.

63. Robert Pagès, "Du reportage psycho-sociologique et du racisme: À propos de la marche civique sur Washington," *Revue Française de Sociologie* 4, no. 4 (October–December 1963): 424–37; Pagès, "Abus racistes de la psychologie et psychologie sociale du racisme," *Droit et Liberté* 382 (1979): supplement, 50–52.

64. Gérard Lemaine and Benjamin Matalon, *Hommes supérieurs, hommes inférieurs? La controverse sur l'hérédité de l'intelligence* (Paris: Colin, 1985), 46.

65. Pagès, "Du reportage," 433.

66. Lemaine and Matalon, *Hommes supérieurs*, 150 (they refer to I. D. McCrone, *Race Attitudes in South Africa* [Oxford: Oxford University Press, 1937]).

67. Lemaine and Matalon, *Hommes supérieurs*, 47. On the interactions (and induced paradoxes) of social and physical kinship, see Ernest Gellner, "Nature and Society in Social Anthropology," *Philosophy of Science* 30 (1963): 236–51; Michael Banton, *Race Relations* (New York: Basic Books, 1967), 55–76.

68. D. Aaron, "The 'Inky Curse': Miscegenation in the White American Literary Imagination," *Social Science* 22 (1983): 169–90 (cited in Lemaine and Matalon, *Hommes supérieurs*, 47).

69. Lemaine and Matalon, *Hommes supérieurs*, 47.

70. E. S. Bogardus, "Measuring Social Distance," *Journal of Applied Sociology* 9

(1925): 299–308; Bogardus, "A Social Distance Scale," *Sociology and Social Research* 17 (1933): 265–71. On Bogardus's scale of social distance, especially destined to measure ethnic attitudes, see Klineberg, *Social Psychology,* 520–21; Banton, *Race Relations,* chapter 13, 315–33; Dana Bramel, "Attrait et hostilité interpersonnels," in *Introduction à la psychologie sociale,* ed. Serge Moscovici (Paris: Larousse, 1972), 1:194–95.

71. Pagès, "Du reportage," 431.
72. Ibid.
73. Gwendolen Carter, *The Politics of Inequality: South Africa since 1948* (London: Thames and Hudson, 1958) (quoted in Pagès, "Du reportage," 431).
74. Pagès, "Du reportage," 432.
75. As proof of this statement, Pagès cites the fact that the unrecognized paternity of a boy tends to be tolerated (ibid.).
76. Ibid.
77. Ibid. The psychosociologist, after recalling this Parisian proverb, "It's better to look like your father than the caretaker" (432 n. 15), refers to a highly illuminating passage from Charles Fourier, "Refus d'analyser la civilisation," in *La Fausse Industrie morcelée, répugnante, mensongère, et l'antidote, l'industrie naturelle, combinée, attrayante, véridique*...(Paris: Bossange, 1836), facsimile edition (Paris: Anthropos, 1967), 551.
78. On the signaling or discriminatory value, for rejection, of pigmentation, among the traits that stand out, are quite visible, and have a high stability (the latter guaranteed inasmuch as it is hereditary), see Pagès, "Du reportage," 434–35; see also Robert Pagès, "La Perception d'autrui," in Paul Fraisse and Jean Piaget, *Traité de psychologie expérimentale,* vol. 9, *Psychologie sociale* (Paris: Presses Universitaires de France, 1969), 164–65. It must nonetheless be specified that these signaling indexes induce unities as much as they do exclusions, certain experiments showing the surprising similarity between the perceptive activity of declared "racists" and those of declared "antiracists." Hence, in the experiment of Secord, Bevan, and Katz, those who judge blacks favorably and those who judge them unfavorably both perceive the black person as more Negroid with respect to physionomic traits than do neutral judges: the racialization of the perception of others is common to those favorable and unfavorable (Paul F. Secord, William Bevan, and Brenda Katz, "The Negro Stereotype and Perceptual Accentuation," *Journal of Abnormal and Social Psychology* 53 [1956]: 78–83; see Pagès, "La Perception d'autrui," 164; Henri Tajfel, "La Catégorisation sociale," in *Introduction à la psychologie sociale,* ed. Serge Moscovici [Paris: Larousse, 1972], 1:286–87). As the tendency to accentuate differences (concerning personality or somatic traits) is imputable to "subjects with prejudices," it functions just as much in the camp of the bearers of "racist" prejudices as in that of the bearers of "antiracist" prejudices. See also Gérard Lemaine and Jeanne Ben Brika, "Identity and Physical Appearance: Stability and Desirability," *Revue Internationale de Psychologie Sociale* 2, no. 3 (July–September 1989): 325–38.
79. Lemaine and Matalon, *Hommes supérieurs,* 34–45.
80. Ibid., 35.
81. Louis Dumont, preface to the French translation of Karl Polanyi, *The Great Transformation* (New York: Farrar and Rinehart, 1944) (*La Grande Transformation,* trans. C. Malamoud and M. Angeno [Paris: Gallimard, 1983], xiv). See also Louis Dumont, *Homo Hierarchicus: An Essay on the Caste System,* trans. Mark Sainsbury (Chicago: University of Chicago Press, 1970), 8–11, 17–19; Dumont, *La Civilisation indienne et nous* (Paris: Colin, 1975), 17, 22–23; Dumont, *Homo aequalis I: Genèse et épanouissement de l'idéologie économique* (Paris: Gallimard, 1977), 12ff.
82. Dumont, *Civilisation indienne et nous,* 16.

83. Ibid., 17.
84. Pagès, "La Perception d'autrui," 164.
85. Pagès, "Du reportage," 433.
86. Cf., for example, Arnold M. Rose, "L'Origine des préjugés," in *Le Racisme devant la science* (Paris: UNESCO, 1960), 429–57. The author describes and refutes the theory of the "horror of differences" (447–48), for differences are themselves perceptible only if one is already prejudiced.
87. Gabriel Tarde was quite optimistic on this point: "The strife of opposition fulfills the rôle of a middle term in the social, as it does in the organic and inorganic, worlds, and that is destined gradually to fade away, exhaust itself, and disappear, as a result of its own growth, which is merely a progress toward its own destruction" (*Social Laws: An Outline of Sociology*, trans. Howard C. Warren [New York: Macmillan, 1899], 132–33). Differences and oppositions have a role only as auxiliaries and intermediaries. A problematic of the same type is also found in André Lalande (see Célestin Bouglé, *Les Maîtres de la philosophie universitaire en France* [Paris: Maloine, 1938], especially 42–45).
88. See Rose, "L'Origine des préjugés," 448–51; Ashley Montagu, *Man's Most Dangerous Myth: The Fallacy of Race* (Oxford: Oxford University Press, 1974), 146–49. The frustration-aggression theory has been formulated in the course of research influenced by psychoanalysis: see especially John Dollard et al., *Frustration and Aggression* (New Haven, Conn.: Yale University Press, 1939). In the same perspective, see Muzafer Sherif and Carolyn Sherif, *Groups in Harmony and Tension* (New York: Harper, 1953). For a discussion of Dollard's hypotheses, see Klineberg, *Social Psychology*, 516–18; Banton, *Race Relations*, 294–99; Michael Banton, *Racial and Ethnic Competition* (Cambridge: Cambridge University Press, 1983), 82–84.
89. Robert E. Park, "The Concept of Social Distance," in *Race and Culture: Essays in the Sociology of Contemporary Man* (Glencoe, Ill.: Free Press, 1950), 257.
90. In his fine book *La Synthèse en histoire: Essai critique et théorique* (Paris: Alcan, 1911), Henri Berr impugns two opposing "errors": on the one hand, the theory of race (there are only collective individualities of sociological order, human races) and, on the other hand, radical sociological individualism (there are only singular individuals) (81–85). One must begin with the historical and social fact that there are "collective characters," implying the existence of one or another "group reality," whose study stems from "collective ethnology" (84–85). Berr justifies a comparative political ethology (86–87). It will especially show "to what point that which may be called *psychological* or historical *race*, through the simple action of secondary contingencies, escapes original destinies, as is commonly said, that is, the primary contingencies of race and environment" (87).

## 9. On Antiracism

1. The ideologization of humanist philosophy is a process homologous to "the ideologization of tradition" studied by Darius Shayegan in the case of the Iranian "Islamic revolution," in his fundamental book *Qu'est-ce qu'une révolution religieuse?* (Paris: Les Presses d'Aujourd'hui, 1982), 179–238.
2. By ideal type *(Idealtypus)* I understand a theoretical construction that plays the role of an interpretive schema of a determined social reality (here of the ideological order), very exactly in the Weberian sense of the term: "An ideal type is formed by the one-sided *accentuation* of one or more points of view and by the synthesis of a great many diffuse, discrete, more or less present and occasionally absent *concrete individual*

phenomena, which are arranged according to those one-sidedly emphasized viewpoints and into a unified *analytical* construct *(Gedankenbild)*. In its conceptual purity, this mental construct *(Gedankenbild)* cannot be found empirically anywhere in reality. It is a *utopia*" (Max Weber, "'Objectivity' in Social Science and Social Policy," in *Max Weber on the Methodology of the Social Sciences,* trans. Edward A. Shils and Henry A. Finch [Glencoe, Ill.: Free Press, 1949], 90).

3. For a critical analysis of the contemporary functioning of the fascism/antifascism pair, in large part transposable to that of the racism/antiracism pair, see Edgar Morin, *Pour sortir du vingtième siècle* (Paris: Nathan, 1981), 61–64. The projection outside history of "fascism" or "Nazism," which have become exemplary foils and objects of ritual moral condemnation, can only nourish a new obscurantism: legitimate horror is then placed in the service of the refusal to understand. Hence the rush to imprecation and conjuration, in spite of their ineffectiveness.

4. This is a shift that does not involve a substitution, but rather the production of transitional forms, such as the following slogan, illustrative of a current condensation: "Apartheid, the new face of Nazism" (communiqué from the MRAP, March 26, 1985). Antiracist rhetoric grafts itself onto this shift, extending the metaphor, the motif of "liberation": "The South African and Namibian peoples will be able to win their freedom; apartheid, the other face of Nazism, will be eliminated from South Africa" (ibid.).

5. The paradoxical "antiracist" racialization of the State of Israel and Zionism in general found its international outcome in the United Nations General Assembly, on November 10, 1975, when a resolution was voted stating that "Zionism is a form of racism and racial discrimination." See Pierre-André Taguieff, *Les Fins de l'antiracisme* (Paris: Michalon, 1995), 435–36.

6. In a book filled with subtle analyses and questionable theses, *Cry of Cassandra: The Resurgence of European Anti-Semitism,* trans. Norman S. Posel (Bethesda, Md.: Zenith, 1985), Simon Epstein has notably shown, with force, how certain propagandistic acts of lumping together (anti-Semitism = racism = fascism, and so on) have paired up with mythical confusions used within the Jewish community in order to engender a system of assuring illusions. Hence the necessity to distinguish clearly three categories of acts, ordinarily confused under and by the polemical etiquette of "anti-Semitism" (and/or "racism"), whose main effect is that of blindness to strategic realities: (1) that which is an international phenomenon and stems from destabilizing terrorism aimed at the Western states (attacks termed "blind"); (2) that which stems from the Israeli-Arab war, waged in France (symbolic attacks with bombs, at symbolic sites); and (3) that which is properly a manifestation of French "anti-Semitism": the small anti-Jewish acts and incidents, the acts of intimidation, and so on, which become massive once they are inventoried. A fourth category is illustrated by the murder of persons "of Jewish origin" committed by isolated, psychopathic, or fanatical "neo-Nazi" individuals.

7. [Let us again remember that Taguieff is writing in 1986. — Trans.]

8. By way of example, we will refer to the *Cahiers de la LICRA* 3 (November 1981) ("If you are different from me, far from doing me wrong, you enrich me"), which presents the general action of the International League against Racism and Anti-Semitism (Ligue Internationale Contre le Racisme et l'Antisémitisme — LICRA). The analysis in chapter 4, on the subject of "the international action of LICRA," illustrates in striking fashion the centering of anticommunist antiracism on the various manifestations of anti-Semitism, symbolic holdovers (Nazism), or sociopolitical realities (the USSR, Arab countries, Argentina). The chapter in fact encompasses the following: "The Hunt for Nazi Criminals" (33–37); "The USSR: Lands of Scorned Freedom" (37–43); "The Right to Life of the State of Israel" (43–46); "Apartheid in South Africa" (47–49);

"A Few Other Hot Spots in the World" (49–57: "A] Racial Segregation in the United States / B] The Fate of Jews in the Arab Countries / C] The Genocide of the Kurdish People / D] The Cambodian Drama / E] Anti-Semitism in Argentina / F] The Extinction of the Indians of the Amazon"). The important corpus of French antiracist texts that have appeared since the early 1930s still awaits its analyst, who will have to be a historian as much as a semanticist, a political scientist and sociologist as much as a psychologist.

9. See Aristotle, *Rhetoric* 1.3, 1358b (2–7; 20–29). We know that the Stagirite distinguished three genres of discourse, involving as many values and different aims to be realized: the deliberative, advising the useful, that is, the best; the forensic, pleading for the just; the epideictic, which treats of praise and blame, and only has to be concerned with what is beautiful or ugly. The argument of epideictic discourse is meant to "increase the intensity of adherence to certain values"; "the speaker tries to establish a sense of communion centered around particular values recognized by the audience, and to this end he uses the whole range of means available to the rhetorician for purposes of amplification and enhancement" (Chaïm Perelman and L. Olbrechts-Tyteca, *The New Rhetoric: A Treatise on Argumentation,* trans. John Wilkinson and Purcell Weaver [Notre Dame, Ind.: Notre Dame University Press, 1969], 51). Epideictic discourse is essentially a stimulant for a disposition to action. But, as Gabriel Tarde noted (in *La Logique sociale* [Paris: Alcan, 1895], 43–44), it recalls a procession more than a struggle; hence it is made to be "practiced by those who, in a society, defend the traditional and accepted values, those which are the object of education, not the new and revolutionary values which stir up controversy and polemics" (Perelman and Olbrechts-Tyteca, *New Rhetoric,* 51). If it is true that "there is an optimistic, lenient tendency in epideictic discourse" (ibid.), it is found with no trouble in commemorative antiracism, whose real political aims are masked by the appeal to values of unanimity, even universality, and declamatory spectacle. In short, its (ideological) strength and its (analytic) weakness stem from the fact that the epideictic tends to be reduced to the exclusive use of techniques favoring a *communion* with the listener.

10. A recurring formula in the press releases of the MRAP that follow racist attacks and incidents. It has various placements in discourse: "For as long as crisis, unemployment, and the latter's corollary, racism, continue to exist, the Le Pen movement has fine days ahead of it" (André Chambraud [Jean-François Kahn], in *L'Événement du Jeudi,* quoted in Olivier Malentraide, "L'Effet Le Pen, c'est le fait Le Pen," *Écrits de Paris* (March 1985): 16–17).

11. Let us recall in passing that René Girard attempted to construct a theory of such a process in his book *The Scapegoat,* trans. Yvonne Freccero (Baltimore: Johns Hopkins University Press, 1986).

12. *Latitudes* 1 (November 1984): 1 (editorial). Editor: Philippe Farine [socialist leader].

13. Madeleine Barot, *Rapport sur le racisme et l'antisémitisme* (Paris, 1982), 8.

14. In the revolutionist vulgate, the standard pair is crisis/transformation; its referential packaging is "this society," with "its contradictions," which appeal to "change" (revolution). The archi-evidence of "crisis" is the representation of an always presupposed state of facts. Cf., for example, the "Présentation" of *Société Française: Cahiers de l'Institut de Recherches Marxistes* (ed. Serge Wolikow) 17 (October–December 1985): second cover page.

15. See *Les Cahiers Rationalistes* 353 (September–October 1979): 9.

16. The crisological formula is an ideologeme whose force of evidence may easily be shown in very different contexts. It illustrates the correlation between economic

Notes to Chapter 9   385

crisis and the emergence of an illegitimate type of practice or conviction (extremism, fascism, racism, and so on). The following opening by Georges Guy-Grand manifests the spontaneous appearance of the stereotype: "The aggravation of the economic crisis, the progress of the extremisms that are its consequence..." (*Problèmes franco-allemands d'après-guerre: Entretiens tenus au siège de l' "Union pour la Vérité" de décembre 1930 à juin 1931* [Paris: Valois, 1932], 14 [foreword]).

17. Françoise Jouet, *Le Bon Usage du mot crise* (Grenoble: Institute of Political Science, 1984), quoted in Frédéric Bon, "Langage et politique," in *Traité de science politique*, ed. Madeleine Grawitz and Jean Leca (Paris: Presses Universitaires de France, 1985), 3:564. See the remarks by Maurice Tournier, in *Mots* 10 (March 1985): 231–35.

18. Jean-Claude Milner, *Les Noms indistincts* (Paris: Seuil, 1983), 80–93. The common core of the arguments of the left and the right is the economistic evidence of "crisis."

19. Weber, *Max Weber on the Methodology of the Social Sciences*, 68–69.

20. Ibid., 69.

21. Ibid.

22. Ibid.

23. I understand by a conspiracy theory of society, following Karl R. Popper, "The view that whatever happens in society — including things which people as a rule dislike, such as war, unemployment, poverty, shortages — are the results of direct design by some powerful individuals or groups" ("Prediction and Prophecy in the Social Sciences," in *Conjectures and Refutations: The Growth of Scientific Knowledge* [New York: Basic Books, 1962], 341). On the specter of plots as "causes" of historical events, see Léon Poliakov, *La Causalité diabolique: Essai sur l'origine des persécutions* (Paris: Calmann-Lévy, 1980), which departs notably from the Popperian analysis (13–27, 241). See also Pierre-André Taguieff, *Les Protocoles des Sages de Sion: Faux et usages d'un faux* (Paris: Berg International 1992), vol. 1.

24. We will note the following paradox: only the apparent "racists," the "noble" or "poor" manipulated people, are legally pursued, whereas the manipulators, the "bigwigs," so to speak, those truly responsible, may not be pursued or condemned. Whence the headlong flight into mythical denunciation, called for by juridical impotence, stimulated and justified by the sense of scandal.

25. Published in the monthly of the MRAP, *Droit et Liberté* 436 (February 1985): 4–5.

26. Let us specify: of "racism" in the singular, in general, as ideological evidence. In short, of "racism" as an operator of lumping together. Here is an example of the diversionary use of antiracism, enabling an effacement of the true nature of the Soviet Union in a unanimist anti-Nazism: "Tuesday, May 7, 1985: all of France against racism. Rallies for memory, solidarity, and hope. Forty years after the victory of *the free peoples* over Nazism, France is confronted with a rise in the ideology of racist violence" (leaflet from the MRAP, April 1985; I underscore the designation that lumps together the victors over Nazism, Stalinist totalitarianism, and pluralist democracies).

27. François Brigneau, *Minute* (April 5–12, 1985): 7.

28. Ibid.

29. Ibid., 6.

30. François Brigneau, "La France aux Français," *Présent* 807 (April 1–2, 1985): 1.

31. Annie Kriegel, "Le Slogan nouveau est arrivé," *Information Juive* (April 1985): 5.

32. Annie Kriegel, *Israël est-il coupable?* (Paris: R. Laffont, 1982), 36–37.

33. Ibid., 37–38.

34. The paradox of egalitarianism was formulated by Julien Freund in his talk at the eighteenth national colloquium of the GRECE (Versailles, November 11, 1984): egalitarianism "has, paradoxically, a hierarchy as its basis, from the fact that it accords the rank of supreme or at least superior value to equality. Stated otherwise, equality itself has value only by the place it is assigned in a hierarchical system of values."

35. On the distinction between "inferior race" and "antirace" in Nazi ideology, see Pierre-André Taguieff, "Les Présuppositions définitionnelles d'un indéfinissable: 'Le Racisme,'" *Mots* 8 (March 1984): 101–2.

36. Ibid., 71ff., 104–5. Every racialization is the inscription of a category of otherized/excluded ones in a dubious humanity or (inferior) subhumanity. But another type of racialization must be noted, which may be either added to or substituted for the first one: the inscription of the Other in a (rival) antihumanity. The ambivalence of the maximally racized one, half-inferior and half-rival, at once beastly (the underman) and dangerous (the mortal enemy), characterized the Jew in Nazi anti-Judaism and today tends to be invested in the demonized type of the Maghrebian, in the nationalist imaginary (the Algerian, especially, rapes, kills, is parasitic, but also prepares the destruction of France). See chapter 4 in this book.

37. In an intellectualist perspective, assuming that no one is wicked voluntarily but only out of ignorance (a mere lack of knowledge), the first two types identified are but one, the second folded over the first. Cf., for example, these remarks by Spinoza: "Finally, Hate comes also from mere report — as we see in the Hate the Turks have against the Jews and the Christians, the Jews against the Turks and the Christians, and the Christians against the Jews and the Turks, etc. For how ignorant most of these are of one another's religion and customs" (Spinoza, *Short Treatise on God, Man, and His Well-Being*, in *The Collected Works of Spinoza*, trans. Edwin Curley [Princeton, N.J.: Princeton University Press, 1985], part 2, chapter 3, 101). Intercommunity hatred would hence derive from the first kind, through sign and hearsay — the realm of rumor.

38. Bernard-Henri Lévy, quoted in *Présent* (February 22, 1985).

39. Bernard-Henri Lévy, in *Globe* 1 (November 1985): 13 (Bloc-notes). The whole argument, which expressly develops an intolerance passed off as antiracist, rests on the norm of the defense of "the democratic order." The democratic system, for humanitarians of atheist or agnostic stripe (those religious spirits unfit for the religious), represents a level of accessible substitutive holiness. Thus is it held up as a supreme transcendent value: the unconditional defenders of democracy in their own way make up a cult on a supraempirical order. They transmute the party of order into the Order of democratic mysticism. It is therefore necessary, in order for Le Pen to be an authentic enemy, one worthy of the name, that he be a guaranteed "real" danger to democracy. This is precisely what Le Pen is in Lévy's rhetoric, because he must be: a "phenomenon" that risks bringing on the "disintegration of the democratic order" (ibid.).

40. Ibid.

41. Leszek Kolakowski, "Diktatur der Wahrheit: Ein quadratischer Kreis," reprinted in his book *Der revolutionäre Geist* (Stuttgart: Kohlhammer, 1972), 85ff.

42. Ibid., 81.

43. Ibid., 97.

44. Ibid. [My translation. — Trans.]

45. Ibid., 97–98.

46. Ibid., 98. [My translation. — Trans.] See also Pierre-André Taguieff, *La République menacée* (Paris: Textuel, 1996), 42–56; Taguieff and Michèle Tribalat, *Face au Front National* (Paris: La Découverte, 1998), 93ff.; Taguieff, "Réflexions sur la ques-

tion antiraciste: Droit, morale et politique," in *Immigration et intégration*, ed. Philippe Dewittte (Paris: La Découverte, 1999), 407–17.

47. Roger Ikor, "La grande question," *La Nef* 19–20 (September–December 1964): 33. Ikor's argument presupposes the basic evidence of the individuo-universalist universe. On the one hand, it offers the affirmation of an immoderate universalism, enveloping a proclaimed intolerance toward any particularism, an attitude representing itself as progressive: "All that is *particular* finds me hostile, or at least on my guard.... I do not dream of breaching the boundaries that separate them (human beings), the artificial and even the natural ones.... Everything that separates seems to me reactionary" (Roger Ikor, *Lettre ouverte aux Juifs* [Paris: Michel, 1970], 16). On the other hand, Ikor's argument interprets the opposition between individualism and racism as that between good and evil: "It is racism that threatens us: it is therefore toward individualism that we must deliberately lean" ("La grande question," 39).

48. Ikor, "La grande question," 34.

49. Ibid.

50. Ibid., 39.

51. There is an antiracist pathos of distance: at issue is keeping away the racist. Contempt may nonetheless not declare itself as such but rather must have reasons: the racist is defined by ignorance coupled with pretentious vulgarity, stupidity mixed with crudeness or brutality. Hence the current usage — for example, in the intellectual class partially followed by the (established) political class — of antipopulist motifs recast in the antifascist-antiracist vulgate. One detests the topics of the "Small Business Café" and "Poujadist" [after Pierre Poujade, the founder, in 1953, of the Union for the Defense of the Tradesman and Artisans of France — Trans.] attitudes, contemporary avatars of contempt for the vulgarity of the "little corporal" of base extraction, a contempt that, detracting from analysis (one is not going to "waste time getting one's hands dirty"), engenders a lack of knowledge of the real danger. Blindness in the face of National Socialism was long nourished by such a contempt. Certainly, sometimes Hitler becomes a Poujade, but sometimes he becomes a Hitler.

52. The racist must be reeducated insofar as she is assumed to be afflicted by a deep evil, endowed with roots, that is, her racist "prejudice." At issue is not only teaching her; at issue is transforming her, uprooting her prejudice, by acting on the structures outside the consciousness of the subject. Reeducation involves a twofold and simultaneous movement: unteaching while teaching. An interview that brought together, on December 17, 1967, at *France-Inter*, four representatives of various trends in antiracist militancy, illustrates the type-argument of the antiracist reeducator: "Les Mécanismes du préjugé," interview with S. Agblemagnon, Albert Memmi, Pierre Paraf, and R. P. Aubert, in *Droit et Liberté* 259 (February 1967): 24. The view of the social therapist is grafted onto the juridico-policing conception of social behaviors and ideological attitudes. But who is going to reeducate the reeducators? And how does one avoid policing minds? How does one limit the development of the seeds of authoritarianism contained in the will to submit opinions and beliefs to a system of values posited as an absolute?

53. Daniel Cohn-Bendit, interview in *L'Arche* (June 1978), quoted in Epstein, *Cry of Cassandra*, 150.

54. Cf. the remarks by Erika Apfelbaum and Ana Vasquez on the reduction of identity: "In the sociopolitical context in which a person finds himself reduced to being no more, for example, than 'the Portuguese,' a label of negative connotation, devalorized and devalorizing, 'cultural identity' is none other than a stigma assigned in order to pin him in a determinate place, to exclude him, and to paralyze him in his attempts to be, as a whole, a man, a father, and a worker, who likes to love, who

knows how to dance, and so on" ("Les réalités changeantes de l'identité," *Peuples Méditerranéens* 24 [July–September 1983]: 98).

55. On this slogan, characteristic of left differentialist and dialogic antiracism, see Pierre-André Taguieff, "Le Néo-racisme différentialiste," *Langage et Société* 34 (December 1985): 69–98.

56. Kriegel, "Le Slogan nouveau est arrivé," 1.

57. "Vivre ensemble avec nos différences," *Appel pour la tenue des assises nationales contre le racisme* (leaflet), March 17–18, 1984, 69–98.

58. See *La Ruée vers l'égalité (Mélanges)* (Paris, 1985), 42. Let us recall that the first march took place at the end of 1983 and that the second (in November 1984) was christened "Convergence 84 for Equality." In November 1985, a third march took place, the "March for Civil Rights."

59. Cf. *La Ruée vers l'égalité*, 8, 28: the origin of the slogan was a handwritten sign carried by a demonstrator in the march of 1983. See Jean-Michel Ollé, "Deux marches, c'est beaucoup," *Différences* 51 (December 1985): 7.

60. See Dominique Garcette, "Super, la France marche au mélange!" reprinted in *La Ruée vers l'égalité*, 29.

61. *La Ruée vers l'égalité*, 8; cf. also 68: "For many the idea of '*mixture*' has had the function of a new idea. But, as F. B. [Farida Belghoul] said, '*mixture is never claimed, but observed.*' And then it is already at work. But we want new conditions of mixture. The inevitable argument of 'mixture' goes in this direction. But we cannot be content with it. It will run dry if we do not feed it with external or internal sources. The '*internal source*' is the recognition of the diversity of supplies, the stabilization in France of cultural and linguistic homes other than French" (Albano Cordeiro, "Grandeurs et misères de Convergence," in *La Ruée vers l'égalité*, 68). From such a rhapsody of militant clichés, three dominant values stand out: "mixture" is valuable in itself, it must be wanted (or desired) for itself; the "new" also represents a value in itself — mixture must be of a new type in order to be fully desirable; finally, "diversity" is good, but insofar as it feeds mixture — there must be difference for there to be mixture. The value of values here remains mixture, a sort of final cause of antiracist action.

62. *La Ruée vers l'égalité*, 11.

63. Ibid.

64. Ibid. "This is the slogan that summarizes our steps," comments the "call" for "Convergence 84 for Equality."

65. Ibid., 17. Mixture, metaphorized by individuals' placement at a "crossroads," is here finalized by "equality": mixture is to equality as the means are to the end.

66. We will not insist on the usual confusion between the strictly bioanthropological motif of "multi*racial*" and the call for the "pluri*cultural*." But the interchangeability of the lexical usages sufficiently indicates that "culturalist" vocabulary intervenes in order to *euphemize* the vocabulary of race. In the ordinary social imaginary, beneath the levels of distinct language in which they are distributed, the field of "race" and that of "culture" have the same connotative effects.

67. "We would like a reciprocal multicultural exchange," declares Jérôme, a marcher in Convergence 84 (quoted in Garcette, "Super, la France marche au mélange!" 29). We see a paradoxical coupling of similarity, reciprocity, and equality with such a "multicultural" ideal: "Sure, differences exist, but the similarities are much greater than the differences," adds Tarek for his part (ibid.). Similarity seems to measure lived proximity: "I feel closer to Jérôme than to a young person living in the Maghrebe [sic]," Tarek goes on to declare (ibid.). See Pierre-André Taguieff, *Les Fins de l'antiracisme* (Paris: Michalon, 1995), 517–62.

68. See Pierre Guiral, "Vue d'ensemble sur l'idée de race et la gauche française," in *L'Idée de race dans la pensée politique française contemporaine*, ed. Pierre Guiral and Émile Temime (Paris: Éditions du CNRS, 1977), 44; the text quoted is excerpted from Élie Faure, *Les Trois Gouttes de sang* (Paris: E. Malfère, 1929), 105 (not 36, as Guiral wrongly indicates).

69. Editorial, *Latitudes* 2 (December 1984): 1 (my emphasis).

70. The differentialist adversaries of the dominant antiracist vulgate have not failed to observe such an inconsequence. Alain de Benoist thus notes: "If we intend to push to term the logic of assimilation, it is evident that it will come back to suppress the plurality inherent in the notions of 'multiracial' or 'multicultural France' " ("Réflexions sur l'identité nationale," in *Une Certaine Idée de la France*, proceedings of the Nineteenth Conference of the GRECE, November 24, 1985 [Paris: Le Labyrinthe, 1985], 81). Guillaume Faye notes a variant on a paradoxical statement: an antiracist biologist "strives...to explain to the French that races do not exist, but does not cease, in order to demonstrate this counterevidence, to act as the apologist of multiracial society. Either they exist, or they do not exist" (*Les Nouveaux Enjeux idéologiques* [Paris: Le Labyrinthe, 1985], 38 n. 10).

71. Norman Podhoretz, "My Negro Problem — and Ours," in *Doings and Undoings: The Fifties and After in American Writing* (New York: Noonday, 1964), 369–70. In a 1931 presentation, Sir Arthur Keith, who believed in the biosocial value of mixophobia, clearly perceived that the logically inferable path of assimilationist antiracism called for "ignoring race": "To obtain universal and perennial peace we must also reckon the price we will have to pay for it. The price is the racial birthright that Nature has bestowed on us. To attain such an ideal world, peoples of all countries and continents must pool their looks. Black, brown, yellows, and white must give and take in marriage and distribute in a common progeny the inheritance which each has come by in their uphill struggle through the leagues of prehistoric time towards the present. If this scheme of universal deracialization ever comes before us as a matter of practical politics — as the sole way of establishing peace and good will in all parts of our world, I feel certain both head and heart will rise against it. There will well up within us an overmastering antipathy to securing peace at such a price. This antipathy or race prejudice Nature has implanted within us for her own ends — the improvement of the human race through racial differentiation" (*The Place of Prejudice in Modern Civilization* [New York: Day, 1931]; quoted in William C. Boyd, *Genetics and the Races of Man: An Introduction to Modern Physical Anthropology* [Boston: Little, Brown, 1950], 12). We will not insist on the obvious finalist reinterpretation of the process of natural selection, no more than on the evolutionist conception of progress founded on the law of differentiation, which reveals Keith's Spencerian orientation.

72. Until 1978, the acronym MRAP designated the Mouvement contre le racisme, l'antisémitisme, et pour la paix (Movement against Racism and Anti-Semitism and for Peace). It was then modified to Mouvement contre le Racisme et pour l'Amitié entre les Peuples (Movement against Racism and for Friendship among Peoples). The transformation of the semantic content of the acronym took place according to two objectives: to erase the specificity of "anti-Semitism" by presupposing it as one form among others of "racism" (that is, racism targeting Jews), to recenter the self-designating formula on the naming of a single enemy to which the prescription for peace, itself defined by "friendship among peoples," is opposed. The antiracist is identified with the party of pacificism and universal brotherhood while attributing to himself the ethical quality par excellence (the respect for the human person), in the face of the racist, identified with the party of warmongering accompanied (indeed founded) by nonrespect for the human

person. The absolute evidence, at the basis of commemorative antiracism, is that *racism is violence,* can be nothing but violence, is essentially violence. But the violence at issue is most often reduced to "the 'sad everyday reality' of the numerous [racist] attacks." Ritualized antiracism cannot move beyond a legal-policing view of violence. Hence it only projects on its Other, the racist, the dominant characteristic of its conceptions and practices: trailing, driving out, denouncing, and condemning the outlaws. It is a legal-policing view of the social world.

73. Raymond Aron, *Peace and War: A Theory of International Relations,* trans. Richard Howard and Annette Fox Baker (New York: Doubleday, 1966), 705; Julien Freund, *L'Essence du politique* (Paris: Sirey, 1965), 598.

74. Aron, *Peace and War,* 705.

75. Freund, *L'Essence du politique,* 598.

76. See Max Scheler, *Ressentiment,* trans. William W. Holdheim (Glencoe, Ill.: Free Press, 1961), 114–36; Scheler, *The Nature of Sympathy,* trans. Peter Heath (London: Routledge and Kegan Paul, 1954), 96–102 (in which the author recognizes that he went "too far" [99] in his reduction of the love of humanity to ressentiment, as he presented it in *Ressentiment*).

77. Freund, *L'Essence du politique,* 599–600.

78. Max Weber, *From Max Weber: Essays in Sociology,* trans. H. H. Gerth and C. Wright Mills (Oxford: Oxford University Press, 1946), 121–22; Freund, *L'Essence du politique,* 599.

79. Freund, *L'Essence du politique,* 499. In all cases of nonrecognition of the enemy, the latter, once encountered, loses his properly human value: "One gives oneself the right to exterminate him as a wrongdoer, a criminal, a pervert, or an unworthy creature" (499). The "superior race" is henceforth implicitly confused with the representatives of humanitarianism, who pose as the only authentic humans worthy of the name.

80. Ibid., 600.

81. If there is agreement on the definitive achievement of peace, disagreement appears concerning the means: lessons from history relayed by an appropriate education (one that is supposed to lead from horror at the effects of war to the will to peace), the legal achievement of a universal federation, the passage from the military age to the age of business, the establishment of the classless society that opens the era of universal brotherhood (see Freund, *L'Essence du politique,* 601). Cf. the typology of pacifisms that Max Scheler proposed in 1927 (*Der Idee des Friedens und der Pazifismus* [Berlin: Neue Geist, 1931]): heroic and individual, Christian, economic, legal (pacifism by law), communist (Marxist socialist), imperialist (the universal empire), capitalist (the international pacifism of the capitalist grand bourgeoisie), cosmopolitanism of the cultural elites (see Aron, *Peace and War,* 704; Freund, *L'Essence du politique,* 598).

82. Freund, *L'Essence du politique,* 482.

83. Ibid.

84. See Scheler, *Ressentiment,* 115.

85. "Antiracism has a meaning only because there is racism, and the two doctrines both cultivate the enemy, without recognition that antiracism is at times reverse racism" (Freund, *L'Essence du politique,* 482).

86. Ibid., 394.

87. Ibid., 499.

88. Scheler, *Ressentiment,* 125–26.

89. Scheler, *Nature of Sympathy,* 100.

90. Scheler, *Der Idee des Friedens,* 61–62.

## 10. Elements of a Theory of Ideological Debate

1. Margaret Mead and James Baldwin, *A Rap on Race* (Philadelphia: Lippincott, 1971), 8. Colette Guillaumin refers to this fragment of conversation because it is exemplary of the reintroduction of "race" into the field of the real and the concrete, of indubitable facts of perception, in the order of the most ordinary evidence (see "The Idea of Race and Its Elevation to Autonomous Scientific and Legal Status," in *Sociological Theories: Race and Colonialism* [Paris: UNESCO, 1980], 41).
2. Malcolm X, *The Autobiography of Malcolm X,* as told to Alex Haley (New York: Grove Press, 1966), 338–40 (quoted in Bernard Lewis, *Race and Color in Islam* [New York: Harper and Row, 1971], 2–3).
3. Lewis, *Race and Color,* 3.
4. Malcolm X, *Autobiography,* 344 (quoted by Lewis, *Race and Color,* 3).
5. Lewis, *Race and Color,* 4.
6. Malcolm X, *Autobiography,* 344 (quoted by Lewis, *Race and Color,* 3).
7. Roger Bastide, "Le Conflit dans le dialogue," preface to the French translation of *A Rap on Race:* Margaret Mead and James Baldwin, *Le Racisme en question* (Paris: Calmann-Lévy, 1972), 19–20.
8. Bastide, "Le Conflit," 24. The famous expression "white man's burden" takes its ordinary meaning from Kipling, who with it intended to evoke the "crushing" responsibility of (the superior) Westerners with respect to the (inferior) peoples they governed.
9. Bastide, "Le Conflit," 24.
10. Ibid., 26. Unfaithfulness to a community culture is a distancing that gives up authenticity and engenders a state of self-dispossession that Marxist influence has proposed to christen *alienation*. For a genealogy and problematization of the term *alienation,* see Paul Siblot, "Le Praxème 'aliénation': Jeux de mots et histoires de fous," in *Questions sur les mots: Analyses sociolinguistiques* (Paris: Didier, 1987), 83–113.
11. Ibid., 24.
12. Cf. Francis Jacques: "Not all conflicts may be resolved through questioning. Far from it. At least they are held up by those who take the time to agree on the nature of the disagreement" (*L'Espace logique de l'interlocution* [Paris: Presses Universitaires de France, 1985], 583).
13. Ibid.
14. Ibid., 574ff. See also Pierre-André Taguieff, *Les Fins de l'antiracisme* (Paris: Michalon, 1995), 42–52, 207–51.

## 11. Pessimism

1. Max Horkheimer, "La Théorie critique hier et aujourd'hui," trans. Luc Ferry, in *Théorie critique* (Paris: Payot, 1978), 369.
2. Ibid.
3. Cf. Lev Shestov: "Our most incontestable, our firmest and most obvious truths, those 'veritates aeternae' as Descartes loved to call them before Pascal's day; those 'reasonable truths' as Leibniz called them later, and after him other lawful guardians of the inherited ideas of the Renaissance, even to our own day—these never weighed with Pascal in his lifetime" ("Gethsemane Night: Pascal's Philosophy," in *In Job's Balances: On the Sources of the Eternal Truths,* trans. Camilla Coventry and C. A. Macartney [Athens: Ohio University Press, 1975], 286).
4. Cf. Emmanuel Lévinas: "Art, essentially disengaged, constitutes, in a world of

initiative and responsibility, a dimension of evasion.... Art brings into the world the obscurity of fate, but it especially brings the irresponsibility that charms as a lightness and a grace.... This is not the disinterestedness of contemplation but of irresponsibility. The poet exiles himself from the city. From this point of view, the value of the beautiful is relative. There is something wicked and egoist and cowardly in artistic enjoyment. There are times when one can be ashamed of it, as of feasting during a plague" ("Reality and Its Shadow," in *Collected Philosophical Papers*, trans. Alphonso Lingis [Dordrecht: Nijhoff, 1987], 12). It must hence be declared, in an epoch of the "hypertrophy of art" in which the latter "is identified with spiritual life" (ibid.), that ethics is above aesthetics. But that is a proposition whose meaning may be understood only beyond nihilism, *our* nihilism.

5. Cf. Jacques Maritain: "Can man know himself only by renouncing at the same time his sacrificing himself to something greater than himself?... It may be that certain forms of heroism permit one to resolve this apparent contradiction.... A humanism disengaged for itself and conscious of itself, which leads man to sacrifice and to a truly superhuman grandeur, because in that case human suffering opens its eyes and is borne in love... Can there be a heroic humanism?... For my part, I answer Yes" (Jacques Maritain, *Integral Humanism: Temporal and Spiritual Problems of a New Christendom*, trans. Joseph W. Evans [New York: Scribner's, 1968], 3–4).

6. André Malraux, *Days of Hope,* trans. Stuart Gilbert (London: Hamish Hamilton, 1968), 195.

7. See Michael Walzer's fine book *Exodus and Revolution* (New York: Basic Books, 1985), 4.

8. Ibid., 149.

9. Ibid.

10. W. D. Davies, *The Territorial Dimension of Judaism* (Berkeley and Los Angeles: University of California Press, 1982), 60 (quoted by Walzer, *Exodus and Revolution,* 149).

11. Walzer, *Exodus and Revolution,* 149.

12. Richard Marienstras, "Réflexions sur le génocide," the opening essay in the collection *Être un peuple en diaspora* (Paris: Maspero, 1975), 21.

13. Ibid., 9.

14. Ibid., 12.

15. Ibid., 19.

16. Ibid., 21.

17. Ibid., 9.

18. Ibid., 35.

19. Ibid., 60.

20. Ibid. Pierre Vidal-Naquet concludes his preface to the book by quoting these remarks (xiii).

21. Ibid., 61.

22. Ibid.

23. Ibid., 35.

24. Ibid., 61.

## 12. Ethics

1. Immanuel Kant, *Groundwork of the Metaphysic of Morals,* trans. H. J. Paton (New York: Harper and Row, 1964), 96.

2. Cf. Éric Weil, *Problèmes kantiens* (Paris: Vrin, 1970), 33: "More precisely: *universalizability*, for universality is a power, in power, in every man, even the most primitive."

3. See Victor Delbos, *La Philosophie pratique de Kant* (Paris: Presses Universitaires de France, 1969), 285-86. Let us recall the fundamental law of pure practical reason: "So act that the maxim of your will could always hold at the same time as a principle establishing universal law" (Immanuel Kant, *Critique of Practical Reason*, trans. Lewis White Beck [Indianapolis: Bobbs-Merrill, 1956], 30).

4. Kant, *Groundwork*, 95.

5. See Delbos, *Philosophie pratique de Kant*, 302.

6. Kant, *Groundwork*, 95.

7. Ibid. On this point, see Gérard Lebrun, *Kant et la fin de la métaphysique* (Paris: Colin, 1970), 492.

8. Kant, *Groundwork*, 92-93; see also the other key passages on the question in the *Groundwork*: 80, 81, 144. Victor Goldschmidt, referring to the text of the *Groundwork* (80), has strongly noted the difference between Stoic axiology, which is ordered on the ontology it assumes, and the axiology of the Moderns that, "especially beginning with Kant," tends to confer on values a normative dignity, by isolating the "metaphysic of morals" from any anthropology and any physics (*Le Système stoïcien et l'idée de temps* [Paris: Vrin, 1969], 69). A remark by Marcus Aurelius will be remembered: "World, I want only what you want" (see André Bridoux, *Le Stoïcisme et son influence* [Paris: Vrin, 1966], 27).

9. Weil, *Problèmes kantiens*, 150. Whereas the "I think" and the formal system of theoretical construction are not an absolute value for every reasonable being, concerning only "the particular constitution of an understanding whose role is to unify a variety that does not emanate in the least from its spontaneity," the moral law is, to the contrary, valid "not only for man, but for every reasonable being, and even for God" (Pierre Lachièze-Rey, *L'Idéalisme kantien* [Paris: Vrin, 1950], 198). It is this removal from the world of real human beings that demands, rather than a reproach of formal ethics for its abstract universality or its "antihumanism," a consideration that it may be achieved only in the order of the juridico-political, which alone allows it to concretize itself, to connect with really living humans.

10. Kant clearly identifies the reasonable subject as noumenon and the empirical human subject as phenomenon. See Immanuel Kant, *Critique of Judgment*, trans. J. H. Bernard (New York: Hafner, 1951), 32-33 n. 2; see also Kant, *Groundwork*, 120, 126-27. On the twofold self-representation (or the twofold "nature") of man, who is at once *phenomenon* and *noumenon*, endowed with sensible *and* intelligible existence, see Delbos, *Philosophie pratique de Kant*, 315ff.; Gottfried Martin, *Kant's Metaphysics and Theory of Science*, trans. P. G. Lucas (Manchester: Manchester University Press, 1955), 189-93 (the author compares the Kantian solution, which he presents as "aporetic" [193], with the traditional principal philosophical solutions: the Platonic, the Aristotelian, and the nominalist).

11. Daniel Christoff, *Le Temps et les valeurs* (Neuchâtel: Baconnière, 1945), 66-67. In the same vein, see Jean-François Lyotard and Jacob Rogozinski, "La Police de la pensée," *L'Autre Journal* (December 1985): 32-33, whose interpretation it is difficult not to follow, at least up to the point where the rigorous reading of the Kantian texts gives way to a reconstruction, in neo-Nietzschean style, of a thought that would thereby think the human and the "all too human." Let us here cite what is essential to the focus, to the point where it slips, under the influence of the polemical will to prove too much. According to Luc Ferry and Alain Renaut, human rights "require that one ground them

on an Idea of Man, of the free and autonomous subject: on this 'nonmetaphysical humanism' that our censors believe they find in Kant and Fichte.... [I]n the face of so much presumptuousness, analysis would be necessary.... When the latter [Kant] proposes to situate the principle of moral duty, he emphasizes that 'it is of the utmost importance' not to seek to 'derive the reality of this principle from *the special characteristics of human nature*' [*Groundwork*, 92]. ... Kant continually repeats that 'Man' is not the addressee of the categorical imperative: the latter is addressed to all 'finite reasonable beings.' As a pure principle of practical reason, the moral Law is, in the strict sense, *inhuman*. What the imperative prescribes to us is a transcendence of our empirical 'humanity,' and what Kant names a 'pathologically affected will.' ... What is 'human' in Man would be that gap, that faulty torsion that turns us away from the Law. To be a man is to be in the wrong: all human is pathological.... The thought of Kant is not a 'humanism' (nor, for that matter, a rationalism). Nor is it an 'antihumanism,' ... because the neutralization of any anthropological given is required in order to confer meaning to human rights. In Kant's perspective, what *gives the right* to human rights, what guarantees their universal, unconditioned character — which defaults on 'rights' and privileges of empirical communities — is their deduction on the basis of the ethical imperative, as an 'exterior' mode of giving of the Law. In order to legitimate the rights of man, one must have uncovered the inhuman agency of the Law, *done right to the inhuman*. From this point of view, Man is never, for Kant, the pure subject of Right." This long quotation shows the authors' insensitivity to the ambiguity of the Kantian texts on the relations between principles of morality and anthropology: if it is undeniable that Kant impugns a certain empirical or "pathological" humanism, an "inhumanism" or an "overhumanism" seems no less excluded. For, of the class of pure reasonable beings, we know only terrestrial reasonable beings, and it is in them, in their persons, that "humanity" must be respected absolutely; thus is founded the dignity of the person and a metaempirical "personalism." The polemical haste of the anti-neo-Kantians is brought to light by their surprising appraisal — surprising because strictly unjustified, except by the intervention of friendship or institutional solidarity — of Jacques Derrida's understanding of Kantianism. After referring to a note in Derrida's "The Ends of Man" (presented in 1968, published in *Margins of Philosophy*, trans. Alan Bass [Chicago: University of Chicago Press, 1982], 109–36; 121–22 n. 15), in which Derrida is for the most part content with quoting the key passages of the *Groundwork* on the question of the status of Man in relation to the end in itself as an unconditioned principle of morality, Lyotard and Rogozinski believe they can add: "This brief note is sufficient to prove that Derrida has understood Kant better than generations of neo-Kantian humanists" (32 n. 6). But it is not in the contemporary precious speculative philosophers that will be found the most profound understanding of Kantian thought enveloped by what is aptly named its "philonomism," a symmetrical inversion of Emerson's "antinomism," a critique linked to the unveiling of his first metaphysical attitude: submission to and obedience of the law. In one of his finest meditations, "The Conquest of the Self-Evident; Dostoievsky's Philosophy," Lev Shestov noted: "Directly Kant hears the word 'law' pronounced he takes his hat off; he neither wishes nor dares to dispute. He who says 'law' says 'power'; he who says 'power' says 'submission' — for man's supreme virtue is to submit himself. "But it is evidently not a living individual who dictates its laws to nature. Such an individual is himself part of nature and therefore subject to it. The supreme, ultimate, definitive power belongs to 'man as such,' that is to say, to an ideal principle equally far removed from the living individual and from inanimate nature. In other words, principle, rule, and law govern everything. Kant's thought could have been expressed as follows, in a more adequate though less striking form: 'It is neither nature nor man who dictates the laws, but the laws are dictated to man and to nature by the laws themselves. In other words: in the beginning was the law.'

"... Kant did not invent this himself; he simply formulated more clearly the general tendencies of scientific thought. The choruses of free, invisible, capricious individual spirits with which mythology had peopled the world were deposed by science and replaced by other phantoms, by immutable principles; and this was declared to be the final rout of antique superstition. Such is the essence of idealism; this is what modern thought looks upon as its supreme triumph" (Lev Shestov, *In Job's Balances: On the Sources of the Eternal Truths,* trans. Camilla Coventry and C. A. Macartney [Athens: Ohio University Press, 1975], 23–24).

12. Kant, *Groundwork,* 96.
13. Ibid.
14. Ibid.
15. Ibid., 95.
16. Ibid., 101: more precisely, a reasonable being "should treat himself and all others, *never merely as a means,* but always *at the same time as an end in himself."* Thus is brought about the possibility of an economic and social life, which implies that reasonable beings may *also* treat one another as means.
17. Ibid., 101.
18. Ibid.
19. On instrumental, utilitarian, and teleological rationality (Max Weber's *Zweckrationalität*) and its limits, see the penetrating study by Ernest Gellner, "The Gaffe-Avoiding Animal or a Bundle of Hypotheses," in *Individualism: Theories and Methods,* ed. Pierre Birnbaum and Jean Leca, trans. John Gaffney (Oxford: Clarendon Press, 1990), 17–32. In this perspective, "conduct is rational if it is optimally effective in attaining a given specified aim" (17). See also Raymond Boudon, *The Analysis of Ideology,* trans. Malcolm Slater (Chicago: University of Chicago Press, 1989), 12–13, 207–8 n. 14.
20. Christoff, *Temps et les valeurs,* 66.
21. Ibid., 67.
22. Victor Delbos, "La Morale de Kant," in Kant, *Fondements de la métaphysique des moeurs,* trans. Victor Delbos (Paris: Delagrave, 1965), 47.
23. Kant, *Groundwork,* 101.
24. Ibid.
25. Delbos, "La morale de Kant," 47; Delbos, *Philosophie pratique de Kant,* 307.
26. Kant, *Groundwork,* 102.
27. Delbos sees in this distinction a "reminiscence of Stoicism, appropriated by Kant to his doctrine" (*Philosophie pratique de Kant,* 160 n. 148), and refers to Seneca, *Letters to Lucilius* 71 and 33, in which the author introduces the difference between price *(pretium)* and dignity *(dignitas).* Let us note in passing, following Émile Bréhier, that in ancient philosophy there exists only "one 'theory of value' presented expressly as such, the Stoicist theory (we translate by *value* the word *axia,* which Cicero rendered as *aestimatio*)" ("Sur une théorie des valeurs dans la philosophie antique," in *Actes du IIIe Congrès des sociétés de philosophie de langue française,* "Values," Brussels-Louvain, September 2–6, 1947 [Paris-Louvain: Vrin-Nauwelaerts, 1947], 229).
28. Kant, *Groundwork,* 102.
29. Ibid.
30. Ibid.
31. Ibid.
32. Ibid.

33. Ibid. At issue of course is the satisfaction engendered by the free and disinterested play of the faculties, the disinterested pleasure in the contemplation of the beautiful.
34. Ibid.
35. Ibid.
36. Ibid.; see also Immanuel Kant, *Anthropology from a Pragmatic Point of View*, trans. Victor Lyle Dowdell (Carbondale: Southern Illinois University Press, 1978), 207.
37. Delbos, *Philosophie pratique de Kant*, 308.
38. Kant, *Groundwork*, 102.
39. Ibid., 61.
40. Ibid., 102.
41. Ibid.
42. Ibid., 103.
43. Ibid.
44. Ibid.
45. Ibid.
46. Ibid.
47. Jean Wahl, *Traité de métaphysique*, 2d ed. (Paris: Vrin, 1970), 140.
48. Ibid., 513–14.
49. Ibid., 514.
50. Delbos, *Philosophie pratique de Kant*, 308 (Delbos here [308 n. 3] refers to Hermann Cohen, *Ethik des reinen Willens* [Berlin: Cassirer, 1904], 302–6).
51. Immanuel Kant, *The Metaphysic of Morals*, trans. Mary Gregor (Cambridge: Cambridge University Press, 1996), 150.
52. And not of "requiring the perfection of *others*," as Lucien Goldmann wrongly interprets it (*Introduction à la philosophie de Kant* [1948], 2d ed. [Paris: Gallimard, 1967], 236).
53. Emmanuel Lévinas, "Judaïsme et révolution," in *Du sacré au saint: Cinq nouvelles lectures talmudiques* (Paris: Minuit, 1977), 19. On this important text, see J. Halperin, "Liberté et responsabilité," in *Textes pour Emmanuel Lévinas*, ed. François Laruelle (Paris: Place, 1980), 67.
54. Lévinas, "Judaïsme et révolution," 19.
55. Ibid.
56. See Emmanuel Lévinas, *Totality and Infinity: An Essay on Exteriority*, trans. Alphonso Lingis (Pittsburgh: Duquesne University Press, 1969), 199; Lévinas, *Otherwise than Being, or Beyond Essence*, trans. Alphonso Lingis (Pittsburgh: Duquesne University Press, 1998), 88–89.
57. Emmanuel Lévinas, *Ethics and Infinity*, trans. Richard A. Cohen (Pittsburgh: Duquesne University Press, 1985), 95.
58. Lévinas, "Judaïsme et révolution," 20. Cf. Emmanuel Lévinas, *Proper Names*, trans. Michael B. Smith (Stanford, Calif.: Stanford University Press, 1996), 37: "It has never been my opinion that the mechanical act of providing food and clothing constituted by itself the fact of the meeting between I and Thou" (letter to Martin Buber, March 11, 1963). [Translation slightly modified. — Trans.]
59. See Vladimir Jankélévitch, *Le Je-ne-sais-quoi et le presque-rien* (Paris: Seuil, 1980), 2:193, 210: "The manner is everything." On this point, see Pierre-André Taguieff, "Vladimir Jankélévitch: Les Apories de l'éthique et la musique de la métaphysique," *Cahiers Bernard-Lazare* 113 (October–December 1985): 81ff.
60. Lévinas, *Proper Names*, 32. A philosophy of dialogue, as such, assumes a relativization of the ego, of its sovereign position, indeed a decentering of the subject. By positing the interlocutive relation as transcendental, Francis Jacques links up with the

Lévinassian thought of the primacy of another. But in one sense only, for the emphasis is placed on the correlation of the "I" and the "Thou," on the relation of interlocution rather than on another as such. The common presupposition is nevertheless the recognition of another in the dialogic situation, in which the addressee receives the status of *person* at the same time as a *personal* status: hence a *"dissymmetry without* a decisive *privilege* among persons" is set up (Francis Jacques, "Les Conditions dialogiques de la référence," Les Études Philosophiques 3 [July–September 1977]: 287). Jacques has developed this dialogic philosophy in two important works: *Dialogiques: Recherches logiques sur le dialogue* (Paris: Presses Universitaires de France, 1979); *L'Espace logique de l'interlocution: Dialogiques II* (Paris: Presses Universitaires de France, 1985).

61. Lévinas, *Proper Names,* 33.
62. Ibid., 32.
63. Ibid., 33.
64. Ibid. Jacques Rolland, one of the most acute of Lévinas's commentators, rightly insists on the centrality of the questioning of the "I" by the Other who is achieved in and as "that shattering of the system because of Another" (Lévinas, *Proper Names,* 73): see Jacques Rolland, "Penser au-delà (notes de lecture)," *Exercices de la Patience* 1 (1980), special issue on Lévinas: 12–14.
65. Lévinas, *Proper Names,* 38.
66. Ibid.
67. Ibid., 73 ("Kierkegaard: Existence and Ethics," which appeared in German in 1963).
68. Ibid.
69. Emmanuel Lévinas, "La Trace de l'autre," in *En découvrant l'existence avec Husserl et Heidegger,* 2d ed. (Paris: Vrin, 1967), 196; see also Lévinas, *Proper Names,* 73–74.
70. Lévinas, *Proper Names,* 73.
71. Ibid.
72. Lévinas, "La Trace de l'autre," 196.
73. Emmanuel Lévinas, "Un Dieu Homme?" *Exercices de la Patience* 1 (1980): 72. For the following citations, ibid.
74. Ibid.
75. Ibid. [The biblical quotation is from the King James Bible.—Trans.]
76. Emmanuel Lévinas, *Difficult Freedom: Essays on Judaism,* trans. Seán Hand (Baltimore: Johns Hopkins University Press, 1990), 21. [Translation slightly modified.—Trans.]
77. Ibid., 21–22.
78. Ibid., 20.
79. Ibid., 22.
80. Ibid., 9.
81. Ibid., 191.
82. Ibid., 177.
83. Ibid., 291.
84. Alain Finkielkraut, "L'Esprit et les racines," in *L'Identité française* (Paris: Tierce, 1985), 41.
85. Rudolf Bultmann, "Der Gottesdanke und der moderne Mensch," in *Glauben und Verstehen* (Tübingen: Mohr, 1965), 125. [My translation.—Trans.]
86. Ibid., 125–26.
87. Ibid., 126.
88. Ibid., 127.

89. Max Scheler, *Man's Place in Nature*, trans. Hans Meyerhoff (Boston: Beacon, 1961), 66.
90. Ibid.
91. Ibid., 68. The "classical theory" is based on the thesis of "the autonomous power of the idea, the view that the (rational) idea has an original power, activity and energy" (62–63). And Scheler specifies that the so-called classical theory "has prevailed almost throughout the whole history of western philosophy" (62). One cannot fail to compare Scheler's critique to the Spinozist position on the idealist fiction of a "free will." In Spinoza, as finite beings are determined by causes foreign to their existence and acting, their will cannot be called a free cause. See Benedict de Spinoza, *Ethics,* trans. William Hale White and Amelia Hutchinson (New York: Hafner, 1949), part 1, proposition 32, corollary 2 (67–68), which draws out the consequences of proposition 32 ("the will cannot be called a free cause, but can only be called necessary" [67]) relative to God. On this point, cf. Martial Guéroult, *Spinoza, I: Dieu (Éthique, I)* (Paris: Aubier Montaigne, 1968), 365: to say that God acts out of the freedom of his will is an absurdity; for God would not "create" the universe by his *free* will, because he would not create it by *his will,* because the latter belongs to the sphere of created things. It follows that the men who believe they are acting by free decree of the soul "are dreaming with their eyes open."
92. Scheler, *Man's Place,* 68.
93. Ibid. Such a perspective in no way excludes the possibility of an increase in the "power of reason" in history: this increase, however, is not due to an energy that belongs to reason but is rather made possible by "the *growing assimilation*" of ideas and values by interests and passions.
94. Ibid., 62.
95. Ibid.
96. Ibid., 68–69.
97. Ibid., 69.
98. Ibid.
99. Ibid.
100. Ibid., 84. This interpretation of Spinozism is of course contestable, but nevertheless based on the text of the *Ethics* (see part 4, propositions 1–4 [191–94], 14 [199], 15 [199–200]; book 5, preface [252–55]). The Spinozist position is that it is useless to rise up against the passions, for it cannot happen that man, as a part of nature, does not have passions. It is not enough to deny the power of the passions in order to free oneself of them: the passions are in no way destroyed by the naive claim of the minds who, through ignorance of the causes, believe themselves free. There is therefore a "truth" of the passions and an irreducibility of human servitude (to follow book 4 alone of the *Ethics*). On this question, Léon Brunschvicg said in a few words what is essential: "In order for the true knowledge of good and evil to be able to act on our passions, it is necessary that it turn itself into a passion, that it become a stronger passion, hence capable of moderating and repressing them [*Ethics,* part 4, proposition 1]. Only at this price will the truth triumph over our passions; but it is not from knowledge of the first kind that such a triumph will ever result" (*Spinoza et ses contemporains* [Paris: Presses Universitaires de France, 1951], 91). On this Spinozist argument, see Alain, *Spinoza* (Paris: Gallimard, 1968), 125–26; Victor Delbos, *Le Spinozisme* (Paris: Vrin, 1968), 137ff.; Ferdinand Alquié, *Servitude et liberté selon Spinoza* (Paris: CDU, 1969), 45ff.; Alexandre Matheron, *Individu et communauté chez Spinoza* (Paris: Minuit, 1969), 223ff.
101. Scheler, *Man's Place,* 69.
102. Ibid.

103. Max Scheler, *Die Idee des Friedens und der Pazifismus* (Berlin: Neue Geist, 1931), 62; see also Scheler, *Formalism in Ethics and Non-formal Ethics of Values: A New Attempt toward the Foundation of an Ethical Personalism*, trans. Manfred S. Frings and Roger L. Funk (Evanston, Ill.: Northwestern University Press, 1973), 493–94.

104. Catherine Kintzler, *Condorcet: L'Instruction publique et la naissance du citoyen* (Paris: Le Sycomore, 1984).

105. Guy Planty-Bonjour, "Le Droit naturel selon Aristote," *Les Études Philosophiques* 2 (April–June 1986): 153.

106. Jacques d'Hondt, "Le Refus des droits de l'homme," *Les Études Philosophiques* 2 (April–June 1986): 217.

107. Ibid.

108. Ibid.

109. Quoted in Célestin Bouglé, "Le Citoyen moderne," in *Du sage antique au citoyen moderne* (Paris: Colin, 1921), 215.

110. Wolfgang Huber, "Les Droits de l'homme: Un Concept et son histoire," *Concilium* 144 (April 1979): 24–25.

111. Nicolas Berdyaev, *Solitude and Society*, trans. George Reavey (London: Centenary, 1938), 193.

112. See Michel Villey, "Polémiques sur les 'droits de l'homme,'" *Les Études Philosophiques* 2 (April–June 1986): 199. Villey nevertheless recognizes, in the various "Declarations of Human Rights," the value of a "defensive weapon" (*Le Droit et les droits de l'homme* [Paris: Presses Universitaires de France, 1983], 9).

113. The "religion of human rights" requires, as such, a mediator for obtaining salvation: the organizations specializing in the defense of human rights are presented as obliged mediators. Let us recall, after Berdyaev, that Plotinus was hostile to religion precisely because of the requirement for legitimate mediators that it involved, he noted, differently from philosophical wisdom, which obtains salvation without mediation (Berdyaev, *Solitude and Society*, 7).

114. Villey, "Polémiques," 191–92; Villey, "Correspondance," *Droits* 2 (1985): 35.

115. Kintzler, *Condorcet*, 249–50. On the contemporary utopia of a universal religion that would bring together without excluding, that is, on the idea of a community of the faithful without infidels, as is suggested by the ethics of human rights, see Pierre-André Taguieff, "Une religion douce," *Légende du Siècle* (May 19, 1987): 1–2.

116. Villey, "Polémiques," 199.

117. Ibid.; Villey, "Correspondance," 39–40.

118. Jan Patočka, *Heretical Essays in the Philosophy of History*, trans. Erazim Kohák (Chicago: Open Court, 1996), 115.

119. Ibid.

120. Ibid.

121. Jean-Pierre Deconchy, "Psychologie sociale expérimentale et exégèse biblique," *Recherches de Psychologie Sociale* 4 (1982): 116 (on Robert P. Carroll, *When Prophecy Failed: Cognitive Dissonance in the Prophetic Traditions of the Old Testament* [New York: Seabury, 1979]). See Joachim Wach, *Sociology of Religion* (Chicago: University of Chicago Press, 1944).

122. Deconchy, "Psychologie sociale," 116.

123. Ibid. The theory of cognitive dissonance assumes that the situation of psychological dissonance, psychologically untenable by the fact that the various elements of the field are no longer in concordance (or in accord) among themselves, involves the aim of a reestablishment of a consonance (a reduction of dissonance), that is, an ef-

fort to bring said elements, one way or another, into better accord. See Leon Festinger and Elliot Aronson, "The Arousal and Reduction of Dissonance in Social Contexts," in *Group Dynamics*, ed. Dorwin Cartwright and Alvin Zander (Evanston, Ill.: Row, Peterson, 1960), 214–32; see also the good overview by Jean-Pierre Poitou, *La Dissonance cognitive* (Paris: Colin, 1974).

## 13. Republican Metapolitics

1. Michael Ignatieff, preface to *La Liberté d'être humain: Essai sur le désir et le besoin*, trans. M. Sissung (Paris: Découverte, 1986), 9–10 (French edition of *The Needs of Strangers* [New York: Viking, 1985]).

2. Paul Ricoeur, "Ethics and Politics," trans. Kathleen Blamey, in *From Text to Action: Essays in Hermeneutics, II* (Evanston, Ill.: Northwestern University Press, 1991), 336–37.

3. The rediscovery comes from the historical studies exemplified by Claude Nicolet's fine book, *L'Idée républicaine en France: Essai d'histoire critique* (Paris: Gallimard, 1982). The debate then shifted and developed on the terrain of political philosophy, especially punctuated by the critical studies of Philippe Raynaud ("Destin de l'idéologie républicaine," *Esprit* [December 1983]: 27–39) and Joël Roman ("L'Idée républicaine," *Intervention* 7 [November 1983–January 1984]: 59–64).

4. The initiator of the rediscovery of the politico-juridical philosophies of Kant and Fichte is, in France, Alexis Philonenko. See Alexis Philonenko, *La Liberté humaine dans la philosophie de Fichte* (Paris: Vrin, 1980); Philonenko, *Théorie et praxis dans la pensée morale et politique de Kant et de Fichte en 1793* (Paris: Vrin, 1968). In the 1970s, the Collège de Philosophie, around Luc Ferry and Alain Renaut, made possible the organization of a school of the trend initiated by Philonenko. See Luc Ferry and Alain Renaut, "D'un retour à Kant," *Ornicar* 20–21 (summer 1980): 191–205.

5. Luc Ferry and Alain Renaut, *Political Philosophy 3: From the Rights of Man to the Republican Idea*, trans. Franklin Philip (Chicago: University of Chicago Press, 1992), 123–28.

6. Shmuel Trigano, *La République et les Juifs après Copernic* (Paris: Aujourd'hui, 1982), 245.

7. Trigano himself recognizes the importance of the distinction: "It is the simulacrum of the universal that collapses, not the universal" (ibid., 263). But he hardly furnishes the philosophical means for conceiving the much-sought-after universal that would not be the simulacrum of universality.

8. Jeanne Hersch, *Idéologies et réalité: Essai d'orientation politique* (Paris: Plon, 1956), 61.

9. Jacques Ellul, *The Betrayal of the West*, trans. Matthew J. O'Connell (New York: Seabury, 1978), 124–25.

10. Robert Brasillach, *Les Sept Couleurs* (Paris: Plon, 1970), 162–64. André Reszler has not failed to note the centrality of the composite myth of the pure, the unitary, and the homogeneous in Nazi ideology, see Reszler, *Mythes politiques modernes* (Paris: PUF, 1981), 149–51. On the relations among "confusionism," "maximalism," "purism," and violence, see the fine analyses by Vladimir Jankélévitch, *Le Pur et l'impur* (Paris: Flammarion, 1978), 164ff.

11. On the contemporary confusion between the concept of community and that of society, see Annie Kriegel, "Une Communauté à double foyer," in *Réflexions sur les questions juives* (Paris: Hachette, 1984), 128–36.

12. We are presupposing that "there cannot be a society that *is* not something for it-

self; that does not *represent* itself *as* being something" — that no society can do without a *self-representation* without entering a "crisis," without there being a "crisis of imaginary social significations" (Cornelius Castoriadis, "La Crise des sociétés occidentales," *Politique Internationale* 15 [spring 1982]: 131–47).

13. Cf. Kriegel, *Réflexions sur les questions juives:* "Every human being, every human group may reach the universal, the general — in short, the human in its plenitude — only through the detour of what makes him or her singular and unique. No one is capable, without mediation, of being entirely of this world: for me this mediation is Judaism" (633). See Pierre-André Taguieff, *Sur la nouvelle droite* (Paris: Descartes et Cie, 1994), passim.

14. Recent texts from the GRECE mark an attempt at integrating the idea of an organic community into the concept of democracy, which involves the distinction between a liberal and an organic democracy. See Alain de Benoist, "Vers une démocratie organique," *Éléments* 52 (winter 1985): 33–35. Democracy as power of the people here assumes the existence of an organic collectivity, a "national and popular community" or a "community of citizens" formally opposed to the nonorganic entity of "society" (Alain de Benoist, "Huit Thèses sur la démocratie," *Éléments* 52 [winter 1985]: 36). "Organic democracy" would be grounded "in reference to the *people* conceived as a collective organism and as the privileged actor in every historical destiny" (35).

15. On the idea of "cultural democracy," see Henri Giordan, *Démocratie culturelle et droit à la différence* (Paris: La Documentation Française, 1982). Such a historical and political presentation of cultural democracy demands to be philosophically rethought. That is one of the theoretical tasks that we propose in the continuation of the present study.

16. André Lalande, "Valeur indirecte de la différence," in *La Raison et les normes: Essai sur le principe et la logique des jugements de valeur* (Paris: Hachette, 1963), 235–60.

17. In the precise sense that Georges Canguilhem gave to this expression, especially in relation to the Spencerian evolutionism that, grounded on the law of differentiation, is strictly inverted in the "involutionist" philosophy of Lalande, the latter grounded on the law of assimilation: "Scientific ideologies are more likely ideologies of philosophers, discourses of scientific pretension" (*Idéologie et rationalité dans l'histoire des sciences de la vie* [Paris: Vrin, 1977], 44).

18. Lalande, *La Raison et les normes*, 236.
19. Ibid., 237.
20. Ibid., 243.
21. Ibid., 245.
22. Ibid., 256.
23. Ibid., 259.

24. Max Horkheimer, afterword to Thilo Koch, *Porträts zur deutsch-jüdischen Geistesgeschichte* (Cologne: Dumont, 1961), 277. [My translation. — Trans.]

25. Cf. Alexis Philonenko: "There must be a neo-Kantianism that is not a return to Kant" (*L'Oeuvre de Kant* [Paris: Vrin, 1972], 2:273). Considering their philosophical self-presentation ("return to ... "), one may wonder if Luc Ferry and Alain Renaut have not gone further than halfway toward such a program.

26. Immanuel Kant, *On the Old Saw: That May Be Right in Theory but It Won't Work in Practice*, trans. E. B. Ashton (Philadelphia: University of Pennsylvania Press, 1974), 57.

27. Immanuel Kant, "Idea for a Universal History from a Cosmopolitan Point of View," trans. Lewis White Beck, in *On History* (Indianapolis: Bobbs-Merrill, 1957), 19;

and the commentary by Carl J. Friedrich, "L'Essai sur la paix: Sa position centrale dans la philosophie politique de Kant," in Institut International de Philosophie Politique, *La Philosophie politique de Kant* (Paris: Presses Universitaires de France, 1962), 41–142.

28. Éric Weil, *Problèmes kantiens* (Paris: Vrin, 1970), 135.

29. Friedrich, "L'Essai sur la paix," 161.

30. Immanuel Kant, *Perpetual Peace and Other Essays on Politics, History, and Morals*, trans. Ted Humphrey (Indianapolis: Hackett, 1983), section 2, first definitive article for perpetual peace: "The only constitution which derives from the idea of the original compact, and on which all juridical legislation of a people must be based, is the republican" (93). Kant says that "the republican constitution...is...the one which is the original basis of every form of civil constitution" (94) and that this origin has "sprung from the pure source of the concept of law" (94). In different terms, the republican character does not apply to one or another form of the state, according to its form of domination: autocratic, aristocratic, democratic—sovereignty of the prince, of the nobility, of the people (95–96). Any state is republican as long as it functions well, as long as it displays wisdom in its administration (Immanuel Kant, *The Metaphysics of Morals*, trans. Mary Gregor [Cambridge: Cambridge University Press, 1996], 112–13). For the forms of a state are only "the *letter* of the original legislation in the civil state" (112). Thus must one be careful not to confuse the republican and the democratic constitutions (*Perpetual Peace*, 95). More precisely, according to the mode the sovereign adopts to govern the people (the form of government), the state is either republican or despotic: "Republicanism is the political principle of the separation of the executive power (the administration) from the legislative; despotism is that of the autonomous execution by the state of laws which it has itself decreed. Thus in a despotism the public will is administered by the ruler as his own will. Of the three forms of the state, that of democracy is...necessarily a despotism, because it establishes an executive power in which 'all' decide for or even against one who does not agree" (96). What is certain is that "the state of peace among men living side by side is not the natural state *(status naturalis)*: the natural state is one of war. A state of peace, therefore, must be *established*" (92). The opposition to Rousseau is on this point unequivocal (see Philonenko, *Théorie et praxis*, 39). On the dangers of democracy according to Kant, see Weil, *Problèmes kantiens*, 121–22; on the Kantian idea of the republic, see ibid., 133ff., and Friedrich, "L'Essai sur la paix," 152ff.

31. The regulative use of the republican Idea, in opposition to its possible constitutive use, which is necessarily productive of illusion. As the Ideas are constructed by reason, they do not have the power to determine Nature, and in the speculative realm have no more than a regulative role. In their legitimate theoretical use, the Ideas depict the ideal of systematization that is to be realized by indicating the way in which the objects of experience may be brought together in the greatest possible unity. On the Kantian distinction between regulative and constitutive uses, see Immanuel Kant, *Critique of Pure Reason*, trans. Norman Kemp Smith (New York: St. Martin's, 1965), 532–49. Among the commentaries: Philonenko, *L'Oeuvre de Kant*, 1:138, 318ff.; Gérard Lebrun, *Kant et la fin de la métaphysique* (Paris: Colin, 1970), 154–55; Gilles Deleuze, *Kant's Critical Philosophy*, trans. Hugh Tomlinson and Barbara Habberjam (Minneapolis: University of Minnesota Press, 1984), 18–21. The illegitimate use of the republican Idea comes down to believing that one may "realize here and now a perfect political constitution and thus...create a wholly rational society" (Ferry and Renaut, *Political Philosophy 3*, 125). Another form of the same type of metaphysical illusion, in which the precritical philosopher and the child, as Plato would have said, "want it both ways"—wants to realize a society in which both social justice and the happiness of all would reign.

32. Ferry and Renaut, *Political Philosophy 3*, 125.
33. Ibid.
34. Ibid., 126.
35. Ibid., 127. See above, trait 3 of the ideal type of racism, pp. 204–6.
36. Ferry and Renaut, *Political Philosophy 3*, 127.
37. Ibid., 126.
38. Ibid., 43–44.
39. Exemplary of the antiuniversalist vulgate that dominated in the French philosophical field of the 1960s and 1970s is this declaration by Michel Foucault: "the search for a moral form that would be acceptable to everyone — in the sense that everyone should be subject to it — seems to me catastrophic" (*Les Nouvelles*, June 28, 1984, quoted in Ferry and Renaut, *Political Philosophy 3*, 127). In the same genre, a testimony to a conformism belonging to the age, is this statement by Michel Serres, as peremptory as it is allusive: "The only philosophy that is possible — that is, vital [?] — consists of repudiating the universal. Pluralism and polymorphism" ("Estime," in *Politiques de la philosophie* [Paris: Grasset, 1976], 120).
40. Ferry and Renaut, *Political Philosophy 3*, 127–28.
41. In an important text, "Pour une sociologie de la démocratie" (1966), Claude Lefort poses the problem (see Claude Lefort, *Éléments d'une critique de la bureaucratie* [Paris: Gallimard, 1979], 343).
42. Ibid., 344.
43. See Jacques Rancière, "La Pensée de l'égalité," seminar at the Collège International de Philosophie, Paris, 1986–87.
44. Lefort, *Éléments*, 344.
45. Claude Lefort, *Democracy and Political Theory*, trans. David Macey (Minneapolis: University of Minnesota Press, 1988). Democracy as the dissolution of the markers of certainty, provoking indefinite attempts to restore said certainty — that defines the labor of ideology (19–20). The disincorporation of power engenders parallel efforts with a view to resubstantialize power, to reincorporate it, and so on (228).
46. We have in mind maximalist pseudo-Platonism, which has been well defined by Vladimir Jankélévitch, in *Le Pur et l'impur*, 173ff. The maximalist is deaf to the intermediaries of whom Plato, in the *Philebus* (17a), recalled the dialectical function: "Your clever modern man, while making his one — or his many, as the case may be — more quickly or more slowly than is proper, when he has got his one proceeds to his unlimited number straightaway, allowing the intermediaries to escape him, whereas it is the recognition of those intermediaries that makes all the difference between a philosophical and a contentious discussion" (*Philebus*, trans. R. Hackforth, in *Plato: The Collected Dialogues*, ed. Edith Hamilton and Huntington Cairns [New York: Pantheon, 1963], 1093).
47. A good example of the simple inversion of the "racist" celebration of differential racial purity is represented in this note by Nietzsche (for whom such an affirmation is customary), which antiracists willingly quote as "proof" of the philosopher's nonracism: "Against [the distinction between] Aryans and Semites: where the races are mixed springs the source of greater civilizations" (Friedrich Nietzsche, *Gesammelte Werke*, vol. 16 [Munich: Musarion, 1928], 374). [My translation. — Trans.] Léon Mis, after quoting this fragment ("Nietzsche et Stefan George, précurseurs du 'Troisième Reich,'" *Revue d'Histoire de la Philosophie et d'Histoire Générale de la Civilisation* 11 [July 15, 1935]: 225), believes he may conclude: "The Germany of today follows paths on which they [Nietzsche and George] would never have set out" (226). In the same perspective: Walter Kaufmann, *Nietzsche: Philosopher, Psychologist, Antichrist* (Princeton,

N.J.: Princeton University Press, 1974), 303; Éric Blondel, *Nietzsche: Le "Cinquième 'Évangile' "?* (Paris: Les Bergers et les Mages, 1980), 59–70; Jean Granier, *Le Problème de la vérité dans la philosophie de Nietzsche* (Paris: Seuil, 1966), 397 n. 3; Léon Poliakov, *The History of Anti-Semitism*, vol. 4, *Suicidal Europe, 1870–1933*, trans. George Klin (Oxford: Oxford University Press, 1985), 8–10; Poliakov, *The Aryan Myth: A History of Racist and Nationalist Ideas in Europe*, trans. Edmund Howard (New York: Basic Books, 1974), 299–300. We will simply point out that a certain praise of a certain *métissage* should not suffice to furnish an absolute criterion of nonracism. Moreover, we have already been warned of the rhetorical facility of the unending plays of reversal into the contrary: from mixophobia to mixophilia and from the latter to the former. Ideological "revolutions" are in large part constituted by such operations. Coming and going in the same element, that of evidence for or against. Alfred Rosenberg was not bothered in the least by the Nietzschean fragments dear to antiracists: "The stock exchange became the idol of the materialistic sickness of the times.... Nietzsche embodied the despairing cry of millions against the latter. The Red standards then joined the banner of Nietzsche and the nomadic wandering Marxist preachers — the sort of men whose doctrine scarcely anyone else had unmasked with such derision as Nietzsche himself. In his name, racial pollution through Syrians and blacks *[Syrier und Nigros]* was sanctified, although Nietzsche, in fact, strove for selective racial breeding. Nietzsche has fallen to the dreams of overheated political whores, which is worse than falling into the hands of robbers" (*The Myth of the Twentieth Century*, trans. Vivan Bird [Torrance, Calif.: Noontide, 1982], 331–32). On Rosenberg's poor knowledge of Nietzsche at the time of his *Myth*, see Yves Guéneau, "Les Idéologues et le philosophe," *Revue d'Allemagne* 16, no. 3 (July–September 1984): 355–56. See also Steven E. Aschheim, *The Nietzsche Legacy in Germany 1890–1990* (Berkeley: University of California Press 1992), 232–307, 316–30.

48. Simone Weil, *Écrits de Londres et dernières lettres* (Paris: Gallimard, 1957), 146.

49. Simone Weil, *Gravity and Grace*, trans. Arthur Wills (New York: Putnam, 1952), 229.

50. Jacques Maritain, *Christianity and Democracy*, trans. Doris C. Anson (New York: Scribner's, 1944), 25.

51. Ibid., 93.

52. Ibid., 98. Cf. 97: "What is asked is that... the climate and the inspiration of common life be an inspiration of generosity and a climate of *heroic hope*" (my emphasis).

53. [Here and throughout this passage, Taguieff is alluding to Pascal's famous "wager" argument, whose purpose is to dispose the addressee to working toward faith in God (Blaise Pascal, *Pensées*, trans. A. J. Krailsheimer [New York: Penguin, 1966], §418, 149–53.—Trans.]

54. See Henri Gouhier, *Blaise Pascal: Commentaires*, 2d ed. (Paris: Vrin, 1971), 254.

55. F. Scott Fitzgerald, *The Crack-Up* (New York: New Directions, 1956), 69.

# Index

*Action Française*, 97–102
Adam, Michel, 22
Adorno, Theodor W., 303, 352 n. 76
Agassiz, Louis, 213, 216, 222
Alembert, Jean Le Rond d', 141
Alleg, Henri, 143
Allport, Gordon W., 50–52, 142, 149
  on discrimination, 161
  on prejudice, 172–76
Ammon, Otto, 23–24, 84, 214
antiracism
  and anti-Semitism, 33–34, 231–32
  and biology, 2–3, 144–45
  and communism, 239–40
  and crisis, 232–35
  and difference, 7–8, 209–12, 232, 248–53
  and economism, 235–36
  and egalitarianism, 29–30, 182–83
  and ethics, 55–58, 296–98
  as heterophilia, 19–30
  and humanity, 258, 273–74
  ideal type of, 230–58 passim
  and ideology, 1–15, 110–37 passim, 141–44, 180–94, 231–32, 238–42, 259–74
  individuo-universalist, 8, 260–74
  and inegalitarianism, 240–41

  Manichaeanism of, 2, 42, 57–58
  and Marxism, 141–43
  and *métissage*, 128, 248–53
  and nationalism, 235, 238–39
  and National Socialism, 233–34, 243–44
  and the New Right, 3–4
  and pacifism, 253–58
  and philosophy of suspicion, 40–43
  and prejudice, 141–79 passim, 185–94
  as racizing practice, 32–36
  and reason, 2–3, 58–63, 263
  and scientism, 2–3, 181–83
  and tolerance, 241–45
  traditio-communitarianist, 8, 260–74
  and universalism, 27–29
  and xenophobia, 233, 237–38
  *See also* racism; prejudice
*Appeal to the Civilized World (Aufruf an die Kulturwelt)*, 97–102
Arendt, Hannah, 147
Aristotle, 7, 232
Aron, Raymond, 21, 255

Bacon, Francis, 158
Bainville, Jacques, 94–95
Baldwin, James, 262–74

Banton, Michael, 145–72 passim
Barot, Madeleine, 233
Barrès, Maurice, 334 n. 8, 336 n. 9
Bastide, Roger, 156–57, 266–74
Bateson, Gregory, 352 n. 73
Benda, Julien, 114
Benoist, Alain de, 49, 326 n. 46
Berdyaev, Nicolas, 230, 300
Bergstraesser, Ludwig, 91
Bérillon, Dr. Edgar, 205, 223
Berr, Henri, 382 n. 90
Boas, Franz, 144–45
  and *métissage*, 218
  on naturalization, 206–7
Bogardus, Emory S., 174, 224–25
Bonnard, Abel, 213, 217, 221
Bouglé, Célestin, 220, 348 n. 20
Boulenger, Jacques, 193
Bourdieu, Pierre, 24, 36, 41, 81, 230, 323 n. 4
Bouthoul, Gaston, 222–23
Braque, Georges, 159
Brasillach, Robert, 306–7
Brigneau, François, 238–39
Brøndal, Viggo, 199
Brunn, Julien, 48–49
Buber, Martin, 292–93
Bultmann, Rudolf, 296
Burke, Edmund: and prejudice, 154
Burns, Sir Alan, 179
Butz, Arthur R., 133

Carnap, Rudolf, 1
Castle, William E., 219
Chakotin, Serge, 180–83
Chaliand, Gérard, 163–64
Chamberlain, Houston Stewart, 192–93, 204, 261
Christen, Yves, 49
Clauss, Ludwig Ferdinand, 261
Club de l'Horloge, 49, 221–22
Cohn-Bendit, Daniel, 247
Comas, Juan, 219
Comte, Auguste, 300
Condorcet, Marquis de, 299
Cornevin, Marianne, 163–64
Cox, Oliver C., 142

Darwin, Charles, 45, 47, 52–54
  and *métissage*, 223

Debray, Régis, 321 n. 21
Dehem, Paul, 347 n. 19
Delacampagne, Christian, 40–43, 328 n. 100, 329 n. 116
Demolins, Edmond, 75–77
Derrida, Jacques, 394 n. 11
Descartes, René: and prejudice, 153, 158–59, 194
difference
  and antiracism, 7–8, 209–12, 232, 248–53
  and egalitarianism, 211–12
  and hierarchy, 209–12
  and the individual, 209–11
  and inegalitarianism, 208
  and *métissage*, 201, 204–5, 220–21
  and the Other, 210–11
  and racialization, 9, 120–33
  and racism, 5–6, 19–30, 198–201, 204–6, 259–61
  and universalism, 284–86, 305–10
  *See also* inegalitarianism; Other, the
Dimier, Louis, 97–102
Dostoyevsky, Fyodor, 283
Dreyfus Affair, the, 9, 85–86, 187
Drumont, Édouard, 85, 129
Dumézil, Georges, 97
Dumont, Louis, 6, 130, 227, 260–61
  on difference, 209–12
Dupréel, Eugène, 259
Dupuy, Bernard, 320 n. 5
Dupuy, Jean-Pierre, 120
Durand ("de Gros"), Joseph-Pierre, 206
Durkheim, Émile, 11–12, 24

Eibl-Eibesfeldt, Irenäus, 27
Ellul, Jacques, 306
Epstein, Simon, 383 n. 6
ethics
  and antiracism, 55–58, 296–98
  and humanity, 287–91
  and the Other, 291–96
  and reason, 288–91
  *See also* humanity; Kant, Immanuel; reason; universalism
ethnocentrism: and racism, 59–67, 154–56
eugenicism
  and *métissage*, 217, 225–29
  and racism, 53–54, 188–90

Evola, Julius, 190–92, 261
Eysenck, Hans J., 75

Fabre-Luce, Alfred, 339–40 n. 53
Faure, Élie, 250
Faurisson, Robert, 133
Favret, Jeanne, 130
Febvre, Lucien: on Oswald Spengler, 106–7
Ferré, Jean, 323 n. 5
Ferry, Jules, 261
Ferry, Luc, 310, 393–94 n. 11
Fichte, Johann Gottlieb, 105, 210
Finch, Earl, 213–14
Finkielkraut, Alain, 295–96
Fitzgerald, F. Scott, 316
Freud, Sigmund, 42–43
Friedrich, Carl J., 310

Galileo, 186–87
Galton, Francis, 148
Ginzburg, Carlo, 113
Giraud, Michel, 363 n. 63
Gobineau, Arthur de, 12–13, 92, 95, 108–9, 116, 186–87, 193, 213, 215, 339–40 n. 53
Grant, Madison, 213, 215, 220
GRECE, the, 48–49
Guillaume, Gustave, 124
Guillaumin, Colette, 23, 41, 78, 79–80, 120, 320 n. 5
Guiral, Pierre, 250

Habermas, Jürgen, 310
Haeckel, Ernst, 261
Hankins, Frank H., 213
Hayek, Friedrich von, 128–29, 151
Herder, Johann Gottfried, 210
Hersch, Jeanne, 121–22
Heschel, Abraham Joshua, 312
Hiernaux, Jean, 72
 on ethnocentrism, 62, 63
 on prejudice, 79
Hitler, Adolf, 95, 104, 105, 118, 125, 132–33, 257. *See also* National Socialism
Hobbes, Thomas, 175
Honoré, Jean-Paul, 353 n. 90
Horkheimer, Max, 114–15, 282, 309, 352 n. 76

humanity
 and antiracism, 258, 273–74, 281–86
 and critical reason, 299
 and ethics, 287–91
 and racism, 55–58
 and universalism, 295–96, 298–302, 303–16
 *See also* ethics; Kant, Immanuel; universalism
Husserl, Edmund, 128–29, 203, 303
Huxley, Thomas, 54

Ignatieff, Michael, 303–4
Ikor, Roger, 245
inegalitarianism
 and antiracism, 240–41
 and difference, 208
 and racism, 141–44, 176–79, 259–61
 *See also* difference

Jacob, François, 2, 73–75
Jacquard, Albert, 2, 73, 75
Jacques, Francis, 396–97 n. 60
Jankélévitch, Vladimir, 24–25, 292
Jensen, Arthur R., 75
Jim Crow, 160–65
Johannet, René, 89–90

Kant, Immanuel, 305, 310–11
 and humanity, 287–91
 *See also* ethics; reason; universalism
Keith, Sir Arthur, 362 n. 56, 389 n. 71
Kintzler, Catherine, 299
Klineberg, Otto, 149
 on discrimination, 160–61
 and *métissage*, 219–20
 on prejudice, 172–74
Kolakowski, Leszek, 197, 242
Kravetz, Marc, 114
Kriegel, Annie, 247–48

Lalande, André, 308–9, 348 n. 20
Langaney, André, 58–59, 324 n. 22
Langmuir, Gavin I., 44–45, 64
Lazare, Bernard, 61–62, 340 n. 58
Le Bon, Gustave, 215, 261
Le Bras–Chopard, Armelle, 333 n. 3
Le Fur, Louis, 87–88
Lemaine, Gérard: on *métissage*, 226–29

Léonard, Jacques, 333 n. 3
Le Pen, Jean-Marie, 33, 241–42
Le Play, Frédéric, 75
Lesseps, Emmanuèle de, 26
Lévinas, Emmanuel, 78, 291–96
Lévi-Strauss, Claude, 20, 154–56
  on ethnocentrism, 60–61, 66
Lévy, Bernard-Henri, 241–43
Lewis, Bernard, 263–64
Lichtenberger, Henri, 88–89
Lorenz, Konrad, 45, 54–55
Ludendorff, Erich, 90
Luschan, Felix von, 215
Lwoff, André, 2
Lyotard, Jean-François, 393–94 n. 11

Malcolm X, 263–64
Malraux, André, 283
Mannheim, Karl, 128, 133
Marienstras, Richard, 284–86
Maritain, Jacques, 172, 314
Martial, Dr. René, 220, 221, 349 n. 28
Marx, Karl, 42–43, 104
Massis, Henri, 31, 106
Matalon, Benjamin, 226–29
Mauco, Georges, 39
Maurras, Charles, 86, 91–96, 120, 339 n. 53
Maybon, A., 86
Mead, Margaret, 262–74
Memmi, Albert, 46, 56–58, 320 n. 2, 320 n. 5, 322 n. 23
Merton, Robert King, 174
Méry, Gaston, 85, 86
*métissage*
  and antiracism, 128, 248–53
  and blood, 216, 218–19
  and difference, 201, 204–5, 220–21
  and equality, 8
  and eugenicism, 217, 225–29
  and fear of difference, 5
  and identity, 224–25
  and psychology, 223–29
  and racism, 117–18, 213–29
Montherlant, Henry de, 283
Mussolini, Benito, 106
Myrdal, Gunnar, 161, 164, 174

National Front, the (le Front National), 4, 171

National Socialism
  and antiracism, 233–34, 243–44
  and *métissage*, 214
  and racism, 3, 5, 8–9, 25, 81–82, 88–96, 102–9, 117–19, 132–33, 142–43, 181–82, 306–7
  *See also* Hitler, Adolf; Rosenberg, Alfred
New Right, the, 3–4, 6, 7, 48–49
Nietzsche, Friedrich, 42–43, 104, 108, 183, 223, 403–4 n. 47

Other, the
  and difference, 210–11
  and ethics, 291–96
  and race, 121–22
  and racialization, 123–26
  and racism, 20–25, 44, 46, 130–36
  *See also* difference

Pagès, Robert, 156, 223–29
Palante, Georges, 336 n. 14
Panoff, Françoise, 129–30
Panoff, Michel, 129–30
Paraf, Pierre, 44
Pareto, Vilfredo, 59, 198–99, 229
Park, Robert E., 229
Parsons, Talcott, 98, 136, 147, 260–61, 267
Pascal, Blaise, 230, 287
Passeron, Jean-Claude, 23
Patočka, Jan, 301
Paul, Saint, 296
Pavlov, Ivan, 181–82
Perelman, Chaïm, 119
Piéron, Henri, 156
Pittard, Eugène, 71–72
Pius XII, Pope, 186
Podhoretz, Norman, 252–53
Poliakov, Léon, 330 n. 122
Popper, Karl R., 299, 330 n. 122
prejudice
  antiracism as, 141–79 passim, 185–94
  and critical reason, 10–11
  and ethnocentrism, 61–63
  and historicism, 184
  racism as, 141–79 passim, 183–94
  and philosophy, 184–85

and reason, 153–54
as term, 144–45
*See also* antiracism; racism
Prenant, Marcel, 343 n. 85
Prévost-Paradol, Lucien-Anatole, 10

Quatrefages de Bréau, Armand de, 206

race
  and biology, 39–40
  and environment, 77
  French, 86–87
  and history, 71–72
  and the Other, 121–22
  and racialization, 77–80
  and racism, 197
  and scientism, 72–80
  and social sciences, 4–5
  and sociology, 75–77
  *See also* racism
racialization
  antiracist, 32–36
  and difference, 120–33
  and identity, 9
  and the individual, 26
  as ideological operation, 4
  and difference, 9
  and the Other, 36–39, 123–26
  and race, 77–80
  and racism, 176–79
racism
  in antiracist discourse, 230–58 passim
  as anti-Semitism, 24–25, 44–45, 46–47, 59, 64, 85–86, 90–91, 114–15, 123–25, 132–33, 173, 175, 193
  and attitude, 148–59
  and barbarism, 97–102
  and biology, 2–3, 39–42, 53–55, 115–16, 146–48
  and colonialism, 173
  and difference, 5–6, 19–30, 198–201, 204–6, 259–61
  as discrimination, 160–72
  and essentialism, 22–24, 74
  and ethnocentrism, 27, 59–67, 154–56
  and ethnology, 129–30
  and eugenicism, 53–54, 188–90
  and evolutionism, 190–93
  French, 186–87
  as heterophilia, 26–27
  as heterophobia, 19–26, 27–30, 43–67
  and history, 180–81
  and humanity, 55–58
  ideal type of, 197–212
  as ideology, 2, 11–15, 80, 82–85, 87–96, 110–37 passim, 141–44, 145–48, 199–212, 259–74
  indeterminate definition of, 9–11, 31–80 passim
  and the individual, 114, 202–4
  individuo-universalist, 260–74
  and inegalitarianism, 141–44, 176–79, 259–61
  and Marxism, 141–43
  and *métissage,* 117–18, 213–29
  as mixophobia, 5
  and the National Front, 4
  and nationalism, 210–11
  and National Socialism, 3, 5, 8–9, 25, 81–82, 88–96, 102–9, 117–19, 132–33, 142–43, 181–82, 306–7
  and nationalism, 88–96, 102–7
  and naturalization, 23–24, 52–58, 206–8
  and the New Right, 3–4, 6, 48
  and the Other, 20, 25, 44, 46, 130–36
  as panekhretism, 44–47
  as prejudice, 141–79 passim, 183–94
  and race, 197
  and racialization, 176–79
  and reason, 2–3
  and scientism, 2–3, 67–80
  and sexism, 26
  and social psychology, 148–59
  and sociobiology, 48
  as term, 36–43, 197–212
  traditio-communitarianist, 192, 260–74
  and universalism, 200–201, 259–74
  and xenophobia, 49, 59–67, 154–56
  *See also* antiracism; prejudice; race
Raphaël, Freddy, 22–23
Rathenau, Walter, 88–89, 102
Rawls, John, 166–67

reason
   and antiracism, 2–3, 10–11, 31–32, 58–63, 263
   critical, and humanity, 299
   critical, and pessimism, 281–86
   critical, and prejudice, 10–11
   and ethics, 288–91
   and prejudice, 153–54
   and racism, 2–3, 10–11
   *See also* ethics; Kant, Immanuel; universalism
Renan, Ernst, 305
Renaut, Alain, 310, 393–94 n. 11
Ribot, Théodule, 213
Richter, Claire, 223
Ricoeur, Paul, 304–5
Rodinson, Maxime, 44–45, 46, 317 n. 4
Rogozinski, Jacob, 393–94 n. 11
Rorty, Richard, 353 n. 92
Rosenberg, Alfred, 105, 117–18, 214. *See also* Hitler, Adolf; National Socialism
Roux, Marie de, 92, 93–94
Royer, Clémence, 261
Ruffié, Jacques, 2, 72, 75, 220
Ruyssen, Théodore, 88

Sageret, Jules, 125–26
Saint-Pierre, Michel de, 39–40
Scheler, Max, 258, 296–98, 299
Schelling, Friedrich W. J., 1
Segalen, Victor, 252
Senghor, Léopold Sédar, 111
Shestov, Lev, 281, 394–95 n. 11
Sombart, Werner, 22–23, 104, 105
Sorokin, Pitirim A., 259
SOS-Racisme, 239
Sowell, Thomas: on discrimination, 163, 167–72
Spengler, Oswald, 102, 106–7, 261, 283, 321 n. 21
Spinoza, Baruch de, 298
Stäglich, Wilhelm, 133
Sternhell, Zeev, 104–5

Stoddard, Lothrop, 213
Stoetzel, Jean, 149–50
Strauss, Leo, 183–85

Taine, Hyppolite, 154
Tarde, Gabriel, 75, 77, 384 n. 9
Tawa, Habib, 49–50
Thomas, Louis, 193
Thuillier, Pierre, 48
Tönnies, Ferdinand, 260–61, 267
Tort, Patrick, 52–54
Trigano, Shmuel, 305

universalism
   and antiracism, 27–29
   and community, 307–8
   and difference, 284–86, 305–10
   and humanity, 295–96, 298–302, 303–16
   and racism, 200–201, 259–74
   *See also* ethics; humanity; Kant, Immanuel

Vacher de Lapouge, Georges, 23–24, 57, 84, 95, 186–90, 261, 334–35 n. 8, 339 n. 53
   and the individual, 203
   and *métissage,* 214, 220
   on naturalization, 207–8
Vallois, Henri-Victor, 71, 323 n. 7
van den Berghe, Pierre L., 163
Vercors, 55–56
Vermeil, Edmond, 89, 102–7
Vigarello, Georges, 318 n. 7
Villey, Michel, 301

Wach, Joachim, 302
Wahl, Jean: on Kant, 287, 291
Wallerstein, Immanuel, 321 n. 21
Wallon, Henri, 115
Walzer, Michael, 283–84
Weber, Max, 70–71, 147, 235–36
Wilson, Edward O., 45, 48
Woltmann, Ludwig, 214
Woodard, James W., 150

**Pierre-André Taguieff,** philosopher and historian of political ideas, is director of research at the Centre National de la Recherche Scientifique, Paris. As a public intellectual, he is a prominent voice in the ongoing debates on racism and antiracism in France. Among his most recent works are *La République menacée* and *Le Racisme.*

**Hassan Melehy** is assistant professor of French and comparative literature at the University of Connecticut. He is the author of *Writing Cogito: Montaigne, Descartes, and the Institution of the Modern Subject* and has translated *Empire of Meaning: The Humanization of the Social Sciences,* by François Dosse, and *The Names of History: On the Poetics of Knowledge,* by Jacques Rancière, both published by the University of Minnesota Press.

www.ingramcontent.com/pod-product-compliance
Lightning Source LLC
Jackson TN
JSHW070312120426
100741JS00007B/33